European SPCs Unravelled

European SPCs Unravelled

A Practitioner's Guide to Supplementary Protection Certificates in Europe

Edited by

Alexa von Uexküll
Oswin Ridderbusch

Wolters Kluwer

Published by:
Kluwer Law International B.V.
PO Box 316
2400 AH Alphen aan den Rijn
The Netherlands
E-mail: international-sales@wolterskluwer.com
Website: lrus.wolterskluwer.com

Sold and distributed in North, Central and South America by:
Wolters Kluwer Legal & Regulatory U.S.
7201 McKinney Circle
Frederick, MD 21704
United States of America
Email: customer.service@wolterskluwer.com

Sold and distributed in all other countries by:
Air Business Subscriptions
Rockwood House
Haywards Heath
West Sussex
RH16 3DH
United Kingdom
Email: international-customerservice@wolterskluwer.com

ISBN 978-90-411-9995-9

e-Book: ISBN 978-90-411-9996-6
web-PDF: ISBN 978-90-411-9601-9

Editors

Oswin Ridderbusch is a German and European patent attorney and a partner at the IP law firm Vossius & Partner, with an academic background in biochemistry. He specializes in the field of supplementary protection certificates, and has more than ten years of professional experience in navigating the intricacies of SPC law and filing strategies. His practice also includes the drafting and prosecution of patent applications, mainly in the fields of medicinal chemistry, pharmaceuticals, biotechnology and diagnostics, as well as post-grant proceedings including opposition, revocation and infringement actions. Oswin further provides counsel in the strategic management of patent portfolios and prepares freedom-to-operate opinions. He is an active member of AIPPI and engages in its standing committee on the Unitary Patent and the UPC.

Dr Alexa von Uexküll has read chemistry, with a focus on biochemistry at the University of London and continued to complete her Master's degree in Pharmacology, followed by a case award funded PhD in the field of central neuropharmacology. She joined Vossius & Partner in 1988 and was admitted to practice as a German Patent Attorney (Patentanwalt) in 1991 and as a European Patent Attorney in 1992. In 1993, Alexa became a partner in the firm. In the same year, the Regulation for Supplementary Protection Certificates came into force, which has been her main focus of interest ever since. Alexa works with clients in the chemical and pharmaceutical fields. In addition to drafting and prosecuting chemical and pharmaceutical patent applications, she has extensive experience in contentious litigation, including oppositions, national nullity actions and infringement.

Contributors

Francis Ahner has worked for over forty years in Regimbeau, an IP Law Firm mainly located in Paris, France and exclusively dedicated to providing a full range of Intellectual Property and technology-related legal services. He is a European and French Patent and Trademark Attorney and is now of counsel for the firm Regimbeau. He has worked in Biology and Chemistry, Physics and Mechanics and is an expert with a worldwide reputation specializing in chemistry, pharmacy, and cosmetology, and acts both for French and foreign public research organizations and for French and international pharmaceutical firms. His legal experience covers all areas of IP law including litigating, negotiating, advising, strategic planning, expert witnessing, opinion-writing, licensing and prosecuting European and French patents. He graduated from Ecole Nationale Supérieure de Chimie de Strasbourg (ENSC) and from the International Center of Intellectual Property Studies (CEIPI) from the Law University of Strasbourg (France). He obtained the 'Master of Intellectual Property Economy, Law and Management'. He has been the President between 2003 and 2006 and is now the President of Honour of FICPI (Fédération Internationale des Conseils en Propriété Industrielle), worldwide representative organization of patent and trademark Attorneys in the free profession. He has been a professor at CEIPI for many years and is President of CEIPI's Education Committee and a member of its Board. He regularly teaches for 'Industrial Property' modules in courses at Grandes Ecoles, Universities and for postgraduate diplomas.

Dr Ann De Clercq is a European & Belgian Patent Attorney at De Clercq & Partners in Sint-Martens-Latem, Belgium. Ann was an Examiner at the EPO in Munich, headed the patent department of Innogenetics and is active as founding partner since 1998 of De Clercq & Partners where she handles prosecution, oppositions, appeals, SPCs, litigation and advises on IP strategy mainly in the field of biotech and related life sciences such as pharmaceuticals, diagnostics, medical chemistry, bioinformatics, agricultural and veterinary sciences. Ann is Chair of the EPI Biotech Committee, member of EPI council for Belgium, frequent lecturer on patents and SPCs, and member of INTA, AIPPI and LES.

Andrea Damonti is an Italian patent attorney and Italian and European trademark attorney at Modiano & Partners, an intellectual property firm with offices in Milan, Italy, as well as in Germany and Switzerland. He holds a university degree in law from the University of Milan, and has more than twenty-five years of experience and assists mostly foreign clients in matters concerning intellectual property in general, supplementary protection certificates, litigation, out of court negotiation, drafting of agreements, due diligence, disputes, as well as confidentiality and contractual issues. He is a frequent lecturer on patents and Community designs.

Ricardo Dijkstra is partner at Vondst, an Amsterdam based, independent boutique law firm that focuses exclusively on contentious intellectual property, pharmaceuticals and life sciences and transactional and contentious IT. He advises and litigates in patent, technology and life sciences matters and has a strong focus on cross-border litigation in the areas of pharmaceuticals & life sciences. His knowledge of pharmaceutical law (e.g., regulatory and marketing issues) is a great advantage in litigation concerning pharmaceutical patents, supplementary protection certificates and paediatric extensions. He also guest lectures on international private law and patent law at the University of Groningen. Ricardo Dijkstra always receives warm praise from his clients that appreciate his strategic approach.

Dr Einar Karl Friðriksson is a partner at Arnason Faktor, an intellectual property firm in Reykjavik, Iceland. He has over nineteen years' experience in the field of IP and advises both domestic and international clients in IP-related matters. He is the current president of the Icelandic Association of Patent and Trademark Representatives (FUVE) and has been an active member in the Council and committees of the European Patent Institute (epi). He has taught courses in patent law in the University of Iceland Continuing Education Institute and given numerous lectures and courses elsewhere. He holds a PhD in chemistry from Cornell University.

Dr Hans Goesaert is a European & Belgian Patent Attorney at De Clercq & Partners in Sint-Martens-Latem, Belgium. Prior to joining De Clercq & Partners in 2015, he worked for almost seven years in the IP and patent domain, as an IP officer at the Technology Transfer Office of the Katholieke Universiteit Leuven, and as a patent counsel in private practice. His areas of practice include prosecution, oppositions, appeals, litigation and advising on IP strategy mainly in the field of biotech and related life sciences such as food technology, (bio)chemistry, chemical engineering and processing, and material science.

Dr José Manuel González is PhD in Biochemistry and Molecular Biology and European Patent Attorney. As associate at Manuel Illescas y Asociados S.L.U., a Spanish IP firm based in Madrid, he focuses his practice on patents and Supplementary Protections Certificates (SPCs), including drafting and prosecuting, client counselling, conducting opinion work and advising on IP protection strategies. He has also acted as technical expert in relation to SPCs before the Madrid High Court of Justice. He has lectured on patents and SPCs related issues before universities and institutions and has authored publications within this area. Before starting working for IP private firms he worked at the Spanish public research institution CSIC (Consejo Superior de Investigaciones Científicas) in matters relating to patents and knowledge transfer.

Nuno Gouveia is an Engineer, Graduated in Automotive Engineering by Polytechnic Institute of Leiria. Nuno has a General Intellectual Property practice, being a Patent expert. With a significant experience in patent drafting, Nuno was a patent Examiner at the Portuguese Patent Office. Presently Nuno is the head of the patent department at J.E. Dias Costa, Lda. He is a member of AIPPI.

Dr Manuel Illescas is PhD in Biochemistry (1992) and European Patent Attorney (2007). He has got a Master degree in Environmental Engineering (1992). He is also Spanish intellectual property attorney, authorized representative before the Spanish Patent and Trademark Office and the European Union Intellectual Property Office (since 1998). He joined, in the past, the body of Spanish Patent and Trademark Office graduates by open examination, where he practiced as an examiner for eight years. In 1993 he joined the firm Elzaburu, which he left in 2007 as a Senior Partner. Since then, Manuel Illescas has his own IP firm MIAPatents (Manuel Illescas y Asociados S.L.U.), wherein he holds the charge of Managing Partner. Manuel Illescas serves as a regular speaker at seminars and frequently lectures on industrial property and innovation. He has combined his experience in the world of intellectual property with his interest in research projects in the field of biotechnology through engagement, as a shareholder or member of the Managing Council, in several seed capital companies such as Inverbio (2005) and Cross Road Biotech (2007), respectively. He has also worked as Scientific Director in other companies, such as SJT Molecular Research (2013). Manuel is member of several organizations and associations, among others: International Association for the Protection of Intellectual Property (AIPPI), Fédération Internationale des Conseils en Propriété Industrielle (FICPI), American Intellectual Property Law Association (AIPLA) and Institute of Professional Representatives before the European Patent Office (EPI). He practices in drafting and prosecution, worldwide, of patents in Biotech and Pharma fields, mainly, including SPCs. He also intervenes, frequently, as patent expert in litigation before Spanish courts related to patents in Pharma and Biotech technical sectors.

Camilla Lidén is a partner at the intellectual property law firm BRANN AB and has fifteen years of experience in the field. Camilla's practice includes assisting clients in all matters involving intellectual property including navigating global patent portfolios, providing strategic legal advice and handling SPCs. Camilla's main technical areas of expertise include molecular biology, microbiology, pharmaceuticals and immunology. Camilla is a European Patent Attorney and an Authorized Swedish Patent Attorney and holds a Master of Science degree with a major in Molecular Biology from Umeå University which included studies at Karolinska Institute and University of Melbourne. In addition to her daily practice, Camilla regularly takes part in intellectual property and industrial conferences and is an active member of AIPPI (Sweden).

Paolo Mimo is an Italian patent attorney and European patent attorney at Modiano & Partners, an intellectual property firm with offices in Milan, Italy, as well as in Germany and Switzerland. After earning a degree in biotechnology from the University of Milan-Bicocca, he began a career in the intellectual property field, assisting both national and foreign clients with the filing and prosecution of patents in the chemistry, pharmaceuticals and biotech sectors, and also focusing on patent and SPC opinion work and related national litigation, also in the context of multinational litigations on behalf of both domestic and foreign clients. He holds the European patent litigation certificate from the Polytechnic University of Milan. He is also a lecturer on patents at the department of industrial chemistry at the University of Bologna.

Micaela Modiano is an Italian and European patent and trademark attorney and a partner and head of the life science department at Modiano & Partners, an intellectual property firm with offices in Milan, Italy, as well as in Germany and Switzerland. She has a B.A. in organic chemistry from Harvard University (US), an M.Sc. in intellectual property law from the University of London (UK) and the European patent litigation certificate from the University of Strasbourg (France). She has twenty plus years of experience in patent and SPC matters, including opinion work and related national litigation on behalf of both domestic and foreign clients, particularly multinationals. She is a member of the epi council and of the epi European Patent Practice Committee. She regularly lectures on patents at various universities, including the European patent litigation course of the Polytechnic University of Milan, as well as at various international conferences, including the yearly Best Practices in IP conference in Tel Aviv, Israel.

Gustaf Örn is a partner at the intellectual property law firm BRANN AB which he joined in 1996. He is a European Patent Attorney and an Authorized Swedish Patent Attorney. Gustaf assists clients in drafting and prosecuting patent applications, in patent portfolio management, defending patents, freedom-to-operate analyses, patentability assessments, and in legal counselling. His main areas of technical expertise are in various fields of chemistry, including pharmaceuticals. He holds a Master of Science degree in chemistry from the Stockholm University.

Gonçalo de Sampaio is a partner at J.E. Dias Costa, Lda., an IP firm based in Lisbon, Portugal. He graduated in Law by the Law School of Portuguese Catholic University. He has been practicing for more than twenty-five years, focusing in the last fifteen on patent litigation. Besides being a lawyer, Gonçalo is also an Official Industrial Property Agent, after passing the examination of the Portuguese PTO and also a European Trade Mark Attorney before the European Union Intellectual Property Office – Trade Marks and Designs (EUIPO). Since 2015 Gonçalo is the President of the Board of AIPPI (Portuguese Group). Prior to that he was the Secretary of the Board of ACPI (Portuguese Group of FICPI), from 2000 to 2015. Gonçalo is a Member of the Portuguese Bar Association, ACPI, FICPI, AIPPI, INTA, ICC and LES.

Charlotte Teall is a UK and European patent attorney and a partner at Forresters IP LLP, a specialist IP firm having a long-standing reputation in delivering clear, sensible and practical advice to clients looking to protect their ideas. Charlotte specializes in biochemistry with a degree in this field from Imperial College London. She is primarily involved in the drafting and prosecution of patent applications in the fields of biotechnology, pharmaceuticals and medical devices. She also has a strong SPC practice and regularly navigates clients through the complex process of securing SPC protection. Charlotte is primarily based in London, but spends several weeks each year in Munich for dealings with the EPO.

Summary of Contents

Table of Contents

CHAPTER 5
The Netherlands
Ricardo Dijkstra 255

Preface

Supplementary Protection Certificates (SPCs) for medicinal and plant protection products were introduced in the European Union just over a quarter of a century ago. As such, the SPC is a relatively new title of intellectual property. As an SPC is only available for a patented product, once the product has passed regulatory marketing approval, an SPC title is of enormous economic importance.

Over the past decades the EU Regulations on SPCs have been subjected to extensive scrutiny and have given rise to complex questions, only some of which have so far been finally resolved by the Court of Justice of the European Union (CJEU), the highest instance court of the EU in SPC matters.

Uncertainties surrounding SPCs have been compounded by the fact that while the current SPC Regulations focus on the substantive requirements for the grant of the certificate, they leave most features of the grant procedure to national laws.

This has resulted in different approaches being adopted by the national patent offices, in particular with respect to formal requirements as well as the level of examination. Thus, some patent offices conduct ex officio examination of the substantive requirements stipulated in the SPC Regulations, while others only check formal requirements; some consult regulatory agencies in relation to data related to the marketing authorization, while others do not. Similarly, there appear to be divergent approaches in terms of how the guidance provided by the CJEU rulings is implemented into the practice of various national patent offices. These seemingly minor divergences and procedural differences may have a substantial impact in the successful prosecution of a national SPC application and may also be of relevance when devising strategic concepts in terms of SPC filings.

This handbook is thus designed to not only provide a practitioner with an easily accessible overview of SPC law in Europe, including the case law of the CJEU and the EFTA Court, as well as the corresponding national case law (including Switzerland), but also to elucidate the at times very different procedural practices of the national patent offices, which need to be considered in detail in order to secure the desired substantive and territorial scope of SPC protection.

Acknowledgments

We are grateful to Dr Michaela Wesse of Vossius & Partner for her valuable support in the preparation of this book.

We wish to thank Dr Jürgen Meier of Vossius & Partner for his support and his encouragement to write this book.

We would like to thank our co-authors Francis Ahner, Dr Ann De Clercq, Andrea Damonti, Ricardo Dijkstra, Dr Einar Karl Friðriksson, Dr Hans Goesaert, Dr José Manuel González, Nuno Gouveia, Dr Manuel Illescas, Camilla Lidén, Paolo Mimo, Micaela Modiano, Gustaf Örn, Gonçalo de Sampaio, and Charlotte Teall for their thorough and dedicated contributions to this book, and for generously sharing their knowledge on SPCs.

We also wish to thank Clare Campbell, Lidija B. Djerić, Tatjana Jeršan, Karel Jůzl, Dr Arne Lund Kvernheim, Dr Luke Maishman, Dr Nataša Marsic, Agnieszka Marszałek, Dr Mária Miskolczi, Dr Martin Müllner, Eva Papa, Dr Jan Mondrup Pedersen, Nikola Petkovski, Dr Cristina Popa, Dr Luigi A. Sansone, Ela Shomo Panidha, and Jasna Zmazek for valuable and stimulating discussions in SPC matters.

We would further like to thank Christine Robben of Wolters Kluwer for her valued support in the conception and preparation of this book.

Alexa von Uexküll
Oswin Ridderbusch

Introduction

I HISTORICAL PERSPECTIVE

[A] Supplementary Protection Certificates: Dysfunctional and Not Fit for Purpose?

On 2 January 1993 the Council Regulation (EEC) No. 1768/92[1] came into force, providing for Supplementary Protection Certificates (SPCs) for medicinal products. This was followed in 1996 by the Regulation (EC) No. 1610/96,[2] with the corresponding provisions for plant protection products.

The SPC system was introduced to compensate for loss in effective patent term due to the increasingly stringent and time-consuming regulatory requirements, as well as the spiralling costs associated with R&D, associated with bringing innovative medicinal and agrochemical products onto the market.

An SPC may provide up to five years of additional proprietary protection once the twenty-year patent term expires (in case of SPCs for medicinal products, the SPC may be subject to a six-month paediatric extension as provided for in the Paediatric Regulation (EC) 1901/2006[3]). As such, an SPC may be the most valuable form of intellectual property in the lifespan of a product, as generally, the sales of the product are the highest towards the end of the patent term.

The SPC system has been in place for more than a quarter of a century. One would expect that any potentially overlooked pitfalls or ambiguities would have been sorted out, and that the system should be fully functional to provide the required level of legal certainty for all players.

1. Council Regulation (EEC) No. 1768/92 of 18 June 1992 concerning the creation of a supplementary protection certificate for medicinal products.
2. Regulation (EC) No. 1610/96 of the European Parliament and of the Council of 23 July 1996 concerning the creation of a supplementary protection certificate for plant protection products.
3. Regulation (EC) No. 1901/2006 of the European Parliament and of the Council of 12 December 2006 on medicinal products for paediatric use.

Unfortunately, the reality is very different. The SPC Regulations were poorly drafted and, as a result, there has been an increasing tendency by the national courts to refer cases to the Court of Justice of the European Union (CJEU, the highest instance court in EU matters). This reflects the struggle of the national judges in implementing the regulations in a fair and meaningful manner.

This course of action has to some extent proven to be counterproductive. Unlike many judges of the national courts of the Member States who deal with intellectual property matters on a daily basis, the CJEU has only limited experience in this regard: As a result, the much-needed guidance provided has at times been unclear and inconsistent, not to mention subject to extensive criticism.

The clarification required by the national courts in relation to the interpretation of the SPC Regulation are diverse and seem to be ever increasing including, e.g., all requirements for obtaining an SPC as set out in Article 3 SPC Regulation; the definition of the 'product' to be protected or the eligibility of certain products; the nature of the first marketing authorization and/or prior approval for the same active ingredient; issues relating to the calculation of the SPC term; the scope of protection of the SPC; and the eligibility of the paediatric extension for patented medicinal products not eligible to SPC protection.

While some of these issues appear to have been resolved, there are still many questions outstanding. The concerns in relation to the rulings of the CJEU are in particular evident by the flood of referrals to the court in an attempt to ascertain the criteria for deciding whether a 'product is protected by a basic patent in force' within the meaning of Article 3(a) of the SPC Regulation.

For example, in *Farmitalia* (C-392/97),[4] the CJEU ruled that in the absence of Community harmonization of patent law, the extent of patent protection can be determined only in the light of the non-Community rules which govern patents. What springs to mind in relation to these 'Extent of Protection Rules' are of course the national equivalent provisions of Article 69 of the European Patent Convention, the EPC.[5]

The seemingly straightforward answer provided by the CJEU in *Farmitalia* has, however, led to divergent interpretation in the Member States as to what test is to be applied to determine whether a product is protected by a basic patent in force within the meaning of Article 3(a) of the SPC Regulation, particularly in relation to combination products.

As a result, some national courts have advocated an 'infringement' test under Article 69 EPC, whereas others have concluded that this test was insufficient and that further considerations should be taken account of.

4. CJEU *Farmitalia Carlo Erba v. Bundesgerichtshof*, C-392/97 of 16 September 1999, paragraph 22.
5. Article 69(1) provides that:

> The extent of the protection conferred by a European patent ... shall be determined by the claims. Nevertheless, the description and drawings shall be used to interpret the claims.

To resolve the issue in a comprehensive manner, the UK courts referred various cases relating to combination products to the CJEU to seek guidance on a number of finely tuned questions (*Medeva* (C-322/10),[6] *Georgetown* (C-422/10),[7] *Yeda* (C-518/10),[8] *Queensland* (C-630/10)[9] and *Daiichi* (C-6/11)[10]).

However, rather than considering the actual questions referred, the CJEU reformulated the questions in the joined cases *Medeva* and *Georgetown* (the three remaining referrals, i.e., *Queensland, Daiichi* and *Yeda*, were disposed of by reasoned orders). The Court simply concluded that an SPC cannot be granted for active ingredients which are not 'specified' or 'identified' in the claims of a patent without providing any additional guidance in this regard.

Thus, in effect, while the 'infringement test' under Article 69 EPC was explicitly thrown overboard by the CJEU, it provided no alternative test to determine the Article 3(a) issue.

The above rulings, collectively referred to as '*Medeva* and its progeny' have resulted in considerable frustration amongst judges and practitioners alike. This is most evident in various subsequent decisions by the UK Patents Court and in the literature, criticizing the CJEU rulings for failing to provide guidance in terms of what tests are to be applied and the consequential need to refer further questions to solve this issue.[11]

This never ending story of referrals in relation to Article 3(a) of the SPC Regulation appears to have culminated in the *Eli Lilly* (C-493/12)[12] case, subsequently handed down by the CJEU, where the claims of the basic patent at bar were directed towards a functionally defined single antibody (as opposed to a combination of active

6. CJEU *Medeva v. Comptroller General of Patents, Designs and Trade Marks*, C-322/10 of 24 November 2011.
7. CJEU *Georgetown University v. Comptroller General of Patents, Designs and Trade Marks*, C-422/10 of 24 November 2011.
8. CJEU *Yeda Research and Development v. Comptroller General of Patents, Designs and Trade Marks*, C-518/10 of 25 November 2011.
9. CJEU *University of Queensland v. Comptroller General of Patents, Designs and Trade Marks*, C-630/10 of 25 November 2011.
10. CJEU *Daiichi Sankyo v. Comptroller General of Patents, Designs and Trade Marks*, C-6/11 of 25 November 2011.
11. High Court of Justice *MedImmune v. Novartis*, [2012] EWHC 181 (Pat) of 10 February 2012, paragraph 53:

> In my view, counsel for MedImmune is also correct to say that the test laid down by the Court of Justice in Medeva and its progeny is unclear save in its rejection of the infringement test in combination cases. In particular, it is unclear precisely what is meant by 'specified (or identified) in the wording of the claims'. Does this mean that it is sufficient for the product to fall within the scope of the claim on its true construction, or is something more required and if so what? For example, is it sufficient, say, for the claim to incorporate a Markush formula which covers a large number of compounds one of which is the product in respect of which an SPC is sought? Is it sufficient for the product to be defined in functional terms? Even in combination cases, it is not clear to me how the test enunciated by the Court should be applied in a case like Gilead. Regrettably, therefore, it is inevitable that there will have to be further references to the CJEU to obtain clarification of the test.

12. CJEU *Eli Lilly v. Human Genome Sciences*, C-493/12 of 12 December 2013.

ingredients as was the case in *Medeva* and its progeny). On this occasion, the CJEU allowed Article 69 EPC to miraculously resurface. The Court concluded in its headnote that Article 3(a) of the SPC Regulation must be interpreted as meaning that, in order for an active ingredient to be regarded as 'protected by a basic patent in force', it is not necessary for the active ingredient to be identified in the claims. Rather it may alternatively be functionally defined 'on condition that it is possible to reach the conclusion on the basis of those claims, interpreted *inter alia* in the light of the description of the invention, as required by Article 69 of the EPC and the Protocol on the interpretation of that provision, that the claims relate, implicitly but necessarily and specifically, to the active ingredient in question, which is a matter to be determined by the referring court'.

As was to be expected, this decision has left practitioners in a state of awe and stupefaction, preventing them from developing any meaningful and much needed advice for their clients. It is, however, comforting to note that even experienced judges have had difficulties in interpreting the guidance provided.[13]

The Rt Hon Professor Sir Robin Jacob, who has unrivalled expertise in intellectual property and is renowned for his outspoken criticism of the CJEU when dealing with IP matters, has taken the opportunity to comment in a plain and direct manner on the headnote of *Eli Lilly* in his anecdotal review of important IP cases 'IP and Other Things: A Collection of Essays and Speeches', concluding that, 'This is close to gibberish.'[14]

While the above-mentioned rulings of the CJEU may not inspire the greatest confidence, one has to bear in mind that the core of the problem is not so much the unclear guidance provided by the CJEU, but rather the SPC legislation itself. Its ambiguous wording has given rise to substantial uncertainty, necessitating the flood of referrals. As evidenced by the diverging positions adopted by the specialized national courts in relation to the Article 3(a) issue of the SPC Regulations, they too had substantial irresolvable struggles in determining which test should be applied in order to determine whether 'a product is protected by a basic patent in force' within the meaning of Article 3(a) of the SPC Regulation.

---

13. High Court of Justice *Teva v. Gilead* [2017] EWHC 13 (Pat) of 13 January 2017, paragraph 81:

> I am bound to say that, in this passage, the Court of Justice has once again failed to give national authorities clear guidance as to the proper interpretation of Article 3(a). Although the Court does clearly state that Article 3(a) does not preclude a product being protected by a basic patent by virtue of a functional definition, it then says that this is only permitted where the claims 'relate, implicitly but necessarily and specifically' to the product in question. What does this mean? How are national authorities supposed to apply this test? The Court does not explain. All that can be said with confidence is that, once again, the Court appears to be suggesting that something more is required than the product falls within the scope of the basic patent applying the Extent of Protection Rules, but without making it clear what more.

14. R. Jacob, *IP and Other Things* (Hart Publishing, ISBN-10: 1849465959).

Moreover, the as yet unresolved practical concerns with regard to the SPC Regulation are not limited to the Article 3(a) issue.

There are various further fundamental concerns in relation to the SPC Regulations, some of which have already been extensively debated in the case law and literature. For example, extensive problems have arisen in relation to the requirement set out in Article 3(d) of the SPC Regulation, i.e., that the marketing authorization supporting an SPC filing must be the first one 'to place the product on the market as a medicinal product'.

As set out in paragraph 28 of the Explanatory Memorandum[15] of the SPC Regulation, it was the legislators' express intention to provide supplementary protection for all pharmaceutical research without discrimination, 'whether it concerns a new product, a new process for obtaining a known product, a new application of a new or known product or a new combination of substances containing new or known products.' (To a certain extent, this is also reflected in Article 1(b) of the SPC Regulation).

By virtue of the requirement of Article 3(d) of the SPC Regulation, this objective can in practice hardly ever be achieved based on a literal interpretation of this provision.

For example, in accordance with the long standing case law of the CJEU (*Pharmacia* (C-31/03),[16] *MIT* (C-431/04),[17] *Yissum* (C-202/05),[18] *Synthon* (C-195/09)[19] and *Synaptech* (C-427/09)[20]), an SPC is precluded where the active ingredient in question had previously been authorized in an earlier marketing authorization within the EU, be it in form of a different formulation, for use in a different species, or for use in a different indication.

It is widely recognized that second medical use inventions may be of great importance, and their patentability under the EPC is well established.[21] Moreover, in the EPC 2000, the patentability of first and second medical use inventions has been codified on a par, as evidenced by Article 54(4) and 54(5) EPC 2000.

The inequity of the SPC system has resulted in considerable frustration. It in effect only rewards first medical use inventions with supplemental protection, rather than being indiscriminately applicable to all medical research leading towards the development of a new medicinal product or new application thereof.

15. COM(90) 101 final.
16. CJEU *Pharmacia Italia v. Bundesgerichtshof*, C-31/03 of 19 October 2004.
17. CJEU *Massachusetts Institute of Technology v. Bundesgerichtshof*, C-431/04 of 4 May 2006.
18. CJEU *Yissum Research and Development Company of the Hebrew University of Jerusalem v. Comptroller-General of Patents*, C-202/05 of 17 April 2007.
19. CJEU *Synthon v. Merz Pharma*, C-195/09 of 28 July 2011.
20. CJEU *Generics (UK) v. Synaptech*, C-427/09 of 28 July 2011.
21. Enlarged Board of Appeal of the EPO, decision G 5/83 (*Eisai*) of 5 December 1984 and decision G 2/08 (*Dosage regime/Abbott*) of 19 February 2010.

In light of the above considerations, it is not surprising that the SPC Regulation has been described as being in a 'dysfunctional state'[22] and 'not fit for purpose'.[23]

The highly controversial decision *Neurim*,[24] where the CJEU adopted a teleological approach in interpreting Article 3(d) of the SPC Regulation and bravely departed from its previous established case law, may have solved some of these issues. In this case, the Court concluded that the prior approval of the product as a veterinary medicinal product was not detrimental for the issue of an SPC for the same product for a different application.

Nevertheless, the CJEU in *Neurim*, in departing from the previous case law, gave rise to many further questions, particularly in terms of the scope of the principles discussed in *Neurim*, and has warranted further referrals to the CJEU.[25]

Thus, it will still take quite some time until all of these uncertainties are resolved.

The dysfunctional state of the SPC system is not limited to the unresolved issues discussed above, i.e., the product definition and its alignment with Article 3(a) and (b) of the SPC Regulation, and the issues relating to the first approval on the market as set out in Article 3(d). Multiple other issues also require clarification. One of these issues is the entitlement to an SPC.

While Article 6 of the SPC Regulation stipulates that an SPC shall be granted to the holder of the basic patent or his successor in title, Article 3(2) of Regulation (EC) 1610/96 for Plant Protection Products (which by virtue of recital 17 is also applicable to the SPC Regulation for Medicinal Products) provides that a specific holder of a patent is only entitled to one SPC per product. On the other hand, in case of multiple holders of different patents, multiple SPCs may issue.

The problems which may arise based on the provisions of Article 3(2) of the SPC Regulation are manifold.

22. Patents Court *GlaxoSmithKline Biologicals SA v. Comptroller-General*, [2013] EWHC 619 (Pat) of 21 March 2013, paragraph 86:

> Finally, I would observe that this is the third time in six months that I have had to refer questions of interpretation of the SPC Regulation to the CJEU. I do so with considerable regret. That this should be necessary demonstrates the dysfunctional state of the SPC system at present. This is primarily due to the poor drafting of the SPC Regulation and to the failure of the European Commission, Council and Parliament to revise it to address the problems which have emerged. Matters have not been assisted, however, by the fact that the Court of Justice's recent case law interpreting the SPC Regulation has not provided the level of clarity and consistency that is required.

23. High Court *Neurim Pharmaceuticals v. Comptroller-General*, [2010] EWHC 976 (Pat) of 6 May 2010, paragraph 30:

> In short, if Neurim are wrong, then the Regulation will not have achieved its key objects for large areas of pharmaceutical research: it will not be fit for purpose. Whether that is so or not is clearly a matter for the EU's highest court.

24. CJEU *Neurim Pharmaceuticals v. Comptroller-General of Patents*, C-130/11 of 19 July 2012.
25. CJEU *Glaxosmithkline Biologicals v. Comptroller-General of Patents, Designs and Trade Marks*, C-210/13 of 14 November 2013 and CJEU *Abraxis Bioscience v. Comptroller General of Patents*, C-443/17, referral of 24 July 2017.

For one, the entitlement to an SPC is not in any way tied to the holder of the marketing approval.

As a consequence of Article 3(2), it has become established practice to issue an SPC for an approved product based on a third party patent as set out in *Biogen* (C-181/95).[26]

In the *Biogen* case, Biogen (the 'third party') had licensed the patent in question to SKB, the holder of the marketing approval. The corresponding technology by Biogen thus contributed to the launch of the medicinal product forming the basis of the SPC, so that one can see some justification in the issue of a separate SPC to the third party.

It is, however, conceivable that the holder of a basic patent may have no relationship whatsoever with the holder of the marketing approval, and its technology may not have in any way contributed to the development of the product.

Theoretically, such a third party could nevertheless apply for an SPC for a product X covered by its patent. The SPC could then be enforced by the third party and prevent the holder of the marketing authorization for product X from marketing this product.[27]

Quite clearly, such a scenario would be completely contrary to the very aim of the SPC Regulation, and it is likely that this issue will need to be resolved by a higher instance court.

Another problem that springs to mind when considering Article 3(2) of the SPC Regulation is that the provision – one SPC per patent per applicant – may, of course, be readily circumvented by transferring the patent to an affiliated entity.

From a patent perspective, such practice is perfectly legitimate and not uncommon. Neither the fact that the holders of the basic patents may belong to the same corporate group nor the degree of affiliation will generally be considered during the prosecution of an SPC. Such a pragmatic approach facilitates legal certainty, as there would not appear to be any justifiable criteria to quantify the degree of affiliation which could be considered acceptable. Moreover, the national patent offices are not in a position to lift the 'cooperate veil' in order to determine any potential affiliation. Accordingly, such considerations will and must be ignored during prosecution when multiple SPCs for a single product are granted to multiple applicants.

In line with this, the presiding judge of the Higher Regional Court of Düsseldorf, Dr T. Kühnen[28] concludes that:

> Since Article 3 (2) is intended to prevent more than one (granted) protection certificate for the same active ingredient being in the hands of one person, a change in the ownership relationships for the basic patent that takes effect by the time of the decision on the grant of the protection certificate must be taken into account.

26. CJEU *Biogen v. SmithKlineBeecham Biologicals*, C-181/95 of 23 January 1997.
27. *See*, e.g., Düsseldorf District Court (Landgericht Düsseldorf), judgment 4a O 143/10 of 10 November 2011 – Ranibizumab, and High Court *Eli Lilly v. HGS* [2012] EWHC 2290 (Pat) of 3 August 2012.
28. Thomas Kühnen: Die Erteilung mehrerer ergänzender Schutzzertifikate für dasselbe Erzeugnis an unterschiedliche Inhaber und die Konsequenzen bei einer Verfolgung von Rechtsverletzungen. Published in: Bender, Schülke, Winterfeldt (eds): Festschrift 50 Jahre Bundespatentgericht, Carl Heymanns Verlag, 2011, ISBN: 9783452275264, pages 361–378.

If originally the same holder has a number of basic patents, with the result that Article 3(2) excludes the grant of multiple protection certificates, the obstacle to the grant ceases to apply if subsequently one of the patents changes the holder before the time of the decision concerning the grant.

Moreover, in his view, even if in a situation where the holders of the basic patents, while being separate legal entities, belong to the same enterprises, the requirement of 'different applicants' in accordance with Article 3(2) of the SPC Regulation should not be an issue. Thus, even controlling relationships that give one basic patent holder a certain influence over the enterprise of the other, or even the fact that all the shares of the holder of the basic patent are held by a second holder of a basic patent, do not generally imply that the persons are not different.

Such a formal approach is also supported by the argument that the parties are in any event at liberty to assign one or more SPCs for the same product immediately after they have been granted. In this way, an applicant can legally acquire possession of a number of SPCs.

This again demonstrates that the current SPC system is dysfunctional in this regard, offering loopholes to circumvent the provisions of Article 3(2).

The above analysis describes just some of the practical problems which practitioners regularly encounter with the SPC regime.

Most, if not all, of these problems should have been foreseeable at the time this enormously important piece of legislation was drafted and, as such, should have been originally considered.

In order to facilitate a better understanding as to why the SPC Regulation for Medicinal Products was called to life (and in analogy the descendant SPC Regulation for Plant Protection Products), with all its apparent deficits, it may be helpful to consider the social-political circumstances within which the SPC system was introduced in the early 1990s.

[B] The Making of the Regulation (EEC) 1768/92

The passing of the SPC legislation was contentious and in no way straightforward.

The legislative process for the introduction of the SPC system for medicinal products was initiated by well-concerted lobbying by the research-based pharmaceutical industry.

In 1988 the European Federation of the Pharmaceutical Industry Association (EFPIA) published a memorandum,[29] pointing out that in light of the increasing costs associated with the R&D and regulatory approval processes, coupled with the ever-decreasing effective patent term, the returns for new medicinal products were insufficient to warrant their development. As a result, the number of new chemical entities being developed and brought to market as a medicinal product was diminishing.

29. Memorandum on the Necessity to restore the effective duration of patents for pharmaceutical products and Explanatory Memorandum COM(90) 101 final.

Moreover, other countries such as the US (1984)[30] and Japan (1988)[31] had already introduced measures to provide for extended patent protection for pharmaceuticals, thereby compromising European competitiveness and its hitherto global dominance in this sector.

The Commission was initially reluctant to support the industry in its call for patent term restoration. In this context, it was also recognized that an amendment of the European Patent Convention (EPC), in order to provide for patent term extension was problematic. The main obstacle was considered to be the revision mechanism of the Munich Convention (*see* Article 172 EPC), according to which the EPC can be amended only if the revised text is approved by three quarters of the contracting states. At the time, more than a quarter of the signatory countries of the Convention were not Community Member States. In light of the very different interests of the EPC contracting states and the potential implications of such measures on domestic health care budgets, it was quite clear that providing for patent term extension via amendment of the EPC would be a very difficult and time-consuming endeavour.

In light of the foreseeable delay in political decision-making at the Community level, France began parliamentary work that eventually led to the unilateral introduction of a national supplementary protection regime (Certificat Complémentaire de Protection),[32] providing for up to seven years of additional protection beyond the twenty-year patent term, which, however, should not exceed seventeen years after the approval of the drug. Italy followed suit,[33] providing up to eighteen years of additional protection beyond the twenty-year patent term.

Bearing in mind that the creation of the single European market by 1992 was a central goal in all Community affairs, the Commission, faced with the risk of heterogeneous development in proprietary protection in this sensitive sector, was under pressure to resolve this issue on a Community-wide level as quickly as possible.

Upon invitation by the Commission in May 1989 the EFPIA submitted a draft directive for a Community legislation for complementary protection for medicinal products for the Commission's consideration, largely based on the French model. However, upon reconsideration the Commission concluded that a directive might not be the most appropriate legal instrument, as the provisions of a directive would first have to be implemented into national law. As such, it would result in further delays in harmonization. Rather, the Commission decided that a Community regulation, having an immediate, uniform and binding effect across the Community would be more appropriate.

30. The 1984 Drug Price Competition and Patent Term Restoration Act (also known as the 'Hatch-Waxman Act').
31. 1988 Patent Law Amendment for Patent Term Restoration.
32. French Law No. 510 (enacted 21 November 1991).
33. Italian Law No. 349/91 (enacted October 1991).

[C] The Commission Proposal

Thus, in April 1990 the Commission made a public proposal for a Council Regulation concerning the creation of a Supplementary Protection Certificate for medicinal products along with an Explanatory Memorandum.[34] The Commission proposal deviated from that of the EFPIA proposal substantively in that it envisaged sixteen years of effective proprietary protection for medicinal products (rather than the twenty years propagated by the pharmaceutical industry).

A further major derogation from the EFPIA draft was that the Commission introduced the requirement that supplemental protection should only be available on the basis of the first approval of the product,[35] thereby de facto precluding any extended protection for second medical use inventions.

As outlined in the Explanatory Memorandum[36] in accordance with the Commission's draft, the SPC had been conceived as a sui generis intellectual property right, sandwiched between two very different administrative procedures – regulatory approval and patent law – which due to their very nature, their aims and approaches in many instances apply different concepts and definitions to certain terms.

This becomes particularly evident if one considers the concept of the definition of the terms 'product' or 'applicant' in these administrative procedures.

For example, in relation to regulatory directives for medicinal products, the notion of a 'global marketing authorization' has been introduced. Thus, Article 6(1) of Directive 2001/83/EC[37] provides that when a medicinal product has been granted an initial marketing authorization, any additional strengths, pharmaceutical forms, administration routes, presentations, as well as any variations (including new indications) to the initial marketing authorization are considered to belong to the same global marketing authorization. Thus, here, the concept of the product is very broad: it encompasses the active ingredient per se, irrespective of any pharmaceutical modifications in terms of, e.g., salt or formulation.

However, in case of patents, a much narrower concept is applied. Modifications such as a new salt, formulation or new indication of the same active ingredient may be subject matter of distinct patents.

Likewise, there are fundamental differences applied in terms of the concept of the 'applicant' or 'holder' of the marketing authorization on the one hand and the 'applicant' or 'holder' of a patent or SPC on the other hand.

Thus, as set out in the Notice to Applicants[38] for the purpose of the application of the pharmaceuticals rules, having a distinct legal personality does not necessarily entail that each entity can be considered as a distinct applicant or marketing authorization holder. Therefore, not only are applicants and marketing authorization holders

34. EEC COM(90) 101 def-syn proposal.
35. *Ibid.* Part Two: Examination of the provisions, paragraph 37.
36. *Ibid.* B. Details and characteristics of the proposed system.
37. Directive 2001/83/EC of the European Parliament and of the Council of 6 November 2001 on the Community code relating to medicinal products for human use.
38. European Commission, Notice to Applicants (Revision 7) Volume 'Procedures for marketing authorisation', Chapter 1 Marketing Authorisation, Section 2.8.

belonging to the same company group (or controlled by the same physical or legal entity) to be considered as one entity, but also other applicants and marketing authorization holders are to be included if they have entered into tacit or explicit agreements concerning the marketing of the same medicinal product for the purposes of the application of the pharmaceuticals rules regarding that medicinal product. This not only includes cases of joint marketing, but also cases where one party licenses to the other party the right to market the same medicinal product.

From a patent perspective the 'applicant' or 'holder' of a patent is construed most narrowly and is limited to the distinct legal entity.[39]

A new intellectual property right positioned somewhere between regulatory matters and patents thus inherently bears the risk that unless it is very carefully drafted, taking all perspectives into consideration, in practice it may give rise to ambiguities, uncertainties and pitfalls.

In the Explanatory Memorandum,[40] the Commission emphasized that in relation to the concept of 'the product' of an SPC in its draft regulation, it chose to rely on the corresponding definition provided in regulatory directives, i.e., the product definition as laid out in Directive 65/65/EEC.[41]

However, on closer scrutiny, it appears that the SPC Regulation was predominantly drafted from the regulator's perspective and that considerations in light of patent law and practice were secondary.

This becomes evident if one closely considers the Explanatory Memorandum and the proposed provisions, such as for example Article 6 'Application for a Certificate', defining the time limits for filing an SPC.[42]

According to this article, an SPC should be filed either within six months of the date of the grant of the authorization, or if the authorization issues before the patent, within six months of 'the date on which the patent is granted'.

The terminology chosen in Article 6(2) of the draft regulation (now Article 7 of the SPC Regulation) is clearly not based on any consideration of the EPC (or the national patent laws), which differentiates between the 'date of the decision to grant a patent' and the 'date of publication of the patent grant', the latter of which may be several months after the former: It is thus prima facie unclear which one of these dates is to apply.

[D] The Adoption of the Regulation

Until this time the Commission and the EFPIA had been working behind closed doors.[43] Thus, it was only at this stage that a public consultation began. In spite of heated

39. *See*, e.g., Boards of Appeal of the EPO, decision T 5/05 of 9 November 2005, point 4.3 of the reasons and decision T 1423/07 of 19 April 2010, point 2.4 of the reasons.
40. EEC COM(90) 101 def-syn proposal, Part Two: Examination of the provisions, paragraph 28.
41. Council Directive 65/65/EEC of 26 January 1965 on the approximation of provisions laid down by Law, Regulation or Administrative Action relating to proprietary medicinal products.
42. *Ibid*. Art. 6. Application for a certificate.
43. G. Permanand, *EU Pharmaceutical Regulation – The politics of the policy-making* (Manchester University press), pp. 131 et seq.

debates and declared opponents to the proposal, the Commission adopted a compromise after consideration of the favourable opinion by the Economic and Social Committee (a Community consultative body),[44] essentially endorsing the proposal. The only substantive changes concerned the period of total effective protection. It established an SPC term of five years maximum and an overall maximum period of exclusivity, resulting from the basic patent and the SPC, of no longer than fifteen years from the first marketing authorization.

The amended draft was then circulated with a broader audience, including the generic industry and national governments. The stakeholders involved appear to have been predominantly concerned with national health budgets and the reconciliation of this legislation with Article 63 EPC, rather than with any substantive, practical issues.

The potential conflicts with Article 63 EPC were resolved by unanimous decision in the diplomatic conference for the revision of the EPC of December 1991. Thus, it was agreed that any EPC contracting state could extend the term of a European patent, if the product in question will have to undergo an administrative authorization procedure prior to marketing.[45]

Once this hurdle was overcome, the European Parliament approved the legislation on the second reading, subject to the introduction of the differential implementation dates (countries which had opposed the legislation outright: Greece, Portugal and Spain) as well as differential transitional periods for the retroactive effect based on the date of the first authorization of the product.

Thus, on 18 June 1992 the EC Council of Ministers adopted the Council Regulation (EEC) No. 1768/92 concerning the creation of a Supplementary Protection Certificate (EEC), without any apparent major public consultation or contentious discussion about its substantive provisions.

The review of the historical development leading to the entry into force of the SPC Regulation for Medicinal Products clearly indicates that the SPC Regulation was enacted in view of the evident needs of the pharmaceutical industry, coupled with the desire to have a harmonized solution on the Community level within a short time frame, and in face of national initiatives by France and Italy to introduce corresponding regulation.

While the passing of the Community legislation may not have been easy, it would appear that the resistance and criticism to this legislation in the course of its drafting focused on issues such as national health budgets and its compatibility with the EPC.

The substantive issues relating to the proper functioning of the Regulation do not appear to have been subject to much public consultation with expert circles, in particular from the patent side, which may account for the problems we are now encountering.

It is comforting to note that there appears to be an increasing tendency for the CJEU to apply a more practical, teleological approach when interpreting the SPC Regulation to meet the industry's and public's needs. Nevertheless, the problems

44. Economic and Social Committee Opinion 91/C96/06, OJEU vol. 34 (1991), p. 22.
45. *See* Art. 63 EPC as amended by the Act revising Art. 63 EPC of 17 December 1991 (OJ EPO 1992).

encountered raise fundamental questions as to whether this legislation, covering this enormously important area of law, should be revised and modernized.

II FUTURE PERSPECTIVE: IS THERE A SILVER LINING?

The idea for a Community patent system with harmonized pan-European rules on substantive patent law, so that a patent may be obtained, maintained and enforced in the form of a single legal title had already been conceived in the 1970s when the EPC was originally enacted, but was then left dormant for decades.

It was abruptly reanimated in 2011 in the wake of a political and legislative initiative that resulted in the birth of the Unitary Patent package, consisting of two EU regulations creating a European patent with unitary effect ('unitary patent') and an international agreement between the corresponding EU Member States, i.e., the Agreement on a Unified Patent Court (UPCA).

Under the terms of the UPCA, SPCs referencing a European patent - with or without unitary effect - as a basic patent should be subject to the exclusive jurisdiction of the UPC for most types of actions.[46]

In October 2015, the Commission in its single market strategic paper[47] addressed the possibility of introducing a unitary SPC title within the framework of the Unitary Patent package and indicated that it will explore a recalibration of certain aspects of patent and SPC protection. It thus initiated a tender project to review the SPC regime in June 2016. As there were only few bidders, the tender was relaunched in December 2016.

The EU Commission also launched a consultation on SPCs and Patent Research Exemptions, the consultation period running from 12 October 2017 to 4 January 2018.

In the light of the above, it is clear that the Commission is considering a major reform of the SPC system. While the focus in the tender and consultation has been the concept of the creation of a unitary European SPC title, the introduction of an SPC manufacturing waiver and an update on the scope of EU patent research exemptions, it will also include a general review of the SPC regime.

In light of the heightened awareness of the problems associated with the current SPC regime, one can expect that in the course of the legislative preparations and public consultations, the new regime will finally address these problems.

At the moment however, the Unitary Patent package appears to have been sent back to hibernation, due to the constitutional complaint[48] filed against the legislation in Germany. In order for the UPC system to come into force, it is however mandatory that Germany, the UK and France have ratified the agreement. So far only France and the UK have done so. To complicate matters further, the UK is on track to leave the EU in March 2019. In order for the UPC in its current version, with the participation of the UK to come into force, the outstanding issues will have to be resolved very quickly. In light

46. *See* Arts 3(b) and 32 UPCA.
47. Upgrading the single market: more opportunities people and business; COM(2015) 550 final of 28 October 2015.
48. Case Reference 2 BvR 739/17.

of the past track record of the speed of grinding of the mills of justice of the German Federal Constitutional Court, it is highly questionable that this will be the case.

Nevertheless, independent from the legislative framework of the Unitary Patent package, there appear to be ongoing discussions by experts from national patent offices from the EU Member States in relation to potential Guidelines for the Examination of SPCs, applicable on the EU level, with the aim of resolving and harmonizing many of the contentious issues which were encountered in the past.

On 28 May 2018, the European Commission published its proposal to amend Regulation (EC) 469/2009 on SPCs for Medicinal Products.[49]

The proposed amendments, however, only focus on the introduction of a manufacturing waiver, to allow manufacturers of generics and biosimilars to manufacture certain pharmaceuticals for export outside the EU during the SPC term.

Thus, in line with the proposal, Article 4 of the SPC Regulation for Medicinal Products will be supplemented with subparagraphs 2–5, exempting from SPC protection, the manufacture of a product covered by a marketing authorization for the exclusive purpose of export of that product outside of the EU and any related strictly necessary act.

The proposal emphasizes the need for transparency and as such requires that the person making the product for the exclusive purpose of export must provide the patent office in the Member State in question with a corresponding twenty-eight day prior notification.

Moreover, according to the proposal, the manufacturing waiver provisions will be applicable to any SPCs granted on or after a specified date after the entry into force of the proposed amendments of the SPC Regulation.

The proposal also stipulates that the manufacturing waiver shall be evaluated by the Commission every five years as set out in Article 21a of the proposed amended SPC Regulation.

The proposal does not address any of the highlighted problems with the SPC regime. Nevertheless, the final report of the study on the legal aspects of SPCs prepared by the Max Planck Institute for Innovation and Competition (accessible online as of 28 May 2018),[50] which critically reviews the SPC system, is of interest in this regard. The review provides a concluding chapter entitled 'Summary and Recommendations' where many of these problematic issues associated with the SPC regime highlighted in this book have been specifically addressed.

It would thus appear likely that the Commission will take account of these considerations in relation to any further amendments to the current SPC legislation or any future legislation for SPCs with unitary effect.

49. European Commission, Proposal for a Regulation of the European Parliament and of the Council amending Regulation (EC) 469/2009 concerning the supplementary protection certificate for medicinal products, COM(2018) 317 final.
50. European Commission. Study on the Legal Aspects of Supplementary Protection Certificates in the EU – Final Report. ISBN: 978-92-79-67756-4. Published in May 2018.

CHAPTER 1

European Union: General Considerations and Case Law of the CJEU and the EFTA Court

Alexa von Uexküll & Oswin Ridderbusch

§1.01 LEGAL BASIS

The EU Member States

The legal basis for SPCs in the European Union is provided primarily by two Regulations, i.e., Regulation (EC) 469/2009[1] (the 'SPC Regulation for Medicinal Products') and Regulation (EC) 1610/96[2] (the 'SPC Regulation for Plant Protection Products'). Further relevant provisions regarding the paediatric extension of SPCs for medicinal products are provided in Regulation (EC) 1901/2006[3] (the 'Paediatric Regulation'). All these Regulations are directly applicable in all EU Member States without requiring transposition into national law.[4]

The current SPC Regulation for Medicinal Products, i.e., Regulation (EC) 469/2009, was preceded by Regulation (EEC) 1768/92[5] (the 'original SPC Regulation for Medicinal Products') which entered into force on 2 January 1993 and has since been

1. Regulation (EC) No. 469/2009 of the European Parliament and of the Council of 6 May 2009 concerning the supplementary protection certificate for medicinal products.
2. Regulation (EC) No. 1610/96 of the European Parliament and of the Council of 23 July 1996 concerning the creation of a supplementary protection certificate for plant protection products.
3. Regulation (EC) No. 1901/2006 of the European Parliament and of the Council of 12 December 2006 on medicinal products for paediatric use and amending Regulation (EEC) No. 1768/92, Directive 2001/20/EC, Directive 2001/83/EC and Regulation (EC) No. 726/2004.
4. Article 288 of the Treaty on the Functioning of the European Union (TFEU). *See also* the summary document 'The direct effect of European law' (EUR-Lex L14547).
5. Council Regulation (EEC) No. 1768/92 of 18 June 1992 concerning the creation of a supplementary protection certificate for medicinal products.

repealed. The legality of its adoption was confirmed by the CJEU in *Spain v. Council* (C-350/92).[6]

The subsequently enacted SPC Regulation for Plant Protection Products, which entered into force on 8 February 1997, is largely identical to the original SPC Regulation for Medicinal Products. However, apart from the differences owing to its focus on plant protection products rather than medicinal products, the SPC Regulation for Plant Protection Products features several notable additions and modifications to the corresponding provisions contained in the original SPC Regulation for Medicinal Products, such as Article 3(2) relating to the grant of more than one SPC for the same product, and Article 17(2) directed to appeals aimed at rectifying the SPC term. The European legislator did not incorporate these same additions and modifications directly into the SPC Regulation for Medicinal Products, but instead chose a rather unusual approach by prescribing in recital 17 of the SPC Regulation for Plant Protection Products that the 'detailed rules' in certain recitals and Articles of this Regulation, reflecting the aforementioned additions and modifications, are also valid for the interpretation of the original SPC Regulation for Medicinal Products.[7] The applicability of the respective provisions of the SPC Regulation for Plant Protection Products to the SPC Regulation for Medicinal Products, via recital 17 of the former, has also been endorsed by the CJEU.[8]

The Paediatric Regulation, i.e., Regulation (EC) 1901/2006, entered into force on 26 January 2007 and amended the original SPC Regulation for Medicinal Products to provide for a possible six-month extension of the SPC term.

The accession of the ten new Member States[9] to the EU on 1 May 2004 as well as the subsequent accession of Bulgaria and Romania on 1 January 2007 prompted further amendments to both the SPC Regulation for Medicinal Products and the SPC Regulation for Plant Protection Products.

Following these successive amendments, a codified version of the original SPC Regulation for Medicinal Products was adopted as Regulation (EC) 469/2009 and came into force on 6 July 2009. This new Regulation does not contain any substantive changes but merely consolidates and codifies the amendments previously made to the

---

6. CJEU *Kingdom of Spain v. Council of the European Union*, C-350/92 of 13 July 1995.
7. Recital 17 of Regulation (EC) No. 1610/96 provides that:

> Whereas the detailed rules in recitals 12, 13 and 14 and in Articles 3 (2), 4, 8 (1) (c) and 17 (2) of this Regulation are also valid, mutatis mutandis, for the interpretation in particular of recital 9 and Articles 3, 4, 8 (1) (c) and 17 of Council Regulation (EEC) No. 1768/92.

8. CJEU *Farmitalia Carlo Erba v. Bundesgerichtshof*, C-392/97 of 16 September 1999, paragraph 20; CJEU *Massachusetts Institute of Technology v. Bundesgerichtshof*, C-431/04 of 4 May 2006, paragraph 24; and CJEU *AHP Manufacturing v. Bureau voor de Industriële Eigendom*, C-482/07 of 3 September 2009, paragraph 23.
9. The ten new Member States that joined the EU on 1 May 2004 are Cyprus, the Czech Republic, Estonia, Hungary, Latvia, Lithuania, Malta, Poland, Slovakia, and Slovenia.

original SPC Regulation for Medicinal Products, in the interests of clarity and transparency,[10] and omits the meanwhile obsolete transitional provisions of Article 3(b) second sentence, Articles 19 and 21 as well as the corresponding recitals 10–12 of the original SPC Regulation. The 'detailed rules' referred to in recital 17 of the SPC Regulation for Plant Protection Products have still not been incorporated directly into the SPC Regulation for Medicinal Products on this occasion, which may be explained by the fact that codification of EU legislative acts follows a simplified legislative procedure and does generally not allow any changes of substance to be made.[11] Recital 17 of the SPC Regulation for Plant Protection Products therefore continues to apply to the current (codified) SPC Regulation for Medicinal Products,[12] which has also been expressly confirmed by the CJEU.[13]

Since the accession of Croatia to the EU on 1 July 2013, the two SPC Regulations have again been amended by introducing transitional and other provisions relating specifically to this state.[14]

On 28 May 2018, the European Commission issued a proposal[15] for a further amendment to the SPC Regulation for Medicinal Products, which will introduce a manufacturing waiver for the export to non-EU/EEA countries and is currently going through the legislative process.

The EEA States

The European Economic Area (EEA) is established by the EEA Agreement between the EU Member States[16] and the EEA-EFTA states Iceland, Liechtenstein and Norway (the EFTA state Switzerland, in contrast, is not an EEA Member State). EU legislative acts

10. *See* recital 1 of Regulation (EC) 469/2009; Explanatory Memorandum to the Commission proposal for a codified version of the SPC regulation for medicinal products, COM(2008) 369 final, paragraph 4; and CJEU *F. Hoffmann-La Roche v. Accord Healthcare*, C-572/15 of 5 October 2016, paragraph 32.
11. Codification of EU legislative acts is based on the Interinstitutional Agreement of 20 December 1994: Accelerated working method for official codification of legislative texts (96/C 102/02). *See also* the Explanatory Memorandum to the Commission proposal for a codified version of the SPC regulation for medicinal products, COM(2008) 369 final, paragraph 3.
12. *See* recital 1 as well as Art. 22 and Annex II of Regulation (EC) 469/2009.
13. CJEU *Incyte Corporation v. Szellemi Tulajdon Nemzeti Hivatala*, C-492/16 of 20 December 2017, paragraphs 33–34.
14. *See* Arts 20(m) and 21(2) of Regulation (EC) 469/2009, and Arts 19a(m) and 20(2) of Regulation (EC) 1610/96.
15. European Commission, Proposal for a Regulation of the European Parliament and of the Council amending Regulation (EC) 469/2009 concerning the supplementary protection certificate for medicinal products, COM(2018) 317 final.
16. Note that new EU Member States do not automatically accede to the EEA Agreement but are obliged to apply for EEA membership. Specifically, Art. 128 of the EEA Agreement stipulates that any European state becoming a member of the EU shall, while Switzerland and any European state becoming a member of EFTA may, apply to become a party to the EEA Agreement. Croatia, for example, joined the EU on 1 July 2013 and signed its accession to the EEA on 11 April 2014, whereby the EEA Agreement has become provisionally applicable to Croatia, pending ratification by all EEA Member States and the EU.

with EEA relevance are continuously incorporated into the EEA Agreement by means of decisions of the EEA Joint Committee, which enter into force once the applicable constitutional requirements in all the EEA-EFTA states, such as approval by parliament or by referendum, have been fulfilled.[17]

The original SPC Regulation for Medicinal Products, i.e., Regulation (EEC) 1768/92, entered into force in the EEA-EFTA states on 1 July 1994, following its incorporation into the EEA Agreement by EEA Joint Committee Decision 7/94 of 21 March 1994.

The SPC Regulation for Plant Protection Products, i.e., Regulation (EC) 1610/96, was subsequently incorporated into the EEA Agreement with EEA Joint Committee Decision 59/97 of 31 July 1997 and entered into force in the EEA-EFTA states on 1 April 1998.

The current (codified) SPC Regulation for Medicinal Products, i.e., Regulation (EC) 469/2009, as well as the Paediatric Regulation, i.e., Regulation (EC) 1901/2006, were finally incorporated into the EEA Agreement with the EEA Joint Committee Decision 92/2017 of 5 May 2017 and entered into force in the EEA-EFTA states on 1 June 2018. The original SPC Regulation for Medicinal Products was thereby repealed under the EEA Agreement.

In view of the patent union between Switzerland and Liechtenstein,[18] the above-mentioned EEA Joint Committee decisions incorporating the current SPC Regulation for Medicinal Products and the SPC Regulation for Plant Protection Products into the EEA Agreement provide that Liechtenstein shall not deliver any SPCs for medicinal products or plant protection products. SPCs granted by Switzerland will instead be effective in Liechtenstein.

Non-EU/EEA States

SPCs are also available under the respective national law in other European states which are not members of the EU or the EEA, particularly in Switzerland (and thereby in Liechtenstein[19]), in the EU candidate or potential candidate countries Albania, Bosnia and Herzegovina, Macedonia, and Serbia, as well as in Armenia, Azerbaijan, Belarus, Georgia, Moldova, Russia, and Ukraine.

17. *See* Arts 97–104 of the EEA Agreement; 'How EU acts become EEA acts and the need for adaptations', Note by Subcommittee V on Legal and Institutional Affairs of 23 May 2013, Ref. 1113623; and 'The Basic Features of the EEA Agreement', Note by Subcommittee V on Legal and Institutional Affairs of 1 July 2013, Ref. 1112099. Information regarding the incorporation of specific EU legislative acts into the EEA Agreement can be found on EEA-Lex (www.efta.int/eea-lex).
18. Treaty between the Swiss Confederation and the Principality of Liechtenstein on Patent Protection (Patent Treaty) of 22 December 1978.
19. Due to the patent union between Switzerland and Liechtenstein, Swiss SPCs are also effective in Liechtenstein.

§1.02 SUBSTANTIVE REQUIREMENTS FOR OBTAINING AN SPC

[A] Types of Products That Can Be Protected

While Article 1 of the SPC Regulations distinguishes between a 'medicinal product' or 'plant protection product' on the one hand and a 'product' on the other hand,[20] SPCs are granted for a 'product'.[21] This term is defined in the SPC Regulations as 'the active ingredient or combination of active ingredients of a medicinal product',[22] and as 'the active substance ... or combination of active substances of a plant protection product',[23] respectively. In the following it will be discussed which types of products can, in principal, be protected by SPCs.

[1] Practical Considerations: What Is the Active Ingredient or Combination of Active Ingredients That Can Form the Basis for an SPC

The Explanatory Memorandums of both SPC Regulations expressly emphasize that the term 'product' is to be construed on the basis of the corresponding definition provided in the regulatory provisions. Thus, in the Explanatory Memorandum for Medicinal Products,[24] reference is made to regulatory Directive 65/65/EEC (now repealed by Directive 2001/83/EC and Directive 2001/82/EC), while in the Explanatory Memorandum for Plant Protection Products,[25] reference is made to Directive 91/414/EEC (now repealed by Regulation (EC) 1107/2009).

In the case of the SPC Regulation for Medicinal Products, the respective definitions provided in Article 1(a) of the SPC Regulation substantially overlap with the definitions applied in the corresponding regulatory provisions in terms of the active ingredient(s) of a medicinal product.

Thus, from a regulatory perspective, an active ingredient is '[a]ny substance or mixture of substances intended to be used in the manufacture of a medicinal product and that, when used in its production, becomes an active ingredient of that product intended to exert a pharmacological, immunological or metabolic action with a view to restoring, correcting or modifying physiological functions or to make a medical diagnosis'.[26]

Moreover, in accordance with the harmonized rules governing medicinal products in Europe, the qualitative composition in terms of the active substance(s) must be

20. Article 1(a) and 1(b) of Regulation (EC) 469/2009, and Art. 1(1) and 1(8) of Regulation (EC) 1610/96.
21. Article 2 of Regulation (EC) 469/2009, and Art. 2 of Regulation (EC) 1610/96.
22. Article 1(b) of Regulation (EC) 469/2009.
23. Article 1(8) of Regulation (EC) 1610/96.
24. Explanatory Memorandum to the Commission proposal for an SPC regulation for medicinal products, COM(90) 101 final – SYN 255, paragraph 28.
25. Explanatory Memorandum to the Commission proposal for an SPC regulation for plant protection products, COM(94) 579 final, paragraph 66.
26. Article 1(3a) of Directive 2001/83/EC.

set out in section 2 of the Summary of Product Characteristics (SmPC) of any drug approved in the EU. The SmPC, on the other hand, is one of the mandatory documents which must be submitted with any SPC request for a medicinal product.[27]

As a logical consequence, most, if not all patent offices take a pragmatic approach and primarily rely on the active ingredient(s) identified in the SmPC when determining the potential active ingredient(s) of an SPC.

In the case of SPCs for plant protection products, the definitions provided in Article 1 of the corresponding SPC Regulation with respect to the terms 'plant protection products' and 'active substances' are based on the literal definitions provided in Article 2(1), 2(3), 2(4), 2(6), 2(7) and 2(8) of Directive 91/414/EEC. While these definitions may be appropriate from the regulatory perspective, the definitions in the SPC Regulation for Plant Protection Products do not appear to facilitate a clear understanding of what a 'product' within the meaning of the SPC Regulation should encompass. Thus, Article 1(8) of the SPC Regulation for Plant Protection Products defines the term 'product' by reference to the active substance or combination of active substances of a plant protection product as defined in Article 1(3) of the SPC Regulation. According to this latter provision, 'active substances' are 'substances or micro-organisms including viruses, having general or specific action: (a) against harmful organisms; or (b) on plants, parts of plants or plant products'.[28] Article 1(8) of this SPC Regulation thus provides a very narrow definition of what should be construed as an active substance, which on a literal interpretation should not include certain active substances, in conflict with the more general definitions used in Article 1(1) and 1(2) of this Regulation.

It would appear difficult to align the above definition of 'active substances' in the SPC Regulation for Plant Protection Products with the provisions and definitions provided in the new plant regulatory Regulation (EC) 1107/2009. Thus, as this regulatory Regulation differentiates between different types of products, such as active substances, safeners, synergistics and co-formulants,[29] the provisions in the SPC Regulation appear to be even more diffused.

Nevertheless, in analogy to the prosecution of SPCs for medicinal products, the national patent offices have pragmatically focused on the active substances which have been identified in the Community approval or subsequent national marketing authorization in order to identify the 'product', that is to say the active substance(s), which may be the subject matter of an SPC.

While a literal interpretation of the two SPC Regulations may have proven to be expedient in terms of clarity and legal certainty, such a restrictive approach undermines the very central purpose of these Regulations, namely to foster innovation in these cost-intensive and substantially self-financing industries.

As a result of the national patent offices' literal and restrictive approach of what products qualify for an SPC, situations have emerged where innovative products, including products of significant scientific, social and economic benefit, which were

27. Article 8(1)(b) of Regulation (EC) 469/2009.
28. Article 1(3) of Regulation (EC) 1610/96.
29. *See* Arts 1(2) and 2 of Regulation (EC) 1107/2009.

associated with very substantial developmental costs and per se should be worthy of supplemental protection, cannot be subsumed under such a restrictive product definition.

[2] *Active Ingredient or Combination of Active Ingredients of a Medicinal Product*

While the SPC Regulation for Medicinal Products does not contain an express and distinct definition of the term 'active ingredient', the meaning of this term would seem to be well derivable from the definition of a 'medicinal product' in Article 1(a) of this Regulation. Thus, a 'medicinal product' is defined as 'any substance or combination of substances presented for treating or preventing disease in human beings or animals and any substance or combination of substances which may be administered to human beings or animals with a view to making a medical diagnosis or to restoring, correcting or modifying physiological functions in humans or in animals'. It would appear to logically follow that the active ingredient(s) is/are the component of the medicinal product responsible for these effects. Nevertheless, the CJEU invoked the lack of an express definition of the term 'active ingredient' in the SPC Regulation in *MIT* (C-431/04) and subsequent decisions[30] and developed its own understanding of this term.

Thus, the CJEU initially found in *MIT*, and confirmed in *Glaxosmithkline Biologicals* (C-210/13), that the term 'active ingredient' does not include any 'substances forming part of a medicinal product which do not have an effect of their own on the human or animal body' and, more specifically, does not cover any 'substance which does not have any therapeutic effect of its own'.[31] This also holds true for therapeutically inactive substances that affect the pharmacokinetic properties of another active ingredient and thereby 'contribute' to (or are even necessary for) the latter's therapeutic efficacy – such as, e.g., a polymeric matrix which enables the controlled release of an active ingredient.[32]

Moreover, insofar as an SPC relates to a 'combination of active ingredients', this same requirement applies to each active ingredient forming part of the respective combination. Under the approach established by the CJEU in *MIT*, a combination of an active ingredient X with a therapeutically inactive substance Y, wherein the inactive substance Y is necessary for the therapeutic efficacy of the active ingredient X, does

30. *See* CJEU *Massachusetts Institute of Technology v. Bundesgerichtshof*, C-431/04 of 4 May 2006, paragraph 17; CJEU *Glaxosmithkline Biologicals v. Comptroller-General of Patents, Designs and Trade Marks*, C-210/13 of 14 November 2013, paragraph 27; and CJEU *Arne Forsgren v. Österreichisches Patentamt*, C-631/13 of 15 January 2015, paragraph 23. The EFTA Court also took this position; *see* EFTA Court, *Pharmaq v. Intervet International*, E-16/14 of 9 April 2015, paragraph 81.
31. CJEU *Massachusetts Institute of Technology v. Bundesgerichtshof*, C-431/04 of 4 May 2006, paragraphs 18 and 25; CJEU *Glaxosmithkline Biologicals v. Comptroller-General of Patents, Designs and Trade Marks*, C-210/13 of 14 November 2013, paragraphs 28, 30 and 35.
32. CJEU *Massachusetts Institute of Technology v. Bundesgerichtshof*, C-431/04 of 4 May 2006.

therefore not constitute a 'combination of active ingredients' which would be eligible for an SPC, either.[33]

Following this same narrow approach, the CJEU concluded in *Glaxosmithkline Biologicals* that an 'active ingredient' does not cover adjuvants either, which do not exert any therapeutic effect of their own. Under this approach, the combination of a therapeutically inactive adjuvant with a therapeutically active antigen in a vaccine, wherein the former enhances the therapeutic efficacy of the latter, does consequently not constitute a 'combination of active ingredients' which could become the subject of an SPC.[34]

The concept of an 'active ingredient' initially endorsed by the CJEU in *MIT* and *Glaxosmithkline Biologicals* thus excludes all substances that do not have any *therapeutic effect of their own*. This very restrictive concept, however, does not appear to do justice to the fact that a number of substances are authorized as medicinal products, and even as monopreparations, even though they do *not* actually exert any therapeutic effect of their own but nevertheless modify physiological functions, thereby indirectly contributing to the therapeutic effect. Therapeutic boosters or adjuncts are one prominent example of such substances. For example, entacapone enhances the therapeutic effect of the active ingredient levodopa in the treatment of Parkinson's disease by inhibiting an enzyme that metabolizes levodopa. Although entacapone alone does not exert any therapeutic effect but merely acts as an adjunct to levodopa, monopreparations containing entacapone as the sole 'active' ingredient have been authorized as medicinal products, and the corresponding SmPCs explicitly refer to entacapone as the 'active substance'.[35] A further example is cobicistat, a cytochrome P450 (CYP) 3A inhibitor which enhances the effects of the HIV drugs atazanavir and darunavir by inhibiting their metabolization. A monopreparation of cobicistat is authorized for combined use with atazanavir or darunavir in the treatment of HIV infection, even though cobicistat itself does not have any therapeutic activity.[36] Similarly, the combination of amoxicillin and clavulanic acid is authorized as a medicinal product for the treatment of certain bacterial infections, and the corresponding SmPCs refer to both amoxicillin and clavulanic acid as active substances, even though clavulanic acid merely prevents the inactivation of amoxicillin and does not exert any therapeutic effect of its own.[37]

Clearly, if substances that do not have any therapeutic effect of their own but enhance the therapeutic effect of another active ingredient can be authorized as medicinal products, there should be no justification to deny them SPC protection. An 'active ingredient' in the sense of the SPC Regulation for Medicinal Products should

33. *Ibid.*

34. CJEU *Glaxosmithkline Biologicals v. Comptroller-General of Patents, Designs and Trade Marks*, C-210/13 of 14 November 2013.

35. *See*, e.g., the SmPCs for the medicinal products Comtan (EMEA/H/C/000171), Comtess (EMEA/H/C/000170), Entacapone Orion (EMEA/H/C/002440) and Entacapone Teva (EMEA/H/C/002075), all of which contain entacapone as the sole 'active substance'.

36. *See* the SmPC for Tybost (EMEA/H/C/002572).

37. *See*, e.g., the SmPCs for Augmentin and Co-Amoxiclav, which state in Section 5.1 under 'mechanism of action' that '*[c]lavulanic acid alone does not exert a clinically useful antibacterial effect*'.

therefore not be required to exert a therapeutic effect of its own, as any such requirement would be at variance with the actual regulatory practice and would unduly disadvantage this type of innovations in the pharmaceutical field. Such an interpretation is also well aligned with the definition provided in Article 1 of the SPC Regulation for Medicinal Products, which also includes substances that modify physiological functions.

Notably, the understanding of what is, or is not, an 'active ingredient' underwent a remarkable refinement in *Forsgren* (C-631/13), where the CJEU took account of the newly introduced definition of the term 'active substance' in Article 1 of Directive 2001/83/EC[38] and concluded on the basis of this new definition that the term 'active ingredient' in the SPC Regulation for Medicinal Products relates to '*substances producing a pharmacological, immunological or metabolic action of their own*'.[39]

It would appear that the types of actions or activities that allow a substance to be qualified as an 'active ingredient' have been considerably expanded under this new definition accepted by the CJEU in *Forsgren* to encompass not only any *pharmacological action*[40] (which already seems broader than the '*therapeutic effect*' required in *MIT* and *Glaxosmithkline Biologicals*) but also any *immunological action* and any *metabolic action*. Arguably, this new definition of 'active ingredients' should also include therapeutic boosters, such as the above-discussed substances entacapone, cobicistat and clavulanic acid which may not have a *therapeutic effect* but do, in fact, exert a *metabolic action* of their own (i.e., entacapone inhibits an enzyme that metabolizes levodopa and thereby enhances and prolongs the action of levodopa; cobicistat inhibits CYP3A enzymes that metabolize atazanavir and darunavir, and thereby enhances their effects; clavulanic acid inhibits bacterial beta-lactamase enzymes and thereby prevents

38. *See* CJEU *Arne Forsgren v. Österreichisches Patentamt*, C 631/13 of 15 January 2015, paragraphs 23–24. By Directive 2011/62/EU of 8 June 2011, the following new definition of the term 'active substance' was introduced in Art. 1 of Directive 2001/83/EC:

    > Any substance or mixture of substances intended to be used in the manufacture of a medicinal product and that, when used in its production, becomes an active ingredient of that product intended to exert a pharmacological, immunological or metabolic action with a view to restoring, correcting or modifying physiological functions or to make a medical diagnosis.

    The intention underlying the introduction of this new definition was acknowledged to consist in ensuring uniform application of Directive 2001/83/EC; *see* recital 5 of Directive 2011/62/EU.
39. CJEU *Arne Forsgren v. Österreichisches Patentamt*, C-631/13 of 15 January 2015, paragraphs 25 and 27. Essentially the same reasoning and the same definition of the term 'active ingredient' were also repeated by the EFTA Court in *Pharmaq v. Intervet International*, E-16/14 of 9 April 2015, paragraphs 81–84.
40. It is noteworthy that the CJEU acknowledged in *Chemische Fabrik Kreussler v. Sunstar Deutschland*, C-308/11 of 6 September 2012 that the term '*pharmacological action*', as used in Art. 1 of Directive 2001/83/EC, does not necessarily require an interaction between the substance under consideration and a cellular constituent of the patient's body, but can also result, e.g., from an interaction of the substance with bacteria, viruses or parasites that are present in the patient's body. While this latter decision (C-308/11) was not directly concerned with SPCs, its relevance for the interpretation of the term 'active ingredient' in Regulation (EC) 469/2009 appears to be confirmed by CJEU *Bayer CropScience v. Deutsches Patent- und Markenamt*, C-11/13 of 19 June 2014, paragraph 33.

the inactivation of amoxicillin). The new definition of 'active ingredients' established in *Forsgren* could possibly even embrace adjuvants for vaccines, provided that they have an *immunological action* of their own, and could thus potentially mark a departure[41] from the CJEU's earlier restrictive approach followed in *Glaxosmithkline Biologicals*. Caution is, however, advisable as the CJEU has not yet had the opportunity to elucidate the ramifications of the new definition of 'active ingredients' endorsed in *Forsgren* and to confirm the broader scope that it would seem to imply.

It is furthermore noteworthy that the definition of a 'product' eligible for an SPC refers to the active ingredient or combination of active ingredients of a *medicinal product*[42] (or of a plant protection product). It may therefore not be sufficient to consider the properties of a given substance in isolation, i.e., without taking into account the corresponding medicinal product, when assessing whether or not it constitutes an active ingredient. The question can thus be raised whether the substance under consideration constitutes an active ingredient of the *specific medicinal product* for which the marketing authorization that the SPC relies upon has been granted.[43,44] For example, even though ascorbic acid (vitamin C) exerts a pharmacological action of its own and could thus be employed in a medicinal product as an active ingredient,[45] it can also be used as an excipient[46] and is indeed contained as such in various medicinal products.[47]

This issue has been clarified in *Forsgren*,[48] in which the CJEU found that an active ingredient whose therapeutic effects do not fall within the therapeutic indications for which a marketing authorization has been granted cannot give rise to the grant of an

41. While it would appear that adjuvants for vaccines which have an immunological action of their own could qualify as 'active ingredients' in view of the CJEU's findings in *Arne Forsgren v. Österreichisches Patentamt*, C-631/13 of 15 January 2015, this understanding has not yet been confirmed. It remains to be seen whether a further referral might become necessary in view of the apparent contradiction to the CJEU's earlier approach taken in *Glaxosmithkline Biologicals v. Comptroller-General of Patents, Designs and Trade Marks*, C-210/13 of 14 November 2013. Note also that the term 'immunological action' is broader than 'immunogenic action' and could be seen to encompass any effects in relation to the immune system.
42. Article 1(b) of Regulation (EC) 469/2009.
43. Article 3(b) of Regulation (EC) 469/2009.
44. Note that this question – i.e., whether a substance constitutes an active ingredient of the medicinal product for which the marketing authorization that the SPC relies upon has been granted – is different from the question addressed in CJEU *Yissum Research and Development Company of the Hebrew University of Jerusalem v. Comptroller-General of Patents*, C-202/05 of 17 April 2007, in which the CJEU effectively found that the definition of the 'product' as an 'active ingredient' cannot include any particular therapeutic use (of the active ingredient) which is protected by a basic patent.
45. For example, the EMA has granted orphan designation for ascorbic acid as an active substance for the treatment of Charcot-Marie-Tooth disease type 1A (EU/3/08/531) and also for the treatment of facioscapulohumeral muscular dystrophy (EU/3/16/1776).
46. EMA, Guideline on excipients in the dossier for application for marketing authorization of a medicinal product (EMEA/CHMP/QWP/396951/2006) of 19 June 2007.
47. For example, the medicinal product Cholib contains fenofibrate and simvastatin as active ingredients, and ascorbic acid as an excipient; *see* the SmPC for Cholib (EMEA/H/C/002559).
48. CJEU *Arne Forsgren v. Österreichisches Patentamt*, C-631/13 of 15 January 2015, paragraphs 34, 35, 38 and 39.

SPC (*see also* §1.02[C][6] below). In the specific case underlying *Forsgren*, the substance in question, Protein D, was seen to have both a therapeutic effect (as a vaccine) and an adjuvant effect of its own, but these effects were not at all reflected in the corresponding marketing authorization which only referred to Protein D as a carrier protein and expressly mentioned that there was no evidence of any independent effect as a vaccine;[49] the CJEU consequently found the grant of an SPC to be precluded under such circumstances, noting that 'since no trial or data concerning the therapeutic effects of Protein D against *Haemophilus influenzae* was integrated into the marketing authorization procedure, that procedure was not able to delay the commercial use of the basic patent'.[50] Ultimately, the CJEU held in *Forsgren* that an SPC can be granted only if the substance at issue produces a pharmacological, immunological or metabolic action of its own, and only if such an effect falls within the therapeutic indications covered by the marketing authorization;[51] it considered this to be a matter for the referring court to determine, which illustrates that a literal designation of the substance under consideration as 'active substance' in the marketing authorization should not be strictly necessary.

It can further be taken from the CJEU decision *Forsgren*[52] that an active ingredient X which is covalently bound to another substance Y, be it another active ingredient or another inactive substance, is still to be considered as the same active ingredient X. In the case underlying this decision, the active ingredient in question was a carrier protein of a conjugate vaccine, which was covalently bound to a bacterial polysaccharide antigen and was therefore not present 'as such' in the corresponding medicinal product, but only in conjugated form. Under these circumstances, the CJEU acknowledged the possibility that, in principle, an active ingredient can give rise to an SPC even if it is covalently bound to other active ingredients. This same reasoning could also be relevant, e.g., for therapeutic proteins or peptides that are covalently modified with polyethylene glycol (PEG) or similar chemical groups. However, it remains to be seen whether and to what extent this approach might be applicable to cases in which it is less clear that one specific part of a larger molecule exerts a pharmacological effect of its own.

[3] Active Substance or Combination of Active Substances of a Plant Protection Product

In contrast to the SPC Regulation for Medicinal Products, the SPC Regulation for Plant Protection Products does, in fact, contain an express definition of the term 'active substance'. Thus, active substances are defined in Article 1(3) of this Regulation as

49. *Ibid.*, paragraphs 13, 16–19 and 37.
50. *Ibid.*, paragraph 38.
51. *Ibid.*, paragraphs 53–54.
52. *Ibid.*, paragraphs 25, 27 and 28.

'substances[53] or micro-organisms including viruses, having general or specific action: (a) against harmful organisms;[54] or (b) on plants, parts of plants or plant products'.

In this regard, the CJEU clarified in its decision *Bayer CropScience* (C-11/13)[55] that the term 'active substances' relates to '*substances which have a toxic, phytotoxic or plant protection action of their own*'; this toxic, phytotoxic or plant protection action does not necessarily have to be a *direct action* but can also be an *indirect action*. Conversely, a substance with no such toxic, phytotoxic or plant protection action cannot be considered to be an 'active substance' within the meaning of the SPC Regulation for Plant Protection Products.[56]

In *Bayer CropScience*, the CJEU furthermore acknowledged that a safener – i.e., a substance that is added to a plant protection product in order to eliminate or reduce the latter's undesired phytotoxic effects on crop plants[57] – can, in principle, constitute an 'active substance', provided that it fulfils the above-mentioned criterion of exerting a toxic, phytotoxic or plant protection action.[58] Specifically, the CJEU did not conclude that all safeners would necessarily be 'active substances', but rather emphasized that the answer to the question whether a safener is an 'active substance' depends on whether the corresponding substance has a toxic, phytotoxic or plant protection action of its own, which has to be ascertained in the light of all the relevant factual and scientific evidence.[59]

[4] Fixed-Dose and Loose Combinations

With respect to a combination of active ingredients, it has already been noted in §1.02[A][2] above that each component of such a combination must individually fulfil the corresponding requirements established by the CJEU in order to be considered an active ingredient.[60]

However, the CJEU has not yet clarified whether SPCs are indeed available for all combinations of active ingredients, including 'loose' combinations in which the individual active ingredients are authorized for combined use but are formulated in

53. The term 'substances' is defined in Art. 1(2) of Regulation (EC) 1610/96 as 'chemical elements and their compounds, as they occur naturally or by manufacture, including any impurity inevitably resulting from the manufacturing process'.
54. Definitions of the terms 'plants', 'plant products', and 'harmful organisms' are provided in Art. 1(5), Art. 1(6) and Art. 1(7) of Regulation (EC) 1610/96, respectively.
55. CJEU *Bayer CropScience v. Deutsches Patent- und Markenamt*, C-11/13 of 19 June 2014, paragraph 33.
56. *Ibid.*, paragraph 34.
57. The CJEU provided an explanation of the term 'safener' in *Bayer CropScience* (C-11/13), paragraph 36, and also referred to the corresponding definition in Art. 2(3)(a) of Regulation (EC) 1107/2009 in this regard.
58. CJEU *Bayer CropScience v. Deutsches Patent- und Markenamt*, C-11/13 of 19 June 2014, headnote.
59. *Ibid.*, paragraphs 35 and 37.
60. CJEU *Massachusetts Institute of Technology v. Bundesgerichtshof*, C-431/04 of 4 May 2006; CJEU *Glaxosmithkline Biologicals v. Comptroller-General of Patents, Designs and Trade Marks*, C-210/13 of 14 November 2013; CJEU *Arne Forsgren v. Österreichisches Patentamt*, C-631/13 of 15 January 2015.

separate compositions, or whether SPC protection should only be available for 'fixed-dose' combinations in which the different active ingredients are all formulated in the same composition. This question stems from the requirement under Article 3(b) of the SPC Regulations[61] that a valid marketing authorization must have been granted for the combination of active ingredients which is the subject of an SPC application.

In the case of a fixed-dose combination, all of the individual active ingredients forming part of the combination will be listed in the corresponding marketing authorization as components of the authorized product. No doubts will therefore arise that this combination of active ingredients is the subject of the marketing authorization.

In the case of a loose combination, however, the corresponding marketing authorization will refer to only one active ingredient (or only several but not all active ingredients of the combination in question) as a component of the *authorized product*, and will list the further active ingredient(s) of the respective combination in the context of the *authorized use* of that product. From a purely formalistic point of view, it may thus be argued that the authorized product contains only one active ingredient, even where the marketing authorization does not allow the use of that product alone but mandatorily requires its use in combination with the other active ingredient. A typical example in this regard is the combination of a small molecule drug, formulated for oral administration, with a large molecule drug (like an antibody) which needs to be formulated for parenteral administration. For pharmacokinetic reasons, it may be practically impossible to formulate such a combination of active ingredients in a single pharmaceutical composition. Furthermore, over the past years the importance of personalized medicine, tailored therapy to the patient's need to ensure the best response and highest safety, has been recognized. Such tailored therapies require dosing flexibility, so that for such therapeutic dosage regimens loose combinations must be available. The development of appropriate treatment regimens for specified patient groups is not trivial and requires considerable research and expenditure. In order to facilitate technological advance in this increasingly important field, it would appear expedient to ensure that SPC protection is also available for such inventions.

Therefore, and in view of the fundamental objective of the SPC Regulations to encourage *all pharmaceutical research and all plant protection research without any discrimination*,[62] it does not seem justifiable to deny supplemental protection to such loose combinations merely because the respective active ingredients are provided in separate compositions and the corresponding marketing authorization refers to the actually authorized combination in the context of the authorized use.

When this issue will eventually be addressed by the CJEU,[63] one can only hope that the Court will take a similarly pragmatic and teleological approach as in *Neurim*

61. Article 3(b) of Regulation (EC) 469/2009, and Art. 3(1)(b) of Regulation (EC) 1610/96.
62. *See* Explanatory Memorandum to the Commission proposal for an SPC regulation for medicinal products, COM(90) 101 final – SYN 255, paragraph 29 as well as Explanatory Memorandum to the Commission proposal for an SPC regulation for plant protection products, COM(94) 579 final, paragraph 66.
63. The corresponding question was already raised in the referral giving rise to the CJEU's decision in *University of Queensland v. Comptroller-General of Patents, Designs and Trade Marks*, C-630/10 of 25 November 2011. In this referral, the UK Patents Court asked, *inter alia*, if there

(C-130/11), where it relied heavily on the objective of the respective SPC Regulation to encourage pharmaceutical research and the intentions expressed in the Explanatory Memorandum as to the type of innovations that should enable an SPC to be granted,[64] and will thus confirm that all combinations of active ingredients *without any discrimination*, including also loose combinations, can benefit from SPC protection. Indeed, the SPC Regulations and the respective Explanatory Memorandums do not give any indication that the grant of SPCs should have been intended only for fixed-dose combinations but not for loose combinations of active ingredients.

[5] Limitation to Products Subjected to a Specific Marketing Authorization Procedure

A further limitation of the type of 'products' that are amenable to SPC protection results from the requirement in Article 2 of the SPC Regulations that the 'product' must have been subject to a specific administrative authorization procedure before it is placed on the market as a medicinal product or as a plant protection product.

Specifically, in the case of SPCs for medicinal products, the 'product' must have been subject to an administrative authorization procedure as laid down in Directive 2001/83/EC (Community code for human medicinal products) or Directive 2001/82/EC (Community code for veterinary medicinal products).[65,66] In the case of SPCs for plant protection products, the 'product' must have been subject to an administrative authorization procedure as laid down in Article 4 of Directive 91/414/EEC (placing on the market of plant protection products), 'or pursuant to an equivalent provision of national law if it is a plant protection product in respect of which the application for authorization was lodged before Directive 91/414/EEC was implemented by the Member State concerned'.[67] It should also be mentioned in this context that Directive 91/414/EEC has meanwhile been repealed and replaced by Regulation (EC) 1107/2009 (placing on the market of plant protection products).

On a literal reading of the SPC Regulations, it could be held that only such products that have been subject to one of the specific administrative authorization procedures expressly mentioned in Article 2 of the respective Regulation can, in principle, become the subject of an SPC, while products that have undergone any other authorization procedure cannot.

---

are any further or different criteria for determining whether a combination of active ingredients is protected by a basic patent, and if one of these further or different criteria is '*whether the active ingredients are admixed together rather than being delivered in separate formulations but at the same time*'; *see* questions 2 and 3. Alas, this specific question remained unanswered.

64. CJEU *Neurim Pharmaceuticals v. Comptroller-General of Patents*, C-130/11 of 19 July 2012, paragraphs 22–25.
65. Article 2 of Regulation (EC) 469/2009.
66. Note that Art. 2 of the previous Regulation (EEC) No. 1768/92 on SPCs for medicinal products, which was repealed and replaced by Regulation (EC) 469/2009, made reference to Directive 65/65/EEC and Directive 81/851/EEC which have been repealed and replaced by Directive 2001/83/EC and Directive 2001/82/EC, respectively.
67. Article 2 of Regulation (EC) 1610/96.

In the case of plant protection products, however, the CJEU found in *Hogan Lovells* (C-229/09) that an SPC could also be granted for a product that has been subject to a 'provisional' marketing authorization procedure according to Article 8(1) of Directive 91/414/EEC,[68] as discussed in more detail in §1.02[C][5] below. In arriving at this conclusion, the CJEU compared the specific conditions under which a 'definitive' marketing authorization may be granted according to Article 4 of Directive 91/414/EEC, which is expressly mentioned in Article 2 of the SPC Regulation for Plant Protection Products, with the corresponding conditions required for a 'provisional' marketing authorization in Article 8(1) of Directive 91/414/EEC,[69] and found that in both cases the same scientific criteria apply, so that a '*link of functional equivalence*'[70] exists between the criteria set out in Article 8(1) and those in Article 4 of Directive 91/414/EEC. When the CJEU had to assess an 'emergency' marketing authorization for plant protection products issued under Article 8(4) of Directive 91/414/EEC in *Sumitomo Chemical* (C-210/12), it again referred to the 'link of functional equivalence' as a decisive requirement. Since functional equivalence between the criteria underlying an emergency marketing authorization under Article 8(4) and a regular marketing authorization under Article 4 of Directive 91/414/EEC was denied, the CJEU concluded that an SPC could not be granted on that basis.[71]

In the case of medicinal products, the CJEU has not yet acknowledged any other administrative authorization procedure to be equivalent to the marketing authorization procedure laid down in Directive 2001/83/EC (Community code for human medicinal products) or in Directive 2001/82/EC (Community code for veterinary medicinal products).

The EFTA Court, however, acknowledged in its decision *Pharmaq* (E-16/14) that also a marketing authorization granted 'in exceptional circumstances' under Article 26(3) of Directive 2001/82/EC constitutes a valid authorization under Directive 2001/82/EC for the purpose of the SPC Regulation.[72] In the same decision, the EFTA Court furthermore found that a provisional permission granted 'in the event of serious epizootic diseases' under Article 8 of Directive 2001/82/EC does not qualify as an administrative authorization procedure and does not constitute a marketing authorization within the meaning of the SPC Regulation. Such a provisional permission does not allow the producer to market the product in question but only to supply it, to the extent necessary to combat the corresponding epizootic disease, with the consequence that such a supply does not constitute a placing on the market as a veterinary medicinal product.[73]

Notably, a referral is currently pending before the CJEU as C-527/17, in which the German Federal Patent Court asked whether an authorization under Directive

68. CJEU *Hogan Lovells International v. Bayer CropScience*, C-229/09 of 11 November 2010.
69. *Ibid.*, paragraphs 33 et seqq.
70. *Ibid.*, paragraph 46.
71. CJEU *Sumitomo Chemical Co. v. Deutsches Patent- und Markenamt*, C-210/12 of 17 October 2013, paragraphs 34–37.
72. EFTA Court, *Pharmaq v. Intervet International*, E-16/14 of 9 April 2015, paragraphs 54–56 and 65.
73. *Ibid.*, paragraphs 57, 58, 64 and 66.

93/42/EEC (medical devices) for a combined medical device and medicinal product in the sense of Article 1(4) of that Directive[74] is, for the purpose of the SPC Regulation for Medicinal Products, equivalent to a marketing authorization under Directive 2001/83/EC, where the medicinal product component of the device/drug combination has been tested, as part of the authorization procedure, for its quality, safety and usefulness by the medicinal products authority of an EU Member State in accordance with Directive 2001/83/EC.[75] The corresponding decision of the CJEU will have profound consequences for the question whether SPCs can be obtained for medical devices, as discussed in more detail in §1.02[A][6] below.

In case a medicinal product can be placed on the market without having to be subjected to any kind of administrative authorization procedure, which applies to certain homeopathic medicinal products and certain herbal medicinal products,[76] such products are evidently not eligible for SPCs.

It is furthermore noteworthy that the SPC Regulations require in Article 2 that the 'product' must have been subject to the corresponding specific marketing authorization procedure '*prior to being placed on the market*'[77] as a medicinal product or as a plant protection product. On the basis of this requirement, the CJEU has concluded that a product which is subjected to such an authorization procedure *only after it had already been placed on the market* as a medicinal product for human or veterinary use cannot be the subject of an SPC – even if the earlier placing on the market occurred under national rules preceding the harmonized European marketing authorization regime, i.e., without having undergone a marketing authorization procedure in accordance with Article 2 of the pertinent SPC Regulation and, in particular, without

74. Article 1(4) of Directive 93/42/EEC provides that:

> Where a device incorporates, as an integral part, a substance which, if used separately, may be considered to be a medicinal product within the meaning of Art. 1 of Directive 65/65/EEC and which is liable to act upon the body with action ancillary to that of the device, that device must be assessed and authorized in accordance with this Directive.

75. *See* German Federal Patent Court decision 14 W (pat) 13/16 of 18 July 2017. The precise wording of the referred question reads as follows (in English translation):

> Must Art. 2 of [the SPC Regulation for Medicinal Products] be interpreted as meaning that, for the purposes of that regulation, an authorization under Directive 93/42/EEC for a combined medical device and medicinal product within the meaning of Art. 1(4) of Directive 93/42/EEC is to be treated as a valid marketing authorization under Directive 2001/83/EC, where, as part of the authorization procedure laid down in Annex I, Section 7.4, first paragraph, to Directive 93/42/EEC, the quality, safety and usefulness of the medicinal product component has been verified by the medicinal products authority of a Member State in accordance with Directive 2001/83/EC?

76. Under Directive 2001/83/EC, the placing on the market of certain homeopathic medicinal products as well as certain herbal medicinal products merely requires a registration but not a marketing authorization; *see* Arts 13 et seq. and Arts 16a et seq. of Directive 2001/83/EC.
77. The 'market' referred to in Art. 2 of the respective SPC Regulation is the EU single market (not the market of the specific Member State for which an SPC is applied); *see* CJEU *Synthon v. Merz Pharma*, C-195/09 of 28 July 2011, paragraph 42.

having undergone safety and efficacy testing.[78] In view of the CJEU's later decision *Neurim* (C-130/11),[79] however, this issue might have largely lost its practical relevance, as discussed in §1.02[C][7][a] below.

[6] Protection of Medical Devices

While medical devices used to be authorized under Directive 90/385/EEC (the 'Active Implantable Medical Devices Directive') or Directive 93/42/EEC (the 'Medical Devices Directive'), which will also be referenced in the following, it must be noted that these two Directives have meanwhile been repealed and replaced by Regulation (EU) 2017/745 (medical devices) which entered into force in May 2017. Under the new Regulation (EU) 2017/745, among many other changes, stricter requirements apply with respect to clinical assessments,[80] and a review of the notified body's assessment through the respective authority responsible for notified bodies in an appropriate number of cases has been prescribed.[81]

Undisputedly, medical devices that do not contain any active ingredient are evidently not eligible for SPCs since the pertinent SPC Regulation for Medicinal Products defines the 'product' to be protected as 'the active ingredient or combination of active ingredients of a medicinal product'.[82]

The question whether SPCs are available for a medical device that includes a medicinal product (such as a drug-releasing stent), however, has been the subject of controversial discussions and divergent national case law. On the one hand, it has been argued that such medical device/drug combinations undergo a CE marking procedure which is, strictly speaking, not an 'administrative' authorization procedure – as it is conducted, at the choice of the device manufacturer, by any one of various accredited entities, referred to as 'notified bodies' (which are typically private companies, not public authorities). A negative decision of a notified body does not have any legally binding effect (in contrast to a negative decision in an administrative procedure), and the device manufacturer is free to commission another notified body with the same conformity assessment in that case (contrary to the situation in an administrative authorization procedure).

On the other hand, it has been pointed out in favour of SPC protection for such medical device/drug combinations that it is required under the Medical Devices Directive that the quality, safety and usefulness of the medicinal product component of the device/drug combination must be verified by analogy with the methods specified in Directive 2001/83/EC (Community code for human medicinal products).[83] To this end, the notified body has to consult the national medicines authority of an EU Member State or the EMA, and has to 'give due consideration to the views expressed in this

78. CJEU *Synthon v. Merz Pharma*, C-195/09 of 28 July 2011, paragraphs 43–51; CJEU *Generics (UK) v. Synaptech*, C-427/09 of 28 July 2011, paragraphs 33–36.
79. CJEU *Neurim Pharmaceuticals v. Comptroller-General of Patents*, C-130/11 of 19 July 2012.
80. *See* Arts 61 et seq. of Regulation (EU) 2017/745.
81. *See* Art. 45 of Regulation (EU) 2017/745.
82. Article 1(b) of Regulation (EC) 469/2009.
83. Directive 93/42/EEC (medical devices), Annex I, Section 7.4 provides that:

consultation when making its decision';[84] the scientific opinion of the competent national authority or the EMA must further be included in the documentation concerning the medical device.[85] It may thus be held that, in effect, an equivalent assessment as required for medicinal products under Directive 2001/83/EC is to be carried out for medical devices that include a medicinal product. Consequently, such medical devices should likewise benefit from SPC protection as a compensation of the loss of effective patent term resulting from the authorization procedure for the medicinal product component of the device.

It has also been argued with reference to the CJEU decision *Laboratoires Lyocentre* (C-109/12)[86] that if the same product can be classified and authorized as a medicinal product under Directive 2001/83/EC in one EU Member State and as a medical device under Directive 93/42/EEC in another EU Member State, this would confirm the equivalence of the respective authorization procedures.

The question whether SPCs are available for medical device/drug combinations is the subject of a referral that is currently pending before the CJEU as C-527/17. Specifically, the German Federal Patent Court asked whether an authorization under the Medical Devices Directive for a combined medical device and medicinal product in the sense of Article 1(4) of that Directive[87] is, for the purpose of the SPC Regulation for Medicinal Products, equivalent to a marketing authorization under Directive 2001/83/EC, where the medicinal product component of the device/drug combination has been tested, as part of the authorization procedure, for its quality, safety and usefulness by the medicinal products authority of an EU Member State in accordance with Directive 2001/83/EC.[88]

> Where a device incorporates, as an integral part, a substance which, if used separately, may be considered to be a medicinal product as defined in Art. 1 of Directive 2001/83/EC and which is liable to act upon the body with action ancillary to that of the device, the quality, safety and usefulness of the substance must be verified by analogy with the methods specified in Annex I to Directive 2001/83/EC.

84. Directive 93/42/EEC (medical devices), Annex II, Section 4.3.
85. *Ibid.*
86. CJEU *Laboratoires Lyocentre v. Lääkealan turvallisuus- ja kehittämiskeskus*, C-109/12 of 3 October 2013.
87. Article 1(4) of Directive 93/42/EEC provides that:

> Where a device incorporates, as an integral part, a substance which, if used separately, may be considered to be a medicinal product within the meaning of Art. 1 of Directive 65/65/EEC and which is liable to act upon the body with action ancillary to that of the device, that device must be assessed and authorized in accordance with this Directive.

88. *See* German Federal Patent Court decision 14 W (pat) 13/16 of 18 July 2017. The precise wording of the referred question reads as follows (in English translation):

> Must Art. 2 of [the SPC Regulation for Medicinal Products] be interpreted as meaning that, for the purposes of that regulation, an authorization under Directive 93/42/EEC for a combined medical device and medicinal product within the meaning of Art. 1(4) of Directive 93/42/EEC is to be treated as a valid marketing authorization under Directive 2001/83/EC, where, as part of the authorization procedure laid down in Annex I, Section 7.4, first paragraph, to Directive 93/42/EEC, the quality, safety and

The guidance which will be provided by the CJEU in this referral may make available SPC protection for a wide range of medical device/medicinal product combinations. Moreover, the decision of the CJEU could also be applicable to the closely related questions whether SPC protection is available for a medical device intended to administer a medicinal product (i.e., a medical device/drug combination in the sense of Article 1(3) of the Medical Devices Directive), and for corresponding active implantable medical device[89]/medicinal product combinations, wherein the medical device either incorporates the medicinal product as an integral part or is intended to administer the medicinal product, and which are authorized under the Active Implantable Medical Devices Directive, given that the pertinent provisions in this Directive are essentially analogous[90] to those in the Medical Devices Directive.

Yet, even if the CJEU were to acknowledge in the pending referral C-527/17 that an SPC may be granted for a combined medical device and medicinal product authorized under the Medical Devices Directive, it would still remain doubtful whether SPC protection could also become available for other medical devices that include a substance which does not have any pharmacological, immunological or metabolic action of its own but, rather, exerts a *physical effect* (such as magnetic nanoparticles which can be injected into a tumour and heated in an alternating magnetic field in order to destroy the tumour cells), given that the definition of an 'active ingredient' as established by the CJEU requires a pharmacological, immunological or metabolic effect of the respective substance (*see* §1.02[A][2] above).

[B] Basic Patent

An SPC has to be filed on the basis of an existing granted patent which, at the date of filing the SPC application, must be in force in the respective state.[91] The basic patent can be a national patent or a European patent validated in that state.[92] It will also be possible to file SPCs on the basis of European unitary patents[93] having effect in the respective state, once such patents became available.

usefulness of the medicinal product component has been verified by the medicinal products authority of a Member State in accordance with Directive 2001/83/EC?

89. An active implantable medical device requires a power source for its functioning (*see* Art. 1(2)(b) of Directive 90/385/EEC) and is intended to be totally or partially introduced into and remain in the human body (*see* Art. 1(2)(c) of Directive 90/385/EEC).
90. *See* Art. 1(3) and 1(4), Annex 1, Section 10, and Annex 2, Section 4.3 of Directive 90/385/EEC (active implantable medical devices) in comparison to Art. 1(3) and 1(4), Annex I, Section 7.4 and Annex II, Section 4.3 of Directive 93/42/EEC (medical devices).
91. Article 3(a) of Regulation (EC) 469/2009, and Art. 3(1)(a) of Regulation (EC) 1610/96.
92. *See*, e.g., recital 8 of Regulation (EC) 469/2009, recital 10 of Regulation (EC) 1610/96, CJEU *Farmitalia Carlo Erba v. Bundesgerichtshof*, C-392/97 of 16 September 1999, paragraph 25, and CJEU *Medeva v. Comptroller General of Patents, Designs and Trade Marks*, C-322/10 of 24 November 2011, paragraph 24. Art. 63(2)(b) EPC enshrines the possibility, in principle, to provide for supplemental protection on the basis of European patents, the subject matter of which is a product, a process for manufacturing a product or a use of a product which has to undergo an administrative authorization procedure before it can be placed on the market.
93. Regulation (EC) 469/2009 and Regulation (EC) 1610/96 do not limit the type of patents that can be relied upon for an SPC; *see also* Rule 5(1)(d) of the Rules of Procedure of the UPC, in the draft

In principle, patents with any type of claims can be used as the basic patent for an SPC filing, i.e., not only patents having product claims directed to the active ingredient (or combination of active ingredients) as such, including product claims directed towards formulations comprising the active ingredient(s), but also patents having process claims directed to the preparation of the active ingredient(s), as well as patents having claims directed to the application of the active ingredient(s). This is reflected in the definition of the term 'basic patent' in the SPC Regulations, which stipulates that the basic patent is 'a patent which protects a product as such, a process to obtain a product or an application of a product',[94] and is furthermore in line with the intention expressed in the Explanatory Memorandums that SPC protection should be available for all types of inventions in the fields of pharmaceutical and plant protection research.[95]

Under Article 3(a) of the SPC Regulations,[96] the basic patent must be 'in force' in the respective state *at the date of the SPC application*. The filing of an SPC application on the basis of a lawfully expired patent is thus clearly barred. However, there is no express requirement in the SPC Regulations that the basic patent would still need to be 'in force' at the point in time when an SPC is actually granted. In line with this, in practice the national patent offices will grant an SPC even if on the date of grant the basic patent has expired due to the lapse of the twenty-year term.

It is conceivable that an SPC may need to be filed at a point of time, where the basic patent is at least temporarily deemed to be not validly pending, e.g., if it has been revoked in first-instance opposition or nullity proceedings. If the corresponding first-instance decision is appealed and the patent is subsequently maintained in the second instance with ex tunc effect, then this should not be detrimental to the filing of the SPC. Under such circumstances, most, if not all patent offices will stay the prosecution of the SPC application.

Similarly, if the patent is deemed to have lapsed due to non-payment of annual renewal fees but is subsequently reinstated, this should not have any impact on the filing of an SPC on the basis of this patent as the legal consequences of failure tripped the time limit shall be deemed not to have ensued.

---

version as of 15 March 2017 (which refers to '*supplementary protection certificates ... based on a European patent with unitary effect*'), and the Explanatory Memorandum to the Commission proposal for an SPC regulation for medicinal products, COM(90) 101 final – SYN 255, paragraphs 30 and 31 as well as the Explanatory Memorandum to the Commission proposal for an SPC regulation for plant protection products, COM(94) 579 final, paragraph 67 ('*...whether this be a national patent, a European patent or, in due course, a Community patent ... whatever the legal source of the patent*'). The CJEU also noted that the Agreement on a Unified Patent Court (UPCA) '*may be applicable in the future, pursuant to Art. 3(b) of that agreement, to SPCs granted on the basis of Regulation (EC) 469/2009*' (*see* CJEU *Eli Lilly v. Human Genome Sciences*, C-493/12 of 12 December 2013, paragraph 30).

94. Article 1(b) of Regulation (EC) 469/2009; a corresponding definition is likewise provided in Art. 1(9) of Regulation (EC) 1610/96.
95. Explanatory Memorandum to the Commission proposal for an SPC regulation for medicinal products, COM(90) 101 final – SYN 255, paragraph 29; and Explanatory Memorandum to the Commission proposal for an SPC regulation for plant protection products, COM(94) 579 final, paragraph 66.
96. Article 3(a) of Regulation (EC) 469/2009, and Art. 3(1)(a) of Regulation (EC) 1610/96.

[1] Requirement for the Product to Be 'Protected' by the Basic Patent

At first glance, the requirement under Article 3(a) of the SPC Regulations that, for obtaining an SPC, the product must be 'protected by a basic patent'[97] appears rather simple and straightforward. Yet, the interpretation of this requirement has caused considerable controversy and has prompted more referrals to the CJEU than any other provision of the SPC Regulations.

It would appear natural that the question what is (or is not) 'protected' by a patent should be answered on the basis of the corresponding principles of patent law, particularly in the absence of any definition or clear indication in the SPC Regulations and the corresponding preparatory documents that a concept different from the one established in patent law should have been intended. From the perspective of patent law, simply put, anything that falls within the scope of the granted claims of a patent is 'protected' by the patent. It has thus been argued that the requirement in the SPC Regulations that the product must be 'protected' by the basic patent should be understood in the sense of an 'infringement test' (or an 'extent of protection test'[98]). This may well be considered justified, not least since, by definition, any product that falls within the scope of the claims of a granted patent makes use of the invention protected by that patent.

This approach has however been criticized, as it would amount to allowing the grant of SPCs on the basis of patents that merely generically encompass a specific product in question, without actually disclosing it and thereby making the specific product directly available. This perceived problem is particularly manifest in the case of combinations of active ingredients, where the use of an 'infringement test' to determine whether a product is 'protected' by the basic patent could allow the grant of an SPC for any conceivable combination of active ingredients A and B on the basis of a patent that claims the active ingredient A but is completely devoid of any disclosure whatsoever relating to the active ingredient B. It has been argued that the grant of an SPC under such conditions would contravene the object of the SPC Regulations to encourage and compensate for long and costly research in the pharmaceutical or plant protection field,[99] particularly for the development of novel products, and that therefore only a product which is specifically disclosed (i.e., identified) and claimed in the basic patent should be regarded as being 'protected' by that patent within the meaning of Article 3(a) of the SPC Regulations. In the past the national patent offices applied conflicting approaches, resulting in divergent national practices and case law.

This controversy and the initial divergence in national case law have since been resolved in favour of an 'identification test' rather than an 'infringement test'. Thus, the

97. *Ibid.*
98. Arguably, an 'infringement test' and an 'extent of protection test' can give different results, e.g., with respect to the question whether a claim requiring (at least) one active ingredient A 'protects' a combination of active ingredients A and B. *See*, e.g., the opinion of Advocate General Wathelet in *Teva UK v. Gilead Sciences*, C-121/17, delivered on 25 April 2018, paragraph 59.
99. *See* recitals 3–5 of Regulation (EC) 469/2009, and recitals 3–7 of Regulation (EC) 1610/96.

CJEU held in *Medeva* (C-322/10)[100] and various subsequent decisions[101] that the product, i.e., the active ingredient or combination of active ingredients, must be '*specified in the wording of the claims*' (or '*identified in the wording of the claims*') of the basic patent. In justifying its conclusion reached in *Medeva*, the CJEU relied primarily on the lack of harmonization of substantive patent law at the EU level and the aim of the SPC Regulation to prevent heterogeneous national developments that could create obstacles to the free movement of goods within the EU's single market.[102] Arguably, the requirement that the product must be 'protected' by the basic patent has thereby effectively been reinterpreted by the CJEU to give it a meaning that could be uniformly applied in all EU Member States and should thus allow for a harmonized European approach, in spite of the lack of harmonization of the national patent laws governing the underlying basic patent. In this sense, the CJEU's endorsement of the 'identification test'[103] has been perceived as overruling – at least to a certain extent – its earlier findings in *Farmitalia* (C-392/97)[104] that in order to determine whether a product is 'protected' by a basic patent, reference would have to be made to the (non-EU) rules governing that patent, which appeared to sanction the application of different approaches in different EU Member States.

In accordance with the 'identification test', in the case of an SPC for a product which is a combination of active ingredients, all active ingredients of the combination must be specified in the wording of the claims of the basic patent.[105] Conversely, if the active ingredient or combination of active ingredients in question is/are specified in the claims of the basic patent *but only together with one or more additional active ingredients* that are not subject of the SPC application, it follows that the patent does not 'protect' (i.e., specify) the corresponding product, so that the grant of an SPC on the basis of that patent is precluded.[106] This approach is consistent with the definition of the term 'product' in the SPC Regulations, which distinguishes between a combination of active ingredients and any of the corresponding individual active ingredients as

100. CJEU *Medeva v. Comptroller General of Patents, Designs and Trade Marks*, C-322/10 of 24 November 2011, headnote 1.
101. CJEU *University of Queensland v. Comptroller-General of Patents, Designs and Trade Marks*, C-630/10 of 25 November 2011, headnote 1; CJEU *Daiichi Sankyo v. Comptroller General of Patents, Designs and Trade Marks*, C-6/11 of 25 November 2011, headnote; CJEU *Yeda Research and Development v. Comptroller General of Patents, Designs and Trade Marks*, C-518/10 of 25 November 2011, headnote and paragraph 37; CJEU *Eli Lilly v. Human Genome Sciences*, C-493/12 of 12 December 2013, paragraph 38.
102. CJEU *Medeva v. Comptroller General of Patents, Designs and Trade Marks*, C-322/10 of 24 November 2011, paragraphs 22–25.
103. Note that the CJEU does not literally use the expression 'identification test' in the referenced case law.
104. CJEU *Farmitalia Carlo Erba v. Bundesgerichtshof*, C-392/97 of 16 September 1999, paragraphs 26–27 and headnote 2.
105. CJEU *Medeva v. Comptroller General of Patents, Designs and Trade Marks*, C-322/10 of 24 November 2011, headnote 1; CJEU *University of Queensland v. Comptroller-General of Patents, Designs and Trade Marks*, C-630/10 of 25 November 2011, headnote 1; CJEU *Daiichi Sankyo v. Comptroller General of Patents, Designs and Trade Marks*, C-6/11 of 25 November 2011, headnote.
106. CJEU *Medeva v. Comptroller General of Patents, Designs and Trade Marks*, C-322/10 of 24 November 2011, paragraph 26; CJEU *Yeda Research and Development v. Comptroller General of Patents, Designs and Trade Marks*, C-518/10 of 25 November 2011, headnote.

different products.[107] The correlation between the active ingredient(s) specified in the claims of the basic patent and the product for which an SPC is obtainable can be illustrated as shown in the following Table 1.1:

Table 1.1 Correlation Between the Active Ingredient(s) Specified in the Claims of the Basic Patent and the Product for Which an SPC Is Obtainable (A, B and C are different active ingredients)

Claims of the Basic Patent	*Subject of the SPC*	*SPC Obtainable?*
A + B	A	no
A + B	A + B	yes
A + B	A + B + C	no

An SPC can also be granted on the basis of a patent claiming a process by which a product is obtained. In this case, too, the product in question must be 'identified' in the wording of the claims of the basic patent. More precisely, as the CJEU explained in *University of Queensland* (C-630/10),[108] the product must be 'identified' in the wording of the claims 'as the product deriving from that process'; in this context, it is irrelevant whether it is possible to obtain the product *directly* as a result of the claimed process.[109]

In practice, however, the application of the 'identification test' has proven far more difficult than it may have originally been envisaged by the CJEU. In particular, its application frequently raises the question just how precisely an active ingredient needs to be specified in the claims of a basic patent in order to be 'protected' by that patent in the sense of Article 3(a) of the SPC Regulations. Thus, in the words of Advocate General Wathelet in his opinion in the CJEU referral *Teva UK v. Gilead Sciences* (C-121/17), the question really is 'what degree of specificity or abstraction' is required for a product to be 'specified' in the claims of the basic patent.[110]

In *Eli Lilly* (C-493/12),[111] the CJEU dealt with claims defining an active ingredient in functional terms (in the case at issue: an antibody that binds specifically to a certain target), and found that an active ingredient does not necessarily have to be specified by a *structural definition* in the claims of the basic patent, but that a *functional definition* may also suffice to specify and thus 'protect' the active ingredient in question. This is possible on the condition that the claims – when interpreted in the light of the description of the basic patent, in accordance with Article 69 EPC and the Protocol on the Interpretation of Article 69 EPC[112] – are found to relate, '*implicitly but necessarily*

107. Article 1(b) of Regulation (EC) 469/2009, and Art. 1(8) of Regulation (EC) 1610/96.
108. CJEU *University of Queensland v. Comptroller-General of Patents, Designs and Trade Marks*, C-630/10 of 25 November 2011.
109. *Ibid.*, paragraphs 40–41 and headnote 3.
110. Opinion of Advocate General Wathelet in *Teva UK v. Gilead Sciences*, C-121/17, delivered on 25 April 2018, paragraph 76.
111. CJEU *Eli Lilly v. Human Genome Sciences*, C-493/12 of 12 December 2013.
112. While Art. 69 EPC and the protocol on its interpretation (which forms an integral part of the EPC; *see* Art. 164 EPC) apply, strictly speaking, only to European patents, the national patent

and specifically', to the active ingredient at issue.[113] Since the CJEU does not have jurisdiction to interpret the provisions of the EPC, including Article 69 EPC and the protocol on its interpretation, it considered itself unable to provide any further guidance how exactly it should be determined whether the claims, when interpreted in the light of the description of the patent, relate 'implicitly but necessarily and specifically' to the corresponding active ingredient.[114]

The significance of these findings in *Eli Lilly* can hardly be overestimated. The CJEU has finally confirmed that the description of the basic patent must be taken into account when determining whether a product is 'protected' by the claims of that patent, which is a welcome clarification. Deciding otherwise, i.e., looking solely at the wording of the claims and ignoring the description of a patent, would have entailed tremendously harsh (and unjust) consequences[115] and would have made the question even more pressing how to deal with basic patents whose claims have been restricted after grant (and possibly only after the filing of an SPC) to recite a specific active ingredient that was not previously mentioned in the claims.[116] By relying on Article 69 EPC and the protocol on its interpretation, and by declaring itself incapable of providing any further guidance how to apply the 'identification test' when considering the description of the basic patent, however, the CJEU has completely evaded the fundamental question how precisely an active ingredient must be identified - be it in the claims or the description - in order to be 'protected' by the basic patent.

Yet, it is remarkable that the CJEU in *Eli Lilly* referred to the rules relating to the extent of protection, particularly Article 69 EPC and the protocol on its interpretation, as being decisive for determining what is 'protected' by the basic patent.[117] While the CJEU emphasized the relevance of the rules relating to the extent of protection in distinction from the 'rules governing infringement proceedings',[118] noting that infringement of the basic patent is 'not a crucial factor' for determining whether a product is 'protected' by the basic patent,[119] this distinction between the extent of protection and the question of infringement seems of limited practical relevance, given that a product (as the subject of an SPC) is not an *act* which could constitute a patent infringement; rather, the question whether the product falls within the extent of

laws of the EU Member States, all of which are also EPC contracting states, contain generally the same or equivalent provisions that also apply to the respective national patents.

113. CJEU *Eli Lilly v. Human Genome Sciences*, C-493/12 of 12 December 2013, headnote.
114. *Ibid.*, paragraph 40.
115. If the wording of the claims alone were decisive (and the description of the basic patent were to be completely disregarded), proprietors of patents that claim an active ingredient in broad terms and identify the specific active ingredient in question in the description would be grossly disadvantaged, particularly as such patents would actually make the specific active ingredient available, just like patents that expressly identify the specific active ingredient in their claims.
116. The restriction of the granted claims of a basic patent by incorporating more specific subject matter disclosed in the description of the patent is generally permissible, e.g., in the course of opposition or voluntary limitation proceedings before the EPO. Notably, if such amendments after grant are made in central proceedings before the EPO, they are deemed to have retroactive effect (*see* Art. 68 EPC).
117. CJEU *Eli Lilly v. Human Genome Sciences*, C-493/12 of 12 December 2013, paragraph 32.
118. *Ibid.*, paragraph 33.
119. *Ibid.*, paragraph 37.

protection of the basic patent is precisely what would normally be assessed in the context of an 'infringement test'.[120]

The CJEU's reference to the 'extent of protection rules' as being decisive for determining what is 'protected' by the basic patent begs the question whether or not the active ingredient under consideration needs to be identified with its full structural details in the description of the basic patent. If the rules relating to the extent of protection are to be applied to assess whether an active ingredient is 'protected' by the basic patent (containing a claim with a functional definition), and if the decisive criterion in this respect is only that it must be possible to reach the conclusion that the claims, when interpreted in the light of the description of the patent, relate 'implicitly but necessarily and specifically' to the active ingredient at issue, does this mean that the corresponding active ingredient must merely be recognizable as being embraced by a functional definition used in the claims? Or should it rather be necessary that the description explicitly identifies this active ingredient, and if so, with which level of detail?

The understanding that the active ingredient must still be *identified* in the description of the basic patent appears to be supported by the CJEU's further comments in *Eli Lilly* to the extent that, in view of the purpose of the SPC Regulation to encourage research and ensure that investments put into such research are covered, 'the refusal of an SPC application for an active ingredient which is not specifically referred to by a patent issued by the EPO ... may be justified ... where the holder of the patent in question has failed to take any steps to carry out more in-depth research and identify his invention specifically, making it possible to ascertain clearly the active ingredient which may be commercially exploited in a medicinal product corresponding to the needs of certain patients'.[121] In particular, the CJEU's reference to a failure to '*identify [the] invention specifically*' and to make it possible to '*ascertain clearly the active ingredient*' as justification for refusing an SPC could be read to mean that the active ingredient in question must be clearly and specifically identified in the patent. On the other hand, since the aforementioned statement of the CJEU in *Eli Lilly* starts from the premise that the active ingredient at issue 'is not specifically referred to by a patent issued by the EPO' – i.e., that the basic patent (not only the wording of the claims) fails to specifically refer to the active ingredient, this statement could likewise be understood as merely providing a rationale for the refusal of an SPC under such conditions, rather than specifying the criteria for determining whether an active ingredient is, or is not, specifically referred to (and thus 'protected') by the basic patent.

The requirement that the active ingredient(s) must be explicitly identified in the description would appear to be an unduly high hurdle in the case of patents identifying

120. Note, however, that an 'infringement test' and an 'extent of protection test' could arguably give different results, e.g., with respect to the question whether a claim requiring (at least) one active ingredient A 'protects' a combination of active ingredients A and B. In this regard, *see*, e.g., the opinion of Advocate General Wathelet in *Teva UK v. Gilead Sciences*, C-121/17, delivered on 25 April 2018, paragraph 59 for illustration.

121. CJEU *Eli Lilly v. Human Genome Sciences*, C-493/12 of 12 December 2013, paragraphs 42 and 43.

a new target for an antibody. This de facto would imply that SPC protection would only be available for more downstream inventions.

In the case at hand the holder of the basic patent had not made any investment in the development of the approved active ingredient. The CJEU in *Eli Lilly* emphasized that under these circumstances, the issue of an SPC to such a third party would undermine the objective of SPC Regulation. As such the guidance provided by the CJEU may also be interpreted to the effect that if the basic patent identifies the active ingredient, the holder of the patent may be entitled to an SPC even if he relies on a third party marketing approval. If, however, the basic patent only provides a functional definition of the active ingredient, an SPC will only be available if the patentee has made investments in the research and development of the product.

The CJEU's reliance on Article 69 EPC and the protocol on its interpretation could pave the way for a more generous 'identification test', particularly as it may allow recourse to be had to the *common general knowledge* of a person skilled in the art when determining the disclosure-content of the basic patent[122] for the purpose of interpreting the claims, and it may possibly even allow the inclusion of *equivalents*[123] that are not expressly disclosed in the patent at all. It is noteworthy in this regard that even though the CJEU found in *Eli Lilly* that the specific active ingredient at issue was not expressly named in the claims and was not otherwise specified in the description of the basic patent either,[124] it could still not determine whether or not the corresponding active ingredient was 'protected' by the patent. This finding does not seem easily reconcilable with a narrow or strict 'identification test', which would require an express and complete identification of the active ingredient at least in the description of the basic patent.

The necessity to interpret the claims of a patent in the light of the description and the drawings, as stipulated in Article 69 EPC, is an absolutely fundamental principle of patent law. The significance of the CJEU's reliance on Article 69 EPC and the protocol on its interpretation in *Eli Lilly* can therefore be expected to extend well beyond the specific case of functional definitions which was addressed in this decision. Thus, it would appear that whenever there is any doubt that the claims of a basic patent identify and hence 'protect' the specific active ingredient in question, it will be necessary to consult the description and interpret the claims in accordance with the principles of Article 69 EPC and the protocol on its interpretation. This, in consequence, would mean that one decisive step in the determination whether a product is 'protected' by a

122. The Enlarged Board of Appeal of the EPO considered the disclosure-content of a European patent or patent application, composed of the description, claims and drawings, as embracing '*what a skilled person would derive directly and unambiguously, using common general knowledge, and seen objectively and relative to the date of filing, from the whole of these documents as filed*', and referred to this as a 'gold standard' (Enlarged Board of Appeal of the EPO, decision G 2/10 of 30 August 2011, item 4.3 of the reasons).

123. Article 2 of the Protocol on the Interpretation of Art. 69 EPC stipulates:

> For the purpose of determining the extent of protection conferred by a European patent, due account shall be taken of any element which is equivalent to an element specified in the claims.

124. CJEU *Eli Lilly v. Human Genome Sciences*, C-493/12 of 12 December 2013, paragraph 36.

basic patent in the sense of Article 3(a) of the SPC Regulations could be systematically excluded from the assessment of the CJEU, which would effectively sanction the (re-)emergence of a certain degree of divergence in the national case law of different EU Member States. To some extent, this could mark an unexpected return to the earlier practice established in *Farmitalia* (C-392/97), in which the CJEU left it to national courts to determine whether the product of an SPC is 'protected' by the basic patent, relying on the respective (non-EU) rules governing that patent.[125]

The CJEU's findings in *Eli Lilly* further raise practical questions regarding the drafting and prosecution of patent applications. As national courts appear to have the final say in the interpretation of functional definitions in the claims of the basic patent and, at least in connection with this particular step, in determining what is 'protected' by the patent, could it make sense to deliberately include a functional definition in the claims, particularly in addition to a generic structural definition of an active ingredient, in order to take advantage of a potentially more generous approach in some EU (or EEA) Member States? One can only hope that the CJEU will clarify the scope of application of its findings in *Eli Lilly* in a consistent manner and confirm that other generic terms or definitions used in the claims of the basic patent must likewise be interpreted in accordance with the principles of Article 69 EPC and the protocol on its interpretation for the purpose of establishing whether they identify and thus 'protect' the active ingredient in question.

In this connection, it should not be left unmentioned that the CJEU in *Actavis v. Sanofi* (C-443/12) – which was issued by the same Chamber on the same day as *Eli Lilly* – referred to the combination of the active ingredient irbesartan with 'an unlimited number of other active ingredients ... referred to in the wording of the claims of the patent in general terms, such as ... "beta-blocking compound", "calcium antagonist", "diuretic", "non-steroidal anti-inflammatory" or "tranquilizer" as being "not protected as such by the basic patent"'.[126] Even though this decision was concerned with a different condition for the grant of an SPC, namely the requirement under Article 3(c) that the product has not already been the subject of an SPC,[127] at first glance it seems surprising that the CJEU could simply conclude that the combination of active ingredients at issue, i.e., irbesartan and hydrochlorothiazide (which is a specific diuretic[128]), was not 'protected' by the claims of the basic patent reciting a pharmaceutical composition containing irbesartan together with a diuretic,[129] without even having to interpret the functional definition 'diuretic' in the light of the description of the basic patent.[130] This seeming inconsistency with the CJEU's findings in *Eli Lilly* is, however, resolved by the fact that the Court took it to be common ground that hydrochlorothiazide (and the combination of irbesartan and hydrochlorothiazide) was not protected 'as such' by the claims of the basic patent, in the sense that it does not embody the 'core inventive advance' of the patent, which was considered to be

125. CJEU *Farmitalia Carlo Erba v. Bundesgerichtshof*, C-392/97 of 16 September 1999, headnote 2.
126. CJEU *Actavis v. Sanofi*, C-443/12 of 12 December 2013, paragraph 41.
127. Article 3(c) of Regulation (EC) 469/2009, and Art. 3(1)(c) of Regulation (EC) 1610/96.
128. CJEU *Actavis v. Sanofi*, C-443/12 of 12 December 2013, paragraph 14.
129. *Ibid.*, paragraph 11.
130. *Ibid.*, paragraph 41.

embodied by irbesartan alone.[131] It thus seems clear that the CJEU did not actually address the question whether the combination of irbesartan and hydrochlorothiazide was *identified* in the basic patent at issue. The relevance of the 'core inventive advance' of the basic patent will be further discussed in §1.02[B][3] below.

In the recent decision *Teva UK v. Gilead Sciences* (C-121/17),[132] the CJEU comprehensively addressed the requirement of Article 3(a) in the context of an SPC directed to an anti-HIV combination product (Truvada) containing the two active ingredients tenofovir disoproxil and emtricitabine. The claims of the basic patent underlying this SPC expressly referred to tenofovir disoproxil as one of the claimed antiviral compounds but did not provide any explicit mentioning of emtricitabine. The patent merely contained a claim directed to a pharmaceutical composition comprising the aforementioned compound 'and optionally other therapeutic ingredients', without however providing any further definition or explanation of the term 'other therapeutic ingredients' anywhere in the description. Moreover, according to the referring court, there was no evidence that emtricitabine would have been known to the person skilled in the art as a therapeutic agent effective against HIV at the priority date of the basic patent.[133]

The CJEU in *Teva UK v. Gilead Sciences* recapitulated that the rules for determining what is 'protected by a basic patent' within the meaning of Article 3(a) are those relating to the extent of the invention covered by a patent, as provided in the case of a European patent in Article 69 EPC and the protocol on its interpretation.[134] It may be noted that the CJEU uses the expression 'extent of the invention' when referring to the 'extent of protection' rules according to Article 69 EPC, which is in line with the corresponding UK terminology.[135]

Referring to its earlier decision *Eli Lilly*, the Court reemphasized that a product cannot be considered to be 'protected' by a basic patent unless the product is either expressly mentioned in the claims of the patent or those claims – when interpreted in the light of the description and drawings of the patent – relate implicitly but necessarily and specifically to the corresponding product.[136]

The CJEU further pointed out that, in view of the protocol on the interpretation of Article 69 EPC, the question whether a product necessarily falls under the invention covered by the basic patent must be assessed from the perspective of a person skilled in the art.[137] Notably, the Court went on to stress that, for this purpose, 'account must be taken exclusively of the prior art at the filing date or priority date of that patent, such that the product must be specifically identifiable by a person skilled in the art in the light of all the information disclosed by that patent',[138] while results that were not yet

131. *Ibid.*, paragraphs 29, 30, 32 and 41.
132. CJEU *Teva UK v. Gilead Sciences*, C-121/17 of 25 July 2018.
133. *Ibid.*, paragraphs 14–20 and 29.
134. *Ibid.*, paragraph 32.
135. Section 125 of the UK Patents Act 1977 is entitled 'Extent of invention' and corresponds essentially to Art. 69 EPC. *See also* CJEU *Teva UK v. Gilead Sciences*, C-121/17 of 25 July 2018, paragraphs 3, 4, 12 and 13.
136. CJEU *Teva UK v. Gilead Sciences*, C-121/17 of 25 July 2018, paragraphs 36–38.
137. *Ibid.*, paragraph 47.
138. *Ibid.*, paragraph 49.

known at the filing date or the priority date of the patent must not be taken into account.[139]

The following understanding of the requirement of Article 3(a) was thus derived by the CJEU in *Teva UK v. Gilead Sciences*:[140]

> Therefore, for the purposes of determining whether a product which is the subject of an SPC is protected by a basic patent, within the meaning of Article 3(a) of [the SPC Regulation], that product must be identifiable specifically by a person skilled in the art in the light of all the information disclosed by the basic patent and of the prior art at the filing date or priority date of that patent.
>
> Having regard to all the foregoing considerations, a product is 'protected by a basic patent in force' within the meaning of Article 3(a) of [the SPC Regulation] in so far as, if that product is not expressly mentioned in the claims of the basic patent, one of those claims relates to it necessarily and specifically. For that purpose, that product must, from the point of view of a person skilled in the art and in the light of the description and drawings of the basic patent, necessarily fall under the invention covered by that patent. The person skilled in the art must be able [to] identify that product specifically in the light of all the information disclosed by that patent, on the basis of the prior art at the filing date or priority date of the patent concerned.

It appears highly significant that the CJEU does not require the product of an SPC to be *actually identified* in the basic patent, but that it suffices for the product to be *identifiable* on the basis of the patent and the prior art available at the effective date of the patent. It may thus be concluded that an SPC can indeed be granted for a product which is not expressly disclosed in the corresponding basic patent, so long as the patent refers to this product using a generic or functional term which makes the corresponding product identifiable from the prior art available at the priority or filing date of the patent.

The CJEU in *Teva UK v. Gilead Sciences* further noted that the above-discussed general understanding of Article 3(a) of the SPC Regulation must also be upheld if, as in the specific case at hand, the product at issue is composed of several active ingredients which have a combined effect. According to the CJEU, it falls to the referring court to determine whether the general expression 'other therapeutic ingredients', associated with the term 'optionally', satisfies the requirement that the claims of the basic patent must relate necessarily and specifically to the product at issue.[141] While it remains to be seen how the UK Patents Court (as the referring court) will assess this question, it is noteworthy that the CJEU did not from the outset exclude the possibility that even a generic term as broad and unspecific as 'other therapeutic ingredients' could potentially make the corresponding product identifiable and could thereby potentially provide a basis for an SPC.

Despite the various above-discussed decisions in which the CJEU has already addressed the requirement under Article 3(a) of the SPC Regulations that the product must be 'protected' by the basic patent, there still remains a high degree of uncertainty

139. *Ibid.*, paragraph 50.
140. *Ibid.*, paragraphs 51–52.
141. *Ibid.*, paragraphs 53–54.

about what this criterion means and how exactly it is to be applied. Two further referrals to the CJEU relating to this requirement are currently pending.[142] Hopefully, these referrals will provide useful answers without raising all too many new questions.

[a] Small Molecules

The question how precisely small molecules need to be specified (or identified) in order to be 'protected' by the basic patent within the meaning of Article 3(a) of the SPC Regulations[143] arises, in particular, in the case of claims reciting a generic chemical formula (so-called Markush formula)[144] which encompasses the specific compound at issue, and where the description of the patent does not explicitly disclose the corresponding specific compound.

A fundamental question in this regard is whether each and every individual compound that is derivable from a generic chemical formula is specified and thus 'protected' by that formula. If that were not always and necessarily the case, a range of further questions would arise, including whether each one of the chemical groups comprised in the active ingredient under consideration needs to be specifically disclosed in the basic patent, or whether it is sufficient that a person skilled in the art, using its common general knowledge, would be aware of the specific chemical group as an exemplary embodiment of the broader term used in the patent.

If, for example, one variable group 'R^1' in a generic chemical formula is defined to be a 'heteroaryl' and thereby encompasses the active ingredient at issue which contains a 'pyridinyl' group (which is a specific type of heteroaryl) in this position, would the patent need to expressly disclose pyridinyl as an example of the heteroaryl group, or would it suffice that pyridinyl is recognizable by a person skilled in the art as a heteroaryl group? In the former case, would the patent also have to disclose the specific point of attachment of the pyridinyl group to the rest of the molecule (e.g., pyridin-2-yl, pyridin-3-yl or pyridin-4-yl)? Would a corresponding disclosure of a pyridinyl group be required specifically in the context of the variable group R^1, or would a general reference to pyridinyl as an example of a heteroaryl group suffice? Alternatively, if an explicit disclosure in the basic patent of the specific chemical groups contained in the active ingredient in question is not necessary, does it make any difference whether these specific groups are common or rather unusual in active ingredients of medicinal products or plant protection products? Does it make any difference whether the particular active ingredient at issue is one of a few or one of

142. Referrals C-650/17 (*QH / Royalty Pharma*) and C-114/18 (*Sandoz v. Searle*).
143. Article 3(a) of Regulation (EC) 469/2009, and Art. 3(1)(a) of Regulation (EC) 1610/96.
144. It is noteworthy that the possibility of relying on '*a patent [that] protects a series of products based on the same formula*' was already acknowledged in the Explanatory Memorandums to the SPC Regulations. *See* the Explanatory Memorandum to the Commission proposal for an SPC regulation for medicinal products, COM(90) 101 final – SYN 255, paragraph 39 and the Explanatory Memorandum to the Commission proposal for an SPC regulation for plant protection products, COM(94) 579 final, paragraph 69.

numerous (possibly a million or a trillion) compounds that are theoretically derivable from the same generic formula?[145]

While these questions have not yet been addressed by the CJEU, there is currently a referral pending, i.e., *Sandoz v. Searle* (C-114/18), which relates specifically to the case of a generic chemical formula (Markush formula). The corresponding question referred to the CJEU by the UK Court of Appeal asks, simply put, whether it is sufficient that the specific compound which is the subject of an SPC would be recognized to be embraced by the Markush formula in the claims of the basic patent, or whether the specific groups/substituents necessary to form this particular compound need to be derivable from the patent by a skilled person using its common general knowledge.[146] In this referral, the UK Court of Appeal suggested that the relevant test to determine whether a basic patent having a Markush formula in its claims 'protects' a specific active ingredient should be 'whether the skilled person, considering the claims of the patent on the one hand and the structure of the product in question on the other, would immediately recognize that the active ingredient in question is one of those specified by the formula'.[147] While this test would have the benefit of avoiding an unduly restrictive assessment of Markush formulae, the subjective qualifying term 'immediately' would

145. The notion that the breadth of a Markush formula could potentially be seen as a relevant factor in this regard appears to be supported by the comments of Advocate General Wathelet in his opinion in the pending CJEU referral *Teva UK v. Gilead Sciences* (C-121/17), paragraph 76 and footnote 39, where he noted that patent claims vary in their degree of specificity or abstraction and quoted an EPO board of appeal decision as saying that '*special problems are caused by the exceptional length of the claims, by the fact that the [Markush] formula consists entirely of variables, and by the number of variables, mostly defined in terms of other variables*'.

146. *See* UK Court of Appeal, *Sandoz Ltd et al. v. G.D. Searle LLC et al.* [2018] EWCA Civ 49. The complete question referred to the CJEU reads as follows:

> Where the sole active ingredient the subject of a supplementary protection certificate issued under [the SPC Regulation] is a member of a class of compounds which fall within a Markush definition in a claim of the patent, all of which class members embody the core inventive technical advance of the patent, is it sufficient for the purposes of Art. 3(a) of the SPC Regulation that the compound would, upon examination of its structure, immediately be recognized as one which falls within the class (and therefore would be protected by the patent as a matter of national patent law) or must the specific substituents necessary to form the active ingredient be amongst those which the skilled person could derive, based on their common general knowledge, from a reading of the patent claims?

147. *See* UK Court of Appeal, *Sandoz Ltd et al. v. G.D. Searle LLC et al.* [2018] EWCA Civ 49, paragraph 114. The corresponding complete observations made by Lord Justice Floyd read as follows:

> In case it would assist the Court of Justice I will express my provisional conclusion. Left to myself, I would have concluded that darunavir was a product protected by the claims of the patent. In the case of a product with a single active ingredient and a patent with a claim which identifies a number of compounds by means of a Markush formula, all of which compounds embody the core inventive technical advance of the patent, the test should be whether the skilled person, considering the claims of the patent on the one hand and the structure of the product in question on the other, would immediately recognize that the active ingredient in question is one of those specified by the formula. On the facts of the present case as found by the judge, that test is satisfied. However, for the reasons I have given, it is not clear that this is the correct approach in EU law.

seem bound to give rise to further questions, divergent national decisions and a lack of legal certainty, if it were adopted by the CJEU.

Until further clarification is provided by the CJEU, it seems advisable to explicitly mention all potentially interesting chemical groups for the variable parts or substituents contained in a generic chemical formula when drafting a patent application. One convenient possibility could be the inclusion, in the description of the patent application, of a definition of each broad term used in the generic chemical formula, together with a comprehensive list of specific chemical groups disclosed as examples of the corresponding broad term, possibly even with various specific points of attachment and various specific stereochemical configurations (where applicable).

[b] Polymers

Polymers are composed of one or more types of structural repeating units (monomeric units). The structural identity of the monomeric units constituting a polymer can be considered as the most fundamental property defining a polymer.[148] However, polymers can be defined more precisely by a number of additional parameters, including the relative amount (molar fraction) of each monomeric unit. Moreover, the monomeric units of a polymer are typically connected in a linear or branched fashion, resulting in a specific type of monomer arrangement (e.g., alternating copolymers, periodic copolymers, statistical copolymers, random copolymers, block copolymers, graft copolymers, etc.) and a specific type of overall architecture (e.g., linear polymers, star polymers, comb polymers, brush polymers, dendrimers, cyclic polymers, etc.). Since a polymer frequently exists as a mixture of macromolecules having different chain lengths, additional physicochemical parameters can be employed to further define the constitution of the polymer, such as the degree of polymerization, number average molecular weight, weight average molecular weight, polydispersity index, and/or glass transition temperature of the polymer.

The question how precisely a polymer as an active ingredient needs to be specified in a basic patent in order to be 'protected' in the sense of the SPC Regulations has not yet been directly addressed in the case law of the CJEU.

Yet, from a practical perspective, it is noteworthy that marketing authorizations for medicinal products typically identify the corresponding active ingredient using an international non-proprietary name (INN), and that, in most cases, SPCs likewise refer to the INN that is indicated in the summary of product characteristics (SmPC) of the authorized medicinal product.

INNs, however, can define polymers with different levels of detail. For example, while many INNs for therapeutic polymers merely specify the structures of their respective constituent monomers, without defining any further properties of the

148. This is also reflected by the fact that the Chemical Abstracts Services (CAS) Registry classifies polymers primarily on the basis of their monomers, and includes many entries for polymers that are identified solely by the structures of their respective constituent monomers.

corresponding polymers, other INNs specify therapeutic polymers via both the structure and the molar fraction of their respective monomers.[149] Moreover, the definition of an INN can specify the structure of each monomer by showing either the actual repeating unit (as it is present in the polymer) or the monomeric starting material (before polymerization), with the consequence that the chemical linkages of the respective monomeric units and the corresponding terminal groups may or may not be defined.[150] Further properties, such as the monomer arrangement, the polymer architecture, the degree of polymerization, the average molecular weight, or the molecular weight distribution are usually not specified in the definitions of INNs for therapeutic polymers, but could potentially also be included.

Arguably, where an SPC (and the underlying marketing authorization) uses an INN to define an active ingredient which is a polymer, the precise definition of that INN and the level of detail it contains could affect the question how precisely the polymer needs to be specified in the basic patent in order to be 'protected' in the sense of Article 3(a) of the SPC Regulations. In principle, it should suffice that the basic patent identifies those features of the polymer that are specified in the definition of the corresponding INN (which is used in the marketing authorization and the SPC), whereas any further characteristics of the actual polymer[151] that are not reflected in the definition of the INN should not necessarily have to be identified in the basic patent, either. To some extent, such considerations and the manner in which a polymer is disclosed in a potential basic patent could already be taken into account when applying for an INN that could later be used in a marketing authorization and an SPC application.

[c] Antibodies, Enzymes and Other Proteins

Although the CJEU already dealt with the question whether a specific antibody was 'protected' by the corresponding basic patent in *Eli Lilly* (C-493/12),[152] which has been discussed in §1.02[B][1] above, the Court did not provide any concrete guidance in this decision how specifically an antibody – or an enzyme or any other protein – would need to be identified in a basic patent in order to be 'protected' by that patent in the sense of Article 3(a) of the SPC Regulations.

149. *See*, e.g., the definitions of the INNs 'sevelamer', 'colesevelam', 'bixalomer', and 'patiromer calcium'. The molar fractions of the constituent monomers of a polymer can also be indicated via the molecular formula defined in an INN.
150. *See* the recommendations of the World Health Organization on INNs in 'The graphic representation of chemical formulae in the publications of international nonproprietary names (INN) for pharmaceutical substances' (WHO/PHARM/95.579), 1995, Chapter 15 – 'Polymers'. For illustration *see*, e.g., the definitions of the INNs 'colesevelam', 'bixalomer' and 'tolevamer'.
151. Further characteristics of the polymer drug actually contained in a medicinal product may be derived, e.g., from the public assessment report established by the European Medicines Agency (EMA) for the corresponding medicinal product.
152. CJEU *Eli Lilly v. Human Genome Sciences*, C-493/12 of 12 December 2013.

In particular, in *Eli Lilly* the claims of the basic patent referred to an isolated antibody or a portion thereof, particularly a monoclonal antibody, that binds specifically to a certain target (without further defining the structure of the antibody).[153] Even though the CJEU noted that the active ingredient in question, i.e., the specific antibody tabalumab, was not expressly named in the claims of the basic patent and was not otherwise specified in the description of the patent either, it could not reach any decision whether or not this specific antibody was 'protected' by the basic patent. In this regard, the CJEU found that the functional definition of the antibody recited in the claims of the basic patent may suffice to specify and thus 'protect' the specific antibody in question, provided that the claims – when interpreted in the light of the description of the basic patent, in accordance with the 'extent of protection rules' of Article 69 EPC and the protocol on its interpretation – relate 'implicitly but necessarily and specifically' to the active ingredient at issue; whether this is the case would have to be determined be the referring court.[154]

While there is no further guidance from the CJEU as to the level of detail required for an antibody, enzyme or other protein to be considered 'specified' or 'identified' in a basic patent, it should be borne in mind that requiring a very high level of detail (such as the complete amino acid sequence) would dramatically reduce the value of patents directed to fundamental innovations in the biomedical field, and would disadvantage patents for entirely new classes of therapeutic proteins over patents that merely provide new specific variants of already known types of therapeutic proteins.

The approach that will eventually be established in this regard may also have implications for the question whether SPCs can be granted for biosimilars (i.e., biological active ingredients that are not structurally identical to the reference drug but have equivalent therapeutic properties) on the basis of a broad patent and the marketing authorization for the corresponding biosimilar.

[d] Nucleic Acids

The therapeutic use of nucleic acids has received growing attention, and examples of nucleic acids as active pharmacological ingredients include antisense oligonucleotides, microRNA (miRNA), short interfering RNA (siRNA), short interfering DNA (siDNA), messenger RNA (mRNA), catalytic nucleic acids (ribozymes and DNAzymes), oligonucleotide decoys, aptamers, and DNA vaccines. Such nucleic acids are characterized primarily by the sequence and chemical constitution of their nucleotide building blocks (e.g., DNA, RNA, or modified forms thereof, such as locked nucleic acids, peptide nucleic acids, etc.), the presence of specific modifications in individual nucleotides, and the provision of single-stranded or double-stranded forms. Analogues (or modified forms) of single nucleotides, nucleosides and nucleobases can also be included in this group or can be regarded as small molecules.

153. *Ibid.*, paragraph 13.
154. *Ibid.*, headnote.

The CJEU has not yet addressed the question how precisely a nucleic acid as an active ingredient needs to be identified in the basic patent in order to be 'protected' by the patent.

[2] Basic Patent Claiming the Product, i.e., the Active Ingredient(s), but Not the Corresponding Authorized Medicinal Product (or Plant Protection Product)

SPCs are not granted for medicinal products or plant protection products as such, but rather for the active ingredient (or the combination of active ingredients) of a medicinal product or a plant protection product.[155] In conformance with this notion, Article 3(a) of the SPC Regulations requires that the 'product', i.e., the active ingredient(s), must be 'protected' by a basic patent in force. There is, however, no explicit requirement in the SPC Regulations that the authorized medicinal product or plant protection product would also need to be 'protected' by the basic patent in the sense of Article 3(a), or that it would need to fall within the scope of protection conferred by the basic patent.

That this must be inevitably the case is immediately evident if one considers Article 4 the SPC Regulations, which provides that the subject matter of the protection conferred by an SPC lies within the limits of the basic patent. The protection conferred by an SPC can thus not exceed the scope of protection of the basic patent. As such, if the basic patent requires, e.g., the presence of a specific excipient (or a specific formulation, a specific dosage form, specific amounts of certain components, etc.), then it follows that the medicinal product which has been approved must also meet these limitations.

In line with this, all national patent offices which carry out a substantive examination of an SPC application will require the applicant to establish that the claims of the patent not only identify the active ingredient(s) as required by Article 3(a), but also that the approved medicinal product falls within the scope of the claims of the basic patent. Therefore, in practice it is not possible to rely on a basic patent, which while identifying the active ingredient(s) does not protect the corresponding medicinal product (or plant protection product).

[3] Requirement for the Product to Constitute 'the Invention' of the Basic Patent

While Article 3(a) of the SPC Regulations,[156] on a literal reading, seems to require nothing more than that the product must be 'protected by a basic patent in force', a potential further criterion has surfaced in the case law of the CJEU on the basis of this same provision, namely that the product (i.e., the active ingredient or combination of

155. Articles 2 and 1(b) of Regulation (EC) 469/2009, and Arts 2 and 1(8) of Regulation (EC) 1610/96.
156. Article 3(a) of Regulation (EC) 469/2009, and Art. 3(1)(a) of Regulation (EC) 1610/96.

active ingredients in question) must constitute the 'subject matter of the invention' covered by the basic patent.[157]

This requirement has been developed in the context of a specific case constellation, in which a patentee has already obtained a first SPC for a single active ingredient A on the basis of a patent claiming this single active ingredient A and then files a second SPC for the combination of the active ingredient A with a further active ingredient B on the basis of the same patent and a new (subsequent) marketing authorization for the combination preparation. The prolongation of protection for combinations of active ingredients under such circumstances has been regarded by the CJEU in a rather critical manner. Thus, in *Actavis v. Boehringer Ingelheim Pharma* (C-577/13), the CJEU resorted to the definition of the term 'basic patent' in Article 1(b) of the SPC Regulation for Medicinal Products, which specifies that this term 'means a patent which protects a product as such…',[158] and concluded from the use of the expression 'as such' in this definition that the product must constitute the 'subject matter of the invention' (or the 'core inventive advance'[159]) of the basic patent in order to be protected 'as such' by the patent.[160]

In arriving at this conclusion, the CJEU reasoned in *Actavis v. Boehringer Ingelheim Pharma* that the expression 'as such' in the definition of the term 'basic patent' in Article 1(b) of the SPC Regulation for Medicinal Products must be given an autonomous interpretation in the light of the objectives of the SPC Regulation.[161] After considering these objectives and the different interests at stake, the Court found that it could not be accepted that the holder of a basic patent could obtain a new SPC 'each time' he places on the market a medicinal product containing an active ingredient that constitutes the subject matter of the invention covered by the basic patent in combination with another active ingredient that does not constitute the subject matter of the invention.[162] The CJEU concluded on this basis that 'in order for a basic patent to protect "as such" an active ingredient within the meaning of Articles 1(c) and 3(a) of [the SPC Regulation for Medicinal Products], that active ingredient must constitute the subject-matter of the invention covered by that patent'.[163]

It must be noted that this requirement is entirely different from the notion that, in order to be 'protected' by the basic patent in the sense of Article 3(a) of the SPC Regulations, an active ingredient (or a combination of active ingredients) has to be 'specified' or 'identified' in the claims of the basic patent (as discussed in §1.02[B][1]

157. CJEU *Actavis v. Boehringer Ingelheim Pharma*, C-577/13 of 12 March 2015, paragraph 38.
158. Article 1(c) of Regulation (EC) 469/2009 in full reads as follows:

> 'basic patent' means a patent which protects a product as such, a process to obtain a product or an application of a product, and which is designated by its holder for the purpose of the procedure for grant of a certificate.

A substantially similar provision is contained in Art. 1(9) of Regulation (EC) 1610/96.
159. CJEU *Actavis v. Sanofi*, C-443/12 of 12 December 2013, paragraph 41.
160. CJEU *Actavis v. Boehringer Ingelheim Pharma*, C-577/13 of 12 March 2015, paragraphs 27 and 38.
161. *Ibid.*, paragraph 32.
162. *Ibid.*, paragraph 37.
163. *Ibid.*, paragraph 38.

above). Thus, in *Actavis v. Boehringer Ingelheim Pharma*, the combination of the two active ingredients in question, telmisartan and hydrochlorothiazide, was explicitly named in the claims of the basic patent (after a post-grant amendment),[164] but the CJEU nevertheless regarded telmisartan alone to be the 'sole subject matter of the invention' covered by the basic patent.[165] Referring to this decision, the Advocate General Wathelet remarked in his opinion in the CJEU referral *Teva UK v. Gilead Sciences* (C-121/17) that 'the fact that a basic patent contains a claim relating to a specifically named active ingredient may, in certain circumstances, not be sufficient'.[166]

This leads to the question what exactly should be understood to be the 'subject matter of the invention' (or the 'core inventive advance') of the basic patent. While it could be held that the claims of a granted patent define the 'invention' that the patent protects, so that, quite simply, the subject matter of any and all claims of the patent should constitute the 'subject-matter of the invention', this is clearly not the understanding on which the CJEU's reasoning in *Actavis v. Boehringer Ingelheim Pharma* was based. Rather, the CJEU's reasoning in this decision seems to imply that the combination of active ingredients in question would need to constitute an invention in its own right, which is separate and independent from the invention consisting in the provision of only one of the corresponding active ingredients – i.e., what was referred to in *Actavis v. Sanofi* (C-443/12) as 'a totally separate innovation'.[167]

Such a narrow understanding of what constitutes the 'subject-matter of the invention' covered by the basic patent, however, would appear to be highly problematic for several reasons. In the case of a patent that contains a broad claim 1 directed to a pharmaceutical composition comprising an active ingredient A, as well as a dependent claim 2 which requires that the pharmaceutical composition of claim 1 further contains an additional active ingredient B, it can be safely assumed that the justification for the grant of the patent was seen in the subject matter of the broader claim 1, and that the question of inventive step was not separately examined for the narrower dependent claim 2. Yet, this does not allow the reverse conclusion that the subject matter of claim 2 (i.e., the combination of active ingredients A and B) could not also constitute an invention. This is, in fact, confirmed by the CJEU's decision *Georgetown University* (C-484/12), in which the Court found that the basic patent under consideration 'protected' not only a specific active ingredient alone (HPV-16) but also various combinations of this active ingredient with further active ingredients (among others the combination of HPV-6, HPV-11, HPV-16 and HPV-18).[168] If a separate independent invention were indeed required, a patent office or a court would seem to be obliged to make its own assessment of inventive step when deciding on the grant of an SPC under such circumstances, which appears challenging, not to say unworkable.

164. *Ibid.*, paragraph 16.
165. *Ibid.*, paragraphs 26 and 37–39.
166. Opinion of Advocate General Wathelet in *Teva UK v. Gilead Sciences*, C-121/17, delivered on 25 April 2018, paragraphs 78–79.
167. CJEU *Actavis v. Sanofi*, C-443/12 of 12 December 2013, paragraph 42.
168. CJEU *Georgetown University v. Octrooicentrum Nederland*, C-484/12 of 12 December 2013.

How exactly should such an assessment of inventive step be made? In patent law, inventive step can only be denied if something is obvious in view of the state of the art, i.e., in view of everything that was made available to the public before the effective date of the patent.[169] If a patent relates to the combination of active ingredients A and B, and if the active ingredient A by itself was novel and non-obvious in view of the state of the art at the effective date of the patent, the same should also hold true for the combination of A and B, simply because this combination would not be rendered obvious by the prior art.

Any other assessment, such as a 'hypothetical' examination of inventive step of a combination of active ingredients A and B on the basis of the – factually wrong – assumption that each of the individual active ingredients was already known in the state of the art, would seem difficult to justify and would entail bizarre consequences. What could be deemed to be known in the 'hypothetical' state of the art about the active ingredient A if that substance was not actually known at the effective date of the patent? Possibly all that the basic patent discloses about the active ingredient A? Moreover, if the basic patent does, in fact, contain experimental data showing that the combination of active ingredients A and B provides certain advantageous effects, would it still be necessary to assess whether these advantageous effects justify the presence of an inventive step in view of a purely 'hypothetical' state of the art (considering both A and B to be individually known)? What if the basic patent includes a mere statement that the combination of active ingredients A and B is particularly advantageous in the treatment of disease X, but does not provide any corresponding experimental evidence – could an SPC applicant rely on such a statement and potentially file further evidence in defence of inventive step of the combination of A and B?

This approach seems all the more absurd when taking into account that voluntary divisional applications can be filed during the prosecution of a European patent application, and that a patentee can thereby legitimately obtain a first (parent) patent directed to a single active ingredient A and a second (divisional) patent directed to the combination of the active ingredient A with another active ingredient B. The corresponding second patent could be limited to refer, both in the claims and the description, exclusively to the combination of A and B.[170] With respect to such a second patent, the sole subject matter of which would be the combination of active ingredients A and B, could it nevertheless be held that the 'subject-matter of the invention' covered by this patent should be something different than what it actually claims?

169. *See*, e.g., Arts 56 and 54(2) EPC.

170. In practice, if the EPO or a national patent office has already granted a (parent) patent to the active ingredient A alone, it would likely consider a divisional patent application claiming the combination of the active ingredients A and B as relating to a narrower subject matter than the parent patent and could directly allow the divisional patent without even discussing the question of inventive step. Therefore, even if recourse could be had to the prosecution history of the divisional patent (which in itself is questionable), this might not provide any insights into the reasons why the claimed combination of active ingredients A and B was found to be inventive by the authority granting the divisional patent.

Further questions arise when the 'subject-matter of the invention' requirement is applied to other case constellations, including cases in which an SPC is filed for a single active ingredient. For example, if an SPC is filed for a specific antibody A on the basis of a patent having a broad claim 1 which relates to a pharmaceutical composition containing *any* therapeutic protein together with specific excipients that improve the absorption of the therapeutic protein, and having a dependent claim 2 which relates specifically to a corresponding pharmaceutical composition in which the therapeutic protein is the aforementioned antibody A, would antibody A constitute the 'subject-matter of the invention' covered by this patent? It seems hardly justifiable to deny an SPC in such a case merely because the invention covered by the basic patent relates not only to the specific antibody A but also, more generally, to *any* therapeutic protein in combination with the specific excipients.

In view of these inconsistencies and seemingly absurd consequences, it may not be inconceivable that the CJEU could still refine its interpretation of the requirement that the product (i.e., the active ingredient or combination of active ingredients which is the subject of an SPC) must be protected 'as such' and must therefore constitute the 'subject-matter of the invention' covered by the basic patent.

A more reasonable approach to the 'subject-matter of the invention' requirement, as referred to in *Actavis v. Boehringer Ingelheim Pharma*, could be based on the assumption that the 'subject-matter of the invention' covered by a patent is simply the subject matter of its claims, which is a fundamental notion in patent law.[171] Thus, if a granted claim of a basic patent relates to the combination of the active ingredients A and B, then this combination forms part of the 'subject-matter of the invention' covered by the patent. This would also be in line with the understanding of Advocate General Wathelet in his opinion in *Teva UK v. Gilead Sciences* (C-121/17), where he noted: 'I confess to a certain amount of difficulty in distinguishing between the "core inventive advance that is the subject of the basic patent" and the invention disclosed by the claims.'[172] Such an approach could effectively bring the 'subject-matter of the invention' requirement back in line with the requirement that the product must be 'specified' or 'identified' in the claims of the basic patent and must fall within the scope of protection of the patent in order to be 'protected' in the sense of Article 3(a) of the SPC Regulations. The above-discussed perceived problem of a patent holder obtaining a new SPC each time he places a new combination product on the market should not speak against such an approach either, since it could still be dealt with under Article 3(c) of the SPC Regulations, given that the CJEU found in *Actavis v. Sanofi* that Article 3(c) would bar the grant of a new SPC under such circumstances even if the requirements of Article 3(a) were satisfied.[173]

In fact, the CJEU was widely expected to clarify the relevance of the potential 'subject matter of the invention' (or 'core inventive advance') requirement in its recent

171. *See*, e.g., Art. 84 EPC and Rule 43(1) EPC.
172. Opinion of Advocate General Wathelet in *Teva UK v. Gilead Sciences*, C-121/17, delivered on 25 April 2018, footnote 30.
173. CJEU *Actavis v. Sanofi*, C-443/12 of 12 December 2013, paragraphs 30 and 44.

decision *Teva UK v. Gilead Sciences* (C-121/17).[174] In the underlying referral, the UK Patents Court – once again – asked what the criteria are for deciding whether a product is protected by a basic patent within the meaning of Article 3(a) of the SPC Regulation, and proposed that the relevant criterion should be that the active ingredient (or combination of active ingredients) at issue must embody the 'inventive advance' of the basic patent.[175]

In *Teva UK v. Gilead Sciences* the CJEU essentially concluded that the requirement under Article 3(a) of the SPC Regulation that the product must be 'protected by a basic patent in force' has to be understood to mean that the product must, from the point of view of a person skilled in the art and in the light of the description and the drawings of the basic patent, necessarily fall under the invention covered by the patent (which, as discussed in §1.02[B][1] above, may be understood to require that the product falls within the extent of protection of the patent), and that each active ingredient contained in the product must be specifically identifiable by the person skilled in the art in the light of all the information disclosed in the patent and in view of the prior art available at the priority date or filing date of the patent.[176] Notably, the CJEU did not impose any additional conditions to be met under Article 3(a) of the SPC Regulation, which could be interpreted as a rejection of the 'subject matter of the invention' (or 'inventive advance') requirement in the form as proposed by the referring court.

Unfortunately, however, the CJEU did not express its view on this issue as clearly and unmistakably as the Advocate General who pointedly rejected the suggestion of the referring court that the product should have to embody the 'inventive advance' of the basic patent in order to be 'protected' in the sense of Article 3(a), noting that such a requirement would 'risk ... giving rise to confusion with the criteria for determining whether an invention is patentable'.[177] In the absence of such a clear and explicit rejection of the proposed 'inventive advance' requirement, and in view of some rather cryptic expressions in the CJEU's judgment (such as the Court's notion that it should be ascertained 'whether a person skilled in the art can understand without any doubt ... that the product to which the claims of the basic patent relate is a specification required for the solution of the technical problem disclosed by that patent'[178]), it remains to be seen how the UK Patents Court and the other national courts will interpret and put into practice the guidance provided by the CJEU in *Teva UK v. Gilead Sciences*, and whether this decision will indeed put an end to the discussion of the 'inventive advance' of the basic patent in the context of Article 3(a).

174. CJEU *Teva UK v. Gilead Sciences*, C-121/17 of 25 July 2018.
175. *See* UK Patents Court, *Teva UK Ltd. et al. v. Gilead Sciences Inc.* [2017] EWHC 13 (Pat), which gave rise to the CJEU referral *Teva UK v. Gilead Sciences* (C-121/17).
176. CJEU *Teva UK v. Gilead Sciences*, C-121/17 of 25 July 2018, paragraphs 51–53 and 57.
177. Opinion of Advocate General Wathelet in *Teva UK v. Gilead Sciences*, C-121/17, delivered on 25 April 2018, paragraph 73.
178. CJEU *Teva UK v. Gilead Sciences*, C-121/17 of 25 July 2018, paragraph 48.

[4] *Criteria for Choosing the Basic Patent among Various Available Patents*

Frequently an SPC applicant holds several different patents, all of which 'protect' the active ingredient (or the combination of active ingredients) in question and could thus potentially serve as the basic patent. Under such circumstances, and in view of the 'one SPC per product per patent holder rule' (which will be discussed in §1.02[D][1][a] below), a choice has to be made as to which one of these patents should be used as the basic patent for the SPC filing.[179]

Simply put, there are three principal criteria that typically affect the choice of the basic patent among several available patents: (i) the SPC term; (ii) the scope of protection of the resulting SPC; and (iii) the strength or validity of the SPC.

The term of an SPC is possibly the single most important factor that determines its economic value. Choosing a basic patent that has a later filing date and can therefore give rise to an SPC having a longer term would clearly be preferable.

Since an SPC confers the same protection and the same rights as the underlying basic patent,[180] albeit confined to the product covered by the respective marketing authorization, choosing a basic patent that has a broad scope of protection will provide an SPC having a correspondingly broad scope.[181] This could be particularly relevant, e.g., if the respective active ingredient (or combination of active ingredients) is expected to be tested for additional therapeutic indications (or additional uses as plant protection product) besides the one specified in the marketing authorization relied upon for the SPC application, and if the SPC applicant does not hold further patents that specifically claim such additional therapeutic indications. In that case, obtaining an SPC on the basis of a patent having product claims or at least first medical use claims would allow to gain protection for all therapeutic indications that will be authorized during the lifetime of the SPC. Conversely, where other uses than the one specified in the marketing authorization relied upon for the SPC filing are clearly not envisaged, it may be sufficient to choose a patent with claims limited to the corresponding specific use defined in the marketing authorization. Similarly, the choice of a patent the claims of which are limited in any particular respect - e.g., to a specific formulation, the presence of specific amounts of active ingredient(s) and/or excipients, a specific dosage form or mode of administration, a specific dosing regimen, or a specific patient group, etc. - may seem acceptable if alternatives to these limitations are unfeasible or economically negligible. In practice, if a patent proprietor holds several patents protecting the same active ingredient(s), the scope of protection of these different

179. *See* the Explanatory Memorandum to the Commission proposal for an SPC regulation for medicinal products, COM(90) 101 final - SYN 255, paragraph 33 as well as the Explanatory Memorandum to the Commission proposal for an SPC regulation for plant protection products, COM(94) 579 final, paragraph 68; *see also*, e.g., CJEU *University of Queensland v. Comptroller-General of Patents, Designs and Trade Marks*, C-630/10 of 25 November 2011, paragraph 35.
180. Articles 4 and 5 of Regulation (EC) 469/2009 and Regulation (EC) 1610/96.
181. *See* in this regard: CJEU *Actavis v. Sanofi*, C-443/12 of 12 December 2013, paragraph 27; and CJEU *Georgetown University v. Octrooicentrum Nederland*, C-484/12 of 12 December 2013, paragraph 28.

patents is often inversely correlated with their respective date of filing and therefore their maximum SPC term. It may thus be necessary to balance the scope of protection against the maximum SPC term when choosing the basic patent for an SPC application.

A further factor to be considered is the validity of an SPC, which is determined by the validity of the underlying basic patent as well as the compliance with the pertinent conditions for SPC grant, particularly the requirement that the product is specified or identified in the claims and thus 'protected' by the basic patent in the sense of Article 3(a) of the SPC Regulations. Obviously, choosing a patent that does not give rise to any concerns in this regard would be preferable. It should be appreciated, however, that this assessment may not necessarily be the same for all European states, even in the case of parallel national patents (or different national parts of the same European patent) having identical claims. Thus, the assessment of patentability and validity of a patent can differ considerably between EU Member States, particularly due to differences in the national practice and case law (regarding, e.g., the treatment of selection inventions, added-matter issues, priority entitlement, etc.), and potentially also due to differences in the prior art situation (e.g., national prior rights may exist in only some states). As a consequence, there may be instances where the choice of the most appropriate patent for an SPC filing may not be the same in all Member States of the Community. At the same time, of course, it is highly undesirable to have SPCs expiring earlier in some EU Member States than in others, not least in view of possible parallel imports.

[C] The Marketing Authorization Forming Basis for an SPC

The conditions which must be fulfilled in order to obtain an SPC are set out in Article 3 of the SPC Regulations. Accordingly, an SPC may only be obtained, if in the Member State where the SPC is applied for, at the application date the product (i.e., the active ingredient or combination of active ingredients) is protected by a basic patent in force (Article 3(a)) and a valid authorization to place the product on the market has been granted (Article 3(b)). It is moreover necessary that the product has not been subject of a Certificate (Article 3(c)) and that the authorization relied upon for the SPC filing is the first authorization to place the product on the market as a medicinal or plant protection product (Article 3(d)), as appropriate.

[1] Combinations of Active Ingredients

If an SPC request is based on a patent claiming a specific active ingredient or a combination of active ingredients and relies on a corresponding first marketing authorization for this active ingredient or combination of active ingredients, the alignment of the SPC to the conditions as set out in Article 3(a) and 3(b) of the SPC Regulations is generally unproblematic.

However, considerable disharmony has emerged amongst the Member States regarding the interpretation of Article 3(a) and 3(b) of the SPC Regulations in case of combination products, where there is a mismatch in terms of the active ingredient(s) identified in the claims of the basic patent or in the SPC request and the active ingredient(s) which are subject to regulatory approval.

The interpretation of Article 3(a) and 3(b) in relation to combination products has been extensively considered by the CJEU in the judgments *Medeva* (C-322/10)[182] and *Georgetown* (C-422/10),[183] as well as in the subsequent reasoned orders *Yeda* (C-518/10),[184] *Queensland* (C-630/10)[185] and *Daiichi* (C-6/11).[186]

[a] The Marketing Authorization Refers to Fewer Active Ingredients than the SPC Application

As set out in Article 3(a) and 3(b) of the SPC Regulations, the product which is subject matter of the marketing authorization must be protected by the basic patent. A patent with claims directed towards a certain combination of active ingredients, without claims to the individual active ingredients, will not extend to the single active ingredient or a combination of fewer active ingredients. As Article 4 of the SPC Regulations provides that the protection conferred by an SPC must lie within the limits of the basic patent, an SPC cannot relate to fewer active ingredients than are required in the claims of the basic patent. If, however, the marketing authorization refers to fewer active ingredients than the claims of the basic patent, the patent does not protect the same product which is the subject matter of the marketing authorization. It follows that an SPC for a combination of active ingredients cannot be based on a marketing authorization for a single active ingredient or fewer active ingredients.

In line with this, the CJEU in *Medeva* ruled that the issue of an SPC relating to active ingredients which are not specified in the wording of the claims of the basic patent is precluded,[187] which it also affirmed in the subsequent reasoned orders *Queensland* and *Daiichi*.[188]

Similarly, the CJEU in *Yeda* by way of a reasoned order with reference to *Medeva* confirmed that an SPC for an active ingredient is not available where the basic patent claims the active ingredient only as an active ingredient forming part of a combination product and is not claimed individually.[189]

182. CJEU *Medeva v. Comptroller General of Patents, Designs and Trade Marks*, C-322/10 of 24 November 2011.
183. CJEU *Georgetown University v. Comptroller General of Patents, Designs and Trade Marks*, C-422/10 of 24 November 2011.
184. CJEU *Yeda Research and Development v. Comptroller General of Patents, Designs and Trade Marks*, C-518/10 of 25 November 2011.
185. CJEU *University of Queensland v. Comptroller General of Patents, Designs and Trade Marks*, C-630/10 of 25 November 2011.
186. CJEU *Daiichi Sankyo v. Comptroller General of Patents, Designs and Trade Marks*, C-6/11 of 25 November 2011.
187. CJEU *Medeva v. Comptroller General of Patents, Designs and Trade Marks*, C-322/10 of 24 November 2011, headnote 1.
188. CJEU *University of Queensland v. Comptroller General of Patents, Designs and Trade Marks*, C-630/10 of 25 November 2011, headnote 1; CJEU *Daiichi Sankyo v. Comptroller General of Patents, Designs and Trade Marks*, C-6/11 of 25 November 2011, headnote.
189. CJEU *Yeda Research and Development v. Comptroller General of Patents, Designs and Trade Marks*, C-518/10 of 25 November 2011, headnote.

Thus, a marketing authorization for fewer active ingredients than those claimed in the basic patent cannot form basis for an SPC relying on this patent.

[b] The Marketing Authorization Refers to More Active Ingredients than the SPC Application

In many therapeutic areas, such as in the field of vaccines or HIV medications, it is very common that active ingredients are approved as fixed combinations with other active ingredients having a different mechanism of action. The basic patent relating to an innovative active ingredient of such a fixed combination typically focuses on the single class of the innovative active ingredient. While in anticipation of how the product may eventually be approved, the patent may also have claims directed towards combinations of the innovative active ingredient with other therapeutic agents, the claims of the basic patent very rarely identify the specific combination of active ingredients which is eventually approved.

According to Article 1 of the SPC Regulation for Medicinal Products, the 'product' that can be the subject matter of an SPC is defined as 'the active ingredient or combination of active ingredients of a medicinal product'. Hence, in terms of SPC law, a product comprising a single active pharmaceutical ingredient and a product comprising the same ingredient in combination with another, are two different products, each being potentially eligible for separate SPCs. Assuming that the term 'product' must have the same meaning in Articles 1, 2 and 3 of the SPC Regulation, it should follow that if the approved medicinal product is a certain combination of active ingredients, the product definition of the SPC (as mirrored by the claims of the basic patent) should be commensurate.

In applying such a literal interpretation of Articles 1–3 of the SPC Regulation, many Member States in the past adopted the position that an SPC should not be available, if the approved medicinal product contains more active ingredients than those applied for in the SPC application (and specified in the claims of the underlying basic patent). Such a restrictive interpretation of the term 'product' within the meaning of Article 3(a) and 3(b) of the SPC Regulation, however, has the consequence of effectively precluding the issue of an SPC for products which need to be approved in combination with other active ingredients (unless the basic patent specifically claims the approved combination).

The issue has been resolved by the CJEU in the *Medeva* and *Georgetown* decisions, where the CJEU ruled that an SPC can be granted for an active ingredient or a combination of active ingredients, even if the medicinal product of the marketing authorization relied upon also contains additional active ingredients.[190] In *Medeva*, the

190. CJEU *Medeva v. Comptroller General of Patents, Designs and Trade Marks*, C-322/10 of 24 November 2011, headnote 2; CJEU *Georgetown University v. Comptroller General of Patents, Designs and Trade Marks*, C-422/10 of 24 November 2011, headnote. *See also* CJEU *University of Queensland v. Comptroller General of Patents, Designs and Trade Marks*, C-630/10 of 25 November 2011, headnote 2.

Advocate-General[191] recognized that a strict approach to Article 3(a) (i.e., the active ingredient(s) having to be 'specified' or 'identified' in the claims of the basic patent) necessitates a balanced, more purposive or 'teleological' approach to interpreting Article 3(b). Otherwise no SPC protection would be available for manufacturers of medicinal products who are obliged, for legal or practical reasons, to market an active ingredient as a fixed combination with other active ingredients. Such an interpretation of the SPC Regulation would run counter to its very aims and the result would not be compatible with the objectives of the Regulation.

The CJEU in *Medeva* endorsed this position. Thus, according to the CJEU, the fundamental objective of the SPC Regulation is to ensure sufficient protection to encourage pharmaceutical research. If the holder of a basic patent relating to an innovative active ingredient were to be refused an SPC on the grounds that, in the commercial version of the medicinal product that active ingredient coexists alongside other active ingredients, this objective would be undermined.

[c] The Marketing Authorization Indicates That a Medicinal Product Containing a Single Active Ingredient Is Authorized for Use in Combination with a Further Active Ingredient

Many therapeutic regimens for the treatment of a disease require the use of a combination of active ingredients. As set out in §1.02[C][1][b] above, the CJEU in *Medeva* and *Georgetown* has recognized that in case of fixed combinations, it is not detrimental that the medicinal product approved contains more active ingredients than those defined in the SPC request or claimed in the basic patent, as any other interpretation of the SPC Regulation would undermine the very purpose of the SPC Regulation.

While in some therapeutic fields, such as in case of vaccines, practical considerations necessitate the approval of multiple active ingredients in a medicinal product as a 'fixed dosage form', in other therapeutic areas combination by way of a fixed dosage form of active ingredients may not be feasible. This is very often the case if very different classes of active ingredients are to be used in conjunction for the treatment of a certain disease, such as the combined use of an antibody and an active ingredient which is a relatively simple chemical compound. These active ingredients differ fundamentally in terms of their pharmacokinetics, the required dosage regimen or formulation requirements and the like. Moreover, there is an increased tendency to tailor therapy to the individual patients' needs in order to optimize response and safety ('personalized medicine'). For these new therapeutic approaches the administration of combination therapies by way of 'loose combinations' offer a great advantage, as they facilitate the required flexibility.

There is thus a practical, therapeutic need for active ingredients, although to be used in conjunction, to be formulated as separate, 'loose' combination dosage form.

191. Opinion of the Advocate General in *Medeva v. Comptroller General of Patents, Designs and Trade Marks*, C-322/10, delivered on 13 July 2011.

The mandatory combined use of the active ingredients may, nevertheless, be reflected in the Summary of Product Characteristics (SmPC) of the medicinal product, which is a central part of the marketing authorization.

The development of such new 'loose' combination therapies is generally just as cost intensive and time consuming as the development of other innovative medicinal products. On a balance of interests, it would appear that there is no logical justification in denying such products additional supplemental protection.

In the past, various national courts[192] have rejected the issue of an SPC on the grounds that the medicinal product which is subject matter of the approval only contains a single active ingredient, whereas the SPC request and the claims of the basic patent are directed towards a mandatory combination of active ingredients, even if the SmPC specifically states that the product must be used in combination with another active ingredient. It should, however, be noted that these national decisions were rendered prior to the *Medeva* ruling, where the CJEU explicitly emphasized that a literal interpretation of the concept of the 'product' in Articles 1–3 of the SPC Regulation is not compatible with the objectives of the Regulation.

Thus, in *Medeva* a teleological interpretation of these provisions was considered to be necessary in order to ensure that medicinal products with multiple active ingredients, only part of which are the subject matter of a patent, can benefit from supplementary protection.

The principles of *Medeva*, as a corollary should be equally applicable to the reverse case, namely where an SPC is sought for a combination of active ingredients as identified in the claims of the basic patent and where the approved medicinal product, while only physically containing one of the claimed active ingredients, is in accordance with the SmPC to be used in conjunction with a further active ingredient.

As evidenced by the more recent guidance provided by the CJEU, the 'fundamental objective' of the SPC Regulation is to ensure sufficient protection to encourage pharmaceutical research. Thus, in *Neurim* (C-130/11)[193] the CJEU has emphasized the value in encouraging research into new applications for known therapeutic agents and not precluding them from the benefits of SPC protection.

Such a purposive interpretation of the SPC Regulation for Medicinal Products is clearly warranted, as it should be applicable to all types of pharmaceutical research without discrimination. Indeed, this legislative goal is expressly stated in the Explanatory Memorandum for the Proposal for a Council Regulation (EEC) concerning the creation of a supplementary protection certificate for medicinal products.[194]

Thus, *Medeva* and *Neurim* clearly establish that the CJEU in the meantime has recognized the need to adopt a teleological approach to the interpretation of the SPC Regulation in order to ensure that it is compatible with its aims.

---

192. *See* e.g., UK High Court, *Yeda Research and Development v. Comptroller General of Patents*, [2010] EWHC 1733 (Pat) of 12 July 2010; and German Federal Supreme Court (Bundesgerichtshof), *Anti-Helicobacter-Präparat*, X ZB 1/08 of 8 July 2008.
193. CJEU *Neurim Pharmaceuticals v. Comptroller-General of Patents*, C-130/11 of 19 July 2012.
194. COM(90) 101 final – SYN 255, paragraph 29.

As a logical consequence, following the guidance provided by the CJEU in *Medeva* and *Neurim*, SPC protection should in principle also be available for a 'loose' combination of active ingredients, in cases where the approved medicinal product contains only a part of the combination, but where the SmPC specifies that it is to be used in conjunction with other active ingredients as identified in the SPC request and the basic patent.

As corresponding cases are pending, it is likely that this issue will be revisited by the national courts, with a possible referral to the CJEU.

[2] The Marketing Authorization Has Not Yet Been Granted at the Time the SPC Application Is Filed

One of the mandatory requirements for filing an SPC is that, at the date of filing of the SPC, a valid marketing authorization has been granted in the Member State in question (Article 3(b)).

This has been confirmed by the CJEU in *Yamanouchi* (C-110/95).[195] In this case, an SPC request was pending in the UK. As it was evident that a national marketing authorization would not issue within the lifespan of the basic patent, the applicant relied upon a marketing authorization obtained for the product in question in France. The CJEU confirmed that the entitlement to the certificate is strictly linked to the existence of a marketing authorization granted in the Member State in which the application is submitted and to the date of that application.

In line with this, in *Merck Sharp & Dohme* (C-567/16)[196] the CJEU ruled that an 'end of procedure notice' issued by a reference Member State in the decentralized procedure under Article 28(4) of Directive 2001/83/EC[197] is not to be treated as being equivalent to a marketing authorization for the purposes of Article 3(b) of the SPC Regulation.

[3] The Holder of the Marketing Authorization

The purpose of the SPC is to compensate a patent holder for the delay in his ability to market a medicinal or plant protection product because of the mandatory requirement that the product has to undergo a stringent regulatory review process prior to being placed on the market. In line with this, Article 6 of the SPC Regulations provides that it is the holder of the basic patent or his successor in title who is entitled to the SPC, rather than the holder of the marketing authorization. Moreover, Article 3(2) of the SPC Regulation for Plant Protection Products (which by virtue of recital 17 is also applicable

195. CJEU *Yamanouchi Pharmaceutical v. Comptroller-General of Patents, Designs and Trade Marks*, C-110/95 of 12 June 1997.
196. CJEU *Merck Sharp & Dohme v. Comptroller General of Patents, Designs and Trade Marks*, C-567/16 of 7 December 2017.
197. Directive 2001/83/EC of the European Parliament and of the Council of 6 November 2001 on the Community code relating to medicinal products for human use.

to the SPC Regulation for Medicinal Products[198]) provides that in case of multiple holders of different patents, multiple SPCs may issue.

Unlike in other jurisdictions (e.g., the US[199] and Japan[200]), where the patentee must furnish proof that he is entitled to rely on a marketing authorization of a third party in order to secure patent term extension, the question of ownership of the marketing authorization is not addressed in the SPC Regulations, nor are there any provisions which tie the entitlement to the SPC in any way to a licence or other form of contractual agreement with the holder of the marketing authorization.

Consequently, questions have arisen concerning the entitlement to an SPC in circumstances where the patentee and the marketing authorization holder are not the same entity, and where the holder of the marketing authorization does not concede to the patentee's reliance on the marketing authorization to secure SPC protection.

In accordance with the current case law of the CJEU, a patentee may rely on a marketing authorization of a third party, even in the absence of the third party's consent.

Thus, in *Biogen* (C-181/95),[201] the approved product was the outcome of a licence agreement and the combined application of several patents held by Biogen and the Institut Pasteur. The holder of the marketing authorization only supported the SPC application filed by Institut Pasteur, but not Biogen's SPC application, arguing that development of the medicinal product was largely due to the research and investment undertaken by those who had finally obtained marketing authorization, and that the marketing authorization holder should therefore be allowed to choose with which patent holder to cooperate in order to enable that patent holder to obtain an SPC.

The CJEU, however, concluded that the SPC Regulation seeks to confer supplementary protection on the holders of such patents, without instituting any preferential ranking amongst them.[202] This position has subsequently also been confirmed by the CJEU in *AHP Manufacturing* (C-482/07).[203]

198. The CJEU has expressly confirmed that Art. 3(2) of the SPC Regulation for Plant Protection Products is, by virtue of recital 17 of this Regulation, also applicable for the interpretation of Art. 3 of the SPC Regulation for Medicinal Products. *See* CJEU *AHP Manufacturing v. Bureau voor de Industriële Eigendom*, C-482/07 of 3 September 2009, paragraph 23. As regards the applicability of recital 17 of the SPC Regulation for Plant Protection Products for the interpretation of the SPC Regulation for Medicinal Products, *see also*: CJEU *Farmitalia Carlo Erba v. Bundesgerichtshof*, C-392/97 of 16 September 1999, paragraph 20; CJEU *Massachusetts Institute of Technology v. Bundesgerichtshof*, C-431/04 of 4 May 2006, paragraph 24; and CJEU *Incyte Corporation v. Szellemi Tulajdon Nemzeti Hivatala*, C-492/16 of 20 December 2017, paragraphs 33 and 34.
199. Manual of Patent Examining Procedure (MPEP), 9th ed., rev. 08.2017 (Jan. 2018), § 2752, 'Patent Term Extension Applicant'.
200. Regulation under the Patent Law (Ordinance No. 10 of the Ministry of International Trade and Industry of 8 March 1959, final revision by Ordinance No. 26 of the Ministry of International Trade and Industry of 30 March 2007), Chapter 4(4) Registration of Extension of the Term of Patent Right, Art. 38-sedecies.
201. CJEU *Biogen v. SmithKlineBeecham Biologicals*, C-181/95 of 23 January 1997.
202. *Ibid.*, paragraph 27.
203. CJEU *AHP Manufacturing v. Bureau voor de Industriële Eigendom*, C-482/07 of 3 September 2009, paragraph 30.

In the *Biogen* case, Biogen (the 'third party') had licensed the patent in question to the holder of the marketing authorization. The corresponding technology by Biogen thus contributed to the launch of the medicinal product forming the basis of the SPC.

If, on the other hand, an SPC is granted to a patent holder who is not the holder of the marketing authorization, has not entered into any collaboration, licence or other agreement with the marketing authorization holder, and could potentially use the SPC to oppose the marketing of the authorized product, the question may be raised if the grant of an SPC under such circumstances would not undermine the very objective of the SPC Regulation.

In this regard, it could still be held that a basic patent which protects the active ingredient(s) of an authorized medicinal product (or plant protection product) is, by definition, the result of precisely the kind of 'long and costly' research that the SPC Regulations intend to encourage, and that the grant of an SPC on the basis of such a patent should compensate the patent holder for the reduced period of effective protection which results from the legal requirement, rather than the practical or financial burden, to undergo an administrative authorization procedure before the respective product can be marketed. It is therefore the patent holder who is entitled to obtain an SPC as recompense for his investment in the research underlying the basic patent, which is separate and independent from the additional efforts and investments, either made by a third party or by the patent holder himself, to obtain regulatory approval. The holder of the marketing authorization, in turn, is rewarded for his efforts by other means, including in particular the periods of data and market exclusivity provided by Article 10 of Directive 2001/83/EC.

It further needs to be appreciated that the possible relationships between the holders of patents and marketing authorizations can be complex and, at times, driven by conflicting interests. For example, if licensing negotiations fail, a marketing authorization applicant might choose to seek regulatory approval while attacking a potentially relevant patent held by a third party. Such a third party holding a potential basic patent, however, might effectively be forced to apply for an SPC on the basis of the first marketing authorization that anyone obtains for the respective product in order to safeguard its rights; even if it intended to independently seek marketing approval for the same product, it might otherwise be barred under Article 3(d) of the SPC Regulations from obtaining an SPC on the basis of its own (later) marketing authorization.

It thus remains to be seen whether, and how, the CJEU might further qualify the conditions under which a patent holder can be granted an SPC on the basis of a marketing authorization held by a different party, particularly where the marketing authorization holder opposes the grant of the SPC.

Notably, in *Eli Lilly* (C-493/12)[204] the CJEU by way of an obiter dictum has suggested that the refusal of an SPC may be justified 'where the holder of the patent in question has failed to take any steps to carry out more in-depth research and identify his invention specifically, making it possible to ascertain clearly the active ingredient

204. CJEU *Eli Lilly v. Human Genome Sciences*, C-493/12 of 12 December 2013, paragraph 43.

which may be commercially exploited in a medicinal product'. In such a situation, according to the CJEU, 'if an SPC were granted to the patent holder, even though – since he was not the holder of the [marketing authorization] granted for the medicinal product developed from the specifications of the source patent – that patent holder had not made any investment in research relating to that aspect of his original invention, that would undermine the objective of [the SPC Regulation]'.

The questions referred to the CJEU in *Eli Lilly* were primarily based on the issue whether a basic patent containing a broad functional definition in its claims can identify and, thus, 'protect' the product at issue within the meaning of Article 3(a) of the SPC Regulation. The CJEU, however, evidently felt it necessary to nevertheless address the 'third-party SPC issue'. As such, the obiter dictum by the CJEU appears to suggest that a functional definition of a product in the basic patent may generally suffice to identify the product for the filing of an SPC. If, however, the SPC applicant has no association with the holder of the marketing authorization, he cannot rely on a patent which only discloses the product by way of a general functional definition, as this would undermine the objectives of the SPC Regulation. Under such circumstances an SPC should issue only if the active ingredient is disclosed specifically in the third-party patent.

[4] Reliance on a Marketing Authorization Granted under a Provision Other than Directive 2001/83/EC or Directive 2001/82/EC

Article 2 of the SPC Regulation for Medicinal Products stipulates that in order to be eligible for an SPC, the product must have been subject to an administrative authorization procedure as laid down in the Medicinal Products Directives, i.e., Directive 2001/82/EC[205] or Directive 2001/83/EC,[206] a requirement which is also reiterated by Article 3(b).

The EEA Agreement[207] further specifies that in relation to SPCs, an authorization to place the product on the market in accordance with the national legislation of an EFTA state shall be treated as an authorization granted in accordance with the appropriate Directives. As such, also national approvals in the EEA-EFTA countries Iceland, Norway and Liechtenstein may be relied upon.

Likewise, to take account of the enlargement of the EU, Article 20 of the SPC Regulation for Medicinal Products sets out that an SPC can also be filed on the basis of a national marketing authorization of the respective new Member States, subject to specific transitional time limits. These, however, have already expired and as such no longer need to be considered.

The approval of therapeutically active ingredients is not limited to 'classical' medicinal products as set out in the above-mentioned Directives. Thus, an active

205. Directive 2001/82/EC of the European Parliament and of the Council of 6 November 2001 on the Community code relating to veterinary medicinal products.
206. Directive 2001/83/EC of the European Parliament and of the Council of 6 November 2001 on the Community code relating to medicinal products for human use.
207. Point 6 of Annex XVII (Intellectual Property) of the EEA Agreement.

ingredient may also be an integral component of an implantable medical device. Such medical devices are approved by way of a CE-marking procedure as governed by Regulation (EU) 2017/745[208] which replaces the previous two Directives on medical devices, i.e., Directive 90/385/EEC[209] and Directive 93/42/EEC.[210]

According to Article 1(8) of Regulation (EU) 2017/745, where a device incorporates, as an integral part, a substance which, if used separately, would be considered to be a medicinal product as defined in Article 1 of Directive 2001/83/EC, and which has an action ancillary to that of the device, shall be assessed and authorized in accordance with this Regulation. Corresponding provisions were likewise contained in the previous two Directives on medical devices, i.e., in Article 1(4) of Directive 90/385/EEC and in Article 1(4) of Directive 93/42/EEC.

Thus, CE-marked medical devices are not authorized according to the Medicinal Products Directives. It has therefore been called into question whether the regulatory hurdle for obtaining a CE-mark may be considered as being equivalent to the standards set out in the Medicinal Products Directive. Nevertheless, the health authorities are involved in the CE-marking procedure by means of a consultation process. In the consultation process the quality, safety and efficacy of the active ingredient of the device is assessed according to the standards of Directive 2001/83/EC. Thus, the applicant for a CE-marked device may be required to submit corresponding evidence on the basis of clinical trials in compliance with Directive 2001/83/EC. As such, the consultation process may be time consuming and may result in a substantial loss of effective patent term.

There has been some controversy as to whether SPCs should also be available for medical devices comprising an active ingredient as an integral component (*see also* §1.02[A][6]). Thus, some national offices have allowed the issue of an SPC for such devices, where the quality, safety and usefulness of a medicinal product component had been verified in analogy with the Medicinal Products Directive. Others, however, have interpreted Articles 2 and 3(b) of the SPC Regulation as strictly precluding an SPC for products that have not been authorized under the Medicinal Products Directive.

In light of the divergent approaches adopted by the Member States, the German Federal Patent Court in case 14 W (pat) 13/16[211] has referred a question to the CJEU, asking essentially whether the SPC Regulation applies to a CE-marked implantable

208. Regulation (EU) 2017/745 of the European Parliament and of the Council of 5 April 2017 on medical devices, amending Directive 2001/83/EC, Regulation (EC) No. 178/2002 and Regulation (EC) No. 1223/2009 and repealing Council Directives 90/385/EEC and 93/42/EEC.

209. Council Directive 90/385/EEC of 20 June 1990 on the approximation of the laws of the Member States relating to active implantable medical devices.

210. Council Directive 93/42/EEC of 14 June 1993 concerning medical devices.

211. German Federal Patent Court (Bundespatentgericht) decision 14 W (pat) 13/16 of 18 July 2017. The precise wording of the referred question reads as follows (in English translation):

> Must Art. 2 of [the SPC Regulation for Medicinal Products] be interpreted as meaning that, for the purposes of that regulation, an authorization under Directive 93/42/EEC for a combined medical device and medicinal product within the meaning of Art. 1(4) of Directive 93/42/EEC is to be treated as a valid marketing authorization under Directive 2001/83/EC, where, as part of the authorization procedure laid down in Annex I, Section 7.4, first paragraph, to Directive 93/42/EEC, the quality, safety and

medical device which incorporates as an integral part an active ingredient which, if used separately, may be considered to be a medicinal product within the meaning of the Medicinal Products Directive. This referral is pending before the CJEU as C-527/17.

With respect to veterinary medicinal products, the EFTA Court acknowledged in *Pharmaq* (E-16/14) that an SPC can also be based on a marketing authorization granted 'in exceptional circumstances' under Article 26(3) of Directive 2001/82/EC, but not on a provisional permission granted 'in the event of serious epizootic diseases' under Article 8 of Directive 2001/82/EC.[212]

[5] The Marketing Authorizations Which Can Be Relied upon for SPC Applications for Plant Protection Products

As set out in the SPC Regulation for Plant Protection Products, in order to secure SPC protection, an authorization must either have been granted in accordance with Article 4 of Directive 91/414/EEC (now repealed by Regulation (EC) 1107/2009[213] with effect from 14 June 2011) or under a relevant provision of national law equivalent to these administrative authorization procedures.[214] In these regulatory provisions several types of authorizations are referred to, including an 'approval regulation' (Article 13 of Regulation (EC) 1107/2009), an 'authorization for placing on the market', (Articles 29 and 40), 'provisional authorizations' (Article 30), 'emergency authorizations' (Article 53) and experimental authorizations 'for research and development' (Article 54). This has led to some confusion as to which authorization may be relied upon for filing an SPC.

In its judgement *Hogan Lovells* (C-229/09),[215] the CJEU confirmed that an SPC may be granted on the basis of a full as well as a provisional marketing authorization granted under Article 8(1) of Directive 91/414/EEC (now Article 30 of Regulation (EC) 1107/2009).

On the other hand, as set out in *Sumitomo Chemical* (C-210/12),[216] an emergency marketing authorization granted in accordance with Article 8(4) of Directive 91/414/EEC (now Article 53 of Regulation (EC) 1107/2009), which is only valid for 120 days, does not amount to a marketing approval within the meaning of Articles 2 and 3(1)(b) of the SPC Regulation for Plant Protection Products.

---

usefulness of the medicinal product component has been verified by the medicinal products authority of a Member State in accordance with Directive 2001/83/EC?

212. EFTA Court, *Pharmaq v. Intervet International*, E-16/14 of 9 April 2015, paragraphs 54–66.
213. Regulation (EC) 1107/2009 of the European Parliament and of the Council of 21 October 2009 concerning the placing of plant protection products on the market and repealing Council Directives 79/117/EEC and 91/414/EEC.
214. The reference to an authorization granted under 'an equivalent provision of national law' in Art. 3(1)(b) of the SPC Regulation for Plant Protection Products must be read, in the light of Art. 2, as relating to plant protection products in respect of which the application for marketing authorization was lodged before Directive 91/414/EEC was implemented by the respective Member State. *See also* CJEU *Bayer CropScience v. Deutsches Patent- und Markenamt*, C-11/13 of 19 June 2014, paragraph 40.
215. CJEU *Hogan Lovells International v. Bayer CropScience*, C-229/09 of 11 November 2010.
216. CJEU *Sumitomo Chemical v. Deutsches Patent- und Markenamt*, C-210/12 of 17 October 2013.

[6] The Product in Question Is Contained in the Authorized Medicinal Product (or the Authorized Plant Protection Product) but Is Not Identified as an Active Ingredient in the Corresponding Marketing Authorization

As set out in Article 2 in conjunction with Article 1(b) of the SPC Regulation for Medicinal Products, an SPC may be granted for a 'product' which is defined as the active ingredient or combination of active ingredients of a medicinal product. While the Regulation does not expressly define the term 'active ingredient', the definition provided in Article 1(a) implies that an active ingredient is a substance which may be administered to human beings or animals with a view to making a medical diagnosis or to restoring, correcting or modifying physiological functions in humans or in animals.

Such an interpretation correlates with the explanations provided in the Explanatory Memorandum for the Proposal for a Council Regulation (EEC) concerning the creation of a supplementary protection certificate for medicinal products, according to which the term 'active ingredient' is to be interpreted in the strict sense, in analogy to the definition provided in Article 1 of the Medicinal Products Directive 65/65/EEC.[217]

Innovation in the pharmaceutical field is not limited to the finding of new active ingredients.

Thus, valuable contributions may also be made, e.g., by way of novel formulations with special excipients and carriers. The approval of such products is subject to the same level of scrutiny under the Medicinal Products Directives, resulting at times in a considerable curtailment of the effective patent term.

Some national patent offices have allowed SPCs to issue for such products, whereas others have applied a more stringent interpretation of the concept of the term 'active ingredient' and have relied on the active ingredients which are designated as such in Section 2 of the Summary of Product Characteristics (SmPC), which is an integral part of the marketing authorization.

The CJEU has addressed this issue in *MIT* (C-431/04).[218] In this case an SPC had been applied for a new dosage form of a prior approved anti-neoplastic agent, carmustine, embedded in an implantable polymeric wafer. While the polymeric wafer has no therapeutic effects on its own, it facilitates the local delivery of the active ingredient, thereby substantially reducing systemic toxicity and thus provides considerable benefits to the patients. The Advocate General[219] recommended that an SPC should be available in this case as 'the necessity for ensuring the therapeutic efficacy of the active ingredient must be the determining factor'. As set out in the headnote of *MIT*, the CJEU, however, ruled that the SPC Regulation 'must be interpreted so as not to include in the concept of "combination of active ingredients of a medicinal product" a combination of two substances, only one of which has therapeutic effects of its own for a specific indication, the other rendering possible a pharmaceutical form of the

217. COM(90) 101 final – SYN 255, paragraph 28.
218. CJEU *Massachusetts Institute of Technology v. Bundesgerichtshof*, C-431/04 of 4 May 2006.
219. Opinion of the Advocate General in *Massachusetts Institute of Technology v. Bundesgerichtshof*, C-431/04, delivered on 24 November 2005.

medicinal product which is necessary for the therapeutic efficacy of the first substance for that indication'.

While the restrictive approach adopted by the CJEU may facilitate legal certainty, the wording of the headnote in the *MIT* decision would appear far too general, as it suggests that only an ingredient having a therapeutic action of its own for the indication in question may be viewed as an active ingredient which may be subject matter of an SPC. This is clearly not appropriate. Many medicinal products contain an ingredient which is identified in the SmPC as being the active ingredient, although it has no direct therapeutic effect, but by modifying physiological functions may potentiate or boost the effect of other therapeutic agents used to treat the underlying disease.

Subsequently, in *GSK* (C-210/13)[220] the CJEU concluded that an SPC cannot be granted for a vaccine formulation comprising a new adjuvant combined with an antigen (an influenza virus component) as the adjuvant has no therapeutic effect of its own and cannot be regarded as an 'active ingredient' of its own. In its reasoning the CJEU relied also on the distinction made in the Medicinal Products Directive[221] between 'active ingredients' and 'adjuvants'.

A similar conclusion was reached by the CJEU in *Forsgren* (C-631/13),[222] where the CJEU ruled that an SPC directed towards Protein D, a carrier protein conjugated to various antigens, is only allowable, if the carrier protein produces a pharmacological, immunological or metabolic action of its own which is covered by the therapeutic indications of the marketing authorization.

The regulatory provisions for plant protection products[223] also expressly distinguish between 'active substances' and other components contained in a plant protection product, such as 'safeners'. In spite of this distinction, the CJEU in *Bayer CropScience* (C-11/13)[224] ruled that the term 'active substances' in the SPC Regulation for Plant Protection Products must be interpreted as meaning to also cover a substance intended to be used as a safener, where that substance has a toxic, phytotoxic or plant protection action of its own. As a consequence, SPCs should be available for new formulations of plant protection products containing a previously approved active ingredient, if they contain a new safener which has a toxic, phytotoxic or plant protection action of its own.

[7] The Notion of the 'First' Marketing Authorization

According to Article 3(d) of the SPC Regulations, an SPC must be filed on the basis of the first authorization, in the Member State concerned, to place the product on the market as a medicinal or plant protection product, as appropriate.

220. CJEU *Glaxosmithkline Biologicals v. Comptroller-General of Patents, Designs and Trade Marks*, C-210/13 of 14 November 2013.
221. *See* Section 3.2.2.1 of Part 1 of Annex I of Directive 2001/83/EC as amended by Directive 2003/63/EC.
222. CJEU *Arne Forsgren v. Österreichisches Patentamt*, C-631/13 of 15 January 2015.
223. *See* Art. 2 of Regulation (EC) 1107/2009.
224. CJEU *Bayer CropScience v. Deutsches Patent- und Markenamt*, C-11/13 of 19 June 2014.

Thus, as set out in the Explanatory Memorandum to the SPC Regulation for Medicinal Products, it often occurs that several authorizations are granted for one and the same product, namely each time a modification is made affecting the pharmaceutical form, dose, composition, indications, etc. In such a case, only the first authorization for the product to be placed on the market should be taken into account for the purposes of the SPC Regulation, in particular for calculating the six-month time limit for filing the SPC.

Furthermore, if the first authorization is also the first authorization to place the product on the market in the Community, it serves as the reference date for all Member States for the purposes of calculating the duration of each of the SPCs granted.

As set out below, the notion of the 'first' marketing authorization has evolved over the past decade, in light of the appreciation by the CJEU that a more teleological interpretation of the SPC Regulation is warranted in order to ensure that the SPC Regulation is compatible with its aims.

[a] *Marketing Authorization for a New Therapeutic Application of a Previously Authorized Product*

The 'first marketing authorization' requirement as set out in Article 3(d) of the SPC Regulations, if literally interpreted, implies that if the active ingredient in question has already been approved for any unrelated therapeutic (or plant protection) application, no SPC extension will be available, even if the basic patent relates to an innovative second medical use (or plant protection use) of the active ingredient. Such a restrictive interpretation of the SPC Regulations would appear to be clearly contrary to the legislative goal as set out in the Explanatory Memorandum for the Proposal for a Council Regulation (EEC) concerning the creation of a supplementary protection certificate for medicinal products, which emphasizes that the SPC Regulation should be applicable to all types of pharmaceutical research without discrimination.[225]

Nevertheless, in *Pharmacia* (C-31/03)[226] the Court ruled 'first, that the decisive factor for the grant of the certificate is not the intended use of the medicinal product and, second, that the purpose of the protection conferred by the certificate relates to any use of the product as a medicinal product without any distinction between use of the product as a medicinal product for human use and as a veterinary medicinal product'.

This position was confirmed by the CJEU in *Yissum* (C-202/05)[227] in a reasoned order, based on its previous case law in *Pharmacia* and *MIT*. Accordingly, the mentioned considerations in relation to the concept of the 'product' of an SPC cannot take account of the therapeutic use protected by a basic patent.

In light of the seemingly established case law of the CJEU in *Pharmacia*, *MIT* and *Yissum*, it was the general consensus at the time that the issue of an SPC was precluded

225. COM(90) 101 final - SYN 255, paragraph 29.
226. CJEU *Pharmacia Italia v. Bundesgerichtshof*, C-31/03 of 19 October 2004, paragraph 20.
227. CJEU *Yissum Research and Development Company of the Hebrew University of Jerusalem v. Comptroller-General of Patents*, C-202/05 of 17 April 2007.

if the active ingredient in question had been authorized in any earlier marketing authorization within the EU, even if the earlier authorization related to a different use in a different species, formulation or second medical use.

In appreciation that such a restrictive literal interpretation of the SPC Regulations in terms of not allowing an SPC for products which had previously been approved would undermine the central objectives of the SPC Regulations, namely to ensure sufficient proprietary protection to encourage all types of pharmaceutical research (or plant protection research) without any discrimination,[228] the CJEU in *Neurim* (C-130/11)[229] departed from its previous guidance. Thus, in *Neurim*, the CJEU applied a teleological approach when interpreting the SPC Regulation for Medicinal Products and concluded that an earlier marketing authorization for a veterinary or human medicinal use does not preclude the grant of an SPC based on a later marketing authorization for a different therapeutic application of the same active ingredient(s), provided that the later marketing authorization falls within the limits of protection of the basic patent relied upon for the SPC filing.

In *Neurim* the CJEU has thus clearly abandoned its earlier rulings provided in *Pharmacia* and *Yissum*, in now allowing an SPC product to extend not just to a new active ingredient, but also to a new use for a known, previously approved active ingredient. As such, the concept of the 'first marketing authorization' now requires a more differential assessment, in that the mere existence of an earlier marketing authorization does not preclude the grant of an SPC for a different application of the same product for which a new marketing authorization has been granted, provided that the application is within the limits of the protection conferred by the basic patent relied upon for the SPC filing.

[b] Marketing Authorization for a New Formulation of a Previously Authorized Product

As set out in §1.02[C][6] above, according to the guidance provided by the CJEU in *MIT*, a new formulation of a previously approved product should not give rise to an SPC for the formulation, as the concept of the 'product' within the meaning of the SPC Regulation must be understood in the strict sense.

Nevertheless, the *Neurim* ruling is difficult to reconcile with the seemingly consistent guidance provided previously by the CJEU in *MIT*, *Pharmacia* and *Yissum*. As such, the scope of the *Neurim* ruling remains unclear. While it has paved the way for SPCs for second medical use inventions of products which had previously been authorized, it is uncertain whether it is also applicable to new formulations of previously approved active ingredients, when the therapeutic use is the same.

In order to resolve these uncertainties the CJEU in *Abraxis* (C-443/17)[230] has again been asked to provide guidance as to whether the SPC Regulation for Medicinal

228. COM(90) 101 final – SYN 255, paragraph 29; COM(94) 579 final, paragraph 66.
229. CJEU *Neurim Pharmaceuticals v. Comptroller-General of Patents, Designs and Trade Marks*, C-130/11 of 19 July 2012.
230. CJEU *Abraxis Bioscience v. Comptroller General of Patents*, C-443/17, referral of 24 July 2017.

Products is to be interpreted as permitting the grant of an SPC where the marketing authorization referred to in Article 3(b) is the first authorization within the scope of the basic patent to place the product on the market as a medicinal product and where the product is a new formulation of an old active ingredient.

[c] Marketing Authorization for a New Specific Salt, Ester or Other Derivative of a Previously Authorized Active Ingredient

As set out in §1.02[C][6] above, in the Explanatory Memorandum for the SPC Regulation for Medicinal Products, the European Commission in relation to the concept of 'the product' of an SPC chose to rely on the definition provided in the Medicinal Products Directive as laid out in Directive 65/65/EEC[231] (now repealed and replaced by Directive 2001/83/EC).[232]

In Article 6(1) of the Medicinal Products Directive 2001/83/EC the concept of the 'global marketing authorization' has been introduced, according to which when a medicinal product has been granted an initial marketing authorization, any additional authorizations granted for other strengths, pharmaceutical forms, administration routes, presentations, as well as any variations and extensions shall be considered as belonging to the same global marketing authorization.

Moreover, the Medicinal Products Directive in Article 10(2)(b) defines a generic product as a medicinal product which has 'the same qualitative and quantitative composition in active substances and the same pharmaceutical form as the reference medicinal product, and whose bioequivalence with the reference medicinal product has been demonstrated by appropriate bioavailability studies. The different salts, esters, ethers, isomers, mixtures of isomers, complexes or derivatives of an active substance shall be considered to be the same active substance, unless they differ significantly in properties with regard to safety and/or efficacy'.

Various national courts have rejected the issue of an SPC based on a marketing authorization for a new salt of a previously approved active ingredient on the grounds that the new salt does not result in a new 'product' within the meaning of the SPC Regulation.

While the CJEU has never been specifically asked to rule on this question head on, the Court on various accounts has taken the opportunity to address the issue. Thus, in *MIT* the CJEU has emphasized that a strict definition of the product of an SPC is called for. According to the CJEU,[233] it would not be acceptable for the total duration of protection granted by an SPC and a basic patent for one and the same product to be

231. Council Directive 65/65/EEC of 26 January 1965 on the approximation of provisions laid down by Law, Regulation or Administrative Action relating to proprietary medicinal products.
232. Directive 2001/83/EC of the European Parliament and of the Council of 6 November 2001 on the Community code relating to medicinal products for human use.
233. CJEU *Massachusetts Institute of Technology v. Bundesgerichtshof*, C-431/04 of 4 May 2006.

exceeded, as may be the case if one and the same product, such as a different salt, a different excipient or a different presentation, were able to be the subject of several successive SPCs. As a consequence, although one and the same substance may be the subject of several patents and several marketing authorizations in one and the same Member State, an SPC should be granted for that substance only on the basis of a single patent and a single authorization, namely the first granted in the Member State concerned.

In light of the above considerations, an SPC should not generally be available based on a new marketing authorization for a specific salt, ester or other simple derivative of a previously authorized product.

This position is in line with the guidance provided by the CJEU in *Farmitalia* (C-392/97),[234] according to which 'where an active ingredient in the form of a salt is referred to in the marketing authorization concerned and is protected by a basic patent in force, the certificate is capable of covering the active ingredient as such and also its various derived forms such as salts and esters, as medicinal products, in so far as they are covered by the protection of the basic patent'.

It is nevertheless conceivable that an SPC may be granted for a new salt or other derivative of a previously approved product.

Thus, the European Commission's Notice to Applicants supplements the list of products falling under the concept of the 'global marketing authorization' and develops the concept of a 'new active substance' (NAS) for regulatory purposes.[235] Accordingly, a product will be considered to be a NAS, even if it is 'an isomer, mixture of isomers, a complex or derivative or salt of a chemical substance previously authorized in a medicinal product for human use in the European Union' as long as it differs 'significantly in properties with regard to safety and/or efficacy from that chemical substance previously authorized'.

It is thus conceivable that a marketing authorization for a new salt, ester or other derivative of a previously approved active ingredient may form the basis of an SPC application, whereby however, the new derivative must exhibit significantly different pharmacological properties from a regulatory perspective in terms of its therapeutic profile.

Such a possibility would also be supported by recital 14 of the SPC Regulation for Plant Protection Products, which is likewise applicable to the SPC Regulation for Medicinal Products[236] and provides that the issue of an SPC for an active substance does not prejudice the issue of other SPCs for derivatives (salts and esters) of that active

234. CJEU *Farmitalia Carlo Erba v. Bundesgerichtshof*, C-392/97 of 16 September 1999, paragraph 21.

235. European Commission, Health and Food Safety Directorate-General. Notice to Applicants, Volume 2A, Procedures for Marketing Authorization, Chapter 1 – Marketing Authorization, Revision 7 of December 2017. Section 2.3 – Notion of 'global marketing authorization' and Annex I – Definition of a new active substance.

236. Recital 14 of Regulation (EC) 1610/96 is, by virtue of recital 17 of this Regulation, also applicable for the interpretation of the SPC Regulation for Medicinal Products. This has been confirmed by the CJEU, e.g., in *Farmitalia Carlo Erba v. Bundesgerichtshof*, C-392/97 of 16 September 1999, paragraph 20.

substance, provided that the derivatives are the subject of patents specifically covering them.

[d] *Marketing Authorization for a New Specific Enantiomer of an Active Ingredient Previously Authorized in Racemic Form*

So far no case relating to an SPC based on a marketing authorization for an enantiomer of an active ingredient previously approved as a racemate has been referred to the CJEU.

Nevertheless, various national courts have addressed this issue in a favourable manner,[237] as here the enantiomers in question were viewed as exhibiting a significantly improved therapeutic profile.

These national decisions would appear to be in line with the guidance provided in the Medicinal Products Directives and the Notice to Applicants, according to which an isomer of a previously authorized chemical substance may be viewed as a new active substance (NAS) if it differs significantly in properties with regard to safety and/or efficacy from that chemical substance previously authorized.

[e] *The Product Has Already Been Placed on the Market Before, but Without an Authorization Granted under Directive 2001/83/EC or Directive 2001/82/EC*

In *Synthon* (C-195/09)[238] and *Generics* (C-427/09),[239] the products of the respective SPC applications were based on approvals granted in accordance with the stringent regulatory requirements as set out in Article 2 of the SPC Regulation for Medicinal Products. However, the products had previously been placed on the market in accordance with national approvals, which were not in compliance with the Directives referred to in the SPC Regulation for Medicinal Products. The CJEU ruled that any product marketed outside of an EU-compliant marketing authorization is outside the SPC system. Moreover, the grant of an SPC for a product which had already been marketed before it was subject to the long and demanding approval procedure would be contrary to the very purpose of the SPC system.

The *Synthon* and *Generics* decisions were rendered prior to *Neurim*. In view of the guidance provided in *Neurim*, a prior approval of the active ingredient(s) under Directive 2001/83/EC or Directive 2001/82/EC or otherwise should not be a bar to an SPC for the same active ingredient(s) if they are to be used for a new therapeutic indication.

237. *See* German Federal Supreme Court (Bundesgerichtshof), *Escitalopram*, Xa ZR 130/07 of 10 September 2009; and UK Court of Appeal, *Daiichi Sankyo v. Generics* [2009] EWCA Civ 646.
238. CJEU *Synthon v. Merz Pharma*, C-195/09 of 28 July 2011.
239. CJEU *Generics (UK) v. Synaptech*, C-427/09 of 28 July 2011.

[f] Prior Marketing Authorization Which Refers to Fewer Active Ingredients than the SPC Application (and the Later Marketing Authorization Relied upon)

In principle, any new combination of active ingredients may be viewed as a new product within the meaning of the SPC Regulations. Therefore, as a rule, if an SPC is filed for a combination product, the first marketing authorization for that product should necessarily relate to all the active ingredients comprised in the combination product, so that any prior marketing authorization for fewer active ingredients should be unproblematic.

In this context, however, account must be taken of the principles set out by the CJEU in *Medeva*. Thus, in *Medeva*[240] the Court emphasized that only the authorization in respect of the first medicinal product placed on the EU market comprising, among its active ingredients, the active ingredient which is the subject of the SPC application may be regarded as the first marketing authorization for that product as a medicinal product within the meaning of Article 3(d) of the SPC Regulation. In other words, if the 'core invention' underlying the basic patent is a certain active ingredient (A) or combination of active ingredients (A + B), the corresponding SPC must be based on the first marketing authorization for this active ingredient or combination of active ingredients. Arguably, if the notion were accepted that an SPC product must embody the 'core inventive advance' of the basic patent (*see* §1.02[B][3] above), it could thus be held that even if the claims of the basic patent allow for further combinations of the core active ingredient(s) with other active ingredients (A + C) or (A + B + C), which are not protected as such by the basic patent, a prior approval of the core active ingredient(s) alone may be detrimental to a later SPC application for a combination of the core active ingredient(s) with other active ingredients, based on a marketing authorization for that combination, unless the combination embodies the inventive advance of the patent.

The above considerations will not apply if the basic patent in question protects the new combination as such, or if the later marketing authorization relates to the use of the active ingredient(s) for a new indication within the meaning of the *Neurim* ruling.

[g] Prior Marketing Authorization Which Refers to More Active Ingredients than the SPC Application (and the Later Marketing Authorization Relied upon)

The considerations as set out in §1.02[C][7][f] above should apply equally to the situation where the prior marketing authorization refers to more active ingredients than the SPC application and the later marketing authorization.

The SPC for a certain innovative product which is the subject matter of a patent (which may be a single active ingredient or a combination of active ingredients) must

240. CJEU *Medeva v. Comptroller General of Patents, Designs and Trade Marks*, C-322/10 of 24 November 2011, paragraph 40.

be based on the first approval of this product, irrespective in what combination it has been approved.

Thus, as explicitly affirmed by the CJEU in *Medeva* and *Georgetown*, the first marketing authorization for the product of an SPC will normally be the first approval of any medicinal product (or plant protection product) comprising, among its active ingredients, the active ingredient(s) referred to in the SPC, even if the corresponding authorized product contains additional active ingredients which are not subject of the SPC.[241]

If, however, the innovation provided by the basic patent is based the use of a specific active ingredient or combination of active ingredients for a new therapeutic application, in light of *Neurim* the prior authorization comprising more active ingredients should not be detrimental to the SPC filing.

[D] Preclusion of New SPCs by an Earlier SPC

The SPC Regulations provide in Article 3(c)[242] that an SPC shall be granted only if, in the Member State in which the SPC application is filed and at the date of that application, 'the product has not already been the subject of a certificate'.

This requirement is further qualified in Article 3(2) of the SPC Regulation for Plant Protection Products, which is also applicable to the SPC Regulation for Medicinal Products.[243] According to Article 3(2), the holder of more than one patent for the same product shall not be granted more than one SPC for that product; however, where two or more SPC applications concerning the same product and emanating from two or more holders of different patents are pending, one SPC for this same product may be issued to each of these patent holders.

As acknowledged by the CJEU in *AHP Manufacturing* (C-482/07),[244] the decisive condition allowing the grant of more than one SPC for the same product is that the corresponding SPC applications emanate from *different holders* of basic patents. In order to determine whether a new SPC can be granted in spite of an earlier existing SPC for the same product, it is thus mandatory to differentiate between the cases of an own earlier SPC and an earlier third-party SPC.

241. *Ibid.* and headnote 2; CJEU *Georgetown University v. Comptroller General of Patents, Designs and Trade Marks*, C-422/10 of 24 November 2011, paragraph 33 and headnote.

242. Article 3(c) of Regulation (EC) 469/2009, and Art. 3(1)(c) of Regulation (EC) 1610/96.

243. Article 3(2) of Regulation (EC) 1610/96 is, by virtue of recital 17 of this Regulation, also applicable for the interpretation of Art. 3 of the SPC Regulation for Medicinal Products. This has been expressly confirmed by the CJEU in *AHP Manufacturing v. Bureau voor de Industriële Eigendom*, C-482/07 of 3 September 2009, paragraph 23. As regards the applicability of recital 17 of the SPC Regulation for Plant Protection Products for the interpretation of the SPC Regulation for Medicinal Products, *see also*: CJEU *Farmitalia Carlo Erba v. Bundesgerichtshof*, C-392/97 of 16 September 1999, paragraph 20; CJEU *Massachusetts Institute of Technology v. Bundesgerichtshof*, C-431/04 of 4 May 2006, paragraph 24; and CJEU *Incyte Corporation v. Szellemi Tulajdon Nemzeti Hivatala*, C-492/16 of 20 December 2017, paragraphs 33 and 34.

244. CJEU *AHP Manufacturing v. Bureau voor de Industriële Eigendom*, C-482/07 of 3 September 2009, paragraphs 25 and 40.

[1] *Consequences of an Earlier Third-Party SPC for the Same Product*

[a] *The 'One SPC per Product per Patent Holder' Rule*

Article 3(2) of the SPC Regulation for Plant Protection Products, which is also applicable to the SPC Regulation for Medicinal Products,[245] expressly allows that different holders of basic patents can each be granted one (and only one) SPC for the same product.[246] While this provision, strictly speaking, only refers to the case that two or more SPC applications for the same product are *pending*, the CJEU clarified in *AHP Manufacturing* (C-482/07)[247] that an SPC can also be granted even if it is filed only after one or more other SPCs for the same product have already been granted to other patent holders, i.e., it is not necessary that the respective SPC applications should be pending at the same time, which is a very sensible approach.[248]

---

245. Article 3(2) of Regulation (EC) 1610/96 is, by virtue of recital 17 of this Regulation, also applicable for the interpretation of Art. 3 of the SPC Regulation for Medicinal Products. This has been expressly confirmed by the CJEU in *AHP Manufacturing v. Bureau voor de Industriële Eigendom*, C-482/07 of 3 September 2009, paragraph 23. As regards the applicability of recital 17 of the SPC Regulation for Plant Protection Products for the interpretation of the SPC Regulation for Medicinal Products, *see also*: CJEU *Farmitalia Carlo Erba v. Bundesgerichtshof*, C-392/97 of 16 September 1999, paragraph 20; CJEU *Massachusetts Institute of Technology v. Bundesgerichtshof*, C-431/04 of 4 May 2006, paragraph 24; and CJEU *Incyte Corporation v. Szellemi Tulajdon Nemzeti Hivatala*, C-492/16 of 20 December 2017, paragraphs 33 and 34.
246. This was already confirmed by the CJEU in respect of the SPC Regulation for Medicinal Products before the SPC Regulation for Plant Protection Products entered into force. *See* CJEU *Biogen v. SmithKlineBeecham Biologicals*, C-181/95 of 23 January 1997, headnote 1.
247. CJEU *AHP Manufacturing v. Bureau voor de Industriële Eigendom*, C-482/07 of 3 September 2009.
248. The CJEU's approach in *AHP Manufacturing* (C-482/07) is sensible for a number of practical reasons. Deciding otherwise, i.e., allowing the grant of further SPCs for the same product only if the corresponding SPC applications are already pending at the time that the first SPC for this product is granted, or possibly allowing only the simultaneous grant of several SPCs but no subsequent grant of any further SPC for the same product (as insinuated in paragraph 32 of *AHP Manufacturing*), would have entailed severely unsatisfactory consequences. This would have meant that the pace of the different national patent offices in granting SPCs would affect the ability of a patent holder to obtain an SPC. Likewise, a slow conduct of proceedings by the authority granting the basic patent would compromise the ability of the patent holder to obtain an SPC on this basis of that patent. The legitimate right of patent holders to be granted SPCs on the basis of their patents would thus have been curtailed in a wholly arbitrary manner by factors that lie (at least partly) beyond their own sphere of influence, such as the pace of the authority granting the respective patent and the pace of the national patent offices in granting SPCs. Under such a hypothetical approach, the differences in pace with which the different national patent offices process SPC applications could furthermore be expected to give rise to the grant (or preclusion) of different SPCs in the different EU Member States and thus result in a fragmentation of the SPC landscape across the Member States, thereby creating obstacles to the free movement of medicinal and plant protection products in the single market, which would be diametrically opposed to the fundamental objectives of the SPC Regulations of creating a uniform solution at EU level and allowing the grant of SPCs under the same conditions in each Member State. On top of that, allowing the grant of several SPCs for the same product only on the basis of simultaneously pending SPC applications would have meant that SPC applicants could no longer rely on their right to make use of the full legal term for filing SPCs established in Art. 7 of the SPC Regulations. For all these reasons, the CJEU's conclusion in *AHP Manufacturing*, confirming that even after the grant of an SPC it is still possible for other

The basic principle resulting from this jurisprudence of the CJEU has become known as the 'one SPC per product per patent holder' rule, meaning that *different holders* of basic patents can each be granted one SPC for the same product, while the *same holder* of several patents cannot be granted more than one SPC for the same product.

[b] Earlier SPC Granted to an Affiliated Third Party

The practice of allowing different patent holders to be each granted an SPC for the same product, while the same patent holder cannot be granted more than one SPC for the same product, prompts the question under which conditions two patent holders are to be considered the same or different. This question arises, in particular, in cases where two patent holders are distinct legal entities but are nevertheless somehow affiliated, e.g., because they both are subsidiaries of the same parent company, or because one patent holder has a certain stake in the other, which may range from a minority interest to a controlling interest or even full ownership. It has not yet been clarified how such cases should be handled.

The SPC Regulations confer entitlement to an SPC to the holder of the basic patent,[249] and the Explanatory Memorandums emphasize that the decision whether to apply for an SPC should be left to the patent holder alone.[250] In view of the central role afforded to the patent holder in the SPC system, it would seem logical to revert to principles of patent law when assessing the identity of the patent holder.

In patent law, the question whether the applicants or proprietors of patents are the same or different arises, for example, in the context of assessing the entitlement to claim priority, the entitlement to file divisional applications, and the prohibition of double patenting. In this connection, a narrow and formal approach has generally been followed, in the sense that any corporate entities that are distinct legal persons are considered to be different applicants/patentees, regardless of any possible affiliation between such entities.[251]

---

patent holders to file new SPCs for the same product, satisfies a basic practical necessity for the proper functioning of the SPC system.

249. Article 6 of both Regulation (EC) 469/2009 and Regulation (EC) 1610/96.
250. Explanatory Memorandum to the Commission proposal for an SPC regulation for medicinal products, COM(90) 101 final - SYN 255, paragraph 37; and Explanatory Memorandum to the Commission proposal for an SPC regulation for plant protection products, COM(94) 579 final, paragraph 71.
251. *See*, e.g., the EPO Board of Appeal decision T 5/05 of 9 November 2005, Sections 4.1-4.3 of the reasons. In this decision, the competent Board of Appeal assessed priority entitlement and found that different legal persons must be regarded as different and independent patent applicants, even if they are subsidiaries fully owned and controlled by the same parent company. Similarly, in the EPO Board of Appeal decision T 1423/07 of 19 April 2010, Section 2.4 of the reasons, the competent Board assessed the question of double patenting between an earlier granted patent and the patent application under examination. While both were originally held by Boehringer Ingelheim Pharma GmbH, the application at issue (but not the earlier patent) was subsequently transferred to Boehringer Ingelheim Vetmedica GmbH. The Board of Appeal concluded that, in view of this transfer, the proprietor of the earlier patent and

Applying this same approach to the question whether a further SPC can be granted despite the existence of an earlier SPC for the same product held by a distinct but affiliated legal entity has the considerable advantages of simplicity and legal certainty. This is not to be underestimated, particularly in view of the plethora of conceivable relationships between different, yet somehow affiliated patent holders.[252] Such an approach would also be in accordance with the fact that the SPC Regulations do not provide any explicit legal basis for treating distinct legal entities - in deviation from their formal legal status - as the 'same' entity under any specific circumstances. Arguably, it may be held that any such deviating treatment of formally distinct legal entities should not even be possible in the absence of a corresponding legal basis.

This approach would furthermore conform with the actual practice of the national patent offices which are not in a position to examine any potential affiliations between different patent holders. Indeed, it is not apparent how this should be possible, particularly where an affiliation is not immediately evident, nor what criteria should possibly be applied to measure and judge the degree of affiliation between such different legal entities. All these reasons support the notion that, in principle, the grant of more than one SPC to different, albeit affiliated patent holders should not be precluded.

Such an interpretation is in line with the fact that the SPC Regulations do not impose any restrictions on the transfer of already granted SPCs and, in particular, do not prevent the transfer of multiple granted SPCs for the same product to the same person. Since the acquisition of multiple SPCs for the same product is legally permissible in this manner, it does not seem justifiable to prohibit the grant of multiple SPCs for the same product to different but affiliated patent holders on the basis of an overly strict interpretation of Article 3(c) and 3(2) of the SPC Regulations, either.

Yet, it should not be left unmentioned that a much broader concept of the identity of a rights holder is applied in pharmaceutical regulatory law, particularly in the specific context of the 'global marketing authorization' according to Article 6(1) of Directive 2001/83/EC (Community code for human medicinal products). Thus, as explained in the European Commission's Notice to Applicants,[253] 'for the purposes of the application of the pharmaceuticals rules, having a distinct legal personality does not necessarily entail that each entity can be considered as a distinct applicant or marketing authorization holder to the other one'. Rather, '[a]pplicants and marketing authorization holders belonging to the same company group or that are controlled by the same physical or legal entity are to be considered as one entity'. Moreover, even

the applicant of the contested patent application were no longer identical and, therefore, double patenting would no longer exist.

252. To give but one example, the seemingly odd question could be raised whether different state-owned public universities or research institutes should be regarded as the 'same' patent holder, for the purpose of the SPC Regulations, on the grounds that they are owned by the same state.

253. European Commission, Health and Food Safety Directorate-General. Notice to Applicants, Volume 2A, Procedures for Marketing Authorization, Chapter 1 - Marketing Authorization, Revision 7 of December 2017. Section 2.8 - Concept of 'applicant' and 'marketing authorization holder'. *See also* the Commission communication on the Community marketing authorization procedures for medicinal products of 22 July 1998 (98/C 229/03).

'[a]pplicants and marketing authorization holders that do not belong to the same company group and are not controlled by the same physical or legal entity are to be considered as one applicant/marketing authorization holder if they have concluded tacit or explicit agreements concerning the marketing of the same medicinal product'. This extremely far-reaching concept of who is to be considered as the 'same' marketing authorization holder applies only in the aforementioned specific context and can evidently not be generalized or transferred to the assessment of identity of rights holders in other circumstances, let alone to the assessment of identity of the holder of a basic patent.

Quite on the contrary, in view of the central position that the SPC Regulations afford to the holder of a basic patent, and particularly the rights conferred to the patent holder in Article 6, it appears mandatory to apply a narrow interpretation of who is (or is not) the holder of a patent. For reasons of consistency, such a necessarily narrow interpretation would likewise be applicable to Article 3(c) and 3(2) of the SPC Regulations, with the consequence that patent holders who are different legal entities, even if they are somehow affiliated, should still be regarded as different patent holders.

The CJEU has not yet provided any guidance in this respect, which would seem to reflect the established practice of the national patent offices that patent holders who are distinct legal entities are simply accepted to be different patent holders, regardless of any potential affiliation. It remains to be seen if this simple and pragmatic approach will be confirmed by the CJEU if a corresponding referral is eventually made.

As a note of caution, if more than one SPC for the same product is sought by affiliated entities, it is advisable to do so openly and disclose the affiliation to the national patent offices where the respective SPC applications are filed, not least in order to reduce the risk of potential antitrust issues (*see* §1.07 below).

[c] *Partial Overlap Between the Holders of the Earlier SPC and the Applicants for the New SPC*

While multiple SPCs for the same product can, in principle, be granted to different holders of basic patents but not to the same patent holder, as discussed in §1.02[D] and §1.02[D][1][a] above, it is controversial how joint patent (or SPC) holders, i.e., two or more natural or legal persons who jointly hold the respective patent (or SPC), should be considered in this regard.

For example, if the joint patent proprietors A + B have obtained a first SPC on the basis of their patent P1, and subsequently the patent proprietor A alone files a second SPC for the same product on the basis of its patent P2, will the grant of the second SPC to A be precluded in view of the first SPC granted to A + B and the 'partial overlap' (in the person of A) between the holders of the respective basic patents P1 and P2?

In patent law, joint applicants or proprietors of patents are generally considered to form a legal unity (i.e., a single party), which is different from any of the individual persons comprised in that legal unity.[254] It could well be argued on this basis that the joint patent holders A + B are different from the sole patent holder A, and that the grant of the second SPC to A alone should therefore not be precluded.

However, even though the holders of the two patents are not completely identical in this example, it seems difficult to deny that the same person A still forms part of both patent holders. When considering the purpose of Article 3(c) of the SPC Regulations, which the Explanatory Memorandums define as preventing the same product from becoming the subject of several successive SPCs which would allow the overall duration of protection to exceed the limits specified in the SPC Regulations,[255] it may also be argued that patent holder A has already obtained a first SPC, albeit in co-ownership with B, and should therefore not be granted the second SPC for the same product.

Moreover, if the situation in this example is reversed and a first SPC based on patent P1 is granted to A alone, before A + B together file a second SPC for the same product on the basis of their jointly owned patent P2, one may ask if this will improve the chances for the second SPC to be granted. It could at least be argued under these circumstances that co-holder B of patent P2 should still be entitled to obtain supplemental protection as recompense for its own investments in the research that led to patent P2, and that the co-holder B could therefore not justifiably be denied the grant of the second SPC, solely because its co-holder A alone has already obtained the first SPC. Even in this scenario, however, it seems far from certain that the grant of the second SPC to A + B together would be considered acceptable under Article 3(c) and 3(2) of the SPC Regulations.

The practices of the national patent offices in assessing such cases seem to differ. Until further guidance is provided by the CJEU, it would seem advisable to take account of the risk that joint patent holders might not be regarded as a legal unity but, to their detriment, might each be considered individually for the purpose of assessing whether the same patent holder has already been granted an SPC for the same product.

[d] Earlier Third-Party SPC Has Been Licensed-In

As a rule, the existence of an earlier third-party SPC does not preclude the grant of a new SPC for the same product to a different patent holder, as explained in §1.02[D][1][a] above. This should likewise hold true in the case where the earlier SPC has been licensed-in by the applicant of the new SPC for the same product, particularly

254. *See*, e.g., the EPO Board of Appeal decisions J 2/01 of 4 February 2004, headnotes 1 and 2, T 788/05 of 8 May 2007, Section 2 of the reasons, and T 755/09 of 27 February 2015, Section 2 of the reasons, as well as the EPO Enlarged Board of Appeal decision G 3/99 of 18 February 2002, Section 15 of the reasons.

255. Explanatory Memorandum to the Commission proposal for an SPC regulation for medicinal products, COM(90) 101 final – SYN 255, paragraph 36; and Explanatory Memorandum to the Commission proposal for an SPC regulation for plant protection products, COM(94) 579 final, paragraph 68. *See also* CJEU *AHP Manufacturing v. Bureau voor de Industriële Eigendom*, C-482/07 of 3 September 2009, paragraph 42.

since the granting of a licence in an SPC does not change the licensor's legal title to the SPC.

This same conclusion will be reached when the provisions of Article 3(c) and 3(2) of the SPC Regulations are subjected to a teleological interpretation. Thus, it should be appreciated that a company wishing to develop a new medicinal or plant protection product will typically need to 'clear the way' and establish freedom to operate before incurring considerable costs for studies required to obtain regulatory approval. Even if the company has filed its own patents for the product in question, it may still be forced to seek an exclusive licence in the existing patent application or patent of a third party, which would include potential future SPCs based on such patent. In this scenario, it may happen that the third party obtains an SPC for the product in question before the company holding the exclusive licence and sponsoring the approval trials is granted its own SPC on the basis of one of its own patents. If that company were precluded from obtaining an SPC on the basis of its own patent merely because it already holds an exclusive licence in the earlier granted third-party SPC, it would effectively be denied the legitimate recompense for its own, independent pharmaceutical or agrochemical research and would be penalized for the timely licensing of third-party IP rights. Obviously, such an outcome would grossly contravene the very purpose of the SPC Regulations of encouraging pharmaceutical (or plant protection) research by providing sufficient protection to cover the investment put into that research. In order to ensure that this fundamental objective can be achieved, licences in earlier third-party SPCs for the same product should generally not preclude the grant of a new SPC on the basis of the licensee's own patent under Article 3(c) and 3(2) of the SPC Regulations.

This is also in line with the actual practice of the national patent offices which do not, and cannot, consider any licence that an SPC applicant might hold in earlier third-party SPCs.

[2] *Consequences of an Own Earlier SPC for the Same Product*

Article 3(c)[256] of the SPC Regulations provides that an SPC shall be granted only if, in the Member State in which the SPC application is filed and at the date of that application, the product in question has not already been the subject of an SPC.

Moreover, according to Article 3(2) of the SPC Regulation for Plant Protection Products, which is also applicable to the SPC Regulation for Medicinal Products,[257] the holder of more than one patent for the same product shall not be granted more than one

256. Article 3(c) of Regulation (EC) 469/2009, and Art. 3(1)(c) of Regulation (EC) 1610/96.

257. Article 3(2) of Regulation (EC) 1610/96 is, by virtue of recital 17 of this Regulation, also applicable for the interpretation of Art. 3 of the SPC Regulation for Medicinal Products. This has been expressly confirmed by the CJEU in *AHP Manufacturing v. Bureau voor de Industriële Eigendom*, C-482/07 of 3 September 2009, paragraph 23. As regards the applicability of recital 17 of the SPC Regulation for Plant Protection Products for the interpretation of the SPC Regulation for Medicinal Products, *see also*: CJEU *Farmitalia Carlo Erba v. Bundesgerichtshof*, C-392/97 of 16 September 1999, paragraph 20; CJEU *Massachusetts Institute of Technology v. Bundesgerichtshof*, C-431/04 of 4 May 2006, paragraph 24; and CJEU *Incyte Corporation v. Szellemi Tulajdon Nemzeti Hivatala*, C-492/16 of 20 December 2017, paragraphs 33 and 34.

SPC for that product (whereas different patent holders may each be granted one SPC for the same product). It is noteworthy that Article 3(2), contrary to Article 3(1), does not refer to the date of filing the SPC application but rather constitutes an absolute bar to the grant of more than one SPC for the same product to the same patent holder.

Thus, as a rule, in the case of an own earlier SPC granted for the same product, the grant of any further SPCs for that product to the same holder is precluded. (For the special case of SPCs based on patents directed to new therapeutic applications of previously approved active ingredients, *see* §1.02[D][3][a] below.)

[a] Own Earlier SPC Application Not Yet Granted

If the same patent holder has filed several SPC applications based on different patents but directed to the same product, he can only be granted one SPC for that product. The filing of several SPC applications per se is nevertheless possible, and the grant of one single SPC for the same product is not precluded by the pendency of other, even earlier-filed, SPC applications emanating from the same patent holder.

In practice, it often occurs that an SPC applicant holds several patents directed to the same product, any of which could potentially serve as a basic patent for an SPC filing. While he eventually has to choose one of these patents (*see* §1.02[B][4] above), it may happen that his preferred patent has not yet been granted whereas the term for filing an SPC on the basis of another potentially suitable patent is about to expire. Under such circumstances, a patent holder may be forced to file an SPC application on the basis of a less preferred patent as a mere precautionary measure, in order to avoid losing the possibility to file such an SPC at all, while he is awaiting the grant of another more preferred basic patent. Similarly, if contentious proceedings, such as opposition or nullity proceedings against one or more potential basic patents are ongoing, it may be desirable for a patent holder to simultaneously file several SPC applications on the basis of different patents directed to the same product and try to await the final outcome of such contentious proceedings before deciding which SPC application should be further pursued to grant.

While most of the national patent offices allow SPC applicants to give priority to one of several pending SPC applications directed to the same product, there are considerable differences in the actual practices of the different patent offices, which affect the strategies available to an SPC applicant. These practical aspects are discussed in more detail in §1.05[F] below.

[b] Revocation, Surrender or Lapse of the Own Earlier SPC after Grant

While the existence of an earlier SPC precludes the grant of any further SPC for the same product to the same rights holder, it is a question of considerable strategic importance what the consequences are if such an earlier SPC ceases to exist.

If an SPC lapses, e.g., because its lawful term expires, the required renewal fees are not paid in time, or its holder voluntarily surrenders it (*see* Article 14 of the SPC Regulations), the effects of the SPC are generally considered to cease ex nunc, i.e., from this point in time.[258] An SPC that takes effect and subsequently lapses will thus still have conferred exclusivity to its holder during its lifetime. As a consequence, even after its lapse the SPC will continue to preclude the grant of any further SPC for the same product to the same holder.

This conclusion should likewise apply in the case where an SPC is surrendered (with ex nunc effect) before the expiry of the lawful term of the underlying basic patent and, thus, before the SPC takes effect. This is supported by the fact that Article 3(c) and 3(2) of the SPC Regulations do not require that an earlier SPC must have taken effect, but simply refer to the existence of an earlier SPC for the same product or the grant of such an SPC to the same patent holder. Clearly, even if an SPC is surrendered before it takes effect, it will still have been granted and existed as such, with the consequence that the preclusive effects of Article 3(c) and 3(2) should still apply.

If, however, an SPC is revoked via an invalidation suit (*see* §1.06 below), the effect of such a revocation will be ex tunc, i.e., retroactive. Even though this is not explicitly stated in the SPC Regulations, the revocation of an SPC must necessarily be retroactive, since otherwise the holder of a revoked SPC could still claim damages for past acts of infringement. Simply put, a revoked SPC may be regarded as if it had never existed.

At first glance, it might thus appear that a retroactively revoked SPC, which is to be treated as if it had never existed, should not preclude the grant of a new SPC for the same product to the same patent holder. Yet, it is highly controversial whether this is indeed the case. Accepting this notion could potentially give the holder of the revoked SPC a 'second chance' to file a new SPC on the basis of another patent and could afford him with a prolonged period of supplemental protection.

In this connection, it is also noteworthy that an SPC holder can have its SPC revoked fairly easily and of its own volition. For example, in the case of an SPC based on a European patent, this is possible using the centralized revocation procedure under Articles 105a and 105b EPC. This procedure allows the proprietor to have its European patent revoked with retroactive effect,[259] and can be initiated even after the expiry of the patent.[260] Since the revocation of the basic patent underlying an SPC is one of the grounds for invalidity of the SPC,[261] and since the SPC Regulations do not preclude an SPC holder from bringing an invalidity suit against its own SPC,[262] it would appear that

258. It should be noted, however, that the question whether the surrender of an SPC under Art. 14(b) of the SPC Regulations may have retroactive effect was already referred to the CJEU but remained answered. *See* CJEU *Georgetown University v. Octrooicentrum Nederland*, C-484/12 of 12 December 2013, paragraphs 24–25, and particularly question 5. The Advocate General in this case supported the notion that the surrender of an SPC should generally be effective ex nunc, i.e., should have no retroactive effect; *see* the opinion of Advocate General Jääskinen in C-484/12, delivered on 14 November 2013, paragraphs 25–42. If the surrender of an SPC should be found to have retroactive effect, the reasoning relating to a retroactive revocation of the SPC provided further below in this chapter would apply.

259. Article 68 EPC. *See also* Guidelines for Examination in the European Patent Office, edition of November 2017, Section D-X, 3.

260. *See* Guidelines for Examination in the European Patent Office, edition of November 2017, Section D-X, 1.

261. Article 15(1)(c) of both Regulation (EC) 469/2009 and Regulation (EC) 1610/96.

262. Article 15(2) of both Regulation (EC) 469/2009 and Regulation (EC) 1610/96.

the holder of an SPC can easily have its own SPC revoked with retroactive effect in this manner.

In principle, an SPC holder could try to follow the 'voluntary revocation' approach outlined above and have its own SPC retroactively revoked, e.g., in order to enable the grant of a new SPC for the same product on the basis of another patent. Whether this is indeed possible has not yet been clarified by the CJEU. A similar question was, in fact, already referred to the CJEU in *Georgetown University v. Octrooicentrum Nederland* (C-484/12)[263] but was not answered by the Court.

If this were indeed possible, the further question would arise whether an SPC granted in violation of Article 3(c) – i.e., a second SPC which was granted even though the SPC applicant already held an earlier first SPC for the same product at the time of filing the corresponding second SPC request – could be 'rescued' by having the earlier SPC retroactively revoked. Such a potential rescue of an SPC granted in violation of Article 3(c) could be problematic, not least for the reason that it could yield systematically different results in different EU Member States. This is because some national patent offices grant SPCs without examining the requirement of Article 3(c)[264] and would thus, in the hypothetical scenario outlined above, always enable the grant and the subsequent 'rescue' of the second SPC, whereas other national patent offices which do examine the requirement of Article 3(c) should normally not even allow the grant of a corresponding second SPC in the first place. Accepting the aforementioned approach could thus result in a fragmentation of the SPC landscape across different EU Member States and could thereby create obstacles to the free movement of medicinal or plant protection products within the single market, contrary to the fundamental objectives of the SPC Regulations. This evidently casts doubt on the validity of such an approach.

In conclusion, it is controversial whether a retroactive revocation of an SPC would remove the obstacle under Article 3(c) and 3(2) of the SPC Regulations precluding the grant of a further SPC for the same product to the same patent holder, and there are some arguments speaking against such a possibility. Nevertheless, in the absence of any clear indication from the CJEU rejecting such an approach, it could still be taken into consideration, at least as a potential (and risk-fraught) last resort.

[c] Transfer of the Own Earlier SPC to a Third Party

The same patent holder cannot be granted more than one SPC for the same product under Article 3(c) and 3(2) of the SPC Regulations. Clearly, this obstacle cannot be overcome simply by transferring an earlier granted SPC to another entity. This notion is also supported by the fact that Article 3(2) precludes the *grant* of more than one SPC for the same product to the same patent holder, without considering the subsequent

263. CJEU *Georgetown University v. Octrooicentrum Nederland*, C-484/12 of 12 December 2013, paragraph 25, questions 4 and 5.

264. The SPC Regulations explicitly allow in Art. 10(5) that Member States may provide that their national patent offices grant SPCs without verifying that the conditions of Art. 3(c) and 3(d) are met. The possibility to grant SPCs without examining the condition of Art. 3(c) is therefore an intrinsic feature of the SPC system.

fate of a corresponding SPC after its grant, including the transfer of the granted SPC to another party.

[d] Acquisition of an SPC Granted to a Third Party

Article 3(c) and 3(2) of the SPC Regulations preclude the grant of more than one SPC for the same product to the same patent holder, but do not prevent the corresponding SPC holder from subsequently acquiring one or more further SPCs which have been granted for the same product to other parties. It may be held that this should likewise be permissible where an SPC applicant acquires an existing SPC from a third party before its own SPC request for the same product is granted, particularly since the respective SPCs would have been originally granted to different patent holders and would be based on independent inventions.

Nevertheless, in the absence of definite guidance from the CJEU as to the assessment of SPCs acquired from third parties, it might be safest for an SPC applicant seeking the grant of its own SPC to adjust the timing of any potential acquisition of another SPC for the same product from a third party, if possible, to occur only after, rather than before the grant of its own SPC.

[3] Consequences of an Own Earlier SPC for a Different Product

In principle, a granted SPC does not preclude the SPC holder from being granted a new SPC for a different product. The decisive question in this regard is, of course, under which conditions the product of the new SPC is to be considered 'different' from the product of the earlier SPC.

[a] Required Distinction from the Product of the Own Earlier SPC

Under Article 3(c) and 3(2) of the SPC Regulations, the grant of a new SPC to the holder of an earlier SPC will be precluded only if the respective products are the same, whereas it may be possible if the products are different. In most cases, it will be uncontroversial whether the product of a new SPC application is different from the product of an own earlier SPC.

This is particularly true in the case of small molecules, where even a slight difference in the chemical structure of two compounds normally means that they will be regarded as different active ingredients and, thus, as different products. An exception in this regard are derivatives, particularly salts and esters, of an active ingredient, which may be considered as the same active ingredient, as discussed in §1.02[D][3][b] below.

Other modifications, which do not affect the structure of an active ingredient, are normally considered to not change the identity of the respective product, as confirmed by the CJEU in *BASF* (C-258/99)[265] with respect to an alteration in the purity of the active ingredient. This holds true regardless of whether the corresponding modification requires that a new marketing authorization must be obtained.[266] With respect to the specific cases of new therapeutic applications or new formulations of previously approved active ingredients, *see* further below.

In the case of large molecules or biologics (such as therapeutic proteins or nucleic acids), however, it can be more difficult to determine whether two such active ingredients should be considered the same or different. For example, two antibodies may have different amino acid sequences but may nevertheless have almost identical three-dimensional structures and may bind to the same epitope with essentially the same affinity. Such biological active ingredients which are structurally similar but not identical and have equivalent therapeutic properties can be summarized under the caption 'biosimilars'.

The question whether biosimilars should be regarded as the same or different active ingredients and, thus, whether the holder of an SPC for a biological active ingredient A can obtain a new SPC for a biosimilar B (which is therapeutically equivalent to the active ingredient A) is effectively the mirror image of the question whether the scope of protection of an SPC for the biological active ingredient A extends to the biosimilar B (assuming, of course, that both A and B fall within the scope of protection conferred by the basic patent underlying the SPC).

If any minor structural difference between biological active ingredients which otherwise have equivalent therapeutic properties could render such active ingredients different from one another, the scope of protection of a corresponding SPC would be drastically reduced to the very specific biological product which is the subject of the respective marketing authorization. Under such a restrictive approach, the SPC would fail to provide effective protection against generic biosimilar competition, which would frustrate the fundamental objectives of the SPC Regulation to encourage pharmaceutical research and provide sufficient protection to cover the investment put into such research. Therefore, and as further discussed in §1.03[B] below, it would seem imperative to avoid an overly narrow approach when determining whether two biological active ingredients are the same or different. It should rather be acknowledged that, at least in principle, it must be possible that similar but non-identical biological active ingredients having equivalent therapeutic properties can be found to constitute the 'same' active ingredient.

This understanding appears to be supported by the findings of the EFTA Court in *Pharmaq* (E-16/14). In this decision, albeit not in the specific context of Article 3(c) and 3(2) of the SPC Regulations, the EFTA Court did not rule out that two different virus strains could constitute the same active ingredient.[267] One important factor to be considered in this regard might be whether the respective active ingredients are 'in

265. CJEU *BASF v. Bureau voor de Industriële Eigendom*, C-258/99 of 10 May 2001, paragraphs 27–29, 34–35 and headnote 2.
266. *Ibid.*, paragraphs 31–32 and headnote 3.
267. EFTA Court, *Pharmaq v. Intervet International*, E-16/14 of 9 April 2015, paragraphs 89, 90 and 92.

principle, therapeutically equivalent'.[268] The need for a separate marketing authorization, in contrast, was not considered to be relevant,[269] which conforms with the CJEU's assessment in *BASF*.[270]

Combinations of Active Ingredients

Special considerations apply in the case of combinations of active ingredients. Due to the 'product' definition in the SPC Regulations,[271] a combination of active ingredients is treated as a product different from each individual active ingredient comprised in the combination. On this basis, it would seem compelling to assume that a first SPC granted for the single active ingredient A relates to a different product than a second SPC for the combination of active ingredients A + B, and that the grant of the first SPC (for A) should therefore never preclude the grant of the second SPC (for A + B) to the same rights holder. Alas, this simple and consistent approach has not been endorsed by the CJEU, apparently as the consequences it entails have been perceived as problematic.

An illustrative example in this regard concerns the case that a basic patent is granted for an active ingredient A, with claims directed to A alone, as well as claims directed to A in combination with an extensive number of further specific active ingredients, including also the combination of A + B. Upon receiving a marketing authorization for A, the patent holder applies for and is granted an SPC for A. This SPC will confer protection, within the limits of protection conferred by the basic patent, for any medicinal product (or plant protection product) containing A alone or in combination with any other active ingredients.[272] If a further marketing authorization is later issued for the combination of A + B, the patent holder may wish to obtain a new SPC for A + B on the basis of the same patent (or, e.g., on the basis of a corresponding divisional patent). Due to the later date of the marketing authorization for A + B, the corresponding SPC for A + B could potentially have a longer term, thereby providing its holder with an additional period of exclusivity for this particular combination of active ingredients.

It is not immediately apparent why the grant of the second SPC for the combination of A + B should pose any problem in the above example, given that this combination of active ingredients is 'protected' by a basic patent in force, it is the subject of a valid marketing authorization which is the first one for this combination product in the respective Member State, and it has not already been the subject of an SPC (because A + B is a different product than A).

Nevertheless, when the CJEU was faced with a similar case in *Actavis v. Sanofi* (C-443/12), it found that 'for the purpose of the application of Article 3(c) of [the SPC

268. *Ibid.*, paragraph 86.
269. *Ibid.*, paragraph 92.
270. CJEU *BASF v. Bureau voor de Industriële Eigendom*, C-258/99 of 10 May 2001, paragraphs 31–32 and headnote 3.
271. *See* Art. 1(b) of Regulation (EC) 469/2009, and Art. 1(8) of Regulation (EC) 1610/96.
272. CJEU *Novartis v. Actavis UK*, C-442/11 of 9 February 2012, headnote; CJEU *Novartis v. Actavis Deutschland*, C-574/11 of 9 February 2012, headnote; CJEU *Actavis v. Sanofi*, C-443/12 of 12 December 2013, paragraphs 33–35.

Regulation for Medicinal Products], it cannot be accepted that the holder of a basic patent in force may obtain a new SPC, potentially for a longer period of protection, each time he places on the market in a Member State a medicinal product containing, on the one hand, the principle active ingredient, protected as such by the holder's basic patent and constituting ... the core inventive advance of that patent, and, on the other, another active ingredient which is not protected as such by that patent'.[273] The CJEU further reasoned that upon expiry of the initial SPC (for A alone), 'it must be possible for third parties to place on the market not only medicinal products consisting of the formerly protected active ingredient but also any medicinal product containing that active ingredient in combination with another active ingredient that is not protected as such by the basic patent or any other patent'.[274] According to the Court, 'the objective of [the SPC Regulation] is not to compensate the holder fully for the delay to the marketing of his invention or to compensate for such delay in connection with the marketing of that invention in all its possible forms, including in the form of combinations based on that active ingredient ... [but rather] to compensate for the delay to the marketing of what constitutes the core inventive advance that is the subject of the basic patent'.[275]

The CJEU's reasoning in *Actavis v. Sanofi* is difficult to follow. It remains rather obscure how the 'core inventive advance' evoked by the Court should relate to the requirement under Article 3(c) that the product in question must not already have been the subject of an SPC. The CJEU derived the notion of an 'inventive advance' requirement from the expression 'as such' in the definition of the term 'basic patent' in Article 1 of the SPC Regulation, where this term is defined as meaning 'a patent which protects a product as such...'. Notwithstanding the fundamental concerns about any such 'inventive advance' requirement (*see* §1.02[B][3] above), even if it were accepted that a basic patent does not necessarily 'protect' all products specified in its claims but only such products that embody the 'inventive advance' of the patent, this should result at most in an issue under Article 3(a) which requires that the product must be 'protected' by the basic patent, but not in an issue under Article 3(c). In *Actavis v. Sanofi*, however, the CJEU explicitly noticed that even if the condition of Article 3(a) were satisfied, the SPC granted for the combination of A + B would still contravene the requirement of Article 3(c).[276] The logic of this reasoning left practitioners dumbfounded. If the condition of Article 3(a) is assumed to be satisfied, this implies that the product must be protected by the basic patent and must therefore, following the CJEU's reasoning, embody the inventive advance of the patent – with the consequence that the requirement of Article 3(c) cannot possibly be violated on the grounds that the product fails to embody the inventive advance of the patent.

While the conclusion in *Actavis v. Sanofi* that the grant of the second SPC (for A + B) was precluded under Article 3(c) by the grant of the earlier SPC (for A alone) may be accepted, it is bewildering that the CJEU did not arrive at this conclusion on the

273. CJEU *Actavis v. Sanofi*, C-443/12 of 12 December 2013, paragraph 30.
274. *Ibid.*, paragraph 36.
275. *Ibid.*, paragraphs 40-41.
276. *Ibid.*, paragraphs 30 and 44.

grounds that the two SPCs would relate to the same product and, consequently, the product of the second SPC (A + B) would already have been the subject of an SPC – but rather on the grounds that A embodies the inventive advance of the basic patent while A + B does not. There is simply no apparent link between Article 3(c) and the 'inventive advance' of the basic patent.

The CJEU's approach in *Actavis v. Sanofi* furthermore begs the question how the reverse situation should be assessed, in which a first SPC is granted for A + B, and only afterwards is a second SPC sought for A alone, on the basis of the same patent claiming both A and A + B. The answer to this question was, in fact, provided in this same decision. According to the Court,[277] the second SPC for A (which constitutes the inventive advance of the basic patent) could not be granted in this hypothetical scenario because it would be precluded under Article 3(c) by the first SPC for A + B (which does not constitute the inventive advance of the patent). Confusingly, it would seem that the grant of a second SPC is somehow precluded in this example, even if the product of the second SPC does embody the 'inventive advance' of the basic patent.

A different conclusion was reached by the CJEU in *Georgetown University v. Octrooicentrum Nederland* (C-484/12).[278] In this decision, the basic patent at issue 'protected', *inter alia*, the single active ingredient A and also the combination of active ingredients A + B + C + D. The patent holder had already been granted an SPC for the combination A + B + C + D on the basis of a marketing authorization for this combination of active ingredients and sought a further SPC for A alone on the basis of the same patent and the same marketing authorization.[279] Remarkably, the CJEU acknowledged that the grant of the second SPC for A alone was not precluded under Article 3(c) by the grant of the first SPC for A + B + C + D. In arriving at this conclusion, the Court initially noted that several SPCs can be obtained for different products on the basis of the same patent if it protects each of these different products as such, and further reasoned that both the combination of A + B + C + D as well as the single active ingredient A are individually 'protected as such' by the basic patent within the meaning of Article 3(a), and '*therefore*' Article 3(c) does not preclude the grant of both the first SPC (for A + B + C + D) and the second SPC (for A alone) on the basis of the same patent and the same marketing authorization.[280] It would thus appear that the CJEU considered the combination of active ingredients A + B + C + D to be a different product than the single active ingredient A because they are each individually 'protected as such' by the basic patent, and for this reason concluded that the earlier SPC for the combination of A + B + C + D does not preclude the grant of a further SPC for A under Article 3(c).

It is also interesting to examine the CJEU's explanations how the case in *Georgetown University v. Octrooicentrum Nederland* differed from that underlying *Actavis v. Sanofi* (which were both decided on the same day). With respect to the latter case, the Court pointed out that the second SPC (for the combination of A + B) was based on the same patent as the first SPC (for A alone) '*but*' on a different, *subsequent*

277. *Ibid.*, paragraph 38.
278. CJEU *Georgetown University v. Octrooicentrum Nederland*, C-484/12 of 12 December 2013.
279. *Ibid.*, paragraphs 30, 32 and 35.
280. *Ibid.*, paragraphs 30 and 35.

marketing authorization for this combination[281] (besides noting that the combination product was not protected as such by the basic patent). In contrast thereto, in the case of *Georgetown University v. Octrooicentrum Nederland*, the two SPCs were based on the same patent and the same marketing authorization. The CJEU found that the grant of these two SPCs was not precluded under Article 3(c), and added that '[e]ven if the protection conferred by two such SPCs were to overlap, they would, in principle, expire on the same date'.[282] Thus, 'upon expiry of such SPCs, the holder thereof may no longer ... oppose the marketing by third parties of the single active ingredient, protected by one of those two SPCs, or the marketing of the combination, protected by the other certificate'.[283] Arguably, the favourable consideration of the two SPCs in *Georgetown University v. Octrooicentrum Nederland* might also have depended on the fact that they both relied on the same patent and the same marketing authorization, and would thus expire on the same date.

As a note of caution, however, it cannot be taken for granted that other such cases, in which SPCs both for a single active ingredient and for a combination of this same active ingredient with one or more other active ingredients are filed on the basis of the same patent and the same marketing authorization, will necessarily be treated in an equally favourable manner. This is because the CJEU took it for granted in *Georgetown University v. Octrooicentrum Nederland* that the products of both SPCs, i.e., the active ingredient A alone and the combination of active ingredients A + B + C + D, were each individually 'protected' as such by the basic patent.[284] Whether or not this will also be acknowledged in other cases may depend on an assessment of the 'inventive advance' of the basic patent which, as explained in §1.02[B][3] above, is an ill-conceived criterion that entails considerable practical difficulties.

In its later decision *Actavis v. Boehringer Ingelheim Pharma* (C-577/13), the CJEU again affirmed that an active ingredient must constitute 'the subject-matter of the invention' covered by the basic patent in order to be protected 'as such' by that patent within the meaning of Article 3(a) of the SPC Regulations.[285] Without further explanations, the Court concluded on this basis that, where a basic patent includes a claim to an active ingredient A which constitutes 'the sole subject-matter of the invention' and a further claim to the combination of this active ingredient A and another active ingredient B, and where the patent holder has already obtained an SPC for the active ingredient A, the patent holder is precluded under Article 3(a) and 3(c) from obtaining a second SPC for the combination of the active ingredients A + B.[286] In this case, similarly as in *Actavis v. Sanofi*, the second SPC (for the combination of A + B) relied on a different, subsequent marketing authorization and would therefore have expired at a later date than the first SPC (for A alone).

281. *Ibid.*, paragraph 33.
282. *Ibid.*, paragraph 35.
283. *Ibid.*, paragraph 40.
284. *Ibid.*, paragraphs 32 and 35.
285. CJEU *Actavis v. Boehringer Ingelheim Pharma*, C-577/13 of 12 March 2015, paragraph 38.
286. *Ibid.*, paragraph 39 and headnote.

Even in view of the above-discussed decisions *Actavis v. Sanofi*, *Georgetown University v. Octrooicentrum Nederland*, and *Actavis v. Boehringer Ingelheim Pharma*, the CJEU's resort to the notion that an SPC for a product which does not embody the 'inventive advance' of the basic patent should be precluded under Article 3(c) remains puzzling. From a dogmatic point of view, it seems incomprehensible how the question what does or does not embody the 'inventive advance' (or the 'subject-matter of the invention') of the basic patent could become relevant for the condition of Article 3(c) of the SPC Regulations.

Under this 'inventive advance' approach, what is required in order to allow the grant of a further SPC for a combination of active ingredients where the SPC applicant already holds an earlier SPC for one of the individual active ingredients comprised in that combination seems to be that the combination of active ingredients must constitute an invention that is separate and independent from the invention embodied by the single active ingredient – or, in the words of the CJEU, a 'totally separate innovation'.[287] For the reasons explained in §1.02[B][3] above, however, this is a plainly unfeasible criterion.

In any event, although the 'inventive advance' criterion may be expected to become relevant under Article 3(c) primarily in those cases in which two SPCs relate to a single active ingredient and a combination involving this active ingredient, respectively, it should be borne in mind that this criterion would not, in principle, be limited to such constellations and could potentially still find application under other circumstances as well.

New Therapeutic Applications of Previously Approved Active Ingredients

Special consideration must furthermore be given to SPCs based on patents directed to new therapeutic applications of previously approved active ingredients.

In its landmark decision *Neurim* (C-130/11),[288] the CJEU established that an SPC can still be obtained in such a case where the basic patent protects a new therapeutic application of a previously approved active ingredient, and that only the marketing authorization of the first medicinal product which comprises the active ingredient in question and relates to a therapeutic use that is within the limits of protection conferred by the basic patent relied upon for the SPC, 'may be considered to be the first [marketing authorization] of "that product" as a medicinal product exploiting that new use within the meaning of Article 3(d) of the SPC Regulation'.

Although this decision was not specifically concerned with the condition of Article 3(c) of the SPC Regulations, if the CJEU allows the grant of an SPC on the basis of a new marketing authorization for a new therapeutic use of a previously authorized active ingredient, it would appear sensible to assume that this should not be precluded

287. CJEU *Actavis v. Sanofi*, C-443/12 of 12 December 2013, paragraph 42.
288. CJEU *Neurim Pharmaceuticals v. Comptroller-General of Patents*, C-130/11 of 19 July 2012, paragraphs 25–27 and headnote 1.

by an earlier SPC based on the earlier marketing authorization either. Thus, an SPC based on the new marketing authorization for the new therapeutic use should, in the words of the CJEU in *Neurim*, constitute the first SPC for 'that product', and should therefore not be precluded by any earlier SPC based on an earlier marketing authorization for a different therapeutic use of the same active ingredient. This should likewise hold true if the earlier SPC was granted to the same patent holder who applies for the new SPC, particularly since the considerations underlying *Neurim* were acknowledged to be independent from any determination of the proprietors of patents and SPCs.[289]

Indeed, in an obiter dictum in *Georgetown University v. Octrooicentrum Nederland* (C-484/12),[290] the CJEU expressly confirmed this understanding derived from *Neurim* in the context of Article 3(c) of the SPC Regulations.

Whether any further case groups warrant such 'special treatment', particularly new formulations of previously approved active ingredients (and possibly also therapeutic applications relying on a new route of administration or a new dosage regimen), is highly controversial. A referral is currently pending before the CJEU, i.e., *Abraxis Bioscience* (C-443/17),[291] which is concerned with such new formulations and might also provide clarification whether a new SPC can be granted under Article 3(c) on the basis of a marketing authorization for a new formulation of a previously authorized active ingredient and a basic patent protecting this new formulation, in spite of the existence of an earlier SPC based on a marketing authorization for a different formulation of the same active ingredient.

[b] SPCs for a Specific Salt, Ester or Other Derivative Where an Own Earlier SPC Has Already Been Granted for the Corresponding Active Ingredient

For the purpose of the SPC Regulations, salts, esters and other derivatives of an active ingredient are normally considered to be specific forms of the *same* active ingredient.

This is a fundamental necessity in order to provide effective supplemental protection for an active ingredient, since otherwise competitors would be free, after the expiry of the basic patent underlying an SPC, to obtain approval and market another salt (or possibly another ester) of the same active ingredient than the specific form which is the subject of the marketing authorization underlying the SPC, thereby frustrating the very purpose of the SPC Regulations. Indeed, this necessity was expressly acknowledged by the CJEU in *Farmitalia* (C-392/97),[292] and is also reflected in recital 13 of the SPC Regulation for Plant Protection Products, which is likewise

289. *Ibid.*, paragraph 34.
290. CJEU *Georgetown University v. Octrooicentrum Nederland*, C-484/12 of 12 December 2013, paragraph 38.
291. Referral to the CJEU from the UK High Court of Justice made on 24 July 2017, *Abraxis Bioscience v. Comptroller General of Patents*, C-443/17.
292. CJEU *Farmitalia Carlo Erba v. Bundesgerichtshof*, C-392/97 of 16 September 1999, paragraphs 18–21.

applicable to the SPC Regulation for Medicinal Products[293] and provides that 'where the basic patent covers an active substance and its various derivatives (salts and esters), the certificate confers the same protection'.

Given that specific derivatives, particularly salts and esters, of an active ingredient are normally considered to be the *same* active ingredient, as a rule, it should not be possible to obtain a new SPC for a specific salt, ester or other derivative of an active ingredient if the patent holder has already been granted an earlier SPC for a different form of the same active ingredient. This also conforms with the treatment of salts and esters envisaged in the Explanatory Memorandum:[294]

> Only one certificate may be granted for any one product, a product being understood to mean an active substance in the strict sense. Minor changes to the medicinal product such as ... the use of a different salt or ester ... will not lead to the issue of a new certificate.

Yet, in deviation from this basic rule, it is acknowledged that the issuance of a new SPC for a specific derivative, particularly a specific salt or ester, of an active ingredient that has already been the subject of an SPC may be possible under Article 3(c), subject to certain conditions. This possibility can be derived directly from recital 14 of the SPC Regulation for Plant Protection Products, which is also applicable to the SPC Regulation for Medicinal Products[295] and provides that the issue of an SPC for an active substance does not prejudice the issue of other SPCs for derivatives (salts and esters) of that active substance, 'provided that the derivatives are the subject of patents specifically covering them'.

The condition imposed in recital 14 of the SPC Regulation for Plant Protection Products, namely that such derivatives must be 'the subject of patents specifically covering them', could be seen to mean simply that the specific derivative in question must be 'protected' (and thus specifically identified) by the basic patent relied upon for the SPC filing. The precise meaning of this condition, however, as well as the question whether it is sufficient to satisfy this condition in order to escape the preclusion under Article 3(c) of the SPC Regulations has been subject to controversy.

In this regard, it has been proposed to rely on the concept of what constitutes the 'same active substance' in pharmaceutical regulatory law, specifically as established in

293. Recital 13 of Regulation (EC) 1610/96 is, by virtue of recital 17 of this Regulation, also applicable for the interpretation of the SPC Regulation for Medicinal Products. This has been expressly confirmed by the CJEU in *Farmitalia Carlo Erba v. Bundesgerichtshof*, C-392/97 of 16 September 1999, paragraph 20. As regards the applicability of recital 17 of the SPC Regulation for Plant Protection Products for the interpretation of the SPC Regulation for Medicinal Products, *see also*: CJEU *Massachusetts Institute of Technology v. Bundesgerichtshof*, C-431/04 of 4 May 2006, paragraph 24; *AHP Manufacturing v. Bureau voor de Industriële Eigendom*, C-482/07 of 3 September 2009, paragraph 23; and CJEU *Incyte Corporation v. Szellemi Tulajdon Nemzeti Hivatala*, C-492/16 of 20 December 2017, paragraphs 33 and 34.

294. Explanatory Memorandum to the Commission proposal for an SPC regulation for medicinal products, COM(90) 101 final – SYN 255, paragraph 11.

295. Recital 14 of Regulation (EC) 1610/96 is, by virtue of recital 17 of this Regulation, also applicable for the interpretation of the SPC Regulation for Medicinal Products. This has been confirmed by the CJEU, e.g., in *Farmitalia Carlo Erba v. Bundesgerichtshof*, C-392/97 of 16 September 1999, paragraph 20.

Article 10(2)(b) of Directive 2001/83/EC in the context of the approval of generic medicinal products:

> The different salts, esters, ethers, isomers, mixtures of isomers, complexes or derivatives of an active substance shall be considered to be the same active substance, unless they differ significantly in properties with regard to safety and/or efficacy.

This same concept is also reflected in the definition of what constitutes a 'new active substance' in the context of the 'global marketing authorization' according to Article 6(1) of Directive 2001/83/EC. Thus, the European Commission's Notice to Applicants[296] explains that:

> A new chemical ... active substance includes: ... an isomer, mixture of isomers, a complex or derivative or salt of a chemical substance previously authorized in a medicinal product for human use in the European Union but differing significantly in properties with regard to safety and/or efficacy from that chemical substance previously authorized.

Arguably, it could thus be held that a specific salt, ester or other derivative of an active ingredient should be regarded as *different* from a previously authorized form of that active ingredient only if it *differs significantly in terms of efficacy and/or safety* from the previously authorized form. As a consequence, only in this case would Article 3(c) not preclude the grant of a new SPC for this specific derivative to the holder of an earlier SPC for another form of the corresponding active ingredient. With respect to the required 'significant difference' in efficacy and/or safety, it may be helpful to consult the EMA's corresponding 'reflection paper' for further guidance.[297]

Resorting to the above-cited concept of what constitutes the 'same active substance' (or, conversely, a 'new active substance') in Directive 2001/83/EC could be justified as being consistent with the CJEU's own reliance on Directive 2001/83/EC in *Forsgren* (C-631/13)[298] when it ascertained the meaning of the term 'active ingredient' in the SPC Regulation for Medicinal Products.

In spite of different perceptions in the national case law, these questions relating to the assessment of salts, esters and other derivatives of active ingredients have not yet been referred to the CJEU.

296. European Commission, Health and Food Safety Directorate-General. Notice to Applicants, Volume 2A, Procedures for Marketing Authorization, Chapter 1 – Marketing Authorization, Revision 7 of December 2017. Section 2.3 – Notion of 'global marketing authorization' and Annex I – Definition of a new active substance.
297. European Medicines Agency. Document EMA/651649/2010 of 18 October 2012. Reflection paper on considerations given to designation of a single stereo isomeric form (enantiomer), a complex, a derivative, or a different salt or ester as new active substance in relation to the relevant reference active substance. *See* particularly Section 2.3 – 'What might constitute a significant difference in safety and/or efficacy to justify new active substance status?'
298. CJEU *Arne Forsgren v. Österreichisches Patentamt*, C-631/13 of 15 January 2015, paragraphs 23–25.

[c] SPCs for a Specific Enantiomer Where an Own Earlier SPC Has Already Been Granted for the Corresponding Racemate

There is no specific guidance in the SPC Regulations or the Explanatory Memorandums how to deal with an SPC for a specific enantiomer of an active ingredient under Article 3(c) and 3(2), where the same patent holder has already been granted an SPC for the racemic form of the corresponding active ingredient. This question is of significant practical relevance, as testified by a range of well-known examples of therapeutic agents that were initially approved as racemates and later as specific enantiomers.[299]

Although different enantiomers of a chiral active ingredient have the same chemical structure, they may exhibit considerable differences in their biological properties, e.g., with respect to their pharmacological, pharmacokinetic, metabolic or toxicological effects.[300] In this respect, different enantiomers of an active ingredient can be regarded as roughly comparable to the case of different salts of an active ingredient.

This notion is also confirmed by the fact that Directive 2001/83/EC refers to 'isomers' (which includes enantiomers) on the same level as salts, esters and other derivatives when specifying what is still to be considered as the 'same active substance' in the context of the approval of generic medicinal products.[301] Indeed, enantiomers are specifically addressed in the EMA's 'reflection paper'[302] relating to the designation of a specific enantiomer (or other derivative) of a previously authorized active ingredient as a 'new active substance'[303] in the context of the 'global marketing authorization' according to Article 6(1) of Directive 2001/83/EC.

For the purpose of Article 3(c) and 3(2) of the SPC Regulations, it would thus seem sensible to treat specific enantiomers of an active ingredient in the same manner as specific salts, esters or other derivatives (*see* §1.02[D][3][b] above).

---

299. For example, the active ingredient ofloxacin has been followed by the specific enantiomer levofloxacin, omeprazole by esomeprazole, citalopram by escitalopram, formoterol by arformoterol, salbutamol by levosalbutamol, ketoprophen by dexketoprophen, and methylphenidate by dexmethylphenidate.
300. *See*, e.g., Nguyen LA et al. Chiral Drugs: An Overview. *Int J Biomed Sci*. 2006. 2(2):85–100.
301. *See* Art. 10(2)(b) of Directive 2001/83/EC (Community code for human medicinal products), which provides in the context of the approval of generic medicinal products that:

> The different salts, esters, ethers, isomers, mixtures of isomers, complexes or derivatives of an active substance shall be considered to be the same active substance, unless they differ significantly in properties with regard to safety and/or efficacy.

302. European Medicines Agency. Document EMA/651649/2010 of 18 October 2012. Reflection paper on considerations given to designation of a single stereo isomeric form (enantiomer), a complex, a derivative, or a different salt or ester as new active substance in relation to the relevant reference active substance. *See* particularly Section 2.3 – 'What might constitute a significant difference in safety and/or efficacy to justify new active substance status?'
303. European Commission, Health and Food Safety Directorate-General. Notice to Applicants, Volume 2A, Procedures for Marketing Authorization, Chapter 1 – Marketing Authorization, Revision 7 of December 2017. Section 2.3 – Notion of 'global marketing authorization' and Annex I – Definition of a new active substance.

[4] *Grant of More than One SPC on the Basis of the Same Patent*

It has been finally clarified by the CJEU that, in principle, several SPCs can indeed be granted on the basis of the same patent, provided that they relate to different products (and that each of these different products is protected as such by the basic patent).[304] Any doubts that might have arisen from earlier case law[305] in this regard have thus been dispelled.

In practice, however, it might still be advantageous to file separate patent applications (or corresponding divisional applications) for each product of interest, particularly in order to avoid complicating any potential discussion whether the product in question constitutes the 'subject-matter of the invention' and is thus 'protected' by the respective patent (*see* §1.02[B][3] and §1.02[D][3][a] above). While the CJEU on one occasion denounced the filing of separate basic patents for each product as potential 'circumvention tactics',[306] it should be appreciated that such considerations form part of the legitimate attempt of SPC applicants to adapt the best possible to a legal system which, despite its conception as 'a simple, transparent system which can easily be applied by the parties concerned',[307] has undergone a substantial and at times radical evolution in the jurisprudence of the CJEU.

§1.03 EXTENT OF PROTECTION AND ENFORCEMENT OF SPCs

[A] The Protection Conferred by an SPC

The relevant provisions governing the extent of protection of an SPC are Article 4 ('Subject matter of protection') and Article 5 ('Effects of the Certificate') of the SPC Regulations.

Accordingly, an SPC provides the same rights as the basic patent, subject to the limitation that the protection conferred extends only to the product covered by the marketing approval, including any further authorized use of the product as a medicinal or plant protection product (as appropriate).

These provisions establish that the limits of protection of an SPC must lie within the scope of the protection of the basic patent. Nevertheless, an SPC does not simply extend the life of a patent on which it is based. It confers the same rights as the patent only insofar as the patent protects the product (i.e., the active ingredient or combination of active ingredients) which is subject matter of the marketing approval. As emphasized in recital 10 of the SPC Regulation for Medicinal Products, the protection granted should be 'strictly confined' to the authorized product.

304. CJEU *Actavis v. Sanofi*, C-443/12 of 12 December 2013, paragraph 29; CJEU *Georgetown University v. Octrooicentrum Nederland*, C-484/12 of 12 December 2013, paragraph 30; CJEU *Actavis v. Boehringer Ingelheim Pharma*, C-577/13 of 12 March 2015, paragraph 33.
305. CJEU *Biogen v. SmithKlineBeecham Biologicals*, C-181/95 of 23 January 1997, paragraph 28.
306. CJEU *Georgetown University v. Octrooicentrum Nederland*, C-484/12 of 12 December 2013, paragraph 31.
307. Explanatory Memorandum to the Commission proposal for an SPC regulation for medicinal products, COM(90) 101 final – SYN 255, paragraph 16.

It thus follows that while the basic patent may protect a plethora of potential active ingredients which could be subject matter of a marketing authorization, the protection conferred by an SPC is limited to the very product approved.

While Article 4 provides a limitation in terms of the subject matter of protection – namely the product which has been subject to regulatory approval – it expressly establishes that the protection is not limited to the specific approved use(s) but also covers any use of the product subsequently approved for as a medicinal or plant protection product, as appropriate.

Within the limits set out in Article 4, Article 5 of the SPC Regulation ensures that the effect of the protection provided by the SPC is aligned to that of the basic patent.

As set out by the CJEU in *Farmitalia* (C-392/97),[308] where a product in the form referred to in the marketing authorization is protected by a basic patent in force, the SPC is capable of covering that product, as a medicinal product, in any of the forms enjoying the protection of the basic patent.

In this decision the CJEU moreover noted that in the absence of Community harmonization of patent law, the extent of patent protection can be determined only in the light of the non-Community rules which govern patents.

It thus follows that the protection afforded by an SPC is to be determined in light of the scope of the patent and the active ingredient(s) as set out in the marketing authorization.

In case of a patent directed towards a product per se (which would afford absolute protection, irrespective of the disclosed or claimed use of the product) the scope of protection afforded by an SPC based on such a patent will inherently be limited to the use of that product as a medicinal or plant protection product (as appropriate). The protection afforded by an SPC is, however, not limited to the specific uses approved in the marketing authorization, but rather encompasses any subsequently approved use of the product as a medicinal or plant protection product.

If the patent is a use patent, directed towards a specific medical indication or application for a specific use as a plant protection product, then the scope of the SPC based on such a patent will be limited accordingly.

Likewise, if the basic patent relied upon is a formulation or method patent for manufacturing a product, the SPC will protect only the patented formulation or method for manufacturing the particular product as claimed in the basic patent and not the product per se.

In the absence of harmonized rules on substantive patent law, it is not possible to provide generalised guidance in terms of the scope of protection afforded by a basic patent, and as such the scope of protection afforded by an SPC. This, of course, may change when the Unified Patent Court (UPC) system enters into force.

Over the past few years, national case law has been generated based on infringement proceedings involving SPCs. However, in most instances the contentious issues addressed in these national proceedings were 'acte clair' and did not warrant clarification from the CJEU.

308. CJEU *Farmitalia Carlo Erba v. Bundesgerichtshof*, C-392/97 of 16 September 1999.

An exception to this, the CJEU has provided guidance in relation to the question whether an SPC granted for a single active ingredient could be asserted against a competitor product comprising this active ingredient in a fixed combination with a further active ingredient. In view of the divergent approaches adopted by the national courts, this issue was referred to the CJEU in *Novartis v. Actavis UK* (C-442/11)[309] and *Novartis v. Actavis Deutschland* (C-574/11).[310] The Court concluded that, in accordance with Articles 4 and 5 of the SPC Regulation, an SPC for an active ingredient confers the same rights as were granted by the basic patent for that active ingredient, within the boundaries of the protection afforded by that patent. Therefore, an SPC that has been granted for a 'product' consisting of a single active ingredient will also confer protection for medicinal products comprising this active ingredient in combination with one or more other active ingredients.[311]

[B] The Scope of an SPC in Relation to Derivatives of an Active Ingredient

Although recital 10 of the SPC Regulation for Medicinal Products specifies that the protection conferred by an SPC should be strictly confined to the authorized product, it has long been recognized that in order for an SPC to fulfil the fundamental objectives of the Regulation, the scope of protection conferred should not be limited to the specific form of the active ingredient which has been authorized.

Thus, in *Farmitalia* (C-392/97),[312] the CJEU confirmed that where an active ingredient in the form of a specific salt has been approved, the SPC is capable of covering the active ingredient as such and also its various derived forms, such as salts and esters, in so far as they are covered by the scope of protection conferred by the basic patent.

This concept has been codified in recital 13 of the SPC Regulation for Plant Protection Products, which expressly provides that the SPC confers the same rights as those conferred by the basic patent, with the result that, where the basic patent covers an active substance and its various derivatives (salts and esters), the SPC confers the same protection.

Recital 14 of the SPC Regulation for Plant Protection Products[313] moreover provides that the issue of an SPC for a product consisting of an active substance does

309. CJEU *Novartis v. Actavis UK*, C-442/11 of 9 February 2012.
310. CJEU *Novartis v. Actavis Deutschland*, C-574/11 of 9 February 2012.
311. CJEU *Novartis v. Actavis UK*, C-442/11 of 9 February 2012, headnote; CJEU *Novartis v. Actavis Deutschland*, C-574/11 of 9 February 2012, headnote; CJEU *Actavis v. Sanofi*, C-443/12 of 12 December 2013, paragraphs 33–35.
312. CJEU *Farmitalia Carlo Erba v. Bundesgerichtshof*, C-392/97 of 16 September 1999.
313. Recitals 13 and 14 are, by virtue of recital 17 of Regulation (EC) 1610/96, also applicable for the interpretation of the SPC Regulation for Medicinal Products. This has also been confirmed by the CJEU; *see*, e.g., CJEU *Farmitalia Carlo Erba v. Bundesgerichtshof*, C-392/97 of 16 September 1999, paragraph 20; CJEU *Massachusetts Institute of Technology v. Bundesgerichtshof*, C-431/04 of 4 May 2006, paragraph 24; CJEU *AHP Manufacturing v. Bureau voor de Industriële Eigendom*, C-482/07 of 3 September 2009, paragraph 23; and CJEU *Incyte Corporation v. Szellemi Tulajdon Nemzeti Hivatala*, C-492/16 of 20 December 2017, paragraphs 33 and 34.

not prejudice the issue of other certificates for derivatives (salts and esters) of the substance, provided that the derivatives are the subject of patents specifically covering them.

The question thus arises as to what standards should be applied in order to determine whether a derivative falls within the scope of an SPC or may be viewed as a new product, which may be subject matter of a separate SPC.

From a regulatory perspective, a new salt or ester of a previously approved active ingredient will be considered to be the same, provided that it is therapeutically equivalent (in terms of its pharmacokinetic, pharmacodynamic and toxicity profile).[314] From a patent perspective, however, a new salt or ester, even if therapeutically equivalent, may be subject matter of a separate patent.

As set out in the chapters relating to the national case law, it appears that the national courts have applied inconsistent standards when determining whether or not a patented, closely related derivative of a previously approved active ingredient may be viewed as a 'new product' which may be subject matter of a separate SPC.

When the SPC Regulations were drafted, the focus of the legislator was on small chemical compounds. In the meantime, however, an increasing number of more complex biological active ingredients, such as vaccines or antibodies are coming to market, which once proprietary protection expires will face biosimilar competition. It is self-speaking that for such products, the fundamental objectives of the SPC Regulation would be frustrated, if the scope of protection conferred by an SPC would be limited to the very product which is subject matter of the marketing approval. The extension of the scope of protection to derivatives, such as salts and esters, may serve its purpose in case of small molecules. It is, however, of limited if any value for more complex biological molecules. Thus, different criteria may need to be applied in order to ascertain whether a biological active ingredient may be viewed as a similar product, falling within the ambit of the scope of protection of an SPC granted for a biological product.

With respect to biological active ingredients, it is noteworthy that the EFTA Court in *Pharmaq* (E-16/14)[315] did not rule out that the scope of protection conferred by an SPC based on the marketing authorization for a virus vaccine could extend to another specific virus strain which was covered by the basic patent, but was not referred to in the marketing authorization. The EFTA Court found that such other specific virus strain could indeed fall within the scope of protection of the SPC, but 'only if the

314. In this regard, *see*, e.g., the definition of the term 'generic medicinal product' in Directive 2001/83/EC:

> '[G]eneric medicinal product' shall mean a medicinal product which has the same qualitative and quantitative composition in active substances and the same pharmaceutical form as the reference medicinal product, and whose bioequivalence with the reference medicinal product has been demonstrated by appropriate bioavailability studies. The different salts, esters, ethers, isomers, mixtures of isomers, complexes or derivatives of an active substance shall be considered to be the same active substance, unless they differ significantly in properties with regard to safety and/or efficacy.

315. EFTA Court, *Pharmaq v. Intervet International*, E-16/14 of 9 April 2015, paragraph 92.

specific strain constitutes the same active ingredient as the authorized medicinal product and has therapeutic effects falling within the therapeutic indications for which the marketing authorization was granted', which would have to be determined by the referring national court. Whether a medicinal product based on such other specific virus strain would require a separate marketing authorization was not considered to be relevant in this regard. While these findings of the EFTA Court are not binding for EU Member States, they suggest that the scope of protection of SPCs for biological active ingredients may indeed extend to other molecules or entities than the one(s) mentioned in the corresponding marketing authorization, provided that they can still be regarded as the 'same active ingredient'. This might dependent on whether such other molecules or entities are 'in principle, therapeutically equivalent'[316] to the product specified in the SPC and the corresponding marketing authorization.

In the absence of any guidance by the CJEU, it remains uncertain to what extent variants of a biological active ingredient are covered by the scope of protection of an SPC. Moreover, so far only very limited national decisions have considered these issues. While the national courts have recognized that the purpose of the SPC system would be frustrated if in case of biologics the scope of protection would not cover therapeutically equivalent products, it appears that the national courts tend to adopt a restrictive approach when construing the scope of protection conferred by an SPC for a biologically active ingredient.

Thus, the general consensus in the national case law appears to be that in view of the complexity of biological products, it cannot be ruled out that a minor difference could have significant effects on the quality, safety and efficacy of the medicinal product.[317] The implications of these decisions appear to suggest that the scope of protection of SPCs for complex biological products is limited to 'therapeutically equivalent' products.

[1] The Relationship Between the Definition of the Active Ingredient(s) in an SPC and Its Scope of Protection

While extensive case law has been generated in relation to the conditions for obtaining an SPC (Article 3 of the SPC Regulations), there is to date only limited guidance available in terms of the significance of the product definition of an SPC.

As set out in *Novartis v. Actavis UK* (C-442/11)[318] and *Novartis v. Actavis Deutschland* (C-574/11),[319] the CJEU has confirmed that the scope of protection conferred by an SPC for a single active ingredient extends to combination products comprising that active ingredient together with one or more further active ingredients.

316. *Ibid.*, paragraph 86.
317. Dutch Council of State, *Yeda v. Dutch Patent Office*, ECLI:NL:RVS:2009:BJ5541 of 19 August 2009; and Norwegian Borgarting Court of Appeal, *Pharmaq v. Intervet International*, 15-170539ASD-BORG/01 of 19 December 2016.
318. CJEU *Novartis v. Actavis UK*, C-442/11 of 9 February 2012.
319. CJEU *Novartis v. Actavis Deutschland*, C-574/11 of 9 February 2012.

It thus follows that an SPC for a single active ingredient A will have a broader scope than an SPC granted for a combination of active ingredients A + B.

The scope of protection of an SPC lies within the scope of the basic patent, limited to the product covered by the marketing approval. To take account of this, SPC applicants frequently formulate the definition of an SPC product, by way of a hypothetical 'SPC claim', so as to include any potential variants of the product in the definition. It should, however, be noted that neither of the SPC Regulations provide any indication that the scope of an SPC is to be determined based on the product definition provided by the applicant.[320] The only provisions guiding the scope of protection are set out in Articles 4 and 5 of the SPC Regulations, and it thus seems questionable whether such an extended definition, beyond the actual approved active ingredient is of any relevance.

Moreover, the practice of the national patent offices in allowing 'patent claim-type' definitions of the SPC product is very divergent.

Thus, some patent offices have allowed generalized definitions, such as 'Compound X[321] in all forms as protected by the basic patent' or 'Compound X, optionally in form of a pharmaceutically acceptable salt or hydrate thereof' or similar more generalized definitions of the product based on the disclosure in the patent. Other patent offices, however, routinely only accept as the product definition the INN of the active ingredient as identified in the marketing authorization.

Thus, in relation to small chemical compounds, as opposed to complex biological products, there is some uncertainty as to whether the product definition of an SPC has any significance in terms of the scope of protection conferred by the SPC.

While the EPO and national patent offices have the competence to determine the breadth of a patent claim, taking into account issues such as patentability, the construction of the scope of protection of an SPC for the purposes of infringement must nevertheless be within the competence of the national civil courts. It therefore follows that if the wording of a generalized SPC product definition, as allowed by some of the national patent offices, were decisive for determining the scope of protection of an SPC, this would substantially undermine the competence of the national courts.

Moreover, in light of the divergent approaches adopted by the national patent offices in terms of allowing such generalized SPC product definitions, the scope of protection conferred by an SPC would differ substantially from Member State to Member State, which would undermine the fundamental objective of the SPC Regulations to provide a uniform solution at the EU level.[322]

In addition, if the product definition in an SPC request were to be decisive for the determination of the scope of protection conferred by an SPC, then logically the product definition should also include other mandatory limitations of the claims of the

320. *See also* Dr Tony Rollins, Nicola Dagg and Steven Baldwin, European Intellectual Property Review 2017, 'The definition of product in the SPC Regulation: (Part 1 of 2) What's in a name?'
321. X usually being the INN designation of the active ingredient as recited in the marketing authorization.
322. *See* recital 7 of Regulation (EC) 469/2009, and recital 9 of Regulation (EC) 1610/96.

basic patent, particularly if the basic patent is a second medical use, formulation or method patent. In most instances, however, this is not the case.

As such, it would appear dogmatically and pragmatically expedient to conclude that the product definition volunteered by the applicant and granted by the national patent office should only be viewed as being of declaratory nature, and that the scope of protection conferred by an SPC must be determined independently by the competent court on a case by case basis, in analogy to any patent infringement case.

This line of reasoning appears to have been adopted at least to a certain extent by the EFTA Court in *Pharmaq* (E-16/14),[323] where the Court ruled that the name given to the product of an SPC is not of relevance when assessing the scope of protection of the SPC.

The *Pharmaq* ruling by the EFTA Court was rendered on the basis of an SPC for a biological product. The SPC had been granted with a broad product definition, namely to a specific inactivated Salmonid pancreatic disease virus, 'or closely related strains which share similar genotypic and/or phenotypic characteristics to said deposited virus strain', whereas the product approved only related to the specific deposited strain.

The EFTA Court indicated that an active ingredient may be covered by the scope of an SPC if it is 'therapeutically equivalent' to the product approved and infringes the patent.[324] In this context it is not of relevance that the active ingredient has been subject matter of a separate marketing authorization. The decision, however, leaves open what criteria are to be applied in order to assess whether a product may be considered to be therapeutically equivalent.

In terms of the definition of the product, the EFTA Court effectively concluded that an SPC, in as far as it covers a broader scope, would be invalid. No further substantiation in terms of the invalidity of an overly broad SPC definition is provided in the decision, so that it would appear that the Court's interpretation of the SPC Regulation was that an SPC with an inappropriately broad worded product definition is partially not enforceable and as such not of relevance.

The EFTA Court decisions are non-binding to the non-EFTA states. Nevertheless, in the absence of any CJEU decision or pertinent national case law in relation to the scope of an SPC for a complex biological active ingredient, this ruling may be of significance, as it may impact future rulings.

The Norwegian Court of Appeal,[325] in light of the guidance provided by the EFTA Court, however, ruled that in the case in question the SPC must be declared invalid in its entirety as the scope of protection sought goes beyond Article 4 of the SPC Regulation, rather than ruling that the SPC can only be effectively enforced within the scope of a reasonable product definition. The Court emphasized that invalidity must be the sanction, even though a wrong product definition is not expressly mentioned as a ground for invalidating an SPC in Article 15 of the SPC Regulation.

323. EFTA Court, *Pharmaq v. Intervet International*, E-16/14 of 9 April 2015.
324. *Ibid.*, paragraph 86.
325. Norwegian Borgarting Court of Appeal, *Pharmaq v. Intervet International*, 15-170539ASD-BORG/01 of 19 December 2016.

While it is uncertain whether other national courts or the CJEU will follow the reasoning of the Norwegian Court of Appeal, the case highlights the risks involved when an SPC is granted with an unduly broad product definition. Thus, if other national courts or the CJEU were to endorse the very restrictive interpretation adopted by the Norwegian Court of Appeal, then this would have a very substantial impact on the prosecution and litigation of SPCs, particularly in case of biological active ingredients. Thus (assuming that the product definition is decisive for the determination of its scope), if the applicant applies for a narrow product definition, the protection afforded may be readily circumvented. If on the other hand, an SPC is granted with a too broad product definition, there is the risk that the SPC may be held invalid.

In this context, however, it appears that in practice most patent offices are reluctant to grant SPCs with such broad product definitions, particularly in case of complex biological products. Thus, in case of an antibody most patent offices will require that the product definition is based on the INN provided for the active ingredient in the marketing authorization relied upon. Such an approach would appear appropriate, as it could lead towards a more harmonized prosecution and grant of SPCs in the EU. In order to ensure that the protection conferred by a corresponding SPC is adequate, such an approach, however, presupposes that upon enforcement of the SPC, its scope is assessed in light of Articles 4 and 5 of the SPC Regulations, without reliance on the actual definition of the SPC product.

[C] Enforcement of an SPC

While the European Commission has suggested that within the framework of the Unitary Patent system, a unitary SPC title should be created,[326] an SPC under the current system is a national right and as such only has effect in the state in which it has been granted.

In the absence of harmonized substantive patent law, the SPC Regulations do not contain any provisions in relation to the enforcement of an SPC, so that the corresponding national provisions are applicable.

As set out in the Explanatory Memorandums for the SPC Regulations,[327] an SPC is a sui generis title of intellectual property. Nevertheless it is ancillary to a previously granted national or European patent. As such an SPC may be enforced on the national level in an analogous manner and via the same instances as are applicable for the enforcement of the corresponding basic patent.

The enforcement of SPCs in order to prevent parallel trade under the 'Specific Mechanism' has been highlighted by a number of referrals to the CJEU.

Prior to the EU enlargement in 2004, many of the accession states did not allow the patenting of pharmaceutical products or did not provide for SPC protection. Nevertheless, pharmaceutical companies were required to market these products in the accession states. The doctrine of exhaustion of patent rights thus implied that they

326. COM(2015) 550 final – Upgrading the Single Market: more opportunities for people and business, Section 3.3.
327. COM(90) 101 final – SYN 255; and COM(94) 579 final.

should not be able to prevent the parallel import of these medicinal products from a new accession state to an 'old' Member State. To remedy this problem and to achieve a balance between effective patent and SPC protection on the one hand, and the free movement of goods on the other hand, the Specific Mechanism was introduced. The legal framework for the Specific Mechanism finds basis in Chapter 2 of Annex IV to the Act of Accession to the EU of 2003,[328] in Chapter 1 of Annex V to the Act of Accession to the EU of 2005,[329] and in Chapter 1 of Annex IV to the Act of Accession to the EU of 2012.[330] It provides that in derogation to the principle of free movement of goods, a holder of a patent or an SPC can assert these rights to prevent such parallel imports.

In accordance with the Specific Mechanism, any person intending to import or market a pharmaceutical product to a Member State where the product enjoys patent or SPC protection must give one month's prior notification to the holder of the patent or SPC as to enable the latter to invoke the rights conferred by the patent or SPC to prevent the importation and marketing of the product concerned. It is only upon expiry of the one-month period that the potential infringer may apply for import licence.

In *Merck Canada* (C-539/13),[331] Sigma Pharmaceuticals, upon notification of the holder of the SPC for the product montelukast imported the product from Poland to the UK. It was only a few months later that the SPC holder objected to the import. While Sigma ceased to import the drug, there was lack of consensus whether the Specific Mechanism automatically applies, or whether the holder of the patent or SPC must give notification of his intention to oppose the import.

The CJEU resolved this issue by concluding that a patent or SPC holder or beneficiary cannot rely on his rights under the first paragraph of the Specific Mechanism until notification is given to an importer of his intention to do so.

Thus, the Specific Mechanism does not go so far as to oblige an importer to obtain the express prior consent of the holder or beneficiary of a patent or SPC. If the holder or beneficiary does not indicate his intention to oppose the parallel import during the applicable one-month period, the importer may legitimately apply for an import license and, where appropriate, import and market the pharmaceutical product. The holder or beneficiary of the patent or SPC, however, has not thereby forfeited his right to rely on the Specific Mechanism and can thus still oppose the future importation and marketing of the protected product, but he cannot obtain compensation for any losses suffered from parallel imports which he failed to oppose in good time.

---

328. Act concerning the conditions of accession of the Czech Republic, the Republic of Estonia, the Republic of Cyprus, the Republic of Latvia, the Republic of Lithuania, the Republic of Hungary, the Republic of Malta, the Republic of Poland, the Republic of Slovenia and the Slovak Republic and the adjustments to the Treaties on which the European Union is founded (OJ 2003 L 236, p. 33, and corrigendum OJ 2004 L 126, p. 2).
329. Act concerning the conditions of accession of the Republic of Bulgaria and Romania and the adjustments to the Treaties on which the European Union is founded (OJ 2005 L 157, p. 203).
330. Act concerning the conditions of accession of the Republic of Croatia and the adjustments to the Treaty on European Union, the Treaty on the Functioning of the European Union and the Treaty establishing the European Atomic Energy Community (OJ 2012 L 112, p. 21).
331. CJEU *Merck Canada & Merck Sharp & Dohme v. Sigma Pharmaceuticals*, C-539/13 of 12 February 2015.

In *Pfizer* (C-681/16),[332] the CJEU was asked to provide guidance in terms of the applicability of the Specific Mechanism, in a case where at the time of filing the SPC in an 'old' Member State, the SPC regime already existed in the respective accession state, but could not be applied for, because no basic patent existed (as it would have been considered to be non-statutory subject matter). A further issue referred was whether the Specific Mechanism also applies to the six-month paediatric extension period of an SPC.

The CJEU concluded in *Pfizer* that the holder of an SPC issued in an 'old' Member State can indeed oppose the parallel importation of a medicinal product under the Specific Mechanism from the corresponding 'new' Member States under such circumstances, i.e. where the legal systems of the 'new' Member States did not yet provide for the possibility of obtaining equivalent protection *at the filing date of the basic patent* underlying the SPC, even if such a possibility was subsequently made available in the 'new' Member States by the time the application for the basic patent was published and/or by the time the SPC was filed in the respective 'old' Member State.[333] The relevant date for the applicability of the Specific Mechanism is thus the filing date of the basic patent underlying an SPC.

Interestingly, in reaching this conclusion the Court effectively considered it inacceptable that a patent holder should be obliged to constantly monitor the legal situation in all potential accession states.[334]

The CJEU in *Pfizer* furthermore acknowledged that the Specific Mechanism also applies to the six-month paediatric extension of an SPC.[335]

Incidentally, the Court in this context endorsed the Advocate General's argument that treating any one of the 'new' Member States differently from the others would allow parallel imports to come in through that particular state, which would ultimately render the protection established by the Specific Mechanism ineffective.[336] This confirms that, at least under such circumstances, the provisions establishing the Specific Mechanism in the Acts of Accession of 2003, 2005 and 2012 are to be interpreted uniformly.

§1.04 DETERMINATION OF THE SPC TERM

[A] The Calculation of the SPC Term

As set out in the recitals of the SPC Regulations,[337] the Certificate should provide adequate effective protection and provide the holder of both a patent and a Certificate with an overall maximum of fifteen years of exclusivity from the time the product in question has obtained its first marketing approval in the Community.

332. CJEU *Pfizer Ireland Pharmaceuticals, Operations Support Group v. Orifarm*, C-681/16 of 21 June 2018.
333. *Ibid.*, paragraphs 51–57 and headnote 1.
334. *Ibid.*, paragraph 56.
335. *Ibid.*, headnote 2.
336. *Ibid.*, paragraph 71.
337. Recital 9 of Regulation (EC) 469/2009 and recital 11 of Regulation (EC) 1610/96.

In line with this, Article 13(1) and 13(2) of the SPC Regulations provide that the Certificate has a duration equal to the period between the filing date of the basic patent and the date of the first marketing authorization in the Community, reduced by five years, whereby the maximum SPC term may not exceed five years.

As the term of the basic patent is twenty years,[338] the maximum overall period of exclusivity (i.e., effective patent term plus SPC term) provided by Article 13 of the SPC Regulations is either:

- fifteen years from the date of the first authorization to place the product on the market in the Community; or
- twenty-five years from the filing date of the basic patent, whichever is the less.

In other words, Article 13 effectively provides that, if the first authorization issues less than five years after the filing date of the patent, no positive SPC term is available, as the effective patent term alone is more than fifteen years. If the first approval in the Community issues only after five years but before ten years from the filing date of the patent, the SPC term is calculated on the basis of the date of the first approval, whereby the overall exclusivity (i.e., effective patent term plus SPC term) may not exceed fifteen years, calculated from the time the first marketing authorization was granted in the Community. If the approval only issues after ten years from the filing date of the patent, the SPC term is the full maximum five years.

It is important to note in this regard that the SPC term is calculated under Article 13(1) of the SPC Regulations on the basis of the first marketing authorization 'in the Community', i.e., in any Member State of the EU or the European Economic Area (EEA),[339] which is not necessarily the same as the marketing authorization according to Article 3(b) and 3(d) which must be valid in the specific Member State in which the SPC is filed.[340]

Thus, by linking the SPC term to the date of the first marketing authorization in the Community, Article 13 ensures that an SPC comes to an end at the same moment in all Member States where the SPC has been obtained, thereby providing for a certain degree of uniformity throughout the Community in line with the objectives expressed in the preamble to the SPC Regulations.[341]

When calculating the SPC term in accordance with Article 13(1), the national patent offices have in the past adopted diverging approaches. Some patent offices have relied on the actual date of the formal decision granting marketing approval, whereas others have calculated the SPC term on the basis of the date on which the holder of the

338. For European patents, *see* Art. 63(1) EPC.
339. As discussed in §1.04[A][1] below, 'the Community' is to be understood as referring to the EU and the EEA.
340. *See*, e.g., CJEU *Yamanouchi Pharmaceutical v. Comptroller-General of Patents, Designs and Trade Marks*, C-110/95 of 12 June 1997, paragraph 24; CJEU *Hässle v. Ratiopharm*, C-127/00 of 11 December 2003, paragraphs 73, 74, 77 and 78; CJEU *Neurim Pharmaceuticals v. Comptroller-General of Patents, Designs and Trade Marks*, C-130/11 of 19 July 2012, paragraph 29; CJEU *Merck Canada v. Accord Healthcare*, C-555/13 of 13 February 2014, paragraph 31; CJEU *F. Hoffmann-La Roche v. Accord Healthcare*, C-572/15 of 5 October 2016, paragraph 38.
341. Recital 7 of Regulation (EC) 469/2009 and recital 9 of Regulation (EC) 1610/96.

marketing authorization was notified of the approval, which usually is a few days afterwards (the notification date is also published in the Official Journal of the EU).

This issue was thus referred to the CJEU, who in *Seattle Genetics* (C-471/14)[342] ruled that the duration of an SPC should be calculated by reference to the date of notification. The Member States, however, again developed divergent practices in allowing SPC holders to rectify Certificates that were granted before and are not in line with *Seattle Genetics*. Thus, as a sequel to the *Seattle Genetics* ruling, the CJEU by way of a preliminary ruling in *Incyte* (C-492/16)[343] found that the holder of an SPC may bring an appeal for rectification of the duration stated in the SPC at any time, provided that the SPC has not yet expired.

[1] The Relevant Marketing Authorization for the Term of an SPC

As set out in Article 13(1) of the SPC Regulations, the date of the first marketing authorization to place the product on the market in the Community is decisive for the determination of the term of an SPC.

In terms of the marketing authorization, the scope of the SPC Regulations is limited to medicinal or plant protection products which have been subjected to an administrative authorization procedure as laid down Article 2 of the SPC Regulations.

In case of medicinal products, the directives in question (Directive 65/65/EEC[344] and Directive 81/851/EEC,[345] now repealed and replaced by Directive 2001/82/EC[346] and Directive 2001/83/EC[347]) cover centralized authorizations issued by the EMA, authorizations issued by way of the mutual recognition procedure or national authorizations.

For plant protection products, the relevant authorization must either have been granted in accordance with Article 4 of Directive 91/414/EEC[348] (now repealed and replaced by Regulation (EC) 1107/2009[349] with effect from 14 June 2011) or under a relevant provision of national law equivalent to these administrative authorization procedures. For the purposes of calculating the SPC term a provisional authorization[350] granted in accordance with the mentioned provisions shall be taken account of, if it is

342. CJEU *Seattle Genetics v. Österreichisches Patentamt*, C-471/14 of 6 October 2015.
343. CJEU *Incyte Corporation v. Szellemi Tulajdon Nemzeti Hivatala*, C-492/16 of 20 December 2017, paragraphs 51, 57 and headnote 2.
344. Council Directive 65/65/EEC of 26 January 1965 on the approximation of provisions laid down by Law, Regulation or Administrative Action relating to proprietary medicinal products.
345. Council Directive 81/851/EEC of 28 September 1981 on the approximation of the laws of the Member States relating to veterinary medicinal products.
346. Directive 2001/82/EC of the European Parliament and of the Council of 6 November 2001 on the Community code relating to veterinary medicinal products.
347. Directive 2001/83/EC of the European Parliament and of the Council of 6 November 2001 on the Community code relating to medicinal products for human use.
348. Directive 91/414/EEC of 15 July 1991 concerning the placing of plant protection products on the market.
349. Regulation (EC) 1107/2009 of the European Parliament and of the Council of 21 October 2009 concerning the placing of plant protection products on the market and repealing Council Directives 79/117/EEC and 91/414/EEC.
350. Article 8(1) of Directive 91/414 and Art. 30 of Regulation (EC) 1107/2009.

followed by a definitive authorization concerning the same product (*see* Article 13(3) of the SPC Regulation for Plant Protection Products).

By virtue of the EEA Agreement,[351] any reference to the 'Community' in the provisions of the SPC Regulations must be read as also referring to the EEA. Moreover, the EEA Agreement[352] specifies that in relation to SPCs, an authorization to place the product on the market in accordance with the national legislation of an EFTA state shall be treated as an authorization granted in accordance with Directive 65/65/EEC and Directive 81/851/EEC. As such, also national approvals in the EFTA/EEA countries Iceland, Norway and Liechtenstein must be taken account of, which has also been expressly confirmed by the CJEU.[353]

Likewise, following the accession of the ten new Member States to the Community on 1 May 2004, and the subsequent enlargements on 1 January 2007 and 1 July 2013, a national authorization granted in one of these states from the accession date is considered to be valid in the Community and must be taken account of when calculating the SPC term.

In view of the notification of the UK of its intention to withdraw from the European Union, all Union primary and secondary law will cease to apply to the UK from 30 March 2019. As set out in the corresponding notification by the European Commission,[354] subject to any transitional arrangement that may be contained in a possible withdrawal agreement, the SPC Regulations for Medicinal Products and Plant Protection Products will no longer apply to the UK. As a consequence, an authorization to place a product on the market in the UK as of the withdrawal date will not be considered a first authorization to place the product on the market in the Community for the purposes of Article 13 of the SPC Regulations.

When the SPC system first came into force, questions were raised as to whether marketing authorizations, in the absence of further mandatory national ancillary requirements, such as pricing requirements, should be viewed as the first authorization within the meaning of Article 13 of the SPC Regulations. This issue was resolved by the CJEU in *Hässle* (C-127/00),[355] where the CJEU confirmed that the relevant marketing authorization is only the authorization in compliance with the respective regulatory provisions, rather than any ancillary national provisions.

In the past the CJEU had also to resolve controversies over what constitutes the first marketing authorization, particularly when the products had already been approved under transitional national legislation, which did not require the same level of testing in terms of safety and efficacy as required by Article 2 of the SPC Regulations.

351. Point 8 of Protocol 1 of the EEA Agreement.
352. Point 6 of Annex XVII 1 of the EEA Agreement.
353. CJEU *Novartis and University College London v. Comptroller-General of Patents, Designs and Trade Marks for the United Kingdom*, C-207/03 and *Millennium Pharmaceuticals v. Ministre de l'Économie*, C-252/03 of 21 April 2005, paragraphs 26 et seq.; CJEU *Astrazeneca v. Comptroller General of Patents, Designs and Trade Marks*, C-617/12 of 14 November 2013, paragraphs 38 et seq.
354. European Commission, *Notice to stakeholders: Withdrawal of the United Kingdom and EU legislation in the field of supplementary protection certificates for medicinal products and plant protection products*, 27 April 2018.
355. CJEU *Hässle v. Ratiopharm*, C-127/00 of 11 December 2003.

Thus, in *Synthon* (C-195/09)[356] and *Generics UK* (C-427/09),[357] the products of the respective SPC applications were based on approvals granted in accordance with the stringent regulatory requirements as set out in Article 2 of the SPC Regulation, however, the products had previously been placed on the market in accordance with national approvals, which were not in compliance with the Directives referred to in the SPC Regulation for Medicinal Products. The CJEU ruled that any product marketed outside of an EU-compliant marketing authorization is outside the SPC system. Moreover, the grant of an SPC to a product which had been marketed before it was subject to the long and demanding approval system would be contrary to the very purpose of the SPC system.

Under the Swiss-Liechtenstein customs union, marketing authorizations granted in Switzerland (which has not ratified the EEA Agreement) are automatically effective in the EFTA state Liechtenstein.[358]

In the joined cases *Novartis & University College London* (C-207/03) and *Millennium Pharmaceuticals* (C-252/03)[359] the CJEU thus ruled that when a Swiss authorization automatically recognized in Liechtenstein was the first in the EEA, it constitutes the first authorization in the Community for the purposes of calculating an SPC term. The potential monetary impact of these decisions is, of course, substantial, bearing in mind that an approval in Liechtenstein, with a market of insubstantial scope will set the clock for the SPC term in the entire European Union.

As a result of these decisions, the agreement between Liechtenstein and Switzerland was amended in terms of the automatic recognition of Swiss approvals in Liechtenstein.[360] According to this agreement a 'negative list' procedure has been installed since 1 June 2005, providing a mechanism for pharmaceutical companies to delay the automatic recognition of marketing authorizations between Switzerland and Liechtenstein for new chemical entities or new active substances by twelve months.

The Liechtenstein issue was, however, revisited in *AstraZeneca* (C-617/12)[361] and in *F. Hoffmann-La Roche* (C-572/15).[362] Here, the facts of the respective cases occurred before the introduction of the negative list, so that it is not surprising that the CJEU confirmed its earlier rulings. It is, however, noteworthy that in *AstraZeneca*, the clinical data upon which the Swiss authorization was granted did not satisfy the

---

356. CJEU *Synthon v. Merz Pharma*, C-195/09 of 28 July 2011.
357. CJEU *Generics (UK) v. Synaptech*, C-427/09 of 28 July 2011.
358. *See* Council Decision 1/95, according to which any marketing authorization granted in Liechtenstein is to be treated as an authorization granted in accordance with Directive 2001/83/EC.
359. CJEU *Novartis and University College London v. Comptroller-General of Patents, Designs and Trade Marks for the United Kingdom*, C-207/03 and *Millennium Pharmaceuticals v. Ministre de l'Économie*, C-252/03 of 21 April 2005.
360. Ergänzungsvereinbarung vom 22. April 2005 zum Notenaustausch betreffend die Geltung der schweizerischen Heilmittelgesetzgebung in Liechtenstein vom 11. December 2001.
361. CJEU *AstraZeneca v. Comptroller General of Patents, Designs and Trade Marks*, C-617/12 of 14 November 2013.
362. CJEU *F. Hoffmann-La Roche v. Accord Healthcare*, C-572/15 of 5 October 2016.

standards applied by the EMA as set out in Regulation (EC) 726/2004.[363] This was considered to be irrelevant as well as the fact that the Swiss marketing authorization was subsequently suspended for these very considerations.

The CJEU has handed down various rulings, addressing questions as to whether an earlier marketing approval as a medicinal product for an unrelated use precludes the issue of a Certificate based on a subsequent approval. These questions are also relevant to the determination of the 'first authorization' referred to in Article 13(1) of the SPC Regulations and hence to the calculation of the SPC term.

Thus, in *Pharmacia* (C-31/03)[364] the Court ruled that 'the decisive factor for the grant of the certificate is not the intended use of the medicinal product and, second, that the purpose of the protection conferred by the certificate relates to any use of the product as a medicinal product without any distinction between use of the product as a medicinal product for human use and as a veterinary medicinal product'.

In *MIT* (C-431/04),[365] the Advocate General recommended that an SPC should be available in case of a new formulation of a previously approved medicinal product, if the new excipient is necessary for the therapeutic efficacy of the active ingredient. The CJEU, however, ruled that the concept of the 'product' within the meaning of the SPC Regulation must be understood in the strict sense, so that a new dose, the use of a different salt or ester or different pharmaceutical form will not lead to a new SPC.[366]

The CJEU in *Yissum* (C-202/05)[367] confirmed in a reasoned order, based on its previous case law, that the mentioned considerations in relation to the concept of the 'product' of an SPC cannot take account of the therapeutic use protected by a basic patent.

In light of the above-summarized case law (*Pharmacia*, *MIT* and *Yissum*), it was the general consensus at the time that the issue of an SPC was precluded if the active ingredient in question had been authorized in any earlier marketing authorization within the EU, even if the earlier authorization related to a different use in a different species, formulation or second medical use.

This restrictive literal interpretation of the SPC Regulation adopted by the CJEU in terms of not allowing an SPC for products which had previously been approved was called into question in *Neurim* (C-130/11).[368] In this decision, the CJEU applied a teleological approach when interpreting the SPC Regulation for Medicinal Products and concluded that an earlier marketing authorization for a veterinary or human use does not preclude the grant of an SPC following a later marketing authorization, provided that the later marketing authorization falls within the limits of the basic patent relied upon for the SPC filing. In line with this reasoning, the CJEU also found that Article

363. Regulation (EC) 726/2004 of the European Parliament and of the Council of 31 March 2004 laying down Community procedures for the authorization and supervision of medicinal products for human and veterinary use and establishing a European Medicines Agency.
364. CJEU *Pharmacia Italia v. Bundesgerichtshof*, C-31/03 of 19 October 2004, paragraph 20.
365. CJEU *Massachusetts Institute of Technology v. Bundesgerichtshof*, C-431/04 of 4 May 2006.
366. *See* paragraph 19 of *MIT* (C-431/04).
367. CJEU *Yissum Research and Development Company of the Hebrew University of Jerusalem v. Comptroller-General of Patents*, C-202/05 of 17 April 2007.
368. CJEU *Neurim Pharmaceuticals v. Comptroller-General of Patents*, C-130/11 of 19 July 2012.

13(1) of the SPC Regulation for Medicinal Products refers only to the marketing authorization of a product that falls within the limits of protection conferred by the basic patent relied upon for the SPC filing.[369]

Thus, in *Neurim* the CJEU has clearly departed from its earlier case law in *Pharmacia* and *Yissum*, in now allowing the 'product' of an SPC to extend not just to a new active ingredient, but also to a new use for a known, previously approved active ingredient. The scope of the *Neurim* ruling, however, remains unclear. While it has paved the way for SPCs for second medical use inventions of products which had previously been authorized, it is questionable whether it is also applicable to new formulations of previously approved active ingredients, when their therapeutic use is the same.

Subsequently, in *Glaxosmithkline Biologicals* (C-210/13)[370] the CJEU concluded that an SPC cannot be granted for a vaccine formulation comprising a new adjuvant combined with an antigen (an influenza virus component) as the adjuvant has no therapeutic effect of its own and cannot be regarded as an 'active ingredient' of its own. In its reasoning the CJEU relied also on the distinction made in the regulatory directive[371] between 'active ingredients' and 'adjuvants'.

In line with this, in *Forsgren* (C-631/13)[372] the CJEU concluded that an SPC directed towards Protein D, a carrier protein conjugated to various antigens, is only allowable if the carrier protein produces a pharmacological, immunological or metabolic action of its own which is covered by the therapeutic indications of the marketing authorization.

The regulatory provisions for plant protection products[373] also expressly distinguish between 'active substances' and other components contained in a plant protection product, such as 'safeners'. In spite of this distinction, the CJEU in *Bayer CropScience* (C-11/13)[374] ruled that the term 'active substances' in the SPC Regulation for Plant Protection Products must be interpreted as also covering a substance intended to be used as a safener, where that substance has a toxic, phytotoxic or plant protection action of its own. As a consequence, SPCs should be available for new formulations of plant protection products containing a previously approved active ingredient, if they contain a new safener.

Thus, the above case law appears to suggest that at least for medicinal products, the principle of *Neurim* is limited to second medical uses of previously approved products, but not to new formulations of old active ingredients.

Nevertheless, in light of the difficulties in reconciling the *Neurim* ruling with the seemingly consistent previous case law of the CJEU, this issue has been subject matter

---

369. *Ibid.*, headnote 2.
370. CJEU *Glaxosmithkline Biologicals v. Comptroller-General of Patents, Designs and Trade Marks*, C-210/13 of 14 November 2013.
371. *See* Section 3.2.2.1 of Part 1 of Annex I of Directive 2001/83/EC as amended by Directive 2003/63/EC.
372. CJEU *Arne Forsgren v. Österreichisches Patentamt*, C-631/13 of 15 January 2015.
373. *See* Art. 2 of Regulation (EC) 1107/2009.
374. CJEU *Bayer CropScience v. Deutsches Patent- und Markenamt*, C-11/13 of 19 June 2014.

of a further referral to the CJEU. Thus, in *Abraxis* (C-443/17)[375] the Court has been asked to provide guidance as to whether the SPC Regulation for Medicinal Products is to be interpreted as permitting the grant of an SPC where the marketing authorization referred to in Article 3(b) is the first authorization within the scope of the basic patent to place the product on the market as a medicinal product and where the product is a new formulation of an old active ingredient.

Provisional Marketing Authorizations

In the regulatory provisions for plant protection products (Directive 91/414/EEC, now repealed and replaced by Regulation (EC) 1107/2009) several types of authorizations are referred to, including an 'approval regulation' (Article 13 of Regulation (EC) 1107/2009), an 'authorization for placing on the market' (Articles 29 and 40), 'provisional authorizations' (Article 30), 'emergency' authorizations (Article 53) and experimental authorizations for research and development (Article 54). This has led to some confusion as to which authorization is of relevance in terms of filing an SPC in accordance with Article 3 as well as the calculation of the SPC term under the SPC Regulation for Plant Protection Products.

As a preliminary remark, it should be noted that an 'approval regulation' for active substances does not allow the product to be placed on the market and as such should not be of relevance for the filing of an SPC or the calculation of an SPC term.

As set out in Article 13(3) of the SPC Regulation for Plant Protection Products, for the purposes of calculating the SPC term account shall be taken of a provisional marketing authorization (if it is directly followed by a definitive authorization for the same product). This provision appears to be in contrast to Article 2 or Article 3(1) of the SPC Regulation for Plant Protection Products, neither of which mentions such provisional authorizations.

In *Hogan Lovells* (C-229/09)[376] and *Sumitomo Chemical* (C-210/12)[377] the CJEU considered authorizations not explicitly mentioned in Article 2 of the SPC Regulation for Plant Protection Products. According to the CJEU, a distinction must be drawn between the various forms of authorizations available for plant protection products.

Thus, an emergency marketing authorization granted in accordance with Article 8(4) of Directive 91/414/EEC (now Article 53 of Regulation (EC) 1107/2009) is only valid for 120 days and does not amount to a marketing approval within the meaning of Article 2 or Article 3(1) of the SPC Regulation for Plant Protection Products.

An SPC can, however, be issued for a product in respect of which a full or provisional marketing authorization has been granted under Article 8(1) of Directive 91/414/EEC (now Article 30 of Regulation (EC) 1107/2009).

The concept of a provisional approval is not limited to plant protection products.

Thus, Article 5(1) of the Medicinal Products Directive, Directive 2001/83/EC, provides a legal basis for Member States to supply unauthorized medicines in response

375. CJEU *Abraxis Bioscience v. Comptroller General of Patents*, C-443/17, referral of 24 July 2017.
376. CJEU *Hogan Lovells International v. Bayer CropScience*, C-229/09 of 11 November 2010.
377. CJEU *Sumitomo Chemical v. Deutsches Patent- und Markenamt*, C-210/12 of 17 October 2013.

to unsolicited requests for individual patients, the so-called compassionate use authorization. According to Article 83 of Regulation (EC) 726/04, such a compassionate use authorization is an exemption to Article 6 of the Medicinal Products Directive. Moreover, Article 83(2) specifies that the product in question must either be subject matter of an ongoing request for marketing authorization or must be undergoing clinical trials. This underscores the fact that a compassionate use authorization is not subject to the same level of scrutiny as a full approval under the Medicinal Products Directive. Therefore, a provisional compassionate use approval should not be considered as a first approval within the Community in accordance with Article 13(1) of the SPC Regulation for Medicinal Products, setting the clock for the calculation of an SPC term.

For veterinary medicinal products, Article 8(1) of Directive 2001/82/EC on veterinary medicinal products allows the Member States to permit provisionally the use of immunological veterinary medicinal products without a marketing authorization, in the absence of a suitable medicinal product.

Directive 2001/82/EC in Article 26(3) also provides for provisional authorizations in 'exceptional circumstances' where the authorization may be granted subject to a requirement for the applicant to introduce specific procedures, in particular concerning the safety of the veterinary medicinal product.

In *Pharmaq* (E-16/14),[378] the EFTA Court, which is the equivalent of the CJEU for matters referred by the national courts of the three EFTA/EEA countries (Iceland, Liechtenstein, and Norway), had to consider the eligibility of successive national authorizations granted in accordance with Article 8(1) or Article 26(3) of Directive 2001/82/EC. The Court concluded that while a provisional allowance under Article 8(1) does not constitute an administrative authorization procedure within the meaning of Article 2 of the SPC Regulation for Medicinal Products, an authorization procedure granted in exceptional circumstances pursuant to Article 26(3) of Directive 2001/82/EC may form basis for an SPC application.

While the EFTA Court ruling is not binding for EU Member States, it is of significance as it suggests that an authorization granted in accordance with Article 26(3) of Directive 2001/82/EC will need to be taken account of when determining the SPC term.

[2] The Expiration Date of an SPC

While an SPC granted on the basis of the same patent and the same marketing approval should theoretically expire on the same day in all EU (and EEA) Member States, in practice there may be a discrepancy by one day, depending on how in accordance with the national provisions the patent term is calculated. Thus, for example, in some countries the full term of a patent is considered to expire on the day before the twentieth anniversary of the filing date of the application for the patent, whereas in others the full term expires on the same day of the twentieth anniversary.

378. EFTA Court, *Pharmaq v. Intervet International*, E-16/14 of 9 April 2015.

[B] Correction of the SPC Term

According to Article 17(2) of the SPC Regulation for Plant Protection Products, the decision to grant an SPC shall be open to an appeal aimed at rectifying the duration of the SPC where the date of the first authorization to place the product on the market in the Community, contained in the SPC application as provided for in Article 8, is incorrect. This same provision likewise applies to SPCs for medicinal products, as recital 17 of the SPC Regulation for Plant Protection Products provides that the detailed rules in Article 17(2) of this Regulation are also valid for the interpretation of Article 17 of Regulation (EEC) 1768/92 which is now Article 18 of the SPC Regulation for Medicinal Products.[379]

The possibility of filing an appeal to correct the duration of an SPC was also specifically acknowledged by the CJEU in *Incyte* (C-492/16),[380] where the Court ruled that the holder of an SPC may bring an appeal for rectification of the duration stated in the SPC at any time, provided that the SPC has not expired.

Such an appeal may be lodged by the SPC holder or a third party.

In the absence of procedural provisions in the SPC Regulations, the procedural provisions applicable under national law to the corresponding basic patent shall apply to the SPC, unless the national law lays down special procedural provisions for SPCs.[381]

[C] Paediatric Extensions

In January 2007 the Paediatric Regulation (EC) 1901/2006[382] came into force, which aims to 'facilitate the development and accessibility of medicinal products for use in the paediatric population'. The Paediatric Regulation mandates that marketing authorizations in the EU for new medicinal products will only be granted if they include the results of paediatric trials, in compliance with an agreed paediatric investigation plan (PIP). A waiver may be granted, if the drug will not be used in children. Likewise, a deferral may be granted if it is appropriate to first carry out adult trials, or if the paediatric trials would bring about substantial delays.

Medicinal products which have been approved in all EU Member States and which are protected by an SPC or by a patent which qualifies for an SPC are eligible for a six-month SPC extension ('the paediatric extension'). A prerequisite for this is that studies in compliance with the PIP are included in the product information, the

379. The applicability of recital 17 of the SPC Regulation for Plant Protection Products for the interpretation of the SPC Regulation for Medicinal Products has also been confirmed by the CJEU. *See*, e.g., CJEU *Farmitalia Carlo Erba*, C-392/97 of 16 September 1999, paragraph 20; CJEU *Massachusetts Institute of Technology v. Bundesgerichtshof*, C-431/04 of 4 May 2006, paragraph 24; CJEU *AHP Manufacturing v. Bureau voor de Industriële Eigendom*, C-482/07 of 3 September 2009, paragraph 23; and CJEU *Incyte Corporation v. Szellemi Tulajdon Nemzeti Hivatala*, C-492/16 of 20 December 2017, paragraphs 33 and 34.
380. CJEU *Incyte Corporation v. Szellemi Tulajdon Nemzeti Hivatala*, C-492/16 of 20 December 2017.
381. Article 19(1) of Regulation (EC) 469/2009, and Art. 18(1) of Regulation (EC) 1610/96.
382. Regulation (EC) 1901/2006 of the European Parliament and of the Council of 12 December 2006 on medicinal products for paediatric use.

Summary of Product Characteristics (SmPC).[383] This paediatric extension is granted even if the studies are negative and do not result in the approval in the paediatric population.

Thus, with the introduction of the Paediatric Regulation (EC) 1901/2006, Article 13 of the SPC Regulation for Medicinal Products was supplemented with a third paragraph, providing for a six-month paediatric extension of an SPC if appropriate paediatric trials have been carried out in accordance with Article 36 of the Paediatric Regulation.

The issue of a paediatric extension, however, presupposes the existence of an SPC. This is unproblematic if the first approval of the product issues after five years from the filing date of the basic patent, as in these instances an SPC with a positive term can issue.

If the approval, however, issues within less than five years after the filing date of the patent, an SPC is normally not available, based on the calculation provided for in Article 13(1) of the SPC Regulation, as this would result in a negative or zero SPC term. An SPC with a zero or negative term by itself would serve no purpose. However, as long as the negative term of the SPC is less than six months, denial of such an SPC would have the consequence that the holder of the basic patent could not obtain supplemental protection and benefit from the paediatric extension, even if appropriate paediatric trials had been completed.

Divergent approaches had initially been adopted by the national patent offices in this regard. Upon referral in *Merck* (C-125/10),[384] the CJEU resolved the issue and ruled that an SPC with a negative SPC term may issue, so that an applicant can benefit from the paediatric extension, whereby the effective term of exclusivity (i.e., effective patent term, negative SPC term plus the six-month paediatric extension) should not exceed fifteen years and six months from the date of the grant of the first marketing authorization for the medicinal product in question in the EU.

As confirmed by the EFTA Court in *Merck* (E-5/17),[385] these principles also apply to the EEA countries.

§1.05 PROCEDURE OF FILING AN SPC APPLICATION

[A] Entitlement to an SPC Application

Article 6 of the SPC Regulations provides that the Certificate shall be granted to the holder of the basic patent or his successor in title. Accordingly, the national patent offices require strict identity of the SPC applicant and the holder of the basic patent.

383. *See* Art. 36 and recitals 26–27 of Regulation (EC) 1901/2006.
384. CJEU *Merck Sharp & Dohme Corp. v. Deutsches Patent- und Markenamt*, C-125/10 of 8 December 2011.
385. EFTA Court, *Merck Sharp & Dohme Corp. v. Icelandic Patent Office*, E-5/17 of 21 December 2017.

The SPC Regulations are, however, silent as to who may file an application for an SPC or a paediatric extension. As set out in the subsequent chapters, divergent approaches have been developed by the national patent offices in this regard.

Thus, some patent offices require that an SPC must be filed in the name of the registered proprietor of the patent, even if the former proprietor who has filed the SPC has subsequently assigned the basic patent and the SPC to a third party. It thus may be expedient to make sure that the patent register reflects the correct proprietor at all times throughout the filing of an SPC.

Questions also arise if the basic patent is held by multiple proprietors. Here, too, divergent approaches have emerged amongst the various Member States. In some countries it suffices if only one of the proprietors of the basic patent applies for an SPC, whereas in others the request must be made jointly by all proprietors. In any case, the SPC must be granted for all patent proprietors jointly in compliance with Article 6 of the SPC Regulations.

[B] The Time Limit for Filing an SPC Application

An SPC must be filed within six months of the authorization referred to in Article 3(b) to place the product on the market as a medicinal or plant protection product in the EU (or EEA) Member State for which the SPC is filed, or within six months of the date on which the patent was granted, whichever date is later (*see* Article 7(1) and 7(2) of the SPC Regulations).

Thus, if the patent was granted prior to the issue of the marketing authorization in the Member State, an SPC must be filed within six months of the issue of the first marketing authorization in that Member State. In view of the CJEU's findings relating to the SPC term in *Seattle Genetics* (C-471/14),[386] the relevant date should most likely be the notification date of the marketing authorization. Until this is expressly confirmed, however, it would be safest to file SPCs within six months of the issue date of the first marketing authorization in the respective Member State.

In this context, it is also important to note that a provisional marketing authorization granted in accordance with Article 26(3) of Directive 2001/82/EC (the Directive for veterinary medicinal products)[387] may constitute the first approval within the meaning of the SPC Regulation for Medicinal Products.[388]

Similarly, a provisional approval issued for a plant protection product under Article 8(1) of Directive 91/414/EEC[389] (now Article 30 of Regulation (EC) 1107/2009[390]) may also constitute a first approval, setting the deadline for filing an SPC

386. CJEU *Seattle Genetics v. Österreichisches Patentamt*, C-471/14 of 6 October 2015.
387. Directive 2001/82/EC of the European Parliament and of the Council of 6 November 2001 on the Community code relating to veterinary medicinal products.
388. EFTA Court, *Pharmaq v. Intervet International*, E-16/14 of 9 April 2015.
389. Directive 91/414/EEC of 15 July 1991 concerning the placing of plant protection products on the market use.
390. Regulation (EC) 1107/2009 of the European Parliament and of the Council of 21 October 2009 concerning the placing of plant protection products on the market and repealing Council Directives 79/117/EEC and 91/414/EEC.

for a plant protection product.[391] On the other hand, an emergency approval granted in accordance with Article 8(4) of Directive 91/414/EEC (now Article 53 of Regulation (EC) 1107/2009) does not amount to a marketing approval within the meaning of Article 2 or Article 3(1) a of the SPC Regulation for Plant Protection Products.[392]

Some uncertainties exist as to how the time limit for filing an SPC is to be determined when the basic patent relied upon is granted only after the issue of the first marketing approval.

Thus, according to Article 7(2) of the SPC Regulations, in such cases the SPC application must be lodged within six months of the 'date on which the patent is granted'. In most instances the basic patent relied upon for an SPC filing is a national part of a European patent. The EPC does not, however, define the date of 'patent grant', but rather distinguishes between the 'decision to grant a European patent' (Article 97(1) EPC) or the 'publication of the mention of the grant in the European Patent Bulletin' (Article 97(3) EPC). While it is very likely that the latter date is of relevance because the decision to grant takes effect on that date, it may be safest to file an SPC on the deadline calculated on the basis of the date of the decision to grant, which may be several months earlier.

Some national patent offices provide for a 'restitutio in integrum' remedy, in analogy to Article 122(1) EPC if the deadline for filing an SPC is missed, whereas others do not provide such a remedy.

In order to file an SPC, it is mandatory that the patent is in force in the corresponding Member State at the date of filing of the SPC. Thus, once the basic patent has expired, it is no longer possible to file an SPC application, even if the pertinent six-month deadline according to Article 7 of the SPC Regulations is still running.

It is likewise mandatory that at the date of filing the SPC, a valid marketing authorization has been granted in the Member State in question. Thus, as set out in *Yamanouchi* (C-110/95),[393] the issue of an SPC is conditional on that, at the date of filing the SPC, a valid authorization to place the product on the market has been granted in the Member State in which the SPC application is submitted.

In line with this, in *Merck Sharp & Dohme* (C-567/16)[394] the CJEU ruled that an end of procedure notice issued by a reference Member State in the decentralized procedure does not amount to the grant of a marketing authorization for the purposes of Article 3(b) of the SPC Regulation.

In *Sumitomo Chemical* (C-210/12)[395] the CJEU likewise confirmed that Article 7(1) is to be interpreted as precluding an application for an SPC being lodged before the date on which the plant protection product has obtained the required marketing authorization referred to in Article 3(1)(b) of the SPC Regulation for Plant Protection Products.

391. CJEU *Hogan Lovells International v. Bayer CropScience*, C-229/09 of 11 November 2010.
392. CJEU *Sumitomo Chemical v. Deutsches Patent- und Markenamt*, C-210/12 of 17 October 2013.
393. CJEU *Yamanouchi Pharmaceuticals v. Comptroller-General of Patents, Designs and Trade Marks*, C-110/95 of 12 June 1997.
394. CJEU *Merck Sharp & Dohme v. Comptroller General of Patents, Designs and Trade Marks*, C-567/16 of 7 December 2017.
395. CJEU *Sumitomo Chemical v. Deutsches Patent- und Markenamt*, C-210/12 of 17 October 2013.

[C] The Filing of an SPC at the National Patent Office

An application for an SPC must be filed with the national patent office of the corresponding Member State, unless that Member State has designated another authority for this purpose[396] (*see* Article 9(1) of the SPC Regulations).

[D] The Documentation Required for an SPC Application

The formal requirements for filing an SPC, including the documentation required, are set out in Article 8 of the SPC Regulations.

Most national patent offices require that the applicant uses the prescribed application form,[397] where the necessary information as set out in Article 8(1) should be provided, such as details in terms of the applicant, the representative, the number and title of the basic patent, as well as details of the first marketing authorization of the product in the Member State in question, including, if appropriate, information about the first authorization to place the product on the market as a medicinal or plant protection product.

In addition, a copy of the marketing authorization,[398] including the Summary of Product Characteristics (SmPC), must be submitted. If there has been a prior approval in the EU or the EEA, then a copy of the notice publishing the authorization in the appropriate official publication must be submitted together with information regarding the identity of the product and the legal provision under which it has been approved. This information is required in order to determine the SPC term in accordance with Article 13 of the SPC Regulations.

If the first approval of the product issued less than ten years after the filing date of the basic patent, and consequently, the duration of the SPC is calculated on the basis of the notification date of the first approval, the publication of the corresponding notification in the official publication must also be submitted.[399]

All national patent offices also require the payment of an SPC application fee.

For those patent offices which carry out a substantive examination, it is pertinent to submit all information necessary to establish that the product in question is

396. With respect to Liechtenstein, *see* Treaty between the Swiss Confederation and the Principality of Liechtenstein on Patent Protection of 22 December 1978.

397. The Italian Patent Office so far has not made available an official SPC application form.

398. While an SPC application needs to include a copy of the marketing authorization relied upon (Art. 8(1)(b) of the SPC Regulations), the CJEU ruled in *Biogen* (C-181/95) that, where the basic patent and the marketing authorization are held by different persons, the SPC application must not be refused on the ground that the patent holder is unable to provide the required copy of the marketing authorization. As noted by the CJEU in this decision, the inclusion of a corresponding copy is a formal requirement, the purpose of which is to demonstrate the existence of the marketing authorization and verify the fulfilment of the conditions for SPC grant. The national authority granting the SPC can obtain a copy of the marketing authorization directly from the authority which issued it 'by simple cooperation'. In the meantime, however, this CJEU decision has largely lost its practical relevance since marketing authorizations, including those issued by the national regulatory authorities, are in general made publicly available.

399. CJEU *Seattle Genetics v. Österreichisches Patentamt*, C-471/14 of 6 October 2015.

protected by the basic patent. This may include an excerpt from the WHO International Nonproprietary Names (INN) List, establishing the link between the INN and the chemical name or structure provided in the patent, or any other documentation suitable to establish that the approved product is protected by the basic patent in force.

[E] The Definition of the Product in an SPC Application

The national patent offices also require that the product for which protection is sought is identified. In this regard, the practices of the patent offices diverge. Some patent offices require the applicant to identify the product in accordance with the INN of the active ingredient specified in the marketing authorization, whereas others allow a more generalized 'patent claim'-like definition.

Broader, patent claim–like definitions, which typically are considered allowable for small chemical compounds are generalizations in terms of salts, esters and hydrates, drafted on the basis of the claims of the basic patent.

In case of more complex biological compounds, the patent offices tend to apply a more restrictive approach, so that in most instances the product is identified by way of its INN.[400]

[F] SPC Examination Procedure and Appeal Procedure

Neither of the SPC Regulations contains any detailed provisions in terms of the examination and appeal procedures for an SPC. The approaches which have been developed by the national patent offices in this regard are divergent. Some patent offices will carry out a formal examination assessing only issues such as whether the application has been filed within the prescribed period, contains the required particulars and is accompanied by the prescribed fee.

Other patent offices carry out a more substantive examination, particularly in terms of whether the SPC request is compliant with the requirements of Article 3(a) and 3(b) of the SPC Regulations, i.e., whether the product is protected by the basic patent and whether a valid marketing authorization within the meaning of the SPC Regulations has been granted.

Some patent offices have installed tight timelines for the prosecution of SPC applications, whereas in others, the prosecution of an SPC may be delayed substantially, particularly if the basic patent is not due to expire in the near future.

From a practical point of view, while in clear-cut cases it may be desirable to have an SPC issue as quickly as possible, it sometimes may be advantageous to delay the prosecution of an SPC.

Thus, an applicant may have multiple patents which could potentially serve as the basis of an SPC filing. The choice of the appropriate patent is usually based on

400. Dutch Council of State, *Yeda v. Dutch Patent Office*, ECLI:NL:RVS:2009:BJ5541 of 19 August 2009.

considerations such as validity, duration and scope of protection afforded by an SPC based on the patent.

In many instances, it may be expedient to await the outcome of contentious proceedings associated with the basic patent, such as opposition or nullity or infringement proceedings, before deciding which patent may be the most appropriate for an SPC filing. In practice, therefore, it may be preferable to delay the final decision on the basis of which patent the SPC prosecution should be moved forward until these issues have been clarified.

Thus, while an applicant is only entitled to be granted a single SPC per product, it is possible to file multiple SPC applications on the basis of different patents protecting the product. Due to the delay in prosecution, the applicant, pending the outcome of any contentious proceedings, can then choose the most appropriate patent to move forward with for the SPC.

If the SPC request, subjected to the substantive and/or formal examination, is deemed to meet the conditions as laid out in the SPC Regulations, a Certificate will be granted. Some patent offices will actually issue a Certificate, whereas in other patent offices only the decision to grant will issue.

Once granted, the patent offices are then required to publish all relevant information as set out in Article 11 of the SPC Regulations in the Official Gazette.

Upon expiry of the basic patent, i.e., when the SPC comes into force, renewal fees (*see* Article 12 of the SPC Regulations) will have to be paid. In some countries these fees must be paid annually, whereas in others they must be paid as a single cumulative amount, before the SPC can take effect.

If, on the other hand, the SPC request upon examination is considered to not meet the requirements as set forth in the SPC Regulations, it must be rejected.

As provided for in the SPC Regulations (Articles 18 and 19 of the SPC Regulation for Medicinal Products, and Articles 17 and 18 of the SPC Regulation for Plant Protection Products), the decisions of the national patent offices may be appealed in accordance with the procedural provisions for appeal provided for in national law in respect of national patents.

[G] Applications for a Paediatric Extension

The formal requirements for filing a request for a paediatric extension are set out in Articles 7–9 of the SPC Regulation for Medicinal Products.

Thus, an application for a paediatric extension must be filed with the national patent office.

If the required paediatric trials have already been carried out and the necessary compliance statement concerning the agreed completed paediatric investigation plan ('PIP') is available at the date of filing of the SPC, the request for a paediatric extension may be filed together with the SPC request. If the compliance statement is only available at a later stage, the request may be filed subsequently, but in any case no later than two years before the expiry of the SPC (*see* Article 7(3) and 7(4) of the SPC Regulation for Medicinal Products).

The formal requirements for filing a paediatric extension, including the documentation required, are set out in Article 8 of the SPC Regulation for Medicinal Products.

Thus, it is necessary to submit the statement of compliance with the agreed and completed PIP.

Moreover, if the product has not been approved centrally by the EMA, it is necessary for the applicant to submit proof of possession of marketing authorizations in all Member States.

The SPC Regulation does not expressly specify that at the date of filing the request for a paediatric extension all required documentation, including the compliance statement must be available, so that these may be submitted at a later stage. This may be of significance, keeping in mind that the request must be filed at the latest two years before the expiry date of the SPC.

Additionally, all Member States require the payment of an application fee for the extension of an SPC.

If the request for an extension of an SPC is rejected, then this decision may be appealed. In accordance with Articles 18 and 19 of the SPC Regulation for Medicinal Products, the appeal procedure should be analogous to the procedure provided for in respect of national patents.

§1.06 PROCEDURE OF INVALIDATING AN SPC

[A] Grounds for the Invalidation of an SPC

According to Article 15 of the SPC Regulations, an SPC shall be invalid for the following grounds:

(a) the SPC was granted contrary to the provisions of Article 3;
(b) the basic patent has lapsed before its full term period; or
(c) the basic patent has been revoked or limited (or if, after expiry of its term, grounds exist which would have justified such action) so that the product for which the SPC was granted would no longer be protected by the patent.

An SPC is ancillary to a patent and, as such, the lapse, invalidity, revocation or limitation of the basic patent will affect the validity of the SPC.

The catalogue of grounds of invalidity as set out in Article 15(1) of the SPC Regulations is not exhaustive, as evidenced by the guidance provided by the CJEU. Thus, in *Hässle* (C-127/00)[401] and *Synthon* (C-195/09),[402] the Court confirmed that even if it is not possible to infer from the wording or the origin of Article 15(1) of the SPC Regulation that the list of grounds of invalidity of an SPC is not exhaustive, the infringement of an Article of that Regulation not referred to in Article 15(1) can still

401. CJEU *Hässle v. Ratiopharm*, C-127/00 of 11 December 2003, paragraphs 90 and 91.
402. CJEU *Synthon v. Merz Pharma*, C-195/09 of 28 July 2011, paragraph 55.

render an SPC invalid 'owing to the connection between the provision in question and Article 3 of the regulation'.

The EFTA Court took this same position in *Pharmaq* (E-16/14)[403] and found that an SPC which was granted with a broader product definition than justified by the marketing authorization relied upon was in breach of Article 4 of the SPC Regulation and – 'owing to the connection between that provision and Article 3 of the SPC Regulation' – would be invalid to the extent that it goes beyond the authorized product. The filing of an SPC with an unduly broad product definition may therefore potentially jeopardize its validity (*see* §1.03[B] above).

Generally speaking, there is thus some uncertainty whether an SPC may also be invalidated if the filing of the SPC was in violation of provisions in the SPC Regulations which have no immediate connection to Article 3, such as Article 7, setting out the time limits for filing an SPC.

[B] The Filing of an Invalidation Suit

The invalidation of an SPC does not occur ex officio. Rather, in accordance with Article 15(2) of the SPC Regulation, it requires a motion for the declaration of invalidity to be filed before the body responsible under national law for the revocation of the corresponding basic patent.

According to Article 15(2) of the SPC Regulations, the request may be filed by any person, suggesting that the person should not need to establish a legal interest in filing the request.

In analogy to the revocation of a patent, the revocation of an SPC should have an ex tunc effect.

The lapse or revocation of an SPC must be published by the competent national authority.[404]

[C] Invalidation Procedure and the Corresponding Appeal Procedure

Neither of the SPC Regulations provides any procedural requirements in terms of invalidation procedure and the corresponding appeal, as set out in Articles 15(2) and 18 of the SPC Regulation for Medicinal Products and Articles 15(2) and 17(1) of the SPC Regulation for Plant Protection Products, respectively.

Thus, Article 19 of the SPC Regulation for Medicinal Products and Article 18 of the SPC Regulation for Plant Protection Products expressly refer to the procedural provisions applicable under national law for the corresponding basic patent, unless the national law provides special procedural provisions for SPCs.

403. EFTA Court, *Pharmaq v. Intervet International*, E-16/14 of 9 April 2015, paragraphs 91 and 93.
404. Article 17(1) of Regulation (EC) 469/2009, and Art. 16 of Regulation (EC) 1610/96.

[D] The Revocation of a Paediatric Extension

The grounds for revocation of a paediatric extension are set out in Article 16 of the SPC Regulation for Medicinal Products. Accordingly, a declaration of invalidity may be filed if the extension was granted contrary to the provisions of Article 36 of Regulation (EC) 1901/2006 (the Paediatric Regulation).

Article 36 of this Regulation stipulates that in order to be entitled to a paediatric extension, all the measures included in the agreed paediatric investigation plan (PIP) must have been complied with and a compliance statement relating to the PIP must be included in the product information, i.e., in the Summary of Product Characteristics (SmPC). Moreover, the product must be authorized in all Member States.

In accordance with Article 36(4) and 36(5) of the Paediatric Regulation, an SPC extension is not available for medicinal products designated as orphan medicinal products pursuant to Regulation (EC) 141/2000 (the Orphan Medicinal Products Regulation) or for medicinal products applied for under Article 8 of the Paediatric Regulation (which leads to the authorization of a new paediatric indication, with a concomitant one-year extension of the period of marketing protection for the medicinal product concerned).

While it is uncertain whether the catalogue of grounds for revocation as set out in Article 16(1) of the SPC Regulation for Medicinal Products is exhaustive, it is possible, in analogy to invalidation of the SPC, that this may not be the case.

Thus, it is conceivable that a paediatric extension may also be revoked if it has been filed in infringement of other Articles of the SPC Regulation, such as the time limits as set out in Article 7(4) and 7(5) of the SPC Regulation for Medicinal Products.

According to Article 16(2) of the SPC Regulation for Medicinal Products, the request for revocation of a paediatric extension may be filed by any person, which suggests that a legal interest in the filing of the request should not be necessary.

From a procedural perspective, in terms of the filing procedure and appeal, the same considerations apply for the revocation of a paediatric extension as set out above for the invalidation of an SPC.

§1.07 UNFAIR COMPETITION LAW

Historically, EU and national competition law has predominately been enforced within the pharmaceutical industry in relation to merger control and prohibiting agreements that restrict parallel trade, particularly through the use of quotas and dual pricing.

Over the past decade, however, increasing tension has emerged between competition law and intellectual property rights, in particular patents and SPCs.

As evidenced by the competition inquiry into the pharmaceutical sector (*see* Final Report of 8 July 2009[405]), the European Commission has become increasingly more sensitive to the competition issues in the pharmaceutical sector. The inquiry was

405. European Commission, Pharmaceutical Sector Inquiry, Final Report, 8 July 2009 (accessible online at: http://ec.europa.eu/competition/sectors/pharmaceuticals/inquiry/).

opened in January 2008 under Article 17 of Regulation (EC) 1/2003,[406] based on information suggesting that competition between innovative and generic medicines manufacturers may be distorted, in light of the decrease of new drugs coming to market (suggesting a decline in innovation) on the one hand and the observed delays in generic market entry on the other.

The main finding of the sector inquiry was that pharmaceutical companies have at their disposal a 'tool box' of strategies designed to prolong patent protection, delay generic market entry and block others' innovation. Of these findings, speed of generic market entry was the Commission's main concern.

While the Commission primarily focused on patent settlements, regulatory strategies and anticompetitive agreements, contravening Article 101 of the Treaty on the Functioning of the European Union (TFEU), it also highlighted strategic patent and SPC filings, that are typically grouped under the heading of 'life cycle management strategies', as being potentially in violation of EU competition law, as such activities may amount to an abuse of a dominant position under Article 102 TFEU.

The exclusive status of intellectual property rights in the EU is manifested in Article 36 TFEU which expressly provides for a derogation from the prohibition of quantitative restrictions on import and export if they are justified on the grounds of 'the protection of industrial and commercial property'.

Beyond this, there are no specific statutory provisions in the interface between intellectual property rights and competition law.

From a patent law perspective, strategic patent and SPC filings in order to maximize and prolong the monopoly for a pharmaceutical product are, of course, generally legitimate and wide-spread. In accordance with the case law of the CJEU, it is, however, settled that the illegality of practice under Article 102 TFEU is unrelated to its compliance with other legal provisions. This situation is best summarized by the statement of the CJEU in paragraph 132 of its judgment in the *AstraZeneca* case (C-457/10 P),[407] namely:

> [T]he illegality of abusive conduct under Article 82 EC [now Article 102 TFEU] is unrelated to its compliance or non-compliance with other legal rules and, in the majority of cases, abuses of dominant positions consist of behaviour which is otherwise lawful under branches of law other than competition law.

Neither the sector inquiry nor the Final Report provides any guidance as to the standard to be applied to the behaviour identified. In the absence of any clear statutory provisions in relation to intellectual property and EU competition law, the statements made by the Commission in this regard are not only disconcerting but have given rise to considerable legal uncertainty.

As a consequence of the inquiry, the pharmaceutical sector must be prepared for a much more rigorous scrutiny of its activities. This is clearly evidenced by the case law of the CJEU in *AstraZeneca* and the decision of the Italian Supreme Administrative

406. Council Regulation (EC) 1/2003 of 16 December 2002 on the implementation of the rules on competition laid down in Arts 81 and 82 of the Treaty.

407. CJEU *AstraZeneca v. European Commission*, C-457/10 P of 6 December 2012.

Court (Consiglio di Stato) in *Pfizer* (693/214),[408] where EU competition law has been enforced against pharmaceutical life cycle management strategies.

As set out in *AstraZeneca*, the mere act of filing SPCs based on a misinterpretation of the provisions of the SPC Regulation may be viewed as abuse of a dominant position, unless all relevant facts are disclosed to the national patent offices.

In this particular case, SPCs had been applied for in 1993 for the medicinal product Losec (comprising the proton pump inhibitor (PPI) omeprazole for use in the treatment of gastrointestinal ulcers) in various Member States, relying on a Luxembourg price approval dated 21 March 1988 as the first marketing authorization in the Community. In support of this, the corresponding 21 March 1988 Luxembourg list of proprietary medicinal products authorized for sale was submitted.

In Germany, the SPC issued and was set to expire fifteen years after the first approval in the Community, i.e., on 21 March 2003. The SPC was challenged by generics for violation of the transitional provisions of Article 19 of the original SPC Regulation for Medicinal Products. While the SPC was held invalid by both the German Federal Patent Court and the Federal Supreme Court, the case was referred to the CJEU (C-127/00, *Hässle*)[409] for clarification as to whether the 'first authorization' as provided for in Article 19 of the SPC Regulation is the date of the actual marketing authorization or whether the concept of the 'first authorization' may be a later authorization such as the pricing authorization for re-imbursement of the medicinal product, without which the product can de facto not be marketed. Thus, the German Federal Supreme Court regarded the issue to not be acte clair, suggesting that it did not consider AstraZeneca's interpretation of Article 19 to be too far-fetched.

This issue was only clarified in December 2003, when the CJEU handed down the *Hässle* decision, confirming that the 'first authorization' within the meaning of the SPC Regulation for Medicinal Products is the date of actual regulatory approval,[410] regardless of the ancillary requirements which may need to be met to actually be able to market the product.

In May 1999, various generic manufacturers filed a complaint to the Commission in relation to AstraZeneca's conduct, which then eventually gave rise to the *AstraZeneca* ruling.

As set out in *AstraZeneca*, the relevant provision which was violated was an abuse of dominance as provided for in Article 102 TFEU and Article 54 of the EEA Agreement[411] (which effectively corresponds to Article 102 TFEU, thereby extending the principle of the prohibition of abuse of a dominant position to the territory covered by this Agreement).

408. Italian Supreme Administrative Court (Consiglio di Stato), *Pfizer*, 693/214 of 12 February 2014.
409. CJEU *Hässle v. Ratiopharm*, C-127/00 of 11 December 2003.
410. *See also* CJEU *Seattle Genetics v. Österreichisches Patentamt*, C-471/14 of 6 October 2015, according to which the relevant date is the date of notification, rather than the actual date of the marketing authorization.
411. *See also* Council Regulation (EC) 2894/94 of 28 November 1994 concerning arrangements for implementing the Agreement on the European Economic Area.

Article 102 TFEU seeks to prohibit a dominant undertaking from impeding a competitor and to thereby strengthen its own position by using methods other than those which come within the scope of competition on the merits.

In order for Article 102 TFEU to be violated, the undertaking must be in a dominant position in the relevant market and the conduct must contravene competition rules. The General Court in the first-instance decision *AstraZeneca* (T-321/05)[412] defined the relevant market very narrowly, so as to include only the market for PPIs, a category of products in which Losec was the leader.

Since conduct which is implemented prior to dominance is in principle not an abuse of a dominant position, AstraZeneca argued that at the relevant time (when filing the SPC applications) it was not in a dominant position, as other medicinal products, in particular histamine H2 receptor blockers (H2 blockers) were prescribed for indications overlapping with those of PPIs. The Commission declined to include H2 blockers in the relevant product market definition, although they were the leading treatment for ulcers when Losec entered the market in 1987/1988 and continued to have a significant share of the market. In the Commission's view, H2 blockers did not exercise a significant competitive constraint on Losec because Losec was considered to be a much better product and the only reason that it did not take over the market completely was the natural inertia in doctors' prescribing practices rather than competition from H2 blockers.

AstraZeneca challenged this very narrow interpretation of the 'relevant market' and emphasized that there was only a very gradual replacement of H2 blockers by PPIs, so that other classes of drugs should have been included in the market definition. The CJEU in the second-instance decision rejected this approach and confirmed that the gradual nature of the increase in sales of a new product substituting an existing product does not necessarily mean that the latter product exercised a significant constraint.

While the mere possession of intellectual property rights in itself does not prove dominance,[413] the General Court agreed with the Commission's findings that first mover status (Losec was the first PPI to be approved and thus had a competitive advantage over later approved PPIs) and the possession of intellectual property rights are capable, in certain circumstances, of creating a dominant position by enabling the undertaking to prevent effective competition on the market.

The *AstraZeneca* case thus vividly establishes that the CJEU in relation to medicinal products applies a very narrow concept of the 'relevant market' in order to assess potential dominance within the meaning of EU competition rules.

SPCs are granted for innovative medicinal products, which per definition are only approved if the balance of benefits and risks for a defined patient population is positive. As such, it follows that the holder of an SPC for an innovative medicinal product is very likely to be viewed as being in a dominant position, irrespective of how small the actual market may be economically.

412. General Court of the European Union, *AstraZeneca v. European Commission*, T-321/05 of 1 July 2010.
413. CJEU *Radio Telefis Eireann and Independent Television Publications v. Commission of the European Communities*, C-241/91 P of 6 April 1995.

In terms of the concept of 'competition on the merits' in *AstraZeneca*, the General Court held that the submission of misleading information to the patent offices and the manifest lack of transparency, *inter alia* in relation to the existence of the earlier Luxembourg and French marketing authorizations, in order to keep for as long as possible its monopoly on the PPI market, fell outside the scope of competition on the merits. The Court emphasized that whether the information is misleading must be assessed on the basis of the specific circumstances of each individual case. Notably, the Court furthermore stressed that it was not necessary to establish a deliberate intent to deceive, although such an intent would be taken into account.

AstraZeneca on appeal argued that the General Court erred in law in holding that the mere act of applying for an SPC was sufficient to constitute an abuse. The CJEU, however, confirmed that it did not matter that the abusive conduct did not actually produce the desired effects, that is, that AstraZeneca was unsuccessful in obtaining SPCs and enforcing them beyond the term of the basic patent. Although the SPCs were filed five to six years before their entry into force, and although, until that time, AstraZeneca's rights were protected by lawful patents, the CJEU held that SPC filings per se are also liable to alter the structure of the market by adversely affecting potential competition even before the expiry of the basic patent.

In the Italian *Pfizer* case, the patentee had inadvertently omitted applying for an SPC for the anti-glaucoma drug latanoprost in Italy. As a divisional patent application was still pending, the SPC for Italy was eventually filed on the basis of the divisional patent. Pfizer made it clear to the generic manufacturers as well as the regulatory authorities that it intended to enforce its SPC and also initiated litigation against generic manufacturers who had already entered the market. In the first instance the Italian Competition Authority (ICA) ruled that Pfizer was in violation of Article 102 TFEU, as Pfizer's divisional patent did not pertain to any additional innovation but simply enabled Pfizer to apply for an SPC. In finding an abuse, the authority criticized Pfizer's actions aimed at enforcing its SPC by sending warning letters and suing generic manufacturers. An analogy to *AstraZeneca* was drawn in terms of providing the patent office with misleading information. As the filing of divisional applications and SPCs, as well as the enforcement of such rights correspond to well-established and legitimate legal instruments, this analogy seems misplaced, particularly as no evidence had been presented indicating that Pfizer may have misled the patent office.

On appeal the decision was overruled by the Italian Administrative Tribunal in September 2012. With regard to the Authority's findings of abuse of dominance and its theory of harm, the Tribunal stated that Pfizer had done nothing more than defend its legitimate interests. In particular, anticompetitive behaviour needed to be supported by evidence of '*clear exclusionary intent and an additional anticompetitive element*' which went beyond legitimate business practices.

In the final instance appeal to the Italian Supreme Administrative Court (Consiglio di Stato) this decision was however overturned. According to the Court, the ICA correctly found that Pfizer, through the use of the parent patent rights, could have extended patent protection in Italy and thus delay the entrance of generic companies in the market, without effectively using the divisional patent – whose object was already protected by the parent patent – and with a purpose different from the proper scope of patent law.

After the decision of the Italian Supreme Administrative Court, the Italian Ministry of Health and the Ministry of Economy and Finances brought a follow-on action against Pfizer before the Civil Court of Rome (Tribunale Civile di Roma), claiming compensation for the economic damage allegedly caused to the public administration by Pfizer's anticompetitive behaviour, as established by the ICA and the Supreme Administrative Court. The Civil Court of Rome, however, rejected the Italian ministries' claim with judgment 15020/2017 of 24 March 2017[414]. Among other considerations, the Court regarded Pfizer's filing of the divisional patent and the corresponding SPC to be legitimate, thereby deviating from the findings of the ICA and the Supreme Administrative Court. An appeal against this judgment of the Civil Court of Rome has been filed by the Italian ministries and is currently pending.

In summary, therefore, according to the current practice of the EU and national competition authorities, the 'relevant market' for an innovative medicinal product tends to be defined narrowly. As such, there is a strong likelihood that the holder of an SPC may be viewed as being in a 'dominant position'.

In light of these considerations, SPC holders and applicants should pay special attention that their conduct comes within the 'scope of competition on the merits'. As some activities, which may be legitimate from a patent perspective, may be considered to be an act of abuse of a dominant position from a competition law perspective, it would appear expedient to ensure that all correspondence with the national patent offices relating to SPCs are fully transparent, in order to avoid any potential accusal of misleading representation.

414. Civil Court of Rome (Tribunale Civile di Roma), *Ministry of Health and Ministry of Economy and Finances v. Pfizer Italia*, 15020/2017 of 24 March 2017.

CHAPTER 2
Germany

Alexa von Uexküll & Oswin Ridderbusch

§2.01 LEGAL BASIS

In German national law,[1] the central legal provisions governing SPCs are contained in Sections 16a and 49a of the German Patent Act (Patentgesetz, 'PatG'), which were introduced with effect of 1 April 1993. Further legal provisions that directly relate to SPCs are Sections 30(1), 81(1) and 142(1) PatG, Sections 19–21 of the German Patent Ordinance (Patentverordnung, 'PatV'), Sections 3(2), 5(2) and 7(1) of the German Patent Costs Act (Patentkostengesetz, 'PatKostG'), Section 2 of the DPMA Ordinance (DPMA-Verordnung, 'DPMAV'), and Article II Section 6a of the German Act on International Patent Treaties (Gesetz über internationale Patentübereinkommen, 'IntPatÜG').

Thus, Section 16a PatG[2] provides that supplementary protection may be applied for on the basis of a patent, pursuant to the pertinent Regulations of the European

1. English translations of most German legal acts and ordinances governing patents and SPCs are provided by the German Patent and Trademark Office at: https://www.dpma.de/english/our_office/law/index.html.
2. Section 16a PatG reads as follows (in English translation):

    (1) An application for supplementary protection for the patent can be filed pursuant to the provisions set out in the Regulations of the European Communities concerning the creation of Supplementary Protection Certificates, reference to which shall be made in the Federal Law Gazette, which supplementary protection shall follow immediately upon expiry of the patent in accordance with Section 16. Annual renewal fees shall be paid for supplementary protection.
    (2) Unless otherwise provided by the law of the European Communities, the provisions of this Act regarding the applicant's entitlement (Sections 6 to 8), regarding the effect of the patent and the exceptions thereto (Sections 9 to 12), regarding an order for use and the compulsory licence (Sections 13 and 24), regarding the extent of protection (Section 14), regarding licences and their registration (Sections 15 and 30), regarding the lapse of the patent (Section 20), regarding revocation (Section 22), regarding the willingness

Union. According to Section 16a PatG, unless provided for otherwise by EU law, the provisions of the German Patent Act are to be applied for SPCs granted on the basis of German and European patents. Accordingly, such SPCs are subject to annuity payments. Moreover, the provisions of the Patent Act in terms of entitlement, the effect of the patent, the extent of protection, licences and their registration (including compulsory licences) and the lapse of the patent and its revocation apply to SPCs, as procedural provisions, including in the appeal instances.

In line with this, according to Section 30(1) PatG, the publicly accessible patent register shall contain the names and addresses of the SPC applicants or proprietors and their representatives as well as details on the term of an SPC, its lapse or invalidity, and the filing of a revocation action. This information is also published in Part 7 of the Patent Gazette (Patentblatt).

Moreover, Section 81(1) PatG provides that an SPC is subject to similar court actions in terms of revocation and compulsory licence proceedings as applicable for patents. According to Section 142(1) PatG, the penal sanctions applicable for patent infringement also apply to the infringement of an SPC.

Section 49a PatG[3] provides detailed rules on the examination, grant and refusal of SPCs.

---

to grant a licence (Section 23), regarding representatives in Germany (Section 25), regarding the Federal Patent Court and proceedings before the Federal Patent Court (Sections 65 to 99), regarding proceedings before the Federal Court of Justice (Sections 100 to 122a), regarding the re-establishment of rights (Section 123), regarding the obligation to tell the truth (Section 124), regarding electronic documents (Section 125a), regarding the official language, notifications and judicial assistance (Sections 126 to 128), regarding legal infringements (Sections 139 to 141a, 142a and 142b), regarding the joinder of actions and arrogation of patent (Sections 145 and 146) shall apply mutatis mutandis to supplementary protection.

(3) Licences and declarations made pursuant to Section 23 which take effect for a patent shall also apply mutatis mutandis to supplementary protection.

3. Section 49a PatG reads as follows (in English translation):

(1) If the person registered as the proprietor of the patent applies for supplementary protection, the Patent Division shall examine whether the application complies with the relevant Regulation of the European Communities as well as with Subsection (5) and Section 16a.

(2) If the application meets these requirements, the Patent Division shall issue the Supplementary Protection Certificate for the duration of its term. Otherwise, it shall invite the applicant to correct any deficiencies within a time limit of at least two months to be set by the Patent Division. If the deficiencies are not corrected, the Patent Division shall take a decision to refuse the application.

(3) If a Regulation of the European Communities provides for the extension of the term of a Supplementary Protection Certificate, Subsections (1) and (2) shall apply mutatis mutandis.

(4) The Patent Division shall take a decision on the requests provided for in Regulations of the European Communities to

1. correct the term of a Supplementary Protection Certificate if the date included in the application for the certificate in respect of the first authorization for placing the invention on the market is incorrect;
2. revoke the extension of the term of a Supplementary Protection Certificate.

(5) Section 34 (6) shall apply. Sections 46 and 47 shall apply to the procedure before the Patent Division.

The German Patent and Trademark Office (GPTO) also issues 'Examination Guidelines for Supplementary Protection Certificates' in German and English language,[4] which provide detailed information on the GPTO's examination practice in SPC matters. Based on the principle of equal treatment of all applicants, the patent divisions of the GPTO are obliged to follow these Guidelines in SPC examination proceedings.[5]

§2.02 SUBSTANTIVE REQUIREMENTS FOR OBTAINING AN SPC

As the guidance provided by the CJEU is binding for all EU Member States, the considerations as set out in Chapter 1 (the 'EU chapter'), specifically in §1.02 above, in relation to the substantive requirements for obtaining an SPC, in as far as they have been addressed by the CJEU, are equally applicable in Germany.

The following discussion will therefore only focus on case law and considerations of interest in Germany beyond the guidance provided by the CJEU.

[A] Types of Products That Can Be Protected

The same considerations as set out in the EU chapter apply.

[1] Practical Considerations: What Is the Active Ingredient or Combination of Active Ingredients That Can Form the Basis for an SPC

The same considerations as set out in the EU chapter apply.

[2] Active Ingredient or Combination of Active Ingredients of a Medicinal Product

As discussed in the EU chapter, the requirement for a substance or a combination of substances to qualify as an 'active ingredient', as elaborated by the CJEU in *Forsgren* (C-631/13),[6] is that the respective substances must produce a pharmacological, immunological or metabolic action of their own.

The German Federal Patent Court effectively acknowledged this definition to be broader than the one previously endorsed by the CJEU, i.e., that the term 'active ingredient' does not include 'substances which do not have any therapeutic effect of

4. German Patent and Trademark Office. Examination Guidelines for Supplementary Protection Certificates. Document number P 2799/2.16 (German version) or P 2799.1/2.16 (English version). Available online at: https://www.dpma.de/english/services/forms/patents/index.html#a11.
5. GPTO Examination Guidelines for SPCs, Section 1.
6. CJEU *Arne Forsgren v. Österreichisches Patentamt*, C-631/13 of 15 January 2015.

their own'.[7] Thus, in *Paliperidonpalmitat* (14 W (pat) 25/16)[8] the Federal Patent Court had to decide upon an SPC application for a specific ester of a previously authorized active ingredient (as discussed in detail in §2.02[C][7][c] and §2.02[D][3][b] below), and found the principles underlying an earlier judgment of the Federal Supreme Court[9] on a closely related question to be no longer applicable because the corresponding judgment had been rendered prior to *Forsgren*. This conclusion would seem to confirm that, also in the view of the Federal Patent Court, the definition of what constitutes an 'active ingredient' has been substantially changed in the CJEU decision *Forsgren*.

Yet, even the broader concept of active ingredients established in *Forsgren* does still not cover all substances used for medicinal purposes, as illustrated by another decision of the Federal Patent Court. In *Aminosilan-beschichtete Eisenoxid-Nanopartikel* (14 W (pat) 45/12),[10] the SPC application at issue was directed to aminosilane-coated iron oxide nanoparticles. These superparamagnetic nanoparticles were approved as a medical device to be used for the magnetic hyperthermia therapy of cancer, i.e., they were to be applied specifically to cancerous tissue and then heated in an alternating external electromagnetic field so as to physically damage or destroy the cancer cells. The Federal Patent Court rejected this SPC application on the grounds that such particles exert an exclusively *physical effect* and do not have any pharmacological, immunological or metabolic action of their own. Consequently, and in accordance with the CJEU's findings in *Forsgren*, these particles were found to not constitute an 'active ingredient' within the meaning of the SPC Regulation for Medicinal Products, and the SPC application was thus rejected.

[3] Active Substance or Combination of Active Substances of a Plant Protection Product

The CJEU decision *Bayer CropScience* (C-11/13),[11] in which the Court acknowledged that a safener can indeed constitute an 'active substance', provided that it exerts a toxic, phytotoxic or plant protection action of its own, was based on a referral from the German Federal Patent Court.[12]

Following the CJEU's ruling in *Bayer CropScience*, the Federal Patent Court in *Isoxadifen II* (15 W (pat) 14/07)[13] found this criterion of exerting a toxic, phytotoxic or

7. CJEU *Massachusetts Institute of Technology v. Bundesgerichtshof*, C-431/04 of 4 May 2006, paragraphs 18 and 25; CJEU *Glaxosmithkline Biologicals v. Comptroller-General of Patents, Designs and Trade Marks*, C-210/13 of 14 November 2013, paragraphs 28, 30 and 35.
8. German Federal Patent Court (Bundespatentgericht), order 14 W (pat) 25/16 of 5 September 2017 – Paliperidonpalmitat, Section II.7 of the reasons.
9. German Federal Supreme Court (Bundesgerichtshof), order X ZB 4/08 of 14 October 2008 – Doxorubicin-Sulfat.
10. German Federal Patent Court (Bundespatentgericht), order 14 W (pat) 45/12 of 8 December 2015 – Aminosilan-beschichtete Eisenoxid-Nanopartikel.
11. CJEU *Bayer CropScience v. Deutsches Patent- und Markenamt*, C-11/13 of 19 June 2014.
12. German Federal Patent Court (Bundespatentgericht), order 15 W (pat) 14/07 of 9 July 2012 – Isoxadifen I.
13. German Federal Patent Court (Bundespatentgericht), order 15 W (pat) 14/07 of 10 December 2014 – Isoxadifen II.

plant protection action to be fulfilled by the specific safener in question and thus granted the SPC. The Court reached this conclusion on the grounds that the safener, in its property as a herbicide antidote, influences the life processes of plants in a manner other than as a nutrient, and thus falls within the corresponding definition of an 'active substance' according to Article 1(1)(b) of the SPC Regulation for Plant Protection Products. The safener's activity as a herbicide antidote having a direct effect of its own on the crop plant's life processes, in turn, was derived by the Federal Patent Court from the description of the basic patent and supporting scientific literature. This 'objective scientific assessment' of the effects of the safener at issue was considered to be solely relevant by the Court, whereas its 'potentially changing, merely transient and merely administrative' classification as an active substance or a co-formulant in the context of the national marketing authorization procedure was held to be irrelevant.

[4] Fixed-Dose and Loose Combinations

The German Federal Supreme Court in *Anti-Helicobacter-Präparat* (X ZB 1/08)[14] found that an SPC for a combination of active ingredients cannot be granted on the basis of a marketing authorization for a medicinal product containing only one of these active ingredients, even where the marketing authorization mandatorily requires the approved product to be used in combination with the other active ingredient(s) that are subject of the SPC application.

In this decision rendered in 2008, however, the Federal Supreme Court could not take into account that the CJEU, contrary to its former practice, has a tendency to apply a more teleological approach when interpreting the provisions of the SPC Regulations in its more recent case law, including *Neurim* (C-130/11).[15] Therefore, and for the reasons detailed in the EU chapter, it does indeed seem conceivable that the restrictive position taken by the Federal Supreme Court in *Anti-Helicobacter-Präparat* could still be overturned, even in future German national jurisprudence. *See also* §2.02[C][1][c] below.

[5] Limitation to Products Subjected to a Specific Marketing Authorization Procedure

The same considerations as set out in the EU chapter apply.

[6] Protection of Medical Devices

Whether or not medical devices containing active ingredients are eligible for SPC protection under the current legislative framework is expected to be clarified by the CJEU's ruling in the pending referral C-527/17.

14. German Federal Supreme Court (Bundesgerichtshof), order X ZB 1/08 of 8 July 2008 – Anti-Helicobacter-Präparat.
15. CJEU *Neurim Pharmaceuticals v. Comptroller-General of Patents*, C-130/11 of 19 July 2012.

Therefore, earlier German case law, particularly *Yttrium-90 Glasmikrokugeln* (14 W (pat) 12/07)[16] and *Hylan A und Hylan B* (15 W (pat) 25/08),[17] can be expected to no longer play any decisive role after the CJEU's decision in this referral.

In *Yttrium-90 Glasmikrokugeln*, the 14th Senate of the German Federal Patent Court granted an SPC for glass microspheres containing the radioactive isotope yttrium-90 on the basis of a CE approval under Directive 90/385/EEC (active implantable medical devices). In contrast thereto, in *Hylan A und Hylan B*, the 15th Senate of the Federal Patent Court dismissed an appeal against the rejection of an SPC application for the combination of hylan A and hylan B approved under Directive 93/42/EEC (medical devices).

In the further decision *Aminosilan-beschichtete Eisenoxid-Nanopartikel* (14 W (pat) 45/12),[18] the Federal Patent Court rejected an SPC application directed to aminosilane-coated iron oxide nanoparticles which were approved as a medical device under Directive 93/42/EEC on the grounds that these particles do not constitute an active ingredient (as discussed in §2.02[A][2] above). It did not have to consider the further question whether an SPC can be based on a marketing authorization under Directive 93/42/EEC in this decision. Undisputedly, medical devices which do not contain any active ingredient within the meaning of the SPC Regulation for Medicinal Products are not eligible for SPC protection.

[B] Basic Patent

As concerns the basic patent underlying an SPC, the same considerations as set out in the EU chapter apply.

Regarding the type of patents that can be used for an SPC filing, the German Federal Patent Court found in *Ranibizumab* (3 Ni 28/11)[19] that a patent with claims to a screening method, which is not a manufacturing method, does generally not qualify as a basic patent for an SPC under Article 1(c) of the SPC Regulation for Medicinal Products.

With respect to the requirement under Article 3(a) of the SPC Regulations that the basic patent must be 'in force' at the date of filing the SPC application, the Federal Patent Court confirmed in *Hexavalenter Impfstoff* (14 W (pat) 10/16)[20] that a basic patent which has been revoked in first-instance opposition proceedings before the EPO is still pending if the decision of revocation has been appealed, so that an SPC can be validly filed on the basis of such a patent.

16. German Federal Patent Court (Bundespatentgericht), order 14 W (pat) 12/07 of 26 January 2010 - Yttrium-90 Glasmikrokugeln.
17. German Federal Patent Court (Bundespatentgericht), order 15 W (pat) 25/08 of 8 March 2010 - Hylan A und Hylan B.
18. German Federal Patent Court (Bundespatentgericht), order 14 W (pat) 45/12 of 8 December 2015 - Aminosilan-beschichtete Eisenoxid-Nanopartikel.
19. German Federal Patent Court (Bundespatentgericht), judgment 3 Ni 28/11 of 2 May 2012 - Ranibizumab, Section II.4 of the reasons.
20. German Federal Patent Court (Bundespatentgericht), order 14 W (pat) 10/16 of 23 January 2018 - Hexavalenter Impfstoff, Section II.4.1 of the reasons.

The condition that the basic patent must be 'in force' at the date of filing the SPC application is not a deadline to be observed but rather a substantive requirement. Therefore, a failure to file the SPC application while the basic patent is still 'in force' cannot be remedied via re-establishment of rights, as also confirmed by the Federal Patent Court in *Abamectin* (15 W (pat) 71/97)[21] and in *Clothianidin I* (15 W (pat) 24/06).[22]

[1] Requirement for the Product to Be 'Protected' by the Basic Patent

Before the CJEU established an 'identification test' in *Medeva* (C-322/10) and subsequent decisions,[23] the German courts used to apply an 'infringement test' to determine whether a product is 'protected' by the basic patent.[24] This earlier approach is no longer applicable, as also acknowledged by the German Federal Patent Court in *Ranibizumab* (3 Ni 28/11).[25]

As a result of this fundamental change of practice, the validity of numerous granted German SPCs was abruptly called into question, including in particular SPCs for combinations of active ingredients (which could previously be granted even on the basis of patents claiming only a single active ingredient). A straightforward attempt to remedy such deficiencies and adapt already granted SPCs to conform with the new standard established by the CJEU in *Medeva* consisted in voluntarily limiting the claims of the basic patent so as to identify the respective active ingredient(s) in the claims, relying on the retroactive effect of amendments made to the patent via either the national German or the centralized European limitation procedure. The feasibility of this approach has since been confirmed in the German case law.

Thus, in *Telmisartan I* (15 W (pat) 25/12)[26] the Federal Patent Court acknowledged that a basic patent underlying a granted SPC, containing a claim directed to a pharmaceutical composition 'comprising' an active ingredient A, can be limited to a pharmaceutical composition comprising the active ingredient A in combination with an active ingredient B, provided of course that this combination is disclosed in the description of the patent as belonging to the invention.

---

21. German Federal Patent Court (Bundespatentgericht), order 15 W (pat) 71/97 of 21 June 1999 – Abamectin.
22. German Federal Patent Court (Bundespatentgericht), order 15 W (pat) 24/06 of 12 December 2011 – Clothianidin I, Section II, fifth paragraph of the reasons.
23. CJEU *Medeva v. Comptroller General of Patents, Designs and Trade Marks*, C-322/10 of 24 November 2011; CJEU *University of Queensland v. Comptroller-General of Patents, Designs and Trade Marks*, C-630/10 of 25 November 2011; CJEU *Daiichi Sankyo v. Comptroller General of Patents, Designs and Trade Marks*, C-6/11 of 25 November 2011; CJEU *Yeda Research and Development v. Comptroller General of Patents, Designs and Trade Marks*, C-518/10 of 25 November 2011.
24. *See*, e.g., German Federal Supreme Court (Bundesgerichtshof), order X ZB 12/01 of 29 January 2002 – Sumatriptan.
25. German Federal Patent Court (Bundespatentgericht), judgment 3 Ni 28/11 of 2 May 2012 – Ranibizumab, headnote 2.
26. German Federal Patent Court (Bundespatentgericht), order 15 W (pat) 25/12 of 31 July 2013 – Telmisartan I.

In the subsequent decision *Telmisartan II* (3 Ni 5/13)[27] relating to a revocation action filed against the corresponding SPC, the Federal Patent Court confirmed that a limitation of the basic patent retroactively takes effect for (and prior to) the filing date of the SPC, and that this is not in any way affected by the provisions of the pertinent SPC Regulation. The retroactive effect of the limitation of the basic patent must therefore also be taken into account when assessing the validity of the SPC. In this context, the Court again confirmed that it is acceptable to limit the claims of the basic patent so as to specifically identify the combination of active ingredients A and B, which was previously disclosed in the description but not explicitly identified in the claims, for the purpose of fulfilling the requirements of Article 3(a) of the SPC Regulation. Notably, the Federal Patent Court furthermore took the position that the retroactive effect of a limitation of the basic patent and its relevance for the assessment of validity of an SPC based on such a patent would be matters of national law and, as such, could not be referred to the CJEU.

With respect to the requirement for the product of an SPC to be identified in the claims of the basic patent in order to be 'protected' by the patent, the same considerations as set out in the EU chapter apply.

It should be noted, however, that the GPTO and the German courts generally apply a relatively broad concept of the disclosure-content of a patent specification, which includes everything that a skilled person 'implicitly reads between the lines'.[28] In accordance with this broad approach,[29] the Düsseldorf District Court in *Irbesartan* (4a O 109/12)[30] did not see any reason to doubt that the generic term 'diuretic' recited in the claims of the basic patent underlying the SPC at issue would indeed identify and, thus, 'protect' the specific active ingredient hydrochlorothiazide (which was part of the product definition of the SPC), even in the absence of a corresponding explicit disclosure in the patent. In reaching this conclusion, the District Court reasoned that the recitation of a generic term in the claims of the basic patent should suffice to identify a specific active ingredient embraced by the generic term, provided that the skilled person reads the specific active ingredient 'between the lines'. This was seen to be true for hydrochlorothiazide since the Court regarded this specific active ingredient as 'the prototype of a diuretic'. While this decision was rendered by the Düsseldorf District Court in preliminary injunction proceedings and does not provide a comprehensive assessment of the requirement of Article 3(a) of the SPC Regulations, it is nevertheless illustrative of some of the factors that German courts may take into consideration when determining whether the product of an SPC is identified and thus 'protected' by the basic patent.

---

27. German Federal Patent Court (Bundespatentgericht), judgment 3 Ni 5/13 of 4 February 2014 – Telmisartan II.
28. *See*, e.g., German Federal Supreme Court (Bundesgerichtshof), judgment X ZR 89/07 of 16 December 2008 – Olanzapin.
29. While the Düsseldorf District Court also referred to the concept of 'reading between the lines' in the discussed decision, it is to be noted that the assessment whether the product of an SPC is identified and thus 'protected' by the basic patent is decidedly different from the evaluation of the admissibility of amendments in patent matters.
30. Düsseldorf District Court (Landgericht Düsseldorf), judgment 4a O 109/12 of 15 August 2012 – Irbesartan.

Conversely, the Munich District Court in its judgment 7 O 11152/17,[31] which was rendered in preliminary injunction proceedings involving an SPC for the combination of tenofovir disoproxil with emtricitabine (Truvada), took the position that the generic functional term 'other therapeutic ingredients' recited in the claims of the basic patent, which was not further characterized in the patent specification, does not identify and thus 'protect' the specific active ingredient emtricitabine. In this respect, the District Court relied on the preliminary opinion of the Federal Patent Court in parallel revocation proceedings instigated against the corresponding SPC, in which the Federal Patent Court suggested that the requirement established by the CJEU in *Eli Lilly* (C-493/12),[32] according to which a functional term used in the claims of the basic patent needs to relate 'implicitly but necessarily and specifically' to the active ingredient at issue, should be understood to mean that the generic functional term in the claims must embrace the corresponding specific active ingredient at issue but, at the same time, must not embrace any other active ingredients which do not share the specific pharmaceutical properties of the active ingredient at issue. On the other hand, the strict standards governing the admissibility of amendments (including limitations) to patents should be of no relevance for determining whether a generic term in the basic patent identifies and thus 'protects' the specific active ingredient which is the subject of an SPC.

The approach proposed in the preliminary opinion of the Federal Patent Court and endorsed by the Munich District Court seems to require that a generic functional term used in the claims of the basic patent must be found, when interpreted in the light of the patent description, to relate exclusively to the specific active ingredient at issue and to exclude any other active ingredients. Such an approach, however, would appear to be unduly restrictive. Pragmatically, it would seem difficult to conceive how a functional definition of an active ingredient could be interpreted to relate to only one single active ingredient.

The Federal Patent Court has meanwhile revoked the above-mentioned SPC for the combination of tenofovir disoproxil with emtricitabine in its yet unpublished judgment 4 Ni 12/17.[33] It remains to be seen how the Federal Supreme Court will interpret the formula 'implicitly but necessarily and specifically' established by the CJEU in *Eli Lilly* and how it will implement the guidance provided in the CJEU's later decision *Teva UK v. Gilead Sciences* (C-121/17),[34] if and when this judgment of the Federal Patent Court is appealed.

[a] Small Molecules

The same considerations as set out in the EU chapter apply.

31. Munich District Court (Landgericht München I), judgment 7 O 11152/17 of 17 August 2017, particularly headnotes 2-4 and paragraphs 70–72, 78–85 and 100–122.
32. CJEU *Eli Lilly v. Human Genome Sciences*, C-493/12 of 12 December 2013.
33. German Federal Patent Court (Bundespatentgericht), judgment 4 Ni 12/17 of 15 May 2018.
34. CJEU *Teva UK v. Gilead Sciences*, C-121/17 of 25 July 2018.

With respect to basic patents claiming and identifying the active ingredient(s) in question via generic chemical formulae, the GPTO has generally taken a liberal approach and has, in practice, accepted the grant of SPCs even in the absence of an explicit and individualized disclosure of the chemical name or structure of the respective active ingredient(s). How such cases will be handled in the future, however, will largely depend on the CJEU's decision in the pending referral *Sandoz v. Searle* (C-114/18).

[b] Polymers

The same considerations as set out in the EU chapter apply.

[c] Antibodies, Enzymes and Other Proteins

The same considerations as set out in the EU chapter apply.

In various recent cases following the CJEU decision *Eli Lilly* (C-493/12),[35] the GPTO has accepted the grant of SPCs for specific therapeutic antibodies on the basis of patents claiming any antibody to the corresponding specific target, without disclosing the sequences of the complementarity-determining regions (CDRs), let alone the full sequence, of the individual antibody which was the subject of the respective SPC.

What level of detail a basic patent must provide in order to identify and thereby 'protect' a specific antibody has not yet been clarified in the German case law.

[d] Nucleic Acids

The same considerations as set out in the EU chapter apply.

[2] Basic Patent Claiming the Product, i.e., the Active Ingredient(s), but Not the Corresponding Authorized Medicinal Product (or Plant Protection Product)

The same considerations as set out in the EU chapter apply.

In the case law of the German Federal Supreme Court preceding the CJEU decision *Medeva* (C-322/10),[36] it was already established that a basic patent with claims directed to the same active ingredient(s) as specified in the SPC application and in the marketing authorization relied upon, but wherein the scope of protection of the patent does not embrace the approved medicinal product (e.g., due to differences in the required amounts of the active ingredients), fails to 'protect' the corresponding product

35. CJEU *Eli Lilly v. Human Genome Sciences*, C-493/12 of 12 December 2013.
36. CJEU *Medeva v. Comptroller General of Patents, Designs and Trade Marks*, C-322/10 of 24 November 2011.

of the SPC as required under Article 3(a) of the SPC Regulations.[37] This finding still holds true.

[3] Requirement for the Product to Constitute 'the Invention' of the Basic Patent

The German courts generally do not require that the product of an SPC must constitute 'the invention' or the 'core inventive advance' of the basic patent in order to be 'protected' by the basic patent in accordance with Article 3(a) of the SPC Regulations.

Thus, the German Federal Patent Court in *Hexavalenter Impfstoff* (14 W (pat) 10/16)[38] emphasized that even if the product of an SPC application does not embody the 'core inventive advance' of the basic patent, this is not a ground to reject the SPC application under Article 3(a) of the SPC Regulations. For the condition of Article 3(a) to be fulfilled, it is sufficient that the active ingredient(s) in question is/are identified in the basic patent. According to the Federal Patent Court, the CJEU decisions dealing with the 'core inventive advance' concept, i.e., *Actavis v. Sanofi* (C-443/12),[39] *Georgetown University* (C-484/12)[40] and *Actavis v. Boehringer Ingelheim Pharma* (C-577/13),[41] are primarily concerned with the condition of Article 3(c) of the SPC Regulations (precluding the grant of a further SPC if the same patent holder has already been granted an SPC for the same product; *see* §2.02[D][3][a] below) and do not impose any additional requirements under Article 3(a).

In *Sitagliptin III* (14 W (pat) 12/17)[42] the Federal Patent Court likewise found that the principles established by the CJEU in *Actavis v. Sanofi* and *Actavis v. Boehringer Ingelheim Pharma* with respect to the 'core inventive advance' concept primarily relate to Article 3(c) of the SPC Regulations and do not impose any further requirements relevant under Article 3(a). The question whether the product of an SPC constitutes an independent innovation can therefore become relevant only under Article 3(c), but not under Article 3(a).

[4] Criteria for Choosing the Basic Patent among Various Available Patents

The same considerations as set out in the EU chapter apply.

37. *See*, e.g., German Federal Supreme Court (Bundesgerichtshof), order X ZB 12/00 of 12 March 2002 – Custodiol I; and German Federal Patent Court (Bundespatentgericht), judgment 3 Ni 49/07 of 16 June 2009 – Piretanid / Ramipril.
38. German Federal Patent Court (Bundespatentgericht), order 14 W (pat) 10/16 of 23 January 2018 – Hexavalenter Impfstoff, particularly Sections II.4.3–II.4.4.3 of the reasons.
39. CJEU *Actavis v. Sanofi*, C-443/12 of 12 December 2013.
40. CJEU *Georgetown University v. Octrooicentrum Nederland*, C-484/12 of 12 December 2013.
41. CJEU *Actavis v. Boehringer Ingelheim Pharma*, C-577/13 of 12 March 2015.
42. German Federal Patent Court (Bundespatentgericht), order 14 W (pat) 12/17 of 17 October 2017 – Sitagliptin III, particularly Sections II.3.3 and II.8 of the reasons.

[C] The Marketing Authorization Forming Basis for an SPC

The considerations in relation to the marketing authorization forming basis for an SPC application as set out in the EU chapter, specifically in §1.02[C], apply equally to Germany.

Thus, in Germany, it is mandatory that at the filing date both the basic patent as well as the marketing authorization relied upon are in force.[43]

[1] Combinations of Active Ingredients

The same considerations as set out in the EU chapter apply.

[a] The Marketing Authorization Refers to Fewer Active Ingredients than the SPC Application

The same considerations as set out in the EU chapter apply.

[b] The Marketing Authorization Refers to More Active Ingredients than the SPC Application

The same considerations as set out in the EU chapter apply.

[c] The Marketing Authorization Indicates That a Medicinal Product Containing a Single Active Ingredient Is Authorized for Use in Combination with a Further Active Ingredient

The German Federal Supreme Court in its decision *Anti-Helicobacter-Präparat* (X ZB 1/08)[44] concluded that an SPC may not be granted on the basis of a 'loose combination of active ingredients', if the marketing authorization relied upon only concerns a single active ingredient, albeit to be used in combination with other active ingredients.

The decision, however, issued prior to the more recent guidance provided by the CJEU where the Court advocated a more teleological approach to interpreting the provisions of the SPC Regulation in order to ensure that all pharmaceutical research is encouraged and, as such, may benefit from SPC protection; *see*, e.g., *Medeva* (C-322/10)[45] and *Neurim* (C-130/11).[46]

In light of the far more differentiated approach adopted nowadays for the treatment of a disease based on a patient's need, and the recognition that a 'one fits all'

43. *See also* GPTO Examination Guidelines for SPCs, Sections 3.3.1.2 and 3.3.3.
44. German Federal Supreme Court (Bundesgerichtshof), order X ZB 1/08 of 8 July 2008 – Anti-Helicobacter-Präparat.
45. CJEU *Medeva v. Comptroller General of Patents, Designs and Trade Marks*, C-322/10 of 24 November 2011.
46. CJEU *Neurim Pharmaceuticals v. Comptroller-General of Patents*, C-130/11 of 19 July 2012.

solution in terms of therapeutic regimens is generally outdated, it would appear that the principles addressed in *Anti-Helicobacter-Präparat* should be revisited.

It is nowadays well recognized that applying a more differential approach in therapy is of paramount importance. Moreover, the development of such special 'personalized medicine' treatment approaches for individual patient groups is generally just as cost intensive and time consuming as the development of other innovative medicinal products. Denying SPC protection for such innovative therapeutic developments would run counter to the very purpose of the SPC regime. On a balance of interests, it would appear that there is no logical justification in denying such products additional supplemental protection.

As the CJEU by now has a track record of applying the SPC Regulation pragmatically, taking into account innovation not envisaged at the time of the initial introduction of the SPC regime, it is conceivable that the earlier case law of the Federal Supreme Court will be overruled, in light of the therapeutic advances made and the need to protect innovation also in the upcoming field of personalized medicine.

[2] The Marketing Authorization Has Not Yet Been Granted at the Time the SPC Application Is Filed

The same considerations as set out in the EU chapter apply.

[3] The Holder of the Marketing Authorization

According to the standing practice of the GPTO, it is unproblematic to file an SPC on the basis of an unrelated third-party marketing authorization.

In the *Ranibizumab* decision (4a O 143/10),[47] the Düsseldorf District Court confirmed that while the purpose of the SPC legislation is to compensate for the delay caused by the requirement to undergo a marketing authorization procedure and the consequential curtailment of the effective patent term, this does not imply that the patent owner is prevented from enforcing an SPC against the holder of the marketing authorization. In this regard, the District Court expressly rejected the corresponding defence put forward by the holder of the marketing authorization and emphasized that (in English translation):[48]

> Insofar as the defendants assert that the plaintiff could not claim injunctive relief for the unlawful use of the subject matter [of the SPC] because the plaintiff, as patent holder, seeks to prohibit the defendant from marketing precisely that medicinal product which is the subject of the marketing authorization that forms the basis of the granted SPC, this does not justify any different assessment. The defendants rightly point out that the introduction of the supplementary protection certificate should make allowance for the fact that administrative regulatory approval procedures which precede the authorization of a substance or procedure

47. Düsseldorf District Court (Landgericht Düsseldorf), judgment 4a O 143/10 of 10 November 2011 – Ranibizumab.
48. *Ibid.*, Section IV of the reasons.

> for marketing, can lead to a curtailment of the effective term of a patent granted for the corresponding product (cf. Benkard, Patentgesetz, 10th edition, § 16a, paragraph 6). However, this does not mean that the holder of the basic patent could not take action, on the basis of the SPC, against the holder of the marketing authorization for the medicinal product. Rather, it may be that the ownership of the SPC does not coincide with that of the marketing authorization. It is therefore possible that the holder of the SPC – as in the present case – can prevent the holder of the marketing authorization, who is different from the SPC holder, from using the SPC (cf. CJEU *Biogen* (C-181/95); Benkard/Grabinski, Patentgesetz, 10th edition, § 16a, paragraph 40).

As a consequence, the holder of a third-party SPC can prohibit the economic use of the subject matter of the SPC by the holder of the marketing authorization.

Such a liberal interpretation of the SPC Regulation would appear to run counter to the very aims of the Regulation, namely to foster the development and marketing of innovative medicinal products, rather than to be used as a tool for competitors to prevent entry to market of an innovative product, particularly if the holder of the SPC based on a third-party marketing approval has not contributed to the research and development of the actual approved product.

In *Ranibizumab*, the case was not heard on appeal, as the Federal Patent Court[49] in the meantime revoked the third-party SPC in question because it was in violation of Article 3(a) of the SPC Regulation for Medicinal Products.

It would appear that in light of the guidance provided by the CJEU in *Eli Lilly* (C-493/12),[50] the GPTO now tends to adopt a more differentiated approach when assessing SPCs based on a third-party marketing authorization. For example, in the *Lipegfilgrastim* case[51] the GPTO rejected an SPC based on a third-party marketing authorization, as the basic patent did not individually disclose the product for which the SPC application was made. The patent office, relying on the guidance provided by the CJEU in *Eli Lilly*, concluded that the issue of an SPC to a third-party patentee who has not identified the active ingredient beyond the general disclosure in the patent, and

49. German Federal Patent Court (Bundespatentgericht), judgment 3 Ni 28/11 of 2 May 2012 – Ranibizumab.
50. CJEU *Eli Lilly v. Human Genome Sciences*, C-493/12 of 12 December 2013, paragraph 43.
51. GPTO, decision of rejection dated 24 April 2014 regarding the SPC application No. 12 2013 000 071.6 – Lipegfilgrastim (accessible online via file inspection of the GTPO register). The corresponding passage of the decision of rejection reads as follows (in English translation):

> The applicant may indeed – as she put forward – have laid the foundations for the approved product. However, the disclosure in the basic patent was not sufficient to make available the actual product. This required further research efforts. To grant a certificate to the patentee, who is not the holder of the marketing authorization for the product lipegfilgrastim, even though the patentee did not promote specifications going beyond the basic patent and therefore did not make any further research investments, would mean to disregard the purpose set out in recital 4 of the SPC Regulation for Medicinal Products (cf. 'Eli Lilly', in particular paragraph 43). The basic objective of the SPC Regulation for Medicinal Products consists in providing a compensation of time for the laborious trials and lengthy authorization procedures that are necessary before the marketing of the medicinal product, and thus creating an incentive for further research and development.

as such has not invested any further research in the development of the product, would be contrary to the objectives of the SPC Regulation.

[4] Reliance on a Marketing Authorization Granted under a Provision Other than Directive 2001/83/EC or Directive 2001/82/EC

The same considerations as set out in the EU chapter apply.

[5] The Marketing Authorizations Which Can Be Relied upon for SPC Applications for Plant Protection Products

The same considerations as set out in the EU chapter apply.

[6] The Product in Question Is Contained in the Authorized Medicinal Product (or the Authorized Plant Protection Product) but Is Not Identified as an Active Ingredient in the Corresponding Marketing Authorization

The same considerations as set out in the EU chapter apply.

[7] The Notion of the 'First' Marketing Authorization

In principle, the same considerations as set out in the EU chapter apply.

[a] *Marketing Authorization for a New Therapeutic Application of a Previously Authorized Product*

In light of the guidance provided by the CJEU in *Neurim* (C-130/11),[52] the GPTO generally also issues SPCs on the basis of a marketing authorization for a new therapeutic application of a previously authorized product. This is also expressly addressed in the Examination Guidelines for SPCs issued by the GTPO.[53]

This issue is unproblematic if the marketing authorization relied upon is a 'stand alone approval', as has been the case in *Neurim*.

To date, it is, however, unresolved whether an SPC in Germany may also be based on a type II variation or extension of an existing marketing authorization.

As discussed in the EU chapter, in most instances the marketing authorization for a new therapeutic application of a previously authorized product will be a type II variation or extension, as the research and development is based on the originator product.

52. CJEU *Neurim Pharmaceuticals v. Comptroller-General of Patents*, C-130/11 of 19 July 2012.
53. GPTO Examination Guidelines for SPCs, Section 3.3.1.3.

This per se should not negate the valuable contribution made by the development of the new therapeutic application, and as such should not be decisive for the eligibility for SPC protection of new therapeutic applications of previously authorized products.

There are cases pending before the GPTO where such issues are of primary concern. As such, it is likely that this matter will be resolved or referred to the CJEU for further clarification.

[b] Marketing Authorization for a New Formulation of a Previously Authorized Product

The same considerations as set out in the EU chapter apply.

[c] Marketing Authorization for a New Specific Salt, Ester or Other Derivative of a Previously Authorized Active Ingredient

As set out by the German Federal Supreme Court in *Sumatriptan* (X ZB 12/01),[54] it follows from the guidance provided in the CJEU decision *Farmitalia* (C-392/97)[55] that an SPC is granted for the active moiety of the approved substance. As such, an SPC protects the active moiety, including other salts and other derivatives within the framework of the basic patent.

As a consequence, the sole reliance on a patent for a new salt or other derivative of a previously approved active moiety is not sufficient to warrant the issue of an SPC for this specific form of the previously authorized active ingredient. The German courts on various accounts have had to consider whether a new salt, ester or other derivative of a previously authorized product may form the basis of an SPC.

Thus, in *Doxorubicin-Sulfat* (X ZB 4/08 and X ZB 5/08)[56] the Federal Supreme Court found that the specific salt for which an SPC was requested, i.e., doxorubicin sulfate, was not a different active ingredient than the previously authorized salt of the corresponding compound, i.e., doxorubicin hydrochloride, because the therapeutic effects mediated by these two salts were based on the activity of the free base and were thus considered to be identical. The Court reached this conclusion even though it acknowledged that doxorubicin sulfate has an improved pharmacological efficacy, reduced toxic effects and different pharmacokinetic properties as compared to the previously authorized doxorubicin hydrochloride. Nevertheless, the Federal Supreme Court considered it decisive in this context that the therapeutic effects of both salts were provided by doxorubicin (the free base), as also pointed out in its subsequent decision *Escitalopram* (Xa ZR 130/07).[57]

---

54. German Federal Supreme Court (Bundesgerichtshof), order X ZB 12/01 of 29 January 2002 – Sumatriptan.
55. CJEU *Farmitalia Carlo Erba v. Bundesgerichtshof*, C-392/97 of 16 September 1999.
56. German Federal Supreme Court (Bundesgerichtshof), order X ZB 4/08 of 14 October 2008 – Doxorubicin-Sulfat; and German Federal Supreme Court (Bundesgerichtshof), order X ZB 5/08 of 14 October 2008. *See*, in particular, paragraphs 11–13 of X ZB 4/08 and paragraphs 13–15 of X ZB 5/08.
57. German Federal Supreme Court (Bundesgerichtshof), judgment Xa ZR 130/07 of 10 September 2009 – Escitalopram, paragraph 77.

A similarly restrictive position was also taken by the German Federal Patent Court in *Triptorelin* (14 W (pat) 9/06),[58] where the Court found that the product of the SPC application at issue, i.e., the pamoate salt of triptorelin, was not a different active ingredient than the previously authorized acetate salt of triptorelin, in spite of the applicant's arguments that the characteristics of the two salts differ and that the pamoate salt provides for a delayed release. The earlier approval of the corresponding medicinal product containing triptorelin acetate, not the later approval of triptorelin pamoate, was consequently regarded as the 'first' marketing authorization within the meaning of Article 3(d).

The relevance of recital 14 of the SPC Regulation for Plant Protection Products, which via recital 17 is also applicable to the SPC Regulation for Medicinal Products, was brushed aside by the Federal Patent Court in *Triptorelin* with the assertion that this recital would have to be taken into account at most in the context of Article 3(c) of the SPC Regulations but not with respect to the requirement of Article 3(d). This narrow appraisal of recital 14 would appear rather questionable, not least in view of the scant reasoning that the Court provided in this regard.

Remarkably, however, the Federal Patent Court in the subsequent decision *Paliperidonpalmitat* (14 W (pat) 25/16)[59] concluded that paliperidone palmitate, the palmitate ester of paliperidone, should be classified as a new product for which an SPC can be granted, even though it was established that the ester is hydrolyzed in vivo and mediates its therapeutic effect by the free base, paliperidone, for which an earlier marketing authorization and an earlier SPC had already been granted.

The Court substantiated its position on the basis of Article 10(2)(b) of Directive 2001/83/EC, according to which an active ingredient and its derivatives are to be considered as the same active ingredient, unless their properties differ significantly with regard to safety and/or efficacy. As the pharmacokinetic differences between paliperidone and paliperidone palmitate were considered to be substantial, they were regarded as different products and the SPC was allowed to issue.

Arguably, these 'significant differences' between paliperidone and its ester paliperidone palmitate invoked by the Federal Patent Court would appear quite comparable to the differences between the two doxorubicin salts, which the Federal Supreme Court disregarded in the above-discussed decision *Doxorubicin-Sulfat*. According to the Federal Patent Court, however, the Federal Supreme Court in *Doxorubicin-Sulfat* could not take into account the later-issued CJEU decision *Forsgren*, in which the relevance of significant differences between the pharmacological, immunological and metabolic effects of different products were highlighted. Therefore, the Federal Patent Court did not consider *Doxorubicin-Sulfat* to stand in conflict with its own reasoning in *Paliperidonpalmitat*.[60]

58. German Federal Patent Court (Bundespatentgericht), order 14 W (pat) 9/06 of 27 November 2008 – Triptorelin.
59. German Federal Patent Court (Bundespatentgericht), order 14 W (pat) 25/16 of 5 September 2017 – Paliperidonpalmitat.
60. *Ibid.*, Section II.7 of the reasons.

The more liberal approach taken by the Federal Patent Court in *Paliperidonpalmitat* appears to do justice to the European legislator's intention expressed in recital 14 of the SPC Regulation for Plant Protection Products, which via recital 17 is also applicable to the SPC Regulation for Medicinal Products and stipulates that the issuance of an SPC for an active ingredient should not preclude the grant of new SPCs for derivatives (salts and esters) of that active ingredient, provided that the derivatives are subject of patents specifically covering them. It remains to be seen whether this approach will be sanctioned by the German Federal Supreme Court (or the CJEU) and where exactly the line should be drawn between significant and insignificant differences in the pharmacological, immunological or metabolic effects of an active ingredient and its derivatives.

A further factor to be considered in this connection is the German Federal Supreme Court's interpretation of recital 14 of the SPC Regulation for Plant Protection Products, as expressed in its decision *Escitalopram*. In this decision, the Court held that recital 14 establishes an exception to the rule that the same product should not become the subject of several successive SPCs, and that this exception requires that a new derivative of a previously authorized active ingredient must be protected by a *product patent*, i.e., a basic patent having *product claims* directed to the respective derivative.[61]

It is not easily comprehensible why such a far-reaching limitation should necessarily follow from recital 14, nor why it should be justified. Derivatives as referred to in recital 14 could well be 'the subject of patents specifically covering them' in the form of second medical use claims. Moreover, in cases where a specific derivative exhibits significantly different pharmacological effects in the treatment of a certain disease, it would seem fitting to draft a patent with second medical use claims focusing on the corresponding treatment.

Nevertheless, in view of the Federal Supreme Court's position taken in *Escitalopram*, it might be safest to rely on a basic patent having product claims directed to a specific derivative of a previously authorized active ingredient when filing a corresponding new SPC application.

[d] Marketing Authorization for a New Specific Enantiomer of an Active Ingredient Previously Authorized in Racemic Form

The German Federal Supreme Court acknowledged in *Escitalopram* (Xa ZR 130/07)[62] that an earlier marketing authorization for an active ingredient in racemic form does not preclude the grant of a new SPC for a specific enantiomer of the corresponding active ingredient on the basis of a later marketing authorization and a basic patent directed to this specific enantiomer. The Court considered that the specific enantiomer in question was a different product from the racemate, where both enantiomers were

61. German Federal Supreme Court (Bundesgerichtshof), judgment Xa ZR 130/07 of 10 September 2009 – Escitalopram, paragraph 76.
62. German Federal Supreme Court (Bundesgerichtshof), judgment Xa ZR 130/07 of 10 September 2009 – Escitalopram, headnote (d).

active, and as such could potentially be considered to be a combination of active ingredients. *See also* the discussion of this decision in §2.02[D][3][c] below.

The later Federal Patent Court decision *Escitalopram II* (3 Ni 22/10)[63] was concerned with another nullity action filed against the same SPC as in the above-mentioned Federal Supreme Court decision. Notably, the Federal Patent Court found that the evidence filed by the nullity plaintiff did not establish beyond reasonable doubt that the enantiomer escitalopram, which was the subject of the attacked SPC, and the previously approved racemate citalopram would have the same therapeutic effects and should therefore be regarded as the same active ingredient within the meaning of the SPC Regulation. The plaintiff's objection under Article 3(d) was consequently rejected.

In the earlier decision *Fusilade* (15 W (pat) 26/98),[64] the Federal Patent Court rejected an SPC application for the (R)-enantiomer of the plant protection agent Fluazifop-P butyl ester in view of an earlier approval of the racemic form of this active substance. This ruling, however, should be of no particular relevance in view of the later-rendered Federal Supreme Court decision *Escitalopram*, and the circumstances of this case, including that the (R)-enantiomer at issue was not specifically claimed in the basic patent.

[e] The Product Has Already Been Placed on the Market Before, but Without an Authorization Granted under Directive 2001/83/EC or Directive 2001/82/EC

The same considerations as set out in the EU chapter apply.

[f] Prior Marketing Authorization Which Refers to Fewer Active Ingredients than the SPC Application (and the Later Marketing Authorization Relied upon)

The same considerations as set out in the EU chapter apply.

[g] Prior Marketing Authorization Which Refers to More Active Ingredients than the SPC Application (and the Later Marketing Authorization Relied upon)

In principle, in accordance with the findings of the CJEU in *Medeva* (C-322/10) and *Georgetown* (C-422/10),[65] the first marketing authorization for the product of an SPC should be the earliest approval of any medicinal product (or plant protection product) comprising, among its active ingredients, the active ingredient(s) referred to in the

63. German Federal Patent Court (Bundespatentgericht), judgment 3 Ni 22/10 of 29 March 2011 – Escitalopram II.
64. German Federal Patent Court (Bundespatentgericht), order 15 W (pat) 26/98 of 27 March 2000 – Fusilade.
65. CJEU *Medeva v. Comptroller General of Patents, Designs and Trade Marks*, C-322/10 of 24 November 2011, paragraph 40 and headnote 2; CJEU *Georgetown University v. Comptroller General of Patents, Designs and Trade Marks*, C-422/10 of 24 November 2011, paragraph 33 and headnote.

SPC, even if the corresponding authorized product contains additional active ingredients which are not included in the product definition of the SPC.

As a rule, the grant of an SPC should therefore be precluded under Article 3(d) of the SPC Regulations if the marketing authorization relied upon was not the first marketing authorization in the respective Member State for a medicinal (or plant protection) product comprising, among its active ingredients, the active ingredient(s) which is/are subject of the SPC application.

Yet, the Düsseldorf District Court deviated from this principle in its *Desogestrel* decisions (4b O 123/12 and 4b O 139/12),[66] both of which were rendered in preliminary injunction proceedings involving the same SPC for a single active ingredient A. The SPC was based on a patent claiming a contraceptive kit comprising desogestrel (active ingredient A) 'as the sole contraceptively effective ingredient', and a corresponding marketing authorization for A alone. Remarkably, the District Court acknowledged the validity of the SPC in spite of the existence of an earlier marketing authorization in the same Member State (Germany) for a combination of the active ingredients A + B. The Court's conclusion was based on the reasoning that the SPC Regulation differentiates between a single active ingredient and a combination of active ingredients as distinct products, so that the earlier approval of A + B was not relevant under Article 3(d) because it did not relate to the same product as the SPC (and the corresponding later marketing authorization) for A alone.

While this finding would appear difficult to reconcile with the CJEU's approach in *Medeva* and *Georgetown*, the Düsseldorf District Court in *Desogestrel* stressed that these CJEU decisions were not concerned with the same constellation as the case at hand, where the basic patent and the marketing authorization relied upon were directed to the single active ingredient A as the sole contraceptively effective agent. According to the District Court, *Medeva* and *Georgetown* would therefore not be in conflict with its conclusion that the earlier marketing authorization for A + B did not relate to the same product as the SPC for A alone.

The District Court's reliance on the differentiation made in the SPC Regulation between single active ingredients and combinations of active ingredients as distinct products would not, by itself, appear to convincingly justify a departure from the principles established by the CJEU in *Medeva* and *Georgetown*. Interestingly, however, the District Court's finding shows striking parallels to the CJEU's approach in *Neurim* (C-130/11),[67] given that the basic patent underlying the SPC in *Desogestrel* was directed to the single active ingredient A 'as the *sole* contraceptively effective ingredient' and should therefore not embrace the product of the earlier marketing authorization for the two contraceptively effective ingredients A + B. In its reasoning, the Düsseldorf District Court made no reference to *Neurim* which had just been delivered a few months before, so that it remains opaque whether the District Court might have taken account of the CJEU's approach in *Neurim*.

66. Düsseldorf District Court (Landgericht Düsseldorf), judgment 4b O 123/12 of 15 November 2012 – Desogestrel; and Düsseldorf District Court (Landgericht Düsseldorf), judgment 4b O 139/12 of 15 November 2012 – Desogestrel.
67. CJEU *Neurim Pharmaceuticals v. Comptroller-General of Patents*, C-130/11 of 19 July 2012.

Alas, the District Court's appreciation of *Medeva* and *Georgetown* as well as the question regarding the applicability of *Neurim* in this specific case have not been further elucidated. The defendant in *Desogestrel* filed a nullity action against the SPC with the Federal Patent Court, arguing that the SPC should be invalidated for lack of compliance with Article 3(d) in view of the earlier marketing authorization in Germany for the active ingredients A + B, and also because grounds existed that would have justified the revocation of the basic patent for lack of inventive step. The Federal Patent Court revoked the SPC with its decision *Desogestrel* (3 Ni 21/12),[68] but merely on the grounds that the basic patent was invalid due to a lack of inventive step, and without deciding on the objection under Article 3(d).

The scope of application of *Neurim* is a matter of ongoing debate, including the question whether the CJEU's approach in this decision should be limited to new therapeutic uses of a previously approved active ingredient, or whether it should also be applicable to other constellations, such as the case underlying *Desogestrel*.

Clearly, however, if the innovation provided by the basic patent underlying an SPC is based on the use of a specific active ingredient or combination of active ingredients for a new therapeutic application, in accordance with *Neurim* the prior authorization comprising more active ingredients should not be detrimental to the SPC filing.

[D] Preclusion of New SPCs by an Earlier SPC

The same considerations as set out in the EU chapter apply.

[1] Consequences of an Earlier Third-Party SPC for the Same Product

[a] The 'One SPC per Product per Patent Holder' Rule

The same considerations as set out in the EU chapter apply.

[b] Earlier SPC Granted to an Affiliated Third Party

The same considerations as set out in the EU chapter apply. The German courts have not yet clarified what relevance an earlier granted SPC might have for a new SPC application filed for the same product by a legally distinct but affiliated patent holder.

Some authority is, however, attributed to the explanations provided in an academic article by Dr Thomas Kühnen[69] who is presiding judge of one of the two patent senates at the Düsseldorf Higher Regional Court and is among the most

68. German Federal Patent Court (Bundespatentgericht), judgment 3 Ni 21/12 of 6 May 2014 – Desogestrel.
69. Thomas Kühnen: Die Erteilung mehrerer ergänzender Schutzzertifikate für dasselbe Erzeugnis an unterschiedliche Inhaber und die Konsequenzen bei einer Verfolgung von Rechtsverletzungen. Published in: Bender, Schülke, Winterfeldt (eds): Festschrift 50 Jahre Bundespatentgericht, Carl Heymanns Verlag, 2011, ISBN: 9783452275264, pages 361–378.

renowned patent judges in Germany. According to Kühnen, an earlier granted SPC does not preclude the grant of a new SPC for the same product to a distinct legal entity, even where both of the respective entities belong to the same parent company or where one of these entities holds some or even all shares and interest in the other.

Yet, Kühnen also advocates that distinct legal entities should nevertheless be regarded as the 'same' entity for the purpose of Article 3(c) of the SPC Regulations in the case of abusive behaviour, particularly if one of the entities has been established for the sole purpose of filing the corresponding SPC and does not conduct any other business activities, and also if one of the distinct legal entities acts as a 'straw man' on behalf of the other. This distinction between justified and abusive SPC filings by distinct but affiliated legal entities seems impractical and highly problematic, particularly when considering that, in practice, the filing of multiple SPCs for the same product by affiliated entities will hardly ever occur without any knowledge or coordination between the respective entities. It would also seem questionable whether the exploitation of a well-known legal loophole in the SPC Regulations that has not been closed by the European legislator despite existing for over twenty years can be regarded as abusive.

In practice, the GPTO typically accepts patent holders who are distinct legal entities as different rights holders, regardless of any potential affiliation. What is decisive in this regard is the formally registered patent holder (Section 30(3) second sentence PatG).

[c] Partial Overlap Between the Holders of the Earlier SPC and the Applicants for the New SPC

The same considerations as set out in the EU chapter apply. It appears that this issue has not yet been specifically addressed in the German case law.

[d] Earlier Third-Party SPC Has Been Licensed-In

The same considerations as set out in the EU chapter apply.

It should be noted in this regard that, as a rule, a licence in a patent will automatically extend to any SPC granted on the basis of that patent under Section 16a(3) PatG, unless the corresponding licence agreement provides otherwise.

[2] Consequences of an Own Earlier SPC for the Same Product

The same considerations as set out in the EU chapter apply.

[a] Own Earlier SPC Application Not Yet Granted

The same considerations as set out in the EU chapter apply.

[b] Revocation, Surrender or Lapse of the Own Earlier SPC after Grant

The same considerations as set out in the EU chapter apply, including with respect to the lapse or surrender of an SPC with ex nunc effect (i.e., without retroactive effect).

Remarkably, the German Federal Patent Court has accepted that the revocation of an SPC with retroactive effect (ex tunc) can indeed remove the obstacle that such an SPC poses under Article 3(c) and 3(2) of the SPC Regulations to the grant of a new SPC for the same product to the same rights holder.

Thus, in the case underlying the Federal Patent Court decision *Clothianidin III* (15 W (pat) 51/05),[70] the SPC applicant had already been granted an earlier SPC for the same product on the basis of the same patent but relying on an emergency marketing authorization for the corresponding plant protection product. The earlier SPC was revoked in nullity proceedings about 4.5 years after it entered into force.[71] Following the revocation of the earlier SPC, the Federal Patent Court in *Clothianidin III* accepted the grant of a new SPC for the same product to the same rights holder (on the basis of the same patent but a new provisional marketing authorization), explaining that the earlier SPC has been revoked with retroactive effect and does therefore no longer preclude the grant of the new SPC under Article 3(1)(c) of the SPC Regulation for Plant Protection Products.

The feasibility of filing a new SPC after the revocation of an earlier SPC for the same product has also been acknowledged in an obiter dictum of the Federal Patent Court in *Iodosulfuron* (3 Ni 16/08).[72] In this decision, the Court referred a question to the CJEU, asking whether an SPC can be based on a provisional marketing authorization for a plant protection product, and in this context noted that even the revocation of the attacked SPC might not constitute a final loss of rights for the SPC holder. This is because, according to the Federal Patent Court, the revocation of the SPC with retroactive effect would enable the SPC holder under Article 3(1)(c) of the SPC Regulation for Plant Protection Products to file a new SPC application (for the same product) relying on its definitive marketing authorization. Since, after the CJEU's ruling in *Hogan Lovells* (C-229/09),[73] the attacked SPC was maintained by the Federal Patent Court,[74] the option of filing a new SPC under such conditions remained hypothetical in this case.

The possibility for an SPC holder to have its own SPC revoked with retroactive effect was further elucidated by the Federal Patent Court in *Trifloxystrobin* (15 W (pat) 22/14).[75] In this decision, the Court confirmed that the invalidation of an SPC can also

70. German Federal Patent Court (Bundespatentgericht), order 15 W (pat) 51/05 of 2 October 2014 - Clothianidin III.
71. German Federal Patent Court (Bundespatentgericht), judgment 3 Ni 60/06 of 24 June 2014 - Clothianidin II.
72. German Federal Patent Court (Bundespatentgericht), order 3 Ni 16/08 of 28 April 2009 - Iodosulfuron, paragraph 47.
73. CJEU *Hogan Lovells International v. Bayer CropScience*, C-229/09 of 11 November 2010.
74. German Federal Patent Court (Bundespatentgericht), judgment 3 Ni 16/08 of 20 March 2012 - Iodosulfuron II.
75. German Federal Patent Court (Bundespatentgericht), order 15 W (pat) 22/14 of 7 December 2016 - Trifloxystrobin.

by requested by the SPC holder himself, given that Article 15(2) of the SPC Regulations allows 'any person' to file an invalidation action or request, which the Court understood to also include the rights holder. The Federal Patent Court concluded that, in analogy to Section 64 PatG, an SPC can be revoked with retroactive effect at the request of its holder in administrative ex parte proceedings before the GPTO. It is also noteworthy that, in this case, the SPC had already expired when it was retroactively revoked.

It should be noted, however, that the Federal Patent Court in *Trifloxystrobin* left it open whether an SPC can under all circumstances be revoked at the request of its holder, or whether this may be possible only if an actual ground of invalidity of the SPC has been established. In the specific case underlying this decision, the SPC was based on an emergency marketing authorization for a plant protection product and was therefore clearly invalid in view of the CJEU decision *Sumitomo Chemical* (C-210/12).[76]

Yet, it would appear that an actual ground of invalidity of an SPC could easily be brought about, for example, by having the basic patent underlying the SPC revoked with retroactive effect at the request of its holder. To this end, the centralized revocation procedure under Articles 105a and 105b EPC before the EPO (as discussed in the EU chapter) and/or the corresponding German revocation procedure under Section 64 PatG before the GPTO could be used, depending on whether the basic patent is a European patent or a national German patent. Notably, a request for the revocation of a patent under Section 64 PatG must be reasoned,[77] and the patentee may have to justify a legitimate interest in the revocation, particularly if the request is filed after the expiry of the patent. In the corresponding European procedure, in contrast, the patentee does not need to provide any reasoning or justification for its request to have its own European patent revoked with retroactive effect, even after the expiry of the patent.[78]

The German courts have not yet provided any guidance whether it might be possible to 'rescue' an SPC that was granted in violation of the requirements of Article 3(c) and 3(2) of the SPC Regulations, i.e., in spite of the existence of an earlier SPC granted for the same product to the same rights holder, by having the earlier SPC revoked with retroactive effect. In light of the guidance provided by the Federal Patent Court in *Clothianidin III*, *Iodosulfuron* and *Trifloxystrobin*, however, it would appear that this could indeed be a viable approach, at least under the current German practice and case law.

[c] Transfer of the Own Earlier SPC to a Third Party

The same considerations as set out in the EU chapter apply.

76. CJEU *Sumitomo Chemical v. Deutsches Patent- und Markenamt*, C-210/12 of 17 October 2013.
77. Section 64(2) PatG.
78. *See* Guidelines for Examination in the European Patent Office, edition of November 2017, Section D-X, 1-3.

[d] *Acquisition of an SPC Granted to a Third Party*

The same considerations as set out in the EU chapter apply.

[3] *Consequences of an Own Earlier SPC for a Different Product*

The same considerations as set out in the EU chapter apply.

[a] *Required Distinction from the Product of the Own Earlier SPC*

In general, the same considerations as set out in the EU chapter apply.

Combinations of Active Ingredients

The German jurisprudence applies the 'core inventive advance' requirement endorsed by the CJEU in *Actavis v. Sanofi* (C-443/12),[79] *Georgetown University v. Octrooicentrum Nederland* (C-484/12)[80] and *Actavis v. Boehringer Ingelheim Pharma* (C-577/13)[81] when assessing the preclusion of a new SPC by a previous SPC granted to the same patent holder under Article 3(c) of the SPC Regulations, specifically in the context of SPCs for combinations of active ingredients.

In particular, the German Federal Patent Court in *Hexavalenter Impfstoff* (14 W (pat) 10/16)[82] extracted the following basic principle from the above-mentioned CJEU case law dealing with the 'core inventive advance' requirement: The grant of a new SPC can be precluded under Article 3(c) of the SPC Regulations in view of an earlier SPC granted on the basis of the *same patent*, even where the respective products are different, if the product of the new SPC is not an *independent innovation* as compared to the product of the earlier SPC. Importantly, according to the Federal Patent Court, this principle applies only to this specific case constellation and cannot be transferred to other cases, such as the one before the Court where the SPC application at issue was directed to a combination of active ingredients which was protected by a *distinct basic patent* and was regarded as an *independent innovation*.

An exemplary decision of the Federal Patent Court, in which the grant of a new SPC for a combination product was found to be precluded by an earlier SPC for a single active ingredient, is *Telmisartan II* (3 Ni 5/13).[83] In this decision, the Court ruled that the grant of a new SPC for the combination of active ingredients A + B is precluded

79. CJEU *Actavis v. Sanofi*, C-443/12 of 12 December 2013.
80. CJEU *Georgetown University v. Octrooicentrum Nederland*, C-484/12 of 12 December 2013.
81. CJEU *Actavis v. Boehringer Ingelheim Pharma*, C-577/13 of 12 March 2015.
82. German Federal Patent Court (Bundespatentgericht), order 14 W (pat) 10/16 of 23 January 2018 – Hexavalenter Impfstoff, Section II.5.2 of the reasons.
83. German Federal Patent Court (Bundespatentgericht), judgment 3 Ni 5/13 of 4 February 2014 – Telmisartan II, headnote 1 and Section II.1 of the reasons. It is also noteworthy that the Federal Patent Court did not consider it necessary to stay the proceedings and await the CJEU's decision in *Actavis v. Boehringer Ingelheim Pharma* (C-577/13), even though the corresponding referral involved the parallel SPC in the UK, which was based on the same European patent as the German SPC application at issue in the Federal Patent Court's judgment.

under Article 3(c) by an earlier SPC granted for the single active ingredient A on the basis of the same patent, if the active ingredient A alone embodies the invention of the basic patent (whereas B is a previously known active ingredient) and if the scope of protection conferred by the earlier SPC already encompassed the combination of active ingredients A + B. In arriving at this conclusion, the Federal Patent Court emphasized that the combination of active ingredients A + B was not shown, or even argued, to have any surprising effect as compared to that of the individual active ingredients, and did therefore not consider this combination of active ingredients to have an independent inventive quality.

New Therapeutic Applications of Previously Approved Active Ingredients

In view of the CJEU's ruling in *Neurim* (C-130/11),[84] the GPTO generally accepts the grant of a new SPC on the basis of a patent specifically claiming a new therapeutic indication of a previously approved active ingredient and a corresponding separate marketing authorization for the new therapeutic application, even where the same patent holder has already obtained an SPC for the same product but on the basis of a different patent and a marketing authorization for a different therapeutic indication.

The grant of a further SPC for a new formulation of a previously approved active ingredient which has already been the subject of an earlier SPC has also been accepted at least in certain cases, but the future practice of the GPTO in this regard can be expected to depend on the decision of the CJEU in the pending referral *Abraxis Bioscience* (C-443/17).

[b] SPCs for a Specific Salt, Ester or Other Derivative Where an Own Earlier SPC Has Already Been Granted for the Corresponding Active Ingredient

The German Federal Supreme Court in *Doxorubicin-Sulfat* (X ZB 4/08 and X ZB 5/08)[85] took a restrictive approach to the question under which circumstances an SPC can be granted for a new specific derivative, particularly a new salt, of a previously authorized active ingredient. While this decision dealt with the requirement of Article 3(d), the same considerations should likewise apply to the requirement under Article 3(c) of the SPC Regulations that the product in question has not already been the subject of an SPC in the respective Member State.

Thus, the Federal Supreme Court in *Doxorubicin-Sulfat* found that the specific salt for which an SPC was requested, i.e., doxorubicin sulfate, was not a different active ingredient than the previously authorized salt of the corresponding compound, i.e., doxorubicin hydrochloride, because in both cases it is doxorubicin (the free base) which provides the therapeutic effects. The two salts, i.e., doxorubicin sulfate and

84. CJEU *Neurim Pharmaceuticals v. Comptroller-General of Patents*, C-130/11 of 19 July 2012.
85. German Federal Supreme Court (Bundesgerichtshof), order X ZB 4/08 of 14 October 2008 – Doxorubicin-Sulfat; and German Federal Supreme Court (Bundesgerichtshof), order X ZB 5/08 of 14 October 2008. *See*, in particular, paragraphs 11–13 of X ZB 4/08 and paragraphs 13–15 of X ZB 5/08.

doxorubicin hydrochloride, were thus regarded as having the same therapeutic effects and, consequently, as constituting the same active ingredient. The Court reached this conclusion even though it acknowledged that doxorubicin sulfate has an improved pharmacological efficacy, reduced toxic effects and different pharmacokinetic properties as compared to the previously authorized doxorubicin hydrochloride. Nevertheless, the Federal Supreme Court considered it decisive in this context that the therapeutic effects of both salts were provided by doxorubicin, as also pointed out in its subsequent decision *Escitalopram* (Xa ZR 130/07).[86]

A similarly restrictive position, again in the context of Article 3(d), was also taken by the German Federal Patent Court in *Triptorelin* (14 W (pat) 9/06).[87] In this decision the Court found that the product of the SPC application at issue, i.e., the pamoate salt of triptorelin, was not a different active ingredient than the previously authorized acetate salt of triptorelin (*see* §2.02[C][7][c] above).

Remarkably, however, the Federal Patent Court in the later case *Paliperidonpalmitat* (14 W (pat) 25/16)[88] accepted the grant of a new SPC for paliperidone palmitate, a specific ester prodrug of paliperidone, on the basis of a patent specifically identifying and claiming this ester and a corresponding marketing authorization, even though an earlier marketing authorization and an earlier SPC had already been granted for paliperidone.

The Federal Patent Court noted in this decision that the new SPC for the ester paliperidone palmitate can be granted under Article 3(c) and 3(d) of the SPC Regulation for Medicinal Products only if paliperidone palmitate and the previously authorized paliperidone are *different products*. For the interpretation of the term 'product' in the SPC Regulation for Medicinal Products, the Court resorted to regulatory pharmaceutical law, specifically to Article 10(2)(b) of Directive 2001/83/EC (providing a definition of the term 'generic medicinal product'), according to which an active ingredient and its derivatives are to be considered as the same active ingredient, unless their properties differ significantly with regard to safety and/or efficacy. Therefore, and in view of the CJEU decision *Forsgren* (C-631/13),[89] for the question whether an active ingredient and its derivatives constitute different products in the sense of the SPC Regulation, the Federal Patent Court considered it decisive whether the properties of the respective substances differ to an extent that results in *different pharmacological, immunological or metabolic effects*.[90]

In the specific case at hand, the Federal Patent Court found that paliperidone and paliperidone palmitate act differently within the human body, particularly due to the specific extended release profile of paliperidone palmitate, which results in a different

86. German Federal Supreme Court (Bundesgerichtshof), judgment Xa ZR 130/07 of 10 September 2009 – Escitalopram, paragraph 77.
87. German Federal Patent Court (Bundespatentgericht), order 14 W (pat) 9/06 of 27 November 2008 – Triptorelin.
88. German Federal Patent Court (Bundespatentgericht), order 14 W (pat) 25/16 of 5 September 2017 – Paliperidonpalmitat.
89. CJEU *Arne Forsgren v. Österreichisches Patentamt*, C-631/13 of 15 January 2015.
90. German Federal Patent Court (Bundespatentgericht), order 14 W (pat) 25/16 of 5 September 2017 – Paliperidonpalmitat, Section II.5 of the reasons.

dosing frequency of the two substances, a different side effect profile and a different duration of the therapeutic effects. On this basis, the Court concluded that paliperidone and paliperidone palmitate show significant, not merely minor, differences in their pharmacological and metabolic effects and are therefore indeed different products.

Arguably, these 'significant differences' between paliperidone and its ester paliperidone palmitate invoked by the Federal Patent Court would appear quite comparable to the differences between the two doxorubicin salts, which the Federal Supreme Court disregarded in the above-discussed decision *Doxorubicin-Sulfat*. According to the Federal Patent Court, however, the Federal Supreme Court in *Doxorubicin-Sulfat* could not take into account the later-issued CJEU decision *Forsgren*, in which the relevance of significant differences between the pharmacological, immunological and metabolic effects of different products were highlighted. Therefore, the Federal Patent Court did not consider *Doxorubicin-Sulfat* to stand in conflict with its own reasoning in *Paliperidonpalmitat*.[91]

The more liberal approach taken by the Federal Patent Court in *Paliperidonpalmitat* appears to do justice to the European legislator's intention expressed in recital 14 of the SPC Regulation for Plant Protection Products, which via recital 17 is also applicable to the SPC Regulation for Medicinal Products and stipulates that the issuance of an SPC for an active ingredient should not preclude the grant of new SPCs for derivatives (salts and esters) of that active ingredient, provided that the derivatives are subject of patents specifically covering them. It remains to be seen whether this approach will be sanctioned by the German Federal Supreme Court (or the CJEU) and where exactly the line should be drawn between significant and insignificant differences in the pharmacological, immunological or metabolic effects of an active ingredient and its derivatives.

A further factor to be considered in this context is the German Federal Supreme Court's interpretation of recital 14 of the SPC Regulation for Plant Protection Products, as expressed in its decision *Escitalopram*. In this decision, the Court held that recital 14 establishes an exception to the rule that the same product should not become the subject of several successive SPCs, and that this exception requires that a new derivative of a previously authorized active ingredient must be protected by a *product patent*, i.e., a basic patent having *product claims* directed to the respective derivative.[92]

It is not easily comprehensible why such a far-reaching limitation should necessarily follow from recital 14, nor why it should be justified. Derivatives as referred to in recital 14 could well be 'the subject of patents specifically covering them' in the form of second medical use claims. Moreover, in cases where a specific derivative exhibits significantly different pharmacological effects in the treatment of a certain disease, it would seem fitting to draft a patent with second medical use claims focusing on the corresponding treatment.

Nevertheless, in view of the Federal Supreme Court's position taken in *Escitalopram*, it might be safest to rely on a basic patent having product claims directed to a

91. *Ibid.*, Section II.7 of the reasons.
92. German Federal Supreme Court (Bundesgerichtshof), judgment Xa ZR 130/07 of 10 September 2009 – Escitalopram, paragraph 76.

specific derivative of a previously authorized active ingredient when filing a corresponding new SPC application.

[c] SPCs for a Specific Enantiomer Where an Own Earlier SPC Has Already Been Granted for the Corresponding Racemate

The German Federal Supreme Court acknowledged in *Escitalopram* (Xa ZR 130/07) that the specific enantiomer under consideration (i.e., escitalopram, which is the (S)-enantiomer of citalopram) is a different product than the racemate of this compound (i.e., citalopram).[93] Consequently, the Court concluded that an earlier marketing authorization for the racemate does not preclude, under Article 3(d) of the pertinent SPC Regulation, the grant of a new SPC for the specific enantiomer on the basis of a corresponding (later) marketing authorization and a basic patent directed to this specific enantiomer.[94]

In arriving at this conclusion, the Federal Supreme Court left the question unanswered whether a specific enantiomer should be regarded – similarly to salts and esters – as a derivative of the corresponding racemate.[95] It rather found that even if this were the case, the condition of Article 3(d) would be fulfilled, because in the case underlying this decision the enantiomer in question was specifically protected by a *product claim* of the basic patent, so that the condition presumably established in recital 14 of the SPC Regulation for Plant Protection Products (*see* the corresponding discussion in §2.02[D][3][b] above) was fulfilled.[96]

Although the condition of Article 3(c) was not explicitly addressed in *Escitalopram*, the Federal Supreme Court's reasoning should likewise apply in this respect. Thus, since the Court acknowledged that the specific enantiomer at issue was a different product than the previously authorized racemate, the grant of the new SPC for that specific enantiomer should not be precluded under Article 3(c) by any earlier SPC that might possibly have been granted for the racemate on the basis of the earlier marketing authorization either.

The later Federal Patent Court decision *Escitalopram II* (3 Ni 22/10)[97] was concerned with another nullity action filed against the same SPC as in the above-mentioned Federal Supreme Court decision. Notably, the Federal Patent Court found that the evidence filed by the nullity plaintiff did not establish beyond reasonable doubt that the enantiomer escitalopram, which was the subject of the attacked SPC, and the previously approved racemate citalopram would have the same therapeutic effects and should therefore be regarded as the same active ingredient within the meaning of the SPC Regulation. The plaintiff's objection under Article 3(d) was consequently rejected.

93. *Ibid.*, paragraphs 69 and 73.
94. *Ibid.*, headnote (d).
95. *Ibid.*, paragraph 75.
96. *Ibid.*, paragraph 76.
97. German Federal Patent Court (Bundespatentgericht), judgment 3 Ni 22/10 of 29 March 2011 – Escitalopram II.

[4] *Grant of More than One SPC on the Basis of the Same Patent*

The same considerations as set out in the EU chapter apply.

§2.03 EXTENT OF PROTECTION AND ENFORCEMENT OF SPCs

[A] The Protection Conferred by an SPC

The considerations in terms of the protection conferred by an SPC outlined in the EU chapter apply equally to Germany. As set out by the Düsseldorf District Court in decision 4b O 280/10[98] and decision 4b O 66/11[99] (the referring decision in the *Novartis* case, C-574/11[100]), while Article 4 of the SPC Regulation stipulates that the protection conferred by an SPC is limited to 'the product covered by the [marketing authorization]', recitals 3–9 of the SPC Regulation for Medicinal Products establish that the Regulation aims at a de facto extension of the patent protection.

Accordingly, Articles 4 and 5 of the SPC Regulations must be interpreted such that while in line with Article 5 the effects of an SPC are identical to the effects of the underlying basic patent, Article 4 determines the object of these effects, namely the approved product, in order to delimit it from other substances which potentially are also encompassed by the basic patent. As such, Article 4 of the SPC Regulations does not aim for a limitation to the specific authorized medicinal (or plant protection) product. The limitation of the subject matter of a certificate in Article 4 of the SPC Regulations as a whole has to be understood in the sense that it has the sole purpose of excluding an 'over-extensive' protection.

The scope of protection of an SPC is thus determined on the basis of the underlying patent, but limited to the product for which the SPC has been granted. Accordingly, as explained by the Düsseldorf Higher Regional Court,[101] if the claims of the basic patent refer to a broader subject matter than the product of the SPC, the corresponding broader definition in the patent specification should be notionally 'replaced' with the product of the SPC for the purposes of claim construction and the determination of the scope of protection in accordance with the general principles established in patent law.

The conformity of the scope of protection of an SPC to that of the respective basic patent has also been confirmed by the Federal Supreme Court in the *Simvastatin* case (X ZR 76/05),[102] according to which an SPC, in analogy to a patent, is infringed by a pre-expiry promotional offer of the product, such as the listing of the medicinal product

98. Düsseldorf District Court (Landgericht Düsseldorf), judgment 4b O 280/10 of 8 March 2011 – Valsartan.
99. Düsseldorf District Court (Landgericht Düsseldorf), order 4b O 66/11 of 8 November 2011 – Valsartan.
100. CJEU *Novartis v. Actavis Deutschland*, C-574/11 of 9 February 2012.
101. Düsseldorf Higher Regional Court (Oberlandesgericht Düsseldorf), judgment I-2 U 21/15 of 6 August 2015 – Ezetimib, paragraph 28.
102. German Federal Supreme Court (Bundesgerichtshof), judgment X ZR 76/05 of 5 December 2006 – Simvastatin.

in the 'Lauer Taxe', which is a usual preparatory step in order to ensure reimbursement for the prescription of the medicament in Germany, particularly if it is to be sold by conventional pharmacies (as opposed to in house, stationary hospital use).

[B] The Scope of an SPC in Relation to Derivatives of an Active Ingredient

So far there have been no German national decisions addressing this point specifically in an infringement case. Nevertheless, the Federal Supreme Court on various accounts has confirmed the guidance provided by the CJEU in *Farmitalia* (C-392/97),[103] according to which, if a product in the form referred to in the marketing authorization is protected by a basic patent in force, the SPC is capable of covering that product, as a medicinal product (or plant protection product), in any of the forms enjoying the protection of the basic patent.

Thus, the Federal Supreme Court emphasized in the decision *Idarubicin II* (X ZB 13/95)[104] that the scope of protection conferred by an SPC based on the free base of an active ingredient will also encompass derivatives of the free base covered by the basic patent, and that such derivatives do not require express incorporation in the product definition of the SPC.

Similarly, in *Sumatriptan* (X ZB 12/01)[105] the Federal Supreme Court noted that the protection conferred by an SPC embraces the corresponding active ingredient as well as its various derivatives insofar as they are covered by the protection of the basic patent; this, however, presupposes that such derivatives are indeed different forms of the *same* active ingredient, i.e., that they provide the same therapeutic effect.[106]

[1] The Relationship Between the Definition of the Active Ingredient(s) in an SPC and Its Scope of Protection

While the GPTO generally allows an SPC to issue with a broader product definition, beyond the specific form of the active ingredient identified in the marketing authorization (e.g., by the inclusion of pharmaceutically acceptable salts of the active ingredient), the practical implications of the product definition of an SPC in terms of the scope of protection conferred by the SPC remain questionable. This issue has not so far been specifically considered by the German courts when assessing the scope of protection of an SPC.

In *Sumatriptan* (X ZB 12/01)[107] the German Federal Supreme Court did not follow the position taken by the Federal Patent Court in the appealed decision, in which the

103. CJEU *Farmitalia Carlo Erba v. Bundesgerichtshof*, C-392/97 of 16 September 1999.
104. German Federal Supreme Court (Bundesgerichtshof), order X ZB 13/95 of 15 February 2000 – Idarubicin II.
105. German Federal Supreme Court (Bundesgerichtshof), order X ZB 12/01 of 29 January 2002 – Sumatriptan.
106. *Ibid.*, Section III.6.(a) of the reasons.
107. *Ibid.*

latter had raised fundamental doubts as to the justification and the legal admissibility of a claim-like definition of the subject of protection of SPCs. The Federal Supreme Court rather found that an SPC must – 'in principle not differently from a patent claim' – concretely identify the product for which the SPC is to be granted, but also acknowledged that the SPC does not establish a distinct subject of protection which would be independent from that of the basic patent.[108] The Court further stressed that it must be possible to request an SPC for an active ingredient in certain forms which might not necessarily be identical to the specific form of that active ingredient in the approved medicinal product.[109] According to the Federal Supreme Court, if an SPC is sought for an active ingredient in broader form than it is identified in the marketing authorization relied upon, then this must be specified in the SPC request; and when an SPC is granted, it must be made clear to what extent such a request has been accepted.[110] Conversely, an applicant should be free to restrict its SPC request vis-à-vis the basic patent to specific forms of the active ingredient.[111]

It would thus appear that the Federal Supreme Court in *Sumatriptan* did not only consider the product definition of an SPC to serve the function of identifying the active ingredient (or combination of active ingredients) for which protection is sought, but also to specify, at least to some extent, the forms of the active ingredient(s) intended to be protected. Still, the reasoning of the Court remains at a rather abstract level and results merely in the conclusion that an SPC must 'concretely identify' the product to be protected. The precise ramifications of the product definition for the scope of protection were not specifically addressed by the Federal Supreme Court in this decision.

The Federal Patent Court in *Hexavalenter Impfstoff* (14 W (pat) 10/16)[112] recapitulated that the scope of protection of an SPC cannot extend beyond that of the underlying basic patent, and added that this holds true even if the product definition of the SPC may appear broader than the invention defined in the claims of the basic patent. While the Federal Patent Court did not further dwell on this aspect, its statement in this decision would appear to conform with the notion that the product definition of an SPC should be merely declaratory and should not allow any extension of the scope protection of the SPC beyond that of the basic patent. This notion would also be supported by the approach taken in *Telmisartan II* (3 Ni 5/13),[113] where the Federal Patent Court resolved an ambiguity in the product definition of the SPC by resorting to the marketing authorization underlying the SPC.

108. *Ibid.*, Section III.4.(b) of the reasons, first and second paragraphs.
109. *Ibid.*, Section III.4.(b) of the reasons, fourth paragraph.
110. *Ibid.*, Section III.4.(b) of the reasons, penultimate paragraph.
111. *Ibid.*, Section III.4.(c) of the reasons.
112. German Federal Patent Court (Bundespatentgericht), order 14 W (pat) 10/16 of 23 January 2018 – Hexavalenter Impfstoff, Section II.4.5 of the reasons.
113. German Federal Patent Court (Bundespatentgericht), judgment 3 Ni 5/13 of 4 February 2014 – Telmisartan II; Section II.3 of the reasons.

[C] Enforcement of an SPC

As set out in Section 16a PatG, the provisions of the German Patent Act in relation to patent infringement (as well as the effect of the patent and exceptions thereto, the scope of protection, and compulsory licences) apply mutatis mutandis to SPCs.

In Germany there is a bifurcated litigation system, whereby patent enforcement and invalidity actions are tried in different courts.

Patent and SPC infringement proceedings are litigated through the twelve district courts that have exclusive jurisdiction in this regard.[114] The most frequented courts for patent and SPC infringement in Germany are the District Courts of Düsseldorf, Munich, Hamburg and Mannheim.

In case of pharmaceutical products, where the infringing activities are generally not only of local nature, any of the twelve district courts may be addressed in an infringement suit at the choice of the plaintiff, whereby the selection of the court is usually based on strategic considerations.

The costs of an infringement action are calculated on a theoretical value of the matter in dispute, on the basis of which the court fees and statutory attorney fees are determined.

The losing party is liable to pay the court fees and reimburse the statutory attorney fees of the other party.

The first-instance decision is typically handed down within ten to fifteen months after the filing of the infringement suit. The appeal proceedings before the higher regional courts typically take about twelve to fifteen months. A further appeal to the Federal Supreme Court, which is strictly limited to legal issues, may take from about eighteen months to four years.

Ex parte injunctive relief is generally also available if there is clear, objective evidence of infringement and if the SPC (and its basic patent) may be presumed to be valid.[115] In such cases the preliminary injunction may issue within a few days.

If the situation is less clear-cut, the district court seized will summon the parties to oral proceedings where the defendant is given the opportunity to submit a written defence pleading, in which case the proceedings will usually take about two to six weeks.

Appeal proceedings relating to preliminary injunctions typically take about three to six months until a final appeal decision is available.

A patent or SPC holder does not forfeit its rights under the Specific Mechanism solely because it replies to a notification regarding parallel imports by invoking the

114. The twelve district courts that have jurisdiction to hear patent and SPC infringement cases are the District Courts of Berlin, Braunschweig, Düsseldorf, Erfurt, Frankfurt am Main, Hamburg, Leipzig, Magdeburg, Mannheim, Munich I, Nuremberg-Fürth, and Saarbrücken.

115. *See*, e.g., Düsseldorf District Court (Landgericht Düsseldorf), judgment 4a O 277/10 of 24 February 2011 – Pramipexoldihydrochloridmonohydrat; and Düsseldorf Higher Regional Court (Oberlandesgericht Düsseldorf), judgment I-2 U 21/15 of 6 August 2015, paragraph 68.

rights conferred by a patent or SPC without specifically identifying the corresponding patent or SPC, as confirmed by the German Federal Supreme Court in *Besonderer Mechanismus* (X ZR 56/09).[116]

Of interest is also the decision of the Düsseldorf Higher Regional Court in the *Ezetimib* case (I-2 U 21/15).[117] In this case, the defendant intended to reimport a medicinal product comprising a combination of active ingredients based on the provisions of the Specific Mechanism from Croatia to Germany. One of the active ingredients of the combination product to be reimported was subject matter of an SPC, which had been filed in Germany in 2003, at a time when SPCs were not available in Croatia. However, as no corresponding patent had been filed in Croatia, the defendant argued that the plaintiff should not be allowed to benefit from the Specific Mechanism.

The Higher Regional Court granted a preliminary injunction as in its view the Specific Mechanism in the Treaty of Accession of the Republic of Croatia[118] is unambiguous in that if at the decisive date, namely when the SPC should have been applied for, the legal instrument of an SPC were not yet available, the importer cannot rely on the principles of patent exhaustion.

A particularly interesting aspect of the decision is that, according to the Higher Regional Court, while a parallel importer should be allowed to reimport a medicinal product from one of the accession states if the product is not protected by a national patent in the accession state, this de facto will constitute an act of infringement once the patent expires and the SPC comes into force in the Member State to which the product is to be reimported.

116. German Federal Supreme Court (Bundesgerichtshof), judgment X ZR 56/09 of 12 July 2011 – Besonderer Mechanismus.
117. Düsseldorf Higher Regional Court (Oberlandesgericht Düsseldorf), judgment I-2 U 21/15 of 6 August 2015 – Ezetimib.
118. Treaty between the Member States of the European Union and the Republic of Croatia concerning the accession of the Republic of Croatia to the European Union, Annex IV, No. 1. The corresponding provision reads as follows:

> SPECIFIC MECHANISM
>
> With regard to Croatia, the holder, or the holder's beneficiary, of a patent or Supplementary Protection Certificate (SPC) for a medicinal product filed in a Member State at the time when such protection could not be obtained in Croatia for that product, may rely on the rights granted by that patent or SPC in order to prevent the import and marketing of that product in the Member State or Member States where the product in question enjoys patent or SPC protection, even if this product was put on the market in Croatia for the first time by the holder or with the holder's consent.
>
> Any person intending to import or market a medicinal product covered by the first paragraph in a Member State where the product enjoys patent or SPC protection shall demonstrate to the competent authorities in the application regarding that import that one month's prior notification has been given to the holder or beneficiary of such protection.

§2.04 DETERMINATION OF THE SPC TERM

[A] The Calculation of the SPC Term

The considerations regarding the calculation of the SPC term as set out in the EU chapter apply equally to Germany.

[1] The Relevant Marketing Authorization for the Term of an SPC

The considerations in terms of the relevant marketing authorization for determining the SPC term as set out in the EU chapter apply equally to Germany.

The GPTO does not, however, carry out a comprehensive search for the verification that the marketing authorization relied upon by the SPC applicant is indeed the first marketing authorization in question.

As such, if it subsequently becomes evident that there is a discrepancy and a prior authorization in the EU (or the EEA) needs to be taken into account, then a correction of the SPC term may be requested by the applicant as well as a third party.

In recent years, the CJEU has effectively liberalized the SPC system, allowing for SPCs to issue for a new therapeutic use of an active ingredient previously authorized as a medicinal product (*see Neurim*, C-130/11[119]). If the product which has been approved for a new therapeutic use has been developed by a party unrelated to the holder of the marketing authorization of the prior approval, then an independent new marketing authorization will issue. If, however, the new therapeutic use is developed by the same originator, then either a type II variation of the previously granted marketing authorization issues, or if the new therapeutic use warrants a different dosage form from the previously approved product, an extension approval, based on the original approval will be issued.

Such type II variations and extensions require the completion of a full approval procedure, with only limited reliance on previously submitted documentation.

In order to adequately take account of the guidance provided by the CJEU in *Neurim*, it would appear expedient to also consider such type II variations and extensions as being the relevant marketing authorization for the determination of the SPC term for a product which has been approved for a new therapeutic use.

There are cases pending before the GPTO where these issues will need to be considered, so that clarification in this regard may be expected in the near future.

[2] The Expiration Date of an SPC

The calculation of the SPC term, in analogy to the calculation of the patent term, is based on the provisions of Section 16 PatG. Thus, the term of a patent shall be twenty years beginning on the day following its filing date. The last day when a patent is in

119. CJEU *Neurim Pharmaceuticals v. Comptroller-General of Patents*, C-130/11 of 19 July 2012.

force is the twentieth anniversary of its filing date. Accordingly, an SPC with a full five-year term will expire on the twenty-fifth anniversary of the filing date of the patent.

For example, a German SPC which is based on a patent filed on 15 June 2000 and a marketing authorization notified on 10 August 2007 (which was the first marketing authorization for this product in the EU and the EEA) will come into effect upon expiry of the basic patent, i.e., on 16 June 2020, and will expire on 10 August 2022 (at the end of the day, i.e., at midnight). If, in this example, the marketing authorization is notified on or after 15 June 2010, the SPC will have the maximum term of 5 years and will thus expire on 15 June 2025 (at the end of the day).

[B] Correction of the SPC Term

As discussed in the EU chapter, Article 17(2) of the SPC Regulation for Plant Protection Products, which via recital 17 is also applicable to the SPC Regulation for Medicinal Products, provides that the decision to grant an SPC shall be open to an appeal aimed at rectifying the duration of the SPC where the date of the first marketing authorization in the Community was incorrectly indicated in the SPC application.

For Germany, the procedure for such an appeal is established by Section 49a(4) No. 1 PatG, which was introduced with effect of 1 October 2009. This provision prescribes that the decision on a request to correct the duration of an SPC, if the date included in the SPC application in respect of the first marketing authorization is incorrect, shall be taken by the patent division of the GPTO. A corresponding request may be filed at any time and by any person, including the SPC holder as well as third parties. The proceedings may be conducted in an adversarial manner.[120] The decision of the patent division on the request for correction can be appealed within one month of service of the decision (Section 73 PatG). It is, strictly speaking, not admissible to request the correction of an erroneous SPC duration resulting from any other error than an incorrect date of the first marketing authorization in the EU via the procedure under Section 49a(4) No. 1 PatG.[121]

Besides the possibility of requesting a correction under Section 49a(4) No. 1 PatG, the SPC holder can also directly appeal the decision of the GPTO granting the SPC, within one month of service of the decision, on the grounds that the duration of the SPC

120. GPTO Examination Guidelines for SPCs, Section 3.8.2.

121. *See also* the explanations provided in the draft act for the simplification and modernization of the German Patent Act (printed documents 757/08 of 17 October 2008 and 16/11339 of 10 December 2008), which indicate (in English translation):

> For these reasons, Section 49a(4) No. 1, which is to be newly introduced, provides for a request which only serves to correct the duration following an incorrect indication of the date of the first marketing authorization. The request does thereby not go beyond the requirements under Community law. Other deficiencies of the supplementary protection certificate, including also errors in the duration based on other reasons, cannot be rectified with this request, but only with the established legal remedies.

is incorrect. The Federal Patent Court acknowledged that this is possible where the appellant is adversely affected in substance by the decision to grant the SPC.[122]

Moreover, for the rectification of an obvious error in the calculation of the SPC duration in a decision of the GTPO, the provisions of Section 95 PatG (relating to the correction of obvious errors in decisions of the Federal Patent Court) are applicable mutatis mutandis,[123] providing for an unbureaucratic correction of the SPC term.

[C] Paediatric Extensions

The considerations in terms of paediatric extensions as set out in the EU chapter apply equally to Germany.

§2.05 PROCEDURE OF FILING AN SPC APPLICATION

[A] Entitlement to an SPC Application

The SPC Regulations stipulate in Article 6 that the SPC shall be granted to the patent holder, but are silent as to who may apply for an SPC. In Germany, it is only the patentee who is entitled to file an SPC application. As such, a licensee of the basic patent may not file the SPC even if the patent owner has given his express authorization to do so.

Likewise, if the basic patent has been transferred, it is only the registered patent owner who may file the SPC.[124]

If there is a discrepancy between the applicant for an SPC and the registered owner of the basic patent, the GPTO will invite the applicant to correct this deficiency.[125]

[B] The Time Limit for Filing an SPC Application

The considerations as set out in the EU chapter apply. It should, however, be noted that in accordance with Section 16a PatG, the provisions for the re-establishment of rights as provided for patents also apply to SPCs.

The fact that the six-month term for filing an SPC application according to Article 7(1) or 7(2) of the SPC Regulations is open to re-establishment of rights has also been

122. German Federal Patent Court (Bundespatentgericht), order 7 W (pat) 1/16 of 6 February 2017; and German Federal Patent Court (Bundespatentgericht), order 7 W (pat) 27/15 of 11 December 2015.
123. GPTO Examination Guidelines for SPCs, Section 5.3.
124. Section 30(3) second sentence PatG.
125. GPTO Examination Guidelines for SPCs, Section 3.2.4.

expressly acknowledged by the German Federal Patent Court in its decisions *Abamectin* (15 W (pat) 71/97)[126] and *Acyclovir-L-valinat* (15 W (pat) 23/99).[127]

Since, however, the requirement under Article 3(a) of the SPC Regulations that the basic patent must be 'in force' at the date of filing the SPC application is not a deadline to be observed but rather a substantive requirement, a failure to file the SPC application while the basic patent is still 'in force' cannot be remedied via re-establishment of rights. This has been specifically confirmed by the Federal Patent Court in *Abamectin*[128] and in *Clothianidin I* (15 W (pat) 24/06).[129]

[C] The Filing of an SPC at the National Patent Office

As set out in the EU chapter, an SPC must be filed before the national patent office within the stipulated time limits, once the basic patent as well as the relevant marketing authorization have issued. The SPC application must be filed in writing, using the prescribed form issued by the GPTO,[130] and must contain all relevant information about the applicant and his representative (names and addresses), as well as details in terms of the basic patent and the marketing authorization (number and date) relied upon for the product in question. The prescribed fee must be paid on filing.[131]

An SPC applicant having neither its residence, principle place of business nor establishment in Germany must appoint a patent attorney or a lawyer as its representative.[132]

No power of attorney is required if the representative is a patent attorney or a lawyer.[133]

[D] The Documentation Required for an SPC Application

The documentation required for filing an SPC application in Germany is based on the requirements as set out in Article 8 of the SPC Regulations.[134]

The SPC request should be supplemented with copies of the marketing authorization to place the product on the market in Germany. While the Examination Guidelines for SPCs of the GPTO stipulate that the documentation does not have to be complete and may be partially redacted, as long as the information provided suffices to

126. German Federal Patent Court (Bundespatentgericht), order 15 W (pat) 71/97 of 21 June 1999 - Abamectin.
127. German Federal Patent Court (Bundespatentgericht), order 15 W (pat) 23/99 of 2 March 2000 - Acyclovir-L-valinat.
128. German Federal Patent Court (Bundespatentgericht), order 15 W (pat) 71/97 of 21 June 1999 - Abamectin, headnote 1.
129. German Federal Patent Court (Bundespatentgericht), order 15 W (pat) 24/06 of 12 December 2011 - Clothianidin I, Section II, fifth paragraph of the reasons.
130. Section 19(1) PatV; *see also* GPTO Examination Guidelines for SPCs, Section 3.2.1.
131. Section 2(1) PatKostG in conjunction the corresponding annex, fee code No. 311 500; and Section 3(1) first sentence PatKostG.
132. Section 16a(2) PatG in conjunction with Section 25(1) PatG.
133. GPTO Examination Guidelines for SPCs, Section 3.2.1.1.
134. *See also* Sections 20 and 21 PatV.

establish the identity of the authorized product, the authorization number, the validity period and the Summary of Product Characteristics (SmPC), such considerations would appear to be redundant in light of the public accessibility of all of these documents nowadays.

In addition, if the first authorization for placing the product on the market is not a German or a central authorization, but was granted in another EU or EEA Member State, the applicant should submit information regarding the identity of the product thus authorized and the legal provision under which the authorization procedure took place, together with a copy of the notice publishing the authorization in the appropriate official publication.

In the case of plant protection products, copies of provisional and/or definitive marketing authorizations must be filed. Where a provisional authorization for placing the plant protection product on the market in Germany is directly followed by a definitive marketing authorization for the plant protection product, copies must be furnished of the provisional authorization as well as of the definitive marketing authorization to prove that there are no gaps. However, if no definitive marketing authorization has been issued, a copy of the provisional authorization(s) is sufficient (*see Hogan Lovells*, C-229/09[135]).

Translations of foreign-language copies of the above-mentioned marketing authorization documents must only be provided where the required data are not identifiable without further explanation.[136]

Unless it is very obvious, the applicant should also provide information as to how the product is protected by the basic patent,[137] as required under Section 19(2) PatV.

[E] The Definition of the Product in an SPC Application

As set out in the Examination Guidelines provided by the GPTO,[138] the product of an SPC should be defined on the basis of the active ingredient(s) as identified in the SmPC, i.e., in Annex 1 of the marketing authorization for the corresponding medicinal product.

In the case of plant protection products, if the identity of the active ingredient cannot be derived from the text of the authorization, the text of the Register of Plant Protection Products (Pflanzenschutzmittelverzeichnis, published by the German Federal Office of Consumer Protection and Food Safety) can be used alternatively.

Moreover, the Examination Guidelines specifically highlight the possibility of using a broader definition of the SPC product, beyond the specifically approved product.[139]

135. CJEU *Hogan Lovells International v. Bayer CropScience*, C-229/09 of 11 November 2010.
136. GPTO Examination Guidelines for SPCs, Section 3.2.1.4.
137. GPTO Examination Guidelines for SPCs, Section 3.2.1.6.
138. GPTO Examination Guidelines for SPCs, Sections 3.2.1.5 and 3.3.1.4.
139. GPTO Examination Guidelines for SPCs, Section 3.2.1.5.

In the past the GPTO has allowed product definitions with a generalized statement 'in all forms as protected by the basic patent', based on the considerations as set out by the CJEU in *Farmitalia* (C-392/97).[140]

This position has changed somewhat in light of the German Federal Supreme Court decision *Sumatriptan* (X ZB 12/01),[141] where it was emphasized that the product of an SPC must be identified concretely.

While in practice some examiners will still allow such general product definitions, there is a tendency by the GPTO to now only allow more specific generalizations of the product definition, which are more closely aligned to the patent claims. In case of small chemical molecules, such SPC product definitions typically focus on minor derivatives, such as pharmaceutically acceptable salts or hydrates of the active ingredient in question.

As affirmed by the Federal Patent Court in *Levofloxacin* (15 W (pat) 15/05),[142] such minor derivatives must, of course, be specifically disclosed and claimed in the basic patent in order to be incorporated into the product definition of an SPC.

In case of more complex biological molecules, such as antibodies, there is a tendency to only allow a product definition based on the International Nonproprietary Name (INN) of the active ingredient as identified in the SmPC.

It is furthermore noteworthy that the Federal Supreme Court in *Idarubicin III* (X ZB 21/00)[143] acknowledged the right of an SPC applicant to have the SPC granted as requested, provided that all corresponding legal conditions are fulfilled. Therefore, if the deciding body in SPC examination proceedings considers another product definition to be *preferable* over the one requested by the applicant, this does not constitute a ground for rejecting the SPC application.

[F] SPC Examination Procedure and Appeal Procedure

In accordance with the practice of the GPTO, an application for an SPC will be subject to a formal examination, followed by a substantive examination.

The formal examination focuses on issues such as the time limits for filing the SPC, the payment of the prescribed fees, the formal entitlement of the applicant, as well as the question as to whether the patent is in force and the documentation submitted is complete. If there are deficits in this regard or if any documentation is missing, the GPTO will invite the applicant to rectify this.

The substantive examination includes the verification that the marketing authorization was granted in accordance with the appropriate directives and is valid at the filing date.

140. CJEU *Farmitalia Carlo Erba v. Bundesgerichtshof*, C-392/97 of 16 September 1999.
141. German Federal Supreme Court (Bundesgerichtshof), order X ZB 12/01 of 29 January 2002 – Sumatriptan.
142. German Federal Patent Court (Bundespatentgericht), order 15 W (pat) 15/05 of 1 December 2005 – Levofloxacin.
143. German Federal Supreme Court (Bundesgerichtshof), order X ZB 21/00 of 17 July 2001 – Idarubicin III.

The GPTO does not generally examine whether the marketing authorization is indeed the first marketing authorization.[144]

Frequently the applicant submits various SPC requests for the same product based on different basic patents in parallel, in which case, however, only a single SPC may issue. The GPTO will therefore check whether a prior SPC for the same product has already been granted to the same applicant.

During the examination the identity of the product is established and it is verified that the product is protected by the basic patent.

If an SPC application is considered to be deficient, the GPTO shall issue an intermediate office action inviting the applicant to correct the deficiencies within an extendable two-month time limit.[145]

According to the Examination Guidelines for SPCs,[146] such an intermediate office action or a direct decision to grant should be served on the applicant within eight months after receipt of the SPC request. In practice, however, the first intermediate office action (or the decision to grant) generally issues much later. The GPTO is usually prepared to unbureaucratically consider accelerating or delaying the examination of an SPC upon informal request by the applicant.

The proceedings can also be stayed, e.g., in order to await the outcome of a pending CJEU referral or pending judicial review proceedings before the German Federal Supreme Court in another case which has a bearing on the case at hand.[147]

As provided for in Section 49a(5) PatG, the provision of Section 46 PatG (relating to examination hearings and minutes) is also applicable for the examination of SPCs. As a consequence, the patent division may summon the parties to a hearing, where witnesses and experts may be heard. A hearing must, however, also take place upon request of the applicant in writing.[148]

If the application for the SPC is in compliance with the statutory requirements as set out in the SPC Regulation and Section 16a PatG, the patent division will issue the decision to grant the certificate for the duration of its term and, if appropriate, its paediatric extension. Alternatively, a reasoned decision to reject the certificate will issue.[149] The decisions of the patent division may be appealed pursuant to Section 73(1) PatG in conjunction with Section 16a PatG.

A substantiated appeal against such a decision must be filed in writing with the GPTO within one month of the service of the decision together with the payment of an

144. GPTO Examination Guidelines for SPCs, Section 3.3.1.3.
145. Section 49a(2) second sentence PatG.
146. GPTO Examination Guidelines for SPCs, Section 3.
147. *See*, e.g., German Federal Patent Court (Bundespatentgericht), order 15 W (pat) 66/97 of 29 May 2001 - Salmeterol; and German Federal Patent Court (Bundespatentgericht), order 15 W (pat) 5/99 of 21 January 2002 - Sertindol.
148. Section 49a(5) PatG in conjunction with Section 46(1) second and third sentences PatG. *See also* GPTO Examination Guidelines for SPCs, Section 3.5.
149. Section 49a(2) third sentence PatG, and Section 49a(5) PatG in conjunction with Section 47(1) PatG.

appeal fee.[150] If the appeal fee is not paid within this time limit, the appeal will be deemed not to have been filed.[151]

If the patent division of the GPTO considers the appeal to be admissible and well founded, it may rectify the decision without further consideration by the Federal Patent Court. If the appeal is not allowed by the patent division, it is remitted to the Federal Patent Court within one month.

A final decision from the Federal Patent Court may be expected within about eighteen months to three years after the filing of the appeal.

[G] Applications for a Paediatric Extension

The formal requirements for filing a paediatric extension correspond to those as outlined in the EU chapter.

The request for a paediatric extension must be filed with the GPTO together with the prescribed fee, using the prescribed form.[152]

If an SPC has already been granted, then the request must be filed no later than two years before the expiry of the SPC.

The required supporting documents are set out in Article 8(1)(d) of the SPC Regulation for Medicinal Products. These include a copy of the statement indicating compliance with the agreed and completed Paediatric Investigation Plan (PIP). Moreover, if the product has not been approved centrally by the EMA, it is necessary for the applicant to submit proof of possession of marketing authorizations for the product in all Member States.

If the statement of compliance is not yet available when filing the request, the GPTO will issue an intermediate office action setting a two-month deadline for filing the missing documents. This deadline may be extended, provided that the applicant can establish upon filing of the request, that he has made every effort to file the statement of compliance before the expiry of the period for filing the application and that he was justified to believe that in the case of proper conduct of procedures for the marketing authorization of medicinal products he would have obtained the statement of compliance in time.[153]

The formal and substantive examination of the request for a paediatric extension includes the verification of the entitlement to lodge the application, the completeness of the documentation in relation to the compliance statement and the verification that the product has been approved in all EU Member States.

In order to be entitled to a paediatric extension the product shall not be designated as an orphan medicinal product, as set out in Article 36(4) of the Paediatric Regulation (EC) 1901/2006. Moreover, no one-year extension of the period of regulatory exclusivity must have been granted, as set out in Article 36(5) of the Paediatric Regulation.

---

150. Sections 2(1), 3(1) and 6(1) first sentence PatKostG.
151. Section 6(2) PatKostG.
152. Section 19(1) PatV; *see also* GPTO Examination Guidelines for SPCs, Section 4.1.2.
153. GPTO Examination Guidelines for SPCs, Section 4.1.5.

§2.06 PROCEDURE OF INVALIDATING AN SPC

Section 16a PatG stipulates that the provisions of the German Patent Act in relation to the revocation of a patent also apply to SPCs.

[A] Grounds for the Invalidation of an SPC

The grounds for invalidating an SPC in Germany correspond to the grounds as set out in Article 15 of the SPC Regulations, as discussed in the EU chapter.

In line with the CJEU's finding that the catalogue of grounds of invalidity set out in Article 15(1) of the SPC Regulations is not exhaustive (*see* the corresponding discussion in the EU chapter), the German Federal Patent Court ruled in *Memantin* (3 Ni 59/05)[154] that non-compliance with the requirement under Article 2 of the SPC Regulations that the product must not have been placed on the market as a medicinal product or a plant protection product before having undergone a specific administrative authorization procedure, also constitutes a ground of invalidity of the SPC.

[B] The Filing of an Invalidation Suit

In Germany there is a bifurcated litigation system, whereby patent enforcement and invalidity actions are tried in different courts. As such for SPCs, in analogy to patents, the German Federal Patent Court has exclusive jurisdiction for invalidation.[155]

An action for the invalidation of an SPC may be filed at any time by any person, independent from any pending infringement proceedings.

According to Section 81(2) second sentence PatG, however, an invalidation action against an SPC is precluded insofar as a request for correction of the SPC term under Section 49a(4) No. 1 PatG or a request to revoke a paediatric extension under Section 49a(4) No. 2 PatG can be filed or proceedings for a decision on these requests are pending. The intention of this provision is to allow the rectification of an incorrectly long SPC term or the revocation of a paediatric extension exclusively via the simplified procedure established by Section 49a(4) PatG, but not also through an invalidation action,[156] in departure from the previous legal situation.[157]

In consideration of Article 15(2) of the SPC Regulations, which provides that the invalidation action or request may be filed by 'any person', the German Federal Patent

154. German Federal Patent Court (Bundespatentgericht), judgment 3 Ni 59/05 (EU) of 11 December 2017 - Memantin, headnote 3 and Section III of the reasons.

155. Section 81 PatG.

156. *See* the corresponding explanations provided in the draft act for the simplification and modernization of the German Patent Act (printed documents 757/08 of 17 October 2008 and 16/11339 of 10 December 2008).

157. *See*, e.g., German Federal Patent Court (Bundespatentgericht), judgment 3 Ni 2/06 of 15 March 2007 - Finasterid; and German Federal Patent Court (Bundespatentgericht), judgment 3 Ni 23/06 of 15 March 2007 - Finasterid.

Court in *Trifloxystrobin* (15 W (pat) 22/14)[158] confirmed that this must be understood to also include the rights holder. The Federal Patent Court concluded that, in analogy to Section 64 PatG, an SPC can be revoked with retroactive effect at the request of its holder in ex parte proceedings before the GPTO. In *Trifloxystrobin*, however, the Federal Patent Court left it open whether the revocation of an SPC at the request of its holder may be possible only if an actual ground of invalidity of the SPC has been established. In the specific case underlying this decision, the SPC for a plant protection product was based on an emergency marketing authorization and was therefore clearly invalid in view of the CJEU decision *Sumitomo Chemical* (C-210/12).[159]

[C] Invalidation Procedure and the Corresponding Appeal Procedure

An invalidation suit against an SPC may be initiated at any time after the expiry of the opposition period, or after the termination of opposition proceedings against the basic patent.

The costs of the proceedings are calculated on a theoretical value of the matter in dispute, on the basis of which the court fees and statutory attorney fees are determined. The losing party is liable to pay the court fees and has to reimburse the statutory attorney fees of the other party.[160]

A first-instance decision is typically handed down within about twelve to eighteen months. A final decision on appeal to the Federal Supreme Court usually issues within about two to three years from lodging the appeal.

In accordance with established case law,[161] an SPC can still be defended on the basis of an amended (restricted) set of claims of the basic patent, even if the patent has already expired. Amended claims of the patent can also be filed in second-instance SPC

158. German Federal Patent Court (Bundespatentgericht), order 15 W (pat) 22/14 of 7 December 2016 – Trifloxystrobin.
159. CJEU *Sumitomo Chemical v. Deutsches Patent- und Markenamt*, C-210/12 of 17 October 2013.
160. The same principles apply in this regard as in patent revocation proceedings. For example, the German Federal Patent Court found that the costs incurred for the 'double representation' of a party by a patent attorney and an attorney-at-law in first-instance invalidation proceedings against an SPC are not reimbursable if no parallel infringement proceedings concerning the same SPC are pending (*see*, e.g., German Federal Patent Court (Bundespatentgericht), order 3 ZA (pat) 33/11 of 28 February 2012 and order 3 ZA (pat) 39/09 of 25 January 2012), which is in line with the corresponding case law regarding patent revocation proceedings (*see* German Federal Supreme Court (Bundesgerichtshof), order X ZB 11/12 of 18 December 2012 – Doppelvertretung im Nichtigkeitsverfahren). In second-instance invalidation proceedings against an SPC before the German Federal Supreme Court, however, the costs for double representation by a patent attorney and an attorney-at-law are considered to be justified, even without parallel infringement proceedings, and can therefore be reimbursed to the prevailing party (*see*, e.g., German Federal Patent Court (Bundespatentgericht), order 3 ZA (pat) 33/11 of 28 February 2012 and order 3 ZA (pat) 39/09 of 25 January 2012). Furthermore, if an invalidation suit is filed only against the basic patent underlying an SPC but not against the SPC itself, this will also affect the value of the matter in dispute and thus the amount of recoverable fees (*see*, e.g., German Federal Patent Court (Bundespatentgericht), order 3 ZA (pat) 35/10 of 14 December 2010).
161. *See*, e.g., German Federal Supreme Court (Bundesgerichtshof), judgment X ZR 68/08 of 9 June 2011 – Memantin, paragraph 30; and German Federal Patent Court (Bundespatentgericht), judgment 3 Ni 36/04 of 27 June 2006 – Alendronsäure, headnote.

invalidation proceedings before the Federal Supreme Court, albeit the same procedural limitations apply in this regard as in regular patent revocation proceedings.[162]

Moreover, according to the Federal Supreme Court, statements made by the holder of the basic patent (or the SPC) in marketing authorization procedures, or by any other party involved in such procedures, do not have any legal significance in invalidation proceedings against the SPC.[163]

First-instance invalidation proceedings against an SPC before the Federal Patent Court can be stayed in view of a pending CJEU referral that concerns a different SPC but the same legal questions.[164]

[D] The Revocation of a Paediatric Extension

As set out in the EU chapter, the grounds for revocation of a paediatric extension correspond to those of Article 16 of the SPC Regulation for Medicinal Products.

The German legislator chose to establish a simplified administrative procedure for the revocation of a paediatric extension. To this end, Section 49a(4) No. 2 PatG was introduced with effect of 1 October 2009. This provision prescribes that the patent division of the GPTO shall take a decision on a request to revoke the extension of the term of an SPC. A corresponding request may be filed with the GPTO at any time by any person. The GPTO may conduct the proceedings in an adversarial manner.[165] The decision of the patent division can be appealed (Section 73 PatG).

The revocation of a paediatric extension cannot, however, be pursued via an invalidation action against the SPC. This follows from Section 81(2) second sentence PatG, which provides that an invalidation action against an SPC is precluded insofar as a request to revoke a paediatric extension under Section 49a(4) No. 2 PatG can be filed or proceedings for a decision on such a request are pending. The legislator thereby intended to allow the revocation of a paediatric extension only via the simplified procedure according to Section 49a(4) No. 2 PatG, but not also via an invalidation action.[166]

Otherwise, the same considerations as set out in §2.06[B] and §2.06[C] above for the revocation of an SPC apply.

§2.07 UNFAIR COMPETITION LAW

The same considerations as set out in the EU chapter apply. Antitrust issues involving SPCs have not yet been specifically addressed in the German case law.

---

162. Section 116(2) PatG.
163. German Federal Supreme Court (Bundesgerichtshof), judgment Xa ZR 130/07 of 10 September 2009 – Escitalopram, paragraph 74.
164. German Federal Patent Court (Bundespatentgericht), order 3 Ni 50/98 of 30 November 2000 – Felodipin.
165. GPTO Examination Guidelines for SPCs, Section 4.5.
166. *See* the corresponding explanations provided in the draft act for the simplification and modernization of the German Patent Act (printed documents 757/08 of 17 October 2008 and 16/11339 of 10 December 2008).

CHAPTER 3
United Kingdom

Charlotte Teall

§3.01 LEGAL BASIS

In UK national law,[1] the central legal provisions governing SPCs are contained in Section 128B and Schedule 4A of the UK Patents Act 1977 (as amended) (the 'Act'). Section 128B was introduced by Regulation 2 of the Patents (Compulsory Licensing and Supplementary Protection Certificates) Regulations 2007 (SI 2007 No. 3293), on 17 December 2007. In combination with Schedule 4A to the Act, it sets out how certain provisions of the Act apply to supplementary protection certificates, and applications for such certificates. Section 128B and Schedule 4A do not implement those provisions of the Regulations (EC) No. 469/2009 and (EC) No. 1610/96 that are directly applicable. The 2007 Patents Rules and 2007 Patents Fees Rules provide specific procedures for UK SPCs and SPC applications which differ from UK patents and applications for patents, including the payment and amount of fees.

Thus, Section 128B[2] provides that supplementary protection may be applied for on the basis of a patent, pursuant to the pertinent Regulations of the European Union.

1. Most of the legal acts and ordinances governing patents and SPCs in the UK are provided by the United Kingdom Intellectual Property Office (UK-IPO) at: https://www.gov.uk/topic/intellectual-property/law-practice.
2. Section 128B reads as follows:

   (1) Schedule 4A contains provision about the application of this Act in relation to supplementary protection certificates and other provision about such certificates.
   (2) In this Act a 'supplementary protection certificate' means a certificate issued under-
   (a) Regulation (EC) No 469/2009 of the European Parliament and of the Council of 6th May 2009 concerning the supplementary protection certificate for medicinal products, or
   (b) Regulation (EC) No 1610/96 of the European Parliament and of the Council of 23 July 1996 concerning the creation of a supplementary protection certificate for plant protection products.

According to Section 128B, unless provided for otherwise by EU law, the provisions of the Act are to be applied for SPCs granted on the basis of UK and European (UK) patents. Accordingly, such SPCs are subject to annuity payments in an accumulated amount. Moreover, the provisions of the Act in terms of entitlement, the effect of the patent, the extent of protection, licences and their registration (including compulsory licences) and the lapse of the patent and its revocation apply to SPCs, as procedural provisions, including in the appeal instances.

In line with this, the publicly accessible patent register contains the names and addresses of the SPC applicants or proprietors and their representatives as well as details on the term of an SPC, its lapse or invalidity, and the filing of a revocation action. This information is also published in the UK Patents Journal.

Article 19 of the SPC Regulation for Medicinal Products and Article 18 of the SPC Regulation for Plant Protection Products are also relevant and provide that where neither Regulation nor the 2007 Patent Rules lays down a special procedure for SPCs, the provisions of the Patents Act 1977 and respective Rules apply to SPCs and applications for SPCs as they do to patents and applications for patents.

The United Kingdom Intellectual Property Office (UK IPO) issues 'Supplementary Protection Certificates Guidance and Forms' in English language, which provides a brief overview of the SPC application process before the UK IPO. The UK IPO also issues a 'Manual of Patent Practice' in English language,[3] which provides more detailed information on the UK IPO's examination practice in both patent and SPC matters. The Manual is not binding on the UK IPO, but provides useful guidance to examiners and applicants on the current accepted practice at the UK IPO.

§3.02 SUBSTANTIVE REQUIREMENTS FOR OBTAINING AN SPC

As the guidance provided by the CJEU is binding for all EU Member States, the considerations as set out in Chapter 1 (the 'EU chapter'), specifically in §1.02 above, in relation to the substantive requirements for obtaining an SPC, in as far as they have been addressed by the CJEU, are equally applicable in the United Kingdom.

The following discussion will therefore only focus on case law and considerations of interest in the United Kingdom beyond the guidance provided by the CJEU.

[A] Types of Products That Can Be Protected

The same considerations as set out in the EU chapter apply. In particular, the patent can protect the active ingredient, a process to obtain the active ingredient or an application of the active ingredient.

3. United Kingdom Intellectual Property Office, Manual of Patent Practice section on Supplementary Protection Certificates for Medicinal and Plant Protection Products, published on 19 February 2016 and last updated on 29 June 2018. Available online at: https://www.gov.uk/guidance/manual-of-patent-practice-mopp/supplementary-protection-certificates-for-medicinal-and-plant-protection-products.

[1] Practical Considerations: What Is the Active Ingredient or Combination of Active Ingredients That Can Form the Basis for an SPC

The same considerations as set out in the EU chapter apply.

[2] Active Ingredient or Combination of Active Ingredients of a Medicinal Product

As discussed in the EU chapter, the requirement for a substance or a combination of substances to qualify as an 'active ingredient', as elaborated by the CJEU in *Forsgren* (C-631/13),[4] is that the respective substances must produce a pharmacological, immunological or metabolic action of their own.

The term 'active ingredient' in Article 1(b) is generally interpreted by the UK IPO as including any closely related derivative, in particular a salt or ester, which has obtained an authorization to be placed on the market and is protected by the basic patent, unless the derivative in question can be regarded as a new active ingredient. The reasoning for this is because of the interpretation of recital 10 of the SPC Regulation for Medicinal Products by recitals 14–17 of the SPC Regulation for Plant Protection Products. The UK IPO will allow the inclusion of salts or esters of the active ingredient in the product definition of the SPC application provided they are also protected by the basic patent.

In relation to combination products, following the CJEU decision in *Massachusetts Institute of Technology* (C-431/04),[5] where the CJEU ruled that a combination of two substances wherein only one substance has a therapeutic effect and the other substance enables a pharmaceutical form of the medicinal product which is necessary for the therapeutic efficacy of the first substance is not 'a combination of active ingredients', the hearing officer at the UK IPO in *Abraxis BioScience LLC* BL O/410/16[6] concluded that the product 'paclitaxel formulated as albumin bound nanoparticles' comprised albumin acting as a carrier and that the product did not qualify as an active ingredient in its own right or as a combination of active ingredients. This view was upheld on appeal in *Abraxis Bioscience LLC v. Comptroller General of Patents* [2017] EWHC 14 (Pat),[7] where Arnold J viewed that Article 1(b) should be strictly interpreted and that it would be inconsistent with such an interpretation for Article 3(d) to permit SPCs to be obtained for new formulations. The UK Patents Court also referred questions to the CJEU (C-443/17),[8] which are currently pending.

In *GlaxoSmithKline Biologicals S.A.* BL O/506/12,[9] the hearing officer at the UK IPO refused SPC applications relating to a product comprising an adjuvant. On appeal

4. CJEU decision in *Arne Forsgren v. Österreichisches Patentamt*, C-631/13 of 15 January 2015.
5. CJEU decision in *Massachusetts Institute of Technology*, C-431/04 of 4 May 2006.
6. UK-IPO decision in *Abraxis BioScience LLC* BL O/410/16 of 26 August 2016.
7. UK Patents Court decision in *Abraxis Bioscience LLC v. Comptroller General of Patents* [2017] EWHC 14 (Pat) of 13 January 2017.
8. CJEU pending referral in *Abraxis BioScience*, C-443/17.
9. UK-IPO decision in *GlaxoSmithKline Biologicals S.A.* BL O/506/12 of 19 December 2012.

in *GlaxoSmithKline Biologicals S.A. v. Comptroller General of Patents* [2013] EWHC 619 [Pat],[10] questions were referred to the CJEU (C-210/13)[11] where it was confirmed that an adjuvant does not fall within the definition of 'product', when considered either alone or in combination with an active ingredient.

As mentioned above, in *Forsgren* (C-631/13),[12] it was determined that a product, which is identified as a 'carrier protein' in a marketing authorization, and is covalently bonded to other active ingredients, can itself be the subject of an SPC if it produces a 'pharmacological, immunological or metabolic action of its own which is covered by the therapeutic indications of the marketing authorization'. The UK Courts have not issued any case law subsequent to this CJEU decision, but in order to determine which components of a medicinal product are active ingredients and which are not, the UK IPO will usually refer to the Summary of Product Characteristics and (if available) European Public Assessment Reports as well as other evidence submitted by the applicant. This practice was approved of in *Abraxis Bioscience LLC v. Comptroller General of Patents* [2017] EWHC 14 (Pat).[13]

Additionally, in *Angiotech Pharmaceuticals Inc. & University of British Columbia* BL O/466/15,[14] the hearing officer at the UK IPO in answering the question of whether the product protected by the SPC application should be Taxol® or Taxol®-eluting stent or both, referred to *Forsgren* (C-631/13)[15] and concluded that the product definition should be Taxol® alone. This case was appealed, but the applicant withdrew their appeal before being heard.

Thus, the UK IPO does not appear to view that the broader concept of active ingredients established in *Forsgren* covers all substances used for medicinal purposes. Unfortunately, this was not one of the questions referred to the CJEU in *Boston Scientific* (C-527/17)[16] also concerning a Taxol®-eluting stent. Therefore, this may be the subject of a future referral.

[3] Active Substance or Combination of Active Substances of a Plant Protection Product

The same considerations as set out in the EU chapter apply. In particular, the CJEU in *Bayer CropScience* (C-11/13),[17] acknowledged that a safener can indeed constitute an

10. UK Patents Court in *GlaxoSmithKline Biologicals S.A. v. Comptroller General of Patents* [2013] EWHC 619 [Pat] of 21 March 2013.
11. CJEU decision in *Glaxosmithkline Biologicals SA and Glaxosmithkline Biologicals, Niederlassung der Smithkline Beecham Pharma GmbH & Co. KG v. Comptroller General of Patents, Designs and Trade Marks* (C-210/13) of 14 November 2013.
12. CJEU decision in *Arne Forsgren v. Österreichisches Patentamt*, C-631/13 of 15 January 2015.
13. UK Patents Court decision in *Abraxis Bioscience LLC v. Comptroller General of Patents* [2017] EWHC 14 (Pat) of 13 January 2017.
14. UK-IPO decision in *Angiotech Pharmaceuticals Inc. & University of British Columbia* BL O/466/15 of 6 October 2015.
15. CJEU decision in *Arne Forsgren v. Österreichisches Patentamt*, C-631/13 of 15 January 2015.
16. CJEU referral pending in *Boston Scientific*, C-527/17.
17. CJEU decision in *Bayer CropScience v. Deutsches Patent- und Markenamt*, C-11/13 of 19 June 2014.

'active substance', provided that it exerts a toxic, phytotoxic or plant protection action of its own.

[4] Fixed-Dose and Loose Combinations

Generally speaking fixed dose combination products are issued a separate marketing authorization to a single product authorization. However, non-fixed dose (loose) combination products are usually issued a marketing authorization by way of a Type-II variation of a single product authorization where there has previously been a single product authorization.

There would not appear to be any logical reason why significant clinical research resulting in a new fixed combination should be awarded extended SPC protection, whereas loose drug combinations which by virtue of kinetic or other therapeutic considerations must be administered separately or sequentially should not be entitled to an SPC. Indeed, such an arbitrary distinction appears contrary to the concept and principles of the SPC Regulation, which are to foster clinical research and to reward the applicant with an SPC where a marketing authorization is obtained following submission of new safety and efficacy data relating to product in question. However, the practice before the UK IPO and UK Courts does not appear to treat loose combinations in the same way as fixed-dose combinations.

For example, in *Imclone Systems Inc. Ltd & Aventis Holdings Inc.* BL O/066/10,[18] the hearing officer at the UK IPO found that a marketing authorization for a single active ingredient which additionally specified the clinical use of that active in conjunction with another active ingredient was not a valid authorization to place a combination product on the market as a medicinal product. The marketing authorization referred to how the active ingredient, cetuximab (Erbitux®), which had cytostatic properties, could be used clinically in conjunction with another active ingredient, irinotecan, with cytotoxic properties, to treat certain types of cancer and that the presence of the cetuximab reduced the amount of irinotecan required to achieve a clinical effect. However, the hearing officer found that the marketing authorization has to be considered in its entirety and not just in respect of the clinical particulars when deciding what is the authorized medicinal product, and hence what is the product that can be protected by an SPC.

On appeal, in *Yeda R&D Company Ltd's v. Comptroller General of Patents* [2010] EWHC 1733 (Pat),[19] the UK Patents Court in paragraph 25 of their judgment, referred to the CJEU case *Massachusetts Institute of Technology* (C-431/04)[20] and in paragraph 18 to the CJEU order in *Yissum* (C-202/05).[21] The UK Patents Court interpreted these CJEU decisions to consider that the concept of 'product' cannot include the therapeutic

18. UK-IPO decision in *Imclone Systems Inc. Ltd & Aventis Holdings Inc.* BL O/066/10 of 23 February 2010.
19. UK Patents Court decision in *Yeda R&D Company Ltd's v. Comptroller General of Patents* [2010] EWHC 1733 (Pat) of 12 July 2010.
20. CJEU decision in *Massachusetts Institute of Technology*, C-431/04 of 4 May 2006.
21. CJEU decision in *Yissum*, C-202/05 of 17 April 2007.

use of an active ingredient protected by a basic patent and that a substance which does not have any therapeutic effect of its own and is used to obtain a certain pharmaceutical form of the medicinal product is not covered by the concept of 'active ingredient'. Following this, the UK Patents Court concluded that the fact that the indication for the therapeutic use of Erbitux™ referred to combination therapy in conjunction with another active ingredient (irinotecan), contained in another medicinal product did not support the conclusion that the marketing authorization granted for Erbitux covered the combination of the active ingredients cetuximab and irinotecan for which SPC protection was sought. The UK Patents Court also took the view that the basic patent protected that therapeutic combination but did not disclose a single active ingredient. Unfortunately, only a question on whether the basic patent also protected the single active ingredient (relevant only to the *Yeda* SPC application for the single active ingredient) was referred to the CJEU in C-518/10.[22] Therefore, the CJEU was not given the opportunity (and has not since) to opine on whether or not the above approach of the UK Patents Court is correct. Also, the UK Patents Court could not take into account that the CJEU, contrary to its former practice, has a tendency to apply a more teleological approach when interpreting the provisions of the SPC Regulations in its more recent case law, including *Neurim* (C-130/11).[23] Therefore, and for the reasons detailed in the EU chapter, it does indeed seem conceivable that the restrictive position taken by the UK Patents Court in respect of the combination SPC application in *Yeda* could still be overturned.

[5] Limitation to Products Subjected to a Specific Marketing Authorization Procedure

The same considerations as set out in the EU chapter apply.

[6] Protection of Medical Devices

Whether or not medical devices containing active ingredients are eligible for SPC protection under the current legislative framework is expected to be clarified by the CJEU's ruling in the pending referral in *Boston Scientific* (C-527/17).[24]

Therefore, earlier UK IPO decisions, particularly *Cerus Corporation* BL O/141/14,[25] *Leibniz-Institut für Neue Materielen Gemeinnützige GmbH* BL O/328/14[26] and *Angiotech Pharmacueticals Inc. and University of British Columbia* BL O/466/15,[27]

22. CJEU decision in *Yeda Research and Development v. Comptroller General of Patents, Designs and Trade Marks*, C-518/10 of 25 November 2011.
23. CJEU decision in *Neurim Pharmaceuticals v. Comptroller-General of Patents*, C-130/11 of 19 July 2012.
24. CJEU referral pending in *Boston Scientific*, C-527/17.
25. UK-IPO decision in *Cerus Corporation* BL O/141/14 of 31 March 2014.
26. UK-IPO decision in *Leibniz-Institut für Neue Materielen Gemeinnützige GmbH* BL O/328/14 of 29 July 2014.
27. UK-IPO decision in *Angiotech Pharmacueticals Inc. and University of British Columbia* BL O/466/15 of 6 October 2015.

can be expected to no longer play any decisive role after the CJEU's decision in this referral.

In all three cases, the hearing officer found that an EC design examination certificate relating to a medical device did not meet the requirements of Article 3(b). The EC design examination certificates were issued having regard to Article 1(4) of Directive 93/42/EEC because the device incorporates as an integral part, a substance which, if used separately, may be considered a medicinal product and which acts upon the body with action ancillary to that of the device. Such 'Class III' devices (as defined in Article 9 and Annex IX of Directive 93/42/EEC) require the safety, quality and usefulness of the substance to be assessed, in an analogous way to authorization under Directive 2001/83/EC. However, this assessment process was not considered by the UK IPO to be the same or equivalent to the process carried out to authorize a medicinal product for human use in accordance with Directive 2001/83/EC. Thus, all three cases resulted in refusal of the SPC application by the UK IPO.

In *Cerus Corporation*, the SPC application concerned a platelet preparation obtainable by addition, and subsequent photoactivation, of amotosalen or its salt, to a suspension of platelets in plasma. In *Leibniz-Institut für Neue Materielen Gemeinnützige GmbH*, the SPC application concerned an aqueous dispersion of iron oxide nanoparticles. In *Angiotech Pharmacueticals Inc. and University of British Columbia*, there were two SPC applications, one for Taxol® and one for a Taxol®-eluting stent.

Interestingly, the product in *Angiotech Pharmacueticals Inc. and University of British Columbia* is the same as the product that is the subject of the pending referral in *Boston Scientific* (C-527/17). Thus, it remains to see whether the CJEU will take the same approach as the UK IPO or instead, find that on a teleological reading of the SPC Regulation, an active ingredient that is required to undergo an authorization process under Directive 93/42/EEC (medical devices) or Directive 90/385/EEC (active implantable medical devices) by virtue of the active ingredient being authorized in combination with a medical device, can be considered to be an authorization process 'in accordance with Directive 2001/83/EC or Directive 2001/82/EC' under Articles 2 and 3(b), and thus subject of an SPC.

Undisputedly, medical devices which do not contain any active ingredient within the meaning of the SPC Regulation for Medicinal Products are not eligible for SPC protection.

[B] Basic Patent

As concerns the basic patent underlying an SPC, the same considerations as set out in the EU chapter apply. The conditions of Article 3 must be satisfied at the date of making an SPC application. Thus, at that date, the basic patent protecting the product must be in force in the UK.

[1] Requirement for the Product to Be 'Protected' by the Basic Patent

As set out in the EU chapter, the CJEU established an 'identification test' in *Medeva* (C-322/10) and subsequent decisions.[28]

The UK IPO will determine whether a product is specified/identified in the wording of the claims of the basic patent if, having regard to the normal cannons of claim interpretation (as confirmed by the CJEU in *Farmitalia* C-392/97), the product is: (i) indicated in a claim; (ii) encompassed by a Markush formula; (iii) shown to result from the process protected by the basic patent; or (iv) encompassed by a functional definition.

In respect of (ii), the UK IPO generally takes a liberal approach and will, in practice, accept the grant of SPCs even in the absence of an explicit and individualized disclosure of the chemical name or structure of the respective active ingredient(s). Recently, the UK Patents Court found in *Sandoz Ltd & Anor v. G.D. Searle & Anor* [2017] EWHC 987 (Pat),[29] that Article 3(a) is satisfied if the product falls within the scope of a Markush formula. In that case, the compound Darunavir was encompassed by the Markush formula, but was neither explicitly recited in the claims, nor explicitly mentioned elsewhere in the patent. On appeal, the UK Court of Appeal referred a question to the CJEU *Sandoz and Hexal* (C-114/18)[30] asking whether this practice in respect of compounds falling within a Markush formula that embody the core inventive technical advance of the patent is correct. How such cases will be handled in the future, will largely depend on the CJEU's decision in C-114/18.

In respect of (iii) and (iv), the UK IPO may ask the applicant to provide evidence, such as in the form of a witness statement, that Article 3(a) is satisfied.

The UK IPO currently indicates in its Manual of Patent Practice that 'in order to meet the requirement that the product is "...in the wording of a claim" an applicant may have recourse to Section 27 of the Patents Act to amend the basic patent accordingly'. Questions concerning the practice of amending a basic patent to render an application compliant with Article 3(a) were referred by the UK Patents Court to the CJEU in *Actavis Group and Actavis UK v. Boehringer Ingelheim Pharma* [2013] EWHC 2927 (Pat) in referral, C-577/13.[31] However, in view of the CJEU's answer to its earlier questions in that referral, those questions were not answered, and are likely to be the subject of a further CJEU referral in the future.

In terms of the UK IPO approach to interpreting the claims, a number of UK IPO decisions confirm that the UK IPO does not take a literal construction of the claims, but

---

28. CJEU decision in *Medeva v. Comptroller General of Patents, Designs and Trade Marks*, C-322/10 of 24 November 2011; CJEU decision in *University of Queensland v. Comptroller-General of Patents, Designs and Trade Marks*, C-630/10 of 25 November 2011; CJEU decision in *Daiichi Sankyo v. Comptroller General of Patents, Designs and Trade Marks*, C-6/11 of 25 November 2011; CJEU decision in *Yeda Research and Development v. Comptroller General of Patents, Designs and Trade Marks*, C-518/10 of 25 November 2011.
29. UK Patents Court decision in *Sandoz Ltd & Anor v. G.D. Searle & Anor* [2017] EWHC 987 (Pat) of 3 May 2017.
30. CJEU referral pending in *Sandoz and Hexal*, C-114/18.
31. CJEU decision in *Actavis Group and Actavis UK v. Boehringer Ingelheim Pharma*, C-577/13 of 12 March 2015.

looks to the description to aid in determining the extent of the claim. This was the UK IPO practice before the 'identification test' in *Medeva* (C-322/10) and subsequent decisions as can be seen by some of the case examples below. Indeed, *Medeva* (C-322/10) and many of the subsequent related CJEU decisions stemmed from referrals from the UK Courts, which have largely confirmed the long-standing UK IPO approach to determining what is protected by the patent.[32]

For example, in *Takeda Chemical Industry's Application* (unreported oral decision on application no. SPC/GB93/017), the UK IPO hearing officer held that a product comprising the acetate salt of a peptide was protected by a basic patent, even though the claims did not on a literal construction include derivatives of the polypeptide, on the grounds that the description made it clear that the polypeptide could be obtained in the form of the acetate.

In *Centocor Inc's SPC Application* [1996] RPC 118,[33] the hearing officer at the UK IPO held that a product consisting of a monoclonal antibody was not protected by claims to a combined preparation of a monoclonal antibody and an anti-microbial agent. In *Takeda Chemical Industries Ltd's Applications* [2004] RPC 1[34] (upheld on appeal to the UK Patents Court [2004] RPC 3[35]) the hearing officer at the UK IPO held that products comprising a combination of ingredients were not protected by patents which related to only one of the ingredients. The basic patents contained no reference to the combinations specified in the SPC applications.

In *Gilead Sciences, Inc.* BL O/006/08,[36] the hearing officer at the UK IPO held that a basic patent which protected a specific active compound and which claimed a combination of the active substance optionally in combination with other (unspecified) therapeutic ingredients did not protect the combination of the active compound with another specific active compound which was the subject of the SPC application. The claim and a corresponding reference in the description were the only indication of a combination of active ingredients in the basic patent. On appeal the UK Patents Court held (*in Re Council Regulation (EEC) No. 1768/92* [2008] EWHC 1902 (Pat)[37]) that although the specific combination was not disclosed in the specification of the basic patent, such a claim did protect the combination within the meaning of Articles 1(c) and 3(a) and therefore that the applicant was entitled to an SPC to the combination of specific active ingredients. This case preceded the 'identification test' in *Medeva*

32. CJEU decision in *Medeva v. Comptroller General of Patents, Designs and Trade Marks*, C-322/10 of 24 November 2011; CJEU decision in *University of Queensland v. Comptroller-General of Patents, Designs and Trade Marks*, C-630/10 of 25 November 2011; CJEU decision in *Daiichi Sankyo v. Comptroller General of Patents, Designs and Trade Marks*, C-6/11 of 25 November 2011; CJEU decision in *Yeda Research and Development v. Comptroller General of Patents, Designs and Trade Marks*, C-518/10 of 25 November 2011.
33. UK-IPO decision in *Centocor Inc's SPC Application* [1996] RPC 118 of 3 May 1995.
34. UK-IPO decision in *Takeda Chemical Industries Ltd's Applications* [2004] RPC 1 of 6 December 2001.
35. UK Patents Court decision in *Takeda Chemical Industries Ltd's Applications (No. 3)* [2004] RPC 3 of 2 April 2003.
36. UK-IPO decision in *Gilead Sciences, Inc.* BL O/006/08 of 10 January 2008.
37. UK Patents Court decision in *Re Council Regulation (EEC) No. 1768/92* [2008] EWHC 1902 (Pat) of 31 July 2008.

(C-322/10) and subsequent decisions of the CJEU,[38] and so it is unclear whether the UK Patents Court would now take the same stance on that case.

In *Astellas Pharma Inc.* BL O/052/09,[39] the hearing officer at the UK IPO similarly found that a patent which disclosed one active ingredient but did not disclose, either specifically or generically, a combination of active ingredients was not a basic patent which protected a combination of active ingredients for the purposes of Article 3(a). On appeal to the UK Patents Court (*Astellas Pharma Inc v. Comptroller-General of Patents* [2009] EWHC 1916 (Pat)[40]), Arnold J upheld the decision of the hearing officer after applying the test articulated in *Gilead*.[41] Arnold J distinguished the facts of *Astellas* from *Gilead* because, unlike in *Gilead*, the basic patent did not specifically disclose and claim a combination of active ingredients.

In *Medeva BV's SPC Applications* BL O/357/09,[42] the hearing officer at the UK IPO, in following the *Astellas* and *Gilead* decisions, found that a basic patent protecting only two particular active ingredients did not protect, for the purposes of Article 3(a), a product containing these two active ingredients in combination with other active ingredients. He also found that a marketing authorization for a medicinal product comprising a combination of active ingredients which included, among others, the two active ingredients was not, for the purposes of Article 3(b), a valid authorization to place a product consisting of these two active ingredients on the market as a medicinal product. On appeal to the UK Patents Court (*Medeva BV v. The Comptroller General of Patents*, [2010] EWHC 68 (Pat), [2010] RPC 20[43]), Kitchin J upheld the decision of the hearing officer and dismissed the appeal, noting that '…It is plain that "product" must have the same meaning in Article 1(b) and Article 3(a). If the product of Article 1(b) is the whole combination of active ingredients then so it remains for the purposes of Article 3(a)… .' On appeal to the UK Court of Appeal (*Medeva's SPC Applications*, [2010] EWCA Civ 700, [2010] RPC 27[44]), the Court referred questions to the CJEU (C-322/10).[45] The CJEU ruled that, for the purposes of Article 3(a), in order to be protected active ingredients needed to be 'specified' in the wording of the claims of the basic patent filed in support of the SPC application, thereby rejecting the so-called infringement test. In relation to Article 3(b), it also ruled that SPCs can be granted for

38. CJEU decision in *Medeva v. Comptroller General of Patents, Designs and Trade Marks*, C-322/10 of 24 November 2011; CJEU decision in *University of Queensland v. Comptroller-General of Patents, Designs and Trade Marks*, C-630/10 of 25 November 2011; CJEU decision in *Daiichi Sankyo v. Comptroller General of Patents, Designs and Trade Marks*, C-6/11 of 25 November 2011; CJEU decision in *Yeda Research and Development v. Comptroller General of Patents, Designs and Trade Marks*, C-518/10 of 25 November 2011.
39. UK-IPO decision in *Astellas Pharma Inc.* BL O/052/09 of 20 February 2009.
40. UK Patents Court decision in *Astellas Pharma Inc v. Comptroller-General of Patents* [2009] EWHC 1916 (Pat) of 31 July 2009.
41. UK-IPO decision in *Gilead Sciences, Inc.* BL O/006/08 of 10 January 2008.
42. UK-IPO decision in *Medeva BV's SPC Applications* BL O/357/09 of 16 November 2009.
43. UK Patents Court in *Medeva BV v. The Comptroller General of Patents*, [2010] EWHC 68 (Pat), [2010] RPC 20 of 27 January 2010.
44. UK Court of Appeal decision in *Medeva's SPC Applications*, [2010] EWCA Civ 700, [2010] RPC 27 of 23 June 2010.
45. CJEU decision in *Medeva v. Comptroller General of Patents, Designs and Trade Marks*, C-322/10 of 24 November 2011.

a combination of active ingredients specified in the wording of the claims of the basic patent relied on where the medicinal product of the marketing authorization submitted in the SPC application also contains other active ingredients in addition to the combination specified in the basic patent. In light of the answers from the CJEU, when the case returned to the UK Court of Appeal, they confirmed that Medeva's applications did not meet these requirements and dismissed their appeal (*Medeva BV v. Comptroller General of Patents* [2012] EWCA Civ 523[46]). In particular, the relevant patent claim referred to a method of preparing a vaccine which 'comprises' the preparation of two specified active ingredients. The claim made no express reference to the other active ingredients of the combination vaccine in respect of which the SPC applications had been made. *Medeva* sought to argue that because the word 'comprises' or 'comprising' in patent claims permits the inclusion of additional elements in addition to those elements expressly referred to, it followed that those additional elements were to be taken as being 'specified' in the wording of the claim. However, the Court of Appeal viewed that the test laid down by the CJEU meant that this was not sufficient for any combination of more than the two active ingredients identified in the claim to be 'specified' in the wording of the claim.

In *Georgetown University, Loyola University of Chicago, and University of Rochester's SPC applications* BL O/401/09,[47] the hearing officer at the UK IPO rejected SPC applications for single active ingredients in the vaccine field on the grounds that they did not satisfy the requirements of Article 3(b) as the marketing authorizations provided in support of these applications related to products with multiple active ingredients. On appeal to the UK Patents Court, Kitchin J referred a question to the CJEU (C-422/10).[48] The question was the same as that referred in *Medeva* in respect of Article 3(b). Consistent with the approach taken in C-322/10,[49] the CJEU ruled that SPCs can be granted for an active ingredient specified in the wording of the claims of the basic patent where the marketing authorization relied upon in the SPC application is for a product that contains other active ingredients in addition to the active ingredient specified in the basic patent.

In *University of Queensland & CSL Limited* BL O/335/10,[50] the hearing officer at the UK IPO followed similar approaches to those in BL O/357/09 (*Medeva*)[51] and BL O/401/09 (*Georgetown*) in relation to Article 3(a) and 3(b) in rejecting multiple SPC applications in the vaccine field for either combinations of active ingredients or single active ingredients. On appeal to the UK Patents Court, Arnold J referred further

46. UK Court of Appeal decision in *Medeva BV v. Comptroller General of Patents* [2012] EWCA Civ 523 of May 2012.
47. UK-IPO decision in *Georgetown University, Loyola University of Chicago, and University of Rochester's SPC applications* BL O/401/09 of 29 December 2009.
48. CJEU decision in *Georgetown University and Others v. Comptroller General of Patents, Designs and Trade Marks*, C-422/10 of 24 November 2011.
49. CJEU decision in *Medeva v. Comptroller General of Patents, Designs and Trade Marks*, C-322/10 of 24 November 2011.
50. UK-IPO decision in *University of Queensland & CSL Limited* BL O/335/10 of 24 September 2010.
51. UK-IPO decision in *Medeva BV's SPC Applications* BL O/357/09 of 16 November 2009.

questions to the CJEU (C-630/10).[52] The CJEU provided its decision by reasoned order with reference to *Medeva* (C-322/10) and *Georgetown* (C-422/10). The CJEU reiterated its answers from its decisions in *Medeva* and *Georgetown*, and clarified that if a basic patent relates to a process by which a product is obtained, Article 3(a) only allows an SPC to be granted for a product which is identified in the wording of the claims of the patent as the product deriving from the process in question. The Court also stated that whether it is possible to obtain the product directly as a result of the process is irrelevant in that regard.

In *Sankyo Company Limited* BL O/271/10,[53] the hearing officer at the UK IPO rejected an SPC application for a combination of active ingredients (olmesartan medoxomil and hydrochlorothiazide) on the basis that it did not meet the requirements of Article 3(a) because the patent only protected the olmeartan medoxomil component. On appeal to the UK Patents Court (*Daiichi Sankyo Company Limited v. Comptroller General of Patents*, [2010] EWHC 2897 (Pat)[54]), Floyd J referred questions to the CJEU (C-6/11)[55] concerning the correct test to apply when deciding whether a product is protected by a basic patent under Article 3(a). The CJEU provided its decision by reasoned order with reference to *Medeva* (C-322/10), confirming that Article 3(a) precludes the grant of an SPC relating to active ingredients which are not identified in the wording of the claims of the basic patent relied upon in the SPC application.

Similarly, in following the approaches taken in *Takeda*,[56] *Gilead*,[57] *Astellas*[58] and *Centocor Inc*,[59] in *Imclone Systems Inc. Ltd & Aventis Holdings Inc.* BL O/066/10,[60] the hearing officer at the UK IPO found that a patent protecting a combination of active ingredients (cetuximab and irinotecan) did not protect a single active ingredient (cetuximab alone) for the purposes of Article 3(a). On appeal to the UK Patents Court (*Yeda Research and Development Company Ltd v. Comptroller General of Patents* [2010] EWHC 1733 (Pat), [2010] RPC 29[61]), Lewison J upheld the decision of the hearing officer to refuse the applications and dismissed the appeal, confirming the approaches taken in previous decisions. On appeal to the UK Court of Appeal (*Yeda Research and Development Company Ltd v. Comptroller General of Patents*[62]), the Court referred a

52. CJEU decision in *University of Queensland and CSL Ltd v. Comptroller General of Patents, Designs and Trade Marks*, C-630/10 of 25 November 2011.
53. UK-IPO decision in *Sankyo Company Limited* BL O/271/10 of 5 February 2010.
54. UK Patents Court decision in *Daiichi Sankyo Company Limited v. Comptroller General of Patents*, [2010] EWHC 2897 (Pat) of 5 November 2010.
55. CJEU decision in *Daiichi Sankyo Company v. Comptroller General of Patents, Designs and Trade Marks*, C-6/11 of 25 November 2011.
56. UK-IPO decision in *Takeda Chemical Industries Ltd's Applications* [2004] RPC 1 of 6 December 2001.
57. UK-IPO decision in *Gilead Sciences, Inc.* BL O/006/08 of 10 January 2008.
58. *UK-IPO decision in Astellas Pharma Inc.* BL O/052/09 of 20 February 2009.
59. UK-IPO decision in *Centocor Inc's SPC Application* [1996] RPC 118 of 3 May 1995.
60. UK-IPO decision in *Imclone Systems Inc. Ltd & Aventis Holdings Inc.* BL O/066/10 of 23 February 2010.
61. UK Patents Court decision in *Yeda Research and Development Company Ltd v. Comptroller General of Patents* [2010] EWHC 1733 (Pat), [2010] RPC 29 of 12 July 2010.
62. UK Court of Appeal in *Yeda Research and Development Company Ltd v. Comptroller General of Patents* of 10 October 2010.

question to the CJEU (C-518/10)[63] concerning whether or not secondary infringement should be part of any proposed infringement test for determining what is protected by the basic patent under Article 3(a). The CJEU provided its decision by reasoned order with reference to *Medeva* (C-322/10), confirming that Article 3(a) precludes the grant of an SPC where the active ingredient specified in the application, even though identified in the wording of the claims of the basic patent as an active ingredient forming part of a combination in conjunction with another active ingredient, is not the subject of any claim relating to that active ingredient alone. Thus, while the 'infringement test' was rejected in favour of an 'identification test', *Medeva* (C-322/10) and subsequent decisions of the CJEU have not greatly altered the practice at the UK IPO. Nonetheless, the UK IPO and UK Courts now have to grapple with the 'identification test' in reasoning their decisions.

The first time the UK Courts had to do this was when the case concerning *University of Queensland, CSL Ltd* (C-630/10)[64] was returned to the UK Patents Court (*University of Queensland and CSL limited v. Comptroller General of Patents*, [2012] EWHC 223 (Pat)[65]). The Court decided that Queensland/CSL's four SPC applications for the individual active ingredients in the Gardasil combination vaccine were allowable based on Queensland/CSL's three basic patents, and granted an order for the SPC applications to proceed to allowance. Neither the Court nor the UK IPO raised the controversial 'one SPC per patent' objection, and so it seems that the UK IPO will allow more than one SPC per patent provided that each SPC is directed towards a different active ingredient i.e., one SPC per product per patent is allowable, provided each active ingredient is different.

University of Queensland, CSL Ltd (C-630/10) was also applied in *Icahn School of Medicine at Mount Sinai* BL O552/14,[66] where the hearing officer at the UK IPO determined that Article 3(a) is complied with if the product identified in the patent claims is the product deriving from the process protected by that patent, but that it is not also necessary to establish that the product is produced by the method of the basic patent.

In *Novartis Pharmaceuticals UK Limited and Medimmune Limited/Medical Research Council* [2012] EWHC 181 (Pat),[67] Arnold J in the UK Patents Court commented at paragraph 53 that 'the test laid down by the CJEU in *Medeva* (C-322/10) and its progeny is unclear save in its rejection of the infringement test in combination cases. In particular, it is unclear precisely what is meant by "specified (or identified) in the wording of the claims"'. Nonetheless, after interpreting and applying *Medeva* and

63. CJEU decision in *Yeda Research and Development Company Ltd and Aventis Holdings Inc. v. Comptroller General of Patents, Designs and Trade Marks*, C-518/10 of 25 November 2011.
64. CJEU decision in *University of Queensland, CSL Ltd*, C-630/10 of 25 November 2011.
65. UK Patents Court in *University of Queensland and CSL limited v. Comptroller General of Patents*, [2012] EWHC 223 (Pat) of 14 February 2012.
66. UK-IPO decision in *Icahn School of Medicine at Mount Sinai* BL O552/14 of 19 December 2014.
67. UK Patents Court decision in *Novartis Pharmaceuticals UK Limited and Medimmune Limited/Medical Research Council* [2012] EWHC 181 (Pat) of 5 July 2011.

subsequent decisions, Arnold J concluded that a claim to a general method of producing a molecule with binding specificity for a particular target did not adequately specify or identify the specific antibody ranibizumab for the purposes of Article 3(a). The appeal against the validity decision on the basic patent failed, and so the appeal on the SPC application was not heard.

In the further UK Patents Court decision in *Actavis Group PTC EHF / Actavis UK Limited and Sanofi and Sanofi Pharma BristolMyers Squibb SNC* [2012] EWHC 2545,[68] Arnold J reiterated his doubt surrounding what is meant by 'specified or identified in the wording of the claims' and that the previous CJEU decisions do not provide a clear test. Therefore, he referred a further question on the interpretation of Article 3(a) to the CJEU in reference C-443/12,[69] which resulted in the CJEU establishing that an SPC is to compensate for delay in marketing 'the core inventive advance' of a patent.

In *Eli Lilly & Company v. Human Genome Sciences Inc* [2012] EWHC 2290 (Pat),[70] the UK Patents Court referred further questions to the CJEU in C-493/12 concerning basic patent claims containing a functional definition. The CJEU determined in C-493/12[71] that a functional definition may suffice for a product to be protected by a basic patent if 'the claims relate, implicitly but necessarily and specifically to the active ingredient in question'.

When the case returned in UK Patents Court in *Eli Lilly & Company v. Human Genome Sciences Inc* [2014] EWHC 2404 (Pat),[72] the UK Patents Court concluded that the question of compliance with Article 3(a) is simply 'does the product fall within the scope of the claims', but in the case of combination products a proviso also exists, in that a product is not protected solely by wording such as 'comprises' that extends the claim beyond its principle scope.

In *Teva UK & Ors v. Gilead* [2017] EWHC 13 (Pat),[73] involving the combination product Tenofovir disproxil and Emtricitabine, Arnold J in the UK Patents Court reviewed the CJEU decisions in respect of how combination products at least may satisfy Article 3(a) and again referred to the CJEU (C-121/17)[74] the question 'what are the criteria for deciding whether "the product is protected by a basic patent in force" in Article 3(a)', which CJEU referral is still pending. At the same time, Arnold J also expressed his view that, to satisfy Article 3(a), a product should fall within the extent of protection of a claim and embody the inventive advance (technical contribution) of the basic patent.

68. UK Patents Court decision in *Actavis Group PTC EHF / Actavis UK Limited and Sanofi and Sanofi Pharma BristolMyers Squibb SNC* [2012] EWHC 2545 of 20 September 2012.
69. CJEU decision in *Actavis Group PTC EHF and Actavis UK Ltd v. Sanofi*, C-443/12 of 12 December 2013.
70. UK Patents Court in *Eli Lilly & Company v. Human Genome Sciences Inc* [2012] EWHC 2290 (Pat) of 3 August 2012.
71. CJEU decision in *Eli Lilly and Company Ltd v. Human Genome Sciences Inc*, C-493/12 of 12 December 2013.
72. UK Patents Court in *Eli Lilly & Company v. Human Genome Sciences Inc* [2014] EWHC 2404 (Pat) of 18 July 2014.
73. UK Patents Court decision in *Teva UK & Ors v. Gilead* [2017] EWHC 13 (Pat) of 13 January 2017.
74. CJEU referral pending in *Teva UK and Others*, C-121/17.

In *Merck Sharp & Dohme Corporation* BL O/117/16,[75] the hearing officer at the UK IPO reviewed *Actavis v. Sanofi* (C-443/12)[76] and *Actavis v. Boehringer* (C-577/13)[77] and concluded that a combination of active ingredients (Ezetimibe and atorvastatin) was protected as such by the patent because it was part of the subject matter or innovation of the patent and fell within the core inventive advance disclosed.

At present, the longstanding UK IPO approach to determining whether the patent protects the product appears to have withstood many CJEU referrals. It remains to be seen whether the CJEU referral in *Teva and others* (C-121/17)[78] will change the UK IPO practice.

[a] Small Molecules

The same considerations as set out in the EU chapter apply.

With respect to basic patents claiming and identifying the active ingredient(s) in question via generic chemical formulae, as mentioned above, the UK IPO generally takes a liberal approach and will, in practice, accept the grant of SPCs even in the absence of an explicit and individualized disclosure of the chemical name or structure of the respective active ingredient(s). How such cases will be handled in the future, will largely depend on the CJEU's decision in *Sandoz v. Searle* (C-114/18).[79]

[b] Polymers

The same considerations as set out in the EU chapter apply.

[c] Antibodies, Enzymes and Other Proteins

The same considerations as set out in the EU chapter apply.

What level of detail a basic patent must provide in order to identify and thereby 'protect' a specific antibody has not yet been clarified in the UK case law following the CJEU decision *Eli Lilly* (C 493/12).[80]

[d] Nucleic Acids

The same considerations as set out in the EU chapter apply.

75. UK-IPO decision in *Merck Sharp & Dohme Corporation* BL O/117/16 of 12 January 2016.
76. CJEU decision in *Actavis v. Sanofi*, C-443/12 of 12 December 2013.
77. CJEU decision in *Actavis v. Boehringer*, C-577/13 of 12 March 2015.
78. CJEU referral pending in *Teva UK and Others*, C-121/17.
79. CJEU referral pending in *Sandoz v. Searle*, C-114/18.
80. CJEU decision in *Eli Lilly and Company Ltd v. Human Genome Sciences Inc*, C-493/12 of 12 December 2013.

[2] Basic Patent Claiming the Product, i.e., the Active Ingredient(s), but Not the Corresponding Authorized Medicinal Product (or Plant Protection Product)

The same considerations as set out in the EU chapter apply.

[3] Requirement for the Product to Constitute 'the Invention' of the Basic Patent

As mentioned above, in a number of UK Court decisions opined by Arnold J, he has made reference to the fact that a product should fall within the extent of protection of a claim and embody the inventive advance (technical contribution) of the basic patent, particularly in view of *Actavis v. Sanofi* (C-443/12).[81]

For example, in *Teva UK & Ors v. Gilead* [2017] EWHC 13 (Pat),[82] involving the combination product Tenofovir disproxil and Emtricitabine, Arnold J referred a question to the CJEU (C-121/17)[83] concerning what the criteria are for deciding whether 'the product is protected by a basic patent in force' in Article 3(a), but also expressed his view that the inventive advance of the basic patent was Tenofovir and not the combination product. In particular, Arnold J viewed that 'the product must infringe because it contains an active ingredient or combination of active ingredients, which embodies the inventive advance (or technical contribution) of the basic patent. Where the product is a combination of active ingredients, the combination, as distinct from one of them, must embody the inventive advance of the basic patent.' Thus, in Arnold J's view, the basic patent did not protect the product because the product did not fall within the extent of protection of the claim and embody the inventive advance (technical contribution) of the basic patent. It remains to be seen whether the CJEU referral will change the outcome on this case.

The UK IPO will also look at the core inventive advance of the patent in determining whether the product is protected by the patent. As mentioned above, in *Merck Sharp & Dohme Corporation* BL O/117/16,[84] the hearing officer at the UK IPO reviewed *Actavis v. Sanofi* (C-443/12)[85] and *Actavis v. Boehringer* (C-577/13)[86] and concluded that a combination of active ingredients (Ezetimibe and atorvastatin) was protected as such by the patent because it was part of the subject matter or innovation of the patent and fell within the core inventive advance disclosed.

It should be noted that in *Merck Sharp & Dohme Corporation* BL O/117/16,[87] Merck had already been granted earlier SPCs on the basis of the same basic patent, one to Ezetimibe alone and one to the combination of Ezetimibe with simvastatin.

81. CJEU decision in *Actavis v. Sanofi*,C-443/12 of 12 December 2013.
82. UK Patents Court decision in *Teva UK & Ors v. Gilead* [2017] EWHC 13 (Pat) of 13 January 2017.
83. CJEU referral pending in *Teva UK and Others*, C-121/17.
84. UK-IPO decision in *Merck Sharp & Dohme Corporation* BL O/117/16 of 12 January 2016.
85. CJEU decision in *Actavis v. Sanofi*, C-443/12 of 12 December 2013.
86. CJEU decision in *Actavis v. Boehringer*, C-577/13 of 12 March 2015.
87. UK-IPO decision in *Merck Sharp & Dohme Corporation* BL O/117/16 of 12 January 2016.

The CJEU decisions dealing with the 'core inventive advance' concept, i.e., *Actavis v. Sanofi* (C-443/12),[88] *Georgetown University* (C-484/12)[89] and *Actavis v. Boehringer* (C-577/13),[90] could be viewed as being primarily concerned with the condition of Article 3(c) of the SPC Regulations (precluding the grant of a further SPC if the same patent holder has already been granted an SPC for the same product; *see* §3.02[D][3][a] below) and do not impose any additional requirements under Article 3(a). However, Arnold J's comments in *Teva UK & Ors v. Gilead* [2017] EWHC 13 (Pat)[91] would indicate that he does not make this distinction and implies that the 'core inventive advance' concept is applicable in his eyes to all SPC applications, and is relevant under both Article 3(a) and (c) (not just Article 3(c)). Time will tell as to whether or not this broader practice will be more limited in future. In particular, hopefully, the CJEU will provide more clarity in C-121/17[92] on whether the 'core inventive advance' concept should apply to Article 3(a) as well as Article 3(c) or be confined only to Article 3(c).

[4] Criteria for Choosing the Basic Patent among Various Available Patents

The same considerations as set out in the EU chapter apply.

[C] The Marketing Authorization Forming Basis for an SPC

The considerations in relation to the marketing authorization forming basis for an SPC application as set out in the EU chapter apply to the UK.

However, the UK IPO views that, while Article 3(b) requires a valid authorization to have been granted, there appears to be no requirement that the authorization should still be in force at the date of making the SPC application (e.g., it may be withdrawn or have lapsed before the date of the application for the SPC).

In some instances the original marketing authorization may have been superseded. In such instances, it is possible to file a chain of marketing authorizations.

[1] Combinations of Active Ingredients

The same considerations as set out in the EU chapter apply.

88. CJEU decision in *Actavis v. Sanofi*, C-443/12 of 12 December 2013.
89. CJEU decision in *Georgetown University v. Octrooicentrum Nederland*, C-484/12 of 12 December 2013.
90. CJEU decision in *Actavis v. Boehringer Ingelheim Pharma*, C-577/13 of 12 March 2015.
91. UK Patents Court decision in *Teva UK & Ors v. Gilead* [2017] EWHC 13 (Pat) of 13 January 2017.
92. CJEU referral pending in *Teva UK and Others*, C-121/17.

[a] The Marketing Authorization Refers to Fewer Active Ingredients than the SPC Application

The same considerations as set out in the EU chapter apply.

[b] The Marketing Authorization Refers to More Active Ingredients than the SPC Application

The same considerations as set out in the EU chapter apply.

[c] The Marketing Authorization Indicates That a Medicinal Product Containing a Single Active Ingredient Is Authorized for Use in Combination with a Further Active Ingredient

As mentioned above, in *Imclone Systems Inc. Ltd & Aventis Holdings Inc.* BL O/066/10,[93] the hearing officer at the UK IPO found that a marketing authorization for a single active ingredient which additionally specified the clinical use of that active in conjunction with another active ingredient was not a valid authorization to place a combination product on the market as a medicinal product. The marketing authorization referred to how the active ingredient, cetuximab (Erbitux®), which had cytostatic properties, could be used clinically in conjunction with another active ingredient, irinotecan, with cytotoxic properties, to treat certain types of cancer and that the presence of the cetuximab reduced the amount of irinotecan required to achieve a clinical effect. However, the hearing officer found that the marketing authorization has to be considered in its entirety and not just in respect of the clinical particulars when deciding what is the authorized medicinal product, and hence what is the product that can be protected by an SPC.

On appeal, in *Yeda R&D Company Ltd's v. Comptroller General of Patents* [2010] EWHC 1733 (Pat),[94] the UK Patents Court in paragraph 25 of their judgment, referred to the CJEU case *Massachusetts Institute of Technology* (C-431/04)[95] and in paragraph 18 to the CJEU order in *Yissum* (C-202/05).[96] The UK Patents Court interpreted these CJEU decisions to consider that the concept of 'product' cannot include the therapeutic use of an active ingredient protected by a basic patent and that a substance which does not have any therapeutic effect of its own and is used to obtain a certain pharmaceutical form of the medicinal product is not covered by the concept of 'active ingredient'. Following this, the UK Patents Court concluded that the fact that the indication for the therapeutic use of Erbitux™ referred to combination therapy in conjunction with another active ingredient (irinotecan), contained in another medicinal product did not

93. UK-IPO decision in *Imclone Systems Inc. Ltd & Aventis Holdings Inc.* BL O/066/10 of 23 February 2010.
94. UK Patents Court decision in *Yeda R&D Company Ltd's v. Comptroller General of Patents* [2010] EWHC 1733 (Pat) of 12 July 2010.
95. CJEU decision in *Massachusetts Institute of Technology*, C-431/04 of 4 May 2006.
96. CJEU decision in *Yissum*, C-202/05 of 17 April 2007.

support the conclusion that the marketing authorization granted for Erbitux covered the combination of the active ingredients cetuximab and irinotecan for which SPC protection was sought. The UK Patents Court also took the view that the basic patent protected that therapeutic combination but did not disclose a single active ingredient. Unfortunately, only a question on whether the basic patent also protected the single active ingredient (relevant only to the *Yeda* SPC application for the single active ingredient) was referred to the CJEU in C-518/10.[97] Therefore, the CJEU was not given the opportunity (and has not since) to opine on whether or not the above approach of the UK Patents Court is correct. Also, the UK Patents Court could not take into account that the CJEU, contrary to its former practice, has a tendency to apply a more teleological approach when interpreting the provisions of the SPC Regulations in its more recent case law in order to ensure that all pharmaceutical research is encouraged and, as such, may benefit from SPC protection; *see*, e.g., *Medeva* (C-322/10)[98] and *Neurim* (C-130/11).[99]

In light of the far more differentiated approach adopted nowadays for the treatment of a disease based on a patient's need, and the recognition that a 'one fits all' solution in terms of therapeutic regimens is generally outdated, it would appear that the principles addressed in *Yeda* should be revisited.

It is nowadays well recognized that applying a more differential approach in therapy is of paramount importance. Moreover, the development of such special 'personalized medicine' treatment approaches for individual patient groups is generally just as cost intensive and time consuming as the development of other innovative medicinal products. Denying SPC protection for such innovative therapeutic developments would run counter to the very purpose of the SPC regime. On a balance of interests, it would appear that there is no logical justification in denying such products additional supplemental protection.

As the CJEU by now has a track record of applying the SPC Regulation pragmatically, taking into account innovation not envisaged at the time of the initial introduction of the SPC regime, it is conceivable that the restrictive position taken by the UK Patents Court in respect of the combination SPC application in *Yeda* could still be overturned, in light of the therapeutic advances made and the need to protect innovation also in the upcoming field of personalized medicine.

[2] The Marketing Authorization Has Not Yet Been Granted at the Time the SPC Application Is Filed

The same considerations as set out in the EU chapter apply.

97. CJEU decision in *Yeda Research and Development v. Comptroller General of Patents, Designs and Trade Marks*, C-518/10 of 25 November 2011.
98. CJEU decision in *Medeva v. Comptroller General of Patents, Designs and Trade Marks*, C-322/10 of 24 November 2011.
99. CJEU decision in *Neurim Pharmaceuticals v. Comptroller-General of Patents*, C-130/11 of 19 July 2012.

In *British Technology Group Ltd's SPC Application* [1997] RPC 118,[100] the hearing officer at the UK IPO found that a letter from the Medicines Control Agency granting permission for a product to be supplied for a proposed clinical trial was not an acceptable marketing authorization because it was not issued in accordance with the Medicinal Products Directive and also did not provide a Summary of Product Characteristics as required by Article 8(1)(b) of the SPC Regulation.

In *Merck Sharp & Dohme Corporation v. Comptroller General of Patents* (C-567/16),[101] the CJEU upheld the view of Arnold J in the Patents Court, who had referred questions to the CJEU, that an end of procedure notice issued by a relevant national competent authority for authorizing medicines (e.g., the MHRA in the UK) under Article 28(4) of the Medicinal Products Directive, is not a valid marketing authorization for the purposes of Article 3(b).

[3] The Holder of the Marketing Authorization

According to the standing practice of the UK IPO, it is unproblematic to file an SPC on the basis of an unrelated third-party marketing authorization.

This practice was confirmed by the UK Patents Court in *Eli Lilly & Company v. Human Genome Sciences Inc* [2012] EWHC 2290 (Pat)[102] where Warren J held that the holder of a basic patent can make an application for an SPC in reliance of a marketing authorization granted to a third party having no connection of any sort with the basic patent holder.

However, in *Novartis Pharmaceuticals UK Ltd v. Medimmune Ltd & Anor* [2012] EWHC 181 (Pat),[103] a point that was not taken up by the parties was made in paragraph 61 of the decision, which stated:

> 'As noted above, in the present case the SPC is based upon a product obtained by means of an allegedly infringing process and upon a marketing authorization obtained by an alleged infringer of the Patent. It might be thought that it was not the purpose of the Regulation to enable a patent owner to obtain an SPC in such circumstances, since the owner has not been delayed in getting the product to market by the need to get a marketing authorization, and therefore no extension to the term of the patent is needed to compensate him for that delay. Counsel for MedImmune accepted that it was not clear from the judgment of the Court of Justice in Case C-181/95 *Biogen Inc v. SmithKline Biologicals SA* [1997] ECR I-386[104] that this was permissible. Nevertheless, counsel for Novartis made it clear that Novartis was not taking this point.' Thus, this may be the subject of a future CJEU referral.

100. UK Patents Court decision in *British Technology Group Ltd's SPC Application* [1997] RPC 118 of 1 January 1997.
101. CJEU decision in *Merck Sharp & Dohme Corporation v. Comptroller General of Patents*, C-567/16 of 7 December 2017.
102. UK Patents Court in *Eli Lilly & Company v. Human Genome Sciences Inc* [2012] EWHC 2290 (Pat) of 3 August 2012.
103. UK Patents Court in *Novartis Pharmaceuticals UK Ltd v. Medimmune Ltd & Anor* [2012] EWHC 181 (Pat) of 10 February 2012.
104. CJEU decision in *Biogen Inc v. SmithKline Biologicals SA*, C-181/95 of 23 January 1997.

The question of whether, having regard to the wording of Article 6, the holder of a marketing authorization may refuse to give a copy to the holder of the basic patent or his successor in title where it is required by Article 8(1)(b) in order to complete the application was referred to the CJEU by the *Tribunal de Commerce, Nivelles, Belgium in Biogen Inc v. SmithKline Beecham Biologicals SA* [1997] RPC 833.[105] The CJEU ruled that the Regulation does not require the holder of the marketing authorization to provide a copy to the patent holder. Such an obligation may, however, be deemed to be inherent in the contractual relationship between the parties. The CJEU also ruled that, where the owner of the basic patent and the holder of the marketing authorization were different persons and the patent owner was unable to provide a copy of the authorization in accordance with Article 8(1)(b), the SPC application could not be refused on that ground alone. It was open to the national authority granting the certificate to obtain a copy of the marketing authorization from the national authority which issued it.

In the light of that ruling, the UK IPO will not reject the SPC application merely because the copy of the authorization is provided by someone other than the applicant, equally the UK IPO will not waive at least the minimum requirements of Article 8(1)(b). Thus, the patent holder must first prove to the UK IPO that he has tried to obtain a copy of the authorization and to provide information available from the authority issuing the authorization (e.g., a gazette notice, a letter or a database printout) that will enable the UK IPO to verify the identity of the product and the date of the authorization stated on the Form SP1 accompanying the SPC application. The UK IPO will then ask the issuing authority to supply a copy of the relevant (usually confidential) Summary of Product Characteristics. If the Summary of Product Characteristics is covered by a request for confidentiality under Rule 53(1) of the Patents Rules 2007 from the authorization authority, it will then be solely for UK IPO use and under no circumstances will be made available to the patent holder or the public. This is somewhat redundant in light of the public accessibility of all of these documents nowadays.

[4] Reliance on a Marketing Authorization Granted under a Provision Other than Directive 2001/83/EC or Directive 2001/82/EC

The same considerations as set out in the EU chapter apply.

As mentioned above, whether medical devices containing active ingredients that are the subject of an EC design examination certificate (not a marketing authorization under Directive 2001/83/EC or Directive 2001/82/EC, but instead under Directive 93/42/EEC (medical devices) or Directive 90/385/EEC (active implantable medical devices)) are eligible for SPC protection under the current legislative framework is expected to be clarified by the CJEU's ruling in the pending referral *Boston Scientific* (C-527/17).[106]

105. UK Patents Court decision in *Tribunal de Commerce, Nivelles, Belgium in Biogen Inc v. SmithKline Beecham Biologicals SA* [1997] RPC 833 of 18 December 1997.

106. CJEU referral pending in *Boston Scientific*, C-527/17.

The current UK IPO practice is to refuse those SPC applications. In *Cerus Corporation* BL O/141/14,[107] *Leibniz-Institut für Neue Materielen Gemeinnützige GmbH* BL O/328/14[108] and *Angiotech Pharmacueticals Inc. and University of British Columbia* BL O/466/15,[109] the hearing officer found that an EC design examination certificate relating to a medical device did not meet the requirements of Article 3(b). The hearing officer considered that the assessment process was not the same or equivalent to the process carried out to authorize a medicinal product for human use in accordance with Directive 2001/83/EC. Thus, all three cases resulted in refusal of the SPC application by the UK IPO.

[5] The Marketing Authorizations Which Can Be Relied upon for SPC Applications for Plant Protection Products

The same considerations as set out in the EU chapter apply.

[6] The Product in Question Is Contained in the Authorized Medicinal Product (or the Authorized Plant Protection Product) but Is Not Identified as an Active Ingredient in the Corresponding Marketing Authorization

The same considerations as set out in the EU chapter apply.

[7] The Notion of the 'First' Marketing Authorization

In principle, the same considerations as set out in the EU chapter apply.

[a] Marketing Authorization for a New Therapeutic Application of a Previously Authorized Product

The CJEU decision in *Neurim* (C-130/11)[110] resulted from a referral from the UK Court of Appeal. In the referral leading up to the CJEU decision, UK IPO and UK Patents Court rejected the SPC application for the product melatonin on the basis that the conditions of Article 3(d) were not met. They determined that an earlier veterinary authorization for the active ingredient melatonin precluded the grant of an SPC based on the later human authorization. After the Court of Appeal referred questions to the CJEU, the CJEU decided that in a case such as Neurim's, Articles 3 and 4 of the Regulation should

107. UK-IPO decision in *Cerus Corporation* BL O/141/14 of 31 March 2014.
108. UK-IPO decision in *Leibniz-Institut für Neue Materielen Gemeinnützige GmbH* BL O/328/14 of 29 July 2014.
109. UK-IPO decision in *Angiotech Pharmacueticals Inc. and University of British Columbia* BL O/466/15 of 6 October 2015.
110. CJEU decision in *Neurim Pharmaceuticals v. Comptroller-General of Patents*, C-130/11 of 19 July 2012.

be interpreted as meaning that: the mere existence of an earlier marketing authorization (obtained for a veterinary medicinal product) does not preclude the grant of an SPC for a different application of the same product for which a marketing authorization has been granted, provided that the application is within the limits of the protection conferred by the basic patent relied upon for the purposes of the application for the SPC. The CJEU went on to state that Article 13(1) must be interpreted as referring to a marketing authorization for a product which falls within the limits of protection conferred by the basic patent relied upon for the purposes of the SPC application.

This decision caused a significant shift in the examination of SPC applications relating to known products for new therapeutic indications at the UK IPO. The UK IPO has found it difficult to reconcile this decision with earlier CJEU decisions in e.g., *Yissum* (C-202/05)[111] and *MIT* (C-431/04),[112] and in practice sought to limit the applicability of the decision to cases with similar fact patterns to *Neurim*. Indeed, this was the position that the UK IPO took in *Abraxis BioScience LLC* BL O/410/16,[113] where the hearing officer held that *Neurim* does not extend to include a new formulation of an existing product, but instead is restricted to a new therapeutic application of an existing product. On appeal to the UK Patents Court in *Abraxis Bioscience LLC v. Comptroller General of Patents* [2017] EWHC 14 (Pat),[114] Arnold J referred questions as to the correct interpretation of Article 3(d) to the CJEU (C-443/17),[115] but nonetheless gave his own opinion that Article 3(d) does not permit SPCs for new formulations of old active ingredients. The decision by the CJEU when issued should shed light on whether the narrow interpretation of *Neurim* taken by the UK IPO and UK Patents Court is correct.

Of course, if the patent holder can explain why marketing authorization is the first for a product which falls within the limits of protection conferred by the basic patent relied upon for the purposes of the SPC application, the UK IPO will accept that such authorization is the first 'relevant' marketing authorization akin to *Neurim*. In such cases, the UK IPO may ask the applicant to show that the indication in the marketing authorization is within the scope of protection of the basic patent, in accordance with paragraph 26 of the judgment. The UK IPO views that the scope of an SPC granted having regard to the *Neurim* judgment will extend only to the authorized use (a view taken from paragraph 25 of the judgment). However, UK IPO practice dictates that it is not necessary to define this use in the product definition at Item 6 of Form SP1. Thus, the product definition in the granted SPC will not include the medical use in line with *Yissum*, where the CJEU found that when a basic patent protects a second medical use of an active ingredient, that use does not form an integral part of the definition of the product. This is an important point to consider when assessing the scope of UK SPCs. For assessing the scope of such SPCs, it is necessary to look beyond

111. CJEU decision in *Yissum*, C-202/05 of 17 April 2007.
112. CJEU decision in *Massachusetts Institute of Technology*, C-431/04 of 4 May 2006.
113. UK-IPO decision in *Abraxis BioScience LLC* BL O/410/16 of 26 August 2016.
114. UK Patents Court decision in *Abraxis Bioscience LLC v. Comptroller General of Patents* [2017] EWHC 14 (Pat) of 13 January 2017.
115. CJEU pending referral in *Abraxis BioScience*, C-443/17.

the product definition given in the SPC to the scope of the marketing authorization and the granted patent.

It is also important to note that the marketing authorization relied upon in *Neurim* was a 'stand alone approval'. To date, it is, however, unresolved whether an SPC in the UK may also be based on a Type-II variation or extension of an existing marketing authorization.

As discussed in the EU chapter, in most instances the marketing authorization for a new therapeutic application of a previously authorized product will be a Type-II variation or extension, as the research and development is based on the originator product.

This per se should not negate the valuable contribution made by the development of the new therapeutic application, and as such should not be decisive for the eligibility for SPC protection of new therapeutic applications of previously authorized products.

Indeed, if one looks at the definition of what the European Commission requires in order for a Type-II variation of a marketing authorization to be granted, then it is clear that a Type-II variation meets these requirements. Commission Regulation (EC) No. 1234/2008 (the Variations Regulation) defines a major variation of Type-II as a variation that is not an extension of the marketing authorization (line extension) and that may have a significant impact on the quality, safety or efficacy of a medicinal product.[116] The European Commission thus determines these changes as major variations and distinguishes them from minor variations of Type IA and IB, which do not require prior examination by the authorities before they can be implemented. In contrast, an application for a major Type-II variation must undergo examination by the authorities and satisfy the authorities that there are not significant safety and efficacy issues due to the major variation.

There are cases pending before the UK IPO where such issues are of primary concern. As such, it is likely that this matter will be resolved or referred to the CJEU for further clarification.

[b] Marketing Authorization for a New Formulation of a Previously Authorized Product

The same considerations as set out in the EU chapter apply.

As mentioned above, in *Abraxis BioScience LLC* BL O/410/16,[117] the hearing officer at the UK IPO held that *Neurim* does not extend to include a new formulation of an existing product, but instead is restricted to a new therapeutic application of an existing product. The patent holder had argued that in *Neurim*, the CJEU had intended that 'different application' could mean either a new indication or a new formulation. On appeal to the UK Patents Court in *Abraxis Bioscience LLC v. Comptroller General of*

116. Guidance on Type-II variations is given by the European medicines agency at: http://www.ema.europa.eu/ema/index.jsp?curl=pages/regulation/q_and_a/q_and_a_detail_000026.jsp.
117. UK-IPO decision in *Abraxis BioScience LLC* BL O/410/16 of 26 August 2016.

Patents [2017] EWHC 14 (Pat),[118] Arnold J referred questions as to the correct interpretation of Article 3(d) to the CJEU (C-443/17),[119] but nonetheless gave his own opinion that Article 3(d) does not permit SPCs for new formulations of old active ingredients. The decision by the CJEU when issued should shed light on whether the narrow interpretation of *Neurim* taken by the UK IPO and UK Patents Court in excluding new formulations of previously authorized products is correct.

[c] Marketing Authorization for a New Specific Salt, Ester or Other Derivative of a Previously Authorized Active Ingredient

The UK IPO follows the guidance provided in the CJEU decision *Farmitalia* (C-392/97)[120] that an SPC is granted for the active moiety of the approved substance. As such, an SPC protects the active moiety, including other salts and other derivatives within the framework of the basic patent. The UK IPO also finds support for this in view of the terms of recitals 14–17 of the SPC Regulation for Plant Protection Products and in the interpretation of recital 10 of the SPC Regulation for Medicinal Products, where the term 'active ingredient' in Article 1(b) is generally interpreted as including any closely related derivative, in particular a salt or ester, which has obtained an authorization to be placed on the market and is protected by the basic patent, unless the derivative in question can be regarded as a new active ingredient.

Thus, provided the basic patent protects the other salts and derivatives of the approved substance, the UK IPO will allow the product definition given in the SPC to optionally include the salts and derivatives. Examples of acceptable wording are 'X optionally in the form of the hydrochloride', 'X optionally in the form of a pharmaceutically acceptable salt such as the hydrochloride', or 'X optionally in the form of a pharmaceutically acceptable salt'.

As a consequence, the sole reliance on a patent for a new salt or other derivative of a previously approved active moiety is not sufficient to warrant the issue of an SPC for this specific form of the previously authorized active ingredient. Of course, if the new salt or derivative can be considered a new active ingredient, then the UK IPO will grant a separate SPC for the new active ingredient or combination of active ingredients.

In the case of *Draco AB's SPC Application* [1996] RPC 417,[121] the patent holder applied for an SPC based on a product licence for an unpressurised asthma inhaler containing the corticosteroid budesonide in the form of agglomerated micronised particles. However, two earlier product licences had been granted for inhalers containing budesonide in the form of micronised particles together with a propellant and surfactant as 'other constituents'. The hearing officer found that the 'product' as defined in Article 1(b) was 'budesonide' in the case of all three inhalers and thus rejected the patent holder's submission that it was 'additive free budesonide in the

118. UK Patents Court decision in *Abraxis Bioscience LLC v. Comptroller General of Patents* [2017] EWHC 14 (Pat) of 13 January 2017.
119. CJEU pending referral in *Abraxis BioScience*, C-443/17.
120. CJEU decision in *Farmitalia Carlo Erba v. Bundesgerichtshof*, C-392/97 of 16 September 1999.
121. UK Patents Court decision in *Draco AB's SPC Application* [1996] RPC 417 of 1 January 1996.

form of agglomerated micronised particles' in the case of the later inhaler and a combination of 'budesonide, a propellant and a surfactant' in the two earlier inhalers. The applicant's alternative submission that the agglomerated form of budesonide was a different 'product' from the non-agglomerated form used in the earlier inhalers was similarly rejected. This decision was upheld by the UK Patents Court, but the patent holder withdrew their appeal to the Court of Appeal before being heard.

The Court reached this conclusion even though 'additive free budesonide in the form of agglomerated micronised particles' had an improved pharmacological efficacy, reduced toxic effects and different pharmacokinetic properties as compared to the previously authorized forms of budesonide; because the Court found that the active ingredient exhibiting the therapeutic effect was confined to 'budesonide'.

Parallels can be drawn to the *Abraxis BioScience LLC* BL O/410/16[122] decision concerning a new formulation of a previously authorized product. The CJEU referral in that case (C-443/17)[123] may shed light on whether the reasoning of *Neurim* can extend to new derivatives or salts of previously authorized products. In particular, the referral may provide some guidance on exactly where the line should be drawn between significant and insignificant differences in the pharmacological, immunological or metabolic effects of an active ingredient and its derivatives.

The CJEU in *Actavis v. Sanofi* (C-443/12)[124] and Arnold J in the UK Patents Court in *Teva UK Limited & Ors v. Merck Sharp & Dohme Corporation* [2017] EWHC 539 (Pat),[125] indicated that dividing products into separate patents would not necessarily assist in an argument that the product of the each patent is 'a totally separate innovation'.

However, careful consideration should still be given to separating out patents to different salts or derivatives, and specifically claiming those salts or derivatives, if it is considered that those salts or derivatives represent a new active ingredient. Prosecution arguments concerning the 'core inventive advance' for each salt or derivative may also assist.

[d] Marketing Authorization for a New Specific Enantiomer of an Active Ingredient Previously Authorized in Racemic Form

The same considerations as set out in the EU chapter apply.

Additionally, the UK Court of Appeal in *Generics (UK) Ltd v. Daiichi Pharmaceutical Co Ltd* [2009] EWCA Civ 646, [2009] RPC 23,[126] upheld the earlier decision of the UK Patents Court ([2008] EWHC 2413 (Pat), [2009] RPC 4[127]) finding that the SPC for levofloxacin, the (-) enantiomer of the racemic mixture, ofloxacin, was correctly

122. UK-IPO decision in *Abraxis BioScience LLC* BL O/410/16 of 26 August 2016.
123. CJEU pending referral in *Abraxis BioScience*, C-443/17.
124. CJEU decision in *Actavis v. Sanofi*,C-443/12 of 12 December 2013.
125. UK Patents Court decision in *Teva UK & Ors v. Gilead* [2017] EWHC 13 (Pat) of 13 January 2017.
126. UK Court of Appeal decision in *Generics (UK) Ltd v. Daiichi Pharmaceutical Co Ltd* [2009] EWCA Civ 646, [2009] RPC 23 of 2 July 2009.
127. UK Patents Court decision in *Generics (UK) Ltd v. Daiichi Pharmaceutical Co Ltd* ([2008] EWHC 2413 (Pat), [2009] RPC 4 of 15 October 2008.

granted despite the existence of earlier marketing authorizations to this racemic mixture. The Courts considered that the specific enantiomer in question was a different product from the racemic mixture.

[e] *The Product Has Already Been Placed on the Market Before, but Without an Authorization Granted under Directive 2001/83/EC or Directive 2001/82/EC*

The same considerations as set out in the EU chapter apply.

[f] *Prior Marketing Authorization Which Refers to Fewer Active Ingredients than the SPC Application (and the Later Marketing Authorization Relied upon)*

The same considerations as set out in the EU chapter apply.

[g] *Prior Marketing Authorization Which Refers to More Active Ingredients than the SPC Application (and the Later Marketing Authorization Relied upon)*

The UK IPO and UK Courts follow the rulings of the CJEU in *Medeva* (C-322/10) and *Georgetown* (C-422/10),[128] which resulted from referrals by the UK Courts, such that the first marketing authorization for the product of an SPC should be the earliest approval of any medicinal product (or plant protection product) comprising, among its active ingredients, the active ingredient(s) referred to in the SPC, even if the corresponding authorized product contains additional active ingredients which are not included in the product definition of the SPC.

As a rule, the grant of an SPC should therefore be precluded under Article 3(d) of the SPC Regulations if the marketing authorization relied upon was not the first marketing authorization in the respective Member State for a medicinal (or plant protection) product comprising, among its active ingredients, the active ingredient(s) which is/are subject of the SPC application.

[D] Preclusion of New SPCs by an Earlier SPC

The same considerations as set out in the EU chapter apply.

128. CJEU decision in *Medeva v. Comptroller General of Patents, Designs and Trade Marks*, C-322/10 of 24 November 2011, paragraph 40 and headnote 2; CJEU decision in *Georgetown University v. Comptroller General of Patents, Designs and Trade Marks*, C-422/10 of 24 November 2011, paragraph 33 and headnote.

[1] Consequences of an Earlier Third-Party SPC for the Same Product

The same considerations as set out in the EU chapter apply.

Recital 17 of the SPC Regulation for Plant Protection Products must be considered in respect of Article 3(c) because, from 8 February 1997 when that Regulation came into force, Article 3 of the SPC Regulation for Medicinal Products is to be interpreted in accordance with Article 3(2) of the SPC Regulation for Plant Protection Products which states 'The holder of more than one patent for the same product shall not be granted more than one certificate for that product. However, where two or more applications concerning the same product and emanating from two or more holders of different patents are pending, one certificate for this product may be issued to each of these holders.'

In *Chiron Corporation and Novo Nordisk A/S* [2005] RPC 24,[129] the hearing officer at the UK IPO concluded that the grant of an SPC for a product to one holder of a basic patent before an application is lodged in relation to the same product by a different holder of a different basic patent on the basis of a common marketing authorization does not provide a ground for rejecting the later application under Article 3(c).

Following this decision, the CJEU in *AHP Manufacturing BV v. Bureau voor de Industriële Eigendom* (C-482/07)[130] held that Article 3(c) does not prevent the grant of an SPC to the holder of a basic patent for a product if, at the time of the submission of the application for the SPC, one or more SPCs have already been granted to one or more holders of one or more other basic patents.

Thus, the UK IPO should allow the grant of a second SPC for a product where an earlier SPC has been granted for that product to a different patent holder on the basis of a different basic patent.

[a] The 'One SPC per Product per Patent Holder' Rule

The same considerations as set out in the EU chapter apply.

When the *University of Queensland, CSL Ltd* (C-630/10)[131] case was returned to the UK Patents Court (*University of Queensland and CSL limited v. Comptroller General of Patents*, [2012] EWHC 223 (Pat)[132]) from the CJEU, the Court decided that Queensland/CSL's four SPC applications for the individual active ingredients in the Gardasil combination vaccine were allowable based on Queensland/CSL's three basic patents, and granted an order for the SPC applications to proceed to allowance. Neither the Court nor the UK IPO raised the controversial 'one SPC per patent' objection, and so it seems that the UK IPO will allow more than one SPC per patent provided that each

129. UK-IPO decision in *Chiron Corporation and Novo Nordisk A/S* [2005] RPC 24 of 16 November 2004.
130. CJEU decision in *AHP Manufacturing BV v. Bureau voor de Industriële Eigendom*, C-482/07 of 3 September 2009.
131. CJEU decision in *University of Queensland, CSL Ltd*, C-630/10 of 25 November 2011.
132. UK Patents Court in *University of Queensland and CSL limited v. Comptroller General of Patents*, [2012] EWHC 223 (Pat) of 14 February 2012.

SPC is directed towards a different active ingredient i.e., one SPC per product per patent is allowable, provided each active ingredient is different.

However, the situation is less clear where an SPC has already been granted for one of the ingredients of a combination product, and an SPC is then sought for the combination. The UK IPO and UK Courts has adapted its approach over the years in line with CJEU rulings.

In *Takeda Chemical Industries Ltd's Applications* [2004] RPC 2,[133] the hearing officer at the UK IPO held that products comprising a combination of ingredients were not precluded from grant of an SPC because one of the ingredients had already been granted an SPC. However, in light of the comment made by the CJEU in *Medeva* (C-322/10)[134] that 'only one certificate may be granted for the basic patent', the UK Patents Court (Arnold J) determined in *Actavis Group PTC EHF / Actavis UK Limited and Sanofi and Sanofi Pharma Bristol-Myers Squibb SNC* [2012] EWHC 2545[135] that the correct interpretation of Article 3(c) was not clear and referred a question to the CJEU (C-443/12)[136] asking whether in the situation in which multiple products are protected by a basic patent does Article 3(c) preclude the patent holder being issued an SPC for each of the products protected? A similar question was referred in *Georgetown University and Octrooicentrum Nederland* (C-484/12).[137] In the resulting decisions, the CJEU determined that it is possible, on the basis of a patent which protects several different products, to obtain several SPCs in relation to each of those products provided that each of those products is protected by the basic patent, (C-484/12, paragraph 30), but that Article 3(c) prohibits successive SPCs based on a single patent for the same active in combination with another active not itself protected by the patent (C-443/12, paragraph 30).

Following this, in *Actavis Group and Actavis UK v. Boehringer Ingelheim Pharma* (C-577/13 - paragraph 39),[138] the CJEU held that, where an SPC has already been granted relating to an active ingredient which constitutes the sole subject matter of the invention, the patent holder is precluded from obtaining an SPC for a combination product claimed in a subsequent claim of the same patent comprising that active ingredient and another substance not constituting the subject matter of the invention.

In reference to this judgment, in *Teva UK Limited & Ors v. Merck Sharp & Dohme Corporation* [2017] EWHC 539 (Pat),[139] Arnold J in the UK Patents Court held that, if the combination represents a distinct invention protected by the patent, it should not matter whether it is protected by the same patent or by a different patent. In other

133. UK-IPO decision in *Takeda Chemical Industries Ltd's Applications* [2004] RPC 1 of 6 December 2001.
134. CJEU decision in *Medeva v. Comptroller General of Patents, Designs and Trade Marks*, C-322/10 of 24 November 2011.
135. UK Patents Court decision in *Actavis Group PTC EHF / Actavis UK Limited and Sanofi and Sanofi Pharma Bristol-Myers Squibb SNC* [2012] EWHC 2545 of 20 September 2012.
136. CJEU decision in *Actavis v. Sanofi*,C-443/12 of 12 December 2013.
137. CJEU decision in *Georgetown University v. Octrooicentrum Nederland*, C-484/12 of 12 December 2013.
138. CJEU decision in *Actavis Group and Actavis UK v. Boehringer Ingelheim Pharma*, C-577/13 of 12 March 2015.
139. UK Patents Court decision in *Teva UK & Ors v. Gilead* [2017] EWHC 13 (Pat) of 13 January 2017.

words, it is the active ingredients found to represent the subject matter of the invention that are critical in determining what the product is, and not if aspects of the subject matter of the invention are found in one or more patents. In that case, the SPC covered a combination of the active ingredient efavirenz together with emtricitabine and tenofovir. The Court found that the SPC failed to comply with the SPC Regulation because: (1) the basic patent did not disclose a combination of all three active ingredients, so the SPC was not protected by the basic patent; and (2) the active ingredient efavirenz had already been the subject of an SPC, and was found to represent the subject matter of the invention, such that a combination comprising efavirenz was not considered to be a distinct invention. Since the combination claimed was not independently valid over the use of efavirenz, it followed that the SPC protected an invention that was already the subject of an SPC, and therefore failed to comply with Article 3(c).

[b] Earlier SPC Granted to an Affiliated Third Party

The same considerations as set out in the EU chapter apply.

The UK Courts have not yet clarified what relevance an earlier granted SPC might have for a new SPC application filed for the same product by a legally distinct but affiliated patent holder.

In practice, if the patent holders appear to be distinct legal entities on the face of the formal register for each basic patent, they will be treated as different rights holders and the two SPCs for the same product granted to the different right holders. In the situation where a relationship between the patent holders appears apparent on the basis of the formal register for each basic patent, the UK IPO would likely ask the second SPC applicant to explain their relationship (if any) to the applicant of the first SPC before the second SPC is granted. However, the boundary as to when the UK IPO would view the second SPC applicant as being different to the first SPC applicant is unclear in such a situation, as this issue does not appear to have been specifically addressed in the UK case law.

[c] Partial Overlap Between the Holders of the Earlier SPC and the Applicants for the New SPC

The same considerations as set out in the EU chapter apply. It appears that this issue has not yet been specifically addressed in the UK case law.

[d] Earlier Third-Party SPC Has Been Licensed-In

The same considerations as set out in the EU chapter apply.

It should be noted in this regard that, as a rule, a licence in a patent will automatically extend to any SPC granted on the basis of that patent, unless the corresponding licence agreement provides otherwise.

In line with this notion, in *Research Corp's SPC* ([1994] RPC 667),[140] the UK Patents Court upheld the decision of the hearing officer at the UK IPO that the endorsement of the basic patent licences of right under the provisions of paragraph 4 of Schedule 1 of the Act was a limitation within the meaning of Article 5. The UK IPO therefore had jurisdiction to entertain an application to settle the terms of licence of right under an SPC, pursuant to Section 46(3) of the Act.

[2] Consequences of an Own Earlier SPC for the Same Product

The same considerations as set out in the EU chapter apply.

[a] Own Earlier SPC Application Not Yet Granted

The same considerations as set out in the EU chapter apply.

The UK IPO will allow a patent holder to withdraw an SPC application (e.g., in favour of a different SPC application) at any time before grant. The withdrawal may not be revoked. The UK IPO does not bar an SPC application being withdrawn before grant and subsequently refiled, provided that the time limit of Article 7 is met.

[b] Revocation, Surrender or Lapse of the Own Earlier SPC after Grant

The same considerations as set out in the EU chapter apply, including with respect to the lapse or surrender of an SPC with ex nunc effect (i.e., without retroactive effect).

One point to note is that lapse of an SPC under Article 14(d) may not be permanent (as it could be restored), whereas once surrendered an SPC cannot be reinstated.

Post-grant amendment of an SPC grant certificate may be permitted under Section 27 of the Patents Act 1977 (which applies by virtue of Schedule 4A to the Patents Act 1977). Questions concerning this practice were referred by the UK Patents Court to the CJEU in *Actavis Group and Actavis UK v. Boehringer Ingelheim Pharma* (C-577/13),[141] but unfortunately these questions were not answered in view of the CJEU's answers to earlier questions. Thus, this issue is not yet resolved.

It is noted that it is possible to correct the SPC expiry date after SPC grant to the 'notification date' rather than the earlier 'decision date' in respect of central marketing authorizations, following the decision of the CJEU in *Seattle Genetics Inc. v. Österreichisches Patentamt* (C-471/14)[142] in line with Article 17(2) of the SPC Regulation for Plant Protection Products, which via recital 17 is also applicable to the SPC Regulation for Medicinal Products.

140. UK Patents Court decision in *Research Corp's SPC* ([1994] RPC 667 of 1994).
141. CJEU decision in *Actavis Group and Actavis UK v. Boehringer Ingelheim Pharma*, C-577/13 of 12 March 2015.
142. CJEU decision in *Seattle Genetics Inc. v. Österreichisches Patentamt*, C-471/14 of 6 October 2015.

Also, the district court of The Hague referred questions concerning whether surrender of a certificate has retrospective effect in *Georgetown University and Octrooicentrum Nederland* (C-484/12),[143] but unfortunately these questions were not answered in view of the CJEU's answers to earlier questions. Thus, this issue is also not yet resolved.

The patent holder could also take advantage of the centralized revocation procedure under Articles 105a and 105b EPC before the EPO (as discussed in the EU chapter) if the basic patent is a European patent. The patentee does not need to provide any reasoning or justification for its request to have its own European patent revoked with retroactive effect, even after the expiry of the patent.[144]

[c] Transfer of the Own Earlier SPC to a Third Party

The same considerations as set out in the EU chapter apply.

[d] Acquisition of an SPC Granted to a Third Party

The same considerations as set out in the EU chapter apply.

[3] Consequences of an Own Earlier SPC for a Different Product

The same considerations as set out in the EU chapter apply.

As mentioned above under §3.02[D][1], when the *University of Queensland, CSL Ltd* (C-630/10)[145] case was returned to the UK Patents Court (*University of Queensland and CSL limited v. Comptroller General of Patents*, [2012] EWHC 223 (Pat)[146]) from the CJEU, the Court decided that Queensland/CSL's four SPC applications for the individual active ingredients in the Gardasil combination vaccine were allowable based on Queensland/CSL's three basic patents, and granted an order for the SPC applications to proceed to allowance. Thus, if the earlier SPC was for a single active ingredient and the later SPC is for a different active ingredient that constitutes a different product, an SPC should be granted in both instances even if both SPC applications are based on the same basic patent.

The situation is less clear where an SPC has already been granted for one of the ingredients of a combination product, and an SPC is then sought for the combination. Here, the UK IPO and UK Courts following CJEU decision *Actavis Group and Actavis UK*

143. CJEU decision in *Georgetown University and Octrooicentrum Nederland*, C-484/12 of 12 December 2013.
144. *See* Guidelines for Examination in the European Patent Office, edition of November 2017, Section D-X, 1–3.
145. CJEU decision in *University of Queensland, CSL Ltd*, C-630/10 of 25 November 2011.
146. UK Patents Court in *University of Queensland and CSL limited v. Comptroller General of Patents*, [2012] EWHC 223 (Pat) of 14 February 2012.

v. Boehringer Ingelheim Pharma (C-577/13),[147] will consider whether the active ingredient of the product of the earlier SPC constitutes the sole subject matter of the invention. If so, the patent holder is precluded from obtaining an SPC for a combination product claimed in a subsequent claim of the same patent comprising that active ingredient and another substance not constituting the subject matter of the invention. The UK Courts also apply this even if the combination is protected by the same patent or a different patent to the single active ingredient (*Teva UK Limited & Ors v. Merck Sharp & Dohme Corporation* [2017] EWHC 539 (Pat)[148]). Their view is that it does not matter if the combination is protected by a different patent if the reason for grant in both patents is because the single active ingredient of the combination that has already been the subject of an SPC is considered to represent the subject matter of the invention. In practice, this places a large burden on the UK IPO to determine what the subject matter of the invention is. Thus, cases may not come to light until litigation.

[a] *Required Distinction from the Product of the Own Earlier SPC*

In general, the same considerations as set out in the EU chapter apply, and the comments under §3.02[D][3] above.

Combinations of Active Ingredients

As mentioned above under §3.02[D][1][a], the UK IPO and UK Courts have adapted their approach over the years in line with CJEU rulings where an SPC has already been granted for one of the ingredients of a combination product, and an SPC is then sought for the combination.

In *Takeda Chemical Industries Ltd's Applications* [2004] RPC 1,[149] the hearing officer at the UK IPO held that products comprising a combination of ingredients were not precluded from grant of an SPC because one of the ingredients had already been granted an SPC. However, in light of the comment made by the CJEU in *Medeva* (C-322/10)[150] that 'only one certificate may be granted for the basic patent', the UK Patents Court (Arnold J) determined in *Actavis Group PTC EHF / Actavis UK Limited and Sanofi and Sanofi Pharma Bristol-Myers Squibb SNC* [2012] EWHC 2545[151] that the correct interpretation of Article 3(c) was not clear and referred a question to the CJEU (C-443/12) asking whether in the situation in which multiple products are protected by a basic patent does Article 3(c) preclude the patent holder being issued an SPC for each of the products protected? A similar question was referred in *Georgetown University*

147. CJEU decision in *Actavis Group and Actavis UK v. Boehringer Ingelheim Pharma*, C-577/13 of 12 March 2015.
148. UK Patents Court decision in *Teva UK & Ors v. Gilead* [2017] EWHC 13 (Pat) of 13 January 2017.
149. UK-IPO decision in *Takeda Chemical Industries Ltd's Applications* [2004] RPC 1 of 6 December 2001.
150. CJEU decision in *Medeva v. Comptroller General of Patents, Designs and Trade Marks*, C-322/10 of 24 November 2011.
151. UK Patents Court decision in *Actavis Group PTC EHF / Actavis UK Limited and Sanofi and Sanofi Pharma Bristol-Myers Squibb SNC* [2012] EWHC 2545 of 20 September 2012.

and Octrooicentrum Nederland (C-484/12).[152] In the resulting decisions, the CJEU determined that it is possible, on the basis of a patent which protects several different products, to obtain several SPCs in relation to each of those products provided that each of those products is protected by the basic patent, (C-484/12, paragraph 30), but that Article 3(c) prohibits successive SPCs based on a single patent for the same active in combination with another active not itself protected by the patent (C-443/12, paragraph 30).

Following this, in *Actavis Group and Actavis UK v. Boehringer Ingelheim Pharma* (C-577/13 - paragraph 39),[153] the CJEU held that, where an SPC has already been granted relating to an active ingredient which constitutes the sole subject matter of the invention, the patent holder is precluded from obtaining an SPC for a combination product claimed in a subsequent claim of the same patent comprising that active ingredient and another substance not constituting the subject matter of the invention.

In reference to this judgment, in *Teva UK Limited & Ors v. Merck Sharp & Dohme Corporation* [2017] EWHC 539 (Pat),[154] Arnold J in the UK Patents Court held that, if the combination represents a distinct invention protected by the patent, it should not matter whether it is protected by the same patent or by a different patent. In other words, it is the active ingredients found to represent the subject matter of the invention that are critical in determining what the product is, and not if aspects of the subject matter of the invention are found in one or more patents. In that case, the SPC covered a combination of the active ingredient efavirenz together with emtricitabine and tenofovir. The Court found that the SPC failed to comply with the SPC Regulation because: (1) the basic patent did not disclose a combination of all three active ingredients, so the SPC was not protected by the basic patent; and (2) the active ingredient efavirenz had already been the subject of an SPC, and was found to represent the subject matter of the invention, such that a combination comprising efavirenz was not considered to be a distinct invention. Since the combination claimed was not independently valid over the use of efavirenz, it followed that the SPC protected an invention that was already the subject of an SPC, and therefore failed to comply with Article 3(c).

New Therapeutic Applications of Previously Approved Active Ingredients

In view of the CJEU's ruling in *Neurim* (C-130/11),[155] the UK IPO generally accepts the grant of a new SPC on the basis of a patent specifically claiming a new therapeutic indication of a previously approved active ingredient and a corresponding separate marketing authorization for the new therapeutic application, even where the same

152. CJEU decision in *Georgetown University v. Octrooicentrum Nederland*, C-484/12 of 12 December 2013.
153. CJEU decision in *Actavis Group and Actavis UK v. Boehringer Ingelheim Pharma*, C-577/13 of 12 March 2015.
154. UK Patents Court decision in *Teva UK & Ors v. Gilead* [2017] EWHC 13 (Pat) of 13 January 2017.
155. CJEU decision in *Neurim Pharmaceuticals v. Comptroller-General of Patents*, C-130/11 of 19 July 2012.

patent holder has already obtained an SPC for the same product but on the basis of a different patent and a marketing authorization for a different therapeutic indication.

The grant of a further SPC for a new formulation of a previously approved active ingredient which has already been the subject of an earlier SPC is more contentious, and usually results in refusal of the SPC application. This practice may change depending on the decision of the CJEU in the pending referral *Abraxis Bioscience* (C-443/17).[156]

[b] SPCs for a Specific Salt, Ester or Other Derivative Where an Own Earlier SPC Has Already Been Granted for the Corresponding Active Ingredient

The UK IPO follows the guidance provided in the CJEU decision *Farmitalia* (C-392/97)[157] that an SPC is granted for the active moiety of the approved substance. As such, an SPC protects the active moiety, including other salts and other derivatives within the framework of the basic patent. The UK IPO also finds support for this in view of the terms of recitals 14–17 of the SPC Regulation for Plant Protection Products and in the interpretation of recital 10 of the SPC Regulation for Medicinal Products, where the term 'active ingredient' in Article 1(b) is generally interpreted as including any closely related derivative, in particular a salt or ester, which has obtained an authorization to be placed on the market and is protected by the basic patent, unless the derivative in question can be regarded as a new active ingredient.

Thus, provided the basic patent protects the other salts and derivatives of the approved substance, the UK IPO will allow the product definition given in the SPC to optionally include the salts and derivatives. Examples of acceptable wording are 'X optionally in the form of the hydrochloride', 'X optionally in the form of a pharmaceutically acceptable salt such as the hydrochloride', or 'X optionally in the form of a pharmaceutically acceptable salt'.

As a consequence, the sole reliance on a patent for a new salt or other derivative of a previously approved active moiety is not sufficient to warrant the issue of an SPC for this specific form of the previously authorized active ingredient. Of course, if the new salt or derivative can be considered a new active ingredient, then the UK IPO will grant a separate SPC for the new active ingredient or combination of active ingredients.

In the case of *Draco AB's SPC Application* [1996] RPC 417,[158] the patent holder applied for an SPC based on a product licence for an unpressurised asthma inhaler containing the corticosteroid budesonide in the form of agglomerated micronised particles. However, two earlier product licences had been granted for inhalers containing budesonide in the form of micronised particles together with a propellant and surfactant as 'other constituents'. The hearing officer found that the 'product' as defined in Article 1(b) was 'budesonide' in the case of all three inhalers and thus rejected the patent holder's submission that it was 'additive free budesonide in the

156. CJEU pending referral in *Abraxis BioScience*, C-443/17.
157. CJEU decision in *Farmitalia Carlo Erba v. Bundesgerichtshof*, C-392/97 of 16 September 1999.
158. UK Patents Court decision in *Draco AB's SPC Application* [1996] RPC 417 of 1 January 1996.

form of agglomerated micronised particles' in the case of the later inhaler and a combination of 'budesonide, a propellant and a surfactant' in the two earlier inhalers. The applicant's alternative submission that the agglomerated form of budesonide was a different 'product' from the non-agglomerated form used in the earlier inhalers was similarly rejected. This decision was upheld by the UK Patents Court, but the patent holder withdrew their appeal to the Court of Appeal before being heard.

The Court reached this conclusion even though 'additive free budesonide in the form of agglomerated micronised particles' had an improved pharmacological efficacy, reduced toxic effects and different pharmacokinetic properties as compared to the previously authorized forms of budesonide; because the Court found that the active ingredient exhibiting the therapeutic effect was confined to 'budesonide'.

Parallels can be drawn to the *Abraxis BioScience LLC* BL O/410/16[159] decision concerning a new formulation of a previously authorized product. The CJEU referral in that case (C-443/17)[160] may shed light on whether the reasoning of *Neurim* (C-130/11)[161] can extend to new derivatives or salts of previously authorized products. In particular, the referral may provide some guidance on exactly where the line should be drawn between significant and insignificant differences in the pharmacological, immunological or metabolic effects of an active ingredient and its derivatives.

The CJEU in *Actavis v. Sanofi* (C-443/12)[162] and Arnold J in the UK Patents Court in *Teva UK Limited & Ors v. Merck Sharp & Dohme Corporation* [2017] EWHC 539 (Pat)[163] indicated that dividing products into separate patents would not necessarily assist in an argument that the product of the each patent is 'a totally separate innovation'.

However, careful consideration should still be given to separating out patents to different salts or derivatives, and specifically claiming those salts or derivatives, if it is considered that those salts or derivatives represent a new active ingredient. Prosecution arguments concerning the 'core inventive advance' for each salt or derivative may also assist.

[c] SPCs for a Specific Enantiomer Where an Own Earlier SPC Has Already Been Granted for the Corresponding Racemate

The UK Court of Appeal in *Generics (UK) Ltd v. Daiichi Pharmaceutical Co Ltd* [2009] EWCA Civ 646, [2009] RPC 23,[164] upheld the earlier decision of the UK Patents Court ([2008] EWHC 2413 (Pat), [2009] RPC 4[165]) finding that the SPC for levofloxacin, the (-)

159. UK-IPO decision in *Abraxis BioScience LLC* BL O/410/16 of 26 August 2016.
160. CJEU pending referral in *Abraxis BioScience*, C-443/17.
161. CJEU decision in *Neurim Pharmaceuticals v. Comptroller-General of Patents*, C-130/11 of 19 July 2012.
162. CJEU decision in *Actavis v. Sanofi*, C-443/12 of 12 December 2013.
163. UK Patents Court decision in *Teva UK & Ors v. Gilead* [2017] EWHC 13 (Pat) of 13 January 2017.
164. UK Court of Appeal decision in *Generics (UK) Ltd v. Daiichi Pharmaceutical Co Ltd* [2009] EWCA Civ 646, [2009] RPC 23 of 2 July 2009.
165. UK Patents Court decision in *Generics (UK) Ltd v. Daiichi Pharmaceutical Co Ltd* ([2008] EWHC 2413 (Pat), [2009] RPC 4 of 15 October 2008.

enantiomer of the racemic mixture, ofloxacin, was correctly granted despite the existence of earlier marketing authorizations to this racemic mixture. The Courts considered that the specific enantiomer in question was a different product from the racemic mixture.

The Court also considered the validity of the basic patent and found that from the point of view of patent law, the specific enantiomer at issue, levofloxacin, was a new product. Thus, that new product was a different product than the previously authorized racemate, and so the grant of the new SPC for that specific enantiomer should not be precluded under Article 3(c) by any earlier SPC that had been granted for the racemate on the basis of the earlier marketing authorization.

[4] Grant of More than One SPC on the Basis of the Same Patent

The same considerations as set out in the EU chapter apply.

When the *University of Queensland, CSL Ltd* (C-630/10)[166] case was returned to the UK Patents Court (*University of Queensland and CSL limited v. Comptroller General of Patents*, [2012] EWHC 223 (Pat)[167]) from the CJEU, the Court decided that Queensland/CSL's four SPC applications for the individual active ingredients in the Gardasil combination vaccine were allowable based on Queensland/CSL's three basic patents, and granted an order for the SPC applications to proceed to allowance. Thus, if the earlier SPC was for a single active ingredient and the later SPC is for a different active ingredient that constitutes a different product, an SPC should be granted in both instances even if both SPC applications are based on the same basic patent.

§3.03 EXTENT OF PROTECTION AND ENFORCEMENT OF SPCs

[A] The Protection Conferred by an SPC

The considerations in terms of the protection conferred by an SPC outlined in the EU chapter apply equally to the UK.

The UK IPO views that Article 4 of the SPC Regulation for Medicinal Products is to be interpreted in the same way as Article 4 of the SPC Regulation for Plant Protection Products in view of recital 17 of the latter. In particular, the UK IPO views that the SPC extends the protection conferred by the basic patent beyond the term of that patent but only in respect of the product covered by the authorization to place the corresponding medicinal product on the market and any use of the product as a medicinal product that has been authorized before expiry of the certificate. It does not, however, extend the term of the patent itself. The UK IPO also takes the view that the plural 'authorizations' makes clear that one SPC will suffice for the first and subsequent authorizations.

166. CJEU decision in *University of Queensland, CSL Ltd*, C-630/10 of 25 November 2011.
167. UK Patents Court in *University of Queensland and CSL limited v. Comptroller General of Patents*, [2012] EWHC 223 (Pat) of 14 February 2012.

However, there is an apparent conflict here with *Neurim* (C-130/11),[168] where a subsequent authorization can be found to be the first 'relevant' authorization.

The UK Courts follow *Novartis AG v. Actavis UK Limited* (C-442/11),[169] which confirmed that Articles 4 and 5 of the SPC Regulation should be interpreted such that SPCs provide patent-like infringement protection for the duration of the SPC.

The scope of protection of an SPC is thus determined on the basis of the underlying patent, but limited to the product for which the SPC has been granted.

Accordingly, if the claims of the basic patent refer to a broader subject matter than the product of the SPC, the corresponding broader definition in the patent specification should be notionally 'replaced' with the product of the SPC for the purposes of claim construction and the determination of the scope of protection in accordance with the general principles established in patent law.

In the case of medical use claims, such as those in *Neurim* (C-130/11),[170] the UK IPO does not allow the therapeutic indication to form part of the product definition. Thus, the product definition in the granted SPC will not include the medical use in line with *Yissum* (C-202/05),[171] where the CJEU found that when a basic patent protects a second medical use of an active ingredient, that use does not form an integral part of the definition of the product. This is an important point to consider when assessing the scope of UK SPCs. For assessing the scope of such SPCs, it is necessary to look beyond the product definition given in the SPC to the scope of the marketing authorization and the granted patent.

[B] The Scope of an SPC in Relation to Derivatives of an Active Ingredient

The UK IPO follows the guidance provided in the CJEU decision *Farmitalia* (C-392/97)[172] that an SPC is granted for the active moiety of the approved substance. As such, an SPC protects the active moiety, including other salts and other derivatives within the framework of the basic patent. The UK IPO also finds support for this in view of the terms of recitals 14–17 of the SPC Regulation for Plant Protection Products and in the interpretation of recital 10 of the SPC Regulation for Medicinal Products, where the term 'active ingredient' in Article 1(b) is generally interpreted as including any closely related derivative, in particular a salt or ester, which has obtained an authorization to be placed on the market and is protected by the basic patent, unless the derivative in question can be regarded as a new active ingredient.

Thus, provided the basic patent protects the other salts and derivatives of the approved substance, the UK IPO will allow the product definition given in the SPC to optionally include the salts and derivatives. Examples of acceptable wording are 'X

168. CJEU decision in *Neurim Pharmaceuticals v. Comptroller-General of Patents*, C-130/11 of 19 July 2012.
169. CJEU decision in *Novartis AG v. Actavis UK Limited*, C-442/11 of 9 February 2012.
170. CJEU decision in *Neurim Pharmaceuticals v. Comptroller-General of Patents*, C-130/11 of 19 July 2012.
171. CJEU decision in *Yissum*, C-202/05 of 17 April 2007.
172. CJEU decision in *Farmitalia Carlo Erba v. Bundesgerichtshof*, C-392/97 of 16 September 1999.

optionally in the form of the hydrochloride', 'X optionally in the form of a pharmaceutically acceptable salt such as the hydrochloride', or 'X optionally in the form of a pharmaceutically acceptable salt'.

If a UK SPC does not include this language in the product definition, arguably in view of *Farmitalia* (C-392/97), the SPC would still be interpreted to include any closely related derivative, in particular a salt or ester, which has obtained an authorization to be placed on the market and is protected by the basic patent. However it is safest to include the language explicitly in the product definition.

[1] The Relationship Between the Definition of the Active Ingredient(s) in an SPC and Its Scope of Protection

While the UK IPO, in view of *Farmitalia* (C-392/97),[173] generally allows an SPC to issue with a broader product definition, beyond the specific form of the active ingredient identified in the marketing authorization (e.g., by the inclusion of pharmaceutically acceptable salts of the active ingredient), the practical implications of the product definition of an SPC in terms of the scope of protection conferred by the SPC remain questionable.

It should also be remembered that according to Article 4, 'within the limits of the protection conferred by the basic patent, the protection conferred by a certificate shall extend only to the product covered by the authorization to place the corresponding medicinal product on the market and for any use of the product as a medicinal product that has been authorized before the expiry of the certificate'.

Thus, in terms of the upper boundary of the scope of protection of an SPC, its scope cannot extend beyond that of the underlying basic patent, even if the product definition of the SPC may appear broader than the invention defined in the claims of the basic patent.

In *Draco AB's SPC Application* [1996] RPC 417,[174] the UK Patents Court held that Article 4 was the operative Article to confer protection on the product, which was the active ingredient as defined in Article 1(b).

In considering recitals 8 and 9 and the operative policy behind the SPC Regulation, Jacob J commented in *Draco* at page 438, lines 30–35: 'It will be noted that the two recitals use both the phrase medicinal product and product. Without more there could be ambiguity. This is because authorizations typically are not for active ingredients as such. They are much more tightly drawn, generally to dosage and formulation or presentation. That has to be so because the actual performance of an active ingredient depends on these matters in addition to the active ingredient itself.' Jacob J went on to note that the authors of the SPC Regulation have thought about the difference between the active ingredient and the actual formulation, and in so doing have defined 'medicinal product' and 'product' in Article 1. Jacob J then stated at page 439, lines 1–5: 'I have no doubt, nor do I think anyone else would have any doubt, that recitals

173. *Ibid.*
174. UK Patents Court decision in *Draco AB's SPC Application* [1996] RPC 417 of 1 January 1996.

8 and 9 must be read as using these definitions. So strictly confined to the product which obtained authorization means: strictly confined to the active ingredient of that which is presented for treatment.'

The definition of the product is thus important not only for determining the scope of protection conferred by a certificate under Article 4 but also for determining whether the conditions for obtaining a certificate, set out in Article 3, are satisfied.

The UK IPO and UK Courts appear to accept that the SPC scope should not be specifically limited to the specific form of the active ingredient identified in the marketing authorization, but to the active ingredient of the marketing authorization in general, which is also protected by the basic patent.

Additionally, in relation to combination product SPCs, in *Novartis AG v. Actavis UK Limited* [2009] EWHC 41 (Ch),[175] the UK Patents Court referred questions concerning the interpretation of Article 4 (and Article 5) to the CJEU (C-442/11).[176] The CJEU decided that SPCs provide patent-like infringement protection for the duration of the SPC. In particular, the SPC for valsartan was found to be infringed by a generic product containing irbesartan in combination with hydrochlorothiazide. The CJEU noted that this combination product would have infringed the basic patent for valsartan (had it been in force), and stated that, '... Articles 4 and 5 of Regulation No. 469/2009 must be interpreted as meaning that, where a "product" consisting of an active ingredient was protected by a basic patent and the holder of that patent was able to rely on the protection conferred by that patent for that "product" in order to oppose the marketing of a medicinal product containing that active ingredient in combination with one or more other active ingredients, a supplementary protection certificate granted for that "product" enables its holder, after the basic patent has expired, to oppose the marketing by a third party of a medicinal product containing that product for a use of the "product", as a medicinal product, which was authorized before that certificate expired.'

Thus if an SPC is granted for product A, the SPC holder will have the right to bring infringement proceedings in respect of a combination product comprising A and B to the extent that this would have been possible under the basic patent.

[C] Enforcement of an SPC

As set out in Section 128B and Schedule 4A, the provisions of the Act in relation to patent infringement (as well as the effect of the patent and exceptions thereto, the scope of protection, and compulsory licences) apply mutatis mutandis to SPCs.

In the UK, the litigation system usually considers patent enforcement and invalidity actions in the same court.

Patent and SPC infringement proceedings are litigated through the UK Patents Court (also generally referred to as the UK High Court), which is a specialist court

175. UK Patents Court decision in *Novartis AG v. Actavis UK Limited* [2009] EWHC 41 (Ch), of 16 January 2009.
176. CJEU decision in *Novartis AG v. Actavis UK Limited*, C-442/11 of 9 February 2012.

within the Chancery Division of the High Court of Justice of England and Wales, with the possibility of appeal to the Court of Appeal and further to the Supreme Court.

The costs of an infringement action are calculated on a theoretical value of the matter in dispute, on the basis of which the court fees and statutory attorney fees are determined.

The losing party is liable to pay the court fees and reimburse the statutory attorney fees of the other party.

The first-instance decision is typically handed down within ten to fifteen months after the filing of the infringement suit. The appeal proceedings before the Court of Appeal typically take about ten to twelve months. A further appeal to the Supreme Court may take from about eighteen months to four years. In the case of SPCs, if any court deems that a point of law is not *acte clair*, they can refer questions to the CJEU and in some instances to the EFTA Court.

Ex parte injunctive relief is available, but is discretionary. A preliminary injunction will be granted depending on whether there is a serious issue to be tried, what the balance of convenience of each party should the order be granted is (in other words, where the balance lies), and whether there are any special factors (*American Cyanamid Co v. Ethicom Ltd* [1975] AC 396[177]). Generally, in UK IP cases, an injunction is granted unless it would be 'grossly disproportionate' to do so.

The UK Court of Appeal has previously referred questions to the CJEU in *Merck Canada Inc, and Merck Sharp & Dohme Ltd v. Sigma Pharmaceuticals plc* (C-539/13)[178] on the interpretation of the Specific Mechanism, a provision which enables holders of patents and supplementary protection certificates (SPCs) of pharmaceutical products to prevent parallel imports of those products into the UK from certain new Member States. The CJEU decided that a patent or an SPC holder or beneficiary cannot rely on his rights under the first paragraph of the Specific Mechanism until notification is given to an importer of his intention to do so. Such notification is, however, not time limited to the one-month period prescribed in the second paragraph of the Specific Mechanism. Consequently, an importer that has followed the procedure under the second paragraph of the Specific Mechanism will not be liable for patent or SPC infringement unless and until the patent holder or beneficiary provides the necessary notification.

§3.04 DETERMINATION OF THE SPC TERM

[A] The Calculation of the SPC Term

The considerations regarding the calculation of the SPC term as set out in the EU chapter apply equally to the United Kingdom.

177. UK HL (now Supreme Court) decision in *American Cyanamid Co v. Ethicom Ltd* [1975] AC 396 of 5 February 1975.
178. CJEU decision in *Merck Canada Inc, and Merck Sharp & Dohme Ltd v. Sigma Pharmaceuticals plc*, C-539/13 of 12 February 2015.

[1] The Relevant Marketing Authorization for the Term of an SPC

The considerations in terms of the relevant marketing authorization for determining the SPC term as set out in the EU chapter apply equally to United Kingdom.

The UK IPO does not, however, carry out a comprehensive search for the verification that the marketing authorization relied upon by the SPC applicant is indeed the first marketing authorization in question. Instead, during substantive examination, the UK IPO includes the following standard request in their exam report:

> The first authorisation within the territories of the existing 'EU Member States and the EFTA states Iceland, Norway and Liechtenstein constitutes the first authorisation in the Community for the purposes of Articles 8(1)(a)(iV), 8(l)(c), 9(2)(e), 11(1)(e) and 13(1) of Regulation 469/2009. Note that marketing authorisations granted in Switzerland can also have effect in Liechtenstein and therefore a first authorisation in Switzerland can also be considered to be effective for the purposes of the above Articles.
>
> You are therefore asked to indicate within the period for reply stated above whether there is any earlier authorisation in Iceland, Norway, Liechtenstein or Switzerland prior to the earliest authorisation specified on Form SP1. If there is such an authorisation, you should specify its State, number and date, the identity of the product authorised and the legal provision under which authorisation took place and supply a copy of its publication in an official gazette pursuant to Article 8(l)(c) together with a translation if necessary. Item 9 of Form SP1 can be amended in the Office if necessary.

If it subsequently becomes evident that there is a discrepancy and a prior authorization in the EU (or the EEA) needs to be taken into account, then a correction of the SPC term may be requested by the applicant as well as a third party.

In recent years, the CJEU has effectively liberalized the SPC system, allowing for SPCs to issue for a new therapeutic use of an active ingredient previously authorized as a medicinal product (*see Neurim*, C-130/11[179]) by considering what is considered to be the first 'relevant' marketing authorization. The UK IPO has found it difficult to reconcile this decision with earlier CJEU decisions in e.g., *Yissum* (C-202/05)[180] and *MIT* (C-431/04),[181] and in practice sought to limit the applicability of the decision to cases with similar fact patterns to *Neurim*. However, in those cases, the UK IPO will consider a later marketing authorization that is the first for a product falling within the scope of the basic patent claims as the first 'relevant' marketing authorization.

It is also important to note that the marketing authorization relied upon in *Neurim* was a 'stand alone approval'. To date, it is, however, unresolved whether an SPC in the UK may also be based on a Type-II variation or extension of an existing marketing authorization.

179. CJEU decision in *Neurim Pharmaceuticals v. Comptroller-General of Patents*, C-130/11 of 19 July 2012.
180. CJEU decision in *Yissum*, C-202/05 of 17 April 2007.
181. CJEU decision in *Massachusetts Institute of Technology*, C-431/04 of 4 May 2006.

If the product which has been approved for a new therapeutic use has been developed by a party unrelated to the holder of the marketing authorization of the prior approval, then an independent new marketing authorization will issue. If, however, the new therapeutic use is developed by the same originator, then either a Type-II variation of the previously granted marketing authorization issues, or if the new therapeutic use warrants a different dosage form from the previously approved product, an extension approval, based on the original approval will be issued.

Such Type-II variations and extensions require the completion of a full approval procedure, with only limited reliance on previously submitted documentation. This per se should not negate the valuable contribution made by the development of the new therapeutic application, and as such should not be decisive for the eligibility for SPC protection of new therapeutic applications of previously authorized products.

Indeed, if one looks at the definition of what the European Commission requires in order for a Type-II variation of a marketing authorization to be granted, then it is clear that a Type-II variation meets these requirements. Commission Regulation (EC) No. 1234/2008 (the Variations Regulation) defines a major variation of Type-II as a variation that is not an extension of the marketing authorization (line extension) and that may have a significant impact on the quality, safety or efficacy of a medicinal product.[182] The European Commission thus determines these changes as major variations and distinguishes them from minor variations of Type IA and IB, which do not require prior examination by the authorities before they can be implemented. In contrast, an application for a major Type-II variation must undergo examination by the authorities and satisfy the authorities that there are not significant safety and efficacy issues due to the major variation.

Thus, in order to adequately take account of the guidance provided by the CJEU in *Neurim*, it would appear expedient to also consider such Type-II variations and extensions as being the relevant marketing authorization for the determination of the SPC term for a product which has been approved for a new therapeutic use.

There are cases pending before the UK IPO where such issues are of primary concern. As such, it is likely that this matter will be resolved or referred to the CJEU for further clarification.

[2] The Expiration Date of an SPC

The calculation of the SPC term, in analogy to the calculation of the patent term, is based on the provisions of Section 25(1) of the Act and a notice in the UK Patents Journal dated 22 July 1992, which makes it clear that from the date of that notice, patent expiry dates recorded on the UK IPO Register, announced in the UK Patents Journal and recorded in official renewal information, are based on the interpretation of

182. Guidance on Type-II variations is given by the European medicines agency at: http://www.ema.europa.eu/ema/index.jsp?curl=pages/regulation/q_and_a/q_and_a_detail_000026.jsp.

the relevant provisions of the legislation that the full term expires on the day before the anniversary of the filing date of the application. Thus, since 1992 the last day when a patent is in force is the day before the twentieth anniversary of its filing date. Accordingly, an SPC with a full five-year term will expire the day before the twenty-fifth anniversary of the filing date of the patent.

For example, a UK SPC which is based on a patent filed on 15 June 2000 and a marketing authorization notified on 10 August 2007 (which was the first marketing authorization for this product in the EU and the EEA) will come into effect upon expiry of the basic patent, i.e., on 15 June 2020, and will expire on 9 August 2022 (at the end of the day, i.e., at midnight). If, in this example, the marketing authorization is notified on or after 15 June 2010, the SPC will have the maximum term of five years (provided the accumulated renewal fees are paid) and will thus expire on 14 June 2025 (at the end of the day).

During examination of the SPC application, the UK IPO will usually invite the applicant to confirm their agreement with the maximum expiry date calculated by the examiner on the basis of the facts presented on Form SP1. The standard paragraph in the examination report usually reads:

> Based on the information presently given, the maximum period expiry date under Article 13 for a certificate granted in respect of your present application is [calculated expiry date]. If you have any observations concerning the accuracy of this date you should include them in the reply to this letter.

[B] Correction of the SPC Term

While the SPC application is pending, it is possible to amend or correct the details on Form SP1 or SP4, including the marketing authorization date (and hence, the SPC expiry date), provided that the time limit of Article 7 is still met.

Post-grant amendment of an SPC grant certificate may be permitted under Section 27 of the Patents Act 1977 (which applies by virtue of Schedule 4A to the Patents Act 1977). Questions concerning this practice were referred by the UK Patents Court to the CJEU in *Actavis Group and Actavis UK v. Boehringer Ingelheim Pharma* (C-577/13).[183] However, these questions were unfortunately not answered in view of the CJEU's answers to the earlier questions. Thus, the general ability to amend the SPC grant certificate in the UK may be the subject of a future CJEU referral.

In any case, as discussed in the EU chapter, Article 17(2) of the SPC Regulation for Plant Protection Products, which via recital 17 is also applicable to the SPC Regulation for Medicinal Products, provides that the decision to grant an SPC shall be open to an appeal aimed at rectifying the duration of the SPC in the specific situation where the date of the first marketing authorization in the Community was incorrectly indicated in the SPC application.

183. CJEU decision in *Actavis Group and Actavis UK v. Boehringer Ingelheim Pharma*, C-577/13 of 12 March 2015.

The UK IPO had already amended its practice in this respect (on 20 November 2013 via a practice notice on their website) before the CJEU decision in *Seattle Genetics* (C-471/14)[184] in view of the hearing officer's decision in *Genzyme Corporation* BL O/418/13.[185] Following that decision, for pending SPC applications, it is necessary to write to the UK IPO providing the SPC application number and a copy of the relevant entry in the OJEU showing the date of notification of the European marketing authorization. The UK IPO will then correct the SPC register to show the corrected maximum SPC expiry date. For granted SPCs, it is necessary to write to the UK IPO providing the SPC number and a copy of the relevant entry in the OJEU showing the date of notification of the European marketing authorization. The UK IPO will then issue a corrected version of the SPC certificate, publish the correction in the UK Patents Journal and correct SPC register to show the corrected maximum SPC expiry date. The same applies to paediatric extensions.

The UK IPO allows the applicant to rectify the duration of an SPC at any point until the SPC (or paediatric extension) expires, in accordance with the practice notice published on their website on 20 November 2013. This practice has been confirmed by the CJEU in *Incyte Corporation v. Szellemi Tulajdon Nemzeti Hivatala* (C-492/16).[186]

[C] Paediatric Extensions

The considerations in terms of paediatric extensions as set out in the EU chapter apply equally to the UK.

§3.05 PROCEDURE OF FILING AN SPC APPLICATION

[A] Entitlement to an SPC Application

The SPC Regulations stipulate in Article 6 that the SPC shall be granted to the patent holder, but are silent as to who may apply for an SPC. In the UK, Article 6 is interpreted as not preventing an SPC application from being lodged by a person other than the patent holder. However, irrespective of who lodged the application, the UK IPO will only grant the SPC to the registered basic patent holder at the time of grant of the SPC.

Additionally, in *Eli Lilly & Company v. Human Genome Sciences Inc* [2012] EWHC 2290 (Pat),[187] Warren J held that the holder of a basic patent can make an application for an SPC in reliance on an MA granted to a third party having no connection of any sort with that holder.

184. CJEU decision in *Seattle Genetics Inc. v. Österreichisches Patentamt* (C-471/14) of 6 October 2015.
185. UK-IPO decision in *Genzyme Corporation* BL O/418/13 of 22 October 2013.
186. CJEU decision in *Incyte Corporation v. Szellemi Tulajdon Nemzeti Hivatala*, C-492/16 of 20 December 2017.
187. UK Patents Court in *Eli Lilly & Company v. Human Genome Sciences Inc* [2012] EWHC 2290 (Pat) of 3 August 2012.

[B] The Time Limit for Filing an SPC Application

The considerations as set out in the EU chapter apply. If the deadline for filing an SPC application has inadvertently been missed, it is possible to obtain an extension to the six-month period of Article 7(1) but this is at the discretion of the UK IPO.

In *Abbott Laboratories* SPC/GB/97/080 (Ex Partes Decision O/302/02),[188] the UK IPO hearing officer considered that the six-month period of Article 7(1) can be extended at the Comptroller's discretion under Rule 110(1) of the 1995 Patent Rules when an application is filed late due to unforeseen circumstances and the applicant acts promptly to rectify the situation.

[C] The Filing of an SPC at the National Patent Office

As set out in the EU chapter, an SPC must be filed before the national patent office within the stipulated time limits, once the basic patent as well as the relevant marketing authorization have issued.

The SPC application must be filed in writing, using the prescribed form issued by the UK IPO, and must contain all relevant information about the applicant and his representative (names and addresses), the EC Regulation (469/2009 or 1610/96) under which the application is made as well as details in terms of product in respect of which the certificate is sought, the basic patent protecting the product, the number and date of the first UK marketing authorization relied upon for the product in question, and (where different from the first UK authorization) the state, number and date of the first authorization in the EU, plus the identity of the authorized product and the legal provision under which the authorization took place (Section 9). The prescribed fee must be paid on filing. Where more than one authorization for the product was granted on the date of the first UK or EU authorization, details of all of the relevant authorizations should be given on the form.

An SPC applicant must provide an address for service in the EEA or Channel Islands. If the applicant does not have its residence, principle place of business nor establishment in the EEA or Channel Islands, they must appoint an agent having a place of business in the EEA or Isle of Man. The agent's ADP number should be given.

No power of attorney is required if the representative is a UK patent attorney.

[D] The Documentation Required for an SPC Application

The documentation required for filing an SPC application in the UK is based on the requirements as set out in Article 8 of the SPC Regulations.

The SPC request should be supplemented by a copy of the first or each UK marketing authorization. This authorization should identify the product, contain the number and date of the authorization and a Summary of the Product Characteristics.

188. UK-IPO Ex Partes decision in *Abbott Laboratories* SPC/GB/97/080 (O/302/02) of 25 July 2012.

Thus, in the case of a pharmaceutical product, it is necessary to file a copy of the Product Licence or Marketing Authorization granted by the UK Medicines and Healthcare Products Regulatory Agency (MHRA), the Veterinary Medicines Directorate or the European Commission following a favourable opinion from the European Medicines Agency (EMA). The copy should include any enclosure or Schedule referred to in the document of grant, such as an attached authenticated copy of the licence application setting out the particulars of the product.

The question of whether, having regard to the wording of Article 6, the holder of a marketing authorization may refuse to give a copy to the holder of the basic patent or his successor in title where it is required by Article 8(1)(b) in order to complete the application was referred to the CJEU by the *Tribunal de Commerce, Nivelles, Belgium in Biogen Inc v. SmithKline Beecham Biologicals SA* [1997] RPC 833.[189] The CJEU ruled that the Regulation does not require the holder of the marketing authorization to provide a copy to the patent holder. Such an obligation may, however, be deemed to be inherent in the contractual relationship between the parties. The CJEU also ruled that, where the owner of the basic patent and the holder of the marketing authorization were different persons and the patent owner was unable to provide a copy of the authorization in accordance with Article 8(1)(b), the SPC application could not be refused on that ground alone. It was open to the national authority granting the certificate to obtain a copy of the marketing authorization from the national authority which issued it.

In the light of that ruling, the UK IPO will not reject the SPC application merely because the copy of the authorization is provided by someone other than the applicant, equally the UK IPO will not waive at least the minimum requirements of Article 8(1)(b). Thus, it the patent holder must first prove to the UK IPO that he has tried to obtain a copy of the authorization and to provide information available from the authority issuing the authorization such information (e.g., a gazette notice, a letter or a database printout) that will enable the UK IPO to verify the identity of the product and the date of the authorization stated on the Form SP1 accompanying the SPC application. The UK IPO will then ask the issuing authority to supply a copy of the relevant (usually confidential) Summary of Product Characteristics. If the Summary of Product Characteristics is covered by a request for confidentiality under Rule 53(1) of the Patents Rules 2007 from the authorization authority, it will then be solely for UK IPO use and under no circumstances will be made available to the patent holder or the public. This is somewhat redundant in light of the public accessibility of all of these documents nowadays.

In addition, if the UK authorization above is not the first authorization for placing the product on the market in the EU or EEA, it is necessary to submit information regarding the identity of the product thus authorized and the legal provision under which the authorization procedure took place, and a copy of the notice publishing the (or each) such first authorization in the appropriate official publication. If no such official publication has been made, a copy of the authorization itself or any other

189. UK Patents Court decision in *Tribunal de Commerce, Nivelles, Belgium in Biogen Inc v. SmithKline Beecham Biologicals SA* [1997] RPC 833 of 18 December 1997.

document proving that the authorization has been issued, such as a confirmatory letter from the authorization authority, should be furnished in lieu.

In the case of plant protection products, copies of provisional and/or definitive marketing authorizations must be filed. Where a provisional authorization for placing the plant protection product on the market in the UK is directly followed by a definitive marketing authorization for the plant protection product, copies must be furnished of the provisional authorization as well as of the definitive marketing authorization to prove that there are no gaps. However, if no definitive marketing authorization has been issued, a copy of the provisional authorization(s) is sufficient (*see Hogan Lovells*, C-229/09[190]).

Any document not in the English language should be accompanied by a translation which only needs to be verified if there is reason to doubt the accuracy of the translation.

Unless it is very obvious, the applicant should also provide information as to how the product is protected by the basic patent. The applicant should also provide whatever information is necessary to enable the UK IPO to confirm that the product is protected by the patent. For example, by specifying a claim of the basic patent which refers to the product or indicating how the product is derived from a general formula in a claim. In the case of chemical compounds, it is common to submit a copy of the chemical structure of the active ingredient from a chemical database, and identify the patent claim(s) that protect the chemical structure.

[E] The Definition of the Product in an SPC Application

As set out in the section of the Manual of Patent Practice concerning SPCs provided by the UK IPO,[191] the product of an SPC should be defined on the basis of the active ingredient(s) as identified in the SmPC, i.e., in Annex 1 of the marketing authorization for the corresponding medicinal product.

In the case of plant protection products, if the identity of the active ingredient cannot be derived from the text of the authorization, the text of the Pesticides Register of UK Authorized Products (published by the Health and Safety Executive) or the EU Pesticides Database (published by the European Commission) can be used alternatively.

The UK IPO follows the guidance provided in the CJEU decision *Farmitalia* (C-392/97)[192] that an SPC is granted for the active moiety of the approved substance. As such, an SPC protects the active moiety, including other salts and other derivatives within the framework of the basic patent. The UK IPO also finds support for this in view of the terms of recitals 14–17 of the SPC Regulation for Plant Protection Products and

190. CJEU decision in *Hogan Lovells International v. Bayer CropScience*, C-229/09 of 11 November 2010.

191. UK-IPO Manual of Patent Practice section on SPCs at: https://www.gov.uk/guidance/manual-of-patent-practice-mopp/supplementary-protection-certificates-for-medicinal-and-plant-protection-products.

192. CJEU decision in *Farmitalia Carlo Erba v. Bundesgerichtshof*, C-392/97 of 16 September 1999.

in the interpretation of recital 10 of the SPC Regulation for Medicinal Products, where the term 'active ingredient' in Article 1(b) is generally interpreted as including any closely related derivative, in particular a salt or ester, which has obtained an authorization to be placed on the market and is protected by the basic patent, unless the derivative in question can be regarded as a new active ingredient.

Thus, provided the basic patent protects the other salts and derivatives of the approved substance, the UK IPO will allow the product definition given in the SPC to optionally include the salts and derivatives. Examples of acceptable wording are 'X optionally in the form of the hydrochloride', 'X optionally in the form of a pharmaceutically acceptable salt such as the hydrochloride', or 'X optionally in the form of a pharmaceutically acceptable salt'.

While the UK IPO, in view of *Farmitalia* (C-392/97),[193] generally allows an SPC to issue with a broader product definition, beyond the specific form of the active ingredient identified in the marketing authorization (e.g., by the inclusion of pharmaceutically acceptable salts of the active ingredient), the practical implications of the product definition of an SPC in terms of the scope of protection conferred by the SPC remain questionable.

It should also be remembered that according to Article 4, 'within the limits of the protection conferred by the basic patent, the protection conferred by a certificate shall extend only to the product covered by the authorization to place the corresponding medicinal product on the market and for any use of the product as a medicinal product that has been authorized before the expiry of the certificate'.

Thus, in terms of the upper boundary of the scope of protection of an SPC, its scope cannot extend beyond that of the underlying basic patent, even if the product definition of the SPC may appear broader than the invention defined in the claims of the basic patent.

In *Draco AB's SPC Application* [1996] RPC 417,[194] the UK Patents Court held that Article 4 was the operative Article to confer protection on the product, which was the active ingredient as defined in Article 1(b).

In considering recitals 8 and 9 and the operative policy behind the SPC Regulation, Jacob J commented in *Draco* at page 438, lines 30–35: 'It will be noted that the two recitals use both the phrase medicinal product and product. Without more there could be ambiguity. This is because authorizations typically are not for active ingredients as such. They are much more tightly drawn, generally to dosage and formulation or presentation. That has to be so because the actual performance of an active ingredient depends on these matters in addition to the active ingredient itself.' Jacob J went on to note that the authors of the SPC Regulation have thought about the difference between the active ingredient and the actual formulation, and in so doing have defined 'medicinal product' and 'product' in Article 1. Jacob J then stated at page 439, lines 1–5: 'I have no doubt, nor do I think anyone else would have any doubt, that recitals 8 and 9 must be read as using these definitions. So strictly confined to the product

193. *Ibid.*
194. UK Patents Court decision in *Draco AB's SPC Application* [1996] RPC 417 of 1 January 1996.

which obtained authorization means: strictly confined to the active ingredient of that which is presented for treatment.'

The definition of the product is thus important not only for determining the scope of protection conferred by a certificate under Article 4 but also for determining whether the conditions for obtaining a certificate, set out in Article 3, are satisfied.

The UK IPO and UK Courts appear to accept that the SPC scope should not be specifically limited to the specific form of the active ingredient identified in the marketing authorization, but to the active ingredient of the marketing authorization in general, which is also protected by the basic patent. Thus, the product definition can be broader than given in the marketing authorization, within the limits of protection conferred by the basic patent.

In the case of medical use claims, such as those in *Neurim* (C-130/11),[195] the UK IPO does not allow the therapeutic indication to form part of the product definition. Thus, the product definition in the granted SPC will not include the medical use in line with *Yissum* (C-202/05),[196] where the CJEU found that when a basic patent protects a second medical use of an active ingredient, that use does not form an integral part of the definition of the product. This is an important point to consider when assessing the scope of UK SPCs. For assessing the scope of such SPCs, it is necessary to look beyond the product definition given in the SPC to the scope of the marketing authorization and the granted patent.

In case of more complex biological molecules, such as antibodies, the UK IPO provides little guidance. A product definition based on the International Nonproprietary Name (INN) of the active ingredient as identified in the SmPC is allowable. Beyond this, it comes down to negotiating a broader product definition with the examiner based on the scope of the basic patent claims and the authorized product.

Additionally, it is important to remember that in relation to combination product SPCs, in *Novartis AG v. Actavis UK Limited* [2009] EWHC 41(Ch),[197] the UK Patents Court referred questions concerning the interpretation of Article 4 (and Article 5) were referred to the CJEU (C-442/11).[198] The CJEU decided that SPCs provide patent-like infringement protection for the duration of the SPC. In particular, the SPC for valsartan was found to be infringed by a generic product containing irbesartan in combination with hydrochlorothiazide. The CJEU noted that this combination product would have infringed the basic patent for valsartan (had it been in force), and stated that, '... Articles 4 and 5 of Regulation No. 469/2009 must be interpreted as meaning that, where a "product" consisting of an active ingredient was protected by a basic patent and the holder of that patent was able to rely on the protection conferred by that patent for that "product" in order to oppose the marketing of a medicinal product containing that active ingredient in combination with one or more other active ingredients, a supplementary protection certificate granted for that "product" enables its holder, after

195. CJEU decision in *Neurim Pharmaceuticals v. Comptroller-General of Patents*, C-130/11 of 19 July 2012.
196. CJEU decision in *Yissum*, C-202/05 of 17 April 2007.
197. UK Patents Court decision in *Novartis AG v. Actavis UK Limited* [2009] EWHC 41 (Ch), of 16 January 2009.
198. CJEU decision in *Novartis AG v. Actavis UK Limited*, C-442/11 of 9 February 2012.

the basic patent has expired, to oppose the marketing by a third party of a medicinal product containing that product for a use of the "product", as a medicinal product, which was authorized before that certificate expired.'

Thus if SPC is granted for product A, the SPC holder will have the right to bring infringement proceedings in respect of a combination product comprising A and B to the extent that this would have been possible under the basic patent.

[F] SPC Examination Procedure and Appeal Procedure

In accordance with the practice of the UK IPO, an application for an SPC will be subject to a formal examination, followed by a substantive examination.

The formal examination focuses on issues such as the use of the correct form, the time limits for filing the SPC, the payment of the prescribed fees, the formal entitlement of the applicant, as well as the question as to whether the patent is in force and the documentation submitted is complete. If there are deficits in this regard or if any documentation is missing, the UK IPO will invite the applicant to rectify this.

The basic patent must be in force and a marketing authorization for the product must have been granted by the date that the SPC application was lodged, it being confirmed by the CJEU in *Merck Sharp & Dohme Corporation* (C-567/16)[199] that the latter requirement is not 'an irregularity' that can be cured during the formalities examination having regard to Article 10(3).

The substantive examination includes the verification that the marketing authorization was granted in accordance with the appropriate directives and is valid at the filing date.

The UK IPO does not generally examine whether the marketing authorization is indeed the first marketing authorization. However, the examiner may consider whether this requirement is met where there is reason to do so (e.g., on the basis of information supplied by the applicant, observations by a third party or information in another application for the same product).

The UK IPO will check that the product identified in the SPC application has not been the subject of a previous UK SPC. Frequently, the applicant submits various SPC requests for the same product based on different basic patents in parallel, in which case, however, only a single SPC may issue.

During the examination the identity of the product is established and it is verified that the product is protected by the basic patent.

Generally, the substantive examination is carried out at the same time as the formalities examination, and all objections arising are reported to the applicant in a single letter. If the basic patent has already expired or is about to expire, substantive examination is carried out as a matter of urgency, in order to avoid delay in the entry into force of the SPC. Substantive examination may however be deferred in cases

199. CJEU decision in *Merck Sharp & Dohme Corporation v. Comptroller-General of Patents, Designs and Trade Marks*, C-567/16 of 7 December 2017.

where the examiner considers it likely that the application may not be able to meet a formal objection.

If an SPC application is considered to be deficient in either formalities or substantive aspects or both, the UK IPO will issue an office action inviting the applicant to correct the deficiencies within a prescribed period, often a four-month time limit which can be extended.

Any observations by a third party concerning whether the application meets the conditions of the SPC Regulation are considered by the examiner as in the case of a patent application. However, as in the case of a patent application, such observations must be in writing and must be made before the SPC is granted.

In reply to the office action, the applicant can submit further documentation and argumentation, such as to show that the patent protects the product, and can amended the details on the Form SP1 or SP4, such as the product definition.

If the applicant wishes to amend Form SP1 or SP4 while the SPC application is pending other than in response to an office action (e.g., to add details of further relevant authorizations that have come to light) the amendment should be formally requested in writing. The applicant can also request correction of the marketing authorization date to the 'notification date' in respect of central European marketing authorizations in view of the CJEU decision in *Seattle Genetics* (C-471/14)[200] using the UK IPO practice in this respect (issued 20 November 2013 via a practice notice on their website). In particular, it is necessary to write to the UK IPO providing the SPC application number and a copy of the relevant entry in the OJEU showing the date of notification of the European marketing authorization. The same applies to paediatric extensions. The UK IPO will then correct the SPC register and Form SP1 accordingly.

Where the applicant has amended or corrected the application, and/or made submissions in response to any objection to formal or substantive matters raised by the examiner, the application is re-examined as soon as possible.

Where the examiner is still not satisfied that the conditions of the SPC Regulation are met, the UK IPO will either issue a further office action outlining the outstanding objection(s), contact the applicant (or his representative) via telephone or for an interview, or initiate the rejection procedure. Unlike the case of patent applications, there is no overall period within which an SPC must be in order for grant. However, where the basic patent has already expired or is about to expire, re-examination is carried out as a matter of urgency.

If the applicant requests to be heard in the matter, the UK IPO, like for patent applications, must appoint an oral hearing before any rejection can be issued. Any decision taken following the oral hearing is subject to appeal to the UK Patents Court.

The applicant can also request a decision to be taken in writing on the current state of the file at any point. Such a decision can also be appealed to the UK Patents Court.

As an example of the UK IPO examination procedure, in *British Technology Group Ltd's SPC Application* [1997] RPC 118, the hearing officer at the UK IPO determined that

200. CJEU decision in *Seattle Genetics Inc. v. Österreichisches Patentamt* (C-471/14) of 6 October 2015.

a valid product licence had not been granted, and so refused permission to keep the application open until the time that the applicants provided a valid authorization in accordance with Article 3(b). To do otherwise would put third parties at a considerable disadvantage. The correct procedure was to file a fresh application when all the requirements of the SPC Regulation could be met, particularly the provision of a valid market authorization. Article 3(c) would not be contravened in such a case because the first filed SPC application had not been granted.

If the application for the SPC is in compliance with the statutory requirements as set out in the SPC Regulation and Section 128B of the Act, the UK IPO will issue the grant certificate for the duration of its term and, if appropriate, its paediatric extension. In this respect, it is noted that in *Merck and Co., Inc.* BL O/108/08, the hearing officer at the UK IPO found that where an application met the requirements of Article 10, an SPC can be granted even if by applying the calculation of Article 13(1) it would never take effect at the end of the lawful term of the basic patent i.e., would have a negative term, because this may give rise to a positive SPC term upon grant of a six-month paediatric extension.

The SPC certificate retains the application number allocated by the UK IPO, states the date of expiry of the maximum possible period of its duration and indicates that entry into force is dependent upon the payment of accumulated renewal fees.

Since the SPC Regulation does not require that grant of the SPC must occur before the basic patent expires, merely that the latter is in force on the date of filing, the UK IPO applies the grant in such a situation as being retrospective to the day after the basic patent expired. Therefore, when details of filing of an SPC application are published in the UK Patents Journal, the public is put on notice that grant of the SPC may occur at any time subsequently.

If the applicant wishes to appeal the decision of the UK IPO concerning their SPC application, a substantiated appeal against such a decision must be filed at the UK Patents Court in writing within twenty-eight days of the service of the decision together with the payment of an appeal fee.[201]

The UK Patents Court will then hear the matter and a final decision from the UK Patents Court may be expected within about twelve months to eighteen months after the filing of the appeal. The UK Patents Court may within this timeframe decide to refer questions to the CJEU on any unclear points of law.

[G] Applications for a Paediatric Extension

The formal requirements for filing a paediatric extension correspond to those as outlined in the EU chapter.

The request for a paediatric extension must be filed with the UK IPO together with the prescribed fee, using the prescribed form.

201. Under the Practice Direction to Part 52 of the Civil Procedure Rules, any appeal must be lodged within twenty-eight days.

If an SPC has already been granted, then the request must be filed no later than two years before the expiry of the SPC.

The required supporting documents are set out in Article 8(1)(d) of the SPC Regulation for Medicinal Products. These include a copy of the statement indicating compliance with the agreed and completed Paediatric Investigation Plan (PIP). Moreover, if the product has not been approved centrally by the EMA, it is necessary for the applicant to submit proof of possession of marketing authorizations for the product in all Member States.

The SPC Regulation does not provide any provisions for extending the Article 7 period, and there are no special provisions under UK law in this respect. Therefore, the applicable provision governing such an extension of time is the appropriate procedural provision under UK law corresponding to the basic patent. In *Merck & Co., Inc.* BL O/035/09,[202] the hearing officer at the UK IPO found that the time limit set by the examiner for rectifying an irregularity in filing the required documents for a paediatric extension was extendable under Rule 108 of the Patents Rules 2007, and further discretionary extensions may be available. The UK Court of Appeal in *E I Du Pont Nemours & Co.* [2009] EWCA Civ 966, [2010] RPC 6[203] also confirmed that the time periods for curing irregularities under Article 10(3) in an application for an extension of the duration of a certificate can be extended.

Thus, if the statement of compliance is not yet available when filing the request, the UK IPO will issue an office action setting a deadline, usually four months, for filing the statement of compliance. According the above case law, that time period is extendable as of right under Rule 108 of the Patents Rules 2007, and further discretionary periods may be available. For example, in *Merck & Co., Inc.* BL O/035/09,[204] the hearing officer viewed that if the applicant was unable to file the statement of compliance because of delays beyond their control, for example, because of the time taken by the competent authority to provide an updated varied marketing authorization, then this is a factor to be taken into consideration in granting a discretionary extension.

The formal and substantive examination of the request for a paediatric extension includes the verification of the entitlement to lodge the application, the completeness of the documentation in relation to the compliance statement and the verification that the product has been approved in all EU Member States.

In order to be entitled to a paediatric extension the product shall not be designated as an orphan medicinal product, as set out in Article 36(4) of the Paediatric Regulation (EC) 1901/2006. Moreover, no one-year extension of the period of regulatory exclusivity must have been granted, as set out in Article 36(5) of the Paediatric Regulation.

202. UK-IPO decision in *Merck & Co., Inc.* BL O/035/09 of 6 February 2009.
203. UK Court of Appeal decision in *E I Du Pont Nemours & Co.* [2009] EWCA Civ 966, [2010] RPC 6 of 17 September 2009.
204. UK-IPO decision in *Merck & Co., Inc.* BL O/035/09 of 6 February 2009.

§3.06 PROCEDURE OF INVALIDATING AN SPC

It is not possible for a third party to oppose the grant of an SPC or a paediatric extension at the UK IPO. It is however possible to file third-party observations during the SPC application procedure, which the UK IPO examiner must take into account.

Additionally, in accordance with Article 15(2) of the SPC Regulations, Section 128B and Schedule 4A of the Act stipulates that the provisions of the Act in relation to the revocation of a patent also apply to SPCs. Such revocation actions can be filed before the UK IPO or the UK Courts, the latter being more common.

In addition to invalidation of the SPC by revocation, declarations of lapse of the SPC can be issued by the UK IPO if the relevant marketing authorization has lapsed or been withdrawn.

If the marketing authorization has lapsed or been withdrawn, the UK IPO will still grant the SPC because the UK IPO views that the SPC Regulation for Medicinal Products does not grant them the power to refuse to grant an SPC on these grounds. However, when the SPC comes into force, the UK IPO may issue a declaration of lapse under Article 14(d) if the marketing authorization has not been reinstated. A third party can also apply to the UK IPO and pay a fee for a declaration of lapse after SPC grant, if the marketing authorization has lapsed or been withdrawn. The UK IPO will then commence proceedings where the SPC holder is informed of the withdrawal in an official letter and that, subject to any observations which the holder may make within a specified period (generally two months), the UK IPO proposes to declare that the certificate has lapsed. Any decision made by the UK IPO in this respect, is subject to appeal to the UK Patents Court.

In the situation where a new authorization is granted, an SPC which has lapsed under Article 14(d) automatically takes effect again from the date of the new authorization, unless the SPC has also been declared invalid or lapsed under any other ground e.g., surrender. The SPC holder must advise the UK IPO of the grant of the new marketing authorization and, if satisfactory, the UK IPO will then issue a notice of termination of the lapse under Article 14(d) in the UK Patents Journal.

[A] Grounds for the Invalidation of an SPC

The grounds for invalidating an SPC in the UK correspond to the grounds as set out in Article 15 of the SPC Regulations, as discussed in the EU chapter.

The UK IPO and UK Courts also adopt the view of the CJEU from *Hässle AB v. Ratiopharm* (C-127/00),[205] that the catalogue of grounds of invalidity set out in Article 15(1) of the SPC Regulations is not exhaustive. For example, as set out in that decision, non-compliance with the requirement under Article 2 of the SPC Regulations that the product must not have been placed on the market as a medicinal product or a plant

205. UK Patents Court decision in *Hässle AB v. Ratiopharm* (C-127/00) [2003] ECR I-14781 of 11 December 2003.

protection product before having undergone a specific administrative authorization procedure, also constitutes a ground of invalidity of the SPC.

[B] The Filing of an Invalidation Suit

In the UK, the UK Patents Court (a specialist IP branch of the UK High Court) will usually hear patent enforcement and invalidity actions at the first instance. As such for SPCs, in analogy to patents, the UK Patents Court has exclusive jurisdiction for invalidation.[206]

An action for the invalidation of an SPC may be filed at any time by any person, independent from any pending infringement proceedings.

Proceedings in relation to the basic patent may also occur at the same time as proceedings in relation to the corresponding SPC, and have a knock on effect on one another. For example, in *Generics (UK) Limited (trading as Mylan) and Novartis AG*, [2011] EWHC 2403 (Pat),[207] Floyd J in the UK Patents Court found the claims of the basic patent filed in support of the SPC were obvious and thus invalid, and consequently also found the associated SPC be invalid.

Also, decisions from the UK Courts or CJEU may result in some previously granted SPCs being invalid. The UK IPO will not re-examine granted SPCs in the period between their dates of grant and coming into force. An interested party may however seek a declaration of invalidity.

Presumably, such an 'interested party' could be the SPC holder in the situation where they had an alternative pending SPC application that would not be rendered invalid by the decision, but this has not been tested before the UK Courts. The SPC holder could alternatively look to surrender their granted SPC and proceed with the pending SPC application.

The District Court of The Hague referred questions to the CJEU in *Georgetown University and Octrooicentrum Nederland* (C-484/12)[208] concerning whether surrender of an SPC has retrospective effect, but given the responses to other questions referred the questions on surrender were not answered. Thus, this may be the subject of a future CJEU referral.

The patent holder could also take advantage of the centralized revocation procedure under Articles 105a and 105b EPC before the EPO (as discussed in the EU chapter) if the basic patent is a European patent. The patentee does not need to provide any reasoning or justification for its request to have its own European patent revoked with retroactive effect, even after the expiry of the patent.[209] Revocation of the basic patent would then result in invalidity and revocation of the corresponding SPC. The

206. Section 128B and Schedule 4A of the Act.
207. UK Patents Court decision in *Generics (UK) Limited (trading as Mylan) and Novartis AG*, [2011] EWHC 2403 (Pat) of 30 September 2011.
208. CJEU decision in *Georgetown University and Octrooicentrum Nederland*, C-484/12 of 12 December 2013.
209. *See* Guidelines for Examination in the European Patent Office, edition of November 2017, Section D-X, 1–3.

patent holder would, of course, not be able to use that basic patent as the basis for an alternative SPC application in such a situation, so this may not be a viable route.

[C] Invalidation Procedure and the Corresponding Appeal Procedure

The SPC Regulations and the Act do not appear to provide any special rules as to the timing of filing an application for a declaration of invalidity of an SPC. Since one of the grounds of invalidity is that the SPC was granted contrary to the provisions of Article 3, presumably, an application for a declaration of invalidity can be filed at any point after grant of the SPC. As mentioned above, opposition to the grant of the SPC is not possible in the UK, but third-party observations are possible before grant. Thus, it would be logical that an application for a declaration of invalidity can be filed at any point after grant of the SPC. However, it is understood that point has not been tested before the UK Courts.

The costs of an application for a declaration of invalidity are calculated on a theoretical value of the matter in dispute, on the basis of which the court fees and statutory attorney fees are determined.

The losing party is liable to pay the court fees and reimburse the statutory attorney fees of the other party.

The first-instance decision is typically handed down within ten to fifteen months after the filing of the application for a declaration of invalidity. The appeal proceedings before the Court of Appeal typically take about ten to twelve months. A further appeal to the Supreme Court may take from about eighteen months to four years. In the case of SPCs, if any court deems that a point of law is not *acte clair*, they can refer questions to the CJEU and in some instances to the EFTA Court.

Any UK Court proceedings against an SPC can be stayed in view of a pending CJEU referral that concerns a different SPC but the same legal questions.

[D] The Revocation of a Paediatric Extension

As set out in the EU chapter, the grounds for revocation of a paediatric extension correspond to those of Article 16 of the SPC Regulation for Medicinal Products.

The procedures for revocation of a paediatric extension and the corresponding appeal procedure are the same as those for an SPC (*see* §3.06[A]–§3.06[C] above).

In *Dr Reddy's Laboratories (UK) Ltd and Dr Reddy's Laboratories Ltd v. Warner-Lambert Company LLC* [2012] EWHC 3715 (Pat),[210] the UK Patents Court decided that it had the power to revoke a paediatric extension having regard to Article 16(1).

210. UK Patents Court decision in *Dr Reddy's Laboratories (UK) Ltd and Dr Reddy's Laboratories Ltd v. Warner-Lambert Company LLC* [2012] EWHC 3715 (Pat) of 20 December 2012.

§3.07 UNFAIR COMPETITION LAW

The same considerations as set out in the EU chapter apply. Antitrust issues involving SPCs have not yet been specifically addressed in the UK case law.

CHAPTER 4
France

Francis Ahner

§4.01 LEGAL BASIS

The Regulations (EC) No. 469/2009 and (EC) No. 1610/96 contain identical provisions with regards to the conditions governing the grant of a certificate for medicinal products and plant protection products.

For all aspects of the SPC prosecution dealt with in said Regulations, national provisions of the French Code de la Propriété Intellectuelle (CPI) with regards to patent prosecution, shall apply.

The French CPI does not contain any specific section exclusively dedicated to SPCs. Some articles are dealing with provisions explicitly relevant to SPCs, namely:

- Article L.611-2 mentions the articles of the French CPI applicable to SPCs and those which are not.
- Articles L.613-17-1 and R.613-25-1 in connection with compulsory licences pursuant to Regulation (EC) No. 816/2006.
- Articles L.614-32–L.614-36 in connection with withholding in customs of suspected infringing products.
- Articles R.617-2-1 and R.617-2-2 in relation with the duration of the grant procedure influenced by the 'silence is deemed refusal' principle enacted by the French decree No. 2015-1436 of 6 November 2015.

The French Industrial Property Office (INPI) also issued specific examination guidelines for SPCs which can be found in both French and English on the INPI's website. Generally speaking, we can say that French examiners scrupulously follow these guidelines.

§4.02 SUBSTANTIVE REQUIREMENTS FOR OBTAINING AN SPC

As a guidance provided by the Court of Justice of the European Union (CJEU) is binding for all EU Member States, the considerations as set out in Chapter 1 (the EU chapter), specifically in §1.02 above in relation to the substantive requirements for obtaining an SPC are equally applicable to France.

The following discussion will therefore only focus on case law and consideration of interest in France beyond the guidance provided by the Court of Justice.

[A] Types of Products That Can Be Protected

No further consideration applies.

[1] Practical Considerations: What Is the Active Ingredient or Combination of Active Ingredients That Can Form the Basis for an SPC

In general, it is clear that both the INPI examiners and the judges of the Appeal Court of Paris employ the strict and rather restrictive application of the concept of active ingredient that emerges from the SPC Regulation and decisions of the CJEU. Accordingly, various pharmaceutical and plant-protection compounds such as excipients, safeners, synergistic additives and controlled release matrices will obviously be excluded from the concept of active ingredient.

It turns out in practice that both INPI and the courts accord particular importance to the Marketing Authorization (MA) and in particular the Summary of Product Characteristics (SmPC). In fact, if a product is mentioned in Section 6 relating to excipients and not specifically cited in paragraph 2 of the Summary of Product Characteristics relating to active ingredients, getting such a product recognized as an active ingredient within the meaning of Article 3(a) becomes unlikely in the extreme.

For a product to be recognized as an active ingredient, it is essential, in the case of a drug, that it be demonstrable, and confirmed by its SmPC, that the drug produces a therapeutic action per se, which is to say that it restores, corrects or modifies the organic functions in humans or animals. In the case of phyto-pharmaceuticals, the same holds and it will be necessary to demonstrate that the product in question produces per se an action on the vital processes of the plants (to the exclusion of growth factors), helps preserve plant products or destroys undesirable plants or parts of plants.

Thus, any light shed by the contents of the MA and in particular the summary of product characteristics, will be determinant in deeming the component of a formula to be an active ingredient. Merely indicating the co-prescription or co-administration of the basic product with another active ingredient will be insufficient to grant an SPC for the combination of those two active ingredients (*see* §4.02[C][1][c]).

[2] Active Ingredient or Combination of Active Ingredients of a Medicinal Product

No further consideration applies.

[3] Active Substance or Combination of Active Substances of a Plant Protection Product

No further consideration applies.

[4] Fixed-Dose and Loose Combinations

No further consideration applies.

[5] Limitation to Products Subjected to a Specific Marketing Authorization Procedure

Both INPI and the French courts have shown themselves to be very strict in how they interpret Article 3(b), which specifically calls for the MA to comply with the Directive 2001/83/EC or Directive 2001/82/EC. For example, one could point to a decision of the Cour de Cassation (Commercial Chamber, of 3 April 2007), which upheld a decision of the Appeal Court of Paris of 15 December 2004 confirming the refusal by the Director of INPI of an SPC application by the Chiron company relative to a test for detecting the AIDS virus in blood samples. Such a diagnostic test, which did not fit the definition of a drug in Article 1(a) of the Regulations and which was not subject to a marketing authorization as set out in Article 3(b) of the same Regulation, accordingly did not lead to the grant of an SPC.

[6] Protection of Medical Devices

To date, there has been no decision or specific provision in the guidance for INPI review concerning therapeutic devices. It turns out in practice, however, that only an active ingredient, if any, which gets combined with the device may be given an SPC.

[B] Basic Patent

No further consideration applies.

[1] Requirement for the Product to Be 'Protected' by the Basic Patent

The basic patent must be a patent in force at the filing of the application for an SPC effective in France. It can therefore be alternatively a French patent, the French part of a European patent or, in the future, a unitary patent. By patent in force is meant a right not definitively cancelled or revoked at the time the SPC application is filed. It will be seen later that in the event of a French patent cancelled by a decision of the Court of First Instance or a European patent revoked before the Opposition Division of the EPO (both of which are appealable), such patents can be validly invoked but with the difficulty pertaining to any request for suspension of procedure that becomes incompatible with Decree No. 2015-1436 of 6 November 2015, which holds that SPCs are governed by the principle of 'silence means refusal'.

In its guidelines, INPI refers explicitly to the decisions of the CJEU and specifically to the *Medeva, Georgetown, Eli Lilly, MIT, GSK, G. Boyer* and *Forsgren* cases. Generally speaking, French practice is to apply the identification test rather than the infringing test. The Review Guidelines specify:

> Whether it concerns medicinal products or plant protection products, the product must be specified in the wording of the claims of the basic patent. Indeed, given that the scope of protection of the patent is defined by these claims, it is not sufficient for the product that is subject to the SPC application to be described in a working example of the invention.
>
> If a patent claims that a product is composed of two active ingredients but does not make any claim in relation to one of those active ingredients individually, an SPC cannot be granted on the basis of such a patent for the one active ingredient considered per se.
>
> An active ingredient which is given a functional definition in the claims of a patent can be regarded as protected by the patent, on condition that it is possible to reach the conclusion on the basis of those claims, interpreted inter alia in the light of the description of the invention, that the claims relate, implicitly but necessarily and specifically, to the active ingredient in question.
>
> In the specific case where the claims of a patent concern a product defined by means of a Markush formula, it is sufficient for the product to fall within the scope of this formula without having to be specifically identified.
>
> However, if the medicinal product is composed of an active substance and a substance that has no therapeutic effect of its own but is used to obtain a pharmaceutical form of the medicinal product necessary for the therapeutic efficacy of the first substance, only the first substance shall be deemed to be the product. The second substance shall be deemed to be an excipient.
>
> Likewise, a combination of two substances – where one is an active ingredient with therapeutic effects of its own and the other is an adjuvant – shall not be considered a 'combination of active ingredients' even though the adjuvant makes it possible to increase these therapeutic effects.
>
> In the more specific case of safeners, it is necessary to verify whether the substance in question has a 'toxic, phytotoxic or plant protection action of its own'.
>
> A SPC cannot be granted for substances having a therapeutic effect of their own where such effect is not set out in the related MA. It must therefore be verified that the 'active ingredient' produces a pharmacological, immunological or metabolic action of its own, which is covered by the therapeutic indications set out in the MA.

[a] Small Molecules

No further comments specific to France as all types of molecules are protectable by an SPC.

[b] Polymers

No further comments specific to France as all types of polymers are protectable by an SPC.

[c] Antibodies, Enzymes and Other Proteins

No further comments specific to France as all types of antibodies and other proteins are protectable by an SPC.

[d] Nucleic Acids

No further comments specific to France as all types of nucleic acids are protectable by an SPC.

[2] Basic Patent Claiming the Product, i.e., the Active Ingredient(s), but Not the Corresponding Authorized Medicinal Product (or Plant Protection Product)

That the patented and medicinal products authorized be identical does not seem to be required or applied in France. Indeed, it seems sufficient that the active ingredient protected by the claim be identical to the active ingredient of the authorized medicinal product as it appears in paragraph 2 of the Summary of Product Characteristics. One must proceed with caution nonetheless, for if the definition of the drug authorized by the MA differs from active ingredient of a possibly infringing drug, Article 4 of the Regulation could make such an SPC not opposable.

[3] Requirement for the Product to Constitute 'the Invention' of the Basic Patent

This is an additional requirement arising from CJEU jurisprudence that goes beyond simply requiring that the product be protected by its claims. More than that, such a product must match the subject matter of the invention protected by the basic patent, or 'the core inventive advance'.

In paragraph (d) which rules out any double protection by the INPI guidelines, one could infer that INPI implicitly includes this additional obligation. In this passage there repeatedly crops up the concept of the innovative active ingredient, which seems to go well beyond the requirements laid down by the SPC Regulations.

As far as combinations of active ingredients are concerned, we feel that the notion of 'inventive advance' should not be taken into consideration to decide about the preclusion of a new SPC by an earlier one, especially when both SPCs are to expire on the same date.

[4] Criteria for Choosing the Basic Patent among Various Available Patents

It is clear that in France the selection of the basic patent is a choice freely made by the applicant, in particular as to the duration of the SPC, the extent of the protection and the presumed validity of the basic patent and of the SPC which will be derived from it.

[C] The Marketing Authorization Forming Basis for an SPC

No further consideration applies.

[1] Combinations of Active Ingredients

The French practice is broadly consistent with the provisions and rules emanating from European jurisprudence.

[a] The Marketing Authorization Refers to Fewer Active Ingredients than the SPC Application

A marketing authorization for fewer active ingredients than those claimed in the basic patent cannot form the basis for an SPC relying on this patent.

[b] The Marketing Authorization Refers to More Active Ingredients than the SPC Application

The INPI guidelines clearly state: 'The fact that an MA additionally covers other active ingredients than those for which the SPC is requested does not rule out that SPC being granted.'

[c] The Marketing Authorization Indicates That a Medicinal Product Containing a Single Active Ingredient Is Authorized for Use in Combination with a Further Active Ingredient

In a ruling made by the Paris Tribunal de Grande Instance on 3 October 2012 in a case between the Sanofi and Teva companies, the question of the conformity of the SPC with Article 3(d) was raised with regard to the combination of the active ingredients Irbesartan and hydrochlorothiazide (HCTZ). In this ruling, the Tribunal points out, 'To the contrary, the two MAs concern different products and simply mentioning in the

Aprovel® SmPC that this product may be prescribed together with HCTZ does not constitute a marketing effort that focuses only on one product and not on this possibility which, even if approved by the health authorities, is not realized by the drug.'

In other words, the MA relating to the combination irbesartan and HCTZ must be regarded as the first marketing authorization, alongside a previous MA relating to medicinal products containing irbesartan as the only active ingredient and mentioning the possibility of co-prescribing or the co-administering it with HCTZ.

[2] The Marketing Authorization Has Not Yet Been Granted at the Time the SPC Application Is Filed

France always made a strict application of Article 3(b) of the SPC Regulation in a way very similar to the grounds expressed in the judgement of the CJEU of 7 December 2017 (Case C-567/16).

[3] The Holder of the Marketing Authorization

For the moment this issue raises no difficulty in France since it is in fact only the apparent holder of the basic patent who may submit an SPC application. Since information about the initial marketing authorization is freely accessible to the public, the patentee may therefore invoke any MA at all, belonging to it or not.

It should be noted, however, that this situation could eventually evolve in the future in that a decision of the CJEU might, making a purposive interpretation, consider that only the holder of the MA and not necessarily the patentee has actually borne the costs of researching and developing the drug. Such a situation could arise in a product protection claim with a functional definition, even if the drug's active ingredient had not been literally described or exemplified in the patent.

[4] Reliance on a Marketing Authorization Granted under a Provision Other than Directive 2001/83/EC or Directive 2001/82/EC

In French practice, it appears that there is no exemption from this obligation, and Article 3(b) is therefore applied stringently. This has been specifically confirmed by the Chiron decision cited above in §4.02[A][5].

[5] The Marketing Authorizations Which Can Be Relied upon for SPC Applications for Plant Protection Products

No further consideration applies.

[6] *The Product in Question Is Contained in the Authorized Medicinal Product (or the Authorized Plant Protection Product) but Is Not Identified as an Active Ingredient in the Corresponding Marketing Authorization*

No further consideration applies.

[7] *The Notion of the 'First' Marketing Authorization*

No further consideration applies.

[a] *Marketing Authorization for a New Therapeutic Application of a Previously Authorized Product*

Both INPI and the French courts apply the *Neurim* decision. The decision of the Appeal Court of 15 February 2013 in *Merck v. INPI* stated: The MA of 2006 in relation with a vaccine for adults to prevent shingles, has to be regarded as the first one in the presence of an MA of 1993 in relation with a paediatric vaccine against chickenpox, since both drugs are intended for two different therapeutical uses of a differently dosed active substance. The Court also noted that the second therapeutical use is protected by the invoked second patent.

Moreover, the INPI Guidelines state: 'A new medical use of an active ingredient may be granted an SPC based on the corresponding MA, even if the product has already been granted an MA for the first medical use. The SPC will be granted provided the basic patent is a patent covering the second medical use of an active ingredient or of a combination of active ingredients for which the MA was granted. The SPC will therefore only cover the new use of the active ingredient subject to the basic patent.

The notion of "new medical use of an active ingredient or of a combination of active ingredients" must be strictly interpreted.'

[b] *Marketing Authorization for a New Formulation of a Previously Authorized Product*

For the moment, it does not seem that a new formulation of a product previously authorized can be issued an SPC. Both INPI and the courts appear to be clearly in favour of such a position.

The *Abraxis* decision could potentially alter this situation in very specific cases where the new formulation led to a new therapeutic effect, opening up the treatment of other diseases. In terms of the current situation, there is the decision by the Paris Tribunal de Grande Instance of 7 October 2009 in *Alk Abello v. Stallergenes*. In this matter the court examined whether the French SPC No. 07C0003 was invalidated by the combined provisions of Articles 15 and 3(d) of Regulation (EEC) 1768/92. French SPC No. 07C0003, issued on the basis of the MA for Grazax® was voided on the grounds that this MA was not the initial marketing authorization issued for this product as a medication. Grazax® contained an allergenic extract in a medium suitable for taking under the tongue, whereas its predecessor drug Alutra® was an injectable suspension of an allergenic extract adsorbed on aluminum hydroxide.

After noting that the active ingredient was identical in the two MAs, namely the allergenic extract, the court concluded that it was in fact the marketing authorization for the Grazax® which should be considered as the initial marketing authorization issued for this product, i.e., the allergenic extract by itself. We see then that the court did take note of the difference in excipient, in formulation and in method of administration allowing a gradual desensitization, but these factors did not alter its position based on the fact that in both drugs and in both MAs there was one and the same active ingredient. The other factors remain inoperative.

[c] Marketing Authorization for a New Specific Salt, Ester or Other Derivative of a Previously Authorized Active Ingredient

More recently, in a judgment of 19 December 2017 opposing *LOYOLA University of Chicago v. INPI*, the Appeal Court of Paris also confirmed the refusal by INPI of an SPC application (No. 07C0065) on the grounds that it did not meet the criterion of Article 3(d) in the SPC Regulations. This case involved the drug Gardasil®, which had received an initial marketing authorization and whose active ingredient was a non-truncated L1 protein of the human papillomavirus type 16, whereas the second MA invoked during the filing of this SPC related to the drug Cervarix®, containing a truncated L1 protein of the human papillomavirus type 16, the truncation pertaining to a sequence of thirty-four amino acids located at the C terminal extremity. The Court recognized that this truncation leading to a protein modified in that way was the consequence of its manufacturing process, involving the use of a cellular line of insects. The Court nevertheless took the view that such changes do not imply the existence of different products. In its opinion, the Court referred to the principle according to which a product can only get one SPC – this resulting primarily from a very strict interpretation of the concept of active ingredient. The Court further held that a second SPC cannot be obtained for a drug which, as compared to a prior drug, presents only minor changes. It cited as examples of such minor changes: a new dosage, the use of a particular salt or ester, or a different pharmaceutical form.

It is worth remembering that the Appeal Court of Paris confirmed the rejection of French SPC application No. 08C0003 based on exactly the same argumentation and it concluded that said SPC application covered a product already the subject matter of an SPC in violation of Article 3(c) of the Regulation (Appeal Court of Paris, April 2016, *LOYOLA v. INPI*).

In decision No. 16-21638 of 16 May 2018, the French Supreme Court upheld the decision of rejection of the Paris Court of Appeal, based on the ascertainment that the L1 protein of HN16 contained in both drugs, is the same.

[d] Marketing Authorization for a New Specific Enantiomer of an Active Ingredient Previously Authorized in Racemic Form

It is likely that the answer to this question will vary according to the particular circumstances of the case.

However, there is in France a decision of the Cour de Cassation of 31 January 2012 on an appeal by the Syngenta and Novartis companies. The application for a supplementary protection certificate (No. 02C0020) related to a combination of benoxacor and S-metolachlor, a combination of active ingredients in a specialty plant-protection product. This application had been denied by the Director of INPI on the grounds that there existed a previous SPC (No. 97C0048) covering the combination of benoxacor and metolachlor. The Court noted that S-metolachlor is only an enantiomer of the substance metolachlor and that it was not shown that the shift of the active substance in question from a racemic form to an enantiomeric form entailed a different activity profile for the product. The Court held therefore that the active ingredients involved were identical and that the denial of an SPC application (No. 02C0020) was for that reason justified.

[e] The Product Has Already Been Placed on the Market Before, but Without an Authorization Granted under Directive 2001/83/EC or Directive 2001/82/EC

No further consideration applies.

[f] Prior Marketing Authorization Which Refers to Fewer Active Ingredients than the SPC Application (and the Later Marketing Authorization Relied upon)

No further consideration applies.

[g] Prior Marketing Authorization Which Refers to More Active Ingredients than the SPC Application (and the Later Marketing Authorization Relied upon)

No further consideration applies.

[D] Preclusion of New SPCs by an Earlier SPC

In France the basic principle resulting from the jurisprudence of the CJEU in *AHP Manufacturing* (C-482/07) is strictly applied by the INPI. That means that only one SPC can normally be granted per product and per patent holder, thus it is essential to make the difference between both situations of an earlier owned SPC and an earlier third-party SPC.

[1] Consequences of an Earlier Third-Party SPC for the Same Product

No further consideration applies.

[a] The 'One SPC per Product per Patent Holder' Rule

Based on decision of the CJEU in cases *AHP Manufacturing* (C-482/07), *Actavis I* (C-577/13) and *Georgetown University* (C-484/12), the French Guidelines for examination expressly state that: 'The product must not already have been the subject of an SPC in the name of the same holder.'

In this framework, the INPI shall carry out a search taking into account all SPCs previously granted in France, irrespective of the date. Consequently, for medicinal products, the check takes into account certificates delivered under French Law No. 90-510 of 25 January 1990 and SPCs granted under Regulation (EEC) No. 1768/92 or Regulation (EC) 496/2009.

[b] Earlier SPC Granted to an Affiliated Third Party

Until a recent past, the INPI applied an extensive interpretation of the concept of patent holders and generally considered that two holders who are different legal entities but are somehow affiliated within the same group, must be considered as the same patent holder. It seems that this interpretation has recently changed. As a matter of fact, an SPC No. 15C0024 was first granted to the BOEHRINGER INGELHEIM PHARMA GmbH and Co. KG on 26 August 2016 and a second SPC No. 15C0046 was recently granted (22 January 2018) to BOEHRINGER INGELHEIM INTERNATIONAL GmbH for the same product based on a different patent and a different marketing authorization.

[c] Partial Overlap Between the Holders of the Earlier SPC and the Applicants for the New SPC

In a recent decision of 19 December 2017 the Appeal Court of Paris has considered such a situation.

The situation was as follows; MEDIVIR AB and JANSSEN IRELAND UC, as co-owner of European patent 1 912 999 obtained SPC No. 14C0076 covering the product Simeprevir based on the Marketing Authorization granted 14 May 2014 for HOLYSID®.

Later on MEDIVIR filed another request for an SPC before the grant of the above-mentioned first SPC. This second request was concerned with the same product based on the same marketing authorization and invoked European patent No. 1 713 823 belonging only to MEDIVIR AB. This second SPC application was rejected by the French Patent Office and the decision was appealed before the Appeal Court of Paris. In its decision, the Appeal Court simply decided that patent owners, MEDIVIR + JANSSEN IRELAND UC on the one hand and MEDIVIR alone on the other hand, both have to be considered as the same owner pursuant to Article 3 of the Regulation concerning the SPC.

This decision does not contain any legal argumentation other than the mere assertion of the fact that it was MEDIVIR's choice to decide to file European patent No. 1 713 823 jointly with JANSSEN IRELAND UC. Thus, this patent could be exploited under the co-ownership regime. Unfortunately, this decision is definitive.

[d] Earlier Third-Party SPC Has Been Licensed-In

The impact of a possible licence of the earlier SPC has never been considered in France in the framework of Article 3(c) and 3(2) of both SPC Regulations. That could nevertheless be potential antitrust issue in very specific circumstances.

[2] Consequences of an Own Earlier SPC for the Same Product

No further consideration applies.

[a] Own Earlier SPC Application Not Yet Granted

In connection with a situation of owned earlier SPC applications which were not yet granted or owned granted SPC which was revoked, nullified, surrendered or subject to restauration procedure, the French Patent Office generally accepted to stay the examination procedure in the past.

Today, for all SPC applications filed after 12 November 2014, the INPI no longer accepts to postpone the application due to the French decree No. 2015-1436 of 6 November 2015 stating that the SPC grant procedure is subject to the 'Silent Is Deemed Refusal' principle (*see* §4.05[F]).

[b] Revocation, Surrender or Lapse of the Own Earlier SPC after Grant

No further consideration applies.

[c] Transfer of the Own Earlier SPC to a Third Party

No further consideration applies.

[d] Acquisition of an SPC Granted to a Third Party

No further consideration applies.

[3] Consequences of an Own Earlier SPC for a Different Product

No further consideration applies.

[a] *Required Distinction from the Product of the Own Earlier SPC*

In order to estimate the minimum required distinction from the product of the owned earlier SPC, it should be possible to develop arguments similar to those presented for distinguishing two products in the framework of Article 3(d) of the Regulation.

In the LOYOLA case cited before, the French court reminded that only minor changes of the product are not sufficient to distinguish two products; different dosage forms, different administration formulations or different derivatives or salts and esters are given for examples as insufficient differences.

In a decision given by the Appeal Court of Paris on 20 January 2017, in relation with a decision of the director of INPI, deciding to appeal against the rejection of an SPC application, such an analysis was made for 'biodrugs' or 'blood products' as far as the first marketing authorization was challenged. The analysis would probably be exactly the same in a case concerning earlier SPC. In the present situation the applicant received several marketing authorizations in which the inhibitor of C1 (human) was subject to some differences leading to a different molecular structure giving different results in terms of specific activity, half-life and specific treated pathologies. In this specific field the court of Paris stated that the SPC Regulation does not contain any exception as far as the product definition and the first marketing authorization are concerned, in the specific case of biodrugs or blood products which would allow to define such kind of products through their manufacturing process. Here again, the analysis of the content of the earlier marketing authorization was decisive since the Court observed that it does not contain any information in connection with the differences resulting from the manufacturing process. In addition, the therapeutic function given in both marketing authorizations, is exactly the same, i.e., treating and preventing crises of angioedema.

In the same way and as discussed before, it would certainly be difficult to demonstrate that a truncated protein is a different product in comparison with a non-truncated one in case it would not be possible to demonstrate specific therapeutic activity in connection with such a truncation of the protein.

[b] *SPCs for a Specific Salt, Ester or Other Derivative Where an Own Earlier SPC Has Already Been Granted for the Corresponding Active Ingredient*

No further consideration applies.

[c] SPCs for a Specific Enantiomer Where an Own Earlier SPC Has Already Been Granted for the Corresponding Racemate

The decision of the Cour de Cassation of 31 January 2012 cited earlier (*see* §4.02[C][7][d]) regarding a comparison between the racemate metolachlor and the enantiomer S-metolachlor, dealt with exactly such a situation, where it was held that the specific enantiomeric structure is insufficient to constitute a major difference between the two structures, the racemate having been issued an initial SPC belonging to the same holder.

[4] Grant of More than One SPC on the Basis of the Same Patent

No further consideration applies.

§4.03 EXTENT OF PROTECTION AND ENFORCEMENT OF SPCs

[A] The Protection Conferred by an SPC

The purpose of the protection and the effects of the Supplementary Protection Certificate are clearly laid out in Articles 4 and 5 of the SPC Regulation. It might be incidentally noted that the corresponding provisions taken in the Unified Patent Court Agreement in its Article 30 have curiously not repeated the reservations found in the Article 4 of the Regulation. It is to be hoped that this difficulty will be easily resolved inasmuch as the Unified Patent Court will apply the law of the European Union and will not therefore be able to ignore the provisions of Article 4 of the Regulation not found in the Agreement.

In its ruling of 19 August 2010 in a case between Aventis Sanofi and Teva, the Paris Tribunal de Grande Instance cited the provisions of Articles 4 and 5 of Regulation (EC) 469/2009 and then drew the following conclusions: 'It follows from these provisions that an SPC which aims to support innovation in the field of healthcare shall protect a product as a drug in all forms covered by the protection of the basic patent. This text does not result in a change to the definition of infringement of a protected invention as found in Article L.613-3a of the French Intellectual Property Code. Consequently, the fact that the rights of Aventis Pharma are based on an SPC and not on a patent does nothing to exclude the product from usual acts of infringement.'

[B] The Scope of an SPC in Relation to Derivatives of an Active Ingredient

The provisions of the *Farmitalia* judgment (C-392/97) are surely relevant to the present matter.

To analyse the materiality of an infringement, however, the Court may first need to determine the extent of the protection conferred by a claim and within that framework, the claim may need to be interpreted in the light of the description. This may lead to a limitation to a few particular salts described sufficiently in the patent and involving an inventive step on the basis of a particular therapeutic activity described. This was notably the case in the *Rosuvastatin* matter. In this case, the Paris Tribunal de Grande Instance interpreted a claim covering a free acid form and pharmaceutically acceptable salts, based on the description, to hold that the scope of the claim was limited to protected salts of alkali-, alkaline earth metals- and ammonium-cations. In such a situation, of course, since what is protected is bounded by the protection conferred by the basic patent, this would result in a limitation to certain specific derivatives of the active ingredient.

[1] The Relationship Between the Definition of the Active Ingredient(s) in an SPC and Its Scope of Protection

To our knowledge, there has been no decision on this particular question. However, one might wonder about invoking the equivalence theory in regard to an SPC. That is, it seems to us that the wording of Article 4 noting that the protection conferred by the SPC extends only to the product covered by the market authorization of the corresponding drug has not to be literally interpreted in a limiting way and so does not appear to restrict the scope of the SPC.

[C] Enforcement of an SPC

Virtually all of the provisions of the Intellectual Property Code applicable to patents of invention are also applicable to SPCs. It is thus possible, for example, to make infringement seizures or require provisional restraints and whatever court-ordered experts are needed to assess the extent of the injury suffered due to infringement of the SPC.

§4.04 DETERMINATION OF THE SPC TERM

[A] The Calculation of the SPC Term

No further consideration applies.

[1] The Relevant Marketing Authorization for the Term of an SPC

The general considerations expressed in Chapter 1 are obviously applicable in France, where such a situation seems never to have been raised in court.

The method for calculating the date of the first marketing authorization is stated in the guidelines for examination before INPI, as follows: 'The "date" of a French MA is the date on which the authorization was granted: in accordance with French administrative law, a decision favorable to the addressee – in particular a decision granting the addressee certain rights – is enforceable upon signature without requiring notification.

Regarding MAs granted by the European Union, the "date" of an MA is defined by EU law. It can be defined as the date on which the applicant was given notification of the decision granting the MA.'

'If the first MA in the EU is a national MA granted by a Member State other than France, the applicant is responsible for providing proof of the date of effect of this MA under the national law of this State.'

[2] The Expiration Date of an SPC

Articles 13 and 8(1)(d) of Regulation (EC) No. 469/2009 shall apply for the calculation of the expiration date.

The French Patent Office considers that a patent expires the day before its last anniversary at midnight, thus the protection conferred by the SPC starts on the anniversary of the patent at 0h00. Accordingly, an SPC with a full five-year term will expire on the twenty-fifth anniversary of the filing date of the patent at 0h00.

For example, a French SPC based on a patent filed on 15 June 2000 and on a Marketing Authorization notified on 10 August 2007 (first Marketing Authorization in the EU and the EEA for this product) will come into effect upon the expiry of the basic patent, i.e., 15 June 2020 at 0h00 and will expire on 10 August 2022, 0h00 or 9 August 2022, midnight. Making reference to the same example, if the Marketing Authorization is notified on or after 15 June 2010, the SPC will have the full five-year term and will thus expire on 15 June 2025, 0h00.

[B] Correction of the SPC Term

Following the *Seattle Genetics, Inc.* decision (C-471/14) and the *Incyte Corporation* decision (C-492/16), it is now possible to request from INPI a rectification of the effective period of an SPC that had originally been calculated using the MA grant date and not the notification date. Such an appeal for rectification, however, is only admissible provided the SPC has not expired.

[C] Paediatric Extensions

No further consideration applies.

§4.05 PROCEDURE OF FILING AN SPC APPLICATION

[A] Entitlement to an SPC Application

It is in fact only the holder of the basic patent who may file an SPC application based on that patent. In the event of a change of ownership, it is therefore essential, prior to filing the SPC application, to make a registration in the National Patents Registry, mentioning such a transfer of ownership of the basic patent.

[B] The Time Limit for Filing an SPC Application

Pursuant to the first criteria, the SPC application must be filed within a period of six months from the date of the first marketing authorization issued in France or covering French territory for the product in question. As previously indicated in §4.04[A][1], the INPI guidelines state how the 'date' of this MA must be determined.

To be safe, however, it seems advisable to file the SPC application bearing in mind the date of the authorization decision rather than that of notification.

[C] The Filing of an SPC at the National Patent Office

Filing an SPC application may only be done electronically. A power of attorney is only required if the representative is not a patent attorney or a lawyer.

[D] The Documentation Required for an SPC Application

Every SPC application must contain a number of documents that are expressly mentioned in the INPI guidelines. It does not seem to us that there are provisions specific to French procedure regarding the content of the documents to be included in the folder.

[E] The Definition of the Product in an SPC Application

As regards the name of the product, INPI recommends mentioning the INN (International Non-proprietary Name) or, failing that, the Usual Common Name or the Chemical Name of the active ingredient(s) of the drug. Of course, a reasonably general product definition, preferably supported by the wording of the claim covering the product, is authorized in the wake of the decision of the Court of Justice in the *Farmitalia* case (C-392/97).

[F] SPC Examination Procedure and Appeal Procedure

The INPI examination procedure includes both a formal review and a substantive review.

INPI, in liaison with the various national or European drug agencies and the Ministry of Agriculture, verifies that the MA mentioned in the request actually matches the initial marketing authorization of the product in France.

INPI also checks that there is no previous SPC already covering the same product.

There is some flexibility in the time limits imposed by INPI to respond to notifications of non-conformance.

However, pursuant to French decree No. 2015-1436 of 6 November 2015, the SPC grant procedure is subject to the 'silence is deemed refusal' principle after a period of one year from the filing date of the application. This period shall be interrupted in the event that the INPI provides notification of an irregularity.

The provisions of this decree shall be applicable to all SPC applications filed after 12 November 2014.

'Consequently, all irregularities relating to the application shall be notified within a period of one year from the filing date of said application.

If the observations presented do not allow for the objection to be lifted or if the irregularities are not rectified within the stated time frame, the SPC application shall be subject to a draft refusal or a letter informing the applicant that their response has not allowed the objection to be lifted. This draft refusal shall be issued within a period of one year from the date of the applicant's response to the notification of irregularity.

Should the applicant fail to rectify the situation following a draft refusal, or if the observations made do not allow for the objection to be lifted, a refusal or a letter shall be addressed to the applicant indicating that their response was not sufficient to lift the objection. This refusal or letter shall be issued within one year of the date of the applicant's response to the draft refusal.

Within the context of the examination, the applicant who has been set a time limit to submit their observations or to rectify their request, may obtain an extension of this response time on written request. This extension may not exceed a maximum of four months.'

It should also be noted that as of the date of the publication of the SPC application, any person may read the documents in the application file and obtain a copy. At the same time, the folders are available in electronic form and can be inspected free of charge online via the patent database at www.inpi.fr.

Lastly, comments by third parties are in principle inadmissible in the procedure for issuing an SPC. However, such comments are nonetheless forwarded to the applicant, though they are excluded from public communications, as are all documents containing confidential data relating to business secrets. Thus, if in connection with the proceedings before INPI, certain documents appear to be confidential, it is preferable to mention that explicitly when they are transmitted and to state that the applicant opposes communicating such documents to the public.

[G] Applications for a Paediatric Extension

The application for a paediatric extension of the duration of the SPC must include among others the copy of the EMA or ANSM statement showing that the MA application complies with a completed paediatric investigation plan (PIP). This statement must also indicate that the summary of the product characteristics reflects the results of studies conducted in compliance with said PIP in each country of the European Union.

Where appropriate, the following items must also be provided:

- the copy of the SPC if it has been granted;

- if the MA application forming the basis of the request was made at a national level, the copy of the corresponding MAs in all of the other Member States making it possible to identify the product subject to the SPC. Where applicable, a translation in French of the information required to examine the application may be requested by the INPI.

The MAs must cover the same active ingredient but not necessarily the same medicinal product. They do not necessarily have to cover a medicinal product for paediatric use.

§4.06 PROCEDURE OF INVALIDATING AN SPC

All provisions of the French Intellectual Property Code applicable to patents in this regard also apply to SPCs. Article L.613-28 lists the conditions that invalidate an SPC.

[A] Grounds for the Invalidation of an SPC

In a large majority, the grounds for invalidation are concerned with the absence of novelty and/or inventive step of the corresponding basic patent.

In a case opposing MSD Somerset, Merck to Arrow Generiques, Eurogenerics and Ratiopharm, the Paris High Court, on 12 February 2008 declared French SPC No. 96C0032 void due to the fact that the grounds for revoking the basic patent justified limiting the claims so that the product for which the SPC was granted was no longer covered by the patent.

[B] The Filing of an Invalidation Suit

SPC invalidation suits may only be brought before the civil courts of Paris, and all the provisions of the French Code of Civil Procedure fully apply.

[C] Invalidation Procedure and the Corresponding Appeal Procedure

In accordance with Article 2224 of the Civil Code, which till now seems to apply to SPC invalidation suits, there is a statutory limitation period of five years from the time when the petitioner was aware of the grounds for invalidation. In terms of patents, this question has been somewhat tricky and been interpreted in a great variety of ways by the French courts, but it arises with even more difficulty with regard to SPCs or paediatric extensions. It is perhaps worth asking whether, if an invalidation suit of a basic patent is unavailable, it might still be possible subsequently, though within five years from the SPC issue date, to seek to invalidate the SPC on the grounds of the lack of validity of the basic patent.

Stay of proceedings was requested in different situations. A ruling was made by the Paris Tribunal de Grande Instance on 7 July 2017 in *Mylan v. Gilead* involving a temporary restraining order, which denied a stay of proceedings and was followed by a second ruling on 5 September 2017 denying the request for a TRO. The SPC cited (No. 05C0032) relates to a product involving the combination of tenofovir disoproxyl and emtricitabine.

Because of an interlocutory question raised with the CJEU by Britain's High Court of Justice, a request for a stay of proceedings was presented to the French court. The question put to the CJEU was precisely whether this combination was expressly covered by the basic patent. In this regard, the Appeal Court cites the *Lilly* decision, which pronounced the rule for interpreting Article 3(a). The Court restated that the claim must pertain implicitly, necessarily and specifically to the combination of tenofovir disoproxyl and emtricitabine, with the question essentially being about emtricitabine. The Court also pointed out that the interpretation of the claim under Article 69(2) EPC (*see* paragraph 4 of the *Lilly* decision) must be made by the lower-court judge in light of the description in the patent. On these conditions, the Paris Tribunal de Grande Instance held that the conditions for requesting a stay were not met. In the second ruling of 5 September 2017, the Tribunal dismissed the request for a preliminary injunction very probably because it viewed as uncertain that this combination was validly covered by the claim of the patent relied on and that, therefore, the conditions set forth in Article 3(a) of the Regulation were not met.

Again concerning a request for a stay, the Cour de Cassation rendered a judgment on 26 November 2013 concerning an SPC application whose underlying basic patent had been the subject of an application for limitation made to INPI, subsequent to the denial of an SPC application. This decision states:

(i) That a stay of proceedings pending a final decision following a request for limitation of the claims of a patent is not called for by French law and that the option to grant one lies solely in the discretion of the lower court judge. The request for a stay was therefore dismissed.
(ii) That the appeal of the decision to deny an SPC application by the Director of INPI is inadmissible given that the request for limitation was made subsequently to the denial and that the Court had to put itself in the conditions existing at the time of the decision, which is to say when the limitation had not yet occurred.

It must therefore be concluded that if a limitation of the basic patent were thought necessary to better cover the product or combination of products in the SPC application, it would be desirable to proceed with such a request for limitation well before the date on which the SPC application might be rejected.

[D] The Revocation of a Paediatric Extension

This involves the same type of procedure as for SPCs based on the grounds for appeal contained in Article 16 of the SPC Regulation.

§4.07 UNFAIR COMPETITION LAW

The antitrust and competition legal system in France is also mainly based on Articles 101 (prohibition of restrictive agreement) and 102 (prohibition of abuse or dominant position) of TFEU (Treaty on the Functioning of the European Union). As a consequence, the considerations of the general Chapter 1 also apply for France.

The well-known PLAVIX® case can be given as an illustration. In this case, the French Competition Authority gave SANOFI a fine of EUR 40.6 million for abuse of dominant position (Article 102 of TFEU) in the framework of a global strategy of defamation comprising on the one hand an incentive for the doctors to specify on their prescription the mention 'non-substitutable' and on the other hand an incentive for pharmacists to substitute in favour of their own generic subsidiary (Winthrop) through reward programs. This decision of the French Competition Authority was upheld by the French Supreme Court in May 2016.

CHAPTER 5

The Netherlands

Ricardo Dijkstra[*]

§5.01 LEGAL BASIS

In Dutch national law,[1] the central legal provisions governing SPCs for medicinal products are contained in Chapter 7 (Articles 90–98) of the Dutch Patent Act of 1995 (Rijksoctrooiwet 1995, 'DPA'), which were introduced with effect of 15 December 1994. The central legal provisions governing SPCs for plant protection products are contained in the Plant Protection Certificate Decree, which were introduced with effect of 8 February 1997 (Besluit certificaat gewasbeschermingsmiddelen, 'PPCD').

The legal provisions relate to definitions (Article 90 DPA, 1 PPCD); the lodging of an application for a certificate with the Dutch Patent Office (Article 91 DPA / 2(1) PPCD); the costs associated with lodging an application (Article 92 DPA / 2(1) and (3) PPCD); the language of the application (Article 93 / 2(2) PPCD in conjunction with Article 24(3) DPA); third-party notifications (Article 93 / 2(2) PPCD in conjunction with Article 38(1) DPA); notification of shortcomings in the application (Article 94 DPA / 2(2) PPCD in conjunction with Article 8 of Regulation 469/2009 or Articles 92 and 93 DPA); maintenance fees (Article 95 DPA / 3 PPCD in conjunction with Articles 61(3) and 62 DPA); notifications regarding the lodging of an application, the grant of an SPC and lapse or invalidity of an SPC (Article 96 DPA / 4(1) and (2) PPCD in conjunction with Articles 9(2), 11 and 14–16 of Regulation 469/2009); and the patent as part of assets (Article 97 DPA / 4(3) PPCD in conjunction with Articles 64–69 DPA).

Subject to the provisions of Articles 4 and 5 of Regulations 469/2009 and 1610/96, the SPC confers the same rights as conferred by the basic patent and shall be

* With special thanks to Carly van der Beek and Berber van der Wansem for their contribution.
1. Unofficial English translation of the Dutch Patent Act ('Rijksoctrooiwet 1995') is provided by the Institute for Information Law ('IViR') at: https://www.ivir.nl/syscontent/pdfs/163.pdf.

subject to the same limitations and the same obligations. The SPC may therefore be enforced on the basis of the same provisions that exist for patents.

The procedural provisions laid down in the General Administrative Law Act (Algemene Wet Bestuursrecht, 'GALA') apply to objections filed against the refusal to grant an SPC before the Board of Appeal (Afdeling van Beroep), appeal against the decision of the Board of Appeal before the Administrative Chamber of the District Court in The Hague (Rechtbank Den Haag, Afdeling Bestuursrecht) and appeal against the decision of the Administrative Chamber of the District Court in The Hague before the Council of State, Department Law (Raad van State, Afdeling Rechtspraak). The Dutch Code of Civil Procedure (Wetboek van Burgerlijke Rechtsvordering, 'DCCP') applies to enforcement and invalidation actions regarding SPCs.

The Dutch Patent Office has not issued any guidelines on the examination of SPCs.

§5.02 SUBSTANTIVE REQUIREMENTS FOR OBTAINING AN SPC

As the guidance provided by the CJEU is binding for all EU Member States, the considerations as set out in Chapter 1 (the 'EU chapter'), specifically in §1.02 above, in relation to the substantive requirements for obtaining an SPC, in as far as they have been addressed by the CJEU, are equally applicable in the Netherlands.

The following discussion will therefore only focus on case law and considerations of interest in the Netherlands beyond the guidance provided by the CJEU.

[A] Types of Products That Can Be Protected

The same considerations as set out in the EU chapter apply.

[1] Practical Considerations: What Is the Active Ingredient or Combination of Active Ingredients That Can Form the Basis for an SPC

The same considerations as set out in the EU chapter apply.

[2] Active Ingredient or Combination of Active Ingredients of a Medicinal Product

The same considerations as set out in the EU chapter apply.

[3] Active Substance or Combination of Active Substances of a Plant Protection Product

The same considerations as set out in the EU chapter apply.

[4] Fixed-Dose and Loose Combinations

The same considerations as set out in the EU chapter apply.

[5] Limitation to Products Subjected to a Specific Marketing Authorization Procedure

The same considerations as set out in the EU chapter apply.

[6] Protection of Medical Devices

Whether or not medical devices containing active ingredients are eligible for SPC protection under the current legislative framework is expected to be clarified by the CJEU's ruling in the pending referral C-527/17.

Therefore, the decision of the District Court of The Hague in *Genzyme Biosurgery Corp. v. Dutch Patent Office*, can be expected to no longer play a role after the CJEU's decision in this referral.

In this District Court decision, the District Court did not object to the grant of SPCs for medical devices. Although both the SPC Regulation and the Explanatory Memorandum to the Regulation appear to restrictively pertain to SPCs for medicinal products only,[2] the District Court in The Hague decided that the Dutch Patent Office had incorrectly assessed the application for an SPC for a medical device. The District Court considered that the mere fact that Article 2 of Regulation 1768/92/EEC[3] did not refer to Directive 93/42/EEC does not mean that Regulation 1768/92/EEC could not be applied. The essential question is whether the medical device that incorporates the active substance has been subjected to the extensive investigation into the safety, quality and usefulness of the active substance as prescribed in Section 7.4 of Annex I to Directive 93/42/EEC. Only then can the marketing authorization under Directive 93/42/EEC be equated with a marketing authorization in accordance with Directive 65/65/EEC (as superseded by Directive 2001/83). As the Dutch Patent Office had, according to the District Court, not sufficiently researched whether the investigation of Section 7.4 of Annex I to Directive 93/42/EEC had been performed, it had insufficiently exercised due care and the Dutch Patent Office had to reconsider its decision.[4]

2. And Regulation 1610/96/EC to plant protection products.
3. Regulation 1768/92/EEC was replaced by the SPC Regulation. In both Regulations Art. 2 relates to the scope of the respective Regulations with similar wording.
4. District Court The Hague *Genzyme Biosurgery Corp. v. Bureau voor de Industriële Eigendom*, ECLI:NL:RBSGR:2004:BH1726 of 3 June 2004 (SPC 960009 for Hylaform). The District Court revoked the decision by the Dutch Patent Office and referred the case back to the Dutch Patent Office to take a new decision. In the following continued objection proceedings, on 14 January 2009, the Dutch Patent Office again denied the SPC application as it turned out that factually the investigation of Section 7.4 of Annex I to Directive 93/42/EEC had not been performed.

[B] Basic Patent

The same considerations as set out in the EU chapter apply.

[1] Requirement for the Product to Be 'Protected' by the Basic Patent

The same considerations as set out in the EU chapter apply.

As a result of changes in CJEU case law, the validity of certain Dutch SPCs may be called into question, including in particular SPCs for combinations of active ingredients. In order to comply with Article 3(a) of the SPC Regulation, the patentee may surrender his basic patent in part by voluntarily limiting the claims so as to identify the respective active ingredient(s) in the claims. The patentee can register a deed to that effect in the Dutch patent register and rely on the retroactive effect of the surrender.[5] As there is no Dutch case law regarding this approach, it remains unclear whether the approach is feasible.

With respect to the requirement for the product of an SPC to be identified in the claims of the basic patent in order to be protected by the patent, the same considerations as set out in the EU chapter apply.

In *X v. Dutch Patent Office*,[6] the District Court had to decide whether the product trastuzumab emtansine was protected by the basic patent. Trastuzumab emtansine was not included (as a structural formula) in claim 1 of the basic patent. The District Court applied the *Eli Lilly*-doctrine and considered that the question is whether the active ingredient trastuzumab emtansine falls under the antibody described under claim 1 of the basic patent based on the functional features and that, on the basis of that claim, interpreted in particular in the light of the description of the invention, as required by Article 69 of the European Patent Convention and the Protocol on the interpretation thereof, it can be concluded that this claim relates, implicitly but necessarily and specifically, to this active ingredient. The District Court considered that, according to the basic patent, the anti-Her2 antibody was, independent of the combination or bond to a cytotoxic agent, itself toxic, which had the advantage that it will lead to significant reduction of undesirable side effects associated with the administration of high dose cytotoxic agents (which are harmful to both healthy cells and cancer cells). Considered in the light of the description of the basic patent, the average skilled person would not conclude from claim 1 of the basic patent that the anti-Her2 antibody according to the invention can also be an anti-Her2 antibody that induces apoptosis due to a cytotoxic agent conjugated thereto. In view of the foregoing, the District Court decided that it cannot be concluded that claim 1 of the basic patent relates, implicitly, but necessarily and specifically, to trastuzumab emtansine.

---

5. Article 63 DPA. The Dutch Patent Office shall not register the deed as long as there are persons who, by virtue of documents entered in the patent register, have registered rights in respect of the patent or have received licences or have commenced legal proceedings concerning the patent and such persons have not consented to the surrender.
6. District Court The Hague *X v. Dutch Patent Office (trastuzumab)*, ECLI:NL:RBDHA:2017:8031 of 19 July 2017, particularly paragraphs 5.1 and 5.2.

On 10 April 2018 the District Court of The Hague rendered judgment in the *Merck Sharp & Dohme Corp. v. Dutch Patent Office* case,[7] where the issue at hand was whether the Dutch Patent Office had rightfully refused the application for an SPC for a combination product of ezetimibe and rosuvastatin on the basis of Article 3 of the SPC Regulation.

The District Court considered that the Dutch Patent Office rightly ruled that Article 3 of the SPC Regulation stands in the way of, in addition to the SPC for the monoproduct ezetimibe, also obtaining an SPC for the combination product ezetimibe and rosuvastatin. In view of the CJEU judgments *Actavis v. Sanofi* and *Actavis v. Boehringer* no supplementary protection can be granted for a situation where a combination product consists of: (i) an active substance protected by a basic patent 'as such', that is the subject matter of the patented invention (in this case ezetimibe); and (ii) an active substance – part of a non-limited group of biosynthesis inhibitors – which is not protected as such by the same basic patent and is not the object of the invention (i.e., rosuvastatin), where the plaintiff has also been able to object within the period of validity of the first SPC for the monoproduct against use of medicinal products consisting of a combination of ezetimibe with a biosynthesis inhibitor (including rosuvastatin) for the same therapeutic application.

The question whether the combination of ezetimibe and rosuvastatin is inventive and whether a separate patent could have been obtained for this combination was not necessary to answer according to the District Court. In paragraph 42 of the *Actavis v. Sanofi* judgment the CJEU considered that a 'new basic patent, in so far as it covered a totally separate innovation', could claim an SPC, but according to the District Court this situation did not occur in this case.

In the preliminary relief case *Merck Sharp & Dohme Corp. v. Teva et al.* (ezetimibe and simvastatin),[8] the preliminary relief judge considered that his decision should be aligned with the relevant parts of the aforementioned decision in the proceedings on the merits case *Merck Sharp & Dohme Corp. v. Dutch Patent Office* (ezetimibe and rosuvastatin).[9] Even though simvastatin was mentioned in claim 17 of the basic patent (opposed to rosuvastatin in the District Court decision), the preliminary relief judge preliminary opined that cholesterol biosynthesis inhibitors do not constitute an 'innovative active ingredient' in the context of the basic patent, and as such, said inhibitors – including simvastatin – are not the 'subject matter' of the patent. The preliminary relief judge therefore concluded that there was a serious, non-negligible chance that the combination SPC shall be invalidated in proceedings on the merits.

7. District Court The Hague *Merck Sharp & Dohme Corp. v. Dutch Patent Office*, ECLI:NL:RB-DHA:2018:4081 of 10 April 2018.
8. Preliminary relief judge of the District Court The Hague *Merck Sharp & Dohme Corp. v. Teva Nederland et al.*, ECLI:NL:RBDHA:2018:6802 of 11 June 2018.
9. District Court The Hague *Merck Sharp & Dohme Corp. v. Dutch Patent Office*, ECLI:NL:RB-DHA:2018:4081 of 10 April 2018.

[a] Small Molecules

The same considerations as set out in the EU chapter apply.

[b] Polymers

The same considerations as set out in the EU chapter apply.

[c] Antibodies, Enzymes and Other Proteins

The same considerations as set out in the EU chapter apply.

In *X v. Dutch Patent Office*,[10] the District Court had to decide whether the product trastuzumab emtansine was protected by the basic patent. Trastuzumab emtansine was not included (as a structural formula) in claim 1 of the basic patent. The District Court applied the *Eli Lilly*-doctrine and considered that the question is whether the active ingredient trastuzumab emtansine falls under the antibody described under claim 1 of the basic patent based on the functional features and that, on the basis of that claim, interpreted in particular in the light of the description of the invention, as required by Article 69 of the European Patent Convention and the Protocol on the interpretation thereof, it can be concluded that this claim relates, implicitly but necessarily and specifically, to this active ingredient. According to the basic patent, the anti-Her2 antibody was, independent of the combination or bond to a cytotoxic agent, itself toxic, which had the advantage that it will lead to significant reduction of undesirable side effects associated with the administration of high dose cytotoxic agents (which are harmful to both healthy cells and cancer cells). Considered in the light of the description of the basic patent, the average skilled person would not conclude from claim 1 of the basic patent that the anti-Her2 antibody according to the invention can also be an anti-Her2 antibody that induces apoptosis due to a cytotoxic agent conjugated thereto. In view of the foregoing, the District Court decided that it cannot be concluded that claim 1 of the basic patent relates, implicitly, but necessarily and specifically, to trastuzumab emtansine.

[d] Nucleic Acids

The same considerations as set out in the EU chapter apply.

[2] Basic Patent Claiming the Product, i.e., the Active Ingredient(s), but Not the Corresponding Authorized Medicinal Product (or Plant Protection Product)

The same considerations as set out in the EU chapter apply.

---

10. District Court The Hague *X v. Dutch Patent Office (trastuzumab)*, ECLI:NL:RBDHA:2017:8031 of 19 July 2017, particularly paragraphs 5.1 and 5.2.

[3] Requirement for the Product to Constitute 'the Invention' of the Basic Patent

The same considerations as set out in the EU chapter apply.

The Dutch cases regarding the rejected SPC for the combination of ezetimibe and rosuvastatin,[11] and the preliminary opinion regarding the invalidity of the SPC for ezetimibe and simvastatin,[12] as discussed earlier in §5.02[B][1], refer to the *Actavis v. Boehringer* case and apply the CJEU's reasoning with regard to the interpretation of 'subject matter of the invention' and the protection 'as such'. With regard to the combination of ezetimibe and rosuvastatin, the District Court found that the 'core inventive advance' of the basic patent is the new group of azetidinone compounds that can be used for the prevention of arteriosclerosis and/or as cholesterol-lowering agents. Ezetimibe is one of those new compounds and is thus deemed as innovative active ingredient, which is protected 'as such' by the basic patent. While on the other hand, cholesterol biosynthesis inhibitors are not protected 'as such' in the basic patent. Therefore, the District Court ruled that said inhibitors are not an 'innovative active ingredient' in the context of the basic patent and as such are not the subject matter of the basic patent.

[4] Criteria for Choosing the Basic Patent among Various Available Patents

The same considerations as set out in the EU chapter apply.

[C] The Marketing Authorization Forming Basis for an SPC

The same considerations as set out in the EU chapter apply.

[1] Combinations of Active Ingredients

The same considerations as set out in the EU chapter apply.

[a] The Marketing Authorization Refers to Fewer Active Ingredients than the SPC Application

The same considerations as set out in the EU chapter apply.

11. District Court The Hague *Merck Sharp & Dohme Corp. v. Dutch Patent Office*, ECLI:NL:RBDHA:2018:4081 of 10 April 2018.
12. Preliminary relief judge of the District Court The Hague *Merck Sharp & Dohme Corp. v. Teva Nederland et al.*, ECLI:NL:RBDHA:2018:6802 of 11 June 2018.

[b] *The Marketing Authorization Refers to More Active Ingredients than the SPC Application*

The same considerations as set out in the EU chapter apply.

[c] *The Marketing Authorization Indicates That a Medicinal Product Containing a Single Active Ingredient Is Authorized for Use in Combination with a Further Active Ingredient*

The same considerations as set out in the EU chapter apply.

[2] *The Marketing Authorization Has Not Yet Been Granted at the Time the SPC Application Is Filed*

The same considerations as set out in the EU chapter apply.

[3] *The Holder of the Marketing Authorization*

The same considerations as set out in the EU chapter apply.

In the case *X v. Dutch Patent Office*,[13] the District Court considered that the Dutch Patent Office, in its contested decision, explicitly did not take a position on whether the refusal to grant an SPC can be based in part on the fact that the claimant in no way contributed to the development of the medicinal product for which a third party obtained a marketing authorization and, from this perspective, the question arises whether the period of effective protection set in this respect was indeed insufficient within the meaning of recital 4 of the preamble of the SPC Regulation. However, as the defendant did not base the refusal to grant a certificate on this fact, the District Court did not comply with the defendant's request to give an opinion in this respect at the hearing, leaving aside the fact that, for that purpose, it may be required to refer these questions to the CJEU with regard to the interpretation of Article 3, preamble and under b of the SPC Regulation.

[4] *Reliance on a Marketing Authorization Granted under a Provision Other than Directive 2001/83/EC or Directive 2001/82/EC*

The same considerations as set out in the EU chapter apply.

The District Court does not seem to object to the grant of SPCs for medical devices as already discussed in §5.02[A][6].

13. District Court The Hague *X v. Dutch Patent Office (trastuzumab)*, ECLI:NL:RBDHA:2017:8031 of 19 July 2017, particularly paragraphs 5.1 and 5.2.

[5] The Marketing Authorizations Which Can Be Relied upon for SPC Applications for Plant Protection Products

The same considerations as set out in the EU chapter apply.

[6] The Product in Question Is Contained in the Authorized Medicinal Product (or the Authorized Plant Protection Product) but Is Not Identified as an Active Ingredient in the Corresponding Marketing Authorization

The same considerations as set out in the EU chapter apply.

[7] The Notion of the 'First' Marketing Authorization

The same considerations as set out in the EU chapter apply.

[a] *Marketing Authorization for a New Therapeutic Application of a Previously Authorized Product*

The same considerations as set out in the EU chapter apply.

In *Bayer Schering Pharma Aktiengesellschaft v. Dutch Patent Office,*[14] the District Court applied the *Neurim* decision. Bayer based an application for an SPC on a basic patent for a multiphase contraceptive based on natural oestrogens that protected the product dienogest and estradiol valerate for which a marketing authorization had been obtained with oral contraception as its therapeutic indication. Previously, however, a marketing authorization had already been obtained for this specific combination for hormone supplementation therapy in the treatment of post-menopausal women suffering from symptoms of oestrogen deficiency. With reference to paragraphs 11 and 35 of the Explanatory Memorandum, CJEU case law *BASF,*[15] *Pharmacia Italia,*[16] *MIT*[17] and *Yissum*[18] as well as Dutch case law *Lundbeck v. Generics,*[19] the Dutch Patent Office argued that 'product' should be interpreted in the strict sense of active ingredient. Therefore, the Dutch Patent Office argued that dienogest and estradiol valerate was not a new product in the sense of Article 1 of the SPC Regulation and that the invoked marketing authorization was not the first marketing authorization for the product as medicinal product in the sense of Article 3(d) of the SPC Regulation. According to the

14. District Court The Hague *Bayer Schering Pharma Aktiengesellschaft v. Dutch Patent Office,* ECLI:NL:RBDHA:2017:793 of 1 February 2017.
15. CJEU *BASF,* C-258/99 of 10 May 2001.
16. CJEU *Pharmacia Italia,* C-31/03 of 19 October 2004.
17. CJEU *MIT,* C-431/04 of 4 May 2006.
18. CJEU *Yissum v. Comptroller-General of Patents,* C-202/05 of 17 April 2007.
19. Court of Appeal The Hague *Lundbeck v. Generics,* ECLI:NL:GHSGR:2012:BV1963 of 24 January 2012.

Dutch Patent Office, the *Neurim* decision[20] does not change this as the prejudicial question in that case was reformulated to a limited legal question in the specific context of the file, more in particular the situation that the first marketing authorization was obtained for a veterinary medicinal product. The District Court in The Hague disagreed with the Dutch Patent Office and held that it follows from considerations twenty-two up to and including twenty-six of the *Neurim* decision that the possibility to obtain an SPC for a new, patented, application of a known active substance, that was already marketed as a medicinal product, also extends to the situation in which the prior marketing authorization pertains to a medicinal product for human use. The District Court added that with regard to the new therapeutic use, also no restriction with respect to veterinary and/or human use can be read in the aforementioned considerations. As the Dutch Patent Office did not put forward other arguments for refusal of the application, the District Court ordered the Dutch Patent Office to issue a new decision by which it would grant Bayer the SPC. The Dutch Patent Office lodged an appeal against this decision before the Council of State and the parties are currently awaiting the decision.

[b] Marketing Authorization for a New Formulation of a Previously Authorized Product

The same considerations as set out in the EU chapter apply.

[c] Marketing Authorization for a New Specific Salt, Ester or Other Derivative of a Previously Authorized Active Ingredient

The same considerations as set out in the EU chapter apply.

In *Yeda v. Dutch Patent Office*,[21] the Council of State considered that it follows from *Farmitalia*[22] that in certain circumstances it may be necessary to define the product in an SPC more broadly than the description of the active ingredient in the relevant marketing authorization. According to the Council of State, the CJEU accepted the argument that the purpose of the SPC Regulation would be frustrated if an SPC could only protect the salt of an active substance mentioned in a marketing authorization in cases where the active substance as such, including the salts derived therefrom are protected by a basic patent. A competitor would then be able to obtain a marketing authorization after expiry of the basic patent in question for another salt of the same active ingredient previously protected by the relevant basic patent. In that case, medicinal products which in principle have the same therapeutic value as the product protected by the SPC could enter into competition with that medicinal product. That would not be compatible with the purpose of the SPC Regulation, which aims to guarantee sufficient protection to encourage pharmaceutical research. The Council of

20. CJEU *Neurim Pharmaceuticals v. Comptroller-General of Patents*, C-130/11 of 19 July 2012.
21. Council of State *Yeda (prev: Aventis) v. Dutch Patent Office*, ECLI:NL:RVS:2009:BI4974 of 27 May 2009.
22. CJEU *Farmitalia Carlo Erba v. Bundesgerichtshof*, C-392/97 of 16 September 1999.

State stated that therefore the CJEU has ruled that an SPC can cover the active ingredient as such and derivatives thereof (such as salts and esters) as medicinal product.

As a consequence, the sole reliance on a patent for a new salt, ester or other derivative of a previously approved active substance is not sufficient to warrant the issue of an SPC for this specific form of the previously authorized active substance with the same therapeutic value (more in particular regarding safety and/or efficacy).

[d] *Marketing Authorization for a New Specific Enantiomer of an Active Ingredient Previously Authorized in Racemic Form*

In *Lundbeck v. Tiefenbacher et al.*,[23] the Court of Appeal decided that the earlier marketing authorization for an active ingredient in racemic form did not preclude the grant of a new SPC for a specific enantiomer of the corresponding active ingredient on the basis of a later marketing authorization and a basic patent directed to this specific enantiomer. It follows from the decision of the Court of Appeal that the enantiomer escitalopram, which was the subject of the attacked SPC, and the previously approved racemate citalopram have different therapeutic effects and should therefore be regarded as different active ingredients within the meaning of the SPC Regulation.

[e] *The Product Has Already Been Placed on the Market Before, but Without an Authorization Granted under Directive 2001/83/EC or Directive 2001/82/EC*

The same considerations as set out in the EU chapter apply.

[f] *Prior Marketing Authorization Which Refers to Fewer Active Ingredients than the SPC Application (and the Later Marketing Authorization Relied upon)*

The same considerations as set out in the EU chapter apply.

[g] *Prior Marketing Authorization Which Refers to More Active Ingredients than the SPC Application (and the Later Marketing Authorization Relied upon)*

The same considerations as set out in the EU chapter apply.

23. Court of Appeal The Hague *Lundbeck v. Tiefenbacher et al.*, ECLI:NL:GHSGR:2012:BV1963 of 24 January 2012.

[D] Preclusion of New SPCs by an Earlier SPC

The same considerations as set out in the EU chapter apply.

[1] Consequences of an Earlier Third-Party SPC for the Same Product

[a] The 'One SPC per Product per Patent Holder' Rule

The same considerations as set out in the EU chapter apply.

The Dutch Patent Office examines whether the same applicant has previously received an SPC for the same product. If so, then the Dutch Patent Office will reject the application as granting a second SPC for the same product to the same applicant would be contrary to the requirement of Article 3(c) of the SPC Regulation.

[b] Earlier SPC Granted to an Affiliated Third Party

The same considerations as set out in the EU chapter apply.

As the Dutch Patent Office does not examine whether another (affiliated) party has previously received an SPC for the same product, the Dutch Patent Office grants SPCs to different patent holders.

[c] Partial Overlap Between the Holders of the Earlier SPC and the Applicants for the New SPC

The same considerations as set out in the EU chapter apply.

[d] Earlier Third-Party SPC Has Been Licensed-In

The same considerations as set out in the EU chapter apply.

As the Dutch Patent Office does not examine whether another (affiliated) party has previously received an SPC for the same product, the Dutch Patent Office grants SPCs to different patent holders.

[2] Consequences of an Own Earlier SPC for the Same Product

The same considerations as set out in the EU chapter apply.

[a] Own Earlier SPC Application Not Yet Granted

The same considerations as set out in the EU chapter apply.

[b] *Revocation, Surrender or Lapse of the Own Earlier SPC after Grant*

The same considerations as set out in the EU chapter apply.

[c] *Transfer of the Own Earlier SPC to a Third Party*

The same considerations as set out in the EU chapter apply.

[d] *Acquisition of an SPC Granted to a Third Party*

The same considerations as set out in the EU chapter apply.

[3] *Consequences of an Own Earlier SPC for a Different Product*

The same considerations as set out in the EU chapter apply.

[a] *Required Distinction from the Product of the Own Earlier SPC*

The same considerations as set out in the EU chapter apply.

Combinations of Active Ingredients

The Dutch courts apply the 'core inventive advance' requirement endorsed by the CJEU in *Actavis v. Sanofi* (C-443/12),[24] *Georgetown University v. Octrooicentrum Nederland* (C-484/12)[25] and *Actavis v. Boehringer Ingelheim Pharma* (C-577/13)[26] when assessing the preclusion of a new SPC by a previous SPC granted to the same patent holder under Article 3(c) of the SPC Regulations, specifically in the context of SPCs for combinations of active ingredients.

On 10 April 2018 the District Court of The Hague rendered judgment in the *Merck Sharp & Dohme Corp. v. Dutch Patent Office* case,[27] where the issue at hand was whether the Dutch Patent Office had rightfully refused the application for an SPC for a combination product of ezetimibe and rosuvastatin on the basis of Article 3 of the SPC Regulation.

The District Court considered that the Dutch Patent Office rightly ruled that Article 3 of the SPC Regulation stands in the way of, in addition to the SPC for the monoproduct ezetimibe, also obtaining an SPC for the combination product ezetimibe and rosuvastatin. In view of the CJEU judgments *Actavis v. Sanofi* and *Actavis v. Boehringer* no supplementary protection can be granted for a situation where a combination product consists of: (i) an active substance protected by a basic patent 'as

24. CJEU *Actavis v. Sanofi*, C-443/12 of 12 December 2013.
25. CJEU *Georgetown University v. Octrooicentrum Nederland*, C-484/12 of 12 December 2013.
26. CJEU *Actavis v. Boehringer Ingelheim Pharma*, C-577/13 of 12 March 2015.
27. District Court The Hague *Merck Sharp & Dohme Corp. v. Dutch Patent Office*, ECLI:NL:RB-DHA:2018:4081 of 10 April 2018.

such', that is the subject matter of the patented invention (in this case ezetimibe); and (ii) an active substance – part of a non-limited group of biosynthesis inhibitors – which is not protected as such by the same basic patent and is not the object of the invention (i.e., rosuvastatin), where the plaintiff has also been able to object within the period of validity of the first SPC for the monoproduct against use of medicinal products consisting of a combination of ezetimibe with a biosynthesis inhibitor (including rosuvastatin) for the same therapeutic application.

The question whether the combination of ezetimibe and rosuvastatin is inventive and whether a separate patent could have been obtained for this combination was not necessary to answer according to the District Court. In paragraph 42 of the *Actavis v. Sanofi* judgment the CJEU considered that a 'new basic patent, in so far as it covered a totally separate innovation', could claim an SPC, but according to the District Court this situation did not occur in this case.

In the preliminary relief case *Merck Sharp & Dohme Corp. v. Teva et al.* (ezetimibe and simvastatin),[28] the preliminary relief judge considered that his decision should be aligned with the relevant parts of the aforementioned decision in the proceedings on the merits case *Merck Sharp & Dohme Corp. v. Dutch Patent Office* (ezetimibe and rosuvastatin).[29] Even though simvastatin was mentioned in claim 17 of the basic patent (opposed to rosuvastatin in the District Court decision), the preliminary relief judge preliminary opined that cholesterol biosynthesis inhibitors do not constitute an 'innovative active ingredient' in the context of the basic patent, and as such, said inhibitors – including simvastatin – are not the 'subject matter' of the patent. The preliminary relief judge therefore concluded that there was a serious, non-negligible chance that the combination SPC shall be invalidated in proceedings on the merits.

New Therapeutic Applications of Previously Approved Active Ingredients

The same considerations as set out in the EU chapter apply.

In *Bayer Schering Pharma Aktiengesellschaft v. Dutch Patent Office*,[30] the District Court applied the *Neurim* decision. Bayer based an application for an SPC on a basic patent for a multiphase contraceptive based on natural oestrogens that protected the product dienogest and estradiol valerate for which a marketing authorization had been obtained with oral contraception as its therapeutic indication. Previously, however, a marketing authorization had already been obtained for this specific combination for hormone supplementation therapy in the treatment of post-menopausal women suffering from symptoms of oestrogen deficiency. With reference to paragraphs 11 and 35 of the Explanatory Memorandum, CJEU case law *BASF*,[31] *Pharmacia Italia*,[32] *MIT*[33] and

28. Preliminary relief judge of the District Court The Hague *Merck Sharp & Dohme Corp. v. Teva Nederland et al.*, ECLI:NL:RBDHA:2018:6802 of 11 June 2018.
29. District Court The Hague *Merck Sharp & Dohme Corp. v. Dutch Patent Office*, ECLI:NL:RBDHA:2018:4081 of 10 April 2018.
30. District Court The Hague *Bayer Schering Pharma Aktiengesellschaft v. Dutch Patent Office*, ECLI:NL:RBDHA:2017:793 of 1 February 2017.
31. CJEU *BASF*, C-258/99 of 10 May 2001.
32. CJEU *Pharmacia Italia*, C-31/03 of 19 October 2004.
33. CJEU *MIT*, C-431/04 of 4 May 2006.

Yissum[34] as well as Dutch case law *Lundbeck v. Generics*,[35] the Dutch Patent Office argued that 'product' should be interpreted in the strict sense of active ingredient. Therefore, the Dutch Patent Office argued that dienogest and estradiol valerate was not a new product in the sense of Article 1 of the SPC Regulation and that the invoked marketing authorization was not the first marketing authorization for the product as medicinal product in the sense of Article 3(d) of the SPC Regulation. According to the Dutch Patent Office, the *Neurim* decision[36] does not change this as the prejudicial question in that case was reformulated to a limited legal question in the specific context of the file, more in particular the situation that the first marketing authorization was obtained for a veterinary medicinal product. The District Court in The Hague disagreed with the Dutch Patent Office and held that it follows from considerations twenty-two up to and including twenty-six of the *Neurim* decision that the possibility to obtain an SPC for a new, patented, application of a known active substance, that was already marketed as a medicinal product, also extends to the situation in which the prior marketing authorization pertains to a medicinal product for human use. The District Court added that with regard to the new therapeutic use, also no restriction with respect to veterinary and/or human use can be read in the aforementioned considerations. As the Dutch Patent Office did not put forward other arguments for refusal of the application, the District Court ordered the Dutch Patent Office to issue a new decision by which it would grant Bayer the SPC. The Dutch Patent Office lodged an appeal against this decision before the Council of State and the parties are currently awaiting the decision.

[b] *SPCs for a Specific Salt, Ester or Other Derivative Where an Own Earlier SPC Has Already Been Granted for the Corresponding Active Ingredient*

The same considerations as set out in the EU chapter apply.

The Council of State[37] considered that it follows from *Farmitalia*[38] that in certain circumstances it may be necessary to define the product in an SPC more broadly than the description of the active ingredient in the relevant marketing authorization. According to the Council of State, the CJEU accepted the argument that the purpose of the SPC Regulation would be frustrated if an SPC could only protect the salt of an active substance mentioned in a marketing authorization in cases where the active substance as such, including the salts derived therefrom are protected by a basic patent. A competitor would then be able to obtain a marketing authorization after expiry of the basic patent in question for another salt of the same active ingredient previously protected by the relevant basic patent. In that case, medicinal products which in

34. CJEU *Yissum v. Comptroller-General of Patents*, C-202/05 of 17 April 2007.
35. Court of Appeal The Hague *Lundbeck v. Generics*, ECLI:NL:GHSGR:2012:BV1963 of 24 January 2012.
36. CJEU *Neurim Pharmaceuticals v. Comptroller-General of Patents*, C-130/11 of 19 July 2012.
37. Council of State *Yeda (prev: Aventis) v. Dutch Patent Office*, ECLI:NL:RVS:2009:BI4974 of 27 May 2009.
38. CJEU *Farmitalia Carlo Erba v. Bundesgerichtshof*, C-392/97 of 16 September 1999.

principle have the same therapeutic value as the product protected by the SPC could enter into competition with that medicinal product. That would not be compatible with the purpose of the SPC Regulation, which aims to guarantee sufficient protection to encourage pharmaceutical research. The Council of State stated that therefore the CJEU has ruled that an SPC can cover the active ingredient as such and derivatives thereof (such as salts and esters) as medicinal product.

[c] SPCs for a Specific Enantiomer Where an Own Earlier SPC Has Already Been Granted for the Corresponding Racemate

In general, the same considerations as set out in the EU chapter apply. This subject matter was addressed in the Dutch escitalopram case.[39]

In *Lundbeck v. Tiefenbacher et al.*,[40] the Court of Appeal decided that the earlier marketing authorization for an active ingredient in racemic form did not preclude the grant of a new SPC for a specific enantiomer of the corresponding active ingredient on the basis of a later marketing authorization and a basic patent directed to this specific enantiomer. It follows from the decision of the Court of Appeal that the enantiomer escitalopram, which was the subject of the attacked SPC, and the previously approved racemate citalopram have different therapeutic effects and should therefore be regarded as different active ingredients within the meaning of the SPC Regulation.

[4] Grant of More than One SPC on the Basis of the Same Patent

The same considerations as set out in the EU chapter apply to the Netherlands.

On 10 April 2018 the District Court of The Hague rendered judgment in the *Merck Sharp & Dohme Corp. v. Dutch Patent Office* case,[41] where the issue at hand was whether the Dutch Patent Office had rightfully refused the application for an SPC for a combination product of ezetimibe and rosuvastatin on the basis of Article 3 of the SPC Regulation.

The District Court considered that the Dutch Patent Office rightly ruled that Article 3 of the SPC Regulation stands in the way of, in addition to the SPC for the monoproduct ezetimibe, also obtaining an SPC for the combination product ezetimibe and rosuvastatin. In view of the CJEU judgments *Actavis v. Sanofi* and *Actavis v. Boehringer* no supplementary protection can be granted for a situation where a combination product consists of: (i) an active substance protected by a basic patent 'as

39. Court of Appeal The Hague *Lundbeck v. Tiefenbacher et al.*, ECLI:NL:GHSGR:2012:BV1963 of 24 January 2012. As far as the part of the judgement concerned with the SPC, the Supreme Court has confirmed that the reasoning of the Court of Appeal in this regard is solid and comprehensible and presents no issues from a legal point of view (apart from the consequences of the invalidity of claims 1-5 to the SPC), *see* Supreme Court, *Lundbeck v. Tiefenbacher et al.*, ECLI:NL:HR:2013:BZ4115 of 7 June 2013.
40. Court of Appeal The Hague *Lundbeck v. Tiefenbacher et al.*, ECLI:NL:GHSGR:2012:BV1963 of 24 January 2012.
41. District Court The Hague *Merck Sharp & Dohme Corp. v. Dutch Patent Office*, ECLI:NL:RB-DHA:2018:4081 of 10 April 2018.

such', that is the subject matter of the patented invention (in this case ezetimibe); and (ii) an active substance – part of a non-limited group of biosynthesis inhibitors – which is not protected as such by the same basic patent and is not the object of the invention (i.e., rosuvastatin), where the plaintiff has also been able to object within the period of validity of the first SPC for the monoproduct against use of medicinal products consisting of a combination of ezetimibe with a biosynthesis inhibitor (including rosuvastatin) for the same therapeutic application.

The question whether the combination of ezetimibe and rosuvastatin is inventive and whether a separate patent could have been obtained for this combination was not necessary to answer according to the District Court. In paragraph 42 of the *Actavis v. Sanofi* judgment the CJEU considered that a 'new basic patent, in so far as it covered a totally separate innovation', could claim an SPC, but according to the District Court this situation did not occur in this case.

In the preliminary relief case *Merck Sharp & Dohme Corp. v. Teva et al.* (ezetimibe and simvastatin),[42] the preliminary relief judge considered that his decision should be aligned with the relevant parts of the aforementioned decision in the proceedings on the merits case *Merck Sharp & Dohme Corp. v. Dutch Patent Office* (ezetimibe and rosuvastatin).[43] Even though simvastatin was mentioned in claim 17 of the basic patent (opposed to rosuvastatin in the District Court decision), the preliminary relief judge preliminary opined that cholesterol biosynthesis inhibitors do not constitute an 'innovative active ingredient' in the context of the basic patent, and as such, said inhibitors – including simvastatin – are not the 'subject matter' of the patent. The preliminary relief judge therefore concluded that there was a serious, non-negligible chance that the combination SPC shall be invalidated in proceedings on the merits.

§5.03 EXTENT OF PROTECTION AND ENFORCEMENT OF SPCs

[A] The Protection Conferred by an SPC

The considerations in terms of the protection conferred by an SPC outlined in the EU chapter apply equally to the Netherlands.

The scope of protection of an SPC is determined on the basis of the underlying patent, but limited to the product for which the SPC has been granted.

In *Sankyo v. Merial*,[44] Sankyo claimed that Merial infringed Sankyo's SPC for the product 'Praziquantel and Ivermectine'. With reference to the Merck-index, Sankyo stated that *all* isomeric forms of praziquantel were included in the SPC. According to Merial, however, it was not clear from the prosecution file of the Dutch SPC nor the marketing authorization for Equimax (the medicinal product of Sankyo) whether praziquantel means the *l*-isomer, the *r*-isomer or the racemic mixture. As it appeared

42. Preliminary relief judge of the District Court The Hague *Merck Sharp & Dohme Corp. v. Teva Nederland et al.*, ECLI:NL:RBDHA:2018:6802 of 11 June 2018.
43. District Court The Hague *Merck Sharp & Dohme Corp. v. Dutch Patent Office*, ECLI:NL:RBDHA:2018:4081 of 10 April 2018.
44. District Court The Hague *Sankyo v. Merial*, ECLI:NL:RBSGR:2005:AU0057 of 7 July 2005.

from literature that for example the *l*-isomer is a very different active ingredient than the racemic mixture of praziquantel (with relevant other activity and toxicity), Merial argued that only the *l*-isomer could be intended in the SPC. Merial further substantiated that with references to the English and German SPC prosecution files and the patent, which would indicate that the *l*-isomer was intended with praziquantel. Furthermore, Merial stated that the Dutch Patent Office attaches great value to the views of authorities that grant marketing authorizations, which considered a purely optically active enantiomer as a new ingredient in addition to a racemic mixture. The *l*-isomer of praziquantel should therefore serve as another product in the sense of Regulation 1768/92 than the racemic mixture. As one SPC can protect only one product according to Article 3(c) of Regulation 1768/92, Merial argued that the SPC related only to the *l*-isomer of praziquantel and that Merial therefore did not infringe the SPC; its product Eqvalan Duo did not contain the *l*-isomer of praziquantel, but the racemic mixture. The preliminary relief judge accepted that reasoning and dismissed the injunction preliminary opining that it was not sufficiently clear that the District Court in the proceedings on the merits would decide that the SPC is infringed.

In the proceedings on the merits in *Merial v. Sankyo*,[45] the District Court reached a different conclusion. With reference to the broad claim in the basic patent and the European pharmacopoeia, the District Court considered that the SPC did not protect the *l*-isomer of praziquantel but praziquantel in general, which means the racemic mixture of praziquantel and not a specific form thereof such as the *l*-isomer.[46]

[B] The Scope of an SPC in Relation to Derivatives of an Active Ingredient

There have not been any national decisions addressing this point specifically in an infringement case.

The issue of a broader product definition in relation to derivatives of an active ingredient has been subject of administrative proceedings regarding the grant of an SPC. In *Yeda v. Dutch Patent Office*[47] – administrative proceedings before the highest instance, the Council of State, regarding the limited grant of an SPC – the Council of State considered as follows. In view of Article 2 of the SPC Regulation, an SPC is issued for a product, which, according to Article 1, preamble and under b, of the SPC Regulation is to be understood as the active ingredient or combination of active ingredients of a medicinal product. In view of Article 3, preamble and under b, of the SPC Regulation, a condition for the obtaining of an SPC is that a marketing authorization has been granted for the product as a medicinal product. The marketing authorization should therefore be used to determine the active ingredient that must be considered for the evaluation of an application for an SPC as the product to be

45. District Court The Hague *Merial v. Sankyo*, ECLI:NL:RBSGR:2005:AZ6590 of 12 October 2005.
46. The District Court invalidated the SPC, because the product was not protected by the basic patent in force. The product did not achieve the synergetic effect in the patent.
47. Council of State *Yeda (prev: Aventis) v. Dutch Patent Office*, ECLI:NL:RVS:2009:BI4974 of 27 May 2009.

protected. This is confirmed in Article 4 of the SPC Regulation in which the protection granted by the certificate is limited to the product that falls under the marketing authorization. In connection with this, Article 8, first paragraph, preamble and under b, of the SPC Regulation stipulates that a certificate application must contain a copy of a marketing authorization, in which the product is identified.

The Council of State further considered that it follows from *Farmitalia*[48] that in certain circumstances it may be necessary to define the product in an SPC more broadly than the description of the active ingredient in the relevant marketing authorization. According to the Council of State, the CJEU accepted the argument that the purpose of the SPC Regulation would be frustrated if an SPC could only protect the salt of an active substance mentioned in a marketing authorization in cases where the active substance as such, including the salts derived therefrom are protected by a basic patent. A competitor would then be able to obtain a marketing authorization after expiry of the basic patent in question for another salt of the same active ingredient previously protected by the relevant basic patent. In that case, medicinal products which in principle have the same therapeutic value as the product protected by the SPC could enter into competition with that medicinal product. That would not be compatible with the purpose of the SPC Regulation, which aims to guarantee sufficient protection to encourage pharmaceutical research. The Council of State considered that therefore the CJEU has ruled that an SPC can cover the active ingredient as such and derivatives thereof (such as salts and esters) as medicinal product.

[1] *The Relationship Between the Definition of the Active Ingredient(s) in an SPC and Its Scope of Protection*

In *Yeda v. Dutch Patent Office*,[49] the Council of State decided on the issue of a broader product definition beyond the specific form of the active ingredient identified in the marketing authorization.

Yeda held a basic patent for human monoclonal antibodies against a cytotoxin, a hybridoma cell line that expresses that and a method for preparing a purified cytotoxin and a marketing authorization for adalimumab. As chemical designation of the product, Yeda included 'human monoclonal antibodies against tumour necrosis factor alpha (TNF-alpha)'. This definition was admitted by the UK IPO with respect to the UK member of the SPC family requested by Yeda.[50]

The Dutch Patent Office granted a certificate for the product adalimumab,[51] which was the active ingredient in the marketing authorization. It refused, however, to grant the certificate with the product definition proposed by Yeda.

Yeda appealed the decision, proposing new and more limited product definitions as main and auxiliary requests. What was common to three of the product definitions

48. CJEU *Farmitalia Carlo Erba v. Bundesgerichtshof*, C-392/97 of 16 September 1999.
49. Council of State *Yeda (prev: Aventis) v. Dutch Patent Office*, ECLI:NL:RVS:2009:BI4974 of 27 May 2009.
50. SPC/GB04/006.
51. SPC 300142 granted by the Dutch Patent Office on 13 June 2005.

filed by the applicant was that they: (i) were not limited to adalimumab; (ii) were extended to antibodies qualified, amongst others, as therapeutic equivalents to adalimumab; and (iii) were protected by the basic patent. A fourth product definition included technical features aimed at delimiting and identifying the group of antibodies that shall be covered together with adalimumab by the SPC.

In support of the appeal before the Administrative Chamber of the District Court, Yeda argued that, based on a reasonable explanation of *Farmitalia*,[52] all therapeutic equivalent variants of the product in the marketing authorization can be included in the product definition of an SPC to the extent that this definition falls under the scope of protection of the basic patent. According to Yeda, a broader product definition should be included in the SPC as the basic patent also protects monoclonal antibodies that are therapeutically equivalent to adalimumab.

In its judgment of 12 November 2008 the Administrative Chamber of the District Court of The Hague[53] upheld the decision of the Dutch Patent Office. According to the District Court, the *Farmitalia* decision could not justify granting a certificate with a broader product definition than that admitted by the Dutch Patent Office. The District Court considered that the premise of *Farmitalia* indeed is that the active ingredient and its chemical derivatives, such as salts and esters, are therapeutic equivalents. However, in the case of antibodies, it is not possible to assume that a change in the amino acid sequence of the polypeptide does not affect its therapeutic effect. For this reason, the District Court concluded that the Dutch Patent Office correctly identified adalimumab as the active ingredient for which the SPC was issued.

The appeal filed against the decision of the Administrative Chamber of the District Court of The Hague was rejected by the Council of State by judgment of 19 August 2009.[54] According to the Council of State, given the molecular complexity of antibodies, it could not be excluded that a minor change to their amino acid structure has no consequence on the safety and efficacy of the medicinal product. The Council of State substantiated this position under reference to the regulatory legal framework. Chemical derivatives of an active ingredient, such as salts and esters, are considered the same active ingredients under Article 10(2)(b) of Directive 2001/83 on the Community code relating to medicinal products for human use ('Directive 2001/83'). For this reason, a marketing authorization for a salt of an active ingredient that has been already authorized may be obtained under the abridged procedure laid down in Article 10 of Directive 2001/83. Such abridged procedure is not available for biological products, since the latter, in consequence of their molecular complexity, are subject to the stricter requirements under Article 10(4) of Directive 2001/83. The Council confirmed the first instance decision not to admit a product definition including further antibodies covered by the patent other than adalimumab.

Thus, considering the case law, the product definition seems to be a necessary feature of the application for a certificate and has a legal impact on the grant of an SPC.

52. CJEU *Farmitalia Carlo Erba v. Bundesgerichtshof*, C-392/97 of 16 September 1999.
53. Administrative Chamber of the District Court of The Hague, *Yeda v. Dutch Patent Office*, ECLI:NL:RBSGR:2008:BG7272 of 12 November 2008.
54. Council of State *Yeda v. Dutch Patent Office*, ECLI:NL:RVS:2009:BJ5541 of 19 August 2009.

The practical implications of the product definition of an SPC in terms of the scope of protection conferred by the SPC remain questionable.

[C] Enforcement of an SPC

Subject to the provisions of Articles 4 and 5 of Regulations 469/2009 and 1610/96, the SPC confers the same rights as conferred by the basic patent and shall be subject to the same limitations and the same obligations. The SPC may therefore be enforced on the basis of the same provisions that exist for patents.

In the Netherlands, the District Court of The Hague has exclusive jurisdiction in first instance proceedings on the merits and preliminary injunction proceedings (kort geding) in respect of patent and SPC enforcement actions and invalidity claims.[55] The Court of Appeal of The Hague hears the appeal proceedings and the Supreme Court the appeal in cassation.

The preliminary relief judge (voorzieningenrechter) – a single judge – may grant an injunction in urgent cases where, in view of the interests of the parties, immediate relief is required.[56] An oral hearing in pharmaceutical preliminary injunction proceedings generally takes place before the actual sale of the alleged infringing medicinal product and the preliminary relief judge may grant an injunction prior to,[57] at[58] or shortly after the oral hearing. An injunction prior to or at the oral hearing will be for the duration until the written decision.

In preliminary injunction proceedings, the preliminary relief judge will preliminary opine on issues such as infringement and validity. The preliminary injunction will be awarded if the (threat of) infringement is made sufficiently plausible and the plaintiff has an urgent interest. The requirement of urgency is relatively easily met, because an infringement of an intellectual property right is considered to be urgent by nature and an injunction is considered to be the most suitable remedy to address such infringement.[59] The preliminary injunction will be dismissed if the preliminary relief judge is of the preliminary opinion that there is no infringement and/or that there is a serious, non-negligible chance that the patent and/or SPC will be invalidated in opposition proceedings or proceedings on the merits.

Although ex parte preliminary injunctions are seldom awarded in SPC and patent cases, Article 1019e DCCP[60] states that an ex parte preliminary injunction may be awarded if the case is urgent and postponement would cause irreparable harm. The preliminary relief judge will decide on the request for an ex parte preliminary injunction within a day or a few days and without hearing the alleged infringer. If the alleged infringer submitted a protective brief, the judge will take those arguments into account before granting or dismissing the request.

55. Article 80 DPA.
56. Article 254 DCCP.
57. Article 1019e DCCP.
58. Article 223 DCCP.
59. Supreme Court *Impag v. Milton*, ECLI:NL:HR:2001:AB2391 of 29 June 2001.
60. Article 9 of the Directive 2004/48/EC on the enforcement of intellectual property rights ('Enforcement Directive').

In case a preliminary injunction is granted (ex parte or inter partes), the preliminary injunction proceedings must be timely followed up by proceedings on the merits according to Article 1019i DCCP. Otherwise, the losing party may request the lapse of the preliminary injunction.

There are two types of patent and SPC proceedings on the merits: normal proceedings on the merits and accelerated proceedings on the merits. In both proceedings, a panel of three specialized judges will handle infringement and validity. Parties generally litigate according to the accelerated regime, which follows a pre-fixed time-schedule that does not allow for extensions and should lead to a decision on the merits (infringement and validity) in about a year.[61] The normal proceedings on the merits take about eighteen months to two years.

Appeal against a decision in preliminary relief proceedings can be lodged within four weeks as from the date of the decision and against a decision on the merits within three months as from the date of the decision.[62] Appeal proceedings in preliminary relief proceedings usually take about six to twelve months and in proceedings on the merits eighteen months to two years.

Appeal in cassation against an appeal decision in preliminary relief proceedings can be lodged within eight weeks as from the date of the decision and against an appeal decision on the merits within three months as from the date of the decision.[63] Appeal in cassation usually takes about eighteen months to two years.

On the basis of Article 1019h DCCP, all costs for legal assistance (including patent attorney fees and expert fees) are fully recoverable in patent and SPC enforcement proceedings to the extent that these costs are reasonable and proportional.[64] The case law in the Netherlands shows that in patent and SPC cases, generally the actual legal costs will be rewarded.

§5.04 DETERMINATION OF THE SPC TERM

[A] The Calculation of the SPC Term

The considerations regarding the calculation of the SPC term as set out in the EU chapter apply equally to the Netherlands.

[1] The Relevant Marketing Authorization for the Term of an SPC

The considerations in terms of the relevant marketing authorization for determining the SPC term as set out in the EU chapter apply equally to the Netherlands.

61. Because of the current backlog, decisions are currently issued later than one year.
62. Article 339 DCCP.
63. Article 402 DCCP.
64. Reasonable and proportional costs for legal assistance in relation to invalidation proceedings cannot be recovered if those proceedings were not initiated in response to a threat to enforce the patent or SPC.

The Dutch Patent Office does not carry out a comprehensive search for the verification that the marketing authorization relied upon by the SPC applicant is indeed the first marketing authorization in question. The Dutch Patent Office will examine the databases of the European Medicines Agency and the Netherlands Medicines Evaluation Board to see if earlier marketing authorizations for the same product have been granted. The Dutch Patent Office may also examine databases in other Member States.

In *Bayer Schering Pharma Aktiengesellschaft v. Dutch Patent Office,*[65] the District Court applied the *Neurim* decision. Bayer based an application for an SPC on a basic patent for a multiphase contraceptive based on natural oestrogens that protected the product dienogest and estradiol valerate for which a marketing authorization had been obtained with oral contraception as its therapeutic indication. Previously, however, a marketing authorization had already been obtained for this specific combination for hormone supplementation therapy in the treatment of post-menopausal women suffering from symptoms of oestrogen deficiency. With reference to paragraphs 11 and 35 of the Explanatory Memorandum, CJEU case law *BASF,*[66] *Pharmacia Italia,*[67] *MIT*[68] and *Yissum*[69] as well as Dutch case law *Lundbeck v. Generics,*[70] the Dutch Patent Office argued that 'product' should be interpreted in the strict sense of active ingredient. Therefore, the Dutch Patent Office argued that dienogest and estradiol valerate was not a new product in the sense of Article 1 of the SPC Regulation and that the invoked marketing authorization was not the first marketing authorization for the product as medicinal product in the sense of Article 3(d) of the SPC Regulation. According to the Dutch Patent Office, the *Neurim* decision[71] does not change this as the prejudicial question in that case was reformulated to a limited legal question in the specific context of the file, more in particular the situation that the first marketing authorization was obtained for a veterinary medicinal product. The District Court in The Hague disagreed with the Dutch Patent Office and held that it follows from considerations twenty-two up to and including twenty-six of the *Neurim* decision that the possibility to obtain an SPC for a new, patented, application of a known active substance, that was already marketed as a medicinal product, also extends to the situation in which the prior marketing authorization pertains to a medicinal product for human use. The District Court added that with regard to the new therapeutic use, also no restriction with respect to veterinary and/or human use can be read in the aforementioned considerations. As the Dutch Patent Office did not put forward other arguments for refusal of the application, the District Court ordered the Dutch Patent Office to issue a new decision by which it would grant Bayer the SPC. The Dutch Patent Office lodged an

65. District Court The Hague *Bayer Schering Pharma Aktiengesellschaft v. Dutch Patent Office,* ECLI:NL:RBDHA:2017:793 of 1 February 2017.
66. CJEU *BASF,* C-258/99 of 10 May 2001.
67. CJEU *Pharmacia Italia,* C-31/03 of 19 October 2004.
68. CJEU *MIT,* C-431/04 of 4 May 2006.
69. CJEU *Yissum v. Comptroller-General of Patents,* C-202/05 of 17 April 2007.
70. Court of Appeal The Hague *Lundbeck v. Generics,* ECLI:NL:GHSGR:2012:BV1963 of 24 January 2012.
71. CJEU *Neurim Pharmaceuticals v. Comptroller-General of Patents,* C-130/11 of 19 July 2012.

appeal against this decision before the Council of State and the parties are currently awaiting the decision.

[2] The Expiration Date of an SPC

The SPC shall take effect at the end of the lawful term of the basic patent.[72] According to Article 37 DPA, a patent granted shall remain in force, barring earlier lapse, waiver or invalidation by the District Court, until the expiry of a term of twenty years from the date of filing. The last day when a patent is in force is the day before the twentieth anniversary of its filing date. Accordingly, an SPC with a full five-year term will expire on the day before the twenty-fifth anniversary of the filing date of the patent.

For example, a Dutch SPC which is based on a patent filed on 15 June 2000 and a marketing authorization notified on 10 August 2007 (which was the first marketing authorization for this product in the EU and the EEA) will come into effect upon expiry of the basic patent, i.e., on 15 June 2020, and will expire on 9 August 2022 (at the end of the day, i.e., at midnight). If, in this example, the marketing authorization is notified on or after 15 June 2010, the SPC will have the maximum term of five years and will thus expire on 14 June 2025 (at the end of the day).

[B] Correction of the SPC Term

As discussed in the EU chapter, Article 17(2) of the SPC Regulation for Plant Protection Products, which via recital 17 is also applicable to the SPC Regulation for Medicinal Products, provides that the decision to grant an SPC shall be open to an appeal aimed at rectifying the duration of the SPC where the date of the first marketing authorization in the Community was incorrectly indicated in the SPC application.

In the preliminary ruling in *Incyte*,[73] the CJEU found that the holder of an SPC may bring an appeal for rectification directly with the authority that granted the SPC at any time, provided that the SPC has not expired. As the Dutch Patent Office is responsible for the grant of SPCs, the holder of the SPC should request the Dutch Patent Office to rectify the SPC term.

[C] Paediatric Extensions

The considerations in terms of paediatric extensions as set out in the EU chapter apply equally to the Netherlands.

72. Article 13 of the SPC Regulations.
73. CJEU *Incyte Corporation v. Szellemi Tulajdon Nemzeti Hivatala*, C-492/16 of 20 December 2017.

§5.05 PROCEDURE OF FILING AN SPC APPLICATION

[A] Entitlement to an SPC Application

The SPC Regulations stipulate in Article 6 that the SPC shall be granted to the holder of the basic patent or his successor in title. In the Netherlands, only the holder of the basic patent or his successor in title can file an SPC application at the Dutch Patent Office.

In the Dutch national administrative objection proceedings that resulted in CJEU *AHP Manufacturing*,[74] the Dutch Patent Office established that by the transfer of the basic patent, on the basis of which the SPC application was filed, from F. Hoffmann-La Roche to AHP Manufacturing, AHP Manufacturing had also replaced F. Hoffmann-La Roche as the applicant in the SPC application.[75] The Dutch Patent Office considered this to be in conformity with Article 6 of the SPC Regulation.

[B] The Time Limit for Filing an SPC Application

The considerations as set out in the EU chapter apply.

Article 8 of the SPC Regulations stipulates that the application for a certificate shall contain a request for the grant of a certificate (including further information), a copy of the authorization to place the product on the market (including further information) and - if the aforementioned marketing authorization is not the first marketing authorization to place the product on the market in the EU and EEA - information regarding the first marketing authorization in another Member State.

According to Article 92 DPA, the applicant must provide proof that an amount has been paid to the Dutch Patent Office in accordance with a rate to be set by general order. Article 93 in conjunction with Article 24(3) DPA stipulates that the application and the other documents shall be in Dutch or in English (with the exception of the claims, which must be in Dutch).

If the provisions contained in Article 8 of the SPC Regulations or Articles 92 and 93 DPA have not been complied with, then Article 94 DPA stipulates that the Dutch Patent Office shall so inform the applicant in writing within two months of the filing of the application for an SPC or the request for an extension of the term of an SPC, stating the requirements that have not been met.

Although the central provisions in the DPA (Chapter 7, Articles 90-98) and the PPCD do not explicitly refer to Article 23(1) DPA and it could be argued that Articles 94 DPA and 2(2) PPCD lay down special procedural provisions for SPCs already, the Dutch Patent Office is of the opinion that Article 18 of the SPC Regulations in conjunction with Article 23(1) DPA provide for a re-establishment of right procedure

74. CJEU *AHP Manufacturing*, C-482/07 of 3 September 2009.
75. Decision of the Board of Appeal of the Dutch Patent Office dated 16 June 2006 in the objection proceedings lodged by *F. Hoffmann-La Roche / AHP Manufacturing* regarding the application for SPC 300129 (etanercept), which decision is published in the Dutch patent register and partly known from the decision of the Administrative Chamber of the District Court The Hague *AHP Manufacturing v. Dutch Patent Office*, ECLI:NL:RBSGR:2009:BK2960 of 4 November 2009.

even if the applicant does not meet the time limit for application under Article 7 of the SPC Regulations.

Article 23(1) DPA stipulates that if, despite taking all due care as required under the circumstances, the applicant for or holder of a patent has not been able to observe a term with respect to the Dutch Patent Office, the Dutch Patent Office can upon request of the applicant restore his rights if the failure to observe the term pursuant to the DPA has directly led to the loss of any right or means of redress. In order to be restored in the previous state, the applicant will still have to request for re-establishment of rights within one year of the date of expiry of the missed time limit and within two months from the date on which the person that is responsible for the SPC or the SPC application knew or could have understood that the time limit has not been met.[76]

[C] The Filing of an SPC at the National Patent Office

As set out in the EU chapter, an SPC must be filed before the national patent office within the stipulated time limits, once the basic patent as well as the relevant marketing authorization have issued. The SPC application must be filed in writing, using the prescribed form available on the website of the Dutch Patent Office, and can only be filed by ordinary mail or facsimile (online filing is not available). The SPC application must contain all relevant information about the applicant and/or his representative (names and addresses), the basic patent, the first marketing authorization for placing the product on the Dutch market (national or central marketing authorization) and the first marketing authorization for placing the product on the market in another Member State.

Upon application for an SPC and for an extension of the term of an SPC, proof must be provided that an amount has been paid to the Dutch Patent Office in accordance with a rate to be set by general order.[77]

SPC applications are published in the electronic Patent Bulletin (Hoofdblad Industriële Eigendom), which appears weekly, and in the online patent register, which is updated daily and also includes the prosecution file. The entry in the online patent register normally takes no more than two weeks and the register also mentions the basic patent and references to the one (or more) SPC applications will be added to the basic patent.

[D] The Documentation Required for an SPC Application

The documentation required for filing an SPC application in the Netherlands is based on the requirements set out in Article 8 of the SPC Regulations. Dutch and English language documents are accepted by the Dutch Patent Office.[78]

76. Administrative Chamber of the District Court The Hague, *BPW Bergische Achsen KG v. Dutch Patent Office*, ECLI:NL:RBDHA:2018:4842 of 16 April 2018.
77. Article 92 DPA / Art. 2(1) PPCD.
78. Article 93 DPA / Art. 2(1) PCCP in conjunction with Art. 24(3) DPA.

The SPC application should be supplemented with copies of the marketing authorization, including the summary of the product characteristics, to place the product on the market in the Netherlands.

In addition, if the first authorization for placing the product on the market is not a Dutch or a central authorization, but was granted in another EU or EEA Member State, the applicant should submit information regarding the identity of the product thus authorized and the legal provision under which the authorization procedure took place, together with a copy of the notice publishing the authorization in the appropriate official publication.

Where the application for an SPC includes a request for an extension of the duration, a copy of the statement indicating compliance with an agreed completed paediatric investigation plan (Article 36(1) of Regulation 1901/2006) and, where necessary, proof of possession of marketing authorizations to place the product on the market of all other Member States (Article 36(3) of Regulation 1901/2006) should be submitted.

A formal Power of Attorney is necessary if the SPC application is filed by a representative, which is generally the case. If the Power of Attorney is not included with the application, the Dutch Patent Office will grant the applicant the opportunity to file the Power of Attorney at a later date.

Also, with the application, an applicant is to either provide proof of payment of the application fees or is to authorize the Dutch Patent Office to take the fees out of a deposit account that the applicant (or its representative) keeps with Dutch Patent Office.[79]

When during the application process it turns out that the documentation required with the application is incomplete, the Dutch Patent Office will, within two months after the application is filed,[80] notify the applicant of the fact that the application was incomplete,[81] indicate which information is missing and set a term within which the applicant will have to supplement the application with the required information.[82] Often, applicants file a so-called dummy application just in time to meet the term limit of Article 7(1) of the SPC Regulation. The Dutch Patent Office then allows the applicant to supplement the pending application with the required documentation at a later stage.

[E] The Definition of the Product in an SPC Application

As set out in §5.03[B] above, the product in an application for an SPC is to be understood as the active ingredient or combination of active ingredients of a medicinal

79. Article 92 DPA / Art. 2(1) PPCD.
80. Article 94 DPA / Art. 2(2) PPCD.
81. This can pertain to the documentation required under Art. 8 of the SPC Regulation, payment of the fee (Art. 92 DPA / Art. 2(1) PCCP) and the language in which documents have been submitted (Art. 93 in conjunction with Art. 24(3) DPA).
82. Article 10(3) of the SPC Regulations.

product and the marketing authorization should be used to determine the active ingredient or combination of active ingredients.

The applicant for an SPC can use a definition of the product that is broader than the active ingredient or combination of active ingredients in the marketing authorization. The Council of State[83] considered that the CJEU has ruled in *Farmitalia*[84] that an SPC can cover the active ingredient as such and derivatives thereof (such as salts and esters) as medicinal product. This typically relates to minor differences and not to differences with consequences on the safety and efficacy of the medicinal product.

[F] SPC Examination Procedure and Appeal Procedure

Although the Dutch Patent Office no longer performs an examination on the substantive requirements for Dutch national patents, it does perform a more substantive examination with regard to SPC applications.

The Dutch Patent Office verifies if all the requirements in the SPC Regulations and Articles 92 and 93 DPA have been complied with. If not, then Article 94 DPA stipulates that the Dutch Patent Office shall so inform the applicant in writing within two months of the filing of the application for an SPC stating the requirements that have not been met.

The Dutch Patent Office does not carry out a comprehensive search for the verification that the marketing authorization relied upon by the SPC applicant is indeed the first marketing authorization in question. The Dutch Patent Office will examine the databases of the European Medicines Agency and the Netherlands Medicines Evaluation Board to see if earlier marketing authorizations for the same product have been granted. The Dutch Patent Office may also examine databases in other Member States.

The Dutch Patent Office examines whether the same applicant has previously received an SPC for the same product. If so, then the Dutch Patent Office will reject the application as granting a second SPC for the same product to the same applicant would be contrary to the requirement of Article 3(c) of the SPC Regulation.

During the examination the identity of the product is established and it is verified that the product is protected by the basic patent in force.

The Dutch Patent Office is generally not too strict with the time lines after the application of an SPC is filed within the term limit. After an office action is dispatched, the period for responding is generally between two and three months after the date on which the office action is dispatched.

The applicant of an SPC can request the acceleration of his application. This is quite uncommon, because the Dutch Patent Office generally processes the application rather quickly if the file is complete.

Prosecution of the application can also be stayed at the request of the applicant if this is not an uncommon request.

83. Council of State *Yeda v. Dutch Patent Office*, ECLI:NL:RVS:2009:BI4974 of 27 May 2009.
84. CJEU *Farmitalia Carlo Erba v. Bundesgerichtshof*, C-392/97 of 16 September 1999.

If so requested, the examiner of the Dutch Patent Office processing an SPC application will hold an (informal) interview with the applicant.

Leading up to a decision by the Dutch Patent Office, there may be a first office action setting out the objections, a written response from the applicant followed by a hearing. The applicant can file objections to the grant or refusal of the application before the Board of Appeal of the Dutch Patent Office within six weeks of the decision, a term set by the General Administrative Law Act.[85] The objections will be handled by a three member panel of the Dutch Patent Office. It usually also includes a hearing. The decision on appeal has to be appealed before the Administrative Chamber of the District Court of the Hague.[86] Finally, the decision of the District Court may be appealed before the Administrative division of the Council of State.[87] The applicant may also request the Dutch Patent Office to agree to skip the objection phase before the Board of Appeal of the Dutch Patent Office and agree to direct appeal before the Administrative Chamber of the District Court.[88]

The Dutch Patent Office allows third-party observations[89] to be filed prior to the decision on SPC applications. These can be filed anonymously, e.g., by representing legal counsel. Third parties, however, cannot file an objection against a decision of the Dutch Patent Office to either grant or deny an SPC application[90] or become a third party in appeal proceedings against the denial of an SPC application.[91]

[G] Applications for a Paediatric Extension

The formal requirements for filing a paediatric extension correspond to those as outlined in the EU chapter.

Upon application for a paediatric extension, proof must be provided that an amount has been paid to the Dutch Patent Office in accordance with a rate to be set by general order.[92]

The required supporting documents are set out in Article 8(1)(d) of the SPC Regulation for Medicinal Products. These include a copy of the statement indicating compliance with the agreed and completed Paediatric Investigation Plan (PIP). Moreover, if the product has not been approved centrally by the EMA, it is necessary for the applicant to submit proof of possession of marketing authorizations for the product in all Member States.

85. Article 6:7 GALA.
86. Article 8:1 GALA.
87. Article 8:105 GALA.
88. Article 7:1 GALA.
89. Article 93 DCCP / Art. 2(2) PCCP in conjunction with Art. 38(1) DPA.
90. District Court The Hague *Actavis v. Dutch Patent Office*, ECLI:NL:RBSGR:2009:29326 of 23 September 2009.
91. District Court The Hague *X v. Dutch Patent Office (trastuzumab)*, ECLI:NL:RBDHA:2017:8031 of 19 July 2017; Council of State *Stichting Bewonersbelangen Kijkduin & the Municipality of The Hague v. State Secretary for Infrastructure and the Environment*, ECLI:NL:RVS:2012:BV6554 of 22 February 2012.
92. Article 92 DPA / Art. 2(1) PPCD.

If any of this information is missing, it is still possible to file the required information at a later date upon request by the Dutch Patent Office in an office action.

A paediatric extension can also be requested simultaneously with the SPC application – the form for the SPC application has a check box for such a situation – but this happens very rarely.

§5.06 PROCEDURE OF INVALIDATING AN SPC

[A] Grounds for the Invalidation of an SPC

The grounds for invalidating an SPC in the Netherlands correspond to the grounds as set out in Article 15 of the SPC Regulations, as discussed in the EU chapter.

[B] The Filing of an Invalidation Suit

Article 15(2) of the SPC Regulations dictates that an action for a declaration of invalidity of a certificate is to be brought before the body responsible under national law for the revocation of the corresponding basic patent.

In the Netherlands, Article 80(2)(a) DPA provides that the District Court in The Hague has the exclusive jurisdiction to decide on actions claiming the absence or lapse of legal effect, invalidity or vindication of patents. Invalidation of SPCs is only possible in proceedings on the merits before the District Court in The Hague.[93] In proceedings on the merits, invalidation may be claimed in the main claim or in a counterclaim.[94]

[C] Invalidation Procedure and the Corresponding Appeal Procedure

There are two types of patent and SPC proceedings on the merits: normal proceedings on the merits and accelerated proceedings on the merits. In both proceedings, a panel of three specialized judges will handle invalidity. Parties generally litigate according to the accelerated regime, which follows a pre-fixed time-schedule that does not allow for extensions and should lead to a decision on the merits (infringement and validity) in about a year.[95] The normal proceedings on the merits take about eighteen months to two years.

93. The preliminary relief judge cannot invalidate an SPC, but may dismiss a preliminary injunction if there is a serious non-negligible chance that the patent and/or SPC will be invalidated in opposition proceedings or proceedings on the merits.
94. Article 80(2)(a) DPA provides that the District Court of The Hague also has the exclusive jurisdiction to decide on enforcement matters as described in Arts 70–72 DPA relating to Dutch and European patents. Patent enforcement and invalidity actions are therefore handled by the same District Court and generally in the same action.
95. Because of the current backlog, decisions are currently issued later than one year.

Appeal against a decision on the merits can be lodged within three months as from the date of the decision.[96] Appeal proceedings in proceedings on the merits usually take about eighteen months to two years.

Appeal in cassation against an appeal decision on the merits can be lodged within three months as from the date of the decision.[97] Appeal in cassation usually takes about eighteen months to two years.

On the basis of Article 1019h DCCP, all costs for legal assistance (including patent attorney fees and expert fees) are fully recoverable in patent and SPC enforcement proceedings to the extent that these costs are reasonable and proportional. Reasonable and proportional costs for legal assistance in relation to invalidation proceedings cannot be recovered if those proceedings were not initiated in response to a threat to enforce the patent or SPC.[98] The case law in the Netherlands shows that in patent and SPC cases, generally the actual legal costs will be rewarded.

[D] The Revocation of a Paediatric Extension

As set out in the EU chapter, the grounds for revocation of a paediatric extension correspond to those of Article 16 of the SPC Regulation for Medicinal Products.

Article 16(2) of the SPC Regulation for Medicinal Products stipulates that any person may submit an application for revocation of the extension of the duration to the body responsible under national law for the revocation of the corresponding basic patent. In the Netherlands, Article 80(2)(a) DPA provides that the District Court in The Hague has the exclusive jurisdiction to decide on actions claiming the absence or lapse of legal effect, invalidity or vindication of patents. Actions for the revocation of SPCs should therefore be brought before the District Court in The Hague.

Otherwise, the same considerations as set out in §5.06[B] and §5.06[C] above for the revocation of an SPC apply.

In *Novartis v. Teva et al.*, the preliminary relief judge had to preliminary opine on the validity of a paediatric extension in view of previous orphan medicinal product exclusivity. The preliminary relief judge considered as follows.

In the Paediatric Regulation, a distinction is made in the rewards and incentives for products protected by the patent (or SPC) foreseen therein between medicinal products that may or may not be designated as orphan medicinal products. In essence, orphan medicinal products are excluded from (the right to) the six-month SPC extension foreseen in Article 36(1) of the Paediatric Regulation. Instead of the SPC extension, (patent-protected) orphan medicinal products obtain an extension of the market exclusivity foreseen in Article 8 of the Orphan Drug Regulation from ten to twelve years based on Article 37 of the Paediatric Regulation. However, the Paediatric

96. Article 339 DCCP.
97. Article 402 DCCP.
98. Court of Appeal The Hague *Danisco v. Home Copy Association*, ECLI:NL:GHSGR:2011:BP9443 of 29 March 2011; Court of Appeal The Hague *Jansen Pharmaceuticals v. Mylan*, ECLI:NL:GHDHA:2016:152 of 2 February 2016; CJEU *Bericap*, C-180/11 of 15 November 2012.

Regulation does not explicitly state for what incentive medicinal products that were designated as orphan medicinal products in the past are eligible.

It is not in dispute that all indications of imatinib (protected by SPC 300086) were withdrawn by the Committee as orphan medicinal product on 16 April 2012 (and therefore long before the application for the extension of the marketing authorization) and were removed from the Register of Orphan Medicinal Products at that time, or at the end of the period of market exclusivity (CML) or at the request of Novartis (all other indications). It was not in dispute either that Novartis did not enjoy the two-year extension of market exclusivity foreseen in Article 37 of the Paediatric Regulation. Finally, it was not in dispute either that Novartis in itself complied with the material terms set in the Paediatric Regulation to qualify for a reward for the paediatric study conducted.

The dispute dividing the parties related to the question whether the paediatric extension for imatinib for the SPC was wrongly granted. In this context, Teva took the position that the exceptional provision of Articles 36(4) and 37 of the Paediatric Regulation also applies if a medicinal product was designated as an orphan medicinal product in the past. Teva's objection was based on the fact that Novartis allegedly enjoyed a double reward because imatinib's designation as orphan medicinal product was withdrawn. For this purpose Teva referred to paragraph 29 of the recital of the Paediatric Regulation and the underlying passages in the European Impact Assessment report. According to Teva, it was for this reason that for imatinib Novartis had to rely on a paediatric reward in the form of a two-year extension of the market exclusivity and it should be for its account and risk that it did not enjoy it by its own doing (withdrawal of the designation as orphan medicinal product). Novartis challenged this defence with reference to, among other things, the European Impact Assessment report to later reports of the Commission and the EMA. In the preliminary opinion of the preliminary relief judge, Teva's position could not be followed. The following was considered in this context.

Based on established case law of the Court of Justice, in the interpretation of a provision of a regulation the wording of the provision should not be the exclusive basis, but the general purpose and the objectives of the regulation of which this provision is part has to be taken into account as well.

In the first place, the wording of Article 36(4) Paediatric Regulation (and the comparable formulations in Article 37 of the Paediatric Regulation) do not provide any evidence for the thought that medicinal products that were designated as orphan medicinal products in the past allegedly do not qualify for SPC extension.

After all, the equally authentic versions of the Paediatric Regulation state 'medicinal products' that 'are designated as orphan medicinal products', 'désignés comme médicaments orphelins', 'als Arzneimittel für seltene Leiden ausgewiesen sind', 'declarados huérfanos', 'als weesgeneesmiddelen zijn aangewezen'. Pursuant to Article 36(1) and (2) of the Paediatric Regulation, the right to SPC extension arises as soon as the application for the marketing authorization contains the results of all studies conducted in accordance with the approved Paediatric Investigation Plan and a statement within the meaning of Article 28 of the Paediatric Regulation is included in the marketing authorization granted.

Based on Article 37(1) of the Paediatric Regulation, the same commencement date applies for the extension of market exclusivity. The formulations of the provision in mutual conjunction with the commencement of the rewards raises the suspicion that the time of the application or the inclusion of the statement of Article 28 of the Paediatric Regulation in the granted marketing authorization is decisive for obtaining the paediatric reward. Even though it could have been achieved with a single addition, Articles 36 and 37 of the Paediatric Regulation in no way express that medicinal products that were designated as orphan medicinal products in the past are excluded from application of the SPC extension.

The explanation provided by Teva is furthermore not supported by paragraph 29 of the recital either. Even though a 'double incentive' is mentioned there, this does not entail that it was intended in the Paediatric Regulation to exclude the reward desired by Novartis. Paragraph 29 of the recital which Teva refers to zooms in on medicinal products that are designated as orphan medicinal products. Here, a distinction is made between patents that are and are not protected by a patent. It is observed in that context that: (i) an SPC extension cannot be granted for medicinal products that are not protected under a patent; (ii) that SPC extension for orphan medicinal products allegedly entails a double incentive; and (iii) that orphan medicinal products are rewarded with extension of the market exclusivity instead of an SPC extension. Nothing can be concluded from this with regard to the status of medicinal products that were designated as orphan medicinal products in the past.

The concerns expressed in the recitals can be found in the market consultation carried out by the Commission that is laid down in the European Impact Assessment report. With regard to the paediatric extension two concerns are distinguished in that report: (1) the concern that the SPC extension is not possible for medicinal products that are not protected by a patent; and (2) the concern that the orphan medicinal products protected by the patent will receive a double incentive: to wit SPC extension and market exclusivity.

It has to be admitted to Teva that with regard to the second concern in the European Impact Assessment report and in the recitals (the double incentive) the combination between the six-month SPC extension and the ten-year market exclusivity (the reward foreseen in Article 8 of the Orphan Medicinal Product Regulation) is referred to. However, it cannot be concluded from this that the Community legislator did not address this second concern (which, incidentally, is not further substantively explained) in his final proposal at all. Like the recitals, with regard to this point the European Impact Assessment report states that (i) it will exclude its orphan medicinal products from SPC extension in its final proposal; and that orphan medicinal products will be rewarded with two extra years of market exclusivity instead (until twelve years instead of ten). The Community legislator has therefore granted the orphan medicinal products an alternative reward. Incidentally, this passage does not say anything about medicinal products that were designated as orphan medicinal product in the past.

The objectives of the Paediatric Regulation (as laid down in marginal No. 6 of the recitals) and the European Impact Assessment report do demonstrate that the starting point of the Paediatric Regulation is that a paediatric study has to be rewarded, also if it concerns orphan medicinal products. Indeed, it can be concluded from the European

Impact Assessment report that the Commission intended to match the reward for orphan medicinal products with the reward for (non-orphan) medicinal products that are protected by the patent. Indeed, with regard to this point the European Impact Assessment report states that instead of granting six months, it was decided to grant two years of additional market exclusivity, since market exclusivity for the orphan designation is deemed less valuable than SPC protection that can include several products. If a medicinal product has lost its designation as orphan medicinal product and the related market exclusivity for whatever reason, extension of the market exclusivity is naturally excluded. If such a former orphan medicinal product would not qualify for SPC extension in that case either, no (extra) reward for a paediatric study would be granted for this category which would be in breach of the aforementioned starting point without there being a justification for this. Furthermore, from a temporal perspective there is no double reward either since – by withdrawing the orphan drug status – the market exclusivity (extension) is not enjoyed simultaneously with the SPC extension. In this context, the preliminary relief judge remarks that Novartis has not enjoyed the full ten-year period of market exclusivity for the ALL indication either. In addition, Article 8 of the Orphan Medicinal Product Regulation determines that this Regulation does not affect intellectual property rights (and other Community rights). When seen from this perspective, there is no objection to SPC extension for (former) orphan medicinal products in this case either.

Given what was considered above, the preliminary relief judge was therefore of the preliminary opinion that the purpose and the objectives of the Paediatric Regulation are no reason to interpret the exception of Article 36 paragraph 4 of that Regulation in such a manner that it has to be concluded that former orphan medicinal products are excluded from SPC extension as well.

Given the foregoing, the preliminary relief judge saw no reason to assume in preliminary relief proceedings that Novartis was not entitled to the paediatric extension for imatinib.

§5.07 UNFAIR COMPETITION LAW

The same considerations as set out in the EU chapter apply. Antitrust issues involving SPCs have not yet been successfully addressed in the Dutch case law.

CHAPTER 6
Belgium

Ann De Clercq & Hans Goesaert

§6.01 LEGAL BASIS

Within the framework of Regulations (EC) 469/2009,[1] (EC) 1610/96[2] and (EC) 1901/2006,[3] the main legal basis for supplementary protection certificates (SPCs) in Belgium[4] is provided by section 'Title 2 – Supplementary Protection Certificates Articles' (Articles XI.92–XI.103) of Book XI of the Belgian Code of Economic Law ('CEL'). Book XI (CEL) consolidated and updated the different provisions related to intellectual property rights under Belgian national law, wherein the part relating to patents and SPCs entered into force on 22 September 2014. Title 2, Book XI, CEL, provides for submitting an SPC application (or a paediatric extension thereof) to the Belgian Office for Intellectual Property (OPRI) and its prosecution, the publication of the SPC application and the granted certificate in the patent register, the fees that are due and a restoration procedure. In addition, in view of Articles 4 and 5 of the SPC Regulations, the sections relating to the scope of protection and infringement of patents are applicable to SPCs as well.

1. Regulation (EC) No. 469/2009 of the European Parliament and of the Council of 6 May 2009 concerning the supplementary protection certificate for medicinal products.
2. Regulation (EC) No. 1610/96 of the European Parliament and of the Council of 23 July 1996 concerning the creation of a supplementary protection certificate for plant protection products.
3. Regulation (EC) No. 1901/2006 of the European Parliament and of the Council of 12 December 2006 on medicinal products for paediatric use and amending Regulation (EEC) No. 1768/92, Directive 2001/20/EC, Directive 2001/83/EC and Regulation (EC) No. 726/2004.
4. Information on SPCs and SPC applications, including a link to the main Belgian legal acts and decrees governing patents and SPCs, is provided by the Belgian Office for Intellectual Property at https://economie.fgov.be/fr/themes/propriete-intellectuelle/brevets/demande-de-brevet/certificats-complementaires-de (for the French version) or https://economie.fgov.be/nl/themas/intellectuele-eigendom/octrooien/octrooiaanvraag/aanvullende (for the Dutch version).

Further national statutory provisions that directly relate to SPCs are provided in the Royal Decree (RD) of 18 December 1986 (as amended by *inter alia* RD of 9 November 2015), specifying the prescribed fees for filing and maintaining SPCs, and the RD of 4 September 2014, specifying the procedural provisions implementing the general legal provisions of Title 2, Book XI (CEL).

§6.02 SUBSTANTIVE REQUIREMENTS FOR OBTAINING AN SPC

The guidance provided by the CJEU is binding for all EU Member States. Consequently, what has been set out in Chapter 1 (the 'EU chapter') in relation to the substantive requirements for obtaining an SPC, in as far as they have been addressed by the CJEU, is equally applicable in Belgium. The following section will therefore mainly focus on further considerations in a Belgian context, beyond the guidance provided by the CJEU.

[A] Types of Products That Can Be Protected

The same considerations regarding the terms 'product' and 'medicinal/plant protection product' as set out in the EU chapter apply in Belgium.

[1] Practical Considerations: What Is the Active Ingredient or Combination of Active Ingredients That Can Form the Basis for an SPC

In general, the same considerations regarding the term 'product' as set out in the EU chapter apply in Belgium. In this context, in an explanatory note for completing the SPC application form,[5] the OPRI provides some guidelines what it considers the 'product' of the SPC application: the name of the product mentioned in the application should correspond to the name of the active ingredient(s) mentioned in the marketing authorization for the corresponding medicinal or plant protection product, and which is covered by the claims of the basic patent, as discussed below in §6.02[B].

[2] Active Ingredient or Combination of Active Ingredients of a Medicinal Product

In general, in Belgium, the same considerations regarding the term 'active ingredient' of a medicinal product as set out in the EU chapter apply.

In Belgian case law, the notions of 'product' and 'active ingredient' or 'active substance' have been discussed as well. In *Escitalopram (I)*,[6] the Brussels Commercial

5. A link to the explanatory note for completing the SPC application form can be found at https://economie.fgov.be/fr/themes/propriete-intellectuelle/brevets/demande-de-brevet/certificats-complementaires-de (for the French version) or https://economie.fgov.be/nl/themas/intellectuele-eigendom/octrooien/octrooiaanvraag/aanvullende (for the Dutch version).
6. Brussels Commercial Court, 2008/AR/07271 of 3 October 2011.

Court believed that Cipramil® (citalopram) and Sipralexa® (escitalopram – the (S)-enantiomer of the racemic mixture citalopram) are products in which the active substance is in both cases escitalopram, and concluded that escitalopram and citalopram are the same product within meaning of Article 1(b) of the SPC Regulation. This decision was later overturned by the Brussels Court of Appeal (in *Escitalopram (II)*).[7] Importantly, in its argumentation, the Brussels Court of Appeal discussed the term 'active ingredient' in the SPC Regulation, referring to the *MIT* (C-431/04)[8] CJEU decision, stating that a substance which does not have any therapeutic effect of its own and which is used to obtain a certain pharmaceutical form of the medicinal product is not covered by the concept of 'active ingredient'. Furthermore, the court indicated that the term 'therapeutic effect' can be more precisely described based on the definition of 'active substance' given in Article 3*bis* of the Directive 2011/62/EU.[9] The court established that an active ingredient is a substance bringing about a pharmaceutical, immunological or metabolic effect in order to restore, improve, or alter physiologic functions. This interpretation by the Brussels Court of Appeal is thus in line with the CJEU's ruling in *Forsgren* (C-631/13).[10]

[3] Active Substance or Combination of Active Substances of a Plant Protection Product

The same considerations regarding the term 'active substance' in a plant protection product as set out in the EU chapter apply in Belgium.

[4] Fixed-Dose and Loose Combinations

The same considerations as set out in the EU chapter apply in Belgium.

[5] Limitation to Products Subjected to a Specific Marketing Authorization Procedure

The same considerations with respect to the product requiring a specific authorization for placing the product on the market as a medicinal or plant protection product as set out in the EU chapter apply in Belgium.

[6] Protection of Medical Devices

Currently, the same considerations regarding the availability of SPC protection for medical devices as set out in the EU chapter apply in Belgium. It is expected that the

7. Brussels Court of Appeal, 2011/AR/02821 of 17 September 2012.
8. CJEU *Massachusetts Institute of Technology v. Bundesgerichtshof*, C-431/04 of 4 May 2006.
9. Directive 2011/62/EU of 8 June 2011, amending Directive 2001/83/EC on the Community code relating to medicinal products for human use.
10. CJEU *Arne Forsgren v. Österreichisches Patentamt*, C-631/13 of 15 January 2015.

CJEU's ruling in the pending referral C-527/17 will clarify the eligibility of medical devices containing active ingredients for SPC protection.

[B] Basic Patent

The same considerations as set out in the EU chapter apply: at the filing date, the basic patent must be in force in Belgium. The basic patent can be a Belgian patent or a European patent which has been validated in Belgium.

In this context, and as a side note, since 1 January 2017 new validation rules apply in Belgium, which aligns the translation requirements in Belgium with the London Protocol. In particular, as Belgium shares a national language with the EPO (i.e., French and German), it is no longer required to file a French, Dutch or German translation of a European patent (that has been filed and granted in English) in order to validate a granted European patent in Belgium. In other words, the European patent will come into effect automatically in Belgium upon grant, and will remain in force as long as the yearly renewal fees are timely paid.

The applicant may request that the OPRI suspend the prosecution of the SPC application in case the basic patent is contested (e.g., via an opposition procedure), and thus the final legal status of the basic patent being unclear.

[1] Requirement for the Product to Be 'Protected' by the Basic Patent

The requirement under Article 3(a) of the SPC Regulations is one of the main aspects that are evaluated during the substantive examination of the SPC application by the OPRI. In practice, the OPRI closely follows the guidelines provided by the CJEU. The Office will cite the relevant CJEU ruling (if any) in case it issues a reasoned intention to reject the application. In addition, it typically also aligns its opinion with other national offices. The OPRI may also propose to suspend the prosecution of the SPC application if it deems a pending referral to the CJEU may affect the examination.

Accordingly, in view of the many CJEU rulings relating to the requirement under Article 3(a) of the SPC Regulations, including the requirement for the product of an SPC to be identified in the claims of the basic patent in order to be 'protected' by the patent, the same considerations as discussed in the EU chapter apply in Belgium as well.

Before the CJEU established a so-called identification test in *Medeva* (C-322/10) and subsequent decisions[11] (wherein the active ingredient or combination of active ingredients must be '*specified (or identified) in the wording of the claims*'), the Belgian courts have been known to apply a so-called infringement test to determine whether a

11. CJEU *Medeva v. Comptroller General of Patents, Designs and Trade Marks*, C-322/10 of 24 November 2011; CJEU *University of Queensland v. Comptroller-General of Patents, Designs and Trade Marks*, C-630/10 of 25 November 2011; CJEU *Daiichi Sankyo v. Comptroller General of Patents, Designs and Trade Marks*, C-6/11 of 25 November 2011; CJEU *Yeda Research and Development v. Comptroller General of Patents, Designs and Trade Marks*, C-518/10 of 25 November 2011.

product is 'protected' by the basic patent. It is to be expected that this earlier approach will no longer be applied.

For instance, in *Valsartan*,[12] the Commercial Court of Antwerp concluded that the SPC for the combination valsartan and HCTZ complied with the requirements under Article 3 of the pertinent SPC Regulation. In its interpretation of Article 3(a) of the SPC Regulation, the court identified the (at that time) different approaches applied in Europe regarding the interpretation of the term 'protected by the basic patent', i.e., essentially, either via an 'infringement test', wherein in case the combination product infringes the basic patent, it can be considered as 'protected by the basic patent', or either via a so-called extent of protection test, wherein in case the combination of active ingredients is explicitly mentioned or identified in the basic patent, it is considered as 'protected by the basic patent'. According to the court, the applied infringement test provided a greater legal certainty (leading to a uniform and transparent system at the European level), in view of Article 69 EPC and the Protocol on the Interpretation of Article 69 EPC.

[a] Small Molecules

The same considerations regarding small molecules specified by a generic chemical formula as set out in the EU chapter apply in Belgium. It may be expected that the CJEU's ruling in the pending referral *Sandoz v. Searle* (C-114/18) will provide further guidelines in case of a basic patent covering an active ingredient by a generic Markush chemical formula.

[b] Polymers

The same considerations for specifying a polymer as active ingredient as set out in the EU chapter apply.

[c] Antibodies, Enzymes and Other Proteins

The same considerations as set out in the EU chapter apply. In this context, in line with the CJEU decision *Eli Lilly* (C-493/12),[13] the OPRI has accepted the grant of an SPC for specific therapeutic antibodies on the basis of a basic patent claiming in a functional manner an antibody to the corresponding specific target.

[d] Nucleic Acids

The same considerations regarding nucleic acids as active ingredients as set out in the EU chapter apply in Belgium.

12. Commercial Court of Antwerp, A/10/06112 of 13 May 2011.
13. CJEU *Eli Lilly v. Human Genome Sciences*, C-493/12 of 12 December 2013.

[2] *Basic Patent Claiming the Product, i.e., the Active Ingredient(s), but Not the Corresponding Authorized Medicinal Product (or Plant Protection Product)*

In general, the same considerations as set out in the EU chapter apply.

[3] *Requirement for the Product to Constitute 'the Invention' of the Basic Patent*

In general, the same considerations as set out in the EU chapter apply.

[4] *Criteria for Choosing the Basic Patent among Various Available Patents*

The EU chapter already addresses the main criteria affecting the choice of a basic patent among several available patents. Accordingly, the same considerations as set out in the EU chapter apply in Belgium as well.

[C] The Marketing Authorization Forming Basis for an SPC

In general, the considerations in relation to the marketing authorization relied upon by an SPC application, as set out in the EU chapter, apply equally in Belgium: at the filing date, the pertinent marketing authorization must be in force in Belgium.

[1] *Combinations of Active Ingredients*

In view of the different CJEU rulings relating to the interpretation of Article 3(a) and 3(b) in case of SPC applications for combination products, the same considerations as set out in the EU chapter apply in Belgium.

[a] *The Marketing Authorization Refers to Fewer Active Ingredients than the SPC Application*

The same considerations as set out in the EU chapter apply in Belgium.

[b] *The Marketing Authorization Refers to More Active Ingredients than the SPC Application*

The same considerations as set out in the EU chapter apply in Belgium.

[c] *The Marketing Authorization Indicates That a Medicinal Product Containing a Single Active Ingredient Is Authorized for Use in Combination with a Further Active Ingredient*

The same considerations as set out in the EU chapter apply in Belgium.

[2] *The Marketing Authorization Has Not Yet Been Granted at the Time the SPC Application Is Filed*

The same considerations relating to a granted marketing authorization as set out in the EU chapter apply in Belgium.

[3] *The Holder of the Marketing Authorization*

In general, the same considerations regarding the holder of the marketing authorization as set out in the EU chapter apply in Belgium. The OPRI does not verify whether or not the patentee and the marketing authorization holder are the same entity and it will not raise an objection when an SPC application is filed on the basis of an unrelated third-party marketing authorization.

[4] *Reliance on a Marketing Authorization Granted under a Provision Other than Directive 2001/83/EC or Directive 2001/82/EC*

In general, the same considerations as set out in the EU chapter apply in Belgium.

[5] *The Marketing Authorizations Which Can Be Relied upon for SPC Applications for Plant Protection Products*

The same considerations as set out in the EU chapter apply in Belgium.

[6] *The Product in Question Is Contained in the Authorized Medicinal Product (or the Authorized Plant Protection Product) but Is Not Identified as an Active Ingredient in the Corresponding Marketing Authorization*

The same considerations as set out in the EU chapter apply in Belgium. As indicated above, in an explanatory note for completing the SPC application form,[14] the OPRI has indicated that the name of the product mentioned in the application should correspond

14. A link to the explanatory note for completing the SPC application form can be found at https://economie.fgov.be/fr/themes/propriete-intellectuelle/brevets/demande-de-brevet/certificats-complementaires-de (for the French version) or https://economie.fgov.be/nl/themas/intellectuele-eigendom/octrooien/octrooiaanvraag/aanvullende (for the Dutch version).

to the name of the active ingredient(s) mentioned in the marketing authorization for the corresponding medicinal or plant protection product.

[7] The Notion of the 'First' Marketing Authorization

In principle, the same considerations regarding the first authorization to place the product on the market in a particular Member State as set out in the EU chapter apply in Belgium.

[a] Marketing Authorization for a New Therapeutic Application of a Previously Authorized Product

In principle, the same considerations regarding a marketing authorization for a new therapeutic use of a previously authorized product as set out in the EU chapter apply in Belgium.

[b] Marketing Authorization for a New Formulation of a Previously Authorized Product

The same considerations as set out in the EU chapter apply. In this context, it may be expected that the CJEU's ruling in the pending referral *Abraxis* (C-443/17)[15] will provide further guidelines in case of a first marketing authorization within the scope of the basic patent to place the product on the market as a medicinal product covering a new formulation of a previously authorized active ingredient.

[c] Marketing Authorization for a New Specific Salt, Ester or Other Derivative of a Previously Authorized Active Ingredient

In principle, the same considerations as set out in the EU chapter apply. A SPC may be obtained covering the active ingredient as such as well as various derived forms thereof (e.g., salts and esters) as medicinal products, to the extent they are covered by the basic patent. A SPC may also be obtained for a new salt or other derivative of an already approved product, based on a marketing authorization of the new salt or other derivative, to the extent it is covered by a basic patent, and provided it exhibits different properties, such as safety or efficacy.

[d] Marketing Authorization for a New Specific Enantiomer of an Active Ingredient Previously Authorized in Racemic Form

The Belgian courts have also addressed the issue of the validity of an SPC based on a marketing authorization for an enantiomer of an active ingredient previously approved as a racemate.

15. CJEU *Abraxis Bioscience v. Comptroller General of Patents*, C-443/17, referral of 24 July 2017.

In *Escitalopram (I)*,[16] the Brussels Commercial Court concluded that Cipramil® (citalopram) and Sipralexa® (escitalopram - the (S)-enantiomer of the racemic mixture citalopram) are the same product within the meaning of Article 1(b) of the SPC Regulation, having the same active substance escitalopram, and revoked the Belgian escitalopram SPC, based on the position that the requirements of Article 3(c) and 3(d) of the SPC Regulation had not been met. This decision was later overturned by the Brussels Court of Appeal (in *Escitalopram (II)*),[17] who found that no conclusive proof had been submitted that the (S)-enantiomer was the only active ingredient in the racemate. On the contrary, the court found that the evidence submitted suggested that the R-enantiomer did have some effect on the activity of the racemate. The court further stated that the marketing authorization for the racemate citalopram did not prevent obtaining a marketing authorization for the enantiomer escitalopram. The Brussels Court of Appeal thus upheld the Belgian escitalopram SPC, bringing the position of the Belgian court in line with the decision of the German, Dutch and French courts related to the escitalopram SPC in those respective countries (*see* §6.02[A][2] above for the interpretation of the term 'active ingredient' by the Brussels Court of Appeal in this case).

[e] The Product Has Already Been Placed on the Market Before, but Without an Authorization Granted under Directive 2001/83/EC or Directive 2001/82/EC

In principle, the same considerations as set out in the EU chapter apply in Belgium.

[f] Prior Marketing Authorization Which Refers to Fewer Active Ingredients than the SPC Application (and the Later Marketing Authorization Relied upon)

The same considerations as set out in the EU chapter apply in Belgium.

[g] Prior Marketing Authorization Which Refers to More Active Ingredients than the SPC Application (and the Later Marketing Authorization Relied upon)

In principle, the same considerations as set out in the EU chapter apply in Belgium.

[D] Preclusion of New SPCs by an Earlier SPC

In general, the same considerations as set out in the EU chapter apply. However, the Belgian law provides that, in line with Article 10(5) of the SPC Regulations, a certificate

16. Brussels Commercial Court, 2008/AR/07271 of 3 October 2011.
17. Brussels Court of Appeal, 2011/AR/02821 of 17 September 2012.

is granted without verifying that the conditions laid down in Article 3(c) and 3(d) of the SPC Regulations are met (Article XI.97 (CEL)). Accordingly, the OPRI is not obliged to assess whether the product of an SPC application has already been the subject of an earlier granted certificate. In this context, the prescribed application form comprises a statement wherein the applicant declares that the product has not already been the subject of a certificate. Nevertheless, during the substantive examination, the OPRI typically checks whether or not the product has already been the subject of a certificate.

[1] Consequences of an Earlier Third-Party SPC for the Same Product

[a] The 'One SPC per Product per Patent Holder' Rule

The same considerations regarding the principle 'one SPC per product per patent holder' as set out in the EU chapter apply in Belgium.

[b] Earlier SPC Granted to an Affiliated Third Party

The same considerations regarding SPCs granted to an affiliated party as set out in the EU chapter apply. In practice, the OPRI typically accepts patent holders who are distinct legal entities as different rights holders, regardless of any potential affiliation. During examination, the OPRI only verifies whether the SPC applicant(s) correspond(s) to the formally registered patent holder(s).

[c] Partial Overlap Between the Holders of the Earlier SPC and the Applicants for the New SPC

The same considerations as set out in the EU chapter apply in Belgium. In practice, the OPRI appears to consider overlapping patent holders as different rights holders to a certificate. The formally registered patent holders are decisive in this regard.

[d] Earlier Third-Party SPC Has Been Licensed-In

The same considerations as set out in the EU chapter apply in Belgium. The licence to a certificate (of an earlier third-party SPC) should be mentioned to the OPRI, who will enter this information in the national register. If the licensee subsequently applies for a new SPC on the basis of his own patent, the licensing of an earlier third-party SPC should not preclude the grant of the new SPC under Article 3(c) and 3(2) of the SPC Regulations, as only the formally registered patent holder is taken into account by the OPRI.

[2] Consequences of an Own Earlier SPC for the Same Product

The same general rule that an own earlier granted certificate granted for the same product precludes the grant of any further SPCs for the same product to the same holder, as set out in the EU chapter, applies in Belgium as well.

[a] Own Earlier SPC Application Not Yet Granted

The same considerations as set out in the EU chapter apply in Belgium. In practice, the OPRI will generally allow SPC applicants to give priority to one of several pending SPC applications directed to the same product.

[b] Revocation, Surrender or Lapse of the Own Earlier SPC after Grant

In principle, the same considerations regarding the revocation or surrender of the applicant's earlier granted SPC as set out in the EU chapter apply in Belgium.

[c] Transfer of the Own Earlier SPC to a Third Party

The same considerations as set out in the EU chapter apply in Belgium.

[d] Acquisition of an SPC Granted to a Third Party

The same considerations as set out in the EU chapter apply in Belgium.

[3] Consequences of an Own Earlier SPC for a Different Product

The same considerations as set out in the EU chapter apply in Belgium.

[a] Required Distinction from the Product of the Own Earlier SPC

In general, the same considerations as set out in the EU chapter apply in Belgium.

Combinations of Active Ingredients

The same considerations as set out in the EU chapter apply. In Belgium, the grant of a first SPC for the single active ingredient A will not preclude the grant of a second SPC for the combination of active ingredients A and B to the same SPC holder, as the combination product A + B is considered different from A, provided the combination is protected by the (same) basic patent in force and is the subject of a valid marketing authorization (which is the first one for this combination). In addition, in principle, the OPRI does not need to establish whether the product of a particular SPC application, such as a combination product, has already been the subject of a certificate, since, as indicated above, Belgian law provides that SPCs are granted without verifying that the conditions laid down in Article 3(c) and 3(d) of the SPC Regulations are met (Article XI.97 (CEL)).

In practice, it will thus be for the competent court to decide, on a case-by-case basis, to what extent an earlier SPC for an active ingredient A precludes or invalidates a second SPC for a combination product A + B. In this context, in *Valsartan*,[18] the Commercial Court of Antwerp concluded that the SPC for the combination valsartan and HCTZ complied with the requirements under Article 3, including Article 3(c) and 3(d), of the pertinent SPC Regulation, although it did not explicitly discuss the requirements of Article 3(c) in light of the SPC for valsartan as the single active ingredient.

At present, it is unclear how the Belgian court will apply the 'core inventive advance' criterion presented by the CJEU in *Actavis v. Sanofi* (C-443/12),[19] *Georgetown University v. Octrooicentrum Nederland* (C-484/12)[20] and *Actavis v. Boehringer Ingelheim Pharma* (C-577/13)[21] when assessing the preclusion of a new SPC by a previous SPC granted to the same patent holder under Article 3(c) of the SPC Regulations, specifically in the context of SPCs for combinations of active ingredients.

New Therapeutic Applications of Previously Approved Active Ingredients

In principle, the same considerations as set out in the EU chapter apply in Belgium.

[b] SPCs for a Specific Salt, Ester or Other Derivative Where an Own Earlier SPC Has Already Been Granted for the Corresponding Active Ingredient

The same considerations as set out in the EU chapter apply to Belgium.

[c] SPCs for a Specific Enantiomer Where an Own Earlier SPC Has Already Been Granted for the Corresponding Racemate

The Brussels Court of Appeal found in *Escitalopram (II)*[22] that the specific enantiomer (i.e., escitalpram, the (S) enantiomer of citalopram) is a different product than the racemate of this product. The Court thus concluded that the earlier SPC for the racemate did not stand in the way of obtaining an SPC for escitalopram (based on a corresponding marketing authorization and basic patent), under Article 3(c) of the pertinent SPC Regulation. The Court's decision was mainly based on the interpretation of the term 'active ingredient' (*see* §6.02[A][2] above), and did not specifically address

18. Commercial Court of Antwerp, A/10/06112 of 13 May 2011.
19. CJEU *Actavis v. Sanofi*, C-443/12 of 12 December 2013.
20. CJEU *Georgetown University v. Octrooicentrum Nederland*, C-484/12 of 12 December 2013.
21. CJEU *Actavis v. Boehringer Ingelheim Pharma*, C-577/13 of 12 March 2015.
22. Brussels Court of Appeal, 2011/AR/02821 of 17 September 2012.

whether a specific enantiomer should be regarded as a derivative of the corresponding racemate.

[4] *Grant of More than One SPC on the Basis of the Same Patent*

The same considerations for the grant of multiple SPCs on the basis of the same patent, provided they relate to different products and are protected by the basic patent, as set out in the EU chapter, apply in Belgium as well.

§6.03 EXTENT OF PROTECTION AND ENFORCEMENT OF SPCs

[A] The Protection Conferred by an SPC

In general, the considerations in terms of the protection conferred by an SPC as outlined in the EU chapter apply equally to Belgium. Thus, the scope of protection of an SPC, as governed by Article 4 and Article 5 of the SPC Regulations, is determined on the basis of the underlying patent, but limited to the product for which the SPC has been granted, including any further authorized use of the product as a medicinal or plant protection product. The Belgian courts have also addressed the issue of the protection conferred by an SPC.

In *Losartan (I)*,[23] the President of the Brussels Commercial Court decided, in first instance summary proceedings, that the scope of protection of the SPC for the active ingredient losartan (whose duration had been extended via a paediatric extension) does not prima facie extend to a generic version of a medicinal product containing the active ingredients losartan and HCTZ. The court reasoned that, since the paediatric extension was applied for and granted only for the 'losartan'-SPC and not for the separately obtained 'losartan + HCTZ'-SPC, the combination product could not benefit from the paediatric extension of the losartan-SPC. This first instance decision was later confirmed by the Brussels Court of Appeal (*Losartan (II)*),[24] likewise in summary proceedings. Referring to recital 10 of the SPC Regulation, in particular the phrase 'the protection granted should furthermore be strictly confined to the product which obtained authorisation to be placed on the market as a medicinal product', and in view of the presence of a separate SPC and marketing authorization for the combination product 'losartan + HCTZ', the Brussels Court of Appeal concluded that the scope of protection of the SPC for a product comprising only one active ingredient (in casu losartan) does prima facie not extend to a medicinal product comprising this active ingredient in combination with another active ingredient (i.e., HCTZ): a medicinal product containing the 'losartan + HCTZ' combination could not infringe the SPC for losartan alone. The Belgian court thus held an opposite view to that of the President of the Paris 'Tribunal de Grande Instance', who was at that time presented with a similar question. In addition, this interpretation of the Brussels court seems in contradiction

23. Brussels Commercial Court, 2010/RK/00014 of 12 February 2010.
24. Brussels Court of Appeal, 2010/KR/00053 of 23 February 2010.

with Article 4 of the SPC Regulation relating to the protection conferred by a certificate to 'any use of the product as a medicinal product'. Nevertheless, in view of the (later) CJEU rulings in *Novartis v. Actavis UK* (C-442/11)[25] and *Novartis v. Actavis Deutschland* (C-574/11),[26] which state that an SPC for a product consisting of a single active ingredient will also cover medicinal products comprising this active ingredient in combination with one (or more) other active ingredient(s), it may be expected that this earlier interpretation will no longer be applied by the Belgian courts.

In *Vinorelbine tartrate*,[27] the Brussels Commercial Court decided in first instance proceedings on the scope of protection conferred by an SPC, particularly whether or not an SPC protects the use of an ingredient as such before it is transformed into a medicinal product. The SPC holder and its exclusive licensee acted against a Belgian company who manufactured vinorelbine ditartrate in Belgium (in raw form) and exported it to a company in the United States. The latter used the active ingredient to manufacture and market a medicinal product for a therapeutic indication identical to that for the drug produced by the exclusive licensee. The Belgian company argued that the scope of protection of an SPC is limited to the use of the product/active ingredient covered by the (Belgian) SPC as a medicinal product in the territory of Belgium, and that, accordingly, manufacturing the ingredient vinorelbine ditartrate and exporting it to the United States where it is transformed into a medicinal product does not infringe the Belgian SPC. The court did not follow this argumentation: in view of *inter alia* the protected active ingredient being essential to manufacture the medicinal product, the court decided that the protection conferred by Article 4 of the SPC Regulations is not limited to the use of the active ingredient when present in a medicinal product (i.e., the finished product), but covers any use of the active ingredient covered by the SPC (basic patent) where that is destined for use as a medicinal product. According to the court, in order for there to be infringement, it is sufficient for a protected product to be produced and sold (or offered for sale) in Belgium and be used in the manufacture of the medicinal product, which may occur outside Belgium.

[B] The Scope of an SPC in Relation to Derivatives of an Active Ingredient

In principle, the same considerations regarding the scope of an SPC extending to a derivative of an active ingredient as set out in the EU chapter apply in Belgium. So far there have been no decisions from the Belgian courts addressing this point specifically in an infringement case. It is to be expected that the guidance provided by the CJEU in *Farmitalia* (C-392/97)[28] will be applied in Belgium as well. According to this CJEU decision, an SPC is capable of covering both the active ingredient in the specific form as approved in the marketing authorization, and also its various derived forms (e.g.,

25. CJEU *Novartis v. Actavis UK*, C-442/11 of 9 February 2012.
26. CJEU *Novartis v. Actavis Deutschland*, C-574/11 of 9 February 2012.
27. Brussels Commercial Court, A/03/11231 of 20 November 2008.
28. CJEU *Farmitalia Carlo Erba v. Bundesgerichtshof*, C-392/97 of 16 September 1999.

salts, esters), provided the latter are covered by the scope of protection of the basic patent as well.

[1] The Relationship Between the Definition of the Active Ingredient(s) in an SPC and Its Scope of Protection

The same considerations regarding the significance of the product definition of an SPC for its scope of protection as set out in the EU chapter apply in Belgium as well.

[C] Enforcement of an SPC

The legal provisions governing the infringement and enforcement of SPCs and patents are set out in Title 9 (CEL) 'Civil Law aspects of the protection of intellectual property rights' (Articles XI.333–XI.335 (CEL)[29]), which implements the Directive 2004/48/EC[30] on the enforcement of intellectual property rights. As set out in Article XI.337 (CEL), as of 1 January 2015, the Brussels Commercial Court has the exclusive jurisdiction over patent and SPC infringement and invalidity proceedings.

In principle, only the SPC holder or an exclusive licensee of the SPC can take legal action against an infringing party. Similar as for patents, an ex parte descriptive seizure procedure ('saisie description') is available. This procedure is specifically intended to enable the holder of an intellectual property right to obtain evidence of the infringement and the extent thereof. Upon authorization by a judge, a bailiff, typically accompanied by an expert appointed by the court, will visit any place where proof of the infringement might be found and to make a detailed description thereof. A preliminary, physical seizure of the presumed counterfeiting goods may be obtained as well, although, typically, only after the court has heard the defending party.

The same measures are available for SPC and patent infringement, such as corrective measures (Article XI.334 (CEL)), injunctions (Article XI.334 (CEL)) and damages (Article XI.335 (CEL)). The losing party is liable to pay the court fees and reimburse the statutory attorney fees of the other party, taking into account that the recoverable legal costs are capped, depending on the value of the proceedings.

§6.04 DETERMINATION OF THE SPC TERM

[A] The Calculation of the SPC Term

In general, the considerations regarding the calculation of the SPC term as set out in the EU chapter apply equally in Belgium.

29. A link to the main Belgian legal acts and decrees governing patents and SPCs, is provided by the Belgian Office for Intellectual Property at https://economie.fgov.be/fr/themes/propriete-intellectuelle/brevets/demande-de-brevet/certificats-complementaires-de (for the French version) or https://economie.fgov.be/nl/themas/intellectuele-eigendom/octrooien/octrooiaan vraag/aanvullende (for the Dutch version).
30. Directive 2004/48/EC of 29 April 2004 on the enforcement of intellectual property rights.

In particular, the CJEU ruling in *Seattle Genetics* (C-471/14)[31] that the relevant date for the calculation of the SPC term is the notification date of the centralized marketing authorization, i.e., the date when the decision is notified to the marketing authorization holder, rather than the decision date, i.e., the date of the European Commission's decision to grant the marketing authorization, confirmed the OPRI's standard practice at that time.

In this context, in March 2018, the OPRI issued a circular letter[32] providing further details on its practice in relation to the relevant date of a marketing authorization, clarifying both the situation of a centralized marketing authorization as well as a national marketing authorization. The main principle applied by the OPRI is that the relevant date of a marketing authorization is the notification date. This main principle is valid for SPCs for medicinal products and for SPCs for plant protection products, and is applicable for both the determination of the due date for filing the SPC application (according to Article 7(1) of the SPC Regulations) as well as for the calculation of the duration of the certificate (as set out in Article 13(1) of the SPC Regulations). As of September 2018, this main principle is implemented in the new SPC application forms, which have been made available by the OPRI.

For a centralized marketing authorization, in line with the *Seattle Genetics* ruling, the relevant date of the marketing authorization is the date of notification of the decision granting the marketing authorization, as published in the Official Journal of the European Union.

Where a national marketing authorization is the first authorization to place the product on the European market, the basic principle is the same as for centralized marketing authorizations, i.e., if there is an official publication it will be the published date of notification of the decision to grant that first marketing authorization. In the absence of an official publication of the notification date, the OPRI will consider the starting date of the period for which that first marketing authorization is valid as the date of the marketing authorization. However, if the applicant was notified later, he has the option to provide evidence of a later notification date.

In case the holder of a certificate believes that a different marketing authorization date (than the one mentioned on the application form) is to be considered for his certificate, he can submit a written motivated request to correct the granted certificate accordingly.

[1] The Relevant Marketing Authorization for the Term of an SPC

In general, the considerations in terms of the relevant marketing authorization for determining the SPC term as set out in the EU chapter apply equally to Belgium. In

31. CJEU *Seattle Genetics v. Österreichisches Patentamt*, C-471/14 of 6 October 2015.
32. A link to the circular letter, dated 8 March 2018, issued by the Belgian Office for Intellectual Property, can be found at https://economie.fgov.be/fr/themes/propriete-intellectuelle/brevets/demande-de-brevet/certificats-complementaires-de (for the French version) or https://economie.fgov.be/nl/themas/intellectuele-eigendom/octrooien/octrooiaanvraag/aanvullende (for the Dutch version).

Aceclofenac,[33] the Brussels courts ruled, both in the first instance and in the appeal proceedings, that the concept 'first authorization to place the market in the Community' is not limited to marketing authorizations granted according to Directive 65/65/EEC[34] (replaced by Directive 2001/82/EC[35]), but that also national marketing authorizations granted under national laws, which have not yet been adapted to the pertinent Directive, need to be taken into account for calculating the SPC term.

The OPRI does not verify that the marketing authorization relied upon by the SPC applicant is indeed the first marketing authorization in question, in line with Article 10(5) of the SPC Regulations and as set out in Article XI.97 (CEL). However, the application form comprises a statement wherein the applicant declares that the marketing authorization (mentioned in the application form as the first marketing authorization in Belgium) is the first marketing authorization in Belgium. The OPRI does not consult regulatory agencies with respect to the data related to the marketing authorization.

[2] The Expiration Date of an SPC

The calculation of the SPC term is in line with the calculation of the patent term under Belgian practice. Subject to the payment of the yearly renewal fees, a patent ends at the end of the twentieth year as from the filing date of the application (Article XI.47 §1 (CEL)). The last day when a patent is in force is thus the day before twentieth anniversary of its filing date. The certificate enters into force on the expiry date of the basic patent. Accordingly, an SPC with a full five-year term will expire the day before the twenty-fifth anniversary of the filing date of the patent.

For example, a Belgian SPC which is based on a patent filed on 15 June 2000 and based on a first marketing authorization notified on 10 August 2007 will come into effect upon expiry of the basic patent, i.e., on 15 June 2020, and will expire on 9 August 2022 at midnight. If, in this example, the marketing authorization is notified on or after 15 June 2010, the SPC will have the maximum term of five years and will thus expire on 14 June 2025 at midnight.

[B] Correction of the SPC Term

In general, the considerations as set out in the EU chapter apply equally in Belgium. Furthermore, the circular letter issued by the OPRI in March 2018 in relation to the relevant date of a marketing authorization explicitly specifies that correction of the SPC term is possible. Should the holder of a certificate believe that a different MA date (than

33. Brussels Commercial Court, A/06/10756, of 15 June 2007; Brussels Court of Appeal, 2007/AR/01841, of 23 June 2009.
34. Council Directive 65/65/EEC of 26 January 1965 on the approximation of provisions laid down by Law, Regulation or Administrative Action relating to proprietary medicinal products.
35. Directive 2001/83/EC of the European Parliament and of the Council of 6 November 2001 on the Community code relating to medicinal products for human use.

the one mentioned on the application form) is to be considered for his certificate, he can submit a written motivated request to correct the granted certificate accordingly.

[C] Paediatric Extensions

The considerations in terms of paediatric extensions as set out in the EU chapter apply equally to Belgium.

§6.05 PROCEDURE OF FILING AN SPC APPLICATION

[A] Entitlement to an SPC Application

In line with Article 6 of the SPC Regulations stipulating that the certificate shall be granted to the patent holder, in Belgium, it is only the registered patent owner(s) who is (are) entitled to file an SPC application. If there is a discrepancy between the applicant(s) for an SPC and the registered owner(s) of the basic patent (such as due to the transfer of the basic patent or a change in address), the OPRI will invite the applicant to correct this deficiency.

[B] The Time Limit for Filing an SPC Application

In general, the considerations as set out in the EU chapter apply equally in Belgium.

The circular letter issued by OPRI in March 2018 (*see* §6.04[A]) establishes the OPRI's main principle to consider the notification date as the relevant date of a marketing authorization. In particular, this letter explicitly specifies that this main principle is also valid for the determination of the due date for filing the SPC application (according to Article 7(1) of the SPC Regulations). Thus, in Belgium, an SPC application is timely filed if submitted within six months of the notification date of the marketing authorization (or within six months of the date on which the patent is granted, if this is the later date).

In addition, the Belgian law provides for a restoration procedure in case, in spite of all due care being taken, the applicant of an SPC or paediatric extension failed to observe a time limit vis-à-vis the OPRI and this non-observance of this time limit resulted in the loss of rights with respect to the SPC or paediatric extension application (Articles XI.102 and XI.103 (CEL)). In particular, the six-month term for filing an SPC application or paediatric extension according to Article 7(1)-7(4) of the SPC Regulations is not excluded from the restoration procedure. Upon a written motivated request submitted by the applicant within two months of the removal of the cause of non-compliance with the time limit, but at the latest within one year of expiry of the unobserved time limit, and provided the OPRI establishes that all due care required under the circumstances has been taken, the OPRI shall grant the request for the re-establishment of rights.

[C] The Filing of an SPC at the National Patent Office

As set out in the EU chapter, an SPC must be filed before the national patent office within the stipulated time limits, once the basic patent as well as the relevant marketing authorization have issued. The SPC application must be filed in writing, using the prescribed form issued by the OPRI, in Dutch, French or German, according to the legislation on the use of languages in the administration. Online filing of SPC applications is currently not yet possible. The application form must contain all relevant information about the applicant and his representative (names and addresses), as well as details in terms of the basic patent (title (or translation thereof), filing date, publication number - as mentioned in the Belgian patent register) and the marketing authorization (number and date, product definition) relied upon for the product in question. An explanatory note (in Dutch and French) providing further clarifications for completing the application form and the required documentation is available.[36] In addition, the payment of a prescribed filing fee is due.

A SPC applicant having neither its residence nor establishment in a Member State of the European Union must appoint a Belgian patent attorney or a lawyer as its representative. In general, no power of attorney is required for filing the SPC application.

[D] The Documentation Required for an SPC Application

The documentation required for filing an SPC application in Belgium is based on the requirements as set out in Article 8 of the SPC Regulations (Article XI.96 (CEL)). The considerations as set out in the EU chapter thus apply equally to Belgium.

Briefly, the SPC application form should be accompanied with a copy of the marketing authorization to place the product on the market in Belgium (in Dutch, French or German), including the Summary of Product Characteristics (SmPC). The documentation should identify the product and mention at least the number and date of the authorization.

In addition, if the first authorization for placing the product on the market is not a Belgian (or a centralized) marketing authorization, the applicant should submit a copy of the first marketing authorization of the pertinent EU or EEA Member State, comprising information regarding the identity of the product thus authorized and the legal provision under which the authorization procedure took place, together with a copy of the notice publishing the authorization in the appropriate official publication. Although it is not required under Belgian law, it is advisable that the applicant provides information as to how the product is protected by the basic patent.

36. A link to the explanatory note for completing the SPC application form can be found at https://economie.fgov.be/fr/themes/propriete-intellectuelle/brevets/demande-de-brevet/certificats-complementaires-de (for the French version) or https://economie.fgov.be/nl/themas/intellectuele-eigendom/octrooien/octrooiaanvraag/aanvullende (for the Dutch version).

[E] The Definition of the Product in an SPC Application

As set out in the explanatory note for completing the application form provided by the OPRI,[37] the product of an SPC should correspond to the name of the active ingredient(s) mentioned in the marketing authorization (or SmPC) for the corresponding medicinal or plant protection product, such as e.g., a product definition based on the International Non-proprietary Name (INN) of the active ingredient as identified in the SmPC. Broader product definitions, e.g., including pharmaceutically acceptable salts of the active ingredient in question, may be found acceptable, to the extent these derivatives are specifically protected by the basic patent as well.

[F] SPC Examination Procedure and Appeal Procedure

In the past, and in line with the purely administrative procedure for the grant of a patent in Belgium, the OPRI primarily carried out a formal examination of the SPC application. In fact, older certificates (issued as a Ministerial Decree) comprise a statement that the certificate was granted without prior examination of the conformity between the product covered by the basic patent and the product that is the subject of the marketing authorization, and at the risk of the applicant. However, since about ten years ago, presumably in view of the different CJEU rulings particularly directed to the interpretation of 'protected by the basic patent' (Article 3(a) of the SPC Regulations), the OPRI carries out a more substantive examination as well.

In accordance with the current practice at the OPRI, an SPC application will be subject to a formal examination, followed by a substantive examination.

The formal examination is carried out by a formality officer. Similarly as provided for patent applications, it is first verified whether the application contains the required information for obtaining a date of filing, as set out in Article XI.93 §1 (CEL), i.e., a request for obtaining a certificate, information identifying the applicant and allowing the applicant to be contacted by the OPRI, and information identifying the basic patent. A suitably completed prescribed application form provides this information. In case these conditions are not met, the OPRI will notify the applicant, who has a period of three months to provide the missing information. The OPRI will also inform the applicant of the date of filing of the SPC application, i.e., the date on which the conditions set out in Article XI.93 §1 (CEL) have been met. In addition, a notification of the filing of an SPC application is published in the patent register, mentioning *inter alia* the applicant, the basic patent, the marketing authorization and the product name (Article XI.95 (CEL)).

The formal examination further focuses on issues such as the formal entitlement of the applicant (i.e., the holder of the basic patent), the time limits for filing the SPC, the payment of the prescribed fees, and whether the submitted documentation is complete. In addition, the information provided by the applicant relating to the basic patent and the legal status thereof are verified as well. The OPRI will invite the

37. *Ibid.*

applicant to rectify any deficiencies observed in the formal examination, within an (extendable) period of two months.

During the substantive examination the OPRI establishes the identity of the product of the marketing authorization and verifies that the product is protected by the basic patent, according to Article 3(a) of the SPC Regulations, taking into account the various CJEU rulings related thereto. The OPRI may also examine whether the product has already been the subject of a certificate, although the Belgian law provides that, in line with Article 10(5) of the SPC Regulations, a certificate is granted without verifying that the conditions laid down in Article 3(c) and (d) of the SPC Regulations are met (Article XI.97 (CEL)) – in this context, the application form also comprises a statement wherein the applicant declares that the product has not already been the subject of a certificate. In addition, any third-party observations (which are not made public) and the status of corresponding SPC applications in other EU Member States are taken into account – the OPRI typically aligns its decision with other national patent offices. A legal officer is involved during the substantive examination as well. The OPRI is usually prepared to consider delaying the examination of an SPC upon informal request by the applicant or to stay the proceedings in view of pending decisions of the CJEU. An informal interview or informal written exchange of information or opinions with the responsible OPRI officer is possible as well.

If the application for the SPC is found to comply with the statutory requirements as set out in the SPC Regulations and the Belgian law, the OPRI will issue the decision to grant the certificate for the duration of its term. Alternatively, the OPRI issues a reasoned intention to reject the application and will invite the applicant to submit his observations thereto, within an (extendable) period of two months. If the objections cannot be overcome, the OPRI will reject the certificate. As also mentioned in the corresponding communication from the OPRI, this decision to reject the certificate can be appealed before the Brussels Commercial Court, in line with Article XI.337 (CEL).

The grant of the certificate (or the rejection of the application) is reported in the register as well (Article XI.98 (CEL)), mentioning the grant date and the expiration date (provided the yearly renewal fees are timely paid).

[G] Applications for a Paediatric Extension

The formal requirements and considerations for filing a paediatric extension in Belgium correspond to those as outlined in the EU chapter.

The request for a paediatric extension must be filed with the OPRI together with the prescribed fee, using the prescribed form, in Dutch, French or German, according to the legislation on the use of languages in the administration. The documentation required for filing a paediatric extension in Belgium is based on the requirements as set out in Article 8 of the SPC Regulation for Medicinal Products (Article XI.96 (CEL)), and include a copy of the statement indicating compliance with the agreed and completed Paediatric Investigation Plan, a copy of the SPC application or the granted certificate, and a copy of the marketing authorization to place the product on the market, including the Summary of Product Characteristics. Moreover, if the product has not been approved centrally by the EMA, it is necessary for the applicant to submit proof of possession of marketing authorizations for the product in all Member States (e.g., by submitting a copy of the marketing authorization of all Member States).

Upon filing the application for a paediatric extension, the OPRI first verifies whether the application contains the required information for obtaining a date of filing, as set out in Article XI.94 §1 (CEL), i.e., a request for obtaining a paediatric extension, information identifying the applicant and allowing the applicant to be contacted by the OPRI, and information identifying the SPC. A suitably completed prescribed application form provides this information. Similar as for SPC applications, the applicant has a period of three months to provide any missing information upon notification by the OPRI. The OPRI will also inform the applicant of the date of filing of the application for the paediatric extension, i.e., the date on which the conditions set out in Article XI.94 §1 (CEL) have been met.

The examination procedure primarily focuses on the formal requirements for obtaining a paediatric extension, and is typically carried out by a legal officer. Examination includes the verification of the completeness of the documentation in relation to the compliance statement and the verification that the product has been approved in all EU Member States. The OPRI will invite the applicant to rectify any deficiencies observed in the formal examination, such as in case the statement of compliance is not yet available when filing the request, within an extendable period of two months.

As for SPC applications, a notification of the filing and the grant of a paediatric extention is published in the patent register. No renewal fee is due in case the paediatric extension extends the term of the certificate beyond five years – the fifth renewal fee for the certificate covers the paediatric extension as well.

§6.06 PROCEDURE OF INVALIDATING AN SPC

[A] Grounds for the Invalidation of an SPC

The grounds for invalidating an SPC in Belgium correspond to the grounds as set out in Article 15 of the SPC Regulations, as discussed in the EU chapter.

[B] The Filing of an Invalidation Suit

As set out in Article XI.337 (CEL), as of 1 January 2015, the Brussels Commercial Court has the exclusive jurisdiction over patent and SPC infringement and invalidity proceedings. Similar as for patent invalidation proceedings, an action for the invalidation of an SPC may be filed at any time by a person who can demonstrate an interest in the matter, independent from any pending infringement proceedings.

[C] Invalidation Procedure and the Corresponding Appeal Procedure

In general, the invalidation procedure and the corresponding appeal procedure follow the same procedural provisions for the corresponding basic patent. Belgian national law does not comprise any special procedural provisions for SPCs.

[D] The Revocation of a Paediatric Extension

As set out in the EU chapter, the grounds for revocation of a paediatric extension correspond to those of Article 16 of the SPC Regulation for Medicinal Products. In addition, the same considerations as set out in §6.06[B] and §6.06[C] above for the revocation of an SPC apply.

§6.07 UNFAIR COMPETITION LAW

The same considerations as set out in the EU chapter apply.

CHAPTER 7
Italy

Andrea Damonti, Paolo Mimo & Micaela Modiano

§7.01 LEGAL BASIS

The Italian Intellectual Property Code (IPC)[1] does not contain any provisions relating to the implementation of Regulation (EC) 469/2009[2] (the 'SPC Regulation for Medicinal Products') and Regulation (EC) 1610/96[3] (the 'SPC Regulation for Plant Protection Products'). As noted in Chapter 1 (the 'EU chapter'), these Regulations are directly applicable in all EU Member States, including Italy, without requiring transposition into national law. Thus, no amendments to the Italian IPC were introduced in order to implement the above Regulations.

§7.02 SUBSTANTIVE REQUIREMENTS FOR OBTAINING AN SPC

Owing to the binding nature on all EU Member States of the decisions issued by the CJEU, it follows that the considerations set out in the EU chapter with respect to the substantive requirements for obtaining an SPC are applicable also to Italy, at least to the extent that such substantive requirements have been addressed by the CJEU.

In view of the above, in the following §7.02[A]–§7.02[D] the discussion will be limited to case law and considerations of relevance only for Italy.

1. Italian Intellectual Property Code (IPC), Legislative Decree No. 30 of 10 February 2005 and subsequent amendments thereof.
2. Regulation (EC) No. 469/2009 of the European Parliament and of the Council of 6 May 2009 concerning the supplementary protection certificate for medicinal products.
3. Regulation (EC) No. 1610/96 of the European Parliament and of the Council of 23 July 1996 concerning the creation of a supplementary protection certificate for plant protection products.

[A] Types of Products That Can Be Protected

The same considerations as set out in the EU chapter apply.

[1] Practical Considerations: What Is the Active Ingredient or Combination of Active Ingredients That Can Form the Basis for an SPC

The same considerations as set out in the EU chapter apply.

[2] Active Ingredient or Combination of Active Ingredients of a Medicinal Product

The same considerations as set out in the EU chapter apply.

[3] Active Substance or Combination of Active Substances of a Plant Protection Product

The same considerations as set out in the EU chapter apply.

[4] Fixed-Dose and Loose Combinations

The same considerations as set out in the EU chapter apply.

[5] Limitation to Products Subjected to a Specific Marketing Authorization Procedure

The same considerations as set out in the EU chapter apply.

[6] Protection of Medical Devices

The same considerations as set out in the EU chapter apply.

[B] Basic Patent

The same considerations as set out in the EU chapter apply.

[1] Requirement for the Product to Be 'Protected' by the Basic Patent

As discussed in the EU chapter, in recent years the CJEU has issued a number of decisions aimed at clarifying the requirement that a product must be 'protected by a basic patent'.

In particular, in *Medeva* (C-322/10)[4] the CJEU ruled out the adoption of an 'infringement test' to determine whether a product, i.e., the active ingredient or combination of active ingredients, is 'protected' by the basic patent, and held that the relevant criteria is that the product must be '*specified in the wording of the claims*' of the basic patent. Subsequently, in *Eli Lilly* (C-493/12),[5] the CJEU addressed the case of an active ingredient defined by way of a *functional definition*, concluding that such product is 'protected' by the basis patent if the claims – when interpreted in the light of the description of the basic patent, in accordance with Article 69 EPC and the Protocol on the Interpretation of Article 69 EPC – are found to relate, '*implicitly but necessarily and specifically*', to the active ingredient at issue.

Possibly as a result of the fact that application of the guidance provided by the CJEU in *Medeva* (and the various subsequent decisions including *Eli Lilly*) has led to divergent decisions throughout Europe and to a perception that further referrals to the CJEU may be necessary to clarify how the 'protected' by the basic patent requirement should be applied, so far Italian courts do not appear to have revised their approach to the assessment of this requirement to any considerable extent in view of *Medeva* and of the subsequent decisions of the CJEU.

As a result, in those circumstances where an active ingredient is not explicitly mentioned in the claims of the basic patent, Italian courts have relied on the patent description as a tool to assess whether the claims might be interpreted to cover the specific active ingredient which is the subject of an SPC. For example, before the issuance of *Medeva* and *Eli Lilly*, the Court of Milan in *Ranbaxy et al. v. Warner-Lambert Company LLC*[6] relied on the fact that the patent description contained several references to the stereochemical configuration of the claimed compounds to conclude that the claims were directed to both a racemate as well as to each of the enantiomers making up the racemate. As a result, the specific enantiomer corresponding to the active ingredient atorvastatin was deemed to be 'protected' by the basic patent. Similarly, following issuance of both *Medeva* and *Eli Lilly*, the Court of Milan in *Roche et al. v. Amgen Inc.*[7] again relied on the patent description for the purpose of interpreting the claims of the basic patent and found that the conjugate active ingredient consisting of the antibody trastuzumab and the cytotoxic agent emtansine was not 'protected' by the claims, since the description made clear that the core of the invention were those antibodies possessing an autonomous apoptotic activity and thus could not encompass a conjugate where the antibody, i.e., trastuzumab, does not have apoptotic activity per se.

Therefore, for the time being in Italy there is still uncertainty regarding how the guidance provided by the CJEU in *Medeva* and *Eli Lilly* will be applied by the national courts. Under such circumstances, resolution of the referrals currently pending before

4. CJEU *Medeva v. Comptroller General of Patents, Designs and Trade Marks*, C-322/10 of 24 November 2011.
5. CJEU *Eli Lilly v. Human Genome Sciences*, C-493/12 of 12 December 2013.
6. Court of Milan, *Ranbaxy et al. v. Warner-Lambert Company LLC*, 7855/2008 of 8 May 2008.
7. Court of Milan, *Roche et al. v. Amgen Inc.*, 6778/2017 of 4 May 2017.

the CJEU may provide more certainty on how the 'protected' by the basic patent requirement will be applied by Italian courts.

[a] Small Molecules

The same considerations as set out in the EU chapter apply.

[b] Polymers

The same considerations as set out in the EU chapter apply.

[c] Antibodies, Enzymes and Other Proteins

The same considerations as set out in the EU chapter apply.

[d] Nucleic Acids

The same considerations as set out in the EU chapter apply.

[2] Basic Patent Claiming the Product, i.e., the Active Ingredient(s), but Not the Corresponding Authorized Medicinal Product (or Plant Protection Product)

The same considerations as set out in the EU chapter apply.

[3] Requirement for the Product to Constitute 'the Invention' of the Basic Patent

Since the Italian Patent and Trademark Office (IPTO) does not carry out a substantive examination of SPC applications with regard to the requirements of Article 3(a), no assessment is carried out with respect to whether the product of an SPC constitutes 'the invention' or the 'core inventive advance' of the basic patent during grant proceedings. On the other hand, in the context of assessing the validity of granted SPCs, Italian courts have commented on several occasions on the relevance of the requirement that the product represent the inventive core of the patent for the purposes of establishing that that product is 'protected' by the basic patent.

In particular, in *Sanofi SA et al. v. Teva Pharma BV et al.*[8] and *Mylan S.p.A. v. Boehringer*[9] the Court of Milan interpreted the considerations expressed by the CJEU at paragraphs 41–42 of *Actavis v. Sanofi* (C-443/12)[10] as meaning that the assessment of

8. Court of Milan, *Sanofi SA et al. v. Teva Pharma BV et al.*, 9855/2014 of 10 July 2014.
9. Court of Milan, *Mylan S.p.A. v. Boehringer*, 4136/2015 of 18 December 2014.
10. CJEU *Actavis v. Sanofi*, C-443/12 of 12 December 2013.

whether an active ingredient is 'protected' as such by the basic patent requires that reference be made to the focus of the inventive core of the patent, i.e., the 'innovative active ingredient that led to the grant of the patent monopoly'. On this basis, the Court of Milan commented that the definition of product 'protected' by the basic patent cannot encompass the combination of an inventive active ingredient together with other known active ingredients where such combination is not inventive per se.

In *Roche et al. v. Amgen Inc.*[11] the Court of Milan found that a conjugate active ingredient consisting of the antibody trastuzumab and the cytotoxic agent emtansine was not 'protected' by the claims, since the description of the basic patent made it clear that the core of the invention were those antibodies possessing an autonomous apoptotic activity, thereby excluding the conjugate where the antibody, i.e., trastuzumab, does not have apoptotic activity per se.

Therefore, in Italy the question whether the product of an SPC embodies the core inventive advance of the basic patent may become relevant for the assessment of compliance of an SPC with the requirement of Article 3(a) of the SPC Regulations carried out by Italian courts.

[4] Criteria for Choosing the Basic Patent among Various Available Patents

The same considerations as set out in the EU chapter apply.

[C] The Marketing Authorization Forming Basis for an SPC

The same considerations as set out in the EU chapter apply.

[1] Combinations of Active Ingredients

The same considerations as set out in the EU chapter apply.

[a] The Marketing Authorization Refers to Fewer Active Ingredients than the SPC Application

The same considerations as set out in the EU chapter apply.

[b] The Marketing Authorization Refers to More Active Ingredients than the SPC Application

The same considerations as set out in the EU chapter apply.

11. Court of Milan, *Roche et al. v. Amgen Inc.*, 6778/2017 of 4 May 2017.

[c] The Marketing Authorization Indicates That a Medicinal Product Containing a Single Active Ingredient Is Authorized for Use in Combination with a Further Active Ingredient

The same considerations as set out in the EU chapter apply.

[2] The Marketing Authorization Has Not Yet Been Granted at the Time the SPC Application Is Filed

The same considerations as set out in the EU chapter apply.

[3] The Holder of the Marketing Authorization

The same considerations as set out in the EU chapter apply.

[4] Reliance on a Marketing Authorization Granted under a Provision Other than Directive 2001/83/EC or Directive 2001/82/EC

The same considerations as set out in the EU chapter apply.

[5] The Marketing Authorizations Which Can Be Relied upon for SPC Applications for Plant Protection Products

The same considerations as set out in the EU chapter apply.

[6] The Product in Question Is Contained in the Authorized Medicinal Product (or the Authorized Plant Protection Product) but Is Not Identified as an Active Ingredient in the Corresponding Marketing Authorization

The same considerations as set out in the EU chapter apply.

[7] The Notion of the 'First' Marketing Authorization

The same considerations as set out in the EU chapter apply.

[a] Marketing Authorization for a New Therapeutic Application of a Previously Authorized Product

The same considerations as set out in the EU chapter apply.

[b] *Marketing Authorization for a New Formulation of a Previously Authorized Product*

The same considerations as set out in the EU chapter apply.

[c] *Marketing Authorization for a New Specific Salt, Ester or Other Derivative of a Previously Authorized Active Ingredient*

The same considerations as set out in the EU chapter apply.

[d] *Marketing Authorization for a New Specific Enantiomer of an Active Ingredient Previously Authorized in Racemic Form*

The same considerations as set out in the EU chapter apply.

[e] *The Product Has Already Been Placed on the Market Before, but Without an Authorization Granted under Directive 2001/83/EC or Directive 2001/82/EC*

The same considerations as set out in the EU chapter apply.

[f] *Prior Marketing Authorization Which Refers to Fewer Active Ingredients than the SPC Application (and the Later Marketing Authorization Relied upon)*

The same considerations as set out in the EU chapter apply.

[g] *Prior Marketing Authorization Which Refers to More Active Ingredients than the SPC Application (and the Later Marketing Authorization Relied upon)*

The same considerations as set out in the EU chapter apply.

[D] Preclusion of New SPCs by an Earlier SPC

The same considerations as set out in the EU chapter apply.

[1] *Consequences of an Earlier Third-Party SPC for the Same Product*

[a] *The 'One SPC per Product per Patent Holder' Rule*

The same considerations as set out in the EU chapter apply.

[b] *Earlier SPC Granted to an Affiliated Third Party*

The same considerations as set out in the EU chapter apply.

It should be noted that in Italy SPC applications for the same product filed by different patent holders are regularly granted by the IPTO, regardless of any affiliation between these different patent holders, and to date no decision was issued by Italian courts impacting such practice of the IPTO.

[c] *Partial Overlap Between the Holders of the Earlier SPC and the Applicants for the New SPC*

The same considerations as set out in the EU chapter apply.

[d] *Earlier Third-Party SPC Has Been Licensed-In*

The same considerations as set out in the EU chapter apply.

[2] ***Consequences of an Own Earlier SPC for the Same Product***

The same considerations as set out in the EU chapter apply.

[a] *Own Earlier SPC Application Not Yet Granted*

The same considerations as set out in the EU chapter apply.

[b] *Revocation, Surrender or Lapse of the Own Earlier SPC after Grant*

The same considerations as set out in the EU chapter apply.

[c] *Transfer of the Own Earlier SPC to a Third Party*

The same considerations as set out in the EU chapter apply.

[d] *Acquisition of an SPC Granted to a Third Party*

The same considerations as set out in the EU chapter apply.

[3] ***Consequences of an Own Earlier SPC for a Different Product***

The same considerations as set out in the EU chapter apply.

[a] Required Distinction from the Product of the Own Earlier SPC

The same considerations as set out in the EU chapter apply.

Combinations of Active Ingredients

The IPTO does not carry out a substantive examination of SPC applications with regard to the requirements of Article 3(c). As a result, in Italy it is generally possible for an applicant to obtain an SPC for a product which is a combination of active ingredients even when such applicant is the holder of an earlier SPC the product of which is one of the active ingredients of the combination.

However, the validity of such a combination SPC is currently questionable, since Italian courts have endorsed the principle established by the CJEU in *Actavis v. Sanofi* (C-443/12)[12] and *Actavis v. Boehringer Ingelheim Pharma* (C-577/13)[13] and found that the grant of an earlier SPC for the active ingredient embodying the inventive core of the patent leads to the invalidity of a further SPC having the same basic patent and directed to the combination of that active ingredient together with another known active ingredient, if such combination is not inventive per se (*see* decisions of the Court of Milan in *Sanofi SA et al. v. Teva Pharma BV et al.*[14] and *Mylan S.p.A. v. Boehringer*[15]).

New Therapeutic Applications of Previously Approved Active Ingredients

The same considerations as set out in the EU chapter apply.

[b] SPCs for a Specific Salt, Ester or Other Derivative Where an Own Earlier SPC Has Already Been Granted for the Corresponding Active Ingredient

The same considerations as set out in the EU chapter apply.

[c] SPCs for a Specific Enantiomer Where an Own Earlier SPC Has Already Been Granted for the Corresponding Racemate

The same considerations as set out in the EU chapter apply.

[4] Grant of More than One SPC on the Basis of the Same Patent

The same considerations as set out in the EU chapter apply.

12. CJEU *Actavis v. Sanofi*, C-443/12 of 12 December 2013.
13. CJEU *Actavis v. Boehringer Ingelheim Pharma*, C-577/13 of 12 March 2015.
14. Court of Milan, *Sanofi SA et al. v. Teva Pharma BV et al.*, 9855/2014 of 10 July 2014.
15. Court of Milan, *Mylan S.p.A. v. Boehringer*, 4136/2015 of 18 December 2014.

§7.03 EXTENT OF PROTECTION AND ENFORCEMENT OF SPCs

[A] The Protection Conferred by an SPC

The same considerations as set out in the EU chapter apply.

As such, in Italy Articles 4 and 5 of the SPC Regulations are understood to mean that while an SPC confers the same rights as conferred by its basic patent, as set out in Article 5, the protection conferred by the SPC is confined to the product which is the subject of the marketing authorization (i.e., it does not include other products that may be encompassed by the basic patent), as set out in Article 4.

[B] The Scope of an SPC in Relation to Derivatives of an Active Ingredient

Consistently with the CJEU's comments in *Farmitalia* (C-392/97),[16] where a marketing authorization refers to a specific derivative (e.g., a salt or an ester) of a product, in Italy the SPC is capable of covering the product as such and also its derivatives, as medicinal products (or plant protection products), subject to the proviso that such derivatives are protected by the basic patent.

Accordingly, the IPTO regularly appends to granted certificates an annotation based on the language of the decision in *Farmitalia*, aimed to explicitly acknowledge that the SPC covers the product, as a medicinal product (or a plant protection product), in any of the forms enjoying the protection of the basic patent.

[1] The Relationship Between the Definition of the Active Ingredient(s) in an SPC and Its Scope of Protection

The IPTO's practice is to grant SPCs where the definition of the product corresponds, in the vast majority of cases, to that adopted for the active ingredient(s) in the marketing authorization for the corresponding medicinal product or plant protection product or in the Summary of Product Characteristics (SmPC). However, the precise relationship between the definition of the active ingredient(s) and the scope of protection of an SPC remains an open issue in Italy in view of a substantial lack of case law on this issue.

So far, the only guidance on this issue comes from a decision[17] rendered by the IPTO Board of Appeal following the appeals filed by Aventis Holdings Inc. and Yeda Research and Development Co. Ltd. against two decisions of the IPTO refusing two SPC applications for panitumumab in combination with other active ingredients for being duplicates of a previously filed SPC application for the same product. Specifically, in this decision the IPTO Board of Appeal concluded that only one SPC could be granted

16. CJEU *Farmitalia Carlo Erba v. Bundesgerichtshof*, C-392/97 of 16 September 1999.
17. IPTO Board of Appeal, *Aventis Holdings Inc. and Yeda Research and Development Co. Ltd*, 11/10 of 27 January 2010.

for the product panitumumab (i.e., where the active ingredient had been defined in accordance with the marketing authorization), noting that in application of the CJEU's decision in *Farmitalia* such SPC would cover the product in all the forms enjoying the protection of the basic patent and that *regardless of the wording used in the definition of the product* the SPC would extend also to subsequently authorized medicinal products 'obtained in application of the technology disclosed and claimed in the basic patent, to the extent that such medicinal product ... are placed on the market within the maximum term of five years'.

On the other hand, the conclusions reached by the IPTO Board of Appeal do not appear to go beyond the considerations expressed by the CJEU in *Novartis v. Actavis UK* (C-442/11)[18] and *Novartis v. Actavis Deutschland* (C-574/11),[19] where the CJEU confirmed that the scope of protection conferred by an SPC for a single active ingredient extends to combination products comprising that active ingredient together with one or more further active ingredients. This, coupled with the fact that the above mentioned appeal decision was issued by the IPTO Board of Appeal, i.e., a governmental body rather than an Italian ordinary court, and the fact that there is no relevant case law from Italian courts, arguably entails that for the time being the issue of the relationship between the definition of the active ingredient(s) and the scope of protection of an SPC remains open for consideration.

[C] Enforcement of an SPC

An Italian SPC can be enforced on the national level exclusively by filing an infringement action or a request for preliminary measures before ordinary courts, specifically those hosting a 'specialized division in company law' (*sezione specializzata in materia di impresa*).

At the time of writing (June 2018), there are twenty-two specialized divisions in company law located in the Courts of Ancona, Bari, Bologna, Bolzano, Brescia, Catania, Catanzaro, Campobasso, Cagliari, Florence, Genoa, L'Aquila, Milan, Naples, Palermo, Perugia, Potenza, Rome, Turin, Trento, Trieste and Venice, but only eleven of these specialized divisions have jurisdiction on cases involving a foreign company (i.e., the divisions located in the Courts of Bari, Bolzano, Cagliari, Catania, Genoa, Milan, Naples, Rome, Trento, Turin and Venice).

For infringement actions and requests for preliminary measures, competence of the court is established on the basis of where the domicile or registered office of the defendant is located or, alternatively, the area where infringement took place. While an infringement action or a request for preliminary measures may be brought in the specialized division of any court which is competent to hear the case, in practice the Courts of Milan, Rome and Turin are the most frequented for patent and SPC litigation in Italy, such that these courts tend to have the most experience.

18. CJEU *Novartis v. Actavis UK*, C-442/11 of 9 February 2012.
19. CJEU *Novartis v. Actavis Deutschland*, C-574/11 of 9 February 2012.

The litigation system in Italy does not entail bifurcation. Since the defendant in infringement proceedings usually files a counterclaim for a declaration of invalidity of the basic patent and/or SPC, both infringement and invalidity are heard and decided by the same court in the same proceedings. In proceedings relating to preliminary measures, the defendant cannot file a counterclaim for a declaration of invalidity, but invalidity arguments may be relied upon as a defence.

The judges of the specialized divisions normally are experienced in patent matters, but they do not have a technical background. As such, a court expert (usually an Italian patent attorney, often also holding the title of European patent attorney) is appointed to assist the judge with the assessment of validity and infringement of patents and SPCs. Court experts are almost invariably appointed in proceedings on the merits, but this is not always the case in proceedings relating to preliminary measures. In fact, some Italian judges feel that the appointment of a court expert in proceedings relating to preliminary measures turns such proceedings into proceedings on the merits, due to the fact that in the view of such judges the assessment carried out by a court expert is always an in-depth analysis which is incompatible with the nature of proceedings relating to preliminary measures where all issues should be reviewed only summarily.

In Italy it also possible to start an infringement action on the basis of a pending SPC application. In fact, the IPC allows to enforce intellectual property rights - thus including SPCs - that have been granted and also those that are still in the process of being granted.[20] However, a decision in an infringement action based on a still pending SPC application may be rendered by the court only after the IPTO has granted that application. In such circumstances, the IPTO examines the SPC application on an urgent basis, in advance of earlier filed applications, and the court orders the suspension of the proceedings, once or repeatedly, as necessary to await the grant of the SPC.

The time required for a first instance decision in an infringement action on the merits is on average between 2.5 and 3 years (including the time required for the court expert phase), depending on the complexity of the case, the court's backlog and possible postponements (e.g., in case a suspension is necessary to allow the IPTO to grant a pending SPC).

An appeal against a first instance decision may be filed within six months from its publication or a shortened period of thirty days from service of the decision. Appeals are heard by a panel of judges from the specialized division of the Court of Appeal located in the same city as the Court of First Instance.

Appeal proceedings usually take between two to three years before a decision is issued. A further appeal to the Italian Supreme Court (*Corte di Cassazione*) is possible and generally takes approximately four years.

For proceedings relating to preliminary measures, a first instance decision is usually issued within one to two months. However, in circumstances where a court

20. Article 120(1) IPC.

expert is appointed by the judge to assist with the assessment of validity and/or infringement, the length of the proceedings will increase by at least four to six months.

First instance decisions issued in proceedings relating to preliminary measures are appealable. The appeal must be filed within fifteen days from issuance of the first instance decision, and the final appeal decision typically issues within about one to two months from the filing of the appeal.

§7.04 DETERMINATION OF THE SPC TERM

[A] The Calculation of the SPC Term

The same considerations as set out in the EU chapter concerning the calculation of the SPC term apply also to Italy.

Recently the IPTO is issuing SPCs with a duration based on the notification date of the marketing authorization rather than on the decision date, as was instead the case in the past. And this is so even in cases where no corresponding request is made in the SPC application.

[1] The Relevant Marketing Authorization for the Term of an SPC

The same considerations as set out in the EU chapter concerning the relevant marketing authorization for determining the SPC term apply also to Italy.

The marketing authorization indicated in the SPC application is not verified by the IPTO to check if it actually is the first marketing authorization for the product in question. This derives from the general approach of the IPTO according to which it has neither the right nor the means to examine the validity of an SPC application on the merits. The validity requirements, if at all, will be dealt with in court, if and when the validity or scope of protection of the SPC will be challenged.

If, after the filing of the SPC application, the applicant becomes aware of a prior marketing authorization - which may occur, for instance, when it turns out that a previous Swiss marketing authorization was automatically effective in Liechtenstein with no postponement due to the delay mechanism - the applicant may bring the matter to the attention of the IPTO, which will then amend the certificate accordingly.

In a very recent case, an SPC application was applied for and granted based on a type II variation of a marketing authorization relating to a product which had already been the subject matter of a granted SPC. As said, the IPTO does not perform an examination of the merits of SPC applications and therefore the actual validity of an SPC on a type II variation will be determined in court, if a third party challenges said SPC.

[2] The Expiration Date of an SPC

The expiration date of an SPC obviously depends on the date on which the SPC becomes effective and, thus, on the date on which the twenty-year duration of the basic patent ended. It is therefore necessary to refer to the national laws on patents to determine this aspect.

In this connection, the Italian IPC[21] simply states that a patent has a duration of twenty years from its filing, but does not specify whether the date of filing must be considered in the twenty-year term or whether the duration of a patent starts from the first day following its filing.

The Italian law provisions which deal with the calculation of terms in other areas exclude the starting day from the calculation. This applies to the Italian civil code with respect to prescription,[22] to the Italian criminal code[23] and to the Italian civil procedure code.[24] However, the position of the IPTO on this aspect is not univocal.

[B] Correction of the SPC Term

The general approach of the IPTO is that once the SPC is granted its term may not be amended, if not through a limitation petition. The IPTO bases this position on the fact that neither the relevant SPC Regulations nor the Italian industrial property code contain any provisions allowing for the correction of any data of the SPC after its grant. However, there are some instances in which it is possible to correct the duration of the granted certificate.

The usual situation in which is possible is when the term of the SPC does not correspond to the documents submitted with the application due to an error of the IPTO. In this case it is possible to have the term corrected and in some cases no particular formality is required. A phone conversation with the Examiner may be sufficient for the latter to correct the IPTO records and to issue a new certificate. Otherwise, the applicant must file a correction petition.

The matter is different when, after the grant of the SPC, the applicant becomes aware of a prior marketing authorization. This usually occurs in cases involving a Swiss marketing authorization, in the situation mentioned above in §7.04[A][1]. On this issue an intervention of the IPTO Board of Appeal was necessary to persuade the IPTO to shift from its general approach and to correct the term of the granted SPC.[25] Specifically, in this case the IPTO Board of Appeal found that the IPC provisions on the national post-grant limitation of patents could be applied to the duration of SPC by analogy, so that if the correction of the SPC expiry date would result in a shortening of the duration of the SPC term then this could be achieved by filing with the IPTO a formal limitation petition (rather than a correction petition) together with a copy of the Swiss marketing authorization.

A further issue that arose recently was triggered by two CJEU decisions.

21. Article 60 IPC.
22. Article 2963(2) of the Italian civil code, Royal Decree No. 262 of 16 March 1942 and subsequent amendments thereof.
23. Article 14(2) of the Italian criminal code, Royal Decree No. 1398 of 19 October 1930 1942 and subsequent amendments thereof.
24. Article 155(1) of the Italian civil procedure code, Royal Decree No. 1443 of 28 October 1940 1942 and subsequent amendments thereof.
25. IPTO Board of Appeal, *F. Hoffmann-La Roche*, 25/17 of 10 April 2017.

The first decision is *Seattle Genetics* (C-471/14),[26] which stated that the duration of an SPC may be recalculated on the basis of the notification date of the marketing authorization instead of the date of the decision. The two dates usually differ for two or three days.

The second decision is *Incyte* (C-492/16),[27] which determined that a granted SPC may be corrected in order to bring it in accordance with the *Seattle Genetics* decision.

Up to the present time, the IPTO automatically applies the *Seattle Genetics* decision to SPC applications, calculating the duration of the SPC on the basis of the notification date. With respect to the possible correction of the duration of granted SPCs, the several correction petitions filed are being kept in a sort of limbo by the IPTO, and so there appears to be nothing to do but wait for the IPTO to determine what approach it wants to take in such connection.

[C] Paediatric Extensions

The same considerations relating to paediatric extensions as set out in the EU chapter apply also to Italy.

§7.05 PROCEDURE OF FILING AN SPC APPLICATION

[A] Entitlement to an SPC Application

The SPC application may be filed only by the patent owner. This applies also if there is an exclusive licensee of the basic patent.

If the basic patent is transferred and the transfer has been duly recorded with the IPTO, it is the assignee who is entitled to apply for an SPC.

In the absence of a correspondence between the patent owner and the SPC applicant, the IPTO will issue an office action requiring clarifications.

[B] The Time Limit for Filing an SPC Application

The same considerations relating to the time limit for filing an SPC application as set out in the EU chapter apply also to Italy.

[C] The Filing of an SPC at the National Patent Office

The SPC application is filed with the IPTO online.

26. CJEU *Seattle Genetics v. Österreichisches Patentamt*, C-471/14 of 6 October 2015.
27. CJEU *Incyte Corporation v. Szellemi Tulajdon Nemzeti Hivatala*, C-492/16 of 20 December 2017.

[D] The Documentation Required for an SPC Application

The documentation required for filing an SPC application in Italy is the one indicated in Article 8 of the SPC Regulation. Therefore, what is needed is a petition providing the name and address of the applicant(s), as well as the details of the basic patent.

The petition must enclose a copy of the first marketing authorization issued for the product in Italy, together with a copy of the SmPC. A power of attorney is required and a filing fee is to be paid.

The applicant is not required to explain how the basic patent covers the product. In very rare cases in which the link between the scope of protection of the basic patent and the SPC product is not clear, the IPTO issues an office action and requires to demonstrate this link.

If the product was previously authorized in another EU state, it is necessary to file a copy of the official gazette on which that earlier marketing authorization was published and to indicate the law provisions according to which that authorization was granted.

If any supporting document is missing at the time of filing of the application, it may be submitted within two months from the filing of the application. A further four-month extension is available, following a reasoned request.

[E] The Definition of the Product in an SPC Application

The Italian IPTO requires the product to be defined as in the marketing authorization or in the SmPC.

When the applicant files the SPC application defining the product in a way which differs from the definition appearing in the marketing authorization or in the SmPC, for instance by adding the wording 'and the pharmaceutically acceptable salts (or derivatives or esters) thereof', the IPTO issues the grant certificate with the wording, 'The SPC protects the product as a medicinal (or a plant protection product), in any of the forms enjoying the protection of the basic patent.'

The same applies in those cases where on the same basic patent and based on the same marketing approval different formulations of the same product were put on the market. A request to obtain an SPC for each of the formulations is usually rejected, with the IPTO issuing a single SPC with the wording mentioned above.[28]

[F] SPC Examination Procedure and Appeal Procedure

Italian SPC applications are examined merely from a formal point of view. In other words, the Examiner checks if the filing was carried out within the due time limit, checks for the presence of all required supporting documents and for the payment of the prescribed official fees.

28. IPTO Board of Appeal, *Aventis Holdings Inc. and Yeda Research and Development Co. Ltd.*, 11/10 of 27 January 2010.

The evaluation of the validity of the SPC and of its scope of protection are left up to the court, should those aspects be challenged by a third party.

If any supporting document is missing or if the application does not provide the necessary information, the IPTO will issue an official letter, setting a term of two months for the applicant to remedy.

This brings with it that that the possibility for the examination procedure to lead to an appeal stage before the Boards of Appeal of the IPTO is extremely rare if not null, of course if all the required documents are timely submitted.

[G] Applications for a Paediatric Extension

The requirements of an application for a paediatric extension are those indicated in Article 8(1)(d) of the SPC Regulation.

Therefore, the applicant will have to submit to the IPTO a copy of the European Commission decision containing the compliance statement relating to the agreed and completed Paediatric Investigation Plan (PIP), a copy of the amended marketing authorization and of the amended SmPC. If the authorization is not an EU one, it is necessary to confirm in the application that the product was authorized in all EU states.

In addition to such documents, applicant will have to provide a copy of the granted SPC and a power of attorney.

No official fees are required.

In case of a granted SPC, the application must be filed no later than two years before the expiry of the SPC.

As is the case for applications for an SPC, applications for a paediatric extension undergo no examination as to the merits and are checked only from a formal point of view.

§7.06 PROCEDURE OF INVALIDATING AN SPC

[A] Grounds for the Invalidation of an SPC

The applicable grounds of invalidity for an SPC in Italy are those listed in Article 15(1) of the SPC Regulations.

As discussed in the EU chapter, the list of grounds of invalidity in Article 15(1) of the SPC Regulations is regarded not to be exhaustive following the CJEU's guidance in *Hässle* (C-127/00)[29] and *Synthon* (C-195/09).[30] However, for the time being no decision was issued by an Italian court finding that an SPC is invalid on a ground which is not one of those explicitly set out in Article 15(1) of the SPC Regulations, such that in practice it remains uncertain what other grounds could be regarded by Italian courts as applicable for invalidating an SPC in Italy.

29. CJEU *Hässle v. Ratiopharm*, C-127/00 of 11 December 2003, paragraphs 90 and 91.
30. CJEU *Synthon v. Merz Pharma*, C-195/09 of 28 July 2011, paragraph 55.

[B] The Filing of an Invalidation Suit

Actions aimed at invalidating an SPC in Italy must be brought before the ordinary courts hosting a 'specialized division in company law' (*sezione specializzata in materia di impresa*).

At the time of writing (June 2018), there are twenty-two specialized divisions in company law located in the Courts of Ancona, Bari, Bologna, Bolzano, Brescia, Catania, Catanzaro, Campobasso, Cagliari, Florence, Genoa, L'Aquila, Milan, Naples, Palermo, Perugia, Potenza, Rome, Turin, Trento, Trieste and Venice, but only eleven of these specialized divisions have jurisdiction on cases involving a foreign company (i.e., the divisions located in the Courts of Bari, Bolzano, Cagliari, Catania, Genoa, Milan, Naples, Rome, Trento, Turin and Venice).

For invalidation actions, competence of the court is established on the basis of where the domicile or registered office of the defendant (i.e., SPC owner) is located. When the domicile or registered office is unknown or when the defendant does not have a domicile or registered office in Italy, the action may be filed before the court where the claimant has its domicile or registered office. If neither the defendant nor the claimant have their domicile or registered office in Italy, then the Court of Rome is competent.

While Article 15(2) of the SPC Regulations states that an invalidation action may be filed by 'any person' without restriction, in Italy it is generally accepted that the standing to sue in proceedings aimed at invalidating a patent (and hence an SPC) lies only with whomever has a commercial interest to obtain a declaration of invalidity of the patent or SPC. Italian case law tends to adopt a broad interpretation of the concept of 'commercial interest', such that a statement by the claimant to the effect that the existence of the patent or SPC is impeding the claimant's own activities is generally regarded enough to establish a commercial interest sufficient to bring an invalidation action against that patent or SPC.

As is also the case with infringement actions, in Italy it is possible to file an invalidation action against a pending SPC application.[31] In such circumstances, a decision may be rendered by the court only after the IPTO has granted the SPC application. In such cases, the IPTO examines the SPC application on an urgent basis and the court orders the suspension of the proceedings for as long as necessary to await the grant of the SPC.

[C] Invalidation Procedure and the Corresponding Appeal Procedure

There is no time limit for starting an invalidation action against an SPC (or a pending SPC application).

Invalidation proceedings begin with the claimant serving a writ of summons on the defendant, followed by the defendant's writ of appearance and counterclaim. This is then followed by a first case management hearing. At the first case management

31. Art. 120(1) IPC.

hearing, the judge may assign to both parties three terms for the submission of further procedural briefs and sets the date for the next case management hearing.

At the next case management hearing, the judge usually decides on the appointment of a court expert who will assist with the assessment of validity (and infringement, if there is a corresponding counterclaim). The assistance of a court expert – who is usually an Italian patent attorney, often also holding the title of European patent attorney – is warranted by the fact that Italian judges do not have a technical background.

Following issuance of the court expert report on validity (and infringement), a further hearing takes place to discuss with the judge the findings of the court expert. Thereafter, the judge will hold a further hearing to hear the parties' final statements, which is followed by the exchange of the parties' conclusive briefs and reply briefs, after which the judge takes a decision on the case. A final hearing to discuss the case before the decision is issued only takes place at the specific request of at least one of the parties.

First instance proceedings in an invalidation action have an average duration of 2.5–3 years (including the time required for the court expert phase), depending on the complexity of the case, the court's backlog and possible postponements (e.g., in case a suspension is necessary to allow the IPTO to grant a pending SPC).

An appeal against a first instance decision may be filed within six months from its publication or a shortened period of thirty days from service of the decision. Procedurally, appeal proceedings begin with the filing of an appeal brief, followed by the respondent's reply brief and a case management hearing. The case management hearing is usually followed by the hearing for the parties' final statements and the exchange of the parties' conclusive briefs and reply briefs, after which the panel takes a decision on the case. The average duration of appeal proceedings is usually between two to three years.

A further appeal to the Italian Supreme Court (*Corte di Cassazione*) is possible and generally takes approximately four years.

[D] The Revocation of a Paediatric Extension

In terms of procedure, the same considerations as set out in §7.06[B] and §7.06[C] above with regard to invalidation actions of an SPC also apply for paediatric extensions.

§7.07 UNFAIR COMPETITION LAW

The same considerations as set out in the EU chapter apply.

CHAPTER 8
Spain

Manuel Illescas & José Manuel González

§8.01 LEGAL BASIS

Spanish patent legislation was amended by entry into force on 1 April 2017 of the new Spanish Patent Law 24/2015. Prior to Spanish Patent Law 24/2015, Spanish patent legislation was governed by Spanish Patent Law 11/1986, which contained almost no specific legal provisions concerning Supplementary Protection Certificates (SPCs). Under Spanish Patent Law 11/1986, the legal basis for SPCs was founded in the legal provisions of Regulation (EC) 469/2009 concerning the SPC for Medicinal Products, and in the legal provisions of Regulation (EC) 1610/96 concerning the creation of an SPC for Plant Protection Products, in combination with the relevant provisions of national Spanish Patent Law 11/1986 which were also applicable to SPCs, in accordance with Article 18 of Regulation 1610/96 and Article 19 of Regulation 469/2009.

This situation changed with the entry into force of the new patent law, which contains legal provisions specifically regulating SPCs in Spain in Articles 45–47 of Spanish Patent Law 24/2015 and Articles 54–57 of Royal Decree 316/2017 approving the Implementing Regulations to Spanish Patent Law 24/2015. Said new Spanish Patent Law and the Implementing Regulations thereof constitute the legal basis for SPCs and SPC paediatric extensions, in Spain, since 1 April 2017. New Spanish Patent Law, however, is fully in line with both of the aforementioned EC Regulations.

To date, no Guidelines for the examination of SPC applications in Spain have been issued by the Spanish Patent and Trademark Office (SPTO).

§8.02 SUBSTANTIVE REQUIREMENTS FOR OBTAINING AN SPC

The guidance provided by the Court of Justice of the European Union (CJEU) is binding for all EU Member States, such that the considerations as set out in Chapter 1 (the 'EU chapter'), above, in particular in §1.02, in relation to the substantive requirements for obtaining an SPC are equally applicable to Spain.

This chapter focuses on case law and considerations of interest in Spain beyond the guidance provided by the CJEU.

[A] Types of Products That Can Be Protected

The same considerations as set out in the EU chapter equally apply here.

[1] Practical Considerations: What Is the Active Ingredient or Combination of Active Ingredients That Can Form the Basis for an SPC

The SPTO relies on the active ingredient identified in the Summary of Product Characteristics (SmPC) of the Marketing Authorization (MA), when determining the active ingredient(s) of an SPC. For certain cases requiring further clarification concerning the determination of the active ingredient(s), the SPTO may also rely on the information disclosed in the European Public Assessment Report (EPAR).

[2] Active Ingredient or Combination of Active Ingredients of a Medicinal Product

With regard to a medicinal product comprising a combination of active ingredients, that combination, as such, must be disclosed in the SmPC (Section 2). Active ingredients that are mentioned in the SmPC in sections other than Section 2 (by way of example, in Section 4, for co-administration) will be regarded as not serving as the basis for an SPC.

[3] Active Substance or Combination of Active Substances of a Plant Protection Product

Analogous to the MA for medicaments, active substances or combinations thereof must be disclosed in the MA issued for plant protection products. MAs for plant protection products are issued in Spain by the Ministry of Agriculture, in particular by the 'Dirección General de la Producción Agraria' an official general section pertaining to the 'Secretaría General de Agricultura y Alimentación'. However, the denomination of the departments in charge of issuing MAs for plant protection products may change with time. Nevertheless, the requirements set out by SPTO remain the same: for an active substance or combinations thereof, which are comprised in a plant protection product to be regarded as disclosed in an MA, and hence for said MA to act as the basis for an SPC, said active substance or combinations must be disclosed in sheet 2 of the MA, along with the name of the plant protection product and its composition.

[4] Fixed-Dose and Loose Combinations

According to the current practice of the SPTO concerning fixed-dose and loose combinations, only SPCs for 'fixed-dose' combinations, in which the different active ingredients are all formulated in the same composition, are granted in Spain.

In contrast, the SPTO currently denies grant of SPCs for loose combinations based on the fact that the corresponding MA refers to only one or several active ingredients as a component of the authorized product but not to all active ingredients of the combination in question.

To date there have been no national case law addressing this point specifically. Clarification in this regard is expected when future decisions are resolved by Spanish national courts.

[5] Limitation to Products Subjected to a Specific Marketing Authorization Procedure

In the case of SPCs for medicinal products, only 'products' that have been authorized under Directives 2001/83/EC and 2001/82/EC are accepted by the SPTO. This practice has been confirmed by the *Cerus*[1] national decision, in which the decision of the Madrid High Court of Justice confirmed the denial of an SPC. In this case, the marketing authorization was authorized under the medical devices Directive 93/42/EEC and the Spanish court decided that an SPC cannot be granted based on this medical device directive and that SPCs can only be granted based on the marketing authorizations referred to in Article 3(b) of SPC Regulation for Medicinal Products.

Special consideration must be given to SPCs based on patents directed to new therapeutic applications of previously approved active ingredients. In the *Neurim* decision of the CJEU, it was established that an SPC can be obtained for a case where the basic patent protects a new therapeutic application of a previously approved active ingredient and which relies on a new MA relating to that new therapeutic application.

However, in some cases, a new MA is not obtained for the new therapeutic application of previously approved active ingredients, since other authorization procedures are available, such as extensions of previously issued MAs, as well as type II variations of formerly issued MAs.

To date, the SPTO takes the position that extensions of MAs and type II variations of MAs are not considered a new MA in the sense of Article 3(b) of the SPC Regulation for Medicinal Products and the SPC Regulation for Plant Protection Products.

[6] Protection of Medical Devices

Only SPCs for medical devices which both contain active ingredients and have been authorized under Directives 2001/83/EC and 2001/82/EC are awarded in Spain. If the

1. Madrid High Court of Justice, decision 166/2013 of 13 February 2013 – Cerus.

medical device is authorized under any other Directive, an SPC will not be awarded, in line with the SPTO practice and the national *Cerus* decision.

[B] Basic Patent

The same considerations as set out in the EU chapter apply here equally.

[1] Requirement for the Product to Be 'Protected' by the Basic Patent

For this requirement, the SPTO applies established CJEU case law. For SPTO, the decisions *Medeva* (C-322/10) and *Eli Lilly* (C-493/12) are particularly relevant.

[a] Small Molecules

The same considerations as set out in the EU chapter apply here equally.

[b] Polymers

The same considerations as set out in the EU chapter apply here equally.

[c] Antibodies, Enzymes and Other Proteins

The definition accepted by the SPTO for these compounds, all of them sharing an amino acid sequence, is the sequence as such. No definitions based on a DNA sequence encoding said amino acid sequence, or an amino acid sequence sharing a certain degree of homology or identity with said amino acid sequence, are accepted as a product definition suitable for SPCs.

[d] Nucleic Acids

Same applies with regard to sequences based on nucleotides (nucleic acid sequences). Only the nucleic acid sequence approved in the MA for being commercially launched and protected in the basic patent, as such, can be used for defining the product subject of the SPC. An amino acid sequence encoded by said nucleic acid sequence, a nucleic acid sequence with a certain percentage of homology or identity with said approved nucleic acid sequence, a nucleic acid sequence degenerate with said approved nucleic acid sequence according to the genetic code, and a nucleic acid sequence hybridizing with said approved nucleic acid sequence, are product definitions not accepted by the SPTO in SPC applications.

[2] *Basic Patent Claiming the Product, i.e., the Active Ingredient(s), but Not the Corresponding Authorized Medicinal Product (or Plant Protection Product)*

Any SPC application filed with the above-mentioned characteristics (basic patent covering the product but not the MA), will be refused by the SPTO.

[3] *Requirement for the Product to Constitute 'the Invention' of the Basic Patent*

The product constitutes the invention if it is claimed in the basic patent. Either literally (explicitly) or implicitly, necessarily and specifically. This means that, even if the product subject of the SPC was not explicitly disclosed in the claims of the basic patent, said product might still constitute the invention of the basic patent, provided that the specification as a whole (description and claims) discloses such a product implicitly (by way of example, when comprised in a Markush formula or when defined functionally), necessarily and specifically (one way direction for selecting the product, without multiple choice from a list of candidate products).

[4] *Criteria for Choosing the Basic Patent among Various Available Patents*

There are no special guidelines for choosing the basic patent from various available patents when applying for an SPC, meaning that this is left up to the applicant and depends on the circumstances surrounding each particular case.

[C] The Marketing Authorization Forming Basis for an SPC

The same considerations as set out in the EU chapter apply here equally.

[1] *Combinations of Active Ingredients*

The same considerations as set out in the EU chapter apply here equally.

[a] *The Marketing Authorization Refers to Fewer Active Ingredients than the SPC Application*

As general principle, in Spain, an SPC cannot be granted for combinations of active ingredients, when the MA submitted with the SPC application has been issued for fewer active ingredients than the ones covered in said SPC application.

[b] The Marketing Authorization Refers to More Active Ingredients than the SPC Application

As general principle, in Spain, an SPC can be granted for combinations of active ingredients, when the MA submitted with the SPC application has been issued for more active ingredients than the ones covered in said SPC application, provided that all the ingredients of the combination for which SPC protection is sought are also comprised in the MA that is issued.

[c] The Marketing Authorization Indicates That a Medicinal Product Containing a Single Active Ingredient Is Authorized for Use in Combination with a Further Active Ingredient

Only if the further active ingredient is identified as such (active ingredient) in the SmPC (Section 2) of the MA can it be used as the basis for an SPC application. If Section 2 of the SmPC discloses, by way of example, only one active ingredient, with a second active ingredient only being mentioned in other sections of the SmPC, but not in Section 2 thereof, an SPC application for the combination of both active ingredients will be refused, even if the combination was protected as such in the basic patent.

[2] The Marketing Authorization Has Not Yet Been Granted at the Time the SPC Application Is Filed

The SPTO will refuse SPC applications based on pending MAs, even if the MA is issued when the SPC application is still pending itself.

[3] The Holder of the Marketing Authorization

The applicant for an SPC need not be the holder of the MA. In this regard, the SPTO approach is in line with *Biogen* (C-181/95), in that a patentee may rely on a third-party MA, even in the absence of the third party's consent.

[4] Reliance on a Marketing Authorization Granted under a Provision Other than Directive 2001/83/EC or Directive 2001/82/EC

In the case of SPCs for medicinal products, only 'products' that have been authorized under Directives 2001/83/EC and 2001/82/EC are accepted by the SPTO. This practice has been confirmed by the national *Cerus* decision which confirmed the denial of the SPC. In this decision, the court concluded that Article 3(b) of the EC Regulation concerning the SPC for Medicinal Products should be interpreted literally and only products authorized under said Directives are eligible for SPC protection.

[5] The Marketing Authorizations Which Can Be Relied upon for SPC Applications for Plant Protection Products

MAs for plant protection products which are issued in Spain by the Ministry of Agriculture (*see* §8.02[A][3]) form a valid basis for requesting SPCs. The only requirement is that the MA must be in force, no matter if the MA is an emergency MA or a provisional MA.

[6] The Product in Question Is Contained in the Authorized Medicinal Product (or the Authorized Plant Protection Product) but Is Not Identified as an Active Ingredient in the Corresponding Marketing Authorization

The SPTO applies a stringent interpretation of the concept of the term 'active ingredient' and does not accept SPCs for products which are not identified explicitly as such (using the wording 'active ingredient') in the corresponding MA. It is particularly important that the term 'active ingredient' is also used to identify products disclosed in the SmPC (Section 2), even though other active compounds might be mentioned therein in the prospect of them being administered jointly with the active ingredients comprised in the MA.

[7] The Notion of the 'First' Marketing Authorization

The SPTO does not examine ex officio whether the MA is the 'first' authorization to place the product on the market as a medicinal product. However, if the existence of a prior MA is subsequently revealed, it will be considered by the SPTO with regard to the compliance with the requirement of Article 3(d) of the SPC Regulation for Medicinal Products.

[a] Marketing Authorization for a New Therapeutic Application of a Previously Authorized Product

In principle, there are no particular difficulties in obtaining an SPC for an active product used in a new medical indication, if an MA covering said new use has been issued. Usually the subsequent MA for the new medical indication is for a different medicament, even though the active ingredient/s may overlap in both the first MA and the subsequent MA.

[b] Marketing Authorization for a New Formulation of a Previously Authorized Product

An SPC cannot be granted for new formulations of the same active compound, unless the formulation is used in a new medical indication. Usually, the new formulation is only considered a new medicament for the purpose of an SPC when it is for a new medical indication authorized by a subsequent MA and protected in a different basic patent.

[c] Marketing Authorization for a New Specific Salt, Ester or Other Derivative of a Previously Authorized Active Ingredient

The SPTO grants SPCs for new specific salts, esters or derivatives (specifically characterized) of previously authorized active ingredients or compounds. The Spanish Supreme Court in *Xeplion*[2] concluded that paliperidone palmitate (the active ingredient of Xeplion) is a different product with respect to paliperidone, which was itself authorized under a prior MA (*Invenga®*) and upon which an SPC has since been granted.

Fully characterized means that no SPC will be granted for general product definitions. Following with the example of paliperidone palmitate: SPC was granted for a specific ester – paliperidone palmitate. However, no SPC would have been granted for a general product definition of the kind: paliperidone esters or derivatives thereof.

[d] Marketing Authorization for a New Specific Enantiomer of an Active Ingredient Previously Authorized in Racemic Form

The SPTO has not reached any final position about this subject matter in so far as no SPC applications have been filed for enantiomers, to date.

[e] The Product Has Already Been Placed on the Market Before, but Without an Authorization Granted under Directive 2001/83/EC or Directive 2001/82/EC

No SPCs are granted in Spain if the product has not been launched in Spanish territory under an MA issued according to Directive 2001/83/EC or 2001/82/EC.

[f] Prior Marketing Authorization Which Refers to Fewer Active Ingredients than the SPC Application (and the Later Marketing Authorization Relied upon)

An SPC can be granted because the SPTO assumes that the product combination covered by the SPC application and the later MA, has not already received a prior MA. That previous MA is understood as covering a different combination wherein not all the active ingredients of the further combination subject of the SPC application were present.

2. Supreme Court, judgment STS 2601/2017 of 27 June 2017 – Xeplion.

[g] *Prior Marketing Authorization Which Refers to More Active Ingredients than the SPC Application (and the Later Marketing Authorization Relied upon)*

In contrast, an SPC cannot be granted when, previously, an MA has been issued which refers to more active ingredients than the subsequent MA upon which said SPC is based, because the SPTO takes the position that the product combination covered by the SPC and the subsequent MA has already received a prior MA. Said prior MA is understood to cover a combination that, although it might differ from that which forms the subject of the SPC application and the subsequent MA, already contains all the active ingredients of the combination which forms the subject of the SPC application.

[D] Preclusion of New SPCs by an Earlier SPC

The same considerations as set out in the EU chapter apply here equally.

[1] *Consequences of an Earlier Third-Party SPC for the Same Product*

No further SPCs can be granted so far.

[a] *The 'One SPC per Product per Patent Holder' Rule*

The SPTO applies the general principle of 'one SPC per product per patent holder' precisely, with the exemption set up in EC Regulation concerning the creation of an SPC for Plant Protection Products (Regulation (EC) 1610/96; Article 3(2)). That exemption would allow to several pending SPC applications, filed in parallel, to be issued in the name of different patent holders, for the same active product.

[b] *Earlier SPC Granted to an Affiliated Third Party*

The SPTO has adopted the pragmatic approach that patent holders who are distinct legal entities are simply accepted to be different SPC applicants, regardless of any potential affiliation between them as subsidiaries or companies belonging to the same group of companies.

[c] *Partial Overlap Between the Holders of the Earlier SPC and the Applicants for the New SPC*

Section 1.02[D][1][c] discloses the following example: the joint patent proprietors A + B have obtained a first SPC on the basis of their patent P1, and subsequently the patent proprietor A alone files a second SPC for the same product on the basis of its patent P2. In this example, the established practice of SPTO is to deny the second SPC to A in view of the first SPC granted to A + B and the 'partial overlap' between the holders of the respective patents P1 and P2.

[d] Earlier Third-Party SPC Has Been Licensed-In

No further SPC will be granted.

[2] Consequences of an Own Earlier SPC for the Same Product

No further SPC will be granted.

[a] Own Earlier SPC Application Not Yet Granted

No further SPC will be granted.

[b] Revocation, Surrender or Lapse of the Own Earlier SPC after Grant

No further SPC will be granted in case of surrender or lapse after grant of an own earlier SPC. However, if an earlier own SPC is revoked, then a further SPC may be granted due to the ex-tunc legal effect of nullity.

[c] Transfer of the Own Earlier SPC to a Third Party

No further SPC will be granted.

[d] Acquisition of an SPC Granted to a Third Party

No further SPC will be granted.

[3] Consequences of an Own Earlier SPC for a Different Product

[a] Required Distinction from the Product of the Own Earlier SPC

As a general statement, distinction of the product of an own earlier SPC and any subsequent SPC must be based on each SPC disclosing different active compounds or, in the case of combinations, different active ingredients.

New Therapeutic Applications of Previously Approved Active Ingredients

Several decisions of the Madrid High Court of Justice have addressed the denial of SPCs directed to new therapeutic applications. Those court decisions were based on earlier

SPCs having been issued for previously approved active ingredients (*Exenatide®*,[3] *HSA-absent Rebif®*,[4] *Botox®*,[5] *Ilaris®*[6] and *Abraxane®*[7] decisions). The decisions of said cases have all confirmed the denial by the SPTO of SPCs directed to combinations of active ingredients for which an SPC was previously approved, because in all cases, the national court understood that the SPCs were not directed to a new medical indication.

In the *Exenatide®* decision, the medical indication of the new and prior MAs was diabetes mellitus type 2 in both cases. The new MA is directed to a new dosage regime of the product and the court alleged that an SPC cannot be granted for a new dosage regime for the same medical indication.

In the *HSA-absent Rebif®* decision, the court decided that the medical indication (multiple sclerosis), was the same medical indication as in the prior MA for the same product (Avonex).

In the *Botox®* decision, the court decided that the medical indication (an urological disease), was the same in both the modification of the MA as well as in the original MA.

In the *Ilaris®* decision, the court reached the conclusion that the indication 'systemic juvenile idiopathic arthritis' was not considered as a new medical indication with respect to 'cryopyrin-associated periodic syndromes'.

In the *Abraxane®* decision, the first SPC was for Abraxane® monotherapy for the treatment of metastatic breast cancer and the second SPC was for Abraxane® for the treatment of metastatic adenocarcinoma of the pancreas. In this latter SPC application, Abraxane® was administered in combination with gemcitabine. The court did not consider that metastatic adenocarcinoma of the pancreas was a new medical indication with respect to metastatic breast cancer.

[b] *SPCs for a Specific Salt, Ester or Other Derivative Where an Own Earlier SPC Has Already Been Granted for the Corresponding Active Ingredient*

It remains possible to obtain a new SPC for a specific salt, ester or other derivative even when an own earlier SPC has already been granted for the corresponding active ingredient, according to recital 14 of Regulation (EC) 1610/96, provided that those salts, esters or other derivatives are protected specifically in a basic patent.

[c] *SPCs for a Specific Enantiomer Where an Own Earlier SPC Has Already Been Granted for the Corresponding Racemate*

A final position has yet to be adopted by the SPTO (neither any SPC applications having been filed for enantiomers so far, nor any Spanish case-law having yet become available).

3. Madrid High Court of Justice, judgment 45/2016 of 27 January 2016 – Exenatide.
4. Madrid High Court of Justice, judgment 630/2016 of 9 September 2016 – HSA-absent Rebif.
5. Madrid High Court of Justice, judgment 44/2017 of 25 January 2017 – Botox.
6. Madrid High Court of Justice, judgment 743/2017 of 31 October 2017 – Ilaris.
7. Madrid High Court of Justice, judgment 135/2018 of 21 February 2018 – Abraxane.

[4] *Grant of More than One SPC on the Basis of the Same Patent*

Perfectly possible.

§8.03 EXTENT OF PROTECTION AND ENFORCEMENT OF SPCs

[A] The Protection Conferred by an SPC

The considerations in terms of the protection conferred by an SPC outlined in the EU chapter apply equally to Spain.

[B] The Scope of an SPC in Relation to Derivatives of an Active Ingredient

The Supreme Court has confirmed the guidance provided in the *Farmitalia* decision of the CJEU (C-392/97),[8] according to which, if a product in the form referred to in the MA is protected by a basic patent in force, the SPC covers that product, as a medicinal product (or plant protection product), in any of the forms enjoying the protection of the basic patent. Thus, the Supreme Court in the decision *Ganirelix*[9] confirmed that the salts of the product Ganirelix are protected by the basic patent and also by the SPC and, in addition, confirmed that the definition of the product should not be limited to the content of the MA.

[1] *The Relationship Between the Definition of the Active Ingredient(s) in an SPC and Its Scope of Protection*

So far there have been no Spanish national decisions specifically addressing this point in an infringement case.

In practical terms, the scope of protection conferred by an SPC would be determined by the competent court on a case-by-case basis by interpreting SPC regulations and patent law. The wording of the SPC product definition would not be decisive for determining the scope of protection of an SPC.

[C] Enforcement of an SPC

The provisions of the Law 24/2015 concerning the scope of protection conferred by a granted patent, apply mutatis mutandis to SPCs.

In Spain patent enforcement and invalidity actions are dealt in the same court, if both grounds are raised by the parties during the same court proceedings. Article 118(2) of Law 24/2015 has established that only certain civil courts are competent for

8. CJEU *Farmitalia Carlo Erba v. Bundesgerichtshof*, C-392/97 of 16 September 1999.
9. Supreme Court, judgment 6573/2012 of 28 September 2012 – Ganirelix.

patent proceedings and, therefore, also for SPC proceedings. This provision has excluded other civil courts who were traditionally competent in patent and SPC proceedings. Currently, the competent civil courts are Madrid, Barcelona and Valencia High Courts. The court will take a decision on costs and the losing party may be liable to pay the statutory attorney fees of the other party.

Once a first-instance decision is handed down, appeal proceedings before second-instance courts are available for the parties. A further appeal to the Supreme Court against a decision handed down by the second-instance court might also be possible, but limited only to certain grounds.

It is also possible to request preliminary injunctions, as well as to file an appeal against court decisions concerning preliminary injunctions.

§8.04 DETERMINATION OF THE SPC TERM

[A] The Calculation of the SPC Term

The considerations regarding the calculation of the SPC term as set out in the EU chapter apply equally to Spain.

[1] The Relevant Marketing Authorization for the Term of an SPC

The considerations in terms of the relevant MA for determining the SPC term as set out in the EU chapter apply equally to Spain.

The SPTO does not examine ex officio if the MA is the 'first' authorization to place the product on the market as a medicinal product. However, if the existence of a prior MA is subsequently revealed and needs to be considered, then a correction of the SPC term may be requested by the applicant as well as by a third party. For doing so, the applicant may file a written request of correction and pay a prescribed fee, as communicated by the SPTO on 19 January 2018 and as provided in Article 49 of Law 24/2015 and Article 109.2 of Law 39/2015.[10]

Currently, Type II variations and extensions of MAs are not considered to constitute a new MA by the SPTO. The SPTO would also not consider variations or extensions as the relevant MA for the determination of the SPC term for a product which has been approved for a new therapeutic use. Clarification in this regard may be expected in the future if the acceptance of extensions and type II variations of MAs is specifically addressed by Spanish national courts or by the CJEU.

[2] The Expiration Date of an SPC

Article 58 of Law 24/2015 establishes that the patent term is twenty years from the date of filing. The calculation of time limits is governed by Article 30(3)–30(5) of Law

10. Law 39/2015 on Common Administrative Procedure of the Public Administration.

39/2015, and according to said provisions, the patent term ends on the same day in the year of expiration, which is the twentieth anniversary of its filing date. Accordingly, an SPC with a full five-year term will expire on the twenty-fifth anniversary of the filing date of the patent.

For example, a Spanish SPC which is based on a patent filed on 15 June 2000 and an MA notified on 10 August 2007 (which was the first MA for this product in the EU and the EEA). Said SPC will come into effect the following day upon expiry of the basic patent, i.e., on 16 June 2020, and the aforesaid SPC will expire on 10 August 2022. If, in this example, the MA is notified on or after 15 June 2010 the SPC will have the maximum term of five years and will thus expire on 15 June 2025.

[B] Correction of the SPC Term

It is possible to correct the duration of an SPC in Spain at any time, provided that the SPC has not expired, as acknowledged by the *Incyte* decision of the CJEU (C-492/16). As communicated by the SPTO on 19 January 2018 and as provided in Article 49 of Law 24/2015 and Article 109.2 of Law 39/2015, it is sufficient for the applicant/owner of the SPC to file a written request of correction and pay a prescribed fee. Thus, it is not mandatory for the applicant/owner of the SPC to file an appeal.

It is also possible to correct the duration in cases of granted SPCs in which a Swiss-Liechtenstein MA was not considered as the first authorization to place the product on the market within the meaning of Article 13 of SPC Regulation for Medicinal Products. The correction can be requested at any time following grant of such an SPC, provided that the SPC has not expired. This is available as provided by the aforementioned *Incyte* decision of the CJEU in conjunction with the *Novartis* decisions of the CJEU (C-207/03 and C-252/03).

[C] Paediatric Extensions

The considerations in terms of paediatric extensions as set out in the EU chapter apply equally to Spain.

However, the SPTO ruled on a case where two different MAs (MA1 and MA2) were held for the same medicament in the name of the same company but with each under different trademarks (this the only difference between the two MAs that were issued), and where MA1, which was used as a basis for the granted SPC, was withdrawn (once the SPC had been issued), while MA2, which was used for requesting the paediatric investigation plan (PIP) approved by European Medicines Agency (EMA), was kept in force. In this case, the SPTO granted the SPC extension, in spite of the fact, that MA1 was different to MA2.

§8.05 PROCEDURE OF FILING AN SPC APPLICATION

[A] Entitlement to an SPC Application

In Spain, it is only the patent owner who is entitled to file an SPC application. As such, a licensee of the basic patent may not file an SPC application even if the patent owner has given his express authorization to do so.

Likewise, if the basic patent has been transferred, it is only the registered patent owner who may file the SPC.

If there is a discrepancy between the applicant for an SPC and the registered owner of the basic patent, the SPTO will invite the applicant to correct this deficiency.

[B] The Time Limit for Filing an SPC Application

The considerations as set out in the EU chapter apply. The provisions for the re-establishment of rights as provided for patents in Article 53 of Law 24/2015 apply to all industrial property rights regulated under Law 24/2015, thus, the provisions for reinstatement of patents also apply to SPCs. In particular, the provisions for the re-establishment of rights apply to the deadline to file an SPC application and the deadline to pay the SPC maintenance fees.

In Spain, all due care must be proven for obtaining re-establishment of rights.

[C] The Filing of an SPC at the National Patent Office

The SPC application must contain all relevant information as specified in Article 8 of the SPC Regulations. Specifically, the SPC applications must contain the name and address of the applicant and his representative, when a representative has been appointed, as well as the number and title of the basic patent, the number, date and European Union (EU) or European Economic Area (EAA) Member State of the first authorization to place the product on the EEA market, when the MA for Spain is not the first authorization, and the number and date of the MA to place the product on the market in Spain.

The product must be specified in the SPC application, as explained in §8.05[E]. The filing fee should also be paid upon filing.

[D] The Documentation Required for an SPC Application

An SPC application must be accompanied by the documents required set out in Article 8 of the SPC Regulations.

The SPC application should be supplemented with a copy of the MA to place the product on the market in Spain together with the Summary of Product Characteristics (SmPC).

In addition, if the first authorization to place the product on the market is not a Spanish or a central authorization, but was granted in another EU or EEA Member

State, the applicant should submit information regarding both the identity of the product thus authorized and the legal provision under which the authorization procedure took place, together with a copy and a translation of the notice publishing the authorization in the appropriate official publication, or a copy and a translation of the first MA.

In addition, information explaining that the product is protected by the basic patent has to be filed, as established by Article 54.1.a).ii) and 54.1.b).ii) Royal Decree 316/2017.[11]

Filing of a power of attorney is not required.

[E] The Definition of the Product in an SPC Application

The product of an SPC should be defined on the basis of the active ingredient(s) as identified in the MA.

The SPTO typically objects to broad product definitions with a generalized statement 'in all forms as protected by the basic patent'. If the product definition is objected too, the applicant will be invited to correct the product definition within a period of two months, extendable for two additional months upon request.

[F] SPC Examination Procedure and Appeal Procedure

Once an SPC application is filed, the SPTO verifies that the application fee has been paid and that the application contains the necessary information for its publication, namely the name and address of the SPC applicant, the number of the basic patent, the title of the invention, the number and date of the first MA to place the product on the market in Spain or the number and date of the first authorization to place the product on the market in the EU or EEA. If any information required for publishing the SPC application is missing, the applicant will be invited to provide said missing information within a non-extendable period of ten days. Although the period is short, providing said missing information appears to be straightforward. Once this formal examination is complete, the SPTO will publish said information in the Spanish Official Industrial Property Gazette within a period of three months.

The SPTO will examine the requirements under Article 3(a), (b) and (c) of the EC Regulation concerning the SPC for Medicinal Products and under Article 3(1)(a), (b) and (c) of the EC Regulation concerning the creation of an SPC for Plant Protection Products. The SPTO does not examine ex officio if the MA is the 'first' authorization to place the product on the market as a medicinal product as set out in Article 46(1) of Law of Patents 24/2015.

If the SPTO finds any deficiency or if the SPC application does not meet any of the requirements of the SPC Regulations, the SPTO will issue an office action inviting the applicant to correct the deficiencies within a period of two months, extendable for two

11. Royal Decree 316/2017 approving the Implementing Regulations for the Law of Patents 24/2015.

additional months upon request. Typically, no more than one or two office actions are issued.

In Spain, the maximum duration of SPC proceedings has been established at ten months from publication of the SPC application to arrive at a final decision if no official action has been issued during prosecution, and fifteen months from publication of the SPC application if an official action has been issued during prosecution. That gives a total of a maximum of twelve to nineteen months from filing to obtain grant (or rejection) of an SPC application.

Prosecution may be stayed under certain circumstances, such as pending proceedings in the European Union which affect the Spanish national proceedings, as provided by Article 22 of Law 39/2015. This provision was introduced in said Law 39/2015, which entered into force on 2 October 2016, and was not available before said date.

Requests for acceleration of proceedings are not available. When an SPC application is filed shortly before expiration of the patent to which it pertains, the SPTO accelerates proceedings in order to reach an examination decision before expiration of the basic patent, whenever possible. This is not always possible, and the examination decision may be reached after expiration of the patent, which is not a desirable situation from the point of view of legal certainty.

Third-party observations are available for patents but are not explicitly foreseen for SPCs under the new Law 24/2015 and implementing regulations thereof. Nevertheless, third-party observations have been filed and are being filed in Spain during SPC examination proceedings and are usually reviewed by the examiners. When a third party files observations, the applicant is not informed of them by the SPTO. If the examiner is of the opinion that any ground of the third-party observations is valid, then the examiner will object to the SPC application on this same ground in an office action, but without explicitly mentioning that it relates to third-party observations.

If the SPTO considers that the SPC application meets the requirements of SPC regulations, the SPTO will issue the decision to grant the certificate for the duration of its term and, if appropriate, its paediatric extension. In contrast, in case objections raised in the office action issued by SPTO have not been overcome by the SPC applicant, a decision to reject the SPC application will be issued.

The decisions of the SPTO may be appealed pursuant to Article 46(2) and the First Additional Provision of Law 24/2015 in conjunction with Articles 121 and 122 of Law 39/2015.

An administrative appeal against such a decision must be lodged in writing with the SPTO within one month of the publication of the decision of grant or rejection of the SPC application, together with the payment of an appeal fee.

If the administrative appeal is dismissed by the SPTO, that decision may be further appealed before national contentious-administrative courts handling contentious-administrative proceedings, as set out in Article 54 of Law 24/2015.

[G] Applications for a Paediatric Extension

The formal requirements for filing a paediatric extension correspond to those as outlined in the EU chapter. The request for a paediatric extension must be accompanied by the payment of a prescribed fee.

If the product has not been approved centrally by the EMA, it is necessary for the applicant to submit proof of possession of MAs for the product in all EU and EEA Member States. The documents submitted as proof of possession must be accompanied by a statement detailing the content of the documentation indicating the EU and EEA Member State to which it corresponds, as provided in Article 54(1)(c) of Royal Decree 316/2017. Translation into Spanish of this documentation is not required.

Prosecution of paediatric extensions with regards to office actions, stay of proceedings, acceleration of proceedings and re-establishment of rights is analogous to the prosecution of SPCs.

§8.06 PROCEDURE OF INVALIDATING AN SPC

In Spain, the patent owner may revoke or limit partially their patent while it is still in force or even later. If an SPC based on said revoked or limited patent is in force, as provided by Article 105(1) of Law 24/2015, that SPC is also considered to be revoked or ultimately limited. If an SPC is considered revoked, this status will be made public in the national register and can, therefore, be verified by consulting said register.

Revocation of an SPC by the patent owner before the SPTO is not possible since it is not foreseen in Spanish national law.

[A] Grounds for the Invalidation of an SPC

In Spain, an SPC can be invalidated on the grounds set out in Article 15 of the SPC Regulations and in the decisions of the CJEU, as discussed in the EU chapter.

[B] The Filing of an Invalidation Suit

As provided in Article 15(2) of the SPC Regulations, any person may file a request for a declaration of invalidity of an SPC before the national courts in Spain.

The provisions for the invalidity of a patent as provided in Articles 102–104 of Law 24/2015 also apply to SPCs. A request for the invalidation of an SPC may be filed from the date on which the SPC enters into force and at any time along its normal or extended duration.

[C] Invalidation Procedure and the Corresponding Appeal Procedure

The procedure for invalidating an SPC may be accomplished, independent of any infringement procedures, via the filing of an invalidation suit before the contentious-administrative courts handling contentious-administrative proceedings (at the end of the administrative proceedings) or any time before civil national courts (nullity proceedings).

It is also possible to claim the invalidity of an SPC in the course of an infringement procedure before a civil court, as a defensive counterclaim.

The court will take a decision on costs and the losing party may be liable to pay the statutory attorney fees of the other party.

Decisions of courts handling contentious-administrative proceedings are appealable before second instance courts as the High Court of Justice (Audiencia Nacional) and up to the Supreme Court.

Decisions of civil courts are appealable at courts of the second instance and, in a third level of proceedings, before the Supreme Court only under specific limited legal grounds.

[D] The Revocation of a Paediatric Extension

As set out in the EU chapter, a paediatric extension can be invalidated on the grounds of Article 16 of the EC Regulation concerning the SPC for Medicinal Products.

Procedurally speaking, the same considerations as set out in §8.06[B] and §8.06[C] above for the revocation of an SPC apply.

§8.07 UNFAIR COMPETITION LAW

The *Aricept*[12] decision of the Barcelona Provincial Court dealt with unfair competition issues. The active ingredient of Aricept is donepezil and Aricept itself is marketed for the palliative treatment of Alzheimer's disease. In this case, a generic medicament was included in the national health system three years before the expiration of the SPC. After inclusion of the medicament in the national health system, a reference price for medicaments with donepezil as an active ingredient was established, after which date Aricept could not be sold at a price exceeding this reference price.

However, the decision in the aforementioned second-instance court, concluded that, including a generic medicament in the national health system three years before expiration of the SPC is an act of unfair competition.

12. Barcelona Provincial Court (Audiencia Provincial de Barcelona), decision of 22 January 2013 – Aricept®.

CHAPTER 9

Portugal

Gonçalo de Sampaio & Nuno Gouveia

§9.01 LEGAL BASIS

In Portuguese national law, the central legal provisions governing SPCs are contained in Articles 115–116 of the Industrial Property Code (Código da Propriedade Industrial), approved by the decree-Law 36/2003, dated 5 March 2003, and modified by Decree-Law No. 318/2007, dated 26 September 2007, No. 360/2007, dated 2 November 2007, No. 142/2008, dated 25 July 2008 and by the Law No. 16/2008, dated 1 April 2008.

These Articles refer to the procedural rules that apply to the application of an SPC, the application for an extension of an SPC, and also the examination and publication phase.

§9.02 SUBSTANTIVE REQUIREMENTS FOR OBTAINING AN SPC

As the guidance provided by the CJEU is binding for all EU Member States, the considerations as set out in Chapter 1 (the 'EU chapter'), specifically in §1.02 above, in relation to the substantive requirements for obtaining an SPC, in as far as they have been addressed by the CJEU, are equally applicable in Portugal.

[A] Types of Products That Can Be Protected

The same considerations as set out in the EU chapter apply.

[1] Practical Considerations: What Is the Active Ingredient or Combination of Active Ingredients That Can Form the Basis for an SPC

The same considerations as set out in the EU chapter apply.

[2] Active Ingredient or Combination of Active Ingredients of a Medicinal Product

The same considerations as set out in the EU chapter apply.

[3] Active Substance or Combination of Active Substances of a Plant Protection Product

The same considerations as set out in the EU chapter apply.

[4] Fixed-Dose and Loose Combinations

The same considerations as set out in the EU chapter apply.

[5] Limitation to Products Subjected to a Specific Marketing Authorization Procedure

The same considerations as set out in the EU chapter apply.

[6] Protection of Medical Devices

The same considerations as set out in the EU chapter apply.

[B] Basic Patent

The same considerations as set out in the EU chapter apply.

[1] Requirement for the Product to Be 'Protected' by the Basic Patent

The same considerations as set out in the EU chapter apply.

[a] Small Molecules

The same considerations as set out in the EU chapter apply.

[b] Polymers

The same considerations as set out in the EU chapter apply.

[c] Antibodies, Enzymes and Other Proteins

The same considerations as set out in the EU chapter apply.

[d] Nucleic Acids

The same considerations as set out in the EU chapter apply.

[2] Basic Patent Claiming the Product, i.e., the Active Ingredient(s), but Not the Corresponding Authorized Medicinal Product (or Plant Protection Product)

The same considerations as set out in the EU chapter apply.

[3] Requirement for the Product to Constitute 'the Invention' of the Basic Patent

The same considerations as set out in the EU chapter apply.

[4] Criteria for Choosing the Basic Patent among Various Available Patents

The same considerations as set out in the EU chapter apply.

[C] The Marketing Authorization Forming Basis for an SPC

The same considerations as set out in the EU chapter apply.

[1] Combinations of Active Ingredients

The same considerations as set out in the EU chapter apply.

[a] The Marketing Authorization Refers to Fewer Active Ingredients than the SPC Application

The same considerations as set out in the EU chapter apply.

[b] The Marketing Authorization Refers to More Active Ingredients than the SPC Application

The same considerations as set out in the EU chapter apply.

[c] The Marketing Authorization Indicates That a Medicinal Product Containing a Single Active Ingredient Is Authorized for Use in Combination with a Further Active Ingredient

The same considerations as set out in the EU chapter apply.

[2] The Marketing Authorization Has Not Yet Been Granted at the Time the SPC Application Is Filed

The same considerations as set out in the EU chapter apply.

[3] The Holder of the Marketing Authorization

The same considerations as set out in the EU chapter apply.

[4] Reliance on a Marketing Authorization Granted under a Provision Other than Directive 2001/83/EC or Directive 2001/82/EC

The same considerations as set out in the EU chapter apply.

[5] The Marketing Authorizations Which Can Be Relied upon for SPC Applications for Plant Protection Products

The same considerations as set out in the EU chapter apply.

[6] The Product in Question Is Contained in the Authorized Medicinal Product (or the Authorized Plant Protection Product) but Is Not Identified as an Active Ingredient in the Corresponding Marketing Authorization

The same considerations as set out in the EU chapter apply.

[7] The Notion of the 'First' Marketing Authorization

The same considerations as set out in the EU chapter apply.

[a] Marketing Authorization for a New Therapeutic Application of a Previously Authorized Product

The same considerations as set out in the EU chapter apply.

[b] Marketing Authorization for a New Formulation of a Previously Authorized Product

The same considerations as set out in the EU chapter apply.

[c] Marketing Authorization for a New Specific Salt, Ester or Other Derivative of a Previously Authorized Active Ingredient

The same considerations as set out in the EU chapter apply.

[d] Marketing Authorization for a New Specific Enantiomer of an Active Ingredient Previously Authorized in Racemic Form

The same considerations as set out in the EU chapter apply.

[e] The Product Has Already Been Placed on the Market Before, but Without an Authorization Granted under Directive 2001/83/EC or Directive 2001/82/EC

The same considerations as set out in the EU chapter apply.

[f] Prior Marketing Authorization Which Refers to Fewer Active Ingredients than the SPC Application (and the Later Marketing Authorization Relied upon)

The same considerations as set out in the EU chapter apply.

[g] Prior Marketing Authorization Which Refers to More Active Ingredients than the SPC Application (and the Later Marketing Authorization Relied upon)

The same considerations as set out in the EU chapter apply.

[D] Preclusion of New SPCs by an Earlier SPC

The same considerations as set out in the EU chapter apply.

[1] Consequences of an Earlier Third-Party SPC for the Same Product

[a] The 'One SPC per Product per Patent Holder' Rule

The same considerations as set out in the EU chapter apply.

[b] Earlier SPC Granted to an Affiliated Third Party

The same considerations as set out in the EU chapter apply.

[c] Partial Overlap Between the Holders of the Earlier SPC and the Applicants for the New SPC

The same considerations as set out in the EU chapter apply. It appears that this issue has not yet been specifically addressed in the Portuguese case law.

[d] Earlier Third-Party SPC Has Been Licensed-In

The same considerations as set out in the EU chapter apply.

[2] Consequences of an Own Earlier SPC for the Same Product

The same considerations as set out in the EU chapter apply.

[a] Own Earlier SPC Application Not Yet Granted

The same considerations as set out in the EU chapter apply.

[b] Revocation, Surrender or Lapse of the Own Earlier SPC after Grant

The same considerations as set out in the EU chapter apply,

[c] Transfer of the Own Earlier SPC to a Third Party

The same considerations as set out in the EU chapter apply.

[d] Acquisition of an SPC Granted to a Third Party

The same considerations as set out in the EU chapter apply.

[3] *Consequences of an Own Earlier SPC for a Different Product*

The same considerations as set out in the EU chapter apply.

[a] *Required Distinction from the Product of the Own Earlier SPC*

The same considerations as set out in the EU chapter apply.

Combinations of Active Ingredients

The same considerations as set out in the EU chapter apply.

New Therapeutic Applications of Previously Approved Active Ingredients

The same considerations as set out in the EU chapter apply.

[b] *SPCs for a Specific Salt, Ester or Other Derivative Where an Own Earlier SPC Has Already Been Granted for the Corresponding Active Ingredient*

The same considerations as set out in the EU chapter apply.

[c] *SPCs for a Specific Enantiomer Where an Own Earlier SPC Has Already Been Granted for the Corresponding Racemate*

The same considerations as set out in the EU chapter apply.

[4] *Grant of More than One SPC on the Basis of the Same Patent*

The same considerations as set out in the EU chapter apply.

§9.03 EXTENT OF PROTECTION AND ENFORCEMENT OF SPCs

[A] The Protection Conferred by an SPC

The considerations in terms of the protection conferred by an SPC outlined in the EU chapter apply equally to Portugal.

Accordingly, Articles 4 and 5 of the SPC Regulations must be interpreted such that while in line with Article 5 the effects of an SPC are identical to the effects of the underlying basic patent, Article 4 determines the object of these effects, namely the approved product, in order to delimit it from other substances which potentially are also encompassed by the basic patent. As such, Article 4 of the SPC Regulations does not aim for a limitation to the specific authorized medicinal (or plant protection) product. The limitation of the subject matter of a certificate in Article 4 of the SPC

Regulations as a whole has to be understood in the sense that it has the sole purpose of excluding an 'over-extensive' protection.

The scope of protection of an SPC is thus determined on the basis of the underlying patent, but limited to the product for which the SPC has been granted.

[B] The Scope of an SPC in Relation to Derivatives of an Active Ingredient

Decisions on this topic are not known.

[1] The Relationship Between the Definition of the Active Ingredient(s) in an SPC and Its Scope of Protection

The Portuguese PTO allows, in general terms, an SPC to be granted with a broader product definition, beyond the specific form of the active ingredient identified in the marketing authorization (e.g., by the inclusion of pharmaceutically acceptable salts of the active ingredient). However, Court Jurisprudence on this topic is not known.

[C] Enforcement of an SPC

As set out in Portuguese Law, the provisions of the Portuguese Industrial Property Code, regarding patents, and namely patent infringement (as well as the effect of the patent and exceptions thereto, the scope of protection, and compulsory licences) apply mutatis mutandis to SPCs.

In Portugal all Portuguese Patent office decisions may be appealed before the Intellectual Property Court (Tribunal da Propriedade Intelectual).

Also, this IP Court is responsible for handling all actions related with IP rights infringements. The IP Court decision may be appealed to the Second Instance Court (Tribunal da Relação de Lisboa).

The costs of an infringement action are calculated always with the legal value of EUR 30,000.01, in order to allow an appeal to be filed. Court fees are calculated on the basis of the value.

The losing party is liable to pay the most relevant part of court fees and reimburse the statutory attorney fees of the other party.

The first-instance decision is typically handed down within ten to fifteen months after the filing of the infringement suit. The appeal proceedings before the Second Instance Court typically take about twelve to fifteen months.

Injunction requests must also be filed before the IP Court. If the infringing product is in the market there is no need to proof 'irreparable harm'. The existence of the right and the strong allegations that it is being infringed should suffice. Injunction decisions are usually taken in few months.

Appeal proceedings relating to preliminary injunctions typically take about six months until a final appeal decision is available.

In parallel with the competence of the IP Court, it was enacted a Decree Law No. 62/2001, dated 12 December 2011, to handle disputes between pharmaceutical patent owners and generics products.

In case of pharmaceutical patents, in which there is a litigation between patent owners and marketing authorizations applicants, it is mandatory to use the arbitration system.

The patent/SPC owner has thirty days, from the publication on the Health Authority website of the MA application, to initiate an arbitration proceeding. If the generic company (owner of the related MA applications) does not answer to said arbitration, it will not be able to use the MA in the market while patent/SPC invoked is in force.

Arbitration Court decisions are possible to appeal to the Second Instance Court (Tribunal da Relação de Lisboa). Current jurisprudence is divided on whether or not the arbitration court may declare the patent/SPC null, and if yes with inter partes effect or erga omnes effect.

§9.04 DETERMINATION OF THE SPC TERM

[A] The Calculation of the SPC Term

The considerations regarding the calculation of the SPC term as set out in the EU chapter apply equally to Portugal.

[1] The Relevant Marketing Authorization for the Term of an SPC

The considerations in terms of the relevant marketing authorization for determining the SPC term as set out in the EU chapter apply equally to Portugal.

[2] The Expiration Date of an SPC

The term of a patent shall be twenty years beginning on the filing date. The last day when a patent is in force is the twentieth anniversary of its filing date. Accordingly, an SPC with a full five-year term will expire on the twenty-fifth anniversary of the filing date of the patent.

[B] Correction of the SPC Term

Legal practice in Portugal allows such a correction, in accordance with EU rules.

[C] Paediatric Extensions

The considerations in terms of paediatric extensions as set out in the EU chapter apply equally to Portugal.

§9.05 PROCEDURE OF FILING AN SPC APPLICATION

[A] Entitlement to an SPC Application

In Portugal, it is only the patentee who is entitled to file an SPC application.

If there is a discrepancy between the applicant for an SPC and the registered owner of the basic patent, the Portuguese PTO may refuse the same, but usually notifies for correction.

[B] The Time Limit for Filing an SPC Application

The considerations as set out in the EU chapter apply to Portugal.

[C] The Filing of an SPC at the National Patent Office

As set out in the EU chapter, an SPC must be filed before the national patent office within the stipulated time limits, once the basic patent as well as the relevant marketing authorization have issued. The SPC application must be filed in writing, using the prescribed form issued by the Portuguese Patent Office, and must contain all relevant information about the applicant and his representative (names and addresses), as well as details in terms of the basic patent and the marketing authorization (number and date) relied upon for the product in question. The prescribed fee must be paid on filing.

No power of attorney is required if the representative is an Industrial Property Official Agent (Agente Oficial da Propriedade Industrial).

[D] The Documentation Required for an SPC Application

The documentation required for filing an SPC application in Portugal is based on the requirements as set out in Article 8 of the SPC Regulations.

The SPC request should be supplemented with copies of the marketing authorization to place the product on the market in the EU.

The applicant should also provide information as to how the product is protected by the basic patent.

[E] The Definition of the Product in an SPC Application

The Portuguese legal practice is that the product of an SPC should be defined on the basis of the active ingredient(s). It must also be filed the SmPC as well as the marketing authorization for the corresponding medicinal product.

[F] SPC Examination Procedure and Appeal Procedure

In line with Portuguese legal practice of the Portuguese PTO, an application for an SPC will be subject to a formal examination, followed by a substantive examination.

The formal examination focuses on issues such as the time limits for filing the SPC, the payment of the prescribed fees, the formal entitlement of the applicant, as well as the question as to whether the patent is in force and the documentation submitted is complete. If there are deficits in this regard or if any documentation is missing, the Portuguese PTO will invite the applicant to rectify this.

The substantive examination includes the verification that the marketing authorization was granted in accordance with the appropriate directives and is valid at the filing date.

During the examination the identity of the product is established and it is verified that the product is protected by the basic patent.

If an SPC application is considered to be deficient, the Portuguese PTO shall issue a notification inviting the applicant to correct the deficiencies within an extendable two-month time limit.

A notification for formal issues is usually issued within three to four months from filing date.

If the application for the SPC is in compliance with the statutory requirements, the Portuguese PTO will issue the decision to grant the certificate for the duration of its term and, if appropriate, its paediatric extension.

Alternatively, a reasoned decision to reject the certificate will issue. The decisions of the patent division may be appealed to the IP Court, within two months.

Also an internal Appeal to the Board of the Portuguese PTO may be filed, with the same two months' term. Said appeal will suspend the deadline for the IP Court Appeal.

A final decision from the IP Court may be expected within about eighteen months to twenty-four months after the filing of the appeal.

[G] Applications for a Paediatric Extension

The formal requirements for filing a paediatric extension correspond to those as outlined in the EU chapter.

The request for a paediatric extension must be filed with the Portuguese PTO together with the prescribed fee, using the prescribed form.

The required supporting documents are set out in Article 8(1)(d) of the SPC Regulation for Medicinal Products. These include a copy of the statement indicating compliance with the agreed and completed Paediatric Investigation Plan (PIP).

The examination procedures follow the steps of an SPC application, seen in §9.05[F] above.

§9.06 PROCEDURE OF INVALIDATING AN SPC

Provisions of the IP Code in relation to the revocation of a patent also apply to SPCs.

[A] Grounds for the Invalidation of an SPC

The grounds for invalidating an SPC in Portugal correspond to the grounds as set out in Article 15 of the SPC Regulations, as discussed in the EU chapter.

[B] The Filing of an Invalidation Suit

The invalidation action must be filed before the IP Court.

An action for the invalidation of an SPC may be filed at any time by any person, independent from any pending infringement proceedings.

[C] Invalidation Procedure and the Corresponding Appeal Procedure

An invalidation suit against an SPC may be initiated at any time after the grant of the SPC.

The IP Court is responsible for handling all actions related with IP rights infringements. The IP Court decision may be appealed to the Second Instance Court (Tribunal da Relação de Lisboa).

The costs of an infringement action are calculated always with the legal value of EUR 30,000.01, in order to allow an appeal to be filed. Court fees are calculated on the basis of the value.

The losing party is liable to pay the most relevant part of court fees and reimburse the statutory attorney fees of the other party.

The first-instance decision is typically handed down within twelve to eighteen months after the filing of the infringement suit. The appeal proceedings before the Second Instance Court typically take about twelve months.

Proceedings could be stayed in view of a pending CJEU referral that concerns the same legal questions.

[D] The Revocation of a Paediatric Extension

As set out in the EU chapter, the grounds for revocation of a paediatric extension correspond to those of Article 16 of the SPC Regulation for Medicinal Products.

The same considerations as set out in §9.06[B] and §9.06[C] above for the revocation of an SPC apply.

§9.07 UNFAIR COMPETITION LAW

The same considerations as set out in the EU chapter apply. Antitrust issues involving SPCs have not yet been specifically addressed in the Portuguese case law.

CHAPTER 10

Sweden

Camilla Lidén & Gustaf Örn

§10.01 LEGAL BASIS

In Swedish national law,[1] legal provisions governing SPCs are contained in Sections 105 and 106 of the Swedish Patents Act (Patentlagen, 'PatL'), which were introduced with effect of 8 February 1997, and 1 January 1995, respectively. Further legal provisions are provided in Sections 67 and 68 of the Decree on Patent Formalities (Patentkungörelsen, 'PatK'), and in Sections 56 and 59 of the Patent Office Regulations (Patentbestämmelserna, 'PB').

Section 105 PatL provides that an application fee is payable for an SPC application, and that renewal fees are payable for a granted SPC. According to Section 106 PatL, the provisions laid down in Chapter 9 of PatL [Liability and Obligation to Pay Compensation, etc.] regarding liability, shall also apply to SPCs.

According to Section 67 PatK an SPC application shall be drafted in Swedish or English. Section 68 PatK [Patent Register] provides that the publicly accessible patent register shall contain the information which has been made publically available according to Articles 9(2), 11, and 16 of Regulation (EEC) 1768/92, and Articles 9(2), 11, and 16 of Regulation (EC) 1610/96, respectively, and also information about annuities paid. A list of fees is appended to PatK, which also includes the relevant application and renewal fees.

1. The Swedish Patents Act (in Swedish) is available from the Swedish Patent and Registration Office webpage: https://www.prv.se/sv/patent/. *See also*: http://www.riksdagen.se/sv/dokument-lagar/dokument/svensk-forfattningssamling/patentlag-1967837_sfs-1967-837. An unofficial English translation of the Swedish Patents Act is also available: https://www.prv.se/globalassets/dokument/patent/informationsmaterial/the-patents-act---unofficial-translation.pdf. The Decree on Patent Formalities and the Patent Office Regulations are not available in English.

Section 56 PB and Section 59 PB both relate to time limits in office actions issued in view of SPC applications.

The patent department of the Swedish Patent and Registration Office (SPRO) also issues guidelines which constitute internal rules on policy and interpretation in cases where the legal provisions allow for different assessments during examination (herein 'guidelines')[2] (Riktlinjer, 'RL').

The guidelines are provided in the Swedish language only and include a chapter on SPCs, i.e., Chapter 10 of Part B ('B10') of the guidelines [SPC for Medicinal Products and Plant Protection Products]. The guidelines are not legally binding and only serve as guidance to the examiners of the patent department.

§10.02 SUBSTANTIVE REQUIREMENTS FOR OBTAINING AN SPC

As the guidance provided by the CJEU is binding for all EU Member States, the considerations as set out in Chapter 1 (the 'EU chapter'), specifically in §1.02 above, in relation to the substantive requirements for obtaining an SPC, in as far as they have been addressed by the CJEU, are equally applicable in Sweden.

The following discussion will therefore focus on case law and considerations of interest in Sweden beyond the guidance provided by the CJEU. In this regard, the intellectual property right court system was reformed, and a new court system was established in Sweden on 1 September 2016, as set out in §10.03[C] below.

In practice, the new court system introduces a new second-instance court and case law from said new second-instance court is gradually evolving, including case law relating to SPCs. Below, reference is also given to case law of the Court of Patent Appeals, which was the first-instance court to which decision from the SPRO was appealed before the court system was reformed in 2016.

[A] Types of Products That Can Be Protected

The same considerations as set out in the EU chapter apply.

[1] Practical Considerations: What Is the Active Ingredient or Combination of Active Ingredients That Can Form the Basis for an SPC

The same considerations as set out in the EU chapter apply.

2. The guidelines (RL), in Swedish only, for SPCs are available at: https://www.prv.se/sv/patent/lagar-och-regler/riktlinjer/.

[2] *Active Ingredient or Combination of Active Ingredients of a Medicinal Product*

Point 1.2 of the guidelines (RL), [Certain Definitions of relevance for the SPC] defines the interpretation of the term 'active ingredient' or 'combination of active ingredients' used by the SPRO. In practice, the SPRO emphasizes a strict interpretation of the term 'active ingredient' with reference to *Forsgren* (C-631/13)[3] 'the respective substances must produce a pharmacological, immunological or metabolic action of their own' with further reference e.g., to *MIT* (C-431/04)[4] and *Glaxo Smithkline* (C-210/13),[5] to which particular weight is given in the aftermath of *Neurim* (C-130/11).[6] This interpretation has also been confirmed by the first-instance Patent and Market Court[7] and previously by the Court of Patent Appeals.[8] Although the SPRO and the first-instance courts have acknowledged the interpretation of 'active ingredient' as brought forward in *Forsgren,* there seem to have been no general reflections on the possible broadened interpretation of this term as compared to CJEU case law preceding *Forsgren.*

In a recent decision from the Patent and Market Court,[9] it was confirmed that an ingredient of a medicinal product, isopropyl myristate, referred to in the Summary of Product Characteristics (SmPC) as an 'excipient', did not qualify as an active ingredient. Therefore, an SPC could not be granted for a combination of active ingredients comprising isopropyl myristate, even though such combination was protected by the basic patent. The fact that the basic patent referred to isopropyl myristate as an active ingredient did not alter the Court's interpretation of isopropyl myristate as being an excipient as set out in the SmPC.

[3] *Active Substance or Combination of Active Substances of a Plant Protection Product*

The same considerations as set out in the EU chapter apply. According to the guidelines (RL), point 1.2 [Certain Definitions of Meaning for Supplementary Protection Certificates] the term 'active substance' as referred to in the SPC Regulation for Plant Protection Products, concerns 'substances having a toxic, phytotoxic or plant protection action on their own' (*Bayer CropScience* (C-11/13),[10] without specific reference thereto). Whether a specific safener may be considered an 'active substance' is decided on a case-by-case basis. As of today's date no relevant national case law is available addressing these matters.

3. CJEU *Arne Forsgren v. Österreichisches Patentamt*, C-631/13 of 15 January 2015.
4. CJEU *Massachusetts Institute of Technology v. Bundesgerichtshof*, C-431/04 of 4 May 2006.
5. CJEU *Glaxosmithkline Biologicals v. Comptroller-General of Patents, Designs and Trade Marks*, C-210/13 of 14 November 2013.
6. CJEU *Neurim Pharmaceuticals v. Comptroller-General of Patents*, C-130/11 of 19 July 2012.
7. The Patent and Market Court, *Plethora Solutions Limited v. Patent- och registreringsverket*, PMÄ 11055-16 of 13 February 2018.
8. The Court of Patent Appeals, *Amylin Pharmaceuticals Inc.*, Case 13-100 of 31 May 2016.
9. The Patent and Market Court, *Medigene AG v. Patent- och registreringsverket*, PMÄ 10829-16 of 30 June 2017.
10. CJEU *Bayer CropScience v. Deutsches Patent- und Markenamt*, C-11/13 of 19 June 2014.

[4] *Fixed-Dose and Loose Combinations*

In the absence of any further guidance from the CJEU and Swedish case law in this respect, the general practice of the SPRO is not to grant an SPC directed to a loose combination, but only to a corresponding fixed-dose combination.

[5] *Limitation to Products Subjected to a Specific Marketing Authorization Procedure*

The same considerations as set out in the EU chapter apply.

[6] *Protection of Medical Devices*

The current position of the SPRO is to not grant an SPC based on a marketing authorization other than as set out in the SPC Regulation for Medicinal Products. An SPC will therefore not be granted based e.g., on Directive 93/42/EEC (medical devices). *See* e.g., the guidelines (RL), point 5.2 [Marketing Authorization for Medical Devices].

[B] Basic Patent

As concerns the basic patent underlying an SPC, the same considerations as set out in the EU chapter apply.

[1] *Requirement for the Product to Be 'Protected' by the Basic Patent*

With respect to the requirement for the product of an SPC to be identified in the claims of the basic patent in order to be 'protected' by the patent, the same considerations as set out in the EU chapter apply.

In addition, already in RÅ 2000 ref. 9,[11] it was confirmed by the Swedish Supreme Administrative Court that an SPC can only be granted for a product protected by the basic patent. The Court effectively denied the application of an 'infringement test' to determine whether a product is protected by a basic patent in force as set out in Article 3(a) of the SPC Regulations.

Hence, already before the establishment of an 'identification test' in *Medeva* and subsequent decisions,[12] the SPRO and the Swedish courts have taken a rather strict view on the terms 'product' and 'active ingredient' and whether such a 'product' or

11. The Supreme Administrative Court, *AB Hässle*, Case No. 3248-96 of 2 February 2000.
12. CJEU *Medeva v. Comptroller General of Patents, Designs and Trade Marks*, C-322/10 of 24 November 2011; CJEU *University of Queensland v. Comptroller-General of Patents, Designs and Trade Marks*, C-630/10 of 25 November 2011; CJEU *Daiichi Sankyo v. Comptroller General of Patents, Designs and Trade Marks*, C-6/11 of 25 November 2011; CJEU *Yeda Research and Development v. Comptroller General of Patents, Designs and Trade Marks*, C-518/10 of 25 November 2011.

'active ingredient' is considered to be protected by the basic patent. As an example, the guidelines (RL), point 6.2.5 (Examination as to whether the Product is Protected by the Basic Patent) set forth that, according to established practice, the SPRO shall take a restrictive approach to granting SPCs to subject matter not fulfilling the wording of the claims, i.a. since the granting of an SPC also includes an assessment of whether the product actually is embraced by the patent protection. However, as referred to above, the SPRO applies established case law of the CJEU including *Eli Lilly* (C-493/12)[13] allowing the active ingredient in some cases to also be identified in functional terms. *See also* §10.02[B][3] below.

[a] Small Molecules

The same considerations as set out in the EU chapter apply.

As mentioned in §10.02[B][1] above, the SPRO follows established case law of the CJEU. However, if not presented with a specific disclosure of the chemical name or structure of the respective active ingredient(s), the SPRO will ask the applicant to submit arguments and/or evidence that the active ingredient is protected by the basic patent. *See also* §10.02[B][3] below.

[b] Polymers

The same considerations as set out in the EU chapter apply.

[c] Antibodies, Enzymes and Other Proteins

The same considerations as set out in the EU chapter apply.

At least following the CJEU decision *Eli Lilly* (C-493/12),[14] the SPRO will in general grant an SPC for a specific therapeutic antibody without disclosing the full sequence of the individual antibody which was the subject of the SPC. The SPRO may also grant an SPC to an antibody defined merely by its function, such as by its binding to a specific target. However, whether such an antibody is considered 'protected by the basic patent', as set out in Article 3(a) of the SPC Regulation for Medicinal Products, will be determined on a case-by-case basis taking into account the content of the basic patent as a whole. If not clear, the SPRO may also ask the applicant to verify and explain the function of the antibody. In general, it is helpful if at least the sequence identity of the complementarity determining regions (CDRs) is disclosed in the basic patent.

However, what level of detail a basic patent must provide in order to identify and thereby 'protect' a specific antibody has not yet been clarified by Swedish case law.

13. CJEU *Eli Lilly v. Human Genome Sciences*, C-493/12 of 12 December 2013.
14. *Ibid.*

[d] *Nucleic Acids*

The same considerations as set out in the EU chapter apply.

[2] *Basic Patent Claiming the Product, i.e., the Active Ingredient(s), but Not the Corresponding Authorized Medicinal Product (or Plant Protection Product)*

The same considerations as set out in the EU chapter apply.

[3] *Requirement for the Product to Constitute 'the Invention' of the Basic Patent*

In *AstraZeneca AB* (12-125)[15] of the Court of Patent Appeals, the Court stated that while the CJEU in *Actavis v. Sanofi* (C-443/12)[16] ruled on the interpretation of Article 3(c) of the SPC Regulations under circumstances where there already was an SPC for a patent protected product as such (to the same applicant), the ruling is also relevant to, and applicable to, the assessment under Article 3(a). In this regard, the Court expressed an opinion on whether a combination product claimed in the basic patent could be considered a result of 'pharmaceutical research' or not.

However, as the specific combination of naproxen and esomeprazole, for which an SPC was sought, was not considered protected by the basic patent, the appeal was rejected on this basis alone with reference to Article 3(a) of the SPC Regulation. This case has since then been followed by the CJEU judgment of *Actavis v. Boehringer Ingelheim Pharma* (C-577/13)[17] setting out additional criteria for determining whether a product is protected 'as such' by the basic patent, which practice, together with e.g., *Actavis v. Sanofi* ('core inventive advance') is also applied by the SPRO when determining whether a product is considered protected by the basic patent. As of today's date, there is no relevant case law applying the judgment of *Actavis v. Boehringer Ingelheim Pharma* in Sweden.

[4] *Criteria for Choosing the Basic Patent among Various Available Patents*

The same considerations as set out in the EU chapter apply.

[C] The Marketing Authorization Forming Basis for an SPC

The considerations in relation to the marketing authorization forming basis for an SPC application as set out in the EU chapter apply equally to Sweden.

15. The Court of Patent Appeals, *AstraZeneca AB*, Case 12-125 of 8 December 2015.
16. CJEU *Actavis v. Sanofi*, C-443/12 of 12 December 2013.
17. CJEU *Actavis v. Boehringer Ingelheim Pharma*, C-577/13 of 12 March 2015.

Thus, in Sweden, it is mandatory that at the filing date of the SPC application, both the basic patent and the marketing authorization relied upon are in force.

[1] Combinations of Active Ingredients

The same considerations as set out in the EU chapter apply.

[a] *The Marketing Authorization Refers to Fewer Active Ingredients than the SPC Application*

The same considerations as set out in the EU chapter apply.

[b] *The Marketing Authorization Refers to More Active Ingredients than the SPC Application*

The same considerations as set out in the EU chapter apply.

[c] *The Marketing Authorization Indicates That a Medicinal Product Containing a Single Active Ingredient Is Authorized for Use in Combination with a Further Active Ingredient*

In the absence of further guidance provided by the CJEU, current SPRO practice is to not grant an SPC on the basis of a 'loose combination of active ingredients'. To this date, there is no relevant Swedish case law on this matter.

[2] The Marketing Authorization Has Not Yet Been Granted at the Time the SPC Application Is Filed

The same considerations as set out in the EU chapter apply.

[3] The Holder of the Marketing Authorization

According to established SPRO practice, the question of who is the holder of the marketing authorization for the product is irrelevant. This is also reflected in point 2 of the guidelines (RL) [Entitlement of the Applicant]. Hence in Sweden, an SPC may be filed on the basis of an unrelated third-party marketing authorization.

[4] Reliance on a Marketing Authorization Granted under a Provision Other than Directive 2001/83/EC or Directive 2001/82/EC

The same considerations as set out in the EU chapter apply.

[5] The Marketing Authorizations Which Can Be Relied upon for SPC Applications for Plant Protection Products

The same considerations as set out in the EU chapter apply.

[6] The Product in Question Is Contained in the Authorized Medicinal Product (or the Authorized Plant Protection Product) but Is Not Identified as an Active Ingredient in the Corresponding Marketing Authorization

The same considerations as set out in the EU chapter apply.

[7] The Notion of the 'First' Marketing Authorization

The same considerations as set out in the EU chapter apply.

[a] Marketing Authorization for a New Therapeutic Application of a Previously Authorized Product

In view of the guidance provided by the CJEU in *Neurim* (C-130/11),[18] the SPRO will generally grant an SPC on the basis of a marketing authorization for a new therapeutic application of a product previously authorized for another therapeutic application, as long as the criteria of the SPC Regulation for Medicinal Products are fulfilled.

In the absence of any further guidance from the CJEU with regard to the term 'therapeutic application' or 'therapeutic use' the current practice of the SPRO is to grant SPCs directed to therapeutic uses that are 'medical conditions' or 'diseases'. The application of *Neurim* has also been set out in the guidelines (RL), point 5.4.3 [Examination as to whether the Marketing Authorization in Question is the First], stating 'according to the practice developed by the CJEU judgment in C-130/11 (the so-called Neurim judgment) the first marketing authorization as set out in Article 3(d) is the first in which the product has been approved for a therapeutic indication, i.e., the treatment of a disease, corresponding to the one protected by the basic patent'.

In *Allergan Inc. v. Patent- och registreringsverket* (PMÄ 10925-16)[19] the appeal was rejected based on Article 3(d) of the SPC Regulation as the marketing authorization was not considered to be the first marketing authorization for the product and the therapeutic indication. This was due to the fact that the therapeutic indication of a previous marketing authorization to the same product overlapped with the therapeutic indication of the subsequent marketing authorization (and with the basic patent). The Patent and Market Court was of the opinion that the judgment in *Neurim*, deviating

---

18. CJEU *Neurim Pharmaceuticals v. Comptroller-General of Patents*, C-130/11 of 19 July 2012.
19. The Patent and Market Court, *Allergan Inc. v. Patent- och registreringsverket*, PMÄ 10925-16 of 23 February 2018.

from the literal interpretation of the SPC Regulation, was not to be interpreted extensively.

[b] *Marketing Authorization for a New Formulation of a Previously Authorized Product*

The same considerations as set out in the EU chapter apply.

Accordingly, based on Article 3(d) of the SPC Regulation and in the absence of further guidance from the CJEU (e.g., *Abraxis Bioscience*, C-443/17) with regard to the scope of *Neurim*, the SPRO will not generally grant an SPC referring to a marketing authorization directed to a pharmaceutical formulation of a product where an earlier marketing authorization already exists directed to the product, or rather the active ingredient, and the sole 'novelty' resides in the pharmaceutical formulation. This has, for example, been confirmed in a judgment from the Court of Patent Appeals, *Amylin Pharmaceuticals Inc.* (13–100)[20] and The Patent and Market Court, *Vectura Limited v. Patent- och registreringsverket* (PMÄ 10815-16).[21]

[c] *Marketing Authorization for a New Specific Salt, Ester or Other Derivative of a Previously Authorized Active Ingredient*

In practice the SPRO, referring to recitals 14 and 17 of the SPC Regulation for Plant Protection Products, requires that a new specific salt, ester or other derivative be protected by a patent specifically protecting such new salt, ester or other derivative to grant an SPC based on such a new salt, ester or other derivative.

In *Genzyme Corporation* (case 11-087)[22] of the Court of Patent Appeals, the product for which an SPC was sought ('sevelamer hydrochloride') was based on the same basic patent as a product for which an SPC had already been granted to the same applicant ('sevelamer carbonate'). The appeal was rejected and the decision of the SPRO not to grant an SPC was affirmed since the Court considered the claims of the basic patent to generally include all salts of sevelamer with a pharmaceutically acceptable anion, i.e., including sevelamer hydrochloride and sevelamer carbonate, and therefore the carbonate could not be considered the subject of a patent specifically covering the salt within the meaning of paragraph 14 of Regulation 1610/96.

As set out in §10.02[B][1] above, the SPRO applies a strict interpretation of the term 'product' or 'active ingredient'. This applies equally to determining whether a new specific salt, ester or other derivative of a previously authorized product qualifies for an SPC.

20. The Court of Patent Appeals, *Amylin Pharmaceuticals Inc.*, Case 13-100 of 31 May 2016.
21. The Patent and Market Court, *Vectura Limited v. Patent- och registreringsverket*, PMÄ 10815-16 of 10 October 2016.
22. The Court of Patent Appeals, *Genzyme Coorporation*, Case 11-087 of 29 August 2013.

[d] Marketing Authorization for a New Specific Enantiomer of an Active Ingredient Previously Authorized in Racemic Form

As of today's date, no case has been considered by a Swedish court relating to a marketing authorization for an enantiomer of an active ingredient previously approved as a racemate.

[e] The Product Has Already Been Placed on the Market Before, but Without an Authorization Granted under Directive 2001/83/EC or Directive 2001/82/EC

The same considerations as set out in the EU chapter apply.

[f] Prior Marketing Authorization Which Refers to Fewer Active Ingredients than the SPC Application (and the Later Marketing Authorization Relied upon)

The same considerations as set out in the EU chapter apply.

[g] Prior Marketing Authorization Which Refers to More Active Ingredients than the SPC Application (and the Later Marketing Authorization Relied upon)

The same considerations as set out in the EU chapter apply.

[D] Preclusion of New SPCs by an Earlier SPC

The same considerations as set out in the EU chapter apply.

[1] Consequences of an Earlier Third-Party SPC for the Same Product

[a] The 'One SPC per Product per Patent Holder' Rule

The same considerations as set out in the EU chapter apply.

[b] Earlier SPC Granted to an Affiliated Third Party

The same considerations as set out in the EU chapter apply. The SPRO will not examine a potential affiliation between patent holders applying for an SPC directed to the same product. Decisive in this regard is the patent holder formally registered in the Swedish Patent Register.

[c] Partial Overlap Between the Holders of the Earlier SPC and the Applicants for the New SPC

The same considerations as set out in the EU chapter apply. In the absence of guidance from the CJEU, the SPRO considers a group of applicants a 'joint applicant', and, as such, a second partially overlapping group of applicants would be considered a different applicant from the first (joint) applicant. Accordingly, as an example, the SPRO may grant an SPC to an applicant A already being in possession of an SPC granted to joint applicants A + B.

[d] Earlier Third-Party SPC Has Been Licensed-In

The same considerations as set out in the EU chapter apply.

[2] Consequences of an Own Earlier SPC for the Same Product

The same considerations as set out in the EU chapter apply.

[a] Own Earlier SPC Application Not Yet Granted

The same considerations as set out in the EU chapter apply.

[b] Revocation, Surrender or Lapse of the Own Earlier SPC after Grant

The same considerations as set out in the EU chapter apply.

[c] Transfer of the Own Earlier SPC to a Third Party

The same considerations as set out in the EU chapter apply.

[d] Acquisition of an SPC Granted to a Third Party

The same considerations as set out in the EU chapter apply.

[3] Consequences of an Own Earlier SPC for a Different Product

The same considerations as set out in the EU chapter apply.

[a] *Required Distinction from the Product of the Own Earlier SPC*

The same considerations as set out in the EU chapter apply.

New Therapeutic Applications of Previously Approved Active Ingredients

In view of the CJEU's ruling in *Neurim* (C-130/11),[23] the SPRO does not generally grant a new SPC on the basis of a patent specifically claiming a new therapeutic indication of a previously approved active ingredient and a corresponding separate marketing authorization for the new therapeutic indication where the same patent holder has already obtained an SPC for the same product but on the basis of a different patent and a marketing authorization for a different therapeutic indication.

In PMÄ 10860-16 of the Patent and Market Court, *Novartis AG*[24] the appeal lied from a decision of the SPRO to reject an SPC for the product 'canakinumab' based on Article 3(c) of the SPC Regulation for Medicinal Products. The basic (European) patent claimed in two separate independent claims new uses of IL1-beta binding antibodies for the treatment of juvenile rheumatoid arthritis, and systemic onset idiopathic juvenile arthritis, respectively. The applicant referred to European Commission Decision C(2013)5600 of 26 August 2013 as being the first marketing authorization within the EEA. This marketing authorization was an amendment of the previous decision C(2009)8375.

The amendment of the marketing authorization comprised the addition of the diseases gouty arthritis and systemic idiopathic juvenile arthritis (SIJA). The applicant had already obtained an SPC for the product 'canakinumab' based on a marketing authorization directed to cryopyrin-associated periodic syndromes. The Court concluded that *Neurim* (C-130/11)[25] did not address Article 3(c) of the SPC Regulation and rejected the appeal based on Article 3(c) considering the applicant had already obtained an SPC for the product 'canakinumab'.

The Court was of the opinion that no further SPC can be granted to an applicant already being in possession of an SPC to a specific product irrespective of the use of the product or whether the products are protected by separate basic patents. As the appeal was rejected based on Article 3(c), the Court did not address the issues in relation to Article 3(d) of the SPC Regulation. The case has been appealed to the second-instance court, the Patent and Market Court of Appeal.

According to current practice, the SPRO takes the view that *Neurim* does not affect the definition of the product, and, hence, that a holder of an SPC for a product for a certain medical condition cannot be granted a further SPC for same product for a different medical condition, even if the basic patents do not overlap in one of their medical conditions.

Awaiting the judgment in *Abraxis Bioscience* (C-443/17), the SPRO will generally not grant a further SPC for a new formulation of a previously approved active

23. CJEU *Neurim Pharmaceuticals v. Comptroller-General of Patents*, C-130/11 of 19 July 2012.
24. The Patent and Market Court, *Novartis AG v. Patent- och registreringsverket*, PMÄ 10860-16 of 27 September 2017.
25. CJEU *Neurim Pharmaceuticals v. Comptroller-General of Patents*, C-130/11 of 19 July 2012.

ingredient which has already been the subject of an earlier SPC, wherein the 'novelty' resides in the pharmaceutical formulation.

[b] SPCs for a Specific Salt, Ester or Other Derivative Where an Own Earlier SPC Has Already Been Granted for the Corresponding Active Ingredient

In practice the SPRO, referring to recital 14 of the SPC Regulation for Plant Protection Products, requires that a new specific salt, ester or other derivative be protected by a patent specifically protecting such new salt, ester or other derivative. *See* §10.02[C][7][c] above for further reference.

[c] SPCs for a Specific Enantiomer Where an Own Earlier SPC Has Already Been Granted for the Corresponding Racemate

As of today's date, no case has been considered by a Swedish court relating to a marketing authorization for an enantiomer of an active ingredient previously approved as a racemate.

[4] Grant of More than One SPC on the Basis of the Same Patent

The same considerations as set out in the EU chapter apply.

§10.03 EXTENT OF PROTECTION AND ENFORCEMENT OF SPCs

[A] The Protection Conferred by an SPC

The considerations in terms of the protection conferred by an SPC outlined in the EU chapter apply equally to Sweden. So far, the Swedish courts have not specifically addressed these issues in an infringement case.

[B] The Scope of an SPC in Relation to Derivatives of an Active Ingredient

The considerations raised in the EU chapter in relation to this subject apply equally to SPCs in Sweden. So far there has been no Swedish national court decision addressing this point specifically in an infringement case.

[1] The Relationship Between the Definition of the Active Ingredient(s) in an SPC and Its Scope of Protection

The considerations raised in the EU chapter in this regard are equally applied in Sweden. While the SPRO generally allows an SPC with a broader product definition beyond the specific form of the active ingredient identified in the marketing authorization (e.g., for small molecules by the inclusion of 'or pharmaceutically acceptable salts or ester of the active ingredient', sometimes also specifically referring to the specific salt or ester form in the product definition), the practical implications of the product definition of an SPC in terms of the scope of protection conferred by the SPC remain questionable, since, arguably, the product definition and scope of protection follow by operation of the SPC Regulations.[26]

The relevance of the product definition has to this date not been specifically addressed in an infringement case in Sweden. Further details regarding the product definitions as generally accepted by SPRO are set out in §10.05[E] below.

[C] Enforcement of an SPC

As set out in Section 106 PatL, the provisions of the Swedish Patents Act in relation to patent infringement (as well as the effect of the patent and exceptions thereto) apply mutatis mutandis to SPCs. The provisions of Section 106 PatL are consequences of provisions laid down in Article 5 of the SPC Regulations.

Sweden has a double track litigation system, wherein patent enforcement and invalidity actions are tried in one and the same court.

As already set out in §10.02 above, on 1 September 2016 a new system of specialized courts was introduced in Sweden. The two courts, the Patent and Market Court and the Patent and Market Court of Appeal, essentially hear all cases and matters in Sweden relating to intellectual property law, competition law and marketing law. These specialized courts also handle appeals against decisions issued by the SPRO in SPC and patent applications (*see* §10.05[F] below).

Accordingly, patent and SPC infringement proceedings are litigated through the Patent and Market Court in Stockholm, which is a part of Stockholm District Court (Stockholms Tingsrätt). A decision from the newly established first-instance court could be expected to be handed down within twelve to eighteen months after the filing of an infringement suit.

A decision from the Patent and Market Court can be appealed to the second-instance court, the Patent and Market Court of Appeal, which is a part of Svea Court of Appeal (Svea Hovrätt). A leave for appeal is required. The appeal proceedings before the second-instance court can be expected to take about twelve months.

It rests with the second-instance court to decide whether its decision should be appealable to the Supreme Court (Högsta Domstolen). A leave for appeal is required.

The costs of an infringement action are calculated based the actual total court costs of a party as specified by the party. The court has a discretionary power to assess the reasonability of the costs as specified by the party if challenged by the counter-party.

The losing party is liable to reimburse the court costs of the other party.

26. Articles 1(b), 4 and 5 of Regulation (EC) 469/2009 and Arts 1(8), 4 and 5 of Regulation (EC) 1610/96.

Ex parte injunctive relief is generally also available if there is probable cause for infringement and the SPC (and its basic patent) may be presumed to be valid, and the claimant deposits a monetary security for any damage that the preliminary injunction may cause the defendant. In such cases the preliminary injunction may issue within a few days.

If the situation is less clear-cut, the Patent and Market Court will summon the parties to oral proceedings where the defendant is given the opportunity to submit a written defence pleading, in which case the proceedings will at the best take about three to four weeks.

§10.04 DETERMINATION OF THE SPC TERM

[A] The Calculation of the SPC Term

The considerations regarding the calculation of the SPC term as set out in the EU chapter apply equally to Sweden.

[1] The Relevant Marketing Authorization for the Term of an SPC

The considerations in terms of the relevant marketing authorization for determining the SPC term as set out in the EU chapter apply equally to Sweden.

The SPRO may carry out a search to verify that the marketing authorization relied upon by the SPC applicant is indeed the first marketing authorization in question.

In recent years, the CJEU has somewhat liberalized the SPC system in the manner that SPCs are now allowed to issue for a new 'therapeutic use' of an active ingredient previously authorized as a medicinal product for another therapeutic use when the basic patent protects said new therapeutic use (*see Neurim* (C-130/11)[27]). However the scope of *Neurim* and particularly the interpretation of the term 'therapeutic use' or 'therapeutic application' remain unclear.

Following the aftermath of *Neurim*, the SPRO seems to take the view that a therapeutic use relying on a different 'medical condition' may justify another SPC for an active ingredient previously having been the subject of an SPC. It has also been confirmed by the Patent and Market Court[28] and the Court of Patent Appeals,[29] that a new pharmaceutical formulation involving such an active ingredient is not a new therapeutic use or therapeutic application within the meaning as set forth in *Neurim*.

Naturally, the other criteria of the SPC Regulation for Medicinal Products need also be fulfilled in the present context, including Article 3(c) which becomes relevant when the applicant for an SPC for a new therapeutic use is the same as the proprietor

27. CJEU *Neurim Pharmaceuticals v. Comptroller-General of Patents*, C-130/11 of 19 July 2012, paragraph 25.
28. The Patent and Market Court, *Vectura Limited v. Patent- och registreringsverket*) PMA 10815-16 of 10 October 2016, The Patent and Market Court, *Alcon laboratories Inc. v. Patent-och registreringsverket*, PMÄ 11089-16 of 20 January 2017.
29. The Court of Patent Appeals, *Amylin Pharmaceuticals Inc.*, Case 13-100 of 31 May 2016.

of the previous SPC directed to the same active ingredient. Such cases are currently pending before the Swedish courts. For further guidance regarding the SPRO and the application of *Neurim* in practice, *see* §10.02[C][7][a] and §10.02[C][7][b] above.

[2] The Expiration Date of an SPC

The calculation of the SPC term is based on the provisions of Article 13 of the SPC Regulations. The term of a patent is based on the provisions of Section 40 PatL, and shall be twenty years beginning on the day following its filing date. The last day when a patent is in force will be the twentieth anniversary of its filing date. An SPC with a full five-year term will expire on the twenty-fifth anniversary of the filing date of the basic patent.

Accordingly, a patent application filed on 1 January 2000 will have a patent term starting on 2 January 2000 and extending to and including 1 January 2020, that is the last day of the term will be the full day of 1 January 2020. The first day of the term of an SPC based on the patent would be 2 January 2020. The last day of the maximum five-year term for such SPC would be the full day of 1 January 2025.

[B] Correction of the SPC Term

Swedish national law does not provide for correction of the term of an SPC.

Following the CJEU decision in *Incyte Corporation* (C-492/16)[30] the SPRO has announced[31] that based on the interpretation of Article 18 of the SPC Regulation for Medicinal Products set forth in the decision, it will upon request from the proprietor of the SPC correct the term of an SPC as long as the SPC has not expired. A decision on a correction requested under Article 18 of the SPC Regulation is typically taken within one to three weeks after the request.

[C] Paediatric Extensions

The considerations in terms of paediatric extensions as set out in the EU chapter apply equally to Sweden.

§10.05 PROCEDURE OF FILING AN SPC APPLICATION

[A] Entitlement to an SPC Application

The SPC Regulations stipulate in Article 6 that the SPC shall be granted to the patent holder, but are silent as to who may apply for an SPC. In Sweden, it is only the patentee who is entitled to file an SPC application. As such, a licensee of the basic patent may not

30. CJEU *Incyte Corporation v. Szellemi Tulajdon Nemzeti Hivatala*, C-492/16 of 20 December 2017.
31. At https://www.prv.se/en/about-us/news/re-examinationrectification-of-the-duration-of-a-supplementary-protection-certificate/.

file an application for an SPC even if the patent owner has given his express authorization to do so.

Likewise, if the basic patent has been transferred, it is only the registered patent proprietor who may file the SPC.

If there is a discrepancy between the applicant for an SPC and the proprietor of the basic patent registered with the Patent Register, the SPRO will invite the SPC applicant to correct this deficiency.

[B] The Time Limit for Filing an SPC Application

The considerations as set out in the EU chapter apply.

The guidelines (RL), point 3.1.2 [Last Day for an Application when the Basic Patent has been Granted by the EPO], clarifies that, since according to Section 82 PatL a European patent must be validated in order to become valid in Sweden, validation is required for the SPRO to start examining an SPC application when the basic patent is a European patent. The time limit in Article 7(2) of the SPC Regulations is therefore counted from the date the basic European patent was validated in Sweden.

In a recent decision,[32] the Patent and Market Court has established that the deadline for filing an SPC application is not a deadline which is amenable to re-establishment of rights, since the omission to apply for an SPC within the deadline does not mean that the applicant has omitted to perform an act prescribed by, or having regard to, the patents act, as required for re-establishment of rights according to Section 72 PatL. Otherwise re-establishment of rights according to Section 72 PatL is also applicable to timely filed SPC applications.

[C] The Filing of an SPC at the National Patent Office

As set out in the EU chapter, an SPC must be filed before the national patent office within the stipulated time limit, once the basic patent as well as the relevant marketing authorization have issued. In instances when the basic patent is a European patent the requirements set out in §10.05[B] above also apply. The SPC application must be filed in writing and must contain all relevant information about the applicant and his representative (names and addresses), as well as details in terms of the basic patent and the marketing authorization (number and date of decision or date of notification in the case of a EU marketing authorization) relied upon for the product in question.

A power of attorney is required for the representative for the SPC applicant. A new power of attorney for the SPC application is not required if there is already a power of attorney on file in view of the basic patent. The power of attorney may be filed subsequently upon invitation from the SPRO if not submitted when filing the SPC application.

32. The Patent and Market Court, *Vanda Pharmaceuticals Inc. v. Patent- och registreringsverket*, PMÄ 322-17 of 27 March 2017.

[D] The Documentation Required for an SPC Application

The documentation required for filing an SPC application in Sweden is based on the requirements as set out in Article 8 of the SPC Regulations.

The SPC request should be supplemented with copies of the marketing authorization to place the product on the market in Sweden and the summary of product characteristics ('SmPC').

In addition, if the first authorization for placing the product on the market is not a Swedish or a central authorization, but was granted in another EU or EEA Member State, the applicant should submit information regarding the identity of the product thus authorized and the legal provision under which the authorization procedure took place, together with a copy of the notice publishing the authorization in the appropriate official publication.

In the case of plant protection products, copies of provisional or definitive marketing authorizations must be filed.

Applicant should also provide information as to how the product is protected by the basic patent.

A power of attorney is also required, if not already on file for the basic patent of the SPC application.

[E] The Definition of the Product in an SPC Application

The guidelines (RL) set forth in point 3.2 [How the Product for which Protection is Sought Shall be Defined] that the product to be defined is the active ingredient or combination of active ingredients. In the guidelines (RL), point 1.2 [Certain Definitions of Importance for SPCs] the term 'active ingredient' is stated to be used synonymously with the term 'active substance' as used in the SPC Regulation for Plant Protection Products.

According to the guidelines (RL), point 6.2.5 [Assessment of whether the Product is Protected by the Basic Patent], the SPRO should adopt a restrictive view when granting SPCs for subject matter not fulfilling the wording of the patent claims, e.g., since the grant of an SPC also entails an establishment as to whether the product is actually embraced by the scope of patent protection.

In general, the SPRO will not accept a product definition which in any way could be perceived as 'unclear or deceptive'. For example, the SPRO will typically not allow a product definition including a reference to 'in all forms as protected by the basic patent', or the like.

In the product definition, the SPRO typically also allows salts and esters of the product, insofar as such salts and esters have been specified in the claims of the basic patent.

[F] SPC Examination Procedure and Appeal Procedure

In accordance with the practice of the SPRO, an application for an SPC will be subject to a formal examination, followed by a substantive examination.

The formal examination focuses on issues such as the time limits for filing the SPC application, the payment of the prescribed fees, if a power of attorney for the applicant's representative is on file, the formal entitlement of the applicant, whether the patent is in force and if the documentation submitted is complete.

If there are any irregularities in this regard, e.g., the required power of attorney is missing, the SPRO will invite the applicant to rectify this by means of a communication (Notice of Irregularities), setting a term of three months for responding to the communication. In principle, all required documents except for the application form can be filed subsequently, as long as the requirements laid down in Article 3 of the SPC Regulations are fulfilled at the date of filing the SPC application.

The substantive examination includes checking the identity of the product and verifying that the product is protected by the basic patent. Accordingly, already with the SPC request, the applicant is requested to provide information with regard to how the product is protected by the basic patent.

In addition, the SPRO will examine the product definition set forth in the application. If the definition is found not to be acceptable to the SPRO, the applicant will be invited to amend the definition accordingly. The SPRO will also verify that the marketing authorization according to Article 3(b) of the SPC Regulation for Medicinal Products and Article 3(1)(b) of the SPC Regulation for Plant Protection Products was granted in accordance with the appropriate directives and that it was valid at the filing date.

Moreover, the SPRO will check whether an SPC for the same product has already been granted to the applicant.

In general, the SPRO will also examine whether the marketing authorization is indeed the first marketing authorization to place the product on the market in accordance with Article 3(d) of the SPC Regulation for Medicinal Products and Article 3(1)(d) of the SPC Regulation for Plant Protection Products.

Sometimes the applicant submits in parallel various SPC requests for the same product based on different basic patents. However, according to Article 3(c) of the SPC Regulation, only one SPC per product may issue to one and the same applicant. If the SPRO identifies various requests directed to the same product, the SPRO will generally invite the applicant to choose which application should proceed to grant if all other requirements of the SPC Regulations are fulfilled.

If during substantive examination by the SPRO an SPC application is found to be deficient, the SPRO will issue an office action (Statement of Remarks) inviting the applicant to correct the deficiencies within a time limit of three months.

According to Section 59 PB the term for filing a reply in view of an SPC application can be extended by two months if there are special reasons. As set out in the guidelines (RL), point 4.3 [Extension of time limits], if the basic patent is a European patent, the SPRO will generally not stay the examination proceedings if the request is based on the fact that opposition or opposition appeal proceedings involving the European patent are pending. Hence, parallel proceedings before the EPO is not an acceptable reason for staying the examination of the SPC application or for requesting an extension of time for responding to an office communication.

According to the guidelines (RL), point 4.1 [Miscellaneous on the Duration of Examination] the examination of the SPC application should if possible be such that a final decision on the application be reached before the expiry of the basic patent. However, this is not generally an issue as usually an application for an SPC is filed well before the expiry of the basic patent. Instead, applicants may experience a delay in receiving substantive office actions from the SPRO.

According to general practise in relation to SPC applications, oral proceedings or an oral conference can be held at applicant's request. Furthermore, a request for an oral conference or oral proceedings may also be requested as a precautionary measure before a negative decision is taken.

If the application for an SPC is in compliance with the statutory requirements as set out in the SPC Regulations, the SPRO will issue a certificate together with a granting decision. The granting decision includes the product definition, the identity of the basic patent and information on the date of publication of the grant in the Swedish Patent Gazette. The SPC granting decision also includes information on the duration of the SPC despite recent EU case law[33] having established that the duration does not form part of the decision to grant an SPC.

Alternatively, if an SPC application cannot be granted, a decision to reject the application will be issued by the SPRO. According to Article 18 of the SPC Regulation for Medicinal Products, and Article 17(1) of the SPC Regulation for Plant Protection Products, respectively, decisions of the patent office may be appealed pursuant to national provisions. The national provisions are laid down in Section 26 PatL.

A formal notice of appeal against such a decision must be filed in writing with the SPRO within two months of the date of the decision. Generally an extension of time (normally two months) for substantiating the grounds of appeal will be granted upon applicant's request.

If the SPRO considers the appeal to be admissible and well-founded, it will rectify the decision. If not, the appeal will be remitted to the Patent and Market Court.

A final decision from the Patent and Market Court could be expected within about twelve months to eighteen months after the filing of the notice of appeal. A negative decision can be appealed to the second-instance court, i.e., the Patent and Market Court of Appeal, provided that a leave for appeal is granted. The court instances are as set out above in §10.03[C].

[G] Applications for a Paediatric Extension

The formal requirements for filing a paediatric extension correspond to those as outlined in the EU chapter.

---

33. CJEU *Incyte Corporation v. Szellemi Tulajdon Nemzeti Hivatala*, C-492/16 of 20 December 2017, paragraph 54.

The request for a paediatric extension must be filed with the SPRO together with the prescribed fee.

A power of attorney is required, unless already on file in view of the basic patent or the SPC.

The required supporting documents are set out in Article 8(1)(d), (2) and (3) of the SPC Regulation for Medicinal Products.

According to the guidelines (RL), point 9.2 [Point of Time for Filing an Application for an Extension of the Duration of an SPC], an application which is filed later than the time limit set forth in Article 7(4), and 7(5), respectively, or that is filed before compliance statements have been issued will be rejected pursuant to Article 10(1) of the SPC Regulation for Medicinal Products. Accordingly, it is required that the marketing authorizations of all EU Member States have been updated with a compliance statement at the latest on the date of application.

According to the guidelines (RL), point 9.4 [Office Communication Inviting the Applicant to Correct Formal Defects], the fact that one or more national medical agencies have not yet updated the marketing authorization with a compliance statement is not a valid reason for extending the term of an office action pointing out such defect, since all updated marketing authorizations must be issued before the date of application for the paediatric extension. Exceptionally, the SPRO may deviate from this strict interpretation, e.g., for reasons of proportionality, such as if the medical agency of one Member State has not updated the marketing authorization within the applicable time limit.

The formal and substantive examination of the application for a paediatric extension includes the verification of the entitlement to lodge the application, the completeness of the documentation in relation to the compliance statement and the verification that the product has been approved in all EU Member States.

In order to be entitled to a paediatric extension the product shall not be designated as an orphan medicinal product, as set out in Article 36(4) of the Paediatric Regulation (EC) 1901/2006. Moreover, no one-year extension of the period of regulatory exclusivity must have been granted, as set out in Article 36(5) of the Paediatric Regulation.

§10.06 PROCEDURE OF INVALIDATING AN SPC

The Swedish Patents Act does not provide any explicit reference to invalidation of an SPC.

[A] Grounds for the Invalidation of an SPC

The grounds for invalidating an SPC in Sweden correspond to the grounds as set out in Article 15 of the SPC Regulations, as set out in the EU chapter.

[B] The Filing of an Invalidation Suit

As set forth above under §10.03[C], in Sweden there is a double track litigation system, wherein patent enforcement and invalidity actions are tried in one and the same court. The Patent and Market Court has exclusive jurisdiction for invalidation.

An action for the invalidation of an SPC may be filed at any time by any person, independently from any pending infringement proceedings.

[C] Invalidation Procedure and the Corresponding Appeal Procedure

An invalidation suit against an SPC may be initiated at any time after the expiry of the opposition period, or after the termination of opposition proceedings against the basic patent.

The costs of the proceedings are calculated based the actual total court costs of a party as specified by the party. The court has a discretionary power to assess the reasonability of the costs as specified by the party if challenged by the counter-party.

The losing party is liable to reimburse the court costs of the other party.

A first-instance decision could be expected to be handed down within about twelve to eighteen months. A final decision on appeal to the Patent and Market Court of Appeal could be expected to issue about twelve months from lodging the appeal.

[D] The Revocation of a Paediatric Extension

As set out in the EU chapter, the grounds for revocation of a paediatric extension correspond to those of Article 16 of the SPC Regulation for Medicinal Products.

Procedurally the same considerations as set out in §10.06[B] and §10.06[C] above for the revocation of an SPC apply.

§10.07 UNFAIR COMPETITION LAW

The same considerations as set out in the EU chapter apply. Antitrust issues involving SPCs have not yet been specifically addressed in the Swedish case law.

CHAPTER 11
Iceland

Einar Karl Friðriksson

§11.01 LEGAL BASIS

The basic national provisions[1] governing SPCs in Iceland are found in the Icelandic Patent Act No. 17/1991 (Lög um einkaleyfi, 'ell') in chapter IX, which contains a single article, Article 65a.[2] The chapter was introduced in 1996, following the incorporation into the EEA Agreement of Council Regulation (EEC) 1768/92, in accordance with the EEA Joint Committee Decision No. 7/94 of 21 March 1994. Further provisions are

1. English translations of patent related laws and regulations are found on the home page of the Icelandic Patent Office at: http://einkaleyfastofan.is/en/acts-and-regulations.
2. Art. 65a ell. reads as follows (English translation as provided by the Patent Office):

> Regulation (EC) No. 469/2009 of the European Parliament and of the Council of 6 May 2009 concerning the supplementary protection certificate for medicinal products, published in the EEA Supplement to the Official Journal of the European Union, No. 31 of 18 May 2017, pp. 542-551, and Art. 36 of Regulation (EC) No. 1901/2006 of the European Parliament and of the Council of 12 December 2006 on medicinal products for paediatric use, published in the EEA Supplement to the Official Journal of the European Union, No. 31 of 18 May 2017, pp. 521-539, have statutory effect with those adaptations resulting from the Decision of the EEA Joint Committee No. 92/2017 of 5 May 2017. Regulation (EC) No. 1610/96 of the European Parliament and of the Council of 23 July 1996 concerning the creation of a supplementary protection certificate for plant protection products, published in the EEA Supplement to the Official Journal of the European Union, No. 48 of 20 November 1997, pp. 98-103, has statutory effect with those adaptations resulting from the decision of the EEA Joint Committee No. 59/97 of 31 July 1997. Provisions of the Regulations also apply to nationals and legal entities of Member States of the European Free Trade Association (EFTA) Treaty and to nationals and legal entities of the Faroe Islands. An application for supplementary protection and applications for extension of such protection shall be submitted in writing to the Patent Office.]1) The applicant shall pay the prescribed application fee. An annual fee shall be paid for each fee year commencing after the patent has lapsed. The same rules which apply to annual fees for patents shall apply in other respects these annual fees. More detailed rules concerning applications for supplementary protection, their processing

found in the Patent Regulation No. 477/2012 (Reglugerð um einkaleyfi 'rg'), in particular Chapter VII, Articles 62–70.

Article 65a ell. was amended in 2018 by Act 40/2018 that entered into force on 1 June 2018, to introduce the possibility to obtain paediatric extension to an SPC, which followed the incorporation into the EEA Agreement of Regulation (EC) 469/2009 by EEA Joint Committee Decision No. 92/2017 of 5 May 2017.[3]

Article 65a ell. specifies that the mentioned Regulation (EC) 469/2009 (the 'new' SPC Regulation) and Article 36 of Regulation (EC) 1901/2006 shall be considered part of the Patent Act, with the transitional provisions as indicated in the mentioned EEA Joint Committee Decision. The Article further specifies that an application shall be filed in writing, that the applicant shall pay the prescribed application fee and that an annual fee shall be paid for each fee year commencing after the patent has lapsed. Amendments to the Patent Regulation No. 477/2012 took effect on 1 July 2018, introducing i.a. provisions relating to paediatric extensions.

§11.02 SUBSTANTIVE REQUIREMENTS FOR OBTAINING AN SPC

The relevant decisions from the CJEU in the interpretation of EU law that is part of the EEA Agreement gives guidance to the EFTA-EEA states and sets precedents that are generally taken into account by courts in these countries as well as the EFTA Court. Thus the considerations discussed in detail in Chapter 1 ('EU chapter') in relation to substantive requirements for obtaining an SPC, in so far as they have been the subject of the CJEU are generally applicable also to Iceland.

[A] Types of Products That Can Be Protected

No further considerations apply in Iceland beyond what is described in the EU chapter. As regards plant protection products it should be noted that so far no applications for an SPC for a plant protection product have been filed in Iceland.

[1] Practical Considerations: What Is the Active Ingredient or Combination of Active Ingredients That Can Form the Basis for an SPC

No further considerations beyond what is described in the EU chapter apply.

and research, the registration of supplementary protection, etc. shall be set in a Regulation. The penalty provisions of Articles 57 and 62 shall also apply to supplementary protection.

3. *See*: http://www.efta.int/sites/default/files/documents/legal-texts/eea/other-legal-documents/adopted-joint-committee-decisions/2017%20-%20English/092-2017.pdf.

[2] Active Ingredient or Combination of Active Ingredients of a Medicinal Product

No further considerations beyond what is described in the EU chapter apply.

[3] Active Substance or Combination of Active Substances of a Plant Protection Product

No further considerations beyond what is described in the EU chapter apply.

[4] Fixed-Dose and Loose Combinations

No further considerations beyond what is described in the EU chapter apply.

[5] Limitation to Products Subjected to a Specific Marketing Authorization Procedure

No further considerations beyond what is described in the EU chapter apply.

[6] Protection of Medical Devices

No further considerations beyond what is described in the EU chapter apply.

[B] Basic Patent

The general considerations discussed in the corresponding EU chapter apply.

[1] Requirement for the Product to Be 'Protected' by the Basic Patent

The ISPTO has been consistent in its practice of objecting to broad product definitions in the cases where such broad protection is not fully covered by the patent. Thus, for example, the Office will generally allow product definition including 'pharmaceutically acceptable salts, hydrates and solvates thereof' but only in so far as such definitions are clearly encompassed by the claims of the basic patent.

Otherwise the considerations described in the corresponding EU chapter apply.

[a] Small Molecules

No publicly available guidelines exist that would provide guidance as to how products of the above-mentioned type could be protected, in other ways than by using the INN name. In some few cases objections are raised for unclear product definition.

[b] Polymers

No publicly available guidelines exist that would provide guidance as to how products of the above-mentioned type could be protected, in other ways than by using the INN name. In some few cases objections are raised for unclear product definition.

[c] Antibodies, Enzymes and Other Proteins

No publicly available guidelines exist that would provide guidance as to how products of the above-mentioned type could be protected, in other ways than by using the INN name. In some few cases objections are raised for unclear product definition. At least in one case, a product definition of a protein was objected to for being unclear, and the Office proposed instead to use the respective INN name.

[d] Nucleic Acids

No publicly available guidelines exist that would provide guidance as to how products of the above-mentioned type could be protected, in other ways than by using the INN name. In some few cases objections are raised for unclear product definition.

[2] Basic Patent Claiming the Product, i.e., the Active Ingredient(s), but Not the Corresponding Authorized Medicinal Product (or Plant Protection Product)

No further considerations beyond what is described in the EU chapter apply.

[3] Requirement for the Product to Constitute 'the Invention' of the Basic Patent

No further considerations beyond what is described in the EU chapter apply.

[4] Criteria for Choosing the Basic Patent among Various Available Patents

No further considerations beyond what is described in the EU chapter apply.

[C] The Marketing Authorization Forming Basis for an SPC

The general considerations discussed in the EU chapter apply.

[1] Combinations of Active Ingredients

No publicly available guidelines or decisions from the Icelandic Patent Office provide any further guidance than what is derived from existing case law from the CJEU and discussed in the corresponding EU chapter.

[a] The Marketing Authorization Refers to Fewer Active Ingredients than the SPC Application

No further considerations beyond what is described in the EU chapter apply.

[b] The Marketing Authorization Refers to More Active Ingredients than the SPC Application

No further considerations beyond what is described in the EU chapter apply.

[c] The Marketing Authorization Indicates That a Medicinal Product Containing a Single Active Ingredient Is Authorized for Use in Combination with a Further Active Ingredient

No further considerations beyond what is described in the EU chapter apply.

[2] The Marketing Authorization Has Not Yet Been Granted at the Time the SPC Application Is Filed

No publicly available guidelines or decisions from the Icelandic Patent Office provide any further guidance than what is derived from existing case law from the CJEU and discussed in the corresponding EU chapter.

[3] The Holder of the Marketing Authorization

At the time of writing, ISPTO has not provided further guidance or decisions beyond what can be derived from present CJEU case law discussed in the corresponding EU chapter indicating how situations might be dealt with where the holder of the marketing authorization is not the same as the holder of the patent and applicant of the SPC. Such applications are however currently pending.

[4] Reliance on a Marketing Authorization Granted under a Provision Other than Directive 2001/83/EC or Directive 2001/82/EC

SPCs have been granted in Iceland referring to a first marketing authorization issued by a national medicinal authority other than the EMA, including at least Sweden, Switzerland, and the Netherlands.

[5] The Marketing Authorizations Which Can Be Relied upon for SPC Applications for Plant Protection Products

No SPC applications for plant protection products have so far been filed in Iceland.

[6] The Product in Question Is Contained in the Authorized Medicinal Product (or the Authorized Plant Protection Product) but Is Not Identified as an Active Ingredient in the Corresponding Marketing Authorization

No decisions or guidelines from the Icelandic Patent Office provide any further guidance than what is derived from existing case law from the CJEU and discussed in the corresponding EU chapters.

[7] The Notion of the 'First' Marketing Authorization

No decisions or guidelines from the Icelandic Patent Office provide any further guidance than what is derived from existing case law from the CJEU and discussed in the corresponding EU chapters.

[a] Marketing Authorization for a New Therapeutic Application of a Previously Authorized Product

The Icelandic Patent Office has granted SPCs that are based on new therapeutic indications, which applications refer to a corresponding basic patent claiming such use in the form of second medical use. In such cases the Icelandic Medicines Agency will not issue a formal approval of certain variations of earlier issued marketing authorizations, rather the practice is that the variations will be considered approved in Iceland when the European Commission issues a decision authorizing a new therapeutic application for a previously authorized product, and there will not be a formal letter or notification from the Icelandic authorities.

[b] Marketing Authorization for a New Formulation of a Previously Authorized Product

No decisions or guidelines from the Icelandic Patent Office provide any further guidance than what is derived from existing case law from the CJEU and discussed in the corresponding EU chapter.

[c] Marketing Authorization for a New Specific Salt, Ester or Other Derivative of a Previously Authorized Active Ingredient

No decisions or guidelines from the Icelandic Patent Office provide any further guidance than what is derived from existing case law from the CJEU and discussed in the corresponding EU chapter.

[d] Marketing Authorization for a New Specific Enantiomer of an Active Ingredient Previously Authorized in Racemic Form

No decisions or guidelines from the Icelandic Patent Office provide any further guidance than what is derived from existing case law from the CJEU and discussed in the corresponding EU chapter.

[e] The Product Has Already Been Placed on the Market Before, but Without an Authorization Granted under Directive 2001/83/EC or Directive 2001/82/EC

No decisions or guidelines from the Icelandic Patent Office provide any further guidance than what is derived from existing case law from the CJEU and discussed in the corresponding EU chapter.

[f] Prior Marketing Authorization Which Refers to Fewer Active Ingredients than the SPC Application (and the Later Marketing Authorization Relied upon)

No decisions or guidelines from the Icelandic Patent Office provide any further guidance than what is derived from existing case law from the CJEU and discussed in the corresponding EU chapter.

[g] Prior Marketing Authorization Which Refers to More Active Ingredients than the SPC Application (and the Later Marketing Authorization Relied upon)

No decisions or guidelines from the Icelandic Patent Office provide any further guidance than what is derived from existing case law from the CJEU and discussed in the corresponding EU chapter.

[D] Preclusion of New SPCs by an Earlier SPC

No decisions or guidelines from the Icelandic Patent Office provide any further guidance than what is derived from existing case law from the CJEU and discussed in the corresponding EU chapters.

[1] Consequences of an Earlier Third-Party SPC for the Same Product

[a] The 'One SPC per Product per Patent Holder' Rule

No further considerations beyond what is described in the EU chapter apply.

[b] Earlier SPC Granted to an Affiliated Third Party

No further considerations beyond what is described in the EU chapter apply.

[c] Partial Overlap Between the Holders of the Earlier SPC and the Applicants for the New SPC

No further considerations beyond what is described in the EU chapter apply.

[d] Earlier Third-Party SPC Has Been Licensed-In

No further considerations beyond what is described in the EU chapter apply.

[2] Consequences of an Own Earlier SPC for the Same Product

No further considerations beyond what is described in the EU chapter apply.

[a] Own Earlier SPC Application Not Yet Granted

No further considerations beyond what is described in the EU chapter apply.

[b] Revocation, Surrender or Lapse of the Own Earlier SPC after Grant

No further considerations beyond what is described in the EU chapter apply.

[c] Transfer of the Own Earlier SPC to a Third Party

No further considerations beyond what is described in the EU chapter apply.

[d] Acquisition of an SPC Granted to a Third Party

No further considerations beyond what is described in the EU chapter apply.

[3] Consequences of an Own Earlier SPC for a Different Product

No further considerations beyond what is described in the EU chapter apply.

[a] *Required Distinction from the Product of the Own Earlier SPC*

No further considerations beyond what is described in the EU chapter apply.

[b] *SPCs for a Specific Salt, Ester or Other Derivative Where an Own Earlier SPC Has Already Been Granted for the Corresponding Active Ingredient*

No further considerations beyond what is described in the EU chapter apply.

[c] *SPCs for a Specific Enantiomer Where an Own Earlier SPC Has Already Been Granted for the Corresponding Racemate*

No further considerations beyond what is described in the EU chapter apply.

[4] *Grant of More than One SPC on the Basis of the Same Patent*

No further considerations beyond what is described in the EU chapter apply.

§11.03 EXTENT OF PROTECTION AND ENFORCEMENT OF SPCs

[A] The Protection Conferred by an SPC

The considerations in terms of the protection conferred by an SPC outlined in the EU chapter apply equally to Iceland. No cases involving the scope of an SPC, such as in a case involving infringement or validity, have come before Icelandic courts. The courts are generally inclined to look at precedents from other European jurisdictions when the underlying legal issues are based on EU-EEA law or legal provisions that are essentially similar in Iceland and other comparable jurisdictions, such as in particular from the other Nordic countries.

[B] The Scope of an SPC in Relation to Derivatives of an Active Ingredient

Again, no national case law exists that gives any guidance beyond and in addition to what is provided by relevant CJEU decisions such as in particular the *Farmitalia* case (C-392/97).[4]

4. CJEU *Farmitalia Carlo Erba v. Bundesgerichtshof*, C-392/97 of 16 September 1999.

[1] *The Relationship Between the Definition of the Active Ingredient(s) in an SPC and Its Scope of Protection*

The ISPTO generally allows an SPC to issue with a broader product definition than the specific form of the active ingredient identified in the marketing authorization (e.g., by the inclusion of pharmaceutically acceptable salts, hydrates and solvates of the active ingredient), with the condition that such broad definition finds basis in the basic patent. The issue has however never come to an Icelandic court if and how such broad definition might affect the scope of the SPC.

[C] Enforcement of an SPC

Article 65a ell. specifies that the penalty provisions of Articles 57 and 62 shall also apply to supplementary protection. In accordance with Article 64 of the Patent Act, patent cases shall be brought in the District Court of Reykjavik; although SPCs are not mentioned it must be presumed that the provision applies as well to them, meaning that infringement cases, invalidity cases, cases relating to the right to the SPC or transfer of rights, etc. shall be dealt with at the first instance by the District Court of Reykjavik.

The court system in Iceland is made up of three stages: district courts (eight courts in eight jurisdictions around the country), appeal trial court Landsréttur and the Supreme Court. Appeals from the District Courts are heard by Landsréttur, only exceptional cases can be appealed further to the Supreme Court, upon approval from the Supreme Court.

An invalidity counter claim by a defendant in an infringement case will be dealt with in the same case.

Costs of an infringement action can vary and will depend on the parties' efforts. Court fees are low (up to ISK 300,000 in the appeals court, approx. EUR 2,400). The winning party can make a claim to obtain costs from the losing party. The judge can decide to award costs and generally if a party loses a case in all major aspects he will be the one bearing the costs. The decision on the amount of costs to be paid is within the powers of the judge, they have in the last few years risen to cover a larger portion of actual costs and in some case full amount of claimed cost.

A first-instance decision is typically handed down within nine to eighteen months after the filing of the suit. Usually a substantial part of the process is to obtain an expert assessment if that is requested. A request for an expert assessment therefore usually delays a final decision in the case.

There is a special procedure before the courts for cases requiring a quick resolution. However, this procedure is generally not available in a typical infringement case. An IP related matter might fall under the category of cases that can fall under this special procedure if the matter relates directly to a decision of governmental authorities.

The time frame of appeal court cases is more difficult to foresee, as the Landsréttur appeals court only started operating 1 January 2018, but can be expected to take twelve to eighteen months. An appeal must be lodged within three months from a court's decision in a first instance case.

The patentee/SPC holder can request preliminary injunction against suspected infringement. Such actions are relatively swift and generally result in a ruling within two to three weeks. If an injunction is granted it must be followed by a court action initiated within a week of the ruling. The necessary conditions for an injunction to be issued is that it is plausible that an act is likely to infringe one's legitimate private rights such as a patent and that the allegedly infringing act has already begun or that it is imminent and that the owners' rights will be wasted or harmed substantially if forced to wait for a court resolution. Furthermore, it is a condition that it is evident that the general rules on torts or punishment will not provide for sufficient protection for the rights holder if the injunction is not granted.

As mentioned above, national case law in the field of patents and SPCs in particular is extremely limited. The courts however are generally inclined to look at and take into account precedents from other European countries, in particular the other Nordic countries, that relate to the same or corresponding legal provisions.

§11.04 DETERMINATION OF THE SPC TERM

[A] The Calculation of the SPC Term

The considerations regarding the calculation of the SPC term as set out in the EU chapter apply equally to Iceland. The Icelandic Patent Office did not allow negative term SPCs under the old SPC Regulation 1768/1992.

In April 2009 the Patent Office rejected an application for an SPC with a calculated negative term. The rejection was appealed to the Patent and Trademark Appeals Board. The Appeals Board upon a request by the appellant stayed the case while awaiting a decision from the CJEU in the case of *Merck Sharp & Dohme v. Deutsches Patent- und Markenamt* (C-125/10).[5] Despite the outcome in that case, in which the CJEU held that an SPC could be granted with a negative term, the Appeals Board decided to maintain the rejection, arguing that since Regulation (EC) 469/2009 had not yet entered into force in Iceland the guidance of the C-125/10 case was not applicable to Iceland. The decision was appealed to the District Court of Reykjavik, which maintained the rejection. The case was appealed to the Supreme Court and the Supreme Court decided to request an opinion from the EFTA Court, since the underlying legal question had to do with interpretation of the EEA Agreement. The EFTA Court issued an opinion[6] in December 2017 stating that Regulation 1768/92 permitted the issuing of an SPC with a negative term. With that opinion, the Supreme Court decided[7] that the Patent Office was obliged to issue the Certificate (the Patent Office had previously stated that other

5. CJEU *Merck Sharp & Dohme Corp. v. Deutsches Patent und Markenamt*, C-125/10 of 8 December 2011.
6. EFTA Court, *Merck Sharp & Dohme Corp. v. the Icelandic Patent Office (Einkaleyfastofan)*, E-5/17 of 21 December 2017.
7. Hæstiréttur, *Merck Sharp & Dohm Corp. v. Einkaleyfastofan*, 506/2016 of 3 May 2018.

requirements were fulfilled). As mentioned above, the new SPC Regulation (EC) 469/2009 finally took effect in Iceland on 1 June 2018 so new SPC applications should in any case be based on the CJEU guidance based on that Regulation.

[1] The Relevant Marketing Authorization for the Term of an SPC

The considerations in terms of the relevant marketing authorization for determining the SPC term as set out in the EU chapter apply equally to Iceland.

The Icelandic Patent Office does not investigate whether the marketing authorization relied upon is in fact the first marketing authorization in question.

[2] The Expiration Date of an SPC

The Icelandic Patent Office calculates the last day of patent protection as the day prior to the twentieth anniversary date. The term of an SPC is calculated in the same manner and this is spelled out in the Patent Regulation Article 96. Thus, as an example, if a patent has a filing date 1 June 2000, the final day of protection is 31 May 2020, and the last date a maximum term SPC is in force is 31 May 2025. If the date of notification of the underlying marketing authorization was within ten years from the patent filing date, for example, 10 October 2008, the last day that an SPC can remain in force is 9 October 2023.

[B] Correction of the SPC Term

There are no provisions specifying how the term of an issued SPC should be corrected. Following decision C-471/14 of the CJEU (*Seattle Genetics*)[8] concerning that calculation of the term of an SPC based on a first market authorization being issued by the EMA and confirming that the calculation be based on the notification date of the market authorization, the Icelandic Patent Office offered to issue corrected certificates if requested by the SPC holder. Based on that precedent, reissue of a Certificate in order to correct the term of an SPC for another reason should as well be possible.

[C] Paediatric Extensions

The considerations relating to the term of paediatric extensions discussed in the EU chapter apply to Iceland except as provided for in transitional provisions. With the EEA Joint Committee Decision No. 92/2017 of 5 May 2017 the Regulation (EC) 469/2009 was incorporated into the EEA Agreement, with transitional provisions. Implementation in Iceland did not take place until 2018, with amendments to the Patent Act (ell.) taking effect on 1 June 2018. The transitional provisions provide that an application for paediatric extension could be filed for an SPC that expired less than six months prior to

8. CJEU *Seattle Genetics v. Österreichisches Patentamt*, C-471/14 of 6 October 2015.

1 June 2018 or in the seven months following 1 June 2018, in both cases the application would have to be lodged within one month after entry into force of the provisions in Iceland, that is prior to 1 July 2018.

§11.05 PROCEDURE OF FILING AN SPC APPLICATION

[A] Entitlement to an SPC Application

The Icelandic Patent Office has interpreted Article 6 of the SPC Regulation, that stipulates that an SPC shall be granted to the patent holder, that only the patent holder can apply for the SPC. Consequently, the Office generally requires that all data concerning the applicant of the SPC (name and address) correspond to the information referring to the patentee in the Patent registry for the basic patent. If the patent has been assigned it is the assignee who has the right to file the application for SPC.

[B] The Time Limit for Filing an SPC Application

The time limits for filing an application for SPC as set out in the EU chapter apply in Iceland. Article 70 of the Patent Regulation provides that the provisions concerning re-establishment of rights according to Article 72 ell. apply also to SPC applications.

[C] The Filing of an SPC at the National Patent Office

The SPC application must be filed using the applicable form, the form should be filled out in Icelandic. The form should be signed by the applicant or his representative. In addition to the information listed in Article 8(1)(a) of the SPC Regulation the application should indicate, if applicants are more than one, to whom notifications should be addressed in writing and must contain all relevant information about the applicant and his representative (names and addresses), as well as details in terms of the basic patent and the marketing authorization (number and date) relied upon for the product in question.

A power of attorney is required unless the representative is on the Patent Office list of exempted representatives.

[D] The Documentation Required for an SPC Application

The documentation required for filing an SPC application in Iceland is based on the requirements as set out in Article 8 of the SPC Regulation and as specified in Article 65 rg.

The SPC request should be supplemented with a copy of the Icelandic marketing authorization. If the Icelandic marketing authorization is not the first authorization then a copy of the official notice of the first marketing authorization should be submitted as well. If the accompanying documentation is not in an accepted language

(Icelandic, Danish, Norwegian, Swedish and English) it must be accompanied by a translation into one of the accepted languages. (The Patent Office may waive the requirement for a translation.)

Article 65 rg. further specifies that the application should be accompanied with 'references to the patent documents concerning the product'. This condition is fulfilled by including a statement explaining how the product is protected by the basic patent.

[E] The Definition of the Product in an SPC Application

The SPC chapter in the Patent Regulation does not include any provisions giving further instructions how the product of an SPC should be defined, in relation to the claims of the basic patent or in the Summary of Product Characteristics in the referenced marketing authorization.

The Patent Office has in the past been liberal in allowing product definitions that are broader than the specific approved product, including terminology such as 'any salts, solvates or hydrates thereof' and also, but not always, a definition including Compound X 'in all forms as protected by the basic patent'. Thus the Office generally follows the CJEU case law from *Farmitalia* (C-392/97).[9] Such broad definitions may however not be broader than what is protected by the claims of the basic patent.

As regards complex biological molecules, few certificates have so far been granted but a number of applications are pending, thus decisions from such applications are too few to provide any guidance as to how the product might be defined in any other way than by referring to the International Nonproprietary Name (INN) of the active ingredient as identified in the SmPC.

[F] SPC Examination Procedure and Appeal Procedure

An application for an SPC is initially subjected to a formality check, in particular checking if any information or documentation is missing.

If the check reveals a deficiency, an invitation is issued providing a term of three months (extendable) for rectifying.

The Patent Regulation provides a one-month term from filing to pay the application fee.

The Icelandic Patent Office will check if corresponding SPC applications have been filed and processed in Denmark, Sweden and/or Norway. If such application has been filed and granted without objections, the Office generally follows that precedent and allows the application in Iceland. If any issues have led to substantive objections and these have been treated differently by the mentioned Nordic Offices, or if no corresponding applications have been filed with these Offices, the Icelandic Patent Office will generally forward the application for substantive examination at the Danish Patent Office, with which the Icelandic Office has a collaboration agreement. Under the agreement, Icelandic SPC applications and also patent applications can be sent for

9. CJEU *Farmitalia Carlo Erba v. Bundesgerichtshof*, C-392/97 of 16 September 1999.

examination by the Danish Office. If the substantive examination reveals any deficiencies an office action is issued with an extendable three-month term limit. The applicant will receive a copy of the examination report as issued by the Danish Patent Office (which is addressed to the Icelandic Patent Office) accompanied with a formal office action by the Icelandic Office notifying the term.

At present, the first office action (or notification of allowance) is issued 1–1.5 years after the filing of an application.

If the office finds that the deficiencies are not adequately resolved by applicant's response another office action may issue or the application may be rejected. Typically, if the application has been examined by the Danish Patent Office, the applicant's response will be forwarded to the Danish examiner for review.

A rejection can be appealed to the Patent and Trademark Board of Appeal. The appeal must be filed within two months from the issue of the rejection. The appeal should set out the appellant's request and indicate the main grounds for the appeal and be accompanied with the appeal fee. The appeal board will issue a term for filing detailed substantive arguments, usually two months from the date of the letter notifying the term. The appellant may request an oral hearing, it is up to the board's discretion however whether such request is allowed. The time span for appeal proceedings varies and typically takes up to one year.

[G] Applications for a Paediatric Extension

The formal requirements for filing a paediatric extension correspond to those as outlined in the EU chapter, except for the transitional provisions set out in the EEA Joint Committee Decision No. 92/2017 of 5 May 2017,[10] as explained above in §11.04[C].

The request for a paediatric extension must be filed with the Patent Office together with the prescribed fee. At the time of writing, updated SPC application forms had not been issued. The official fee (June 2018) for a request for paediatric extension is ISK 47,800 (approx. EUR 380).

Transitional provisions allow that if an SPC has expired less than six months prior to the entering into force in Iceland of the Regulation (EC) 469/2009 which was on 1 June 2018, or will expire within seven months of that date, an application for paediatric extension may be filed within one month from said date.

After 1 July 2018, the general transitional provision of the Regulation will apply, providing that for five years following the entry into force of Regulation 1901/2006 in Iceland (until 1 June 2023) an application for paediatric extension of a granted SPC must be filed no later than six months prior to the expiry of the SPC. After the terminal provisions have expired the regular term applies meaning that an application for paediatric extension of a granted SPC must be filed no later than two years prior to the expiry of the SPC.

10. *See*: http://www.efta.int/sites/default/files/documents/legal-texts/eea/other-legal-documents/adopted-joint-committee-decisions/2017%20-%20English/092-2017.pdf.

For a pending SPC application, an application for paediatric extension can be filed at any time provided that other requirements are met.

The required supporting documents are set out in Article 8(1)(d) of the SPC Regulation for Medicinal Products. These include a copy of the statement indicating compliance with the agreed and completed Paediatric Investigation Plan (PIP). Moreover, if the product has not been approved centrally by the EMA, it is necessary for the applicant to submit proof of possession of marketing authorizations for the product in all Member States.

At the time of writing it is not known how applications for paediatric extension will be handled in practice, but likely these will be handled in collaboration with the Danish Patent Office. Amendments to the Patent Regulation No. 477/2012 took effect on 1 July 2018, introducing and amending relevant provisions relating to paediatric extension.

§11.06 PROCEDURE OF INVALIDATING AN SPC

Article 70 rg. states that a decision to issue an SPC cannot be appealed and further states that anyone can file a lawsuit for invalidation of a granted SPC. The party filing the invalidation lawsuit shall notify the Patent Office. Provisions of Article 63 ell. apply in so far as they are applicable; this article sets conditions for the party requesting invalidation that he shall inform any registered licensees. If the plaintiff does not prove on the day on which the case comes up for trial that notification under paragraph 1 has been effected, the court may fix a time limit for compliance with the requirements of paragraph 1. If the said time limit is not observed, the case shall be dismissed.

[A] Grounds for the Invalidation of an SPC

The grounds for invalidating an SPC in Iceland correspond to the grounds as set out in Article 15 of the SPC Regulations, as discussed in the EU chapter. No national decisions or case law exist that deal with this issue.

[B] The Filing of an Invalidation Suit

A lawsuit for the invalidation of an SPC must be filed in the District Court of Reykjavik. An SPC invalidation suit has to date not been filed in Iceland, nor has a suit for invalidating a patent. The Patent Act or Patent Regulation give no further conditions or requirements for the filing of an invalidation suit than what is mentioned above.

[C] Invalidation Procedure and the Corresponding Appeal Procedure

For general details on court procedures we refer to §11.03[C] above.

[D] The Revocation of a Paediatric Extension

An action for revocation of a Paediatric Extension would have to be brought before the District Court of Reykjavik. The grounds for revocation of a paediatric extension are those of Article 16 of the SPC Regulation, national provisions provide no further details.

The same considerations as set out in §11.03[C], §11.06[B] and §11.06[C] above for the revocation of an SPC apply.

§11.07 UNFAIR COMPETITION LAW

The same considerations as set out in the EU chapter apply in general for Iceland, as Icelandic competition law is generally in harmony with EU law. Antitrust issues involving SPCs have not yet been addressed by Icelandic courts.

The competition rules in the EEA Agreement are equivalent to the competition rules in the EU. The rules prohibit agreements and conduct that distort or restrict competition (Article 53).[11] The competition rules also prohibit dominant firms from abusing their market power (Article 54).[12]

The Icelandic Competition Authority ('Samkeppniseftirlitið') is the national body designated to enforce the requirements and prohibitions of the Icelandic Competition

---

11. Article 53 EEA Agreement:

    1. The following shall be prohibited as incompatible with the functioning of this Agreement:
       all agreements between undertakings, decisions by associations of undertakings and concerted practices which may affect trade between Contracting Parties and which have as their object or effect the prevention, restriction or distortion of competition within the territory covered by this Agreement, and in particular those which:
       a) directly or indirectly fix purchase or selling prices or any trading conditions;
       b) limit or control production, markets, technical development, or investment;
       c) share markets or sources of supply;
       d) apply dissimilar conditions to equivalent transactions with other trading parties, thereby placing them at a competitive disadvantage;
       e) make the conclusion of contracts subject to acceptance by the other parties of supplementary obligations which, by their nature or according to commercial usage, have no connection with the subject of such contracts.
    2. Any agreements or decisions prohibited pursuant to this Article shall be automatically void.
    3. The provisions of paragraph 1 may, however, be declared inapplicable in the case of:
       - any agreement or category of agreements between undertakings;
       - any decision or category of decisions by associations of undertakings;
       - any concerted practice or category of concerted practices;

         which contributes to improving the production or distribution of goods or to promoting technical or economic progress, while allowing consumers a fair share of the resulting benefit, and which does not:
         a) impose on the undertakings concerned restrictions which are not indispensable to the attainment of these objectives;
         b) afford such undertakings the possibility of eliminating competition in respect of a substantial part of the products in question.

12. Article 54 EEA Agreement:

Act[13] and, as applicable, Articles 53 and 54 of the EEA Agreement, and to permit exceptions pursuant to the Competition Act.

The EFTA Surveillance Authority (ESA) has the role of monitoring the compliance with the EEA competition rules in the EFTA states. ESA accordingly enforces the prohibitions in Iceland, Liechtenstein and Norway and undertakings active in those EFTA States must comply with the EEA competition rules. ESA has equivalent powers and similar functions to those of the European Commission. ESA is, like the Commission, independent from the States over which it has jurisdiction. National courts may also apply the two prohibitions in order to protect the individual rights conferred on citizens by the EEA Agreement.

A system for co-operation with national competition authorities and national courts has been put in place to ensure uniform interpretation of the EEA competition rules. The rules on co-operation are set out in ESA's Notices of cooperation:[14]

- Notice on co-operation within the EFTA Network of Competition Authorities;
- Notice on the co-operation between the EFTA Surveillance Authority and the courts of the EFTA States in the application of Articles 53 and 54 of the EEA Agreement.

More generally, ESA seeks to develop and maintain uniform surveillance throughout the EEA and to promote homogeneous implementation, application and interpretation of the EEA competition rules. ESA and the Commission co-operate to that effect, both formally and informally. As Articles 53 and 54 are identical in substance to the corresponding rules of the Treaty on the Functioning of the European Union (TFEU), the case law of the Court of Justice of the European Union and the General Court (Court of First Instance) is relevant for the interpretation of those Articles.

Any abuse by one or more undertakings of a dominant position within the territory covered by this Agreement or in a substantial part of it shall be prohibited as incompatible with the functioning of this Agreement in so far as it may affect trade between Contracting Parties.

1. Such abuse may, in particular, consist in:
   a) directly or indirectly imposing unfair purchase or selling prices or other unfair trading conditions;
   b) limiting production, markets or technical development to the prejudice of consumers;
   c) applying dissimilar conditions to equivalent transactions with other trading parties, thereby placing them at a competitive disadvantage;
   d) making the conclusion of contracts subject to acceptance by the other parties of supplementary obligations which, by their nature or according to commercial usage, have no connection with the subject of such contracts.

13. Icelandic Competition Act No. 44/2005. Unofficial translation provided by the Competition Authority is found here: http://en.samkeppni.is/media/en-news/Competition_law_no_44_2005.pdf.
14. The text of the Notices is found here: http://www.eftasurv.int/competition/notices-and-guidelines/.

CHAPTER 12
Switzerland

Alexa von Uexküll & Oswin Ridderbusch

§12.01 LEGAL BASIS

As Switzerland is not a member of the EU or EEA, the corresponding EU Regulations on SPCs are not applicable. Nevertheless, the Swiss Patent Act ('SPA')[1] has been amended so as to harmonize Swiss law with the corresponding European legislation regarding SPCs. Thus, SPCs for medicinal products were introduced in Switzerland in September 1995,[2] followed by SPCs for plant protection products in May 1999.[3] Further provisions on SPCs can be found in the Swiss Patent Ordinance ('SPO').[4]

In light of the Supplemental Agreement to the Patent Union Treaty with Switzerland,[5] SPCs granted here are also effective in Liechtenstein. The SPCs are unitary and have the same effect in both states. Nevertheless, as set out in Articles 3 and 4 of the Supplemental Agreement, exhaustion in Liechtenstein in accordance with EEA law does not imply exhaustion in Switzerland. Similarly, nullity based on EEA law does not affect the validity of the Swiss part of the SPC.

1. An English translation of the Swiss Patent Act (Bundesgesetz über die Erfindungspatente; Patentgesetz) is accessible online at: https://www.admin.ch/opc/en/classified-compilation/19540108/index.html.
2. Articles 140a et seq. of the Swiss Patent Act.
3. Articles 140n, 146 and 147 of the Swiss Patent Act.
4. *See*, in particular, Arts 3(3) and 127a–127m of the Swiss Patent Ordinance (Verordnung über die Erfindungspatente; Patentverordnung). The corresponding legal text is accessible online (in German, French and Italian only) at: https://www.admin.ch/opc/de/classified-compilation/19770250/index.html.
5. Complementary Agreement to the Treaty of 22 December 1978 between the Swiss Confederation and the Principality of Liechtenstein on Patent Protection (Ergänzungsvereinbarung zwischen der Schweizerischen Eidgenossenschaft und dem Fürstentum Liechtenstein zum Vertrag vom 22. Dezember 1978 über den Schutz der Erfindungspatente) which entered into force on 1 May 1995. Accessible online at: https://www.admin.ch/opc/de/classified-compilation/19940306/index.html.

Currently no paediatric extensions are available in Switzerland. However, following the enactment of amendments to the Federal Therapeutics Act and the Patent Act,[6] respectively, which have been passed by Parliament in March 2016, paediatric extensions will become available.

The amended legislation will not only provide for a six-month paediatric extension based on existing SPCs, but also a novel six-month 'Paediatric Certificate' for patents for which no SPCs have (or could have) been applied for.

The Swiss Patent Office (Eidgenössisches Institut für Geistiges Eigentum, 'IGE') is expected to implement the provisions for the paediatric extensions and the novel Paediatric Certificates in the beginning of 2019.

The Guidelines for the Substantive Examination of National Patent Applications ('Guidelines for Examination')[7] issued by the IGE also contain a section on the examination of SPCs and are binding for the examiners of the IGE.[8]

§12.02 SUBSTANTIVE REQUIREMENTS FOR OBTAINING AN SPC

The Swiss system for SPCs closely mirrors the corresponding legislation of the European Union. Moreover, while judgments of the CJEU on the interpretation and application of the EU legislation on SPCs are not binding in Switzerland, the Swiss authorities, including the Patent Office and the Courts strive to harmonize and align their practice to be compatible with the practice of the Community.

[A] Types of Products That Can Be Protected

Article 140a paragraphs 1 and 2 SPA define the 'product' within the meaning of the provisions relating to SPCs for medicinal products as the 'active ingredient or combination of active ingredients' which have been approved as medicinal products in Switzerland.

Moreover, Article 140n provides that an SPC may issue for an 'active ingredient or combination of active ingredients' of plant protection products.

[1] Practical Considerations: What Is the Active Ingredient or Combination of Active Ingredients That Can Form the Basis for an SPC

As set out in the EU chapter, the Explanatory Memorandum to the original SPC Regulation for Medicinal Products[9] indicates that the 'product' of an SPC should be

6. Botschaft zur Änderung des Heilmittelgesetzes 12.080 of 7 November 2012.
7. IGE, Guidelines for the Substantive Examination of National Patent Applications (Richtlinien für die Sachprüfung der nationalen Patentanmeldungen), 1 April 2017.
8. IGE, Guidelines for the Substantive Examination of National Patent Applications (Richtlinien für die Sachprüfung der nationalen Patentanmeldungen), 1 April 2017, Section 1.1.
9. Explanatory Memorandum to the Commission proposal for an SPC regulation for medicinal products, COM(90) 101 final - SYN 255, paragraph 28.

narrowly construed, based on the EU regulatory provisions for medicinal products. While there is no equivalent detailed memorandum documenting the background for introducing Swiss SPCs, one must bear in mind that the SPC provisions in Switzerland have been established in an attempt to seek legal harmonization with the provisions of the EU.

Thus, as confirmed in the Federal Administrative Court decisions *Etanercept* (B-3064/2008)[10] and *Panitumumab* (B-3245/2010),[11] it was the Swiss legislator's express intention to copy the statutory provisions of EU law and, accordingly, the Swiss national SPC provisions should be interpreted in conformity with EU law and practice. It thus follows that many of the practical considerations voiced in the EU chapter also apply to Switzerland.

[2] Active Ingredient or Combination of Active Ingredients of a Medicinal Product

The current SPA provides no definition of the terms 'active ingredient' or 'combination of active ingredients' of a medicinal product which may be subject matter of an SPC.

Moreover, the guidance provided in the Explanatory Message of 1993 relating to the introduction of SPC provisions in Switzerland[12] merely states that the product of an SPC is not the (human or veterinary) medicinal product which has been approved but rather the active ingredient(s) used in such products.

The Swiss Council of States has thus decided that within the framework of the planned amendments in the Patent Act so as to provide for paediatric extensions, the product definition in the SPA in relation to SPCs for medicinal products should be amended to take account of the guidance provided by the CJEU in the decision *MIT* (C-431/04).[13]

Thus, as discussed in the Explanatory Message of 2012 concerning the Amendment of the Federal Therapeutics Act,[14] new Article 140a paragraph 1*bis* SPA is to read as follows:

> An active ingredient is a component of a medicinal product composition of chemical or biological origin, which exhibits a medicinal effect on an organism. A combination of active ingredients is a combination of multiple components, which all have a medicinal effect on the organism.

As outlined, it is expected that this amendment, together with the provisions for paediatric extensions will enter into force in early 2019.

10. Swiss Federal Administrative Court (Bundesverwaltungsgericht), judgment B-3064/2008 of 13 September 2010 – Etanercept; *see*, in particular, Section 3 of the reasons.
11. Swiss Federal Administrative Court (Bundesverwaltungsgericht), judgment B-3245/2010 of 18 August 2011 – Panitumumab.
12. Botschaft zu einer Änderung des Bundesgesetzes betreffend die Erfindungspatente sowie zu einem Bundesbeschluss über eine Änderung des Übereinkommens über die Erteilung Europäischer Patente 93.061 of 18 August 1993.
13. CJEU *Massachusetts Institute of Technology v. Bundesgerichtshof*, C-431/04 of 4 May 2006.
14. Botschaft zur Änderung des Heilmittelgesetzes 12.080 of 7 November 2012.

According to its established practice, the IGE only allows active ingredients which exert a medicinal effect on their own to be included in the definition of the 'product' of an SPC.

[3] Active Substance or Combination of Active Substances of a Plant Protection Product

The current SPA provides no definition of the terms 'active ingredient' or 'combination of active ingredients' of a plant protection product.

In the Explanatory Message of 1998 relating to the Amendment of the Patent Act[15] introducing the proposed amendments for the implementation of SPCs for plant protection products in Switzerland, reference is made to the Swiss Directive for Plant Protection Products.[16] According to this Explanatory Message, the definition provided in this Directive for Plant Protection Products is also applicable to SPCs for plant protection products. While the definition provided here is not identical to the corresponding definition in EU regulatory law, the Swiss authorities also acknowledge foreign marketing authorizations, which would not be covered by the Swiss Directive, if they have been assessed based on equivalent conditions and are agriculturally and environmentally acceptable.[17] As such, according to the Explanatory Message, the compatibility of Swiss law with the EU provisions has been provided for.

Within the framework of the planned changes in the Patent Act so as to provide for paediatric extensions, a further amendment of the SPA has been proposed,[18] advocating an analogous definition for the concept of the product of an SPC for plant protection products as used in the SPC Regulation for Plant Protection Products (Regulation (EC) 1610/96[19]). Accordingly, in the future the definition of the active ingredient(s) of a plant protection product in Switzerland as set out in Article 140t paragraph 3 SPA will be as follows:

> Active ingredients are substances and micro-organisms including viruses, having general or specific action:
>
> (a) against harmful organisms;
> (b) on plants, parts of plants or plant products.

[4] Fixed-Dose and Loose Combinations

While SPCs are clearly available for fixed-dose combinations in Switzerland, no further information is available in terms of how the IGE deals with SPCs based on medicinal or

15. Botschaft zur Änderung des Patentgesetzes 98.008 of 19 January 1998.
16. Verordnung über das Inverkehrbringen von Pflanzenbehandlungsmitteln und Mitteln zum Schutz von Erntegütern of 26 January 1994.
17. Bundesgesetz über die Förderung der Landwirtschaft und die Erhaltung des Bauernstandes of 3 October 1951.
18. Botschaft zur Änderung des Heilmittelgesetzes 12.080 of 7 November 2012.
19. Regulation (EC) No. 1610/96 of the European Parliament and of the Council of 23 July 1996 concerning the creation of a supplementary protection certificate for plant protection products.

plant protection products which have been approved as loose combinations, i.e., where the approved formulation contains only one active ingredient, which however is to be administered or applied jointly with another active agent formulated as a separate composition.

[5] Limitation to Products Subjected to a Specific Marketing Authorization Procedure

In order to secure SPC protection in Switzerland, the product must have been authorized by the competent Swiss authorities. No further information beyond this is available.

[6] Protection of Medical Devices

The Swiss Federal Therapeutics Act (Heilmittelgesetz) and the Swiss Medical Devices Ordinance (Medizinprodukteverordnung) transpose requirements of the European Medical Device Directives into Swiss law and specify additional national requirements. The Swiss therapeutic product regulation is enforced by the Swiss Agency for Therapeutic Products (Swissmedic) and by the Cantonal Authorities in specific areas.

Moreover, there is a bilateral agreement with the EFTA states on the mutual recognition of conformity assessment of medical devices.[20]

In the *Taxol-Stent* decision (B-3026/2015)[21] the Federal Administrative Court concluded that a Conformity Assessment Certificate for a paclitaxel (Taxol®) eluting stent may not be viewed as the first approval of a product within the meaning of Article 140a SPA, as the active ingredient 'paclitaxel' cannot be classified as an embodiment which together with the stent forms an integral unitary product. As paclitaxel had already been previously approved, the SPC request was rejected.

As set out in the EU chapter, the question whether SPCs are available for medical device/drug combinations is the subject of a referral by the German Federal Patent Court that is currently pending before the CJEU (case C-527/17).[22] It is conceivable that the Swiss authorities will take account of the guidance provided by the CJEU in this regard in the future.

[B] Basic Patent

The considerations as set out in the EU chapter also apply to Switzerland. Thus, the basic patent which may be relied upon in Switzerland for an SPC filing is either a Swiss national patent or a European patent validated in Switzerland.[23]

20. Abkommen zwischen der Schweizerischen Eidgenossenschaft und der Europäischen Gemeinschaft über die gegenseitige Anerkennung von Konformitätsbewertungen of 21 June 1999.
21. Swiss Federal Administrative Court (Bundesverwaltungsgericht), judgment B-3026/2015 of 21 December 2016 – Taxol-Stent.
22. German Federal Patent Court decision 14 W (pat) 13/16 of 18 July 2017.
23. IGE, Guidelines for the Substantive Examination of National Patent Applications (Richtlinien für die Sachprüfung der nationalen Patentanmeldungen), 1 April 2017, Section 13.2.1.

According to Article 140b(1)(a) SPA, a basic patent must either protect the product as such, a process for its manufacture or its use.

The patent must be in force at the date of filing.

[1] Requirement for the Product to Be 'Protected' by the Basic Patent

The Swiss authorities have traditionally applied the so-called infringement test in order to determine whether a product is protected by a basic patent. This practice has been confirmed in the Federal Supreme Court decision *Fosinopril* (Case 124 III 375).[24] In accordance with this decision an SPC may be granted for a combination of active ingredients, even if only one of the active ingredients is subject matter of the claims of the basic patent. In this context, according to the Court it does not matter that the corresponding mono-product had already been subject matter of an SPC.

The 'infringement test' approach, which up until the Federal Supreme Court decision *Truvada* (4A_576/2017)[25] had been adopted in Switzerland, differs fundamentally from the by now well-established 'identification test' applied in the EU based on the guidance provided by the CJEU. Thus, in *Medeva* (C-322/10)[26] and various subsequent decisions[27] the CJEU has held that the product of an SPC, i.e., the active ingredient or combination of active ingredients, must be 'specified in the wording of the claims' (or 'identified in the wording of the claims') of the basic patent. In justifying its conclusion reached in *Medeva*, the CJEU relied primarily on the lack of harmonization of substantive patent law at the EU level and the aim of the SPC Regulation to prevent heterogeneous national developments that could create obstacles to the free movement of goods within the EU's single market.

The validity of the 'infringement test' approach, being in divergence with EU practice, has since been put under scrutiny. In recognition of the resulting divergent development in the practice of the IGE and EEA Member States, the IGE in 2016 initiated amendments of its Guidelines for Examination[28] for SPCs in order to take account of the CJEU *Medeva* ruling, so as to facilitate harmonization.

Subsequently, however, in the first-instance *Truvada* decision (O2017_001),[29] where the validity of the 'infringement test' was the primary contentious issue, the Swiss Federal Patent Court took the opportunity to carefully review the guidance

24. Swiss Federal Supreme Court (Bundesgericht), judgment 124 III 375 of 10 July 1998 – Fosinopril.
25. Swiss Federal Supreme Court (Bundesgericht), judgment 4A_576/2017 of 11 June 2018 – Truvada (Tenofovir Disoproxilfumarat + Emtricitabin).
26. CJEU *Medeva v. Comptroller General of Patents, Designs and Trade Marks*, C-322/10 of 24 November 2011, headnote 1.
27. CJEU *University of Queensland v. Comptroller-General of Patents, Designs and Trade Marks*, C-630/10 of 25 November 2011, headnote 1; CJEU *Daiichi Sankyo v. Comptroller General of Patents, Designs and Trade Marks*, C-6/11 of 25 November 2011, headnote; CJEU *Yeda Research and Development v. Comptroller General of Patents, Designs and Trade Marks*, C-518/10 of 25 November 2011, headnote and paragraph 37; CJEU *Eli Lilly v. Human Genome Sciences*, C-493/12 of 12 December 2013, paragraph 38.
28. IGE, Guidelines for the Substantive Examination of National Patent Applications (Richtlinien für die Sachprüfung der nationalen Patentanmeldungen), 1 April 2017.
29. Swiss Federal Patent Court (Bundespatentgericht), judgment O2017_001 of 3 October 2017 – Truvada (Tenofovir Disoproxilfumarat + Emtricitabin).

provided by the CJEU in the relevant decisions in relation to the requirement that 'the product is protected by the basic patent' in accordance with Article 3(a) of the SPC Regulation. The Court summarized the 'core messages' in the CJEU decisions in a table[30] which is reproduced below as Table 12.1:

Table 12.1 Core Messages of CJEU Decisions as Summarized by the Swiss Federal Patent Court in Truvada (O2017_001)

CJEU Decision	*Core Message*
Medeva	which are not specified in the wording of the claims of the basic patent
Yeda	is not the subject of any claim relating to that active ingredient alone
Actavis/Sanofi	core inventive advance that is the subject of the basic patent
University of Queensland and Daiichi Sankyo	which are not identified in the wording of the claims of the basic patent
Eli Lilly	the claims relate, implicitly but necessarily and specifically, to the active ingredient in question
Actavis/Boehringer Ingelheim	the subject matter of the invention covered which constitutes the sole subject matter of the invention

The Federal Patent Court concluded that the guidance provided by the CJEU in these decisions is unclear, amounting to a 'terminological mess' ('terminologisches Durcheinander'[31]), giving rise to more questions than answers. As a consequence the Court considered a harmonization of the Swiss SPC case law in this regard to be premature as long as the CJEU does not provide comprehensible and clearly implementable guidance. As the established 'infringement test' as applied in Switzerland in accordance with the *Fosinopril* decision is simple, comprehensible, and provides legal certainty, the Court saw no reason to change the practice in Switzerland in terms of how to assess whether a product is protected by a basic patent in force in order to be entitled to an SPC.

On appeal, however, the Swiss Federal Supreme Court in *Truvada* emphasized the paramount importance of a harmonized interpretation of the SPC rules.[32] According to the Federal Supreme Court, the historically different approaches adopted in Switzerland versus the EU in terms of how to determine whether a product is protected by a basic patent according to Article 140b(1)(a) SPA and Article 3(a) of the EU SPC Regulation, respectively, do not affect just isolated cases. As such, in order to ensure

30. *Ibid.*, paragraph 44.
31. *Ibid.*, paragraph 45.
32. Swiss Federal Supreme Court (Bundesgericht), judgment 4A_576/2017 of 11 June 2018 – Truvada (Tenofovir Disoproxilfumarat + Emtricitabin), Section 2.2.3 of the reasons.

conformity of the Swiss practice with the EU, it is necessary that coherent and harmonized considerations are applied. In light of the legislator's intended alignment of Swiss SPC law to EU law, the Swiss authorities cannot ignore the case law and practice in the EU when interpreting the Swiss SPC provisions. To this effect it is immaterial that the case law of the CJEU is not always very clear in all its details.

The Federal Supreme Court thus ruled that the infringement test as applied in *Fosinopril* can no longer be maintained in Switzerland.[33] Thus, if a basic patent only claims one active ingredient, then an SPC may not issue on the basis of a marketing authorization for a medicinal product comprising two active ingredients. Article 140b(1)(a) SPA must be interpreted based on the EU paradigm developed by the CJEU, namely that the active ingredients must be recited in the claims of the basic patent or must implicitly and necessarily be derivable from the disclosure of the patent, taking into account the description in accordance with Article 51(3) SPA (corresponding to Article 69 EPC).

The Court, however, also concluded that this change of practice does not have a retroactive effect.[34] Thus, as Gilead's SPC for the combination of tenofovir disoproxil fumarate with emtricitabine had been legally issued on the then applicable infringement test, the SPC cannot now be revoked as at the time the conditions for granting the SPC were fulfilled. The Court emphasized that due to the requirement of legal certainty as a general rule, the grant of an SPC may not be revoked due to a later change in practice when interpreting the SPC provisions.

In summary, therefore, while according to the Federal Supreme Court in *Truvada* the infringement test is no longer applicable in order to determine whether a product is protected by a basic patent within the meaning of Article 140b(1)(a) SPA, this change in practice does not affect the validity of SPCs which have already been granted in light of the infringement test.

There is still some uncertainty in terms of how pending SPC applications will be dealt with. While the Swiss Federal Supreme Court does not expressly address this, it would appear that from now on not only all future SPC applications, but also all pending cases must be examined in accordance with the CJEU's identification test. This is, in fact, in accordance with the approach as set out in the Guidelines for Examination (as of 1 April 2017)[35] which already reflect the guidance provided by the CJEU in *Medeva*.

[a] Small Molecules

With respect to basic patents claiming and identifying the active ingredient(s) in question via generic chemical formulae, the IGE has generally taken a liberal approach and has, in practice, accepted the grant of SPCs even in the absence of an explicit and

33. *Ibid.*, Section 2.2.6 of the reasons.
34. *Ibid.*, Sections 3–3.7 of the reasons.
35. IGE, Guidelines for the Substantive Examination of National Patent Applications (Richtlinien für die Sachprüfung der nationalen Patentanmeldungen), 1 April 2017, Section 13.2.2.

individualized disclosure of the chemical name or structure of the respective active ingredient(s).

In light of the Federal Supreme Court ruling in *Truvada* (4A_576/2017),[36] it is however very likely that the IGE will closely follow and apply the standards established by the CJEU in this regard.

[b] Polymers

No special considerations apply.

[c] Antibodies, Enzymes and Other Proteins

No special considerations apply.

[d] Nucleic Acids

No special considerations apply.

[2] Basic Patent Claiming the Product, i.e., the Active Ingredient(s), but Not the Corresponding Authorized Medicinal Product (or Plant Protection Product)

The same considerations as set out in the EU chapter apply.

[3] Requirement for the Product to Constitute 'the Invention' of the Basic Patent

The IGE generally does not require that the product of an SPC must constitute 'the invention' or the 'core inventive advance' of the basic patent in order to be 'protected' by the basic patent in accordance with Article 140b(1)(a) SPA.

[4] Criteria for Choosing the Basic Patent among Various Available Patents

In principle, the same considerations apply as set out in the EU chapter. In this context, it should however be noted that contrary to the practice of many patent offices in the EU, according to the Federal Administrative Court decision *Exenatide* (case B-1019/2010),[37] the applicant must decide early on which patent he wishes to rely

36. Swiss Federal Supreme Court (Bundesgericht), judgment 4A_576/2017 of 11 June 2018 – Truvada (Tenofovir Disoproxilfumarat + Emtricitabin).
37. Swiss Federal Administrative Court (Bundesverwaltungsgericht), judgment B-1019/2010 of 20 October 2010 – Exenatide.

upon as a basic patent for an SPC application, as the IGE will not grant a stay of the prosecution of an SPC, e.g., pending the outcome of opposition proceedings.

[C] The Marketing Authorization Forming Basis for an SPC

The considerations in relation to the marketing authorization forming basis for an SPC application as set out in the EU chapter, specifically in §1.02[C], apply equally to Switzerland, with the exception that the marketing authorization relied upon must be the first one in Switzerland (not in the EU or the EEA) under Article 140b(2) SPA.

Thus, in Switzerland, it is mandatory that at the filing date both the basic patent as well as the marketing authorization relied upon are in force. As set out in the Guidelines for Examination,[38] the marketing authorization does not necessarily have to be identical with the first authorization. Thus it may be a variation of the original authorization, due to changes in the galenic formulation or the like.

[1] Combinations of Active Ingredients

[a] The Marketing Authorization Refers to Fewer Active Ingredients than the SPC Application

The considerations as set out in the EU chapter also in principle apply in Switzerland.

Thus, in the decision *Panitumumab* (B-3245/2010),[39] the Federal Administrative Court ruled that an SPC can only be granted if the product falls within the scope of protection of the basic patent. As a consequence, if the basic patent claims a combination of active ingredients such as a monoclonal antibody in conjunction with an anti-neoplastic agent, this combination is the patent's contribution to the art. An individual component of this combination is not an equivalent embodiment to the patented combination and does not fall within the scope of protection of the basic patent.

[b] The Marketing Authorization Refers to More Active Ingredients than the SPC Application

As outlined, up until recently the 'infringement test' has been applied in Switzerland in order to determine whether a product is protected by a basic patent. As such, as a combination product will infringe a patent protecting an individual component of the combination, it logically follows that an SPC may also be obtained on the basis of a marketing authorization comprising more active ingredients than the SPC application. This has been confirmed by the Federal Supreme Court in the *Fosinopril* case (124 III

38. IGE, Guidelines for the Substantive Examination of National Patent Applications (Richtlinien für die Sachprüfung der nationalen Patentanmeldungen), 1 April 2017, Section 13.2.2.
39. Swiss Federal Administrative Court (Bundesverwaltungsgericht), judgment B-3245/2010 of 18 August 2011 – Panitumumab.

375).[40] These considerations also apply if for the mono-product an SPC has already been granted.

As outlined in *Truvada* (4A_576/2017),[41] the Swiss Federal Supreme Court has ruled that Switzerland must depart from the infringement test approach and align its SPC granting practice to that of the EU. In *Medeva* the CJEU however ruled that an SPC can be granted for an active ingredient or a combination of active ingredients, even if the medicinal product of the marketing authorization relied upon also contains additional active ingredients.

According to the Guidelines for Examination (as of 1 April 2017),[42] if an SPC application is pending on the basis of the patent claiming active ingredient A, but the marketing authorization relied upon relates to a combination of active ingredients (e.g., A + B), then the certificate will be granted for the product A. As such, the current Swiss practice is de facto already in line with EU practice. It thus follows that the considerations as set out in the EU chapter also apply here.

[c] The Marketing Authorization Indicates That a Medicinal Product Containing a Single Active Ingredient Is Authorized for Use in Combination with a Further Active Ingredient

No information in this regard is currently available. The Swiss authorities are likely to adapt their practice to that of the EU.

[2] The Marketing Authorization Has Not Yet Been Granted at the Time the SPC Application Is Filed

The same considerations as set out in the EU chapter apply.

[3] The Holder of the Marketing Authorization

In accordance with the established practice of the IGE, the SPC applicant does not have to be the holder of the marketing authorization. It is thus unproblematic to file an SPC on the basis of a third-party marketing authorization.

Indeed, the Federal Administrative Court in *Etanercept* (B-3064/2008)[43] explicitly acknowledged that a patent holder may apply for an SPC on the basis of a third-party marketing authorization. In this regard, the Court stressed (in English translation):

> The right to the SPC follows the right to the patent (Article 140c(1) SPA) and not any 'ownership' of the marketing authorization. For the issue of an SPC, the law

40. Swiss Federal Supreme Court (Bundesgericht), judgment 124 III 375 of 10 July 1998 – Fosinopril.
41. Swiss Federal Supreme Court (Bundesgericht), judgment 4A_576/2017 of 11 June 2018 – Truvada (Tenofovir Disoproxilfumarat + Emtricitabin).
42. IGE, Guidelines for the Substantive Examination of National Patent Applications (Richtlinien für die Sachprüfung der nationalen Patentanmeldungen), 1 April 2017, Section 13.2.3.
43. Swiss Federal Administrative Court (Bundesverwaltungsgericht), judgment B-3064/2008 of 13 September 2010 – Etanercept, Section 5.4 of the reasons.

does not take into account who applies for the marketing authorization of a medicinal or plant protection product, who has provided the often complex, necessary evidence and paid the fees incurred. Even someone who has not been granted the first authorization or has not been granted any authorization for the placing on the market of a medicinal or plant protection product can request an SPC on the basis of the first authorization granted to a third party.

[4] Reliance on a Marketing Authorization Granted under a Provision Other than Directive 2001/83/EC or Directive 2001/82/EC

In Switzerland the marketing authorization which can be relied upon must be the first marketing authorization for the active ingredient(s) as a medicinal product for human or veterinary use. The marketing authorization must be issued by Swissmedic or the Federal Veterinary Office.

[5] The Marketing Authorizations Which Can Be Relied upon for SPC Applications for Plant Protection Products

The marketing authorization which can be relied upon must be the first marketing authorization for the active ingredient(s) as a plant protection product by the Swiss Federal Office of Agriculture.

[6] The Product in Question Is Contained in the Authorized Medicinal Product (or the Authorized Plant Protection Product) but Is Not Identified as an Active Ingredient in the Corresponding Marketing Authorization

No further considerations apply.

[7] The Notion of the 'First' Marketing Authorization

In Switzerland the concept of the first marketing authorization has evolved over time. Initially, the legislator appears to have had a narrow concept of the notion of the 'first marketing authorization' in mind. However, in accordance with the current practice of the IGE, a more liberal, differential approach is applied.

Thus, the Explanatory Message of 1993 relating to the introduction of SPC provisions into Swiss law explains that Article 140b(2) SPA (which provides that an SPC will only issue on the basis of the first marketing authorization) ensures that an SPC cannot issue for further medicinal indications for the product.[44]

44. Botschaft zu einer Änderung des Bundesgesetzes betreffend die Erfindungspatente sowie zu einem Bundesbeschluss über eine Änderung des Übereinkommens über die Erteilung Europäischer Patente 93.061 of 18 August 1993.

In the meantime, however, as evidenced by the practice of the IGE, SPCs may generally speaking issue if the new approval is based on a separate later invention, in spite of the fact that the same active ingredient(s) has been subject matter of a prior Swiss approval.

This is also reflected in the case law available as well as the Guidelines for Examination.[45]

[a] *Marketing Authorization for a New Therapeutic Application of a Previously Authorized Product*

As discussed in §12.02[C][7] above, in accordance with the 1993 Explanatory Message introducing SPCs into Swiss law,[46] SPCs should not issue for new therapeutic indications.

Further, as is evident from the Council of States winter session 2014 paper,[47] in accordance with the initial proposal of the Federal Council of 7 November 2012, Article 140b(2) SPA was to be amended to the effect that a certificate is granted 'on the basis of the marketing authorization for the first medical indication (first marketing authorization)', suggesting that SPCs should not be available for new therapeutic applications of a previously authorized active ingredient (or combination of active ingredients). The National Council, however, revised the draft so that Article 140b(2) SPA in the current proposal provides that the certificate will be granted 'on the basis of the first marketing authorization', which merely amounts to an editorial amendment.[48] The Swiss Council of States has in the meantime endorsed the proposal of the National Council.

In accordance with the Guidelines for Examination (as of 1 April 2017),[49] as an SPC is not granted for the approved medicinal product, different dosages and indications may not serve as the basis for an SPC. Nevertheless, the mere fact that the approved product contains the same active ingredient(s) does not necessarily imply that it is the same product. If a new invention is made on the basis of a known product (i.e., the same active ingredient or combination of active ingredients), such as the use of the product for the treatment of a new medical indication, then the product may be viewed as an independent product which may be subject matter of an SPC; *see also* the

45. IGE, Guidelines for the Substantive Examination of National Patent Applications (Richtlinien für die Sachprüfung der nationalen Patentanmeldungen), 1 April 2017, Section 13.2.2.
46. Botschaft zu einer Änderung des Bundesgesetzes betreffend die Erfindungspatente sowie zu einem Bundesbeschluss über eine Änderung des Übereinkommens über die Erteilung Europäischer Patente 93.061 of 18 August 1993.
47. Ständerat, 12.080 *n*, Heilmittelgesetz Änderung, Wintersession 2014.
48. The German term currently used for the marketing authorization in Art. 140b(2) SPA, i.e., 'Genehmigung', was considered old-fashioned and should be replaced by 'Zulassung'; *see also* Botschaft zur Änderung des Heilmittelgesetzes 12.080 of 7 November 2012.
49. IGE, Guidelines for the Substantive Examination of National Patent Applications (Richtlinien für die Sachprüfung der nationalen Patentanmeldungen), 1 April 2017, Section 13.1.

Ciclosporin decision (PA 03/97),[50] handed down by the Swiss Appeals Commission for Intellectual Property.[51]

In light of these considerations, the IGE has allowed SPCs to issue on the basis of a marketing authorization for a new therapeutic use. Thus, for example, the SPC for the product 'melatonin' (C00518468/01), which was subject matter of the CJEU *Neurim* (C-130/11)[52] referral, was allowed by the IGE.

The practice of the IGE thus appears to be in line with the practice in the EU in this regard.

[b] Marketing Authorization for a New Formulation of a Previously Authorized Product

The Swiss authorities apply a differential approach in relation to SPCs for a new formulation of a previously authorized product.

This position is evident from the Federal Supreme Court decision *Arzneimittel* (4A.7/1998),[53] where an SPC was allowed to issue for a new dosage form of the previously approved combination of active ingredients comprising 'deogestrel and ethinyl estradiol'. According to the Court, more differential considerations need to be applied in order to assess whether a product may be considered to be new within the meaning of the SPC provisions. In this context it was considered to be of significance that the claim of the basic patent relied upon for the new dosage of the active ingredients was a product claim.

In contrast, however, a new marketing authorization based on a new formulation of a previously authorized product having the same mode of application, e.g., a topical formulation as a gel versus a cream, are viewed as the same product (*see* e.g., the Swiss Appeals Commission for Intellectual Property decision *Differin Gel* (PA 02/03)[54] and the Federal Administrative Court decision *Etanercept* (B-3064/2008)[55]), so that no SPC may issue.

In light of the desired alignment of the Swiss implementation of the SPC provisions, it is conceivable that the Swiss practice in this regard will change, depending on the guidance provided by the CJEU in the *Abraxis* referral (C-443/17),[56]

50. Swiss Appeals Commission for Intellectual Property (Eidgenössische Rekurskommission für geistiges Eigentum), decision PA 03/97 of 30 April 1999 – Ciclosporin.
51. With effect of 1 January 2007, the Swiss Appeals Commission for Intellectual Property (Eidgenössische Rekurskommission für geistiges Eigentum) was dissolved and replaced by the newly established Federal Administrative Court (Bundesverwaltungsgericht).
52. CJEU *Neurim Pharmaceuticals v. Comptroller-General of Patents*, C-130/11 of 19 July 2012.
53. Swiss Federal Supreme Court (Bundesgericht), judgment 4A.7/1998 of 17 November 1998 – Arzneimittel.
54. Swiss Appeals Commission for Intellectual Property (Eidgenössische Rekurskommission für geistiges Eigentum), decision PA 02/03 of 21 January 2005 – Differin Gel.
55. Swiss Federal Administrative Court (Bundesverwaltungsgericht), judgment B-3064/2008 of 13 September 2010 – Etanercept.
56. CJEU *Abraxis Bioscience v. Comptroller General of Patents*, C-443/17, referral of 24 July 2017.

where the Court has been asked to provide guidance as to whether an SPC may issue where the approved medicinal product is a new formulation of an old active ingredient.

[c] *Marketing Authorization for a New Specific Salt, Ester or Other Derivative of a Previously Authorized Active Ingredient*

According to the Guidelines for Examination (as of 1 April 2017),[57] different salts or esters of an active ingredient are regarded as one and the same chemical substance, and thus as the same product, unless the specific salt or ester has an influence on the pharmacological effect. If the new salt, ester or other derivative is subject matter of a patent, then a corresponding marketing authorization may form basis for an SPC.

[d] *Marketing Authorization for a New Specific Enantiomer of an Active Ingredient Previously Authorized in Racemic Form*

The IGE has issued SPCs on the basis of a new enantiomer of a previously authorized racemic active ingredient (*see* e.g., the Swiss SPC for escitalopram, C00347066/01).

[e] *The Product Has Already Been Placed on the Market Before, but Without an Authorization Granted under Directive 2001/83/EC or Directive 2001/82/EC*

These considerations do not apply to Switzerland.

[f] *Prior Marketing Authorization Which Refers to Fewer Active Ingredients than The SPC Application (and the Later Marketing Authorization Relied upon)*

In accordance with the current practice of the IGE, as an approved medicinal product with more active ingredients (e.g., A + B + C) clearly differs from a previously approved medicinal product comprising fewer active ingredients (e.g., A + B), it is a new product which as such may be subject matter of an SPC (*see also* the Federal Supreme Court decision *Fosinopril*, Case 124 III 375[58]). An SPC may thus be granted for the corresponding combination of active ingredients (A + B + C) on the basis of the later marketing authorization. This is also in accordance with the approach as set out in the Guidelines for Examination.[59]

57. IGE, Guidelines for the Substantive Examination of National Patent Applications (Richtlinien für die Sachprüfung der nationalen Patentanmeldungen), 1 April 2017, Section 13.1.
58. Swiss Federal Supreme Court (Bundesgericht), judgment 124 III 375 of 10 July 1998 – Fosinopril.
59. IGE, Guidelines for the Substantive Examination of National Patent Applications (Richtlinien für die Sachprüfung der nationalen Patentanmeldungen), 1 April 2017, Section 13.2.4.

[g] Prior Marketing Authorization Which Refers to More Active Ingredients than the SPC Application (and the Later Marketing Authorization Relied upon)

Under Swiss practice, a single active ingredient and a combination of active ingredients (as well as distinct combinations of active ingredients) are considered to be different products, which is also acknowledged in the Guidelines for Examination.[60] An SPC may thus issue on the basis of a later approval of the corresponding active ingredient(s), even where an earlier approval of a medicinal product containing more active ingredients exists.

It is, however, conceivable that in light of the Federal Supreme Court decision *Truvada* (4A_576/2017),[61] the Swiss practice in this regard might change, so as to be in conformity with EU practice.

[D] Preclusion of New SPCs by an Earlier SPC

As set out in Article 140c(2) SPA, only one certificate may issue for each product. Nevertheless, as provided for in Article 140c(3) SPA, if multiple SPC applications based on patents held by different patentees are pending and no SPC has yet been issued, then an SPC may issue for each applicant.

[1] Consequences of an Earlier Third-Party SPC for the Same Product

[a] The 'One SPC per Product per Patent Holder' Rule

Article 140c SPA has been amended (*see* Explanatory Message of 1998 relating to the Amendment of the Patent Act[62]) to align the Swiss provisions with the EU SPC Regulations. Accordingly, Article 140c(2) SPA provides that only one SPC may issue per product. Article 140c(3) SPA provides that if multiple SPCs are filed for the same product based on patents held by different patentees and no SPC has issued, then a certificate may issue to each applicant.

The requirement in Article 140c(3) SPA that 'no certificate has yet been granted' would seem to imply that it should be possible to obtain an SPC only if any earlier SPC application directed to the same product is still pending at the time of filing.

In the *Etanercept* decision (B-3064/2008),[63] however, the Federal Administrative Court ruled that Article 140c(3) SPA, contrary to the literal wording of this provision, must be interpreted as meaning that each applicant may obtain one SPC for the same

60. *Ibid.*
61. Swiss Federal Supreme Court (Bundesgericht), judgment 4A_576/2017 of 11 June 2018 – Truvada (Tenofovir Disoproxilfumarat + Emtricitabin).
62. Botschaft zur Änderung des Patentgesetzes 98.008 of 19 January 1998.
63. Swiss Federal Administrative Court (Bundesverwaltungsgericht), judgment B-3064/2008 of 13 September 2010 – Etanercept; *see*, in particular, Section 8 of the reasons.

product, even if other SPCs for that product have already been granted to other patent holders at the filing date of the respective SPC application.

[b] *Earlier SPC Granted to an Affiliated Third Party*

Under Swiss practice, legally distinct but affiliated entities can each be granted one SPC for the same product. This practice is explicitly sanctioned by the Guidelines for Examination[64] which stipulate (in English translation):

> If several affiliated companies each file an SPC application based on a different patent, they can be granted. Affiliated companies are legally independent entities and thus 'two or more patentees'.[65]

Notwithstanding this liberal approach, the Federal Administrative Court in *Etanercept* (B-3064/2008)[66] held that the IGE should be allowed to reject SPC applications in cases of abusive behaviour, including where an applicant seeks to surreptitiously obtain a second SPC for the same product using a straw man. There is no case law specifically addressing this aspect.

[c] *Partial Overlap Between the Holders of the Earlier SPC and the Applicants for the New SPC*

The same considerations as set out in the EU chapter apply.

[d] *Earlier Third-Party SPC Has Been Licensed-In*

The same considerations as set out in the EU chapter apply.

[2] *Consequences of an Own Earlier SPC for the Same Product*

In light of the 'one SPC per patent per holder' concept as provided for in Article 140c(2) and 140c(3) SPA, as a general rule, a prior issued SPC precludes the issue of a further SPC for the same product to the same applicant. If the product, however, has been modified, e.g., by the inclusion of a further active ingredient, a second SPC may issue (*see* the Federal Supreme Court decision *Fosinopril*, 124 III 375[67]). The same considerations should apply if a second SPC is based on a patent directed towards a new

64. IGE, Guidelines for the Substantive Examination of National Patent Applications (Richtlinien für die Sachprüfung der nationalen Patentanmeldungen), 1 April 2017, Section 13.2.4, penultimate paragraph.
65. The original German expression translated as 'two or more patentees' is identical to the corresponding expression used in Art. 140c(3) SPA.
66. Swiss Federal Administrative Court (Bundesverwaltungsgericht), judgment B-3064/2008 of 13 September 2010 – Etanercept, Section 8.2 of the reasons.
67. Swiss Federal Supreme Court (Bundesgericht), judgment 124 III 375 of 10 July 1998 – Fosinopril.

therapeutic indication or substantially new galenic formulation (*see* e.g., the Federal Administrative Court decision *Etanercept*, B-3064/2008[68]).

[a] Own Earlier SPC Application Not Yet Granted

In light of the fact that only one SPC may be granted for the same applicant, the patentee will be required to make a choice in terms of which patent should be extended. Unlike other patent offices, the IGE will generally not allow SPC applicants to delay prosecution of an SPC, in order to e.g., await the outcome of an opposition (*see* Federal Administrative Court decision *Exenatide*, B-1019/2010[69]).

[b] Revocation, Surrender or Lapse of the Own Earlier SPC after Grant

The same considerations as set out in the EU chapter apply.

[c] Transfer of the Own Earlier SPC to a Third Party

The same considerations as set out in the EU chapter apply.

[d] Acquisition of an SPC Granted to a Third Party

The same considerations as set out in the EU chapter apply.

[3] Consequences of an Own Earlier SPC for a Different Product

The same considerations as set out in the EU chapter apply.

[a] Required Distinction from the Product of the Own Earlier SPC

The same considerations as set out in the EU chapter in principle apply. If the product, however, has been modified, e.g., by the inclusion of a further active ingredient, a second SPC may issue (*see* the Federal Supreme Court decision *Fosinopril*). As noted above, the same considerations should apply if a second SPC is based on a patent directed towards a new therapeutic indication or new galenic formulation (*see* e.g., the Federal Administrative Court decision *Etanercept*).

68. Swiss Federal Administrative Court (Bundesverwaltungsgericht), judgment B-3064/2008 of 13 September 2010 – Etanercept, Section 5.1 of the reasons.
69. Swiss Federal Administrative Court (Bundesverwaltungsgericht), judgment B-1019/2010 of 20 October 2010 – Exenatide.

[b] SPCs for a Specific Salt, Ester or Other Derivative Where an Own Earlier SPC Has Already Been Granted for the Corresponding Active Ingredient

The same considerations as set out in the EU chapter in principle apply. The IGE, however, appears to adopt a slightly more liberal approach, in that if the new salt, ester or derivative by virtue of a special property is subject matter of a patent, then an SPC may issue.

[c] SPCs for a Specific Enantiomer Where an Own Earlier SPC Has Already Been Granted for the Corresponding Racemate

The same considerations as set out in the EU chapter apply.

[4] Grant of More than One SPC on the Basis of the Same Patent

As has been confirmed by the Federal Supreme Court in *Fosinopril* (124 III 375),[70] if the basic patent protects multiple products, multiple SPCs may be granted on the basis of the same patent.

This is also affirmed in the Guidelines for Examination which provide that the issue of an SPC for active ingredient A does not preclude the issue of a further SPC for a combination of active ingredients including A, and vice versa, and that this also holds true if the respective SPCs are based on the same patent.[71]

§12.03 EXTENT OF PROTECTION AND ENFORCEMENT OF SPCs

[A] The Protection Conferred by an SPC

The considerations as set out in the EU chapter substantially also apply to Switzerland. As such, an SPC in Switzerland provides the same rights as the basic patent,[72] subject to the limitation that the protection conferred extends only to the product covered by the marketing approval, including any further authorized use of the product as a medicinal or plant protection product[73] (as appropriate).

Moreover, as has been confirmed in the decision *Fluoxetin* (Case 4P. 11/1999)[74] by the Federal Supreme Court, the scope of protection of an SPC may not exceed that of the basic patent. Thus, an SPC based on a process claim cannot be relied upon to

70. Swiss Federal Supreme Court (Bundesgericht), judgment 124 III 375 of 10 July 1998 – Fosinopril.
71. IGE, Guidelines for the Substantive Examination of National Patent Applications (Richtlinien für die Sachprüfung der nationalen Patentanmeldungen), 1 April 2017, Section 13.2.4, last paragraph.
72. Article 140d(2) SPA.
73. Article 140d(1) SPA.
74. Swiss Federal Supreme Court (Bundesgericht), judgment 4P. 11/1999 of 27 May 1999 – Fluoxetin.

prohibit a third party from using a process for making the product which does not make use of the central feature of the process claim.

[B] The Scope of an SPC in Relation to Derivatives of an Active Ingredient

In accordance with the standing practice of the IGE, derivatives such as salts or esters of an active ingredient are viewed as the 'same active ingredient' in as far as they do not exhibit a different pharmacological effect.[75]

In line with this, the Swiss Federal Patent Court in *Kombinationspräparat* (S2017_006)[76] has granted ex parte interim injunctive relief prohibiting the marketing of the *phosphate salt* of tenofovir in combination with emtricitabine, on the basis of an SPC granted for the *fumarate salt* of tenofovir in combination with emtricitabine. The approval for tenofovir phosphate was an abridged, generic approval, establishing that the pharmacological effects of the two salt forms were equivalent.

[1] The Relationship Between the Definition of the Active Ingredient(s) in an SPC and Its Scope of Protection

As set out in the *Kombinationspräparat* decision,[77] the Federal Patent Court has confirmed that while the definition of the product of an SPC must be clear, it has per se no effect on the scope of protection. As such, an SPC will cover any derivative of the respective active ingredient(s) as covered by the basic patent, provided that the derivative has the same pharmacological effect.

[C] Enforcement of an SPC

The Federal Patent Court has exclusive jurisdiction in civil matters relating to both the validity and the infringement of patents as well as SPCs.[78] The Federal Patent Court's decisions can be appealed within thirty days to the Federal Supreme Court.[79]

The Federal Patent Court began operating on 1 January 2012. The seat of the Federal Patent Court is in St. Gallen.

75. *See also* IGE, Guidelines for the Substantive Examination of National Patent Applications (Richtlinien für die Sachprüfung der nationalen Patentanmeldungen), 1 April 2017, Section 13.1.
76. Swiss Federal Patent Court (Bundespatentgericht), judgment S2017_006 of 12 October 2017 – Kombinationspräparat.
77. *Ibid.*
78. Article 26 of the Swiss Federal Act on the Federal Patent Court (Bundesgesetz über das Bundespatentgericht) of 20 March 2009.
79. Articles 72(2)(b), 75(1), 90 and 100(1) of the Swiss Federal Act on the Federal Supreme Court (Bundesgesetz über das Bundesgericht) of 17 June 2005.

If the Federal Patent Court agrees, the parties may also plead in English language.[80] All decisions and procedural notifications will, however, be issued in the language of the proceedings.

§12.04 DETERMINATION OF THE SPC TERM

[A] The Calculation of the SPC Term

The SPC term in Switzerland is calculated in accordance with the provisions of Article 140e SPA. In analogy to the EU Regulations on SPCs, the certificate has a duration equal to the period between the filing date of the basic patent and the date of the first marketing authorization in Switzerland, reduced by five years, whereby the maximum SPC term may not exceed five years.

As set out in the Guidelines for Examination,[81] the relevant date for the calculation of the SPC term is the date of issue of the authorization.

[1] The Relevant Marketing Authorization for the Term of an SPC

In accordance with the current practice, the relevant marketing authorization decisive for the determination of the SPC term is the Swiss national marketing authorization.

It should, however, be noted that in accordance with Article 140e(3) SPA, the Federal Council may decide that the date of the first marketing authorization to place the product on the market may be the first authorization issued within the EEA (if it is earlier than the date of the first marketing authorization in Switzerland). No such decision has been taken to date.

[2] The Expiration Date of an SPC

The calculation of the SPC term, in analogy to the calculation of the patent term, is based on the provisions of Articles 14 and 140e SPA. Thus, the term of a patent shall be twenty years beginning on its filing date. The last day when a patent is in force is the day before the twentieth anniversary of its filing date. Accordingly, an SPC with a full five-year term will expire on the day before the twenty-fifth anniversary of the filing date of the basic patent.

[B] Correction of the SPC Term

As set out in the Guidelines for Examination,[82] the SPC term may be corrected. If, however, the term is corrected, it must be examined whether the SPC has been filed

80. Article 36(3) of the Swiss Federal Act on the Federal Patent Court (Bundesgesetz über das Bundespatentgericht) of 20 March 2009.
81. IGE, Guidelines for the Substantive Examination of National Patent Applications (Richtlinien für die Sachprüfung der nationalen Patentanmeldungen), 1 April 2017, Section 13.2.3.
82. *Ibid.*

within the statutory time limits. Thus, in the decision *Differin Gel* (PA 02/03)[83] the Swiss Appeals Commission for Intellectual Property rejected an SPC request for having been filed late. Here the applicant corrected the marketing authorization in light of the 'first marketing authorization requirement'. The SPC application was then in violation of Article 140f(1)(a) SPA, setting out the time limits for filing an SPC.

[C] Paediatric Extensions

The calculation of the term of a paediatric extension in Switzerland will essentially correspond to that discussed in the EU chapter.

The current Guidelines for Examination[84] also indicate that a negative SPC term, in analogy to the principles discussed in the CJEU decision *Merck* (C-125/10),[85] will be applicable. This option was introduced in anticipation of the forthcoming changes to the Swiss Patent Act allowing for paediatric extensions, but has never been codified and would now appear to be redundant, given that a six-month paediatric extension will also be available on the basis of a patent protecting a product that has been approved in Switzerland in compliance with a PIP, even in the absence of an SPC. There should thus be no legal interest in securing an SPC with a negative term.

§12.05 PROCEDURE OF FILING AN SPC APPLICATION

[A] Entitlement to an SPC Application

Article 140c(1) SPA stipulates that the patentee is entitled to the certificate, but is silent as to who may apply for an SPC. In accordance with the practice of the IGE, it is only the patentee who is entitled to file an SPC application. As such, a licensee of the basic patent may not file the SPC even if the patent owner has given his express authorization to do so.

Likewise, if the basic patent has been transferred, it is only the registered patent owner who may file the SPC.

[B] The Time Limit for Filing an SPC Application

In analogy to the time limits provided in the EU SPC Regulations, an application for an SPC in Switzerland must be filed within six months of the issue of the first marketing authorization to place the product on the market as a medicinal or plant protection product in Switzerland, or within six months of the date on which the patent was granted, whichever date is later (*see* Article 140f SPA).

83. Swiss Appeals Commission for Intellectual Property (Eidgenössische Rekurskommission für geistiges Eigentum), decision PA 02/03 of 21 January 2005 – Differin Gel.
84. IGE, Guidelines for the Substantive Examination of National Patent Applications (Richtlinien für die Sachprüfung der nationalen Patentanmeldungen), 1 April 2017, Section 13.4.
85. CJEU *Merck Sharp & Dohme Corp. v. Deutsches Patent- und Markenamt*, C-125/10 of 8 December 2011.

Further processing is not available if this term has been missed; a request for re-establishment of rights is however possible (*see* Articles 46a(4)(h) and 47 SPA).

[C] The Filing of an SPC at the National Patent Office

The filing requirements for an SPC are set out in the Swiss Patent Ordinance (SPO), particularly in Articles 127b and 127c SPO. Thus, an SPC must be filed at the IGE within the stipulated time limits, once the basic patent as well as the relevant marketing authorization have issued. The SPC application must be filed in writing, using the prescribed form issued by the IGE in one of the official languages (German, French or Italian). The request must contain all relevant information about the applicant and his representative (names and addresses), as well as details in terms of the basic patent and the marketing authorization (number and date) relied upon for the product in question. The prescribed fee must be paid on filing.

[D] The Documentation Required for an SPC Application

The documentation required for filing an SPC application in Switzerland is based on the requirements as set out in Articles 127b and 127c SPO.

The SPC request should be supplemented with copies of the marketing authorization to place the product on the market in Switzerland, including a copy of the Summary of Product Characteristics or the instructions for use in case of plant protection products.

[E] The Definition of the Product in an SPC Application

As set out in the Guidelines for Examination,[86] the definition of the active ingredient or combination of active ingredients provided for the product of an SPC must be clear. Typically systematic chemical nomenclature (e.g., as used by the Chemical Abstracts Service (CAS) or the International Union of Pure and Applied Chemistry (IUPAC)) or the International Non-proprietary Name (INN) may be relied upon, as well as the designation of the active ingredient(s) as used in the Swiss marketing authorization.

[F] SPC Examination Procedure and Appeal Procedure

In accordance with the practice of the IGE, an application for an SPC will be subject to a formal examination, followed by a substantive examination.

The formal examination focuses on issues such as the time limits for filing the SPC, the payment of the prescribed fees, the formal entitlement of the applicant, as well

86. IGE, Guidelines for the Substantive Examination of National Patent Applications (Richtlinien für die Sachprüfung der nationalen Patentanmeldungen), 1 April 2017, Section 13.1.

as the question as to whether the patent is in force and the documentation submitted is complete.

If deficits are found in the course of the formal examination, the applicant will be given a two-month deadline to rectify the application (Article 127e(2) SPO).

The substantive examination includes the verification that the marketing authorization was granted in accordance with the pertinent regulatory law and is valid at the filing date. During the examination the identity of the product is established and it is verified that the product is protected by the basic patent.

If multiple SPC requests for the same product based on different basic patents are pending in the name of the same applicant, then the IGE will require the applicant to make a choice on the basis of which patent the SPC is to be prosecuted (*see Exenatide* (B-1019/2010)[87]). The IGE will also check whether a prior SPC for the same product has already been granted to the same applicant.

If an SPC application is considered to be deficient, the IGE shall issue an office action inviting the applicant to correct the deficiencies within an extendable three-month time limit. According to the Guidelines for Examination, in exceptional cases the IGE may issue a second office action setting a shorter time limit of two months.[88] In practice, however, the IGE frequently sets longer terms for responding to office actions and may be prepared to conduct the examination proceedings in a more flexible manner.

If the application for the SPC is in compliance with the statutory requirements the certificate will be granted by way of a notification in the patent register (Article 127g SPO).

Decisions of the IGE may be appealed to the Swiss Federal Administrative Court,[89] and the corresponding decisions of the Swiss Federal Administrative Court may be appealed to the Swiss Federal Supreme Court.[90]

[G] Applications for a Paediatric Extension

To date no paediatric extensions are available in Switzerland. The Swiss Patent Act is, however, to be amended within the framework of the revision of the Therapeutic Products Act. It is expected that the revised Patent Act will come into force in 2019.

87. Swiss Federal Administrative Court (Bundesverwaltungsgericht), judgment B-1019/2010 of 20 October 2010 – Exenatide.
88. IGE, Guidelines for the Substantive Examination of National Patent Applications (Richtlinien für die Sachprüfung der nationalen Patentanmeldungen), 1 April 2017, Section 13.3.
89. Article 31 of the Swiss Federal Act on the Federal Administrative Court (Bundesgesetz über das Bundesverwaltungsgericht) of 17 June 2005 and Art. 5 of the Swiss Federal Act on Administrative Procedure (Bundesgesetz über das Verwaltungsverfahren) of 20 December 1968. *See also* IGE, Guidelines for the Substantive Examination of National Patent Applications (Richtlinien für die Sachprüfung der nationalen Patentanmeldungen), 1 April 2017, Section 13.3.
90. Articles 72(2)(b), 75(1) and 90 of the Swiss Federal Act on the Federal Supreme Court (Bundesgesetz über das Bundesgericht) of 17 June 2005.

The proposed amendments in the Therapeutic Products Act incorporate provisions which largely correspond to those of the Paediatric Regulation (EC) 1901/2006.[91]

Thus, paediatric extensions will be provided for in new Articles 140n–140y of the amended SPA.

In Switzerland a paediatric extension may in the future be applied for either on the basis of an SPC (paediatric SPC extension) or on the basis of a patent protecting the approved medicinal product (paediatric certificate), i.e., in the absence of an SPC. As such, paediatric extensions are available for medicinal products which have been approved in Switzerland and which are protected by an SPC or by a patent which is eligible for a six-month SPC extension, if the Swiss marketing authorization contains a compliance statement, confirming that paediatric trials, in compliance with an agreed paediatric investigation plan (PIP) have been completed.

In order to safeguard that a medicinal product for paediatric use is made available in Switzerland with the minimum delay, it is mandatory that the requests for marketing authorization must be filed in Switzerland within six months of the corresponding EEA marketing authorization (new Article 140n SPA). If the marketing authorization with the corresponding PIP has been filed before the amended Patent Act has come into force, this six-month term does not apply.

In case of the new paediatric certificate based on a patent (as opposed to an SPC) the marketing authorization relied upon with the compliance statement does not necessarily have to be the first marketing authorization for the product. The marketing authorization may also relate to a new indication, a new dosage form or a new mode of administration of a medicinal product. The applicant must, however, seek the consent from the holder of the marketing authorization comprising the PIP compliance statement (new Article 140*ster* SPA).

As set out in the current Guidelines for Examination,[92] in analogy to the situation in the EU (*see Merck* (C-125/10)[93]), an SPC with a negative term may issue. This option, which was introduced in anticipation of the forthcoming changes to the Swiss Patent Act, providing for paediatric extensions, has never been codified and now would appear to be redundant. Thus, as in Switzerland a six-month paediatric extension will be available on the basis of a patent protecting a product which has been approved in Switzerland in compliance with a PIP, even in the absence of an SPC, there should be no legal interest in securing an SPC with a negative term.

According to new Article 140s SPA, the Swiss Federal Council will govern the paediatric extension of an SPC, its registration in the patent register and its corresponding publication. Moreover, the provisions of the European Union are to be considered.

A paediatric extension for an SPC must be filed at the earliest together with the SPC request and no later than two years before the expiry of the SPC (new Article 140o).

---

91. Regulation (EC) 1901/2006 of the European Parliament and of the Council of 12 December 2006 on medicinal products for paediatric use.
92. IGE, Guidelines for the Substantive Examination of National Patent Applications (Richtlinien für die Sachprüfung der nationalen Patentanmeldungen), 1 April 2017, Section 13.4.
93. CJEU *Merck Sharp & Dohme Corp. v. Deutsches Patent- und Markenamt*, C-125/10 of 8 December 2011.

According to new Article 127 SPO, the documentation required to the filing of a paediatric extension includes proof as to when the Swiss marketing authorization with the PIP compliance statement was applied for. It is also necessary to submit a corresponding confirmation from Swissmedic as well as proof that the Swiss marketing authorization was filed within six months of the corresponding EEA approval comprising the PIP compliance statement.

A paediatric extension on the basis of the patent (i.e., in the absence of an SPC) must be filed at least two years prior to the expiry of the patent (new Article 140s*quarter* SPA). The existence of an SPC precludes the grant of a paediatric certificate.

According to the transitional provisions as set out in new Article 149 SPA, up until five years after entry into force of the provisions for paediatric extensions in Switzerland, a paediatric extension based on an SPC must be filed at least six months before the expiry of the SPC (new Article 149(1) SPA). The same time limit applies for a paediatric extension based on a patent (new Article 149(1) SPA).

If the medicinal product with the PIP compliance statement is authorized within six months after the entry into force of the Swiss provisions for a paediatric extension, the deadlines as set out in new Article 140s SPA do not apply. Similarly, the six-month time limit between the first marketing authorization with the PIP compliance statement in the EEA and the corresponding Swiss marketing authorization filing date as set out in Article 140n(1)(b) do not apply.

The question of entitlement is governed in a new Article 140 SPA.

Accordingly, the patentee is entitled to the paediatric certificate, and in principle only one extension per product may issue. If, however, there are several basic patents held by different patentees covering the same product, then an extension may be granted to each holder of the basic patents, provided that a statement of consent from the holder of the marketing authorization with the PIP compliance statement is submitted.

Finally, for an SPC paediatric extension as well as a paediatric extension for a patent, the prescribed fee must be paid as set out in new Articles 140q and 140s SPA.

§12.06 PROCEDURE OF INVALIDATING AN SPC

[A] Grounds for the Invalidation of an SPC

The grounds for invalidating an SPC are set out in Article 140(k)(1) SPA and correspond to those of the EU SPC Regulations.

The Federal Patent Court in the *Sevelamer* decision (Case O2017_016)[94] found that the enumeration of the grounds for invalidation in Article 140(k)(1) SPA is exhaustive. Thus, the Court rejected the argument raised by the alleged infringer of the invoked SPC that the certificate was invalid because the IGE had wrongly granted a

94. Swiss Federal Patent Court (Bundespatentgericht), judgment O2017_016 of 12 June 2018 – Sevelamer, Section 4.3 of the reasons.

request for re-establishment of rights with respect to the time limit for filing the SPC application which gave rise to the invoked SPC.

[B] The Filing of an Invalidation Suit

As provided for in Article 140(k)(2) SPA, a request for the invalidation of an SPC may be filed by any person.

[C] Invalidation Procedure and the Corresponding Appeal Procedure

An invalidation procedure against an SPC may be initiated before the specialized patent court, the Swiss Federal Patent Court, which has exclusive jurisdiction in this regard in Switzerland, or before the courts in Liechtenstein. In both cases, a final appeal is possible to the Swiss Federal Supreme Court.

[D] The Revocation of a Paediatric Extension

New Article 140r SPA governs the revocation of a paediatric SPC extension in Switzerland. Thus, the IGE may revoke an SPC extension if it was granted in violation of new Article 140n SPA and or if it retrospectively violates new Article 140n SPA. Any person may request the revocation of an SPC extension. New Article 140*sexies* SPA provides for the revocation of a paediatric certificate based on a patent. Such an extension may be revoked if it has been granted in violation of Article 140s*bis* or if it retrospectively is in violation of this provision.

§12.07 UNFAIR COMPETITION LAW

In Switzerland, the statutory provisions in relation to unfair competition law largely correspond to those of the EU. Thus, the Federal Act on Cartels and other Restraints of Competition (Cartel Act)[95] contains provisions which are analogous to those of Articles 101 and 102 of the Treaty on the Functioning of the European Union (TFEU). The competent administrative authority for the enforcement of Swiss competition law is the Swiss Competition Commission (ComCo), which may act on its own accord upon complaint by any third party.

In the pharmaceutical sector, up until now the focus of attention of ComCo has been on anticompetitive agreements, merger controls and the like. Anticompetitive conduct of an enterprise having a dominant position is also of major concern. So far, however, there have not been any unfair competition issues in Switzerland involving SPCs.

95. Federal Act on Cartels and other Restraints of Competition (Bundesgesetz über Kartelle und andere Wettbewerbsbeschränkungen) of 6 October 1995.

In light of the intended alignment of the laws in Switzerland with those of the EEA, it would appear that the considerations as set out in the EU chapter likely also apply in Switzerland.

CHAPTER 13
Further European Countries

Alexa von Uexküll & Oswin Ridderbusch

In this chapter, specific aspects of practical relevance regarding the filing of SPCs in further European countries will be discussed, particularly with respect to the EU Member States Austria, Croatia, Cyprus, the Czech Republic, Denmark, Greece, Hungary, Ireland, Malta, Poland, Romania, Slovakia, and Slovenia, the EFTA-EEA Member State Norway, and the EU candidate countries Albania and Macedonia.

§13.01 AUSTRIA

In Austria, an SPC application has to be filed in the name of the proprietor of the basic patent. A divergence between the name of the SPC applicant and the holder of the basic patent (e.g., due to a transfer of the basic patent) can still be corrected before a decision on the SPC application is taken.

If the deadline for filing an SPC has inadvertently been missed, it will, in principle, be possible to request re-establishment of rights in order to have the case reinstated. This also holds true with respect to the deadline for filing a request for a paediatric extension.

For filing an SPC application, the documents required under Article 8 of the SPC Regulations have to submitted, including a copy of the marketing authorization in Austria with *all* its enclosures. These documents can still be filed at a later stage during the grant procedure. The filing of a power of attorney is not strictly necessary but is recommendable.

For requesting a paediatric extension, the corresponding documents required under Article 8 of the SPC Regulation for Medicinal Products can still be supplemented after the filing of the corresponding request.

SPC applications undergo a substantive examination procedure. In this context, the Austrian patent office examines whether the product of the SPC is protected by the basic patent. However, in accordance with Section 3(1) of the Austrian Federal Act on

Supplementary Protection Certificates (Bundesgesetz betreffend ergänzende Schutzzertifikate, 'SchZG'), the Austrian patent office does not check whether prior SPCs filed in the name of the same applicant exist, nor whether the marketing authorization relied upon is the first approval of the corresponding product in Austria.

Austrian law does not provide for the possibility of filing third-party observations in SPC examination proceedings. The informal submission of such observations is further complicated by the fact that SPC applications are kept secret until they are granted.

With respect to the timeframe for the examination of SPC applications, while there is a directive requiring that a first office action should be issued within a reasonable time, it can in practice take years until the first office action issues. Examiners may flexibly react to an applicant's informal request to accelerate or delay the SPC examination proceedings. It may also be possible to conduct an informal interview with the competent examiner.

In practice, a broader product definition may be used than the specific form of the active ingredient indicated in the marketing authorization. The inclusion of salts and esters of the active ingredient in the product definition of the SPC is typically accepted.

With respect to the duration of the SPC, it is to be noted that the basic patent expires at the end of the day of the twenty-year anniversary of its filing date. An SPC with a full five-year term will thus expire at the end of the day of the twenty-five-year anniversary of the filing date of the basic patent.

Under Section 3(2) SchZG, a contractual licence agreement in a basic patent will automatically extend to an SPC granted on the basis of such a patent, unless the parties involved have agreed otherwise.

§13.02 CROATIA

In Croatia, an SPC application has to be filed in the name of the registered proprietor of the basic patent. A deficiency in this regard can normally not be rectified after filing the SPC application.

If the deadline for filing an SPC has inadvertently been missed, it will not be possible to file an SPC anymore, i.e., re-establishment of rights is not available. This also holds true with respect to the deadline for filing a request for a paediatric extension.

Besides the documents required for filing an SPC application under Article 8 of the SPC Regulations, a power of attorney has to be submitted. The required documents can still be filed at a later stage during the grant procedure. In particular, the power of attorney has to be filed within an inextensible deadline of sixty days from the receipt of a corresponding official action.

For requesting a paediatric extension, most of the documents required under Article 8 of the SPC Regulation for Medicinal Products can still be submitted at a later stage of proceedings. However, at least some of the required documents must be filed together with the request for a paediatric extension.

SPC applications undergo a substantive examination procedure. The Croatian patent office checks whether the product is protected by the basic patent, and also whether prior SPCs filed in the name of the same applicant exist.

Third-party observations filed during the examination procedure may be taken into account by the competent examiner.

There is no fixed timeframe for the SPC examination proceedings, except that they should be concluded before the expiry of the basic patent. Examiners may flexibly react to an applicant's informal request to accelerate or delay the SPC examination proceedings. It is normally also possible to conduct an informal interview with the competent examiner.

In practice, a broader product definition may be used than the specific form of the active ingredient indicated in the marketing authorization. For example, product definitions such as 'Compound X and derivatives thereof' or 'Compound X and salts thereof' are normally accepted, provided of course that they are covered by the claims of the basic patent.

SPC applications for products based on a CE approval of a medical device are not accepted. The future practice in this regard can, however, be expected to depend on the CJEU's ruling in the pending referral C-527/17.

With respect to the duration of the SPC, it is to be noted that the last day of validity of the basic patent is the day of the twenty-year anniversary of its filing date. An SPC with a full five-year term will thus expire at the end of the day of the twenty-five-year anniversary of the filing date of the basic patent.

For a contractual licence agreement in a basic patent to extend to an SPC granted on the basis of such a patent, a corresponding provision in the licence agreement is required. Licences in patents and SPCs have to be recorded with the Croatian patent office.

§13.03 CYPRUS

In Cyprus, an SPC application has to be filed in the name of the proprietor of the basic patent. A deficiency in this regard can still be rectified during the prosecution of the SPC application.

If the deadline for filing an SPC has inadvertently been missed, it will not be possible to file an SPC anymore, i.e., re-establishment of rights is not available. This also holds true with respect to the deadline for filing a request for a paediatric extension.

Besides the documents required for filing an SPC application under Article 8 of the SPC Regulations, a power of attorney has to be submitted. Under current practice, the required documents can still be filed at a later stage during the grant procedure.

Likewise, for requesting a paediatric extension, the corresponding documents required under Article 8 of the SPC Regulation for Medicinal Products and a power of attorney can still be submitted at a later stage of proceedings.

The Cypriot patent office merely conducts a formal examination of SPC requests but no substantive examination. Thus, the patent office does not check whether the product is protected by the basic patent, nor whether prior SPCs granted to the same applicant exist.

The patent office may, however, take into account third-party observations filed during the grant procedure.

The SPC grant proceedings can be conducted relatively flexibly, and the patent office has a discretionary power to delay or stay the proceedings at the request of the applicant. Conversely, it is typically not possible to accelerate the SPC grant procedure. An informal interview may be conducted with the competent examiner.

SPC applications for products based on a CE approval of a medical device are not accepted. The future practice in this regard can, however, be expected to depend on the CJEU's ruling in the pending referral C-527/17.

With respect to the duration of the SPC, it is to be noted that the basic patent expires at the end of the day *before* the twenty-year anniversary of its filing date. An SPC with a full five-year term will thus expire at the end of the day *before* the twenty-five-year anniversary of the filing date of the basic patent.

For a contractual licence agreement in a basic patent to extend to an SPC granted on the basis of such a patent, a corresponding provision in the licence agreement is required.

§13.04 CZECH REPUBLIC

In the Czech Republic, an SPC application has to be filed in the name of the proprietor of the basic patent. A deficiency in this regard can still be rectified during the prosecution of the SPC application.

If the deadline for filing an SPC has inadvertently been missed, it will not be possible to file an SPC anymore, i.e., re-establishment of rights is not available. This also holds true with respect to the deadline for filing a request for a paediatric extension.

Besides the documents required for filing an SPC application under Article 8 of the SPC Regulations, a power of attorney has to be submitted. The required documents can still be filed at a later stage during the grant procedure.

Likewise, for requesting a paediatric extension, the corresponding documents required under Article 8 of the SPC Regulation for Medicinal Products can still be submitted at a later stage of proceedings.

SPC applications undergo a substantive examination procedure. The Czech patent office checks whether the product is protected by the basic patent, and also whether prior SPCs filed in the name of the same applicant exist.

Third-party observations filed during the examination procedure will be taken into account.

There is no fixed timeframe for the SPC examination proceedings. Examiners may flexibly react to an applicant's informal request to accelerate or delay the SPC examination proceedings. It is normally also possible to conduct an informal interview with the competent examiner by telephone.

While an SPC applicant can indicate a broader product definition in the request, the Czech patent office tends to specify the product in the granted SPC exactly as indicated in the marketing authorization, even without giving prior notice to the applicant.

With respect to the duration of the SPC, it is to be noted that the last day of validity of the basic patent is the day of the twenty-year anniversary of its filing date. An SPC with a full five-year term will thus expire at the end of the day of the twenty-five-year anniversary of the filing date of the basic patent.

For a contractual licence agreement in a basic patent to extend to an SPC granted on the basis of such a patent, a corresponding provision should be included in the licence agreement.

§13.05 DENMARK

In Denmark, an SPC application has to be filed in the name of the registered proprietor of the basic patent. If the SPC applicant is different from the registered proprietor of the patent, the Danish patent office will raise an objection, allowing for the rectification of the corresponding deficiency during the prosecution of the SPC.

If the deadline for filing an SPC has inadvertently been missed, it will, in principle, be possible to request re-establishment of rights in order to have the case reinstated.

The documents required for filing an SPC application under Article 8 of the SPC Regulations can still be submitted after filing the SPC request. A filing date is accorded if the product that the SPC application seeks to protect can be identified. It is, however, recommended to file at least the marketing authorization for Denmark together with the application form when applying for an SPC.

A power of attorney is generally not required by the Danish patent office. If requested, however, a power of attorney can still be filed subsequently.

For requesting a paediatric extension, the corresponding documents required under Article 8 of the SPC Regulation for Medicinal Products can still be submitted after filing the request.

SPC applications undergo a substantive examination procedure. The Danish patent office checks whether the product is protected by the basic patent, and also whether prior SPCs filed in the name of the same applicant exist.

Third-party observations can be filed in SPC examination proceedings and will be taken into account by the examiner.

There is no prescribed timeframe for the examination of SPC applications. Examiners may flexibly react to an applicant's informal request to accelerate or delay the SPC examination procedure. It is often also possible to conduct an informal interview with the competent examiner.

In practice, a broader product definition may be used than the specific form of the active ingredient indicated in the marketing authorization. However, product definitions such as 'Compound X in all forms as protected by the basic patent' or 'Compound X and derivatives thereof' are generally not accepted.

It is possible to rely on the description of the basic patent for the assessment whether an active ingredient is identified and thus 'protected' by the basic patent. An unspecific term such as 'a further active ingredient' is normally not considered sufficient in this regard.

With respect to the duration of the SPC, it is to be noted that the basic patent expires at the end of the day of the twenty-year anniversary of its filing date. An SPC with a full five-year term will thus expire at the end of the day of the twenty-five-year anniversary of the filing date of the basic patent.

§13.06 GREECE

In Greece, an SPC application has to be filed in the name of the proprietor of the basic patent. A deficiency in this regard can normally not be rectified after filing the SPC application.

If the deadline for filing an SPC has inadvertently been missed, it will not be possible to file an SPC anymore, i.e., re-establishment of rights is not available. This also holds true with respect to the deadline for filing a request for a paediatric extension.

Besides the documents required for filing an SPC application under Article 8 of the SPC Regulations, a power of attorney has to be submitted. The required documents can still be submitted within four months from the filing date of the SPC application.

For requesting a paediatric extension, the corresponding documents required under Article 8 of the SPC Regulation for Medicinal Products and a power of attorney have to be submitted. These documents can still be filed at a later stage of proceedings.

The Greek patent office merely conducts a formal examination of SPC requests but no substantive examination. Thus, it does not check whether the product is protected by the basic patent, nor whether prior SPCs granted to the same applicant exist.

Third-party observations filed during the grant procedure are normally not taken into account.

There is no fixed timeframe for the SPC grant proceedings. It is not possible to delay or stay, nor to accelerate the grant proceedings at the request of the applicant. It may, however, be possible to conduct an informal interview with the competent examiner.

SPC applications for products based on a CE approval of a medical device are not accepted. The future practice in this regard can, however, be expected to depend on the CJEU's ruling in the pending referral C-527/17.

With respect to the duration of the SPC, it is to be noted that the basic patent expires at the end of the day *after* the twenty-year anniversary of its filing date. An SPC with a full five-year term will thus expire at the end of the day *after* the twenty-five-year anniversary of the filing date of the basic patent.

For a contractual licence agreement in a basic patent to extend to an SPC granted on the basis of such a patent, a corresponding provision in the licence agreement is required.

§13.07 HUNGARY

In Hungary, an SPC application has to be filed in the name of the registered proprietor of the basic patent. In the case of a transfer of the patent, it is strongly advisable to request the recordal of the transfer before filing the SPC application.

If the deadline for filing an SPC has inadvertently been missed, it will not be possible to file an SPC anymore, i.e., re-establishment of rights is not available. This also holds true with respect to the deadline for filing a request for a paediatric extension.

Among the documents and data required for filing an SPC application according to Article 8 of the SPC Regulations, the following must be submitted in order to establish a valid SPC filing date: name and address of the applicant; name and address of the legal representative (if any); definition of the product; number and title of the basic patent relied upon; number and date of the first marketing authorization in Hungary and, if this authorization is not the first one in the EU and the EEA, the number, date and state of the first marketing authorization in the EU or EEA.

The further documents and data required under Article 8 of the SPC Regulations, particularly a copy of the first marketing authorization in Hungary and the additional information regarding the first marketing authorization in the EU or EEA, as well as a power of attorney can still be submitted later in the course of the SPC grant proceedings. The power of attorney does not need to be notarized or legalized, but the signatory's authority to sign should be confirmed, e.g., by filing an excerpt of the company register.

For requesting a paediatric extension, it is necessary to file the following documents and data in order to establish a valid filing date: name and address of the applicant; name and address of the legal representative (if any); definition of the product; number and title of the basic patent relied upon; and number of the already granted SPC (or a reference to a corresponding SPC request). The further documents referred to in Article 8(1)(d) of the SPC Regulation for Medicinal Products, particularly a copy of the statement indicating compliance with an agreed completed paediatric investigation plan and, where applicable, proof of possession of marketing authorizations for all other Member States, as well as a copy of the SPC certificate (if already issued) can still be filed subsequently.

SPC applications undergo a substantive examination procedure. The Hungarian patent office checks whether the product is protected by the basic patent, and also whether prior SPCs filed in the name of the same applicant exist.

Third-party observations filed during the examination procedure will be taken into account.

There is no fixed timeframe for the SPC examination proceedings. The term set in an office action for rectifying a deficiency is normally extendible. Examiners may, at their discretion, react to an applicant's informal request to accelerate, delay or stay the SPC examination procedure. It may also be possible to conduct an informal interview with the competent examiner.

In practice, a broader product definition may be used than the specific form of the active ingredient indicated in the marketing authorization. In particular, the inclusion of salts and hydrates of the active ingredient in the product definition of the SPC is typically accepted.

With respect to the duration of the SPC, it is to be noted that the basic patent expires at the end of the day of the twenty year anniversary of its filing date. A maximum five year SPC term will thus expire at the end of the day of the twenty-five-year anniversary of the filing date of the basic patent.

For a contractual licence agreement in a basic patent to extend to an SPC granted on the basis of such a patent, a corresponding provision in the licence agreement is required.

§13.08 IRELAND

In Ireland, an SPC application has to be filed in the name of the registered proprietor of the basic patent. If the basic patent has been transferred, however, it is normally acceptable to file the SPC application in the name of the new proprietor of the basic patent simultaneously with the request to record the transfer of ownership in the patent. The same considerations apply to changes in the name or address of the patent proprietor.

If the deadline for filing an SPC has inadvertently been missed, it will not be possible to file an SPC anymore, i.e., re-establishment of rights is not available. This also holds true with respect to the deadline for filing a request for a paediatric extension.

Besides the documents required for filing an SPC application under Article 8 of the SPC Regulations, the applicant typically has to provide evidence showing how the product in question is protected by the basic patent. Such evidence can still be supplemented after the filing date of the SPC.

A power of attorney further needs to be submitted within three months from the SPC filing date, unless the agent is already representing the patent proprietor in respect of the basic patent.

For requesting a paediatric extension, the corresponding documents required under Article 8 of the SPC Regulation for Medicinal Products must be submitted on filing.

SPC applications undergo a substantive examination procedure. The Irish patent office checks whether the product is protected by the basic patent, and typically also whether prior SPCs exist that were filed in the name of the same applicant or rely on the same basic patent.

It is possible to file third-party observations in SPC examination proceedings, which will be forwarded to the SPC applicant and may be considered by the examiner.

The timeframe for the examination of SPC applications is rather flexible, and examiners may, at their discretion, react to an applicant's informal request to accelerate or delay the SPC examination procedure. It is often also possible to conduct an informal interview with the competent examiner by telephone.

In practice, a broader product definition may be used than the specific form of the active ingredient indicated in the marketing authorization.

The Irish patent office, however, takes a rather strict approach when assessing whether an active ingredient is identified and thus 'protected' by the basic patent, expecting the active ingredient(s) to be explicitly specified in the claims or the description of the patent.

Moreover, the Irish patent office typically rejects SPC applications for products based on a CE approval of a medical device. The future practice in this regard can, however, be expected to depend on the CJEU's ruling in the pending referral C-527/17.

With respect to the duration of the SPC, it is to be noted that the basic patent expires on the day *before* the twenty-year anniversary of its filing date. An SPC with a full five-year term will thus expire at the end of the day *before* the twenty-five-year anniversary of the filing date of the basic patent.

§13.09 MALTA

Under current Maltese law and practice, an SPC application can not only be filed by the proprietor of the basic patent but, remarkably, can also be filed by the holder of the marketing authorization relied upon.

Thus, the Maltese Patents (Medicinal Products) Regulations[1] and the Patents (Plant Protection Products) Regulations,[2] which were enacted to implement the provisions on SPCs of the Maltese Patents and Designs Act, both provide in Article 4(1):

> Any person who has obtained a market authorization in relation to a product may apply for a certificate to the Comptroller.

This provision is unique among the EU Member States. While the holder of a marketing authorization may thus *apply* for an SPC under Maltese law, the corresponding SPC will still have to be *granted* to the holder of the basic patent relied upon, in accordance with Article 6 of the SPC Regulations.

The fact that Maltese law allows the holder of a marketing authorization to apply for an SPC but does not explicitly refer to the patent holder in this context, begs the question whether there can be any doubt as to the patent holder's entitlement to file an SPC application – as opposed to its entitlement to be granted the SPC. While it would hardly seem reconcilable with Article 6 of the SPC Regulations to deny the patent holder the right to apply for an SPC on the basis of its patent, there is no case law specifically addressing this aspect. In practice, the Maltese patent office grants SPCs filed by the patent holder, even if the patent holder is different from the holder of the marketing authorization relied upon.

If the deadline for filing an SPC has inadvertently been missed, it will not be possible to file an SPC anymore, i.e., re-establishment of rights is not available. This is because Article 46(1) of the Maltese Patents and Designs Act provides for re-establishment of rights in respect of 'a time limit set by the Comptroller' but does not

1. Maltese Patents (Medicinal Products) Regulations, 2002 (entry into force on 1 March 2003). Accessible online at: http://www.wipo.int/wipolex/en/details.jsp?id=8174.
2. Maltese Patents (Plant Protection Products) Regulations, 2002 (entry into force on 1 January 2003). Accessible online at: http://www.wipo.int/wipolex/en/details.jsp?id=8175.

apply to any statutory time limits. For the same reason, re-establishment of rights is not available in respect of the deadline for filing a request for a paediatric extension either.

Besides the documents required for filing an SPC application under Article 8 of the SPC Regulations, a power of attorney has to be submitted. While the power of attorney can still be filed at a later stage, the other required documents have to be submitted on the filing date of the SPC. It is recommended that the power of attorney should be notarized and legalized.

For requesting a paediatric extension, the corresponding documents required under Article 8 of the SPC Regulation for Medicinal Products must be submitted on filing.

SPC applications undergo a substantive examination procedure. The Maltese patent office checks whether the product is protected by the basic patent, and typically also whether prior SPCs filed in the name of the same applicant exist.

There is no fixed timeframe for the examination of SPC applications. The examination proceedings may be delayed or stayed at the request of the applicant, but can typically not be accelerated. It may be possible to conduct an informal interview with the competent examiner by telephone.

With respect to the duration of the SPC, it is to be noted that the basic patent expires at the end of the day of the twenty-year anniversary of its filing date. An SPC with a full five-year term will thus expire at the end of the day of the twenty-five-year anniversary of the filing date of the basic patent.

A contractual licence agreement in a basic patent should automatically extend to an SPC granted on the basis of such a patent, unless the corresponding licence agreement provides otherwise.

§13.10 POLAND

In Poland, an SPC application has to be filed in the name of the proprietor of the basic patent. The SPC applicant must be identical to the registered patent proprietor when filing the SPC. A deficiency in this regard can normally not be rectified during the prosecution of the SPC application.

If the deadline for filing an SPC has inadvertently been missed, it will not be possible to file an SPC anymore, i.e., re-establishment of rights is not available. In this regard, Article 75-5(2) of the Polish Industrial Property Act[3] specifically provides that the term for lodging an SPC application shall not be restorable. This has also been confirmed by the Polish Supreme Administrative Court in its decision II GSK 288/07 of 18 December 2007.

With respect to the deadline for filing a request for a paediatric extension, however, the Industrial Property Act does not contain any provisions which would specifically allow or exclude re-establishment of rights.

3. An English translation of the Polish Industrial Property Act is accessible online at: http://www.wipo.int/wipolex/en/details.jsp?id=16993.

Besides the documents required for filing an SPC application under Article 8 of the SPC Regulations, a power of attorney has to be submitted. The required documents can still be filed at a later stage during the grant procedure. All these documents have to be filed in Polish translation.

Moreover, in accordance with Article 8(1)(c) of the SPC Regulations, if the marketing authorization relied upon is not the first marketing authorization for the respective product in the EU or the EEA, information regarding the identity of the product thus authorized and the legal provision under which the authorization procedure took place must be submitted. This information should be submitted in the form of a declaration signed by the SPC applicant.

For requesting a paediatric extension, the corresponding documents required under Article 8 of the SPC Regulation for Medicinal Products can also still be submitted at a later stage of proceedings. Here, too, all documents to be filed with the Polish patent office must be translated into Polish.

SPC applications undergo a substantive examination procedure. The Polish patent office checks whether the product is protected by the basic patent, and also whether prior SPCs filed in the name of the same applicant exist.

Following the publication of an SPC filing in the official gazette, it is possible to file third-party observations against the grant of the SPC, which will be considered by the competent examiner.

There is no fixed timeframe for the SPC examination proceedings. Examiners may flexibly react to an applicant's informal request to accelerate or delay the SPC examination proceedings. It is normally also possible to conduct an informal interview with the competent examiner.

In practice, a broader product definition may be used than the specific form of the active ingredient indicated in the marketing authorization. In particular, the inclusion of salts of the active ingredient in the product definition of the SPC is typically accepted.

Notably, however, if the SPC is based on a patent with second medical use claims or a patent with process of manufacture claims, the Polish patent office requires the product definition of the SPC to recite a corresponding use or process limitation. For example, if the claims of the basic patent relate to compound X for use in the treatment of a specific disease, the product definition of the SPC must include a corresponding reference, such as 'compound X for use in accordance with patent no. Y'.

The Polish patent office furthermore takes a rather strict approach when assessing whether an active ingredient is identified and thus 'protected' by the basic patent, expecting the active ingredient(s) to be expressly specified in the claims of the patent. So far, the CJEU decision *Eli Lilly* (C-493/12) has not affected the practice of the patent office in this regard.

Moreover, the Polish patent office typically rejects SPC applications for products based on a CE approval of a medical device. The future practice in this regard can, however, be expected to depend on the CJEU's ruling in the pending referral C-527/17.

With respect to the duration of the SPC, it is to be noted that the basic patent expires at the end of the day of the twenty-year anniversary of its filing date. An SPC with a full five-year term will thus expire at the end of the day of the twenty-five-year anniversary of the filing date of the basic patent.

For a contractual licence agreement in a basic patent to extend to an SPC granted on the basis of such a patent, a corresponding provision in the licence agreement is required.

§13.11 ROMANIA

In Romania, an SPC application has to be filed in the name of the proprietor of the basic patent. A deficiency in this regard can still be rectified during the prosecution of the SPC application, i.e., at the latest before a decision on the SPC application is taken by the Romanian patent office.

If the deadline for filing an SPC has inadvertently been missed, it will, in principle, be possible to request re-establishment of rights in order to have the case reinstated. This also holds true with respect to the deadline for filing a request for a paediatric extension.

Besides the documents required for filing an SPC application under Article 8 of the SPC Regulations, a copy of the basic patent, a power of attorney (the original document) and a proof of payment of the official filing fee have to be submitted. The indications required under Article 8 of the pertinent SPC Regulation have to be submitted on filing, while the corresponding documents may still be submitted at a later stage, subject to the payment of a late-filing fee. The required power of attorney can still be submitted within four months from the filing date of the SPC application.

SPC applications undergo a substantive examination procedure. The Romanian patent office checks whether the product is protected by the basic patent, whether the marketing authorization relied upon is the first marketing authorization for that product in Romania, and also whether prior SPCs for the same product filed by the same applicant exist.

There is no fixed timeframe for the SPC examination proceedings. The time limit set for responding to an office action can be extended on serious grounds, whereby prosecution may be delayed. Moreover, if the basic patent is subject to pending opposition or limitation proceedings before the EPO, or national revocation or limitation proceedings before the Romanian patent office, the SPC examination proceedings will normally be suspended until the protection conferred by the patent can be definitely established. Conversely, the applicant may request an acceleration of the SPC examination proceedings. It is typically also possible to conduct an informal interview with the competent examiner by telephone.

In practice, a broader product definition may be used than the specific form of the active ingredient indicated in the marketing authorization. In particular, the inclusion of salts of the active ingredient in the product definition of the SPC is typically accepted, whereas definitions like 'compound X in all forms as protected by the basic patent' have often been objected to.

With respect to the duration of the SPC, it is to be noted that the last day of validity of the basic patent is the day of the twenty-year anniversary of its filing date. An SPC with a full five-year term will thus expire at the end of the day of the twenty-five-year anniversary of the filing date of the basic patent.

For a contractual licence agreement in a basic patent to extend to an SPC granted on the basis of such a patent, a corresponding provision in the licence agreement is required.

§13.12 SLOVAKIA

In Slovakia, an SPC application has to be filed in the name of the proprietor of the basic patent. A deficiency in this regard can still be rectified during the prosecution of the SPC application.

If the deadline for filing an SPC has inadvertently been missed, it will not be possible to file an SPC anymore, i.e., re-establishment of rights is not available. This also holds true with respect to the deadline for filing a request for a paediatric extension.

Besides the documents required for filing an SPC application under Article 8 of the SPC Regulations, a power of attorney has to be submitted. The required documents can still be filed at a later stage during the grant procedure.

Likewise, for requesting a paediatric extension, the corresponding documents required under Article 8 of the SPC Regulation for Medicinal Products can still be submitted at a later stage of proceedings.

SPC applications undergo a substantive examination procedure. The Slovak patent office checks whether the product is protected by the basic patent, and also whether prior SPCs filed in the name of the same applicant exist.

Third-party observations filed during the examination procedure will be taken into account.

There is no fixed timeframe for the SPC examination proceedings. Examiners may flexibly react to an applicant's informal request to accelerate or delay the SPC examination proceedings. It is normally also possible to conduct an informal interview with the competent examiner by telephone.

While an SPC applicant can indicate a broader product definition in the request, the Slovak patent office tends to specify the product in the granted SPC exactly as indicated in the marketing authorization, even without giving prior notice to the applicant.

With respect to the duration of the SPC, it is to be noted that the last day of validity of the basic patent is the day of the twenty-year anniversary of its filing date. An SPC with a full five-year term will thus expire at the end of the day of the twenty-five-year anniversary of the filing date of the basic patent.

For a contractual licence agreement in a basic patent to extend to an SPC granted on the basis of such a patent, a corresponding provision should be included in the licence agreement.

§13.13 SLOVENIA

In Slovenia, an SPC application has to be filed in the name of the proprietor of the basic patent. A divergence between the name of the SPC applicant and the holder of the basic patent (e.g., due to a transfer of the basic patent) can still be corrected during the prosecution of the SPC.

If the deadline for filing an SPC has inadvertently been missed, it will, in principle, be possible to request re-establishment of rights in order to have the case reinstated in accordance with Article 68 of the Slovenian Industrial Property Act. This also holds true with respect to the deadline for filing a request for a paediatric extension.

Besides the documents required for filing an SPC application under Article 8 of the SPC Regulations, a power of attorney has to be submitted. The required documents can still be filed within three months from a corresponding invitation by the Slovenian patent office.

Likewise, for requesting a paediatric extension, the corresponding documents required under Article 8 of the SPC Regulation for Medicinal Products can still be submitted within three months from a corresponding invitation by the Slovenian patent office.

SPC applications undergo a substantive examination procedure. In this context, the Slovenian patent office examines whether the product of the SPC is protected by the basic patent, and it also checks whether prior SPCs filed in the name of the same applicant exist.

Slovenian law does not provide for the possibility of filing third-party observations in SPC examination proceedings, but the competent examiner may take into account any such informally filed observations.

With respect to the timeframe for the examination of SPC applications, the first office action is typically issued within about two months from the filing of the SPC request. Prosecution may be delayed or stayed at the request of the applicant, but only on the grounds referred to in the Slovenian General Administrative Procedure Act. The prosecution can furthermore be accelerated at the request of the applicant. It may also be possible to conduct an informal interview with the competent examiner.

Under the current practice of the Slovenian patent office, a broader product definition such as 'Compound X in all forms as protected by the basic patent' or 'Compound X and derivatives thereof' will normally not be allowed.

The product must furthermore be identified in the claims, not merely in the description, in order to be 'protected' by the basic patent under current practice.

Under current practice, SPC applications can also be based on a CE approval of a medical device. Whether this practice continues may, however, depend on the CJEU's ruling in the pending referral C-527/17.

With respect to the duration of the SPC, it is to be noted that the basic patent expires at the end of the day of the twenty-year anniversary of its filing date. A maximum five-year SPC term will thus expire at the end of the day of the twenty-five-year anniversary of the filing date of the basic patent.

For a contractual licence agreement in a basic patent to extend to an SPC granted on the basis of such a patent, a corresponding provision in the licence agreement is required.

§13.14 NORWAY

In Norway, an SPC application has to be filed in the name of the proprietor of the basic patent. A deficiency in this regard can still be rectified during the prosecution of the SPC application.

If the deadline for filing an SPC has inadvertently been missed, it should, in principle, be possible to request re-establishment of rights in order to have the case reinstated. This should also hold true with respect to the deadline for filing a request for a paediatric extension. However, there appears to be no case law specifically confirming this possibility.

For filing an SPC application, it is necessary to submit a copy of the decision from the Norwegian Medicines Agency granted a marketing authorization in Norway and, if that marketing authorization is not the first one within the EEA, a copy of the corresponding first marketing authorization within the EEA. Instead of a copy of the fist marketing authorization within the EEA (where this is not also the first approval in Norway), the applicant can alternatively submit information on the identity of the approved product and the legal provision under which the corresponding authorization procedure took place, together with a copy of the notice publishing the authorization in the respective official publication. The documents required in accordance with Article 8 of the SPC Regulations can still be submitted at a later stage during the SPC examination procedure.

A power of attorney has to be filed, unless the representative is an attorney-at-law. The required power of attorney can still be submitted after filing the SPC application.

For requesting a paediatric extension, the corresponding documents required under Article 8 of the SPC Regulation for Medicinal Products can likewise still be submitted at a later stage of proceedings. However, if a missing marketing authorization or compliance statement is subsequently filed, the corresponding document must have been issued by the respective competent authority within the prescribed time limit for filing the request for a paediatric extension.

SPC applications undergo a substantive examination procedure. The Norwegian patent office checks whether the product is protected by the basic patent, and also whether prior SPCs filed in the name of the same applicant exist. In the examination procedure, the patent office furthermore consults the Norwegian Medicines Agency in order to confirm that the marketing authorization relied upon for the SPC application is indeed the first marketing authorization for the respective product in Norway.

Third-party observations can be filed during the examination procedure and will be taken into account.

There is no fixed timeframe for the SPC examination proceedings, and examiners can flexibly react to an applicant's informal request to accelerate or delay the SPC examination proceedings. A request to delay or stay the proceedings must, however, be justified. It is also possible to conduct an informal interview with the competent examiner.

In practice, a broader product definition may be used than the specific form of the active ingredient indicated in the marketing authorization. In particular, the inclusion of salts of the active ingredient in the product definition of the SPC is normally accepted.

Moreover, the Norwegian patent office normally rejects SPC applications for products based on a CE approval of a medical device. The future practice in this regard might, however, be affected by the CJEU's ruling in the pending referral C-527/17.

With respect to the duration of the SPC, it is to be noted that the basic patent expires on the day *after* the twenty-year anniversary of its filing date. An SPC with a full five-year term will thus expire at the end of the day *after* the twenty-five-year anniversary of the filing date of the basic patent.

For a contractual licence agreement in a basic patent to extend to an SPC granted on the basis of such a patent, a corresponding provision should be included in the licence agreement. However, there appears to be no case law specifically addressing this point.

Further information on the examination of SPC applications is provided in the Patent Guidelines (Part C, Chapter V) issued by the Norwegian patent office.[4]

§13.15 ALBANIA

Albania has been granted official candidate status for accession to the EU, but is not yet an EU (or EEA) Member State. As such, the pertinent EU legislation on SPCs is not applicable in Albania. SPCs are, however, available under national Albanian law, and the corresponding provisions in Articles 96–111 of the Albanian Law on Industrial Property[5] closely resemble those of the EU Regulations on SPCs. Albanian law does not yet provide for paediatric extensions.

An SPC is granted to the holder of the basic patent or his successor in title (Article 102 of the Albanian Law on Industrial Property). If there is a discrepancy between the SPC applicant and the proprietor of the basic patent, this can still be rectified during the SPC examination proceedings.

If the deadline for filing an SPC has inadvertently been missed, it will, in principle, be possible to request re-establishment of rights in order to have the case reinstated.

For filing an SPC application, the following documents have to be submitted to the Albanian patent office: the application form; an official payment receipt; a power of attorney (which should be sealed or notarized); a copy of the Albanian marketing authorization relied upon, including the summary of product characteristics; and a document proving the relationship between the holder of the basic patent and the holder of the marketing authorization (unless they are identical). The application form and the payment receipt should be submitted on filing, while at least the other required

4. Accessible online at: https://www.patentstyret.no/tjenester/patent/patentretningslinjer/utvalg/del-c/del-c-realitetsbehandling-kap-v---supplerende-beskyttelsess/ (in Norwegian only).
5. Albanian Law No. 9947 of 7 July 2008 on Industrial Property, as last amended by Law No. 55/2014 of 29 May 2014. Accessible online at: http://www.wipo.int/wipolex/en/details.jsp?id=16292 (in English translation).

documents can still be filed during the SPC grant proceedings in response to a corresponding official communication.

The Albanian patent office merely conducts a formal examination of SPC requests but no substantive examination. Thus, the patent office does not check whether the product is protected by the basic patent, nor whether prior SPCs granted to the same applicant exist.

The examination of SPC applications should be commenced within three months from their filing date, but the overall procedure can be flexibly conducted. It is normally not possible to accelerate, delay or stay the SPC examination proceedings at the request of the applicant. It may, however, be possible to conduct an informal interview with the competent examiner.

The product definition of the SPC must correspond exactly to the indication of the active substance(s) in the marketing authorization.

The grant of SPCs should not be possible on the basis of the regulatory approval of a medical device.

With respect to the duration of the SPC, it is to be noted that the basic patent expires at the end of the day of the twenty-year anniversary of its filing date. An SPC with a full five-year term will thus expire at the end of the day of the twenty-five-year anniversary of the filing date of the basic patent.

§13.16 MACEDONIA

Macedonia has been granted official candidate status for accession to the EU, but is not yet an EU (or EEA) Member State. As such, the pertinent EU legislation on SPCs is not applicable in Macedonia. SPCs are, however, available under national Macedonian law. The corresponding provisions in Articles 75–86 of the Macedonian Law on Industrial Property and in Articles 32–34 of the Macedonian Patent Regulation[6] are largely similar to those of the EU Regulations on SPCs. Macedonian law does not yet provide for paediatric extensions.

The holder of the basic patent or his legal successor is entitled to an SPC (Article 78(1) of the Macedonian Law on Industrial Property). If there is a discrepancy between the SPC applicant and the proprietor of the basic patent, it should be possible to rectify this during the SPC examination proceedings.

If the deadline for filing an SPC has inadvertently been missed, it should, in theory, be possible to request re-establishment of rights in order to have the case reinstated under Articles 265–270 of the Macedonian Law on Industrial Property. There appears to be no case law specifically addressing this point.

For filing an SPC application, the following documents have to be submitted to the Macedonian patent office: the official request form; proof of payment of the official fee; the Macedonian marketing authorization (as original or in notarized copy); a certified copy of the first marketing authorization of the corresponding product in any

6. Both accessible online at: http://www.ippo.gov.mk/EN/Legislation.aspx (in English translation).

state of the Paris Union or the World Trade Organization; and a power of attorney. The required documents may still be submitting after the filing date.

The Macedonian patent office merely conducts a formal examination of SPC requests but no substantive examination. Thus, the patent office does not check whether the product is protected by the basic patent, nor whether prior SPCs granted to the same applicant exist.

There is no fixed timeframe for the SPC examination proceedings, and examiners should, in principle, be able react to an applicant's informal request to accelerate or delay the SPC examination proceedings. It may also be possible to conduct an informal interview with the competent examiner.

There appears to be no established practice or case law regarding the acceptable degree of generalization of the product definition of an SPC as compared to the specific form of the active ingredient(s) indicated in the marketing authorization.

With respect to the duration of the SPC, it is to be noted that the basic patent expires at the end of the day of the twenty-year anniversary of its filing date. An SPC with a full five-year term will thus expire at the end of the day of the twenty-five-year anniversary of the filing date of the basic patent.

Appendices

APPENDIX I

Legal Text of Regulation (EC) 469/2009 on SPCs for Medicinal Products

In the following, the complete text of the 'SPC Regulation for Medicinal Products', i.e. Regulation (EC) 469/2009, is reproduced[1] in its consolidated version as of 1 July 2013, i.e. as last amended by the Treaty of Accession of Croatia (2012).

REGULATION (EC) No 469/2009 OF THE EUROPEAN PARLIAMENT AND OF THE COUNCIL

of 6 May 2009

concerning the supplementary protection certificate for medicinal products

(Codified version)

(Text with EEA relevance)

THE EUROPEAN PARLIAMENT AND THE COUNCIL OF THE EUROPEAN UNION,

Having regard to the Treaty establishing the European Community, and in particular Article 95 thereof,

Having regard to the proposal from the Commission,

Having regard to the opinion of the European Economic and Social Committee([2]),

Acting in accordance with the procedure laid down in Article 251 of the Treaty([3]),

Whereas:

1. The consolidated text of Regulation (EC) 469/2009 has been obtained from EUR-Lex, © European Union, http://eur-lex.europa.eu/, 1998-2018.
2. OJ C 77, 31.3.2009, p. 42.
3. Opinion of the European Parliament of 21 October 2008 (not yet published in the Official Journal) and Council Decision of 6 April 2009.

(1) Council Regulation (EEC) No 1768/92 of 18 June 1992 concerning the creation of a supplementary protection certificate for medicinal products([4]) has been substantially amended several times([5]). In the interests of clarity and rationality the said Regulation should be codified.
(2) Pharmaceutical research plays a decisive role in the continuing improvement in public health.
(3) Medicinal products, especially those that are the result of long, costly research will not continue to be developed in the Community and in Europe unless they are covered by favourable rules that provide for sufficient protection to encourage such research.
(4) At the moment, the period that elapses between the filing of an application for a patent for a new medicinal product and authorisation to place the medicinal product on the market makes the period of effective protection under the patent insufficient to cover the investment put into the research.
(5) This situation leads to a lack of protection which penalises pharmaceutical research.
(6) There exists a risk of research centres situated in the Member States relocating to countries that offer greater protection.
(7) A uniform solution at Community level should be provided for, thereby preventing the heterogeneous development of national laws leading to further disparities which would be likely to create obstacles to the free movement of medicinal products within the Community and thus directly affect the functioning of the internal market.
(8) Therefore, the provision of a supplementary protection certificate granted, under the same conditions, by each of the Member States at the request of the holder of a national or European patent relating to a medicinal product for which marketing authorisation has been granted is necessary. A regulation is therefore the most appropriate legal instrument.
(9) The duration of the protection granted by the certificate should be such as to provide adequate effective protection. For this purpose, the holder of both a patent and a certificate should be able to enjoy an overall maximum of 15 years of exclusivity from the time the medicinal product in question first obtains authorisation to be placed on the market in the Community.
(10) All the interests at stake, including those of public health, in a sector as complex and sensitive as the pharmaceutical sector should nevertheless be taken into account. For this purpose, the certificate cannot be granted for a period exceeding five years. The protection granted should furthermore be strictly confined to the product which obtained authorisation to be placed on the market as a medicinal product.
(11) Provision should be made for appropriate limitation of the duration of the certificate in the special case where a patent term has already been extended under a specific national law,

4. OJ L 182, 2.7.1992, p. 1.
5. *See* Annex I.

HAVE ADOPTED THIS REGULATION:

Article 1

Definitions

For the purposes of this Regulation, the following definitions shall apply:

(a) 'medicinal product' means any substance or combination of substances presented for treating or preventing disease in human beings or animals and any substance or combination of substances which may be administered to human beings or animals with a view to making a medical diagnosis or to restoring, correcting or modifying physiological functions in humans or in animals;
(b) 'product' means the active ingredient or combination of active ingredients of a medicinal product;
(c) 'basic patent' means a patent which protects a product as such, a process to obtain a product or an application of a product, and which is designated by its holder for the purpose of the procedure for grant of a certificate;
(d) 'certificate' means the supplementary protection certificate;
(e) 'application for an extension of the duration' means an application for an extension of the duration of the certificate pursuant to Article 13(3) of this Regulation and Article 36 of Regulation (EC) No 1901/2006 of the European Parliament and of the Council of 12 December 2006 on medicinal products for paediatric use([6]).

Article 2

Scope

Any product protected by a patent in the territory of a Member State and subject, prior to being placed on the market as a medicinal product, to an administrative authorisation procedure as laid down in Directive 2001/83/EC of the European Parliament and of the Council of 6 November 2001 on the Community code relating to medicinal products for human use([7]) or Directive 2001/82/EC of the European Parliament and of the Council of 6 November 2001 on the Community code relating to veterinary medicinal products([8]) may, under the terms and conditions provided for in this Regulation, be the subject of a certificate.

6. OJ L 378, 27.12.2006, p. 1.
7. OJ L 311, 28.11.2001, p. 67.
8. OJ L 311, 28.11.2001, p. 1.

Article 3

Conditions for obtaining a certificate

A certificate shall be granted if, in the Member State in which the application referred to in Article 7 is submitted and at the date of that application:

(a) the product is protected by a basic patent in force;
(b) a valid authorisation to place the product on the market as a medicinal product has been granted in accordance with Directive 2001/83/EC or Directive 2001/82/EC, as appropriate;
(c) the product has not already been the subject of a certificate;
(d) the authorisation referred to in point (b) is the first authorisation to place the product on the market as a medicinal product.

Article 4

Subject matter of protection

Within the limits of the protection conferred by the basic patent, the protection conferred by a certificate shall extend only to the product covered by the authorisation to place the corresponding medicinal product on the market and for any use of the product as a medicinal product that has been authorised before the expiry of the certificate.

Article 5

Effects of the certificate

Subject to the provisions of Article 4, the certificate shall confer the same rights as conferred by the basic patent and shall be subject to the same limitations and the same obligations.

Article 6

Entitlement to the certificate

The certificate shall be granted to the holder of the basic patent or his successor in title.

Article 7

Application for a certificate

1. The application for a certificate shall be lodged within six months of the date on which the authorisation referred to in Article 3(b) to place the product on the market as a medicinal product was granted.

2. Notwithstanding paragraph 1, where the authorisation to place the product on the market is granted before the basic patent is granted, the application for a certificate shall be lodged within six months of the date on which the patent is granted.
3. The application for an extension of the duration may be made when lodging the application for a certificate or when the application for the certificate is pending and the appropriate requirements of Article 8(1)(d) or Article 8(2), respectively, are fulfilled.
4. The application for an extension of the duration of a certificate already granted shall be lodged not later than two years before the expiry of the certificate.
5. Notwithstanding paragraph 4, for five years following the entry into force of Regulation (EC) No 1901/2006, the application for an extension of the duration of a certificate already granted shall be lodged not later than six months before the expiry of the certificate.

Article 8

Content of the application for a certificate

1. The application for a certificate shall contain:
   (a) a request for the grant of a certificate, stating in particular:
      (i) the name and address of the applicant;
      (ii) if he has appointed a representative, the name and address of the representative;
      (iii) the number of the basic patent and the title of the invention;
      (iv) the number and date of the first authorisation to place the product on the market, as referred to in Article 3(b) and, if this authorisation is not the first authorisation for placing the product on the market in the Community, the number and date of that authorisation;
   (b) a copy of the authorisation to place the product on the market, as referred to in Article 3(b), in which the product is identified, containing in particular the number and date of the authorisation and the summary of the product characteristics listed in Article 11 of Directive 2001/83/EC or Article 14 of Directive 2001/82/EC;
   (c) if the authorisation referred to in point (b) is not the first authorisation for placing the product on the market as a medicinal product in the Community, information regarding the identity of the product thus authorised and the legal provision under which the authorisation procedure took place, together with a copy of the notice publishing the authorisation in the appropriate official publication;
   (d) where the application for a certificate includes a request for an extension of the duration:

(i) a copy of the statement indicating compliance with an agreed completed paediatric investigation plan as referred to in Article 36(1) of Regulation (EC) No 1901/2006;

(ii) where necessary, in addition to the copy of the authorisation to place the product on the market as referred to in point (b), proof of possession of authorisations to place the product on the market of all other Member States, as referred to in Article 36(3) of Regulation (EC) No 1901/2006.

2. Where an application for a certificate is pending, an application for an extended duration in accordance with Article 7(3) shall include the particulars referred to in paragraph 1(d) of this Article and a reference to the application for a certificate already filed.
3. The application for an extension of the duration of a certificate already granted shall contain the particulars referred to in paragraph 1(d) and a copy of the certificate already granted.
4. Member States may provide that a fee is to be payable upon application for a certificate and upon application for the extension of the duration of a certificate.

Article 9

Lodging of an application for a certificate

1. The application for a certificate shall be lodged with the competent industrial property office of the Member State which granted the basic patent or on whose behalf it was granted and in which the authorisation referred to in Article 3(b) to place the product on the market was obtained, unless the Member State designates another authority for the purpose.
   The application for an extension of the duration of a certificate shall be lodged with the competent authority of the Member State concerned.
2. Notification of the application for a certificate shall be published by the authority referred to in paragraph 1. The notification shall contain at least the following information:
   (a) the name and address of the applicant;
   (b) the number of the basic patent;
   (c) the title of the invention;
   (d) the number and date of the authorisation to place the product on the market, referred to in Article 3(b), and the product identified in that authorisation;
   (e) where relevant, the number and date of the first authorisation to place the product on the market in the Community;
   (f) where applicable, an indication that the application includes an application for an extension of the duration.
3. Paragraph 2 shall apply to the notification of the application for an extension of the duration of a certificate already granted or where an application for a

certificate is pending. The notification shall additionally contain an indication of the application for an extended duration of the certificate.

Article 10

Grant of the certificate or rejection of the application for a certificate

1. Where the application for a certificate and the product to which it relates meet the conditions laid down in this Regulation, the authority referred to in Article 9(1) shall grant the certificate.
2. The authority referred to in Article 9(1) shall, subject to paragraph 3, reject the application for a certificate if the application or the product to which it relates does not meet the conditions laid down in this Regulation.
3. Where the application for a certificate does not meet the conditions laid down in Article 8, the authority referred to in Article 9(1) shall ask the applicant to rectify the irregularity, or to settle the fee, within a stated time.
4. If the irregularity is not rectified or the fee is not settled under paragraph 3 within the stated time, the authority shall reject the application.
5. Member States may provide that the authority referred to in Article 9(1) is to grant certificates without verifying that the conditions laid down in Article 3(c) and (d) are met.
6. Paragraphs 1 to 4 shall apply mutatis mutandis to the application for an extension of the duration.

Article 11

Publication

1. Notification of the fact that a certificate has been granted shall be published by the authority referred to in Article 9(1). The notification shall contain at least the following information:
   (a) the name and address of the holder of the certificate;
   (b) the number of the basic patent;
   (c) the title of the invention;
   (d) the number and date of the authorisation to place the product on the market referred to in Article 3(b) and the product identified in that authorisation;
   (e) where relevant, the number and date of the first authorisation to place the product on the market in the Community;
   (f) the duration of the certificate.
2. Notification of the fact that the application for a certificate has been rejected shall be published by the authority referred to in Article 9(1). The notification shall contain at least the information listed in Article 9(2).

3. Paragraphs 1 and 2 shall apply to the notification of the fact that an extension of the duration of a certificate has been granted or of the fact that the application for an extension has been rejected.

Article 12

Annual fees

Member States may require that the certificate be subject to the payment of annual fees.

Article 13

Duration of the certificate

1. The certificate shall take effect at the end of the lawful term of the basic patent for a period equal to the period which elapsed between the date on which the application for a basic patent was lodged and the date of the first authorisation to place the product on the market in the Community, reduced by a period of five years.
2. Notwithstanding paragraph 1, the duration of the certificate may not exceed five years from the date on which it takes effect.
3. The periods laid down in paragraphs 1 and 2 shall be extended by six months in the case where Article 36 of Regulation (EC) No 1901/2006 applies. In that case, the duration of the period laid down in paragraph 1 of this Article may be extended only once.
4. Where a certificate is granted for a product protected by a patent which, before 2 January 1993, had its term extended or for which such extension was applied for, under national law, the term of protection to be afforded under this certificate shall be reduced by the number of years by which the term of the patent exceeds 20 years.

Article 14

Expiry of the certificate

The certificate shall lapse:

(a) at the end of the period provided for in Article 13;
(b) if the certificate holder surrenders it;
(c) if the annual fee laid down in accordance with Article 12 is not paid in time;
(d) if and as long as the product covered by the certificate may no longer be placed on the market following the withdrawal of the appropriate authorisation or authorisations to place on the market in accordance with Directive 2001/83/EC or Directive 2001/82/EC. The authority referred to in Article 9(1)

of this Regulation may decide on the lapse of the certificate either of its own motion or at the request of a third party.

Article 15

Invalidity of the certificate

1. The certificate shall be invalid if:
   (a) it was granted contrary to the provisions of Article 3;
   (b) the basic patent has lapsed before its lawful term expires;
   (c) the basic patent is revoked or limited to the extent that the product for which the certificate was granted would no longer be protected by the claims of the basic patent or, after the basic patent has expired, grounds for revocation exist which would have justified such revocation or limitation.
2. Any person may submit an application or bring an action for a declaration of invalidity of the certificate before the body responsible under national law for the revocation of the corresponding basic patent.

Article 16

Revocation of an extension of the duration

1. The extension of the duration may be revoked if it was granted contrary to the provisions of Article 36 of Regulation (EC) No 1901/2006.
2. Any person may submit an application for revocation of the extension of the duration to the body responsible under national law for the revocation of the corresponding basic patent.

Article 17

Notification of lapse or invalidity

1. If the certificate lapses in accordance with point (b), (c) or (d) of Article 14, or is invalid in accordance with Article 15, notification thereof shall be published by the authority referred to in Article 9(1).
2. If the extension of the duration is revoked in accordance with Article 16, notification thereof shall be published by the authority referred to in Article 9(1).

Article 18

Appeals

The decisions of the authority referred to in Article 9(1) or of the bodies referred to in Articles 15(2) and 16(2) taken under this Regulation shall be open to the same appeals as those provided for in national law against similar decisions taken in respect of national patents.

Article 19

Procedure

1. In the absence of procedural provisions in this Regulation, the procedural provisions applicable under national law to the corresponding basic patent shall apply to the certificate, unless the national law lays down special procedural provisions for certificates.
2. Notwithstanding paragraph 1, the procedure for opposition to the granting of a certificate shall be excluded.

Article 20

Additional provisions relating to the enlargement of the Community

Without prejudice to the other provisions of this Regulation, the following provisions shall apply:

(a) any medicinal product protected by a valid basic patent and for which the first authorisation to place it on the market as a medicinal product was obtained after 1 January 2000 may be granted a certificate in Bulgaria, provided that the application for a certificate was lodged within six months from 1 January 2007;

(b) any medicinal product protected by a valid basic patent in the Czech Republic and for which the first authorisation to place it on the market as a medicinal product was obtained:

  (i) in the Czech Republic after 10 November 1999 may be granted a certificate, provided that the application for a certificate was lodged within six months of the date on which the first market authorisation was obtained;

  (ii) in the Community not earlier than six months prior to 1 May 2004 may be granted a certificate, provided that the application for a certificate was lodged within six months of the date on which the first market authorisation was obtained;

(c) any medicinal product protected by a valid basic patent and for which the first authorisation to place it on the market as a medicinal product was obtained in

Estonia prior to 1 May 2004 may be granted a certificate, provided that the application for a certificate was lodged within six months of the date on which the first market authorisation was obtained or, in the case of those patents granted prior to 1 January 2000, within the six months provided for in the Patents Act of October 1999;

(d) any medicinal product protected by a valid basic patent and for which the first authorisation to place it on the market as a medicinal product was obtained in Cyprus prior to 1 May 2004 may be granted a certificate, provided that the application for a certificate was lodged within six months of the date on which the first market authorisation was obtained; notwithstanding the above, where the market authorisation was obtained before the grant of the basic patent, the application for a certificate must be lodged within six months of the date on which the patent was granted;

(e) any medicinal product protected by a valid basic patent and for which the first authorisation to place it on the market as a medicinal product was obtained in Latvia prior to 1 May 2004 may be granted a certificate. In cases where the period provided for in Article 7(1) has expired, the possibility of applying for a certificate shall be open for a period of six months starting no later than 1 May 2004;

(f) any medicinal product protected by a valid basic patent applied for after 1 February 1994 and for which the first authorisation to place it on the market as a medicinal product was obtained in Lithuania prior to 1 May 2004 may be granted a certificate, provided that the application for a certificate was lodged within six months from 1 May 2004;

(g) any medicinal product protected by a valid basic patent and for which the first authorisation to place it on the market as a medicinal product was obtained after 1 January 2000 may be granted a certificate in Hungary, provided that the application for a certificate was lodged within six months from 1 May 2004;

(h) any medicinal product protected by a valid basic patent and for which the first authorisation to place it on the market as a medicinal product was obtained in Malta prior to 1 May 2004 may be granted a certificate. In cases where the period provided for in Article 7(1) has expired, the possibility of applying for a certificate shall be open for a period of six months starting no later than 1 May 2004;

(i) any medicinal product protected by a valid basic patent and for which the first authorisation to place it on the market as a medicinal product was obtained after 1 January 2000 may be granted a certificate in Poland, provided that the application for a certificate was lodged within six months starting no later than 1 May 2004;

(j) any medicinal product protected by a valid basic patent and for which the first authorisation to place it on the market as a medicinal product was obtained after 1 January 2000 may be granted a certificate in Romania. In cases where the period provided for in Article 7(1) has expired, the possibility of applying for a certificate shall be open for a period of six months starting no later than 1 January 2007;

(k) any medicinal product protected by a valid basic patent and for which the first authorisation to place it on the market as a medicinal product was obtained in Slovenia prior to 1 May 2004 may be granted a certificate, provided that the application for a certificate was lodged within six months from 1 May 2004, including in cases where the period provided for in Article 7(1) has expired;

(l) any medicinal product protected by a valid basic patent and for which the first authorisation to place it on the market as a medicinal product was obtained in Slovakia after 1 January 2000 may be granted a certificate, provided that the application for a certificate was lodged within six months of the date on which the first market authorisation was obtained or within six months of 1 July 2002 if the market authorisation was obtained before that date;

(m) any medicinal product protected by a valid basic patent and for which the first authorisation to place it on the market as a medicinal product was obtained after 1 January 2003 may be granted a certificate in Croatia, provided that the application for a certificate is lodged within six months from the date of accession.

Article 21

Transitional provisions

1. This Regulation shall not apply to certificates granted in accordance with the national legislation of a Member State before 2 January 1993 or to applications for a certificate filed in accordance with that legislation before 2 July 1992.
   With regard to Austria, Finland and Sweden, this Regulation shall not apply to certificates granted in accordance with their national legislation before 1 January 1995.
2. This Regulation shall apply to supplementary protection certificates granted in accordance with the national legislation of the Czech Republic, Estonia, Croatia, Cyprus, Latvia, Lithuania, Malta, Poland, Romania, Slovenia and Slovakia prior to their respective date of accession.

Article 22

Repeal

Regulation (EEC) No 1768/92, as amended by the acts listed in Annex I, is repealed. References to the repealed Regulation shall be construed as references to this Regulation and shall be read in accordance with the correlation table in Annex II.

Article 23

Entry into force

This Regulation shall enter into force on the 20th day following its publication in the *Official Journal of the European Union.*
This Regulation shall be binding in its entirety and directly applicable in all Member States.

ANNEX I

REPEALED REGULATION WITH LIST OF ITS SUCCESSIVE AMENDMENTS

(referred to in Article 22)

Council Regulation (EEC) No 1768/92
(OJ L 182, 2.7.1992, p. 1)
Annex I, point XI.F.I, of the 1994 Act of Accession
(OJ C 241, 29.8.1994, p. 233)
Annex II, point 4.C.II, of the 2003 Act of Accession
(OJ L 236, 23.9.2003, p. 342)
Annex III, point 1.II, of the 2005 Act of Accession
(OJ L 157, 21.6.2005, p. 56)
Regulation (EC) No 1901/2006 of the European Parliament and of the Council
(OJ L 378, 27.12.2006, p. 1) Only Article 52

ANNEX II

CORRELATION TABLE

Regulation (EEC) No 1768/92	This Regulation
—	Recital 1
Recital 1	Recital 2
Recital 2	Recital 3
Recital 3	Recital 4
Recital 4	Recital 5
Recital 5	Recital 6
Recital 6	Recital 7
Recital 7	Recital 8
Recital 8	Recital 9
Recital 9	Recital 10

Regulation (EEC) No 1768/92	This Regulation
Recital 10	—
Recital 11	—
Recital 12	—
Recital 13	Recital 11
Article 1	Article 1
Article 2	Article 2
Article 3, introductory wording	Article 3, introductory wording
Article 3, point (a)	Article 3, point (a)
Article 3, point (b), first sentence	Article 3, point (b)
Article 3, point (b), second sentence	—
Article 3, points (c) and (d)	Article 3, points (c) and (d)
Articles 4 to 7	Articles 4 to 7
Article 8(1)	Article 8(1)
Article 8(1a)	Article 8(2)
Article 8(1b)	Article 8(3)
Article 8(2)	Article 8(4)
Articles 9 to 12	Articles 9 to 12
Article 13(1), (2) and (3)	Article 13(1), (2) and (3)
Articles 14 and 15	Articles 14 and 15
Article 15a	Article 16
Articles 16, 17 and 18	Articles 17, 18 and 19
Article 19	—
Article 19a, introductory wording	Article 20, introductory wording
Article 19a, point (a), points (i) and (ii)	Article 20, point (b), introductory wording, points (i) and (ii)
Article 19a, point (b)	Article 20, point (c)
Article 19a, point (c)	Article 20, point (d)
Article 19a, point (d)	Article 20, point (e)
Article 19a, point (e)	Article 20, point (f)
Article 19a, point (f)	Article 20, point (g)
Article 19a, point (g)	Article 20, point (h)
Article 19a, point (h)	Article 20, point (i)
Article 19a, point (i)	Article 20, point (k)
Article 19a, point (j)	Article 20, point (l)
Article 19a, point (k)	Article 20, point (a)
Article 19a, point (l)	Article 20, point (j)
Article 20	Article 21
Article 21	—
Article 22	Article 13(4)

Regulation (EEC) No 1768/92	This Regulation
—	Article 22
Article 23	Article 23
—	Annex I
—	Annex II

APPENDIX II

Legal Text of Regulation (EC) 1610/96 on SPCs for Plant Protection Products

In the following, the complete text of the 'SPC Regulation for Plant Protection Products', i.e. Regulation (EC) 1610/96, is reproduced[1] in its consolidated version as of 1 July 2013, i.e. as last amended by the Treaty of Accession of Croatia (2012).

REGULATION (EC) No 1610/96 OF THE EUROPEAN PARLIAMENT AND OF THE COUNCIL

of 23 July 1996

concerning the creation of a supplementary protection certificate for plant protection products

THE EUROPEAN PARLIAMENT AND THE COUNCIL OF THE EUROPEAN UNION,

Having regard to the Treaty establishing the European Community, and in particular Article 100a thereof,

Having regard to the proposal from the Commission([2]),

Having regard to the opinion of the Economic and Social Committee([3]),

Acting in accordance with the procedure referred to in Article 189b of the Treaty([4]),

1. The consolidated text of Regulation (EC) 1610/96 has been obtained from EUR-Lex, © European Union, http://eur-lex.europa.eu/, 1998-2018.
2. OJ C 390, 31.12.1994, p. 21 and OJ C 335, 13.12.1995, p. 15.
3. OJ No C 155, 21.6.1995, p. 14.
4. Opinion of the European Parliament of 15 June 1995 (OJ C 166, 3.7.1995, p. 89), common position of the Council of 27 November 1995 (OJ C 353, 30.12.1995, p. 36) and decision of the European Parliament of 12 March 1996 (OJ C 96, 1.4.1996, p. 30).

(1) Whereas research into plant protection products contributes to the continuing improvement in the production and procurement of plentiful food of good quality at affordable prices;
(2) Whereas plant protection research contributes to the continuing improvement in crop production;
(3) Whereas plant protection products, especially those that are the result of long, costly research, will continue to be developed in the Community and in Europe if they are covered by favourable rules that provide for sufficient protection to encourage such research;
(4) Whereas the competitiveness of the plant protection sector, by the very nature of the industry, requires a level of protection for innovation which is equivalent to that granted to medicinal products by Council Regulation (EEC) No 1768/92 of 18 June 1992 concerning the creation of a supplementary protection certificate for medicinal products([5]);
(5) Whereas, at the moment, the period that elapses between the filing of an application for a patent for a new plant protection product and authorization to place the said plant protection product on the market makes the period of effective protection under the patent insufficient to cover the investment put into the research and to generate the resources needed to maintain a high level of research;
(6) Whereas this situation leads to a lack of protection which penalizes plant protection research and the competitiveness of the sector;
(7) Whereas one of the main objectives of the supplementary protection certificate is to place European industry on the same competitive footing as its North American and Japanese counterparts;
(8) Whereas, in its Resolution of 1 February 1993([6]) on a Community programme of policy and action in relation to the environment and sustainable development, the Council adopted the general approach and strategy of the programme presented by the Commission, which stressed the interdependence of economic growth and environmental quality; whereas improving protection of the environment means maintaining the economic competitiveness of industry; whereas, accordingly, the issue of a supplementary protection certificate can be regarded as a positive measure in favour of environmental protection;
(9) Whereas a uniform solution at Community level should be provided for, thereby preventing the heterogeneous development of national laws leading to further disparities which would be likely to hinder the free movement of plant protection products within the Community and thus directly affect the functioning of the internal market; whereas this is in accordance with the principle of subsidiarity as defined by Article 3b of the Treaty;

5. OJ No L 182, 2.7.1992, p. 1.
6. OJ No C 138, 17.5.1993, p. 1.

(10) Whereas, therefore, there is a need to create a supplementary protection certificate granted, under the same conditions, by each of the Member States at the request of the holder of a national or European patent relating to a plant protection product for which marketing authorization has been granted is necessary; whereas a Regulation is therefore the most appropriate legal instrument;

(11) Whereas the duration of the protection granted by the certificate should be such as to provide adequate, effective protection; whereas, for this purpose, the holder of both a patent and a certificate should be able to enjoy an overall maximum of fifteen years of exclusivity from the time the plant protection product in question first obtains authorization to be placed on the market in the Community;

(12) Whereas all the interests at stake in a sector as complex and sensitive as plant protection must nevertheless be taken into account; whereas, for this purpose, the certificate cannot be granted for a period exceeding five years;

(13) Whereas the certificate confers the same rights as those conferred by the basic patent; whereas, consequently, where the basic patent covers an active substance and its various derivatives (salts and esters), the certificate confers the same protection;

(14) Whereas the issue of a certificate for a product consisting of an active substance does not prejudice the issue of other certificates for derivatives (salts and esters) of the substance, provided that the derivatives are the subject of patents specifically covering them;

(15) Whereas a fair balance should also be stuck with regard to the determination of the transitional arrangements; whereas such arrangements should enable the Community plant protection industry to catch up to some extent with its main competitors, while making sure that the arrangements do not compromise the achievement of other legitimate objectives concerning the agricultural policy and environment protection policy pursued at both national and Community level;

(16) Whereas only action at Community level will enable the objective, which consists in ensuring adequate protection for innovation in the field of plant protection, while guaranteeing the proper functioning of the internal market for plant protection products, to be attained effectively;

(17) Whereas the detailed rules in recitals 12, 13 and 14 and in Articles 3 (2), 4, 8 (1) (c) and 17 (2) of this Regulation are also valid, mutatis mutandis, for the interpretation in particular of recital 9 and Articles 3, 4, 8 (1) (c) and 17 of Council Regulation (EEC) No 1768/92,

HAVE ADOPTED THIS REGULATION:

Article 1

Definitions

For the purposes of this Regulation, the following definitions shall apply:

1. 'plant protection products': active substances and preparations containing one or more active substances, put up in the form in which they are supplied to the user, intended to:
   (a) protect plants or plant products against all harmful organisms or prevent the action of such organisms, in so far as such substances or preparations are not otherwise defined below;
   (b) influence the life processes of plants, other than as a nutrient (e.g. plant growth regulators);
   (c) preserve plant products, in so far as such substances or products are not subject to special Council or Commission provisions on preservatives;
   (d) destroy undesirable plants; or
   (e) destroy parts of plants, check or prevent undesirable growth of plants;
2. 'substances': chemical elements and their compounds, as they occur naturally or by manufacture, including any impurity inevitably resulting from the manufacturing process;
3. 'active substances': substances or micro-organisms including viruses, having general or specific action:
   (a) against harmful organisms; or
   (b) on plants, parts of plants or plant products;
4. 'preparations': mixtures or solutions composed of two or more substances, of which at least one is an active substance, intended for use as plant protection products;
5. 'plants': live plants and live parts of plants, including fresh fruit and seeds;
6. 'plant products': products in the unprocessed state or having undergone only simple preparation such as milling, drying or pressing, derived from plants, but excluding plants themselves as defined in point 5;
7. 'harmful organisms': pests of plants or plant products belonging to the animal or plant kingdom, and also viruses, bacteria and mycoplasmas and other pathogens;
8. 'product': the active substance as defined in point 3 or combination of active substances of a plant protection product;
9. 'basic patent': a patent which protects a product as defined in point 8 as such, a preparation as defined in point 4, a process to obtain a product or an application of a product, and which is designated by its holder for the purpose of the procedure for grant of a certificate;
10. 'certificate': the supplementary protection certificate.

Article 2

Scope

Any product protected by a patent in the territory of a Member State and subject, prior to being placed on the market as a plant protection product, to an administrative authorization procedure as laid down in Article 4 of Directive 91/414/EEC([7]), or pursuant to an equivalent provision of national law if it is a plant protection product in respect of which the application for authorization was lodged before Directive 91/414/EEC was implemented by the Member State concerned, may, under the terms and conditions provided for in this Regulation, be the subject of a certificate.

Article 3

Conditions for obtaining a certificate

1. A certificate shall be granted if, in the Member State in which the application referred to in Article 7 is submitted, at the date of that application:
   (a) the product is protected by a basic patent in force;
   (b) a valid authorization to place the product on the market as a plant protection product has been granted in accordance with Article 4 of Directive 91/414/EEC or an equivalent provision of national law;
   (c) the product has not already been the subject of a certificate;
   (d) the authorization referred to in (b) is the first authorization to place the product on the market as a plant protection product.
2. The holder of more than one patent for the same product shall not be granted more than one certificate for that product. However, where two or more applications concerning the same product and emanating from two or more holders of different patents are pending, one certificate for this product may be issued to each of these holders.

Article 4

Subject-matter of protection

Within the limits of the protection conferred by the basic patent, the protection conferred by a certificate shall extend only to the product covered by the authorizations to place the corresponding plant protection product on the market and for any use of the product as a plant protection product that has been authorized before the expiry of the certificate.

7. OJ L 230, 19.8.1991, p. 1. Directive as last amended by Directive 95/36/EC (OJ L 172, 22.7.1995, p. 8).

Article 5

Effects of the certificate

Subject to Article 4, the certificate shall confer the same rights as conferred by the basic patent and shall be subject to the same limitations and the same obligations.

Article 6

Entitlement to the certificate

The certificate shall be granted to the holder of the basic patent or his successor in title.

Article 7

Application for a certificate

1. The application for a certificate shall be lodged within six months of the date on which the authorization referred to in Article 3 (1) (b) to place the product on the market as a plant protection product was granted.
2. Notwithstanding paragraph 1, where the authorization to place the product on the market is granted before the basic patent is granted, the application for a certificate shall be lodged within six months of the date on which the patent is granted.

Article 8

Content of the application for a certificate

1. The application for a certificate shall contain:
   (a) a request for the grant of a certificate, stating in particular:
      (i) the name and address of the applicant;
      (ii) the name and address of the representative, if any;
      (iii) the number of the basic patent and the title of the invention;
      (iv) the number and date of the first authorization to place the product on the market, as referred to in Article 3 (1) (b) and, if this authorization is not the first authorization to place the product on the market in the Community, the number and date of that authorization;
   (b) a copy of the authorization to place the product on the market, as referred to in Article 3 (1) (b), in which the product is identified, containing in particular the number and date of the authorization and the summary of the product characteristics listed in Part A.I (points 1-7) or B.I (points 1-7) of Annex II to Directive 91/414/EEC or in equivalent national laws of the Member State in which the application was lodged;

(c) if the authorization referred to in (b) is not the first authorization to place the product on the market as a plant protection product in the Community, information regarding the identity of the product thus authorized and the legal provision under which the authorization procedure took place, together with a copy of the notice publishing the authorization in the appropriate official publication or, failing such a notice, any other document proving that the authorization has been issued, the date on which it was issued and the identity of the product authorized.

2. Member States may require a fee to be payable upon application for a certificate.

Article 9

Lodging of an application for a certificate

1. The application for a certificate shall be lodged with the competent industrial property office of the Member State which granted the basic patent or on whose behalf it was granted and in which the authorization referred to in Article 3 (1) (b) to place the product on the market was obtained, unless the member State designates another authority for the purpose.
2. Notification of the application for a certificate shall be published by the authority referred to in paragraph 1. The notification shall contain at least the following information:
   (a) the name and address of the applicant;
   (b) the number of the basic patent;
   (c) the title of the invention;
   (d) the number and date of the authorization to place the product on the market, referred to in Article 3 (1) (b), and the product identified in that authorization;
   (e) where relevant, the number and date of the first authorization to place the product on the market in the Community.

Article 10

Grant of the certificate or rejection of the application

1. Where the application for a certificate and the product to which it relates meet the conditions laid down in this Regulation, the authority referred to in Article 9 (1) shall grant the certificate.
2. The authority referred to in Article 9 (1) shall, subject to paragraph 3, reject the application for a certificate if the application or the product to which it relates does not meet the conditions laid down in this Regulation.
3. Where the application for a certificate does not meet the conditions laid down in Article 8, the authority referred to in Article 9 (1) shall ask the applicant to rectify the irregularity, or to settle the fee, within a stated time.

4. If the irregularity is not rectified or the fee is not settled under paragraph 3 within the stated time, the application shall be rejected.
5. Member States may provide that the authority referred to in Article 9 (1) is to grant certificates without verifying that the conditions laid down in Article 3 (1) (c) and (d) are met.

Article 11

Publication

1. Notification of the fact that a certificate has been granted shall be published by the authority referred to in Article 9 (1). The notification shall contain at least the following information:
   (a) the name and address of the holder of the certificate;
   (b) the number of the basic patent;
   (c) the title of the invention;
   (d) the number and date of the authorization to place the product on the market referred to in Article 3 (1) (b) and the product identified in that authorization;
   (e) where relevant, the number and date of the first authorization to place the product on the market in the Community;
   (f) the duration of the certificate.
2. Notification of the fact that the application for a certificate has been rejected shall be published by the authority referred to in Article 9 (1). The notification shall contain at least the information listed in Article 9 (2).

Article 12

Annual fees

Member States may require the certificate to be subject to the payment of annual fees.

Article 13

Duration of the certificate

1. The certificate shall take effect at the end of the lawful term of the basic patent for a period equal to the period which elapsed between the date on which the application for a basic patent was lodged and the date of the first authorization to place the product on the market in the Community, reduced by a period of five years.
2. Notwithstanding paragraph 1, the duration of the certificate may not exceed five years from the date on which it takes effect.

3. For the purposes of calculating the duration of the certificate, account shall be taken of a provisional first marketing authorization only if it is directly followed by a definitive authorization concerning the same product.

Article 14

Expiry of the certificate

The certificate shall lapse:

(a) at the end of the period provided for in Article 13;
(b) if the certificate-holder surrenders it;
(c) if the annual fee laid down in accordance with Article 12 is not paid in time;
(d) if and as long as the product covered by the certificate may no longer be placed on the market following the withdrawal of the appropriate authorization or authorizations to place it on the market in accordance with Article 4 of Directive 91/414/EEC or equivalent provisions of national law. The authority referred to in Article 9 (1) may decide on the lapse of the certificate either on its own initiative or at the request of a third party.

Article 15

Invalidity of the certificate

1. The certificate shall be invalid if:
   (a) it was granted contrary to the provisions of Article 3;
   (b) the basic patent has lapsed before its lawful term expires;
   (c) the basic patent is revoked or limited to the extent that the product for which the certificate was granted would no longer be protected by the claims of the basic patent or, after the basic patent has expired, grounds for revocation exist which would have justified such revocation or limitation.
2. Any person may submit an application or bring an action for a declaration of invalidity of the certificate before the body responsible under national law for the revocation of the corresponding basic patent.

Article 16

Notification of lapse or invalidity

If the certificate lapses in accordance with Article 14 (b), (c) or (d) or is invalid in accordance with Article 15, notification thereof shall be published by the authority referred to in Article 9 (1).

Article 17

Appeals

1. The decisions of the authority referred to in Article 9 (1) or of the body referred to in Article 15 (2) taken under this Regulation shall be open to the same appeals as those provided for in national law against similar decisions taken in respect of national patents.
2. The decision to grant the certificate shall be open to an appeal aimed at rectifying the duration of the certificate where the date of the first authorization to place the product on the market in the Community, contained in the application for a certificate as provided for in Article 8, is incorrect.

Article 18

Procedure

1. In the absence of procedural provisions in this Regulation, the procedural provisions applicable under national law to the corresponding basic patent and, where appropriate, the procedural provisions applicable to the certificates referred to in Regulation (EEC) No 1768/92, shall apply to the certificate, unless national law lays down special procedural provisions for certificates as referred to in this Regulation.
2. Notwithstanding paragraph 1, the procedure for opposition to the granting of a certificate shall be excluded.

TRANSITIONAL PROVISIONS

Article 19

1. Any product which, on the date on which this Regulation enters into force, is protected by a valid basic patent and for which the first authorization to place it on the market as a plant protection product in the Community was obtained after 1 January 1985 under Article 4 of Directive 91/414/EEC or an equivalent national provision may be granted a certificate.
2. An application made under paragraph 1 for a certificate shall be submitted within six months of the date on which this Regulation enters into force.

Article 19a

Provisions relating to the enlargement of the Community

Without prejudice to the other provisions of this Regulation, the following shall apply:

(a) (i) any plant protection product protected by a valid basic patent in the Czech Republic and for which the first authorisation to place it on the market as a plant protection product was obtained in the Czech Republic after 10 November 1999 may be granted a certificate, provided that the application for a certificate was lodged within six months of the date on which the first market authorisation was obtained,

(ii) any plant protection product protected by a valid basic patent in the Czech Republic and for which the first authorisation to place it on the market as a plant protection product was obtained in the Community not earlier than six months prior to the date of accession may be granted a certificate, provided that the application for a certificate was lodged within six months of the date on which the first market authorisation was obtained;

(b) any plant protection product protected by a valid basic patent and for which the first authorisation to place it on the market as a plant protection product was obtained in Estonia prior to the date of accession may be granted a certificate, provided that the application for a certificate was lodged within six months of the date on which the first market authorisation was obtained or, in the case of those patents granted prior to 1 January 2000, within the six month period provided for in the Patents Act of October 1999;

(c) any plant protection product protected by a valid basic patent and for which the first authorisation to place it on the market as a plant protection product was obtained in Cyprus prior to the date of accession may be granted a certificate, provided that the application for a certificate was lodged within six months of the date on which the first market authorisation was obtained; notwithstanding the above, where the market authorisation was obtained before the grant of the basic patent, the application for a certificate must be lodged within six months of the date on which the patent was granted;

(d) any plant protection product protected by a valid basic patent and for which the first authorisation to place it on the market as a plant protection product was obtained in Latvia prior to the date of accession may be granted a certificate. In cases where the period provided for in Article 7(1) has expired, the possibility of applying for a certificate shall be open for a period of six months starting no later than the date of accession;

(e) any plant protection product protected by a valid basic patent applied for after 1 February 1994 and for which the first authorisation to place it on the market as a plant protection product was obtained in Lithuania prior to the date of accession may be granted a certificate, provided that the application for a certificate is lodged within six months of the date of accession;

(f) any plant protection product protected by a valid basic patent and for which the first authorisation to place it on the market as a plant protection product was obtained after 1 January 2000 may be granted a certificate in Hungary, provided that the application for a certificate is lodged within six months of the date of accession;

(g) any plant protection product protected by a valid basic patent and for which the first authorisation to place it on the market as a plant protection product was obtained in Malta prior to the date of accession may be granted a certificate. In cases where the period provided for in Article 7(1) has expired, the possibility of applying for a certificate shall be open for a period of six months starting no later than the date of accession;

(h) any plant protection product protected by a valid basic patent and for which the first authorisation to place it on the market as a plant protection product was obtained after 1 January 2000 may be granted a certificate in Poland, provided that the application for a certificate is lodged within six months starting no later than the date of accession;

(i) any plant protection product protected by a valid basic patent and for which the first authorisation to place it on the market as a plant protection product was obtained in Slovenia prior to the date of accession may be granted a certificate, provided that the application for a certificate is lodged within six months of the date of accession, including in cases where the period provided for in Article 7(1) has expired;

(j) any plant protection product protected by a valid basic patent and for which the first authorisation to place it on the market as a plant protection product was obtained in Slovakia after 1 January 2000 may be granted a certificate, provided that the application for a certificate was lodged within six months of the date on which the first market authorisation was obtained or within six months of 1 July 2002 if the market authorisation was obtained before that date;

(k) any plant protection product protected by a valid basic patent and for which the first authorisation to place it on the market as a plant protection product was obtained after 1 January 2000 may be granted a certificate in Bulgaria, provided that the application for a certificate is lodged within six months of the date of accession;

(l) any plant protection product protected by a valid basic patent and for which the first authorisation to place it on the market as a plant protection product was obtained after 1 January 2000 may be granted a certificate in Romania. In cases where the period provided for in Article 7(1) has expired, the possibility of applying for a certificate shall be open for a period of six months starting no later than the date of accession;

(m) any plant protection product protected by a valid basic patent and for which the first authorisation to place it on the market as a plant protection product was obtained after 1 January 2003 may be granted a certificate in Croatia, provided that the application for a certificate is lodged within six months from the date of accession.

Article 20

1. In those Member States whose national law did not, on 1 January 1990, provide for the patentability of plant protection products, this Regulation shall apply from 2 January 1998.
   Article 19 shall not apply in those Member States.
2. This Regulation shall apply to supplementary protection certificates granted in accordance with the national legislation of the Czech Republic, Estonia, Croatia, Cyprus, Latvia, Lithuania, Malta, Poland, Romania, Slovenia and Slovakia prior to their respective date of accession.

FINAL PROVISION

Article 21

Entry into force

This Regulation shall enter into force six months after its publication in the *Official Journal of the European Communities*.
This Regulation shall be binding in its entirety and directly applicable in all Member States.

APPENDIX III

Excerpt of Regulation (EC) 1901/2006 on Medicinal Products for Paediatric Use

In the following, an excerpt[1] of the 'Paediatric Regulation', i.e. Regulation (EC) 1901/2006, is reproduced[2] in its consolidated version as of 26 January 2007, i.e. as last amended by Regulation (EC) 1902/2006.

This excerpt encompasses only recitals 11 and 26 to 29 as well as Articles 1, 2, 7 to 9 and 36 to 38 of the Paediatric Regulation.

REGULATION (EC) No 1901/2006 OF THE EUROPEAN PARLIAMENT AND OF THE COUNCIL

of 12 December 2006

on medicinal products for paediatric use and amending Regulation (EEC) No 1768/92, Directive 2001/20/EC, Directive 2001/83/EC and Regulation (EC) No 726/2004

(Text with EEA relevance)

THE EUROPEAN PARLIAMENT AND THE COUNCIL OF THE EUROPEAN UNION,

Having regard to the Treaty establishing the European Community, and in particular Article 95 thereof,

Having regard to the proposal from the Commission,

1. The complete text of Regulation (EC) 1901/2006 is accessible online at: https://eur-lex.europa.eu/legal-content/EN/ALL/?uri=celex:32006R1901. The consolidated version as of 26 January 2007 is directly accessible at: https://eur-lex.europa.eu/legal-content/EN/TXT/?uri=CELEX:02006R1901-20070126.
2. The consolidated text of Regulation (EC) 1901/2006 has been obtained from EUR-Lex, © European Union, http://eur-lex.europa.eu/, 1998-2018.

Having regard to the Opinion of the European Economic and Social Committee(3),

Having consulted the Committee of the Regions,

Acting in accordance with the procedure referred to in Article 251 of the Treaty(4),

Whereas:

(11) It is necessary to introduce a requirement for new medicinal products and for authorised medicinal products covered by a patent or a supplementary protection certificate to present either the results of studies in the paediatric population in accordance with an agreed paediatric investigation plan or proof of having obtained a waiver or deferral, at the time of filing a marketing authorisation application or an application for a new indication, new pharmaceutical form or new route of administration. The paediatric investigation plan should be the basis upon which compliance with that requirement is judged. However, that requirement should not apply to generics or similar biological medicinal products and medicinal products authorised through the well-established medicinal use procedure, nor to homeopathic medicinal products and traditional herbal medicinal products authorised through the simplified registration procedures of Directive 2001/83/EC of the European Parliament and of the Council of 6 November 2001 on the Community code relating to medicinal products for human use(5).

(26) For products falling within the scope of the requirement to submit paediatric data, if all the measures included in the agreed paediatric investigation plan are complied with, if the product is authorised in all Member States and if relevant information on the results of studies is included in product information, a reward should be granted in the form of a 6-month extension of the supplementary protection certificate created by Council Regulation (EEC) No 1768/92(6). Any decisions by Member States' authorities as regards the setting of prices for medicinal products or their inclusion in the scope of national health insurance schemes have no bearing on the granting of this reward.

(27) An application for an extension of the duration of the certificate pursuant to this Regulation should only be admissible where a certificate is granted pursuant to Regulation (EEC) No 1768/92.

(28) Because the reward is for conducting studies in the paediatric population and not for demonstrating that a product is safe and effective in the

3. OJ C 267, 27.10.2005, p. 1.
4. Opinion of the European Parliament of 7 September 2005 (OJ C 193 E, 17.8.2006, p. 225), Council Common Position of 10 March 2006 (OJ C 132 E, 7.6.2006, p. 1) and Position of the European Parliament of 1 June 2006 (not yet published in the Official Journal). Council Decision of 23 October 2006.
5. OJ L 311, 28.11.2001, p. 67. Directive as last amended by Directive 2004/27/EC (OJ L 136, 30.4.2004, p. 34).
6. OJ L 182, 2.7.1992, p. 1. Regulation as last amended by the 2003 Act of Accession.

paediatric population, the reward should be granted even when a paediatric indication is not authorised. However, to improve the information available on the use of medicinal products in the paediatric population, relevant information on use in paediatric populations should be included in authorised product information.

(29) Under Regulation (EC) No 141/2000 of the European Parliament and of the Council of 16 December 1999 on orphan medicinal products([7]), medicinal products designated as orphan medicinal products gain ten years of market exclusivity on the granting of a marketing authorisation for the orphan indication. As such products are frequently not patent-protected, the reward of supplementary protection certificate extension cannot be applied; when they are patent-protected, such an extension would provide a double incentive. Therefore, for orphan medicinal products, instead of an extension of the supplementary protection certificate, the ten-year period of orphan market exclusivity should be extended to twelve years if the requirement for data on use in the paediatric population is fully met.

HAVE ADOPTED THIS REGULATION:

TITLE I

INTRODUCTORY PROVISIONS

CHAPTER 1

Subject matter and definitions

Article 1

This Regulation lays down rules concerning the development of medicinal products for human use in order to meet the specific therapeutic needs of the paediatric population, without subjecting the paediatric population to unnecessary clinical or other trials and in compliance with Directive 2001/20/EC.

Article 2

In addition to the definitions laid down in Article 1 of Directive 2001/83/EC, the following definitions shall apply for the purposes of this Regulation:

1) 'paediatric population' means that part of the population aged between birth and 18 years;

7. OJ L 18, 22.1.2000, p. 1.

2) 'paediatric investigation plan' means a research and development programme aimed at ensuring that the necessary data are generated determining the conditions in which a medicinal product may be authorised to treat the paediatric population;
3) 'medicinal product authorised for a paediatric indication' means a medicinal product which is authorised for use in part or all of the paediatric population and in respect of which the details of the authorised indication are specified in the summary of the product characteristics drawn up in accordance with Article 11 of Directive 2001/83/EC;
4) 'paediatric use marketing authorisation' means a marketing authorisation granted in respect of a medicinal product for human use which is not protected by a supplementary protection certificate under Regulation (EEC) No 1768/92 or by a patent which qualifies for the granting of the supplementary protection certificate, covering exclusively therapeutic indications which are relevant for use in the paediatric population, or subsets thereof, including the appropriate strength, pharmaceutical form or route of administration for that product.

TITLE II

MARKETING AUTHORISATION REQUIREMENTS

CHAPTER 1

General authorisation requirements

Article 7

1. An application for marketing authorisation under Article 6 of Directive 2001/83/EC in respect of a medicinal product for human use which is not authorised in the Community at the time of entry into force of this Regulation shall be regarded as valid only if it includes, in addition to the particulars and documents referred to in Article 8(3) of Directive 2001/83/EC, one of the following:
   (a) the results of all studies performed and details of all information collected in compliance with an agreed paediatric investigation plan;
   (b) a decision of the Agency granting a product-specific waiver;
   (c) a decision of the Agency granting a class waiver pursuant to Article 11;
   (d) a decision of the Agency granting a deferral.

   For the purposes of point (a), the decision of the Agency agreeing the paediatric investigation plan concerned shall also be included in the application.
2. The documents submitted pursuant to paragraph 1 shall, cumulatively, cover all subsets of the paediatric population.

Article 8

In the case of authorised medicinal products which are protected either by a supplementary protection certificate under Regulation (EEC) No 1768/92, or by a patent which qualifies for the granting of the supplementary protection certificate, Article 7 of this Regulation shall apply to applications for authorisation of new indications, including paediatric indications, new pharmaceutical forms and new routes of administration.
For the purposes of the first subparagraph, the documents referred to in Article 7(1) shall cover both the existing and the new indications, pharmaceutical forms and routes of administration.

Article 9

Articles 7 and 8 shall not apply to products authorised under Articles 10, 10a, 13 to 16 or 16a to 16i of Directive 2001/83/EC.

TITLE V

REWARDS AND INCENTIVES

Article 36

1. Where an application under Article 7 or 8 includes the results of all studies conducted in compliance with an agreed paediatric investigation plan, the holder of the patent or supplementary protection certificate shall be entitled to a six-month extension of the period referred to in Articles 13(1) and 13(2) of Regulation (EEC) No 1768/92.
   The first subparagraph shall also apply where completion of the agreed paediatric investigation plan fails to lead to the authorisation of a paediatric indication, but the results of the studies conducted are reflected in the summary of product characteristics and, if appropriate, in the package leaflet of the medicinal product concerned.
2. The inclusion in a marketing authorisation of the statement referred to in Article 28(3) shall be used for the purposes of applying paragraph 1 of this Article.
3. Where the procedures laid down in Directive 2001/83/EC have been used, the six-month extension of the period referred to in paragraph 1 shall be granted only if the product is authorised in all Member States.
4. Paragraphs 1, 2 and 3 shall apply to products that are protected by a supplementary protection certificate under Regulation (EEC) No 1768/92, or under a patent which qualifies for the granting of the supplementary protection certificate. They shall not apply to medicinal products designated as orphan medicinal products pursuant to Regulation (EC) No 141/2000.

5. In the case of an application under Article 8 which leads to the authorisation of a new paediatric indication, paragraphs 1, 2 and 3 shall not apply if the applicant applies for, and obtains, a one-year extension of the period of marketing protection for the medicinal product concerned, on the grounds that this new paediatric indication brings a significant clinical benefit in comparison with existing therapies, in accordance with Article 14(11) of Regulation (EC) No 726/2004 or the fourth subparagraph of Article 10(1) of Directive 2001/83/EC.

Article 37

Where an application for a marketing authorisation is submitted in respect of a medicinal product designated as an orphan medicinal product pursuant to Regulation (EC) No 141/2000 and that application includes the results of all studies conducted in compliance with an agreed paediatric investigation plan, and the statement referred to in Article 28(3) of this Regulation is subsequently included in the marketing authorisation granted, the ten-year period referred to in Article 8(1) of Regulation (EC) No 141/2000 shall be extended to twelve years.
The first paragraph shall also apply where completion of the agreed paediatric investigation plan fails to lead to the authorisation of a paediatric indication, but the results of the studies conducted are reflected in the summary of product characteristics and, if appropriate, in the package leaflet of the medicinal product concerned.

Article 38

1. Where a paediatric use marketing authorisation is granted in accordance with Articles 5 to 15 of Regulation (EC) No 726/2004, the data and marketing protection periods referred to in Article 14(11) of that Regulation shall apply.
2. Where a paediatric use marketing authorisation is granted in accordance with the procedures laid down in Directive 2001/83/EC, the data and marketing protection periods referred to in Article 10(1) of that Directive shall apply.

Table of Cases

Belgium

European Union and European Economic Area

European Patent Office

France

Germany

Iceland

Italy

The Netherlands

Norway

Poland

Spain

Sweden

Switzerland

United Kingdom

www.ingramcontent.com/pod-product-compliance
Lightning Source LLC
LaVergne TN
LVHW020647300926
849161LV00004B/857